DATE DUE

Printed
in USA

JUN 06 1938

DEALERS
AND DREAMERS

A WORLD OF LOVE: ELEANOR ROOSEVELT AND HER FRIENDS,
1943–62

LOVE, ELEANOR: ELEANOR ROOSEVELT AND HER FRIENDS

DAG HAMMARSKJÖLD: CUSTODIAN OF THE BRUSHFIRE PEACE

ELEANOR ROOSEVELT: A FRIEND'S MEMOIR

ELEANOR AND FRANKLIN

ELEANOR: THE YEARS ALONE

FROM THE DIARIES OF FELIX FRANKFURTER

ROOSEVELT AND CHURCHILL

HELEN AND TEACHER

Joseph P. Lash

——⋙⟶✦✦⟵⋘——

DEALERS

AND

DREAMERS

A New Look at the New Deal

Doubleday

NEW YORK

1988

Library of Congress Cataloging-in-Publication Data
Lash, Joseph P., 1909–
    Dealers and dreamers.
    Includes index.
    1. New Deal, 1933–1939.   2. Cohen, Benjamin V.
3. Corcoran, Thomas G.   4. United States—History—
1933–1945. I. Title.
E806.L32   1987   973.917   87-6706
ISBN 0-385-18716-5

Acknowledgments

This book originated with a suggestion of Harrison Salisbury to Evan Thomas who, after his retirement from W.W. Norton, passed it on to Kenneth McCormick at Doubleday where it ended up in the competent and helpful hands of Carolyn Blakemore.

Salisbury's suggestion was a natural. I had been interviewing Ben Cohen all during the postwar years on New Deal matters with which he had been involved and even had persuaded this genuinely modest man to talk about his life. He was a rare spirit and this book will have failed if its readers do not come away from it persuaded, as the author is, that he should have been on the Supreme Court.

Thomas Corcoran was a name indissolubly linked with Cohen's and one to conjure with in the thirties. I first met him in the 1940 presidential campaign. By then Tom, in the service of Roosevelt, had become a whipping boy of the party regulars and though this had come about largely because of his work for Roosevelt, the President who needed the support of the party machine thought it prudent to get Tommy out of Washington. So he was sent to New York, the headquarters of the Norris-La Guardia Committee for the reelection of the President, where he functioned almost anonymously. I, too, was there as director of the Youth Division, having broken with the Left during the Nazi-Soviet pact. On a considerably lesser scale my name too made the regulars uncomfortable. "I'm the treasurer of the irregulars," Tommy introduced himself to me. The words were meant consolingly. Like him the greatest service I could offer to the reelection of the President was to keep out of sight.

Although I never served in a New Deal agency, I had a firsthand knowledge of the men and women who make up this chronicle.

That knowledge has been supplemented by early access to Ben Cohen's papers which the executors of his will, Joseph L. Rauh and David Ginsberg, gave me. Cohen kept few of his papers. Much of his correspondence was in longhand without carbons. Corcoran, on the other hand, kept everything including an unfinished autobiography, *Rendezvous with Destiny,* and the drafts of many of its chapters. His papers were made available to me by his son Thomas G. Corcoran, Jr., and I have made liberal use of the recollections therein.

In addition, I talked with many New Deal survivors, as the contents make clear, who helped with papers as well as with interviews. I am particularly indebted to Joseph Rauh, Lauchlin Currie, Robert Nathan, Walter Salant, and Ida Klaus.

Most of the material discussed in this book is now in library collections, first of all the manuscript division of the Library of Congress, where I had the particular help of Dr. David Wigdor and Paul Ledvina who was the archivist assigned to processing the Corcoran papers. The collections at the Franklin D. Roosevelt Library (FDRL) at Hyde Park were indispensable, as were the Homer Cummings Diary at the University of Virginia, the Jerome Frank papers at Yale University, the Cohen, Corcoran, James Rowe papers at the Lyndon Johnson Presidential Library in Austin. New Dealer oral histories at Columbia University (COH) proved a unique resource and, as a researcher without a university connection, I do not know what I would have done without the privilege to use the Bobst Library at New York University, which was extended to me by Dean Carlton Rochelle, its director.

There was an unexpected treat for me in the Zionist Archives in New York and in reliving through them the early years of the Balfour Declaration.

Several talks with Professor Robert Solow of the Massachusetts Institute of Technology constituted a quick course in how today's economists view the achievements of the thirties.

As with all my books, I am indebted to the careful reading given them by my son, Jonathan, and especially my wife, Trude.

At lunch one day with Susan Brownmiller, I was telling her about the remarkable friendship between Irishman and Jew, Corcoran and Cohen. "How pedestrian," was her reaction to my working title, "The New Deal Revisited." "Why don't you call it 'Dealers and Dreamers'?" she suggested. I knew she was right. I had been trying to use a line of Cohen's as a subtitle, "Some came to Washington to make the system better, some came to make it work." In two words Susan's suggestion summed up that influx of young men and women into Roosevelt's Washington that gave it, second only to the Roosevelts themselves, its special savor.

In the thirties I was a member of the Left, working in the American

Student Union and the American Youth Congress. Our agitation on behalf of young people's needs brought us in touch with New Dealers like Eleanor Roosevelt, Aubrey Williams, Will Alexander. We beat the drums on Capitol Hill for huge appropriations for youth and that enabled Aubrey to get larger sums for the NYA. It was a useful function but not mainstream politics as I began to learn when I went to work for the Norris-La Guardia Committee. I have learned it anew in the course of writing this book. What distinguished the New Dealers was their sixth-sense feeling for the programs that were politically feasible not simply ideally desirable.

Contents

DEALERS
AND DREAMERS

Prologue

In 1932 Franklin D. Roosevelt was reelected governor of New York by a record-shattering margin and declared for the presidency. Samuel I. Rosenman, one of his advisers and speech writers, speaking with him about the need to bring in experts on national issues, suggested that he try the universities for a change since the usual advisers, the financiers and politicians, had been discredited by the economic disaster that was afflicting the country. Although not philosophically minded, certainly not an original thinker, Roosevelt, a master politician, knew the importance of ideas in government, was comfortable in the presence of the people who produced them, and was adept at the use of these people for public purposes. He gave Rosenman the green light to get in touch with Raymond Moley, a professor of political science at Columbia, who recruited two other Columbia professors, Rexford G. Tugwell, an economist, and Adolph A. Berle, a specialist in the laws of credit and finance, and the three soon began to journey regularly to Albany to brief an eager and demanding governor. Thus the "brains trust," or as it quickly became, the "Brain Trust," was born and the use of brains which the New Dealers exemplified became a feature of the Roosevelt presidency.[1]

Some five years later, toward the end of 1937, much to the dismay of Roosevelt and the New Dealers, the recovery from the Great Depression that until then had been sensational, ground to a halt. From the 14 million unemployed that Roosevelt inherited in March 1933, the figure fell to 5 million by mid-1937 only to start climbing again, so that by early 1938 it stood at 9,600,000.[2] As Roosevelt desperately cast about him for the reasons, consulting the leading lights of government, banking, commerce, and labor, one of them, Harry Hopkins, the head of the Works Progress Administration, advised him to talk directly "to the boys" who actually wrote the memos of his cabinet members and hear from them what should be done.

This is a book about the 350-odd men and women, the New Dealers, who helped Roosevelt put through the social transformation of the thirties. In early July 1932 Roosevelt had flown to Chicago to accept the presidential nomination and had ended his speech with the words, "I pledge you, I pledge myself, to a new deal for the American people." "New Deal" was an inspired choice of words but they were inserted without much thought and a Roosevelt radio broadcast a month later expounding the Democratic National Platform did not mention the term. A Rollin Kirby cartoon in the New York *World,* nevertheless, which showed a plane enroute to Chicago with New Deal on its wings and a farmer leaning on his hoe looking up at it, caught the candidate's and public's mood of a readiness for new beginnings so that seven months later editorialists could write of Roosevelt's inauguration with no fear of misunderstanding, "The New Deal Begins."

Some called it the Roosevelt *Revolution* for though it was democratic it transferred the power from Wall Street to Washington, ended a judicial blockade of the popular will, and established government-wielded economic tools that Roosevelt and successive presidents could use to advance the general welfare if they and the people so wished.

Within the compass of that New Deal revolution this book is also an account of two of its leaders, Benjamin V. Cohen and Thomas G. Corcoran. They constituted one of history's great friendships. "If it hadn't been for Tom, I would never have been heard of," Cohen told *Time* in 1938 and the magazine added, "Tom thinks Ben ought to get Cardozo's place on the Supreme Court."[3]

Although the two were much in the headlines of the thirties and did for Roosevelt what hundreds now do for the presidents who succeeded, their names have faded from current memory—but not from that of the thousand or so diners who assembled in Washington, D.C., to commemorate Roosevelt's inaugural speech of 1933 and to remind President Jimmy Carter who was then in office of a moment in American history almost as eventful as the gathering in 1887 in Philadelphia of the Founding Fathers.

Thin and somewhat bent, Benjamin V. Cohen's nasal drawl cut through the quietness of the Mayflower ballroom. "For most of us our New Deal years were the best years of our lives." It was March 4, 1977, forty-four years from the day Franklin D. Roosevelt was inaugurated President of a stricken country and proclaimed that the nation which wanted action, and action now, would get it. The men and women had come together to recall the past in order to hearken the present and to honor such Roosevelt era figures as Cohen, Corcoran, and Tugwell.[4]

Portents that the meeting might accomplish this were not good even though Jimmy Carter, a Democrat, was President. He had not himself been invited, and no prominent members of his administration thought it prudent to come. His Vice President, Walter Mondale, who had accepted, felt obliged at the last minute to withdraw, citing a need to do some ice fishing in Minnesota. His mentor, Hubert H. Humphrey, gaunt and ailing, filled in for him.

An administration's heroes are an earnest of its purposes and methods. Roosevelt and the New Dealers had identified themselves with Jefferson and Jackson, with Abraham Lincoln and Theodore Roosevelt. Carter as a candidate had sought to benefit from the party's traditions, arising at dawn to begin his campaign for election at Warm Springs, Georgia, with Roosevelt's sons at his side. Once elected President, however, in a campaign in which he had made a virtue of being an outsider who ran against Washington, he snubbed the establishment, including the Democratic Party. Tugwell, one of the original Brain Trusters, bolstered the impression that Carter wanted political Washington to know that his administration had hatched without fathers. He had written to a president-elect Carter, he disclosed, to caution him that the first few months were the most favorable time in which to reorganize a government's structure and to make "a more serious effort at planning the use of resources" than Carter's speeches had thus far indicated.

Carter's reply had been perfunctory. He did not seem to recognize who Tugwell was. He referred the letter to Jack Watson "who [was] helping to plan the transition between administrations . . ." Tugwell heard nothing further from Carter or his lieutenants.

Marquis Childs, the columnist, was master of ceremonies. He was a man of balanced views and quiet sympathies, and the absence of Carter people startled him. "We don't have a single Carter [person] here tonight," he noted, "so in a sense this is a clean break between the past and the present."

"Having worked several years at the White House in my youth," an equally astonished Arthur Schlesinger, Jr., chronicler of the Roosevelt years and a guest at the dinner, wrote to Fritz Mondale, "I know how these things operate. Every time five Bessarabians get together in Waco, Texas, and request a presidential message, they get one. How in the world do you suppose a Democratic President, on the forty-fourth anniversary of the first inauguration of the greatest Democratic President of this century, could not manage a few words expressing his sense of the occasion?"[5]

People in the White House realized they had blundered. Several weeks later Corcoran wrote a friend, "You will be amused that Ben and I were invited to the White House for lunch yesterday to meet Hamilton Jordan, Frank Moore and Jack Watson to hear their protestations that they would have loved to come to dinner if asked."

There was another behind-the-scenes drama the evening of the New Deal reunion. The friends of Tugwell were indignant that he had been allowed only three minutes. Leon Keyserling, one of Tugwell's Columbia students whom he had brought to Washington in early 1933 and who later served as chairman of Truman's Council of Economic Advisers, took the dinner's organizers to task for perpetrating a mythology about the relative weight of various New Dealers in the thirties. The closeness of Tugwell to FDR, he went on, should have been recognized by giving him a big place on the program.

In the three minutes Chairman Marquis Childs did allot to the still-handsome Tugwell, he touched on the basic issue, as he saw it, that had divided the New Dealers—"we don't know whether we are populists or planners . . ." A letter that he wrote to Keyserling after the dinner disagreed with his former pupil's faith in the Humphrey-Hawkins Full Employment Bill as able to ensure full production. The letter went to the heart of his controversies with the Brandeis-Frankfurter progressives in the thirties. "I have always felt that only making the production system more orderly by substituting concentration for fractionalization can strengthen productivity." He feared that the resistance to planning preserved an obsolete structure.

When President Carter spoke at our Center [for Democratic Institutions] when he was beginning his campaign for the Presidency, he deplored the growth of corporate power and said it resulted from "lack of fervent and undeviating enforcement of the anti-trust laws." I have seen nothing to indicate a change from this free market syndrome. Apparently we are to go on with a large part of the bureaucracy devoted to preventing any movement toward national concentration of industries or comprehensive management of direction. I see bad signs everywhere. For instance the FTC [Federal Trade Commission] now has a Bureau of Competition— very active, too. If one thing is clear to me, and always has been, it is that competition is costly, that a system based on it is disjointed and that a substitute is so easily visualized that I cannot understand the resistance of good people to what I conceive to be reform.[6]

There was little awareness, the night of the New Dealers' reunion, of Tugwell's anguish or any sense of the controversy that had gripped progressives in the thirties between collectivist-planners of Tugwell's persuasion and Keynesian planners of the Frankfurter-Corcoran-Cohen variety. The thousand-odd guests, many of whom served in the New Deal, were content to have Benjamin V. Cohen speak for all of them that evening.

To introduce him another legendary figure of the thirties was present, Thomas G. "Tommy the Cork" Corcoran. Ben called him "my brother." He had steadfastly refused to allow dinners to be held in his honor because their organizers would not also honor Tom. Washington controversies were set aside this evening, and in a few words Tom demonstrated anew a felicity of pen, an Irish brio, a feeling for essentials that had made him a favorite of Justice Oliver Wendell Holmes, whose law clerk he had been, and that had elevated Ben and him to *primus inter pares* among the younger men who had staffed the New Deal. The words almost sang as Tom introduced Ben:

Without bloodshed the New Deal defanged our most dangerous internal crisis since the crisis of 1861. This it accomplished by institutionalizing compassion and recognizing the political indispensability for a democracy of hope in all its people.

The genius of Roosevelt, Tom said of the President against whom both Ben and he, in the privacy of their offices, sometimes had railed but whom they had always called "Boss," was his ability to read the popular mind . . ." [he] could summon the spirits from the vast deeps and they would come."

"If we could organize the government in the first hundred days," he told newsmen before the speech, "they [the Carter people] can summon the energy to reorganize it." He wanted to remind Mr. Carter that when something had to be done, it can be done. "You just have to summon the spirit of the people."

Unlike Tugwell, with whom, as will be clear from this narrative, they had feuded in Roosevelt's first term, both Corcoran and Cohen that evening seemed less interested in specific statutes and programs than in the spirit of governance that had enabled Roosevelt to lead the American people through the great crises of depression and war. There was the lesson for democracy, they emphasized. "He could draft laws in terms even an antagonistic Supreme Court could not disturb. In the largest sense his legal victories were the most important defense of the whole New

Deal" and by the time of Roosevelt's third term "we were sure the New Deal was safely on high ground where not even a tidal wave would wash it away."

For many years he and Ben had lived together, their relationship so close that the columnists had dubbed them "the Gold Dust Twins." Ben's most important political victories, Tom went on, were against "the money markets and the utility holding companies, the only concentrations of political power which could organize a political counter-revolution."

Always Ben eschewed administrative office with its perquisites and high-visibility social honor. His influence did not grow from command of a big office and hosts of assistants. His power seeped from many little offices in which he seemed a titular assistant or adviser to some more visible figure—and the frugality of his social life in which he escaped all pleasures except that of functioning so he might concentrate as no other New Dealer concentrated on devotion to what he saw as a cause. No one from the President down did not seek and benefit from Ben's advice. Never was there a more harmonious relationship with the Judiciary and Congress than was exhibited in Ben's own work. And he infused all he touched with the energy of moral purpose . . .

"He is the high priest, he is the saint," Tom ended, and the moment came for Ben to speak. He arose, slightly stooped, and walked forward from his table to the platform, stood behind the lectern, shuffling his feet slightly as was the wont of this modest man when he became the cynosure of other eyes. "We were the lucky ones," he began as the applause subsided. "For us it was a time when 'to be alive was joy and to be young was very Heaven.' Indeed," he smiled, "if we were not young then we would not be here tonight."

Many in his audience, he noted, had come to Washington in the early days of the New Deal because "Washington was the center of action and most of us wanted to be part of the action . . . The New Dealers brought to Washington new energies, new ideas, and the fruitful clashing of ideas, both new and old."

Ben picked up Tom's theme of how an administration can mobilize a people's energies to meet a great nation's "pressing and long neglected needs." He recalled the "Winter of Despair," the winter of 1933, and with the nation in a state of paralysis how Roosevelt promised action, "and action came," and how Walter Lippmann, who earlier had been a critic of Roosevelt, wrote, "In one week, the nation, which had lost confidence in everything and everybody, has regained confidence in the government and in itself."

He read the roll of the fifteen New Deal programs and actions which Congress authorized during The First Hundred Days.

Never before in American history was so much accomplished by the Congress in so little time . . . The time called for enthusiasm and energy both from those who wanted to make the world a better world and from those who just hoped it could be made to work. Roosevelt encouraged both groups while he steered a middle course.

Roosevelt's leadership was guided, said Cohen, by the principle of consensual, not confrontational, politics. He did not move "until he had some idea of the support he might expect and the opposition he might encounter" and refrained from irreversible committal until he had explored what was possible. In these probes, as will be indicated in these pages, Tom was one of his main scouts on the Hill, and Ben the draftsman of the bills that were sent up. "I recall how smoothly and effectively Roosevelt worked with the Congress when Jim Landis, Tom and I were asked to work on our first assignment, i.e., the Securities Act of 1933." "The one exception," Ben noted ruefully, "occurred after the 1936 election sweep in the presentation of the Supreme Court plan without adequate consultation."

Ever since 1934 when a Republican, Representative Fred A. Britten, had dubbed the house in which Ben and Tom lived "the little red house in Georgetown," the two had made headlines across the nation and been considered slightly subversive. In that "little red house," said Britten, "ten to eighteen" young men—"they call them Felix Frankfurter's hot dogs"— met nightly to "promote Communistic legislation."

Despite the phantoms of subversion that Britten and his cohorts had conjured up against them in the thirties, the two men that evening portrayed Roosevelt and his New Dealers as dedicated strategists of the democratic process.

Roosevelt was an activist, said Cohen, but ready to reconcile his own viewpoints and interests with those represented in Congress. He was ready, if necessary, "to educate constituents in order to alter any negative reaction of members of Congress," but "as a reasonable leader of a democracy, he was careful not to get too far behind or too far ahead of public opinion."

He saw himself as the leader not only of a party but of a nation. "He recognized his responsibility and accountability to the Congress as a whole and the people as a whole." He did not attach himself to "any dogma or school of thought" and his first cabinet included "not only Hull, Woodin and Roper with conservative leanings, but Progressives Wallace and Ickes with their early ties to the Republican Party," and he knew "he would need support from both parties, for rarely without some support from both parties can an important measure get through Congress intact."

"It was a Republican, Senator Vandenberg of Michigan," who, in the first hundred days, proposed a plan to guarantee bank deposits for which Vice President Garner and RFC chief Jesse Jones informed Roosevelt there was support in Congress. Roosevelt accepted it and it became "a jewel in the crown of New Deal legislation."

He hoped, he ended his speech, that President Carter and Vice President Mondale would establish "their own 'New Deal' in their own way and style." For himself, and for "most of us" in the audience, "our New Deal years were the best years of our lives." He sounded a note once struck by Elihu Root, "to be part of great things—that is life."

This book is an account of how a band of young men and women helped shape the "Roosevelt Revolution."

I

An Unusual Scholar

The Jewish peddler of the nineteenth century lived a grubby yet informed existence. An adventurous soul, he had avoided the crowded ghettos of the East Coast, particularly New York City, to build a life for himself and his family in the Midwest and South. Traveling with his cart and pack, he bought and sold, exchanged the news, and learned at firsthand the diversity and promise of rural and small-town America.

Benjamin V. Cohen was the son of an immigrant peddler from Grajewo, Poland, who came to the United States in 1874. Within eight years Moses Cohen had graduated from peddling and with the help of his in-laws started a scrap-iron shop in Muncie, Indiana. He had originally been drawn to Indianapolis by relatives who had settled there. Circumstances forced him to be a peddler, but he also tried to make his way as a melamed, a teacher of Hebrew. Soon he married Sarah Ringolsky and joined his father-in-law in the scrap-iron enterprise. The latter had emigrated from Lithuania in 1866 when Sarah was still a baby. In the 1880s the two families moved to Muncie.

"The Moses Cohen household was not kosher," Ben's nephew recalled.[1] "One Orthodox visitor would eat only hard-boiled eggs there—but Moses helped his sons and perhaps other Jewish boys in Muncie to learn Hebrew and Jewish history." Another kinsman reports a visit to Ben's mother, Sarah. "I wondered what would be safe to order in case Sarah was kosher, but your grandmother set me at ease by ordering a ham sandwich." Later she became a follower of Mary Baker Eddy and Christian Science.

Muncie, Indiana, is the town the Robert E. Lynds, the sociologists later made famous with their study of "Middletown," as they called Muncie, meaning that it was representative of America's small towns demographically, culturally, and geographically. Ben was born there in 1893, a depression year. At the time it numbered roughly fourteen thousand,* mostly Protestant. There were thirty to forty Jewish families. Most were assimilationist in outlook. They constituted a Reform congregation that held services twice a month. These were led by a student rabbi from Hebrew Union College of Cincinnati, Ohio, a hotbed of the Reform faith.

The Lynds give an intriguing account of Midwestern Jewish life in *Middletown,* then a city of some thirty-five thousand.[2] Although the Jewish population was so small "as to be numerically negligible," this predominantly Protestant community was mildly anti-Semitic. Jews were accepted socially but with "just enough qualification to make them aware that they do not entirely 'belong.'" The Lynds were struck, nevertheless, by the account of a speech in the 1920s by a Russian Jew, speaking in broken English at a "citizenship" dinner at Middletown's chamber of commerce. Fifty new citizens were the guests of the city's businessmen. Perhaps Ben's father, by then a successful dealer in scrap iron, was there. He had just gotten his own citizenship papers. The speech exemplified the sentiments of the Jewish newcomer bent upon becoming an American.

I came to this country expecting to find it a land of gold. But the gold I found in New York was carefully locked up in other people's banks. Slowly I came to realize that America is rich in another kind of gold. I was a peddler with a horse and wagon and one night I asked a farmer if I could stay on his farm. He himself unhitched my horse. I thought he was trying to take it away from me. Then he gave the horse real oats—the first it had ever eaten!—with his own horses; he took me in and fed me with his family—chicken and everything. When I came to leave I asked him what I owed and pulled out half a dollar. He shook his head and I saw my week's savings going. He said, "Young man, if you want to pay me, give up this wandering life, settle down, and when men and women come to you for help, pass on to them what I've done if you think it is worth anything!" The little Jew paused in embarrassment, wiped the perspiration from his forehead, and said: "I'm sorry I cannot speak better. I honor your schools that are teaching us. But I do want to say that you have gold in America—not paving your streets, but gold of this sort in the heart of your citizens, the gold which, too, makes each of us able to go all over the world with respect and safety as American citizens. We who have come to your land have left behind us our own ways of living and things dear to us; we gladly take yours and offer you all we possess—our fortunes and our children."

* U.S. Census, 1890, 11,345; 1900, 20,942.

No doubt the speaker, like other members of the small Jewish congregation in Muncie, intoned the traditional Jewish prayer, "Next year in Jerusalem," but it had a different meaning, one of sympathy and benevolence rather than inner hopes as when it was said in Eastern Europe.

The American Jews had fled torture, persecution, death in the lands of their birth. They had found "Zion" in the United States. It was no wonder, said a Jewish bicentennial speaker in Fort Wayne, Indiana, "that to the Jews America, a country in which equal justice would be meted out on the basis of personal merit and without intolerance, had a powerful appeal."[3]

Ben's mother's parents lived next door and they kept a kosher home. He went to Seder there and, taught by his father as well as the itinerant student rabbi, was able to read Hebrew. But he was always most conscious of being an American. He reached the age of confirmation believing, as he had been taught, that the only thing that distinguished him and his family "from our neighbors was our religion."[4]

Ben was the baby in the family, and an item in the local paper when he arrived reported, "another Republican was born." His father was fiercely Republican and Ben's childhood hero was Albert Beveridge, the Republican senator from Indiana, a "bit more" of an imperialist, "than I can accept in my later and less enterprising years," Ben said in the 1970s.

He attended public school and took great pride in it, but he was a "homebody" and spent most of his time at his studies. He considered himself a Hoosier American and when he was denied a part in a school play in which most of his schoolmates were given parts, he ascribed it to his manner of speech. Only later did it occur to him that it might have been anti-Semitism. His memories of life in Muncie were all good and he always thought there was "a great advantage in living in so small a town because you got in some way the benefit of an integrated and American society within a small compass."[5]

The Cohens moved to Chicago in the early twentieth century because of the success of two of their sons in the scrap-metal business there. Another period began in Ben's life.

"Added to this is the spirit of ambition which pervades your very being, and seems to make the day's work like a happy child at play," wrote Albert Einstein, then in Germany, in a New Year's greeting to America. Every young native American, other observers noted, is eligible to become president. "Bennie Cohen," as he signed himself in his boyhood years, had such an ambition as an earliest memory.

Whether the spark came from Ben's father or his mother, whether it was a function of a powerful mind that from early years on astonished his parents, or from the circumstance of being a young Jew in a largely Christian community, we do not know. In any event his parents enrolled him in University High, an elite high school in Chicago that was oriented toward the University of Chicago, which was located near its two buildings.

"Probably when I was young I said I wanted to be President," Ben recalled in his late eighties. "But even as a child I dropped the idea of becoming President, but still wanted a public career."[6] University High was hospitable to academic achievement. It was also coeducational with a lively social life of weekly dance classes and interclass activities. Ben did not participate in these. A classmate remembers him as "very quiet and good-looking too. He must have had some inferiority complex." He was self-effacing but quietly determined.[7]

Despite a voice that was high-pitched and nasal, he sought to master the art of public speaking by joining the school's Clay Club and made its debating team. The Clay Club reflected the interests of its namesake, law and political oratory. That drew Ben. Perhaps the spirit of Henry Clay, what it represented in American history in light of Ben's later career in politics, also attracted him. Though Clay never achieved the presidency, his career in law, which included a university professorship, fortified him for public activity. Even more presageful of Ben's future was the unique stamp Clay left on American politics, for he was famous before the Civil War for his ability to come up with solutions in the most intractable controversies. His name is linked with the Missouri Compromise in 1820, the Compromise Tariff of 1833, and the Compromise of 1850, again in the interests of saving the Union. Men called him the Great Pacificator or the Great Compromiser.

Henry Clay was a good aegis under which to begin. Said the school's *Daily* of its team's defeat in an interschool debate on the proposition, "RESOLVED: That the commission form of government should be adopted in Chicago," that although U High lost, "Cohen, the original 'Henry Clay' took all the honors." He made "an excellent speech and proved that the commission form of government was of no use for such a large city." Aside from debates, the Clay Club's meetings were filled with extemporaneous oratory and readings. The club held mock trials and visited the circuit court. Because of his high-pitched voice, Cohen was not the star in the club, but what Ben was unable to achieve there, not to mention on the dance floor and sports field, he more than made up for in the classroom. As graduation approached in May 1911, *The Correlator*, the school's yearbook, published the photographs of the senior class and next to Ben's portrait, that of a neat-looking boy, wrote:

At the early age of four, Ben Victor Cohen was discovered by his parents munching an algebra. They at once entered him in U. High, where he has continued to devour books, becoming a prize student and a delight unto his teachers. We like Ben even if he does study. It takes all kinds of people to make a school, so Ben is in the right place. Senior year—Debating Team; Clay Club.[8]

There were twenty-one students in the graduating class. He alone listed his prospective occupation as "lawyer."

He matriculated at the University of Chicago when he was sixteen. His ambition was clear:

When I found out that I couldn't be President I wanted to be prepared for any public job in the domestic or foreign field that might come along. In preparation for such readiness I didn't want to stop at the University of Chicago. The last two years at Chicago I spent on Law studies. I took more courses than was required and went to summer school every summer. I got scholarships.[9]

A demon for work he finished college in three years. The first summer he took algebra and trigonometry, in which he received A's, but a course in public speaking brought him only a B. That was to be the pattern in his undergraduate studies—all A's, except public speaking. "I didn't speak well because I had trouble with breathing—otherwise my record was all A's." In 1913 he was elected to Phi Beta Kappa and in June 1914, at the age of twenty-one, he received his Ph.D, with honors in Law, Political Economy, and Political Science. In 1915 the Chicago University Law School awarded him a J.D. Again he had made all A's and was graduated cum laude.

His undergraduate language had been German, which he thought of as the language of Goethe and also the lingua franca of serious scholarship. He was no radical, but it was the mark of a progressive spirit that he elected to take a course in Trade Unionism in 1913 which he followed with a seminar on Research in Labor Problems.

For someone interested in politics as Ben was, 1912 was the year of dramatic events in Chicago. It was an unusual presidential year. Theodore Roosevelt had bolted the Republican Party after a GOP steamroller in June had renominated William Taft, the incumbent president. Around a defiant TR a new host had arisen, the Bull Moose or Progressive Party. Roosevelt accepted its designation in August on a militant platform that called for women's suffrage, the direct election of senators, reduced tariffs, and advanced social welfare measures. For fifty-two minutes fifteen thousand men and women stood on their feet, "wildly waving red bandannas" as they roared their welcome to TR. He did not disappoint them. "We stand at Armageddon and we battle for the Lord," his fiery speech ended.

Few liberal spirits in Chicago were not touched by the Bull Moosers. At the university Ben helped organize the progressive club. His heroes were Harold Ickes, a militant reformer who had emerged as a leader of the Illinois progressives, and a university professor, Charles Merriam. Roosevelt lost with 4,119,538 votes to Woodrow Wilson's 6,293,454 while Taft trailed with 3,484,980. Ben's part in it, although small, showed the direction of his sympathies.

There was another candidate in that election, Eugene Victor Debs, the leader of America's socialists. He polled close to a million votes, the highest the socialists ever would receive. Although Ben shared the middle name of Victor with Debs, he was not among his supporters despite the pressures on him to become such. One of his professors thought it "too bad that I had decided to go into law rather than one of the radical movements." Even at that time Ben was a practitioner of mainstream politics.[10]

Despite his unique academic record at the university and law school, he had another infirmity in addition to weakness in public speaking. He did not have a commanding presence, and, as a classmate said, "Ben was very awkward physically."

Man as incomplete, searching for the other, is a frequent theme in poetry and philosophy. George Eliot in *Daniel Deronda* cites the Cabalah to explain the consumptive Mordecai's search for another, more beautiful, more executive self to incorporate and fulfill his vision of a reunited Jewish people in a new Jerusalem:

Certain incapacities of his own had made the sentence of exclusion; and hence it was that his imagination had constructed another man who would be something more than the second soul bestowed, according to the notion of the Cabalists, to help out the insufficient first . . .[11]

There already was in young Ben Cohen a haunting sense of insufficiency. To the natural striving of most people to find another who will bring out the better angels in their nature, there was added the realization that he lacked a presence that dominated and commanded. He read, analyzed, understood better than everyone around him and his sweet nature made him a delight to those who appreciated intelligence and sensitivity, but the ideas and visions that thronged his brain required others to bring them to fruition.

II

Harvard and World War I

"My family was not wealthy," Ben said of the period after he was graduated from the University of Chicago, "but when I went on to Harvard to do graduate work I brought my tuition money with me." At the Harvard Law School he fell into the golden embrace of Professor Felix Frankfurter.

For a man who wished to immerse himself in the public's business via the law, the encounter with the dazzling Frankfurter was providential. Frankfurter had been appointed to teach at the law school the year before in 1914 when he was only thirty-two. A wealth of practical experience informed his teaching. He had been assistant U.S. attorney under Henry Stimson, joined the latter's gubernatorial campaign in 1910 to draft position papers and write speeches, and moved on with him when he became President Taft's Secretary of War.

But Frankfurter's heart really was in law and, though neither the law school nor the bench was ever able to contain his bubbling energies, the law was his mistress. Five feet five, with bluish gray eyes that were alive with intelligence, Frankfurter had accepted appointment in Cambridge in the profound belief that the world's problems were amenable to reason, an advocate of the "Wisconsin idea" that politics should be administered by the intelligence and rationality of university-trained men.[1]

Ben took to Felix and Felix took to the gifted Ben. For many years the relationship was to be a dominant one in Ben's life. Frankfurter's aim at the law school was to fix the attention of his students on the legislative and administrative processes.

"Law students leave the Law Schools," he had written Justice Oliver Wendell Holmes, "ignorant and indifferent to legislation," and he proposed to change that. Ben's temperament was melancholic. That, too, on the principle that opposites attract each other, drew him to Felix. The latter was buoyant and optimistic, so much so that Harold J. Laski, a budding political scientist doing graduate work at Harvard, described his friend Felix to Holmes as "nervously restless . . . dashing here and there in a kind of creative fertility that drives me to despair."

"Felix liked to arrange things—mainly good things," commented Ben laconically in 1982.[2] "I think I have a clearer idea now of his outlook than when I was younger." Ben arrived in Cambridge in September 1915, just twenty-one. Frankfurter, the friend of Holmes and Louis D. Brandeis, awed him. Felix talked like forked electricity but it was informed talk, always to a purpose. He already was on the lookout for young intellects that his creative energies might fertilize, and while he was partial to young men who were from "good" families, providing they had brains, he prized intelligence above all. When he heard that Ben had made the highest record ever at the University of Chicago, he took him to his heart, telling his good friend Brandeis, then practicing law in Boston and soon to be appointed by Woodrow Wilson to the Supreme Court, about this intellectual prodigy.

The courses Ben took at Harvard were equity, jurisprudence, and Roman Law, in all of which he scored in the high 70s, where 75 and up equaled an A. Felix gave him his highest grade in Public Utilities, an 81. Felix had not yet begun to supply law clerks to Holmes and Brandeis, but Julian W. Mack, a judge on the court of appeals, the most influential Jew among Harvard's alumni, was a good friend. On Felix's recommendation Ben became Mack's law clerk.

The genial Mack became devoted to him, as he became to Mack, but after a year Ben was ready to move on. He consulted the dean of the law school, Roscoe Pound. The Nebraskan, who had been appointed to the faculty in 1909, like Felix and Ben had "a sociological conception of jurisprudence." Ben asked Pound about a teaching post. Pound wrote Mack:

I have just heard of a very attractive opening in a New York law office which I really think would be worth Cohen's while. Even if he intends to teach ultimately it would do him no harm to have a certain [period of] apprenticeship in an office.

Ben evidently demurred. As he said later, "I never thought of going into private law practice. My decision was for a public career in matters relating to the law." In this spirit he seems to have written the dean, who replied:

Dear Cohen:

I think on the whole you probably have to go into the office for a few years if only [because] the University Presidents and Trustees are inclined to demand what they are pleased to call "practical experience." As to the matter of "punch," that is born in men not acquired. I think you have sufficient latent in your system, but what you need is a little of the self-confidence which comes from experience, and enables one to use his latent punch effectively.[3]

A few weeks after Ben received this letter the United States entered the war. Ben's attitude toward the United States' involvement is nowhere recorded but in the absence of other evidence one may assume that he shared the attitude of his mentors—Mack, Brandeis, and Frankfurter, all of whom accepted the necessity, nay, welcomed United States entry. "I'm at rest that we are in it," Frankfurter wrote Learned Hand. "No other way, I believe, could we have had a responsible opportunity for a hand in European, and therefore, world ordering. That's the objective of all my dreaming."[4]

Frankfurter, like Ben, had supported TR and the progressives in 1912, but Brandeis had been for Wilson. He supported Wilson in 1916. So did Frankfurter who held it in Wilson's favor that in addition to his advocacy of a League to Enforce the Peace he had appointed Brandeis to the Supreme Court. "I can't get Father to admit any regret over our entrance into the war," wrote Brandeis's daughter Elizabeth. "He calls it highly desirable, and thinks the world more hopeful than at any time since 1848 with more basis of permanent gain now than then."[5]

By the summer of 1917 Frankfurter was in Washington as assistant to the Secretary of War, Newton D. Baker. "Mr. Wilson has charge of foreign policy and Felix seems to sponsor the rest of the government," Laski reported to Holmes. "To my certain knowledge he directs the War Department . . . I saw that he has almost annexed the Shipping Board . . ." Laski's hyperbole reflected Frankfurter's growing talent for finding and placing young lawyers in the many new wartime agencies. Among the latter was Ben who had gone to work for the Shipping Board. Its chief counsel was a fatherly figure, Edward B. Burling of the distinguished Washington law firm Covington Burling.

Like most young Americans Ben did not want to stay out of uniform. He was almost twenty-five and eligible, so far as age went, for military service. But repeated efforts to go into the service brought from the draft board a firm rejection, "not qualified for active military duty because of eyes." In July 1918 he tried to circumvent the disqualification by application for Officers Training School. Burling urged the school to admit him. "He has for more than a year past been one of the attorneys for the United States Shipping Board of which I am Chief Counsel . . . His chief characteristic, I should say, is an active and complete devotion to whatever duty is placed upon him." Everyone at the Shipping Board felt his place was there.

But he now feels that the demand for men in France is so great that in spite of his special fitness for the work he has been doing here, he feels he ought to get into active service. In this decision of his I can only acquiesce, although if there were any supreme authority capable of assigning to each man the work for which he is best fitted, I believe Mr. Cohen, in view of his peculiar fitness for his work here, would be ordered to continue his present task.[6]

Again Ben failed his medical. "Physically unfit for active military duty," the examiner recorded, because of "very defective vision in both eyes." Barred from military service, Ben was determined to get closer to where decisive events were taking place. The eyes of most progressives were turned toward Russia where the Tsar had been overthrown and the Bolsheviks had seized power. Again Burling interceded on Ben's behalf. "I understand that Mr. Cohen has applied for any service in Russia that the Government may see fit to assign him," he wrote the Secretary of State. "Mr. Cohen is a man of extraordinarily brilliant intellect." The State Department was not interested. The name "Cohen" may have automatically disbarred him.

Which was the department's loss—it deprived itself of a man of rare analytical talents. As the commissioner of the Shipping Board wrote Cohen in September 1918 about a new schedule of rates of compensation for refrigerated vessels that Ben had drafted:

It gives me great pleasure to be able to advise you that the very clear manner in which the entire matter was prepared, greatly facilitated the Board in arriving at its conclusion, which was to adopt the rate therein worked out.[7]

Less than two months later the armistice that ended the war was signed, and at the end of December Ben was on a ship bound for London.

III

The
Zionist Experience

Among the hidden threads of history, the Balfour Declaration that
pledged the British government to the creation of a Jewish homeland in
Palestine is one of the most important in the weaving of the New Deal
fabric. It first brought together in intense collaboration a group of talented
American Jews who would play pivotal roles in the New Deal's regeneration of American politics and economics. And the group's experience with
the practical problems of re-creating a state out of Zionist longings and
rhetoric predisposed them to the pragmatic, step-by-step approach of
Roosevelt's revolution.

"In January 1919, at the request of Justice Brandeis and Judge Julian
W. Mack, I, then a young lawyer and a novice in the Zionist movement,"
wrote Ben in 1971, when he was disenchanted with Felix Frankfurter or he
surely would have included him, "embarked for London and Paris to help
the Zionist leaders present their case at the Peace Conference and at the
conferences to follow, concerning the Palestine mandate. I was also to
serve as a sort of liaison officer between the American and European Zionists."[1] Without power or authority except what his intellect gave him, the
twenty-five-year-old Cohen suddenly found himself at the center of things.

London and Versailles in 1919 were magnets to which all statesmen were attracted. Mankind hoped the four years of destruction might indeed lead to an organized effort to prevent future wars. Jews throughout the world shared in such hopes with an added awareness, almost electric in intensity, that after centuries of pogroms, persecutions, and dispersions, the Balfour Declaration which pledged the British in 1917 to establish in Palestine a national home for the Jewish people suddenly made "Next year in Jerusalem" an issue of practical politics.

The Jewish delegation at Versailles had its hearing before the Big Four on February 4, 1919. Its leader, Chaim Weizmann, presented the classic Jewish case for a homeland in Palestine. The document he presented had been drafted earlier in London in the Savoy Hotel room of a European Zionist leader, Julius Simon, who was to become a lifelong friend of Ben's.[2] The small meeting included Ahad ha-Am, the venerable spokesman for Zionist humanism, as well as the twenty-five-year-old Ben. "We agreed to state the Zionist cause in two short paragraphs," said Simon.

From London Ben went on to Paris to sit with the American Jewish delegation to the peace conference, which included Judge Mack, Rabbi Stephen Wise, and Felix Frankfurter. When the Americans left for home Ben remained behind as the representative of American Zionism at the Zionist offices in London that Simon had set up at 77 Great Russell Street.

Ben's ability to break down a complicated political and economic problem into manageable components already was recognized and Weizmann handed him the job of working with representatives of the British Foreign Office to spell out the mandate that would be incorporated in the Turkish treaty with Great Britain confirmed as the mandatory power.

The political institutions that were to replace the British military power in Palestine had to be established and the Jewish role in the government of Palestine under the mandatory described. Arab ambitions had to be conciliated, boundaries agreed to. Everything was in motion.

Confronted by a snake pit of ambitions and rivalries, Ben quickly became known in the Zionist offices for his readiness to work around the clock as well as for his analytical talents. In addition, he regularly sent Brandeis and Mack voluminous reports that were models of order, clarity, and detailed exposition.[3]

He also led an intense private life. In Washington one of his high school classmates had vainly tried to get him to go out on a double date. He ascribed Ben's refusal to do so to his shyness with girls; moreover, he was too high-minded to undertake romance casually.[4] In London he fell deeply in love with Ella Winters. She had been Frankfurter's secretary in Versailles, having just graduated from the London School of Economics with a first. Graham Wallas had sent her to Felix and when the latter's sister Stella came to London to attend the London School of Economics, Felix sent cables to Ella and Ben about her coming. Ben greeted Stella with a "bed and breakfast" list. He had to patronize "economic" eating places. Judge Mack was underwriting his expenses and he lived abstemiously. Fortunately, he was indifferent to food and to clothes. He often saw Stella and his twenty-two-year-old secretary Margery Abrahams. Her father was a distinguished surgeon, her mother a concert pianist, and she had a flat in Queen Ann's Gate. She had read history at Oxford and never even heard of Herzl, the founder of Zionism, when she went to work in the Zionist offices. Ben was, she recalled in 1983, "brilliant, absolutely honest. His virtue was his legal knowledge. Things had to be just right. He was devoted to Brandeis and Frankfurter and committed to the idea of a Jewish homeland." Had she loved him? "Oh yes. It was quite natural when you meet a young man of that caliber, but he had no emotional interest in me."

"He was devoted to someone else who wasn't interested in him. It was Ella Winter." Later Margery Abrahams wrote this author from Sussex: "It was Professor Cannon of the London School of Economics who described the frills and furbelows Ella Winter hung on the staff pegs to those of the Queen of Sheba. She was very attractive, with a fresh pink complexion, though not really beautiful, but she had a ready wit."[5] Her lack of interest hit Ben hard and accentuated misgivings about his want of forcefulness. "Ben was not made for marriage," said Stella. "His rising inflection kept women off . . . I couldn't imagine anyone being in love with Ben." Ella had set her cap for "greatness," Stella believed, and soon thereafter married Lincoln Steffens. The temperamentally melancholic young lawyer became even more so.

In subsequent years Ben never spoke of his love for Ella. But the two years he spent in the London Zionist offices were shadowed by a weltschmerz that Ella's unresponsiveness only deepened.

Apart from these few women, Ben's friends at the time were largely Frankfurter's former law students who came through London, among them Max Lowenthal who had clerked for Mack the year before Ben did and Louis Harris who had worked his way through Harvard and salvaged the family's substantial raincoat business. A note to Ben from Lowenthal:

Lou Harris is planning to leave here in February for a visit to Palestine, and will undoubtedly see you in London. Lord knows when I'm to be freed from bondage [of his private practice]. I haven't the courage of, let us say, Felix Frankfurter. Frida Laski said the other day that [the thing] she most admired in Felix [was] that he doesn't care for money.[6]

Where did Ben get his feeling about Zionism? What did being a Jew mean to him? What he said about the men who were his mentors, in particular Brandeis, Mack, and Frankfurter, shed some light about his own feelings. "Mack identified with his fellow Jews, whether Russian, Polish, or German; they were his people, so he had to work with them and for them. He felt responsible."[7]

Mack began as an assimilationist but became a Zionist whose guiding star was the re-creation of a Jewish homeland, although he showed no interest in settling in Palestine.

Ben's parents were somewhere in between the assimilationists and the Zionists. They came from Poland, then under the Russian yoke, and had settled in Muncie, Indiana. The farther west Jews went from New York, the less involved they were with Judaism as a religion and Palestine as a cause. The greatest spur to Jewish fellow-feeling was the attitude of the non-Jewish world. "What is a Jew, anyway?" a youthful Walter Lippmann asked an equally young Felix Frankfurter, who replied, "A Jew is a person whom non-Jews regard as a Jew."

"Frankfurter was not an observant Jew," Ben wrote in two pages of notes in 1965 for Professor Paul Freund, "but he was very proud of his Jewish heritage. He did not profess to be learned in the Torah or Talmud but he would frequently amaze his friends with the bits and pieces of Jewish wit and lore he somehow managed to acquire. He became active in the Zionist movement for a Jewish homeland in Palestine in the early days of the first World War when his friends, Mr. Louis D. Brandeis and Judge Julian W. Mack, assumed positions of leadership in the movement."[8]

A few years later Ben responded to Freund's request for notes on Brandeis's Jewish activities. That was "much more difficult to deal with . . . than F.F.'s . . . more involved and complex but more significant." He noted that Brandeis's parents, who had settled in the United States after the failure of the 1848 revolution in Germany, "observed no formal religion," were partisans of no particular formula or religious belief although they believed in God. Brandeis himself "never disavowed being a Jew but until past fifty he took no significant part in any Jewish activities." In those years he condemned what President Theodore Roosevelt had called "hyphenated Americanism." Brandeis's Jewish consciousness was first awakened in 1910 when he was called in to mediate a garment workers' strike in New York and was surprised to feel "a genuine kinship with these Jewish workers and their employers and was struck by their great capacity for placing themselves in the other fellows' shoes." That same year Brandeis met Jacob de Haas, a Jewish journalist, who stimulated his interest in Zionism. He came to recognize "the value of pluralism in American life," wrote Ben, "and in contrast to his 1905 dictum against hyphenated Americanism wrote: 'My approach to Zionism was through Americanism. In time practical experience and observation convinced me that Jews were by reason of their tradition and their character peculiarly fitted for the attainment of American ideals. Gradually it became clear to me that to be good Americans, we must be better Jews, and to be better Jews, we must become Zionists.' "

In the matter of Zionism, Judge Mack was considered Brandeis's "prime minister," and as such at Versailles: "He always sought to calm the ruffled feelings of egotists and prima donnas with whom he worked and thus gave them credit not only for their own work, but (also) for his. Even saints history remembers had much more of an ego than he had."[9]

Ben appreciated people who kept the machinery of great movements oiled and functioning. In London he worked with most of the major spokesmen for the Zionist cause, and he was "particularly drawn to a thoughtful, soft-spoken gentleman," Julius Simon, a German Zionist and a close friend of Chaim Weizmann. Ben's affection for Simon was reminiscent of his praise of Mack. They were both modest and selfless men. Neither secured the recognition he deserved, Ben wrote, and Ben's friends in later years would feel the same about him. His friendship with Julius Simon and his beautiful wife, Joanna, became one of his closest ones. He remembered Simon's children in his will.

At the beginning of World War I, Simon got no farther than Holland when the Zionists coopted him to move Zionist headquarters from Berlin to neutral territory. At the Hague, he met Nehemiah de Lieme, the spiritual leader of the Zionist organization in Holland as well as its president. De Lieme was a hardheaded businessman who laid the foundations for a farsighted land policy in Palestine. Through Simon, de Lieme also became a good friend of Ben and an ally in the struggle to keep Brandeis and Weizmann together.

Weizmann "relied on Ben and said proudly he was of East European origin," recalled Margery Abrahams.[10] And Ben admired Weizmann. "He was not only the head of the Zionist Organization but the confidant of Balfour and his government," he said. His experiments with alcohol "were so advanced, they're only beginning to show effect now—his ideas that power and energy could be used to create food and his dreams of the way to multiply crops in the tropical zone."

In the summer of 1919, at the close of the Supreme Court session,

Brandeis visited London, Paris, and Palestine. Ben gave a brief account of the visit in the notes he prepared for Paul Freund:

In London he met Dr. Weizmann for the first time. Both were favorably impressed with one another, but both felt a certain reserve in the company of the other. In London and Paris he met and conferred with President Wilson, Lord Balfour and other high American, British and French statesmen attending the Peace Conference.* In Palestine he was enthusiastic about the beauty of the country and its latent possibilities and the indomitable spirit of the Jewish settlers. But he found their problems and difficulties even more serious than he had anticipated. He was greatly disturbed by the lack of business methods and budgetary controls in the handling of Zionist funds. He saw that malaria was sapping the energies of the settlers and he urged that priority be given to an all-out effort to stamp it out.

On Brandeis's way back through London he startled most of the Zionist leaders who had been assembled to hear him, especially the East Europeans, by his plea that immigration be suspended until malaria was stamped out.

At the same meeting of the "Actions Committee," as the directing group of the world organization was called, a behind-the-scenes episode foreshadowed trouble ahead. Simon drafted a resolution on the composition of the Jewish Agency that the Zionists were proposing for inclusion in the mandate as the Jewish directing body under the British mandatory in Palestine. Brandeis to whom he showed it said, "Okay." Weizmann, however, amended the draft to include wider representation. In particular, he wanted to include the Jewish Minority Councils of Eastern Europe. That, said Brandeis, would make the agency unmanageable. Moreover, unstated, but no doubt present, was his belief it would feed the idea of "Diaspora Nationalism," the conviction that *all* Jews the world over owed political and national loyalty to a Jewish peoplehood, a concept to which the Americans were opposed. When the amendment was shown to Brandeis, he wrote tersely "No L.D.B." Whereupon Weizmann passionately opposed the resolution and the resulting tie vote was broken only when Brandeis summoned de Haas, who had accompanied him to Palestine, to cast his ballot. The vote, said Simon, left Weizmann "white with rage." Simon went to Weizmann's room. The latter almost wept. "You have left me without arms to fight," he said, meaning East European Jews would be less enthusiastic in their support of the Zionist cause. The next day Vera Weizmann told Simon, "You have wounded Chaim to the heart," and later

* In April 1917 Lord Balfour headed an extraordinary British delegation to Washington after America's entry into the war. He had met Brandeis at a dinner given by President Wilson and said after his return to London, "Mr. Brandeis, in some ways, was the most remarkable man I met in the United States."

he learned that Weizmann had told his wife, "He shall never pass my door again."

Brandeis returned to the United States aware that Simon and de Lieme were two European Zionist leaders sympathetic to his tough-minded approach to Palestine's economic problems and that in Ben he had a rare collaborator whose views were balanced and poised.

The effort to reconcile Brandeis and Weizmann became part of Ben's task in London. He was too young, too much the newcomer to consider himself a leader of the movement. Yet gradually a group emerged in the London office which had Weizmann's confidence and also shared the pragmatic viewpoint of the American Zionists led by Brandeis and Mack. Its members, in addition to Ben, were Julius Simon, the prewar leader of German Zionism, de Lieme of the Hague, young Robert Szold, a Frankfurter protégé who was sent to Palestine to represent the American viewpoint, and Paul Singer, a Viennese Zionist who became treasurer of the London organization.

"I don't know whether your letters to LDB are official or unofficial," Judge Mack wrote Ben in a discussion of financial developments in Palestine. "I rather think that you regard them as unofficial inasmuch as you have read only parts of them to Simon."[11] "Dear Judge," Ben replied in longhand, "It is not always easy to retain a calm spirit and clear mind over here but I suppose it is my duty to keep on trying for awhile." He warned de Haas of "the almost emotional feelings of Eastern Jewry." He hoped such passions would not "unduly influence" the proceedings of a world Zionist meeting slated for the summer . . . "I am in deep distress over the political outlook. . . ."

Despite Zionist alarums the Allied powers—notably Britain and France —were moving toward conclusion of a peace treaty with Turkey. Ben was at the hub of the negotiations with the British Foreign Office over the terms of the mandate.

"Situation critical but not unhopeful," Ben cabled New York as he left for San Remo. Weizmann on his way back from Palestine had summoned him. Weizmann had gone to Jerusalem to check the depth and extent of Arab riots. The Jewish leader was under a twofold pressure—from the East Europeans in particular and some of the militants in Palestine who urged a more aggressive policy toward the Arabs, the British, and the American Zionists; and, secondly, from the British including Lord Balfour, the great friend of the Zionists, that he keep his adherents in Palestine under control. Occasionally Weizmann lashed out at the American Zionists, rejecting their impatience with his taking into account British imperial interests, a British position, he dryly noted, that was not unlike United States operations under the Monroe Doctrine.

Such comparisons created trouble, Felix Frankfurter warned "Dear Weitzie":

I shudder to think where we would have been or would be without you. But you must restrain your impatience with us—and really trust us to know things in America better than you can possibly know them. After all, whatever your dissatisfaction with us here do remember that it was Brandeis and the others who have brought American Zionism where it is—that have aroused American Jewry as it has been aroused.

Frankfurter ended that he would see Weizmann the following summer in Basel, "And this time, as you know, I shall have a wife with me. Yes, I know you must be sad that she is a *shikse,* but that's one of those ultimates which are beyond discussion."

Brandeis and Frankfurter relied on Cohen because of his sense of responsibility and intelligence, but that young man was impatient to return to the United States and begin his career in law and politics. He favored Palestine as a refuge for Jews without a homeland but he did not consider settling there himself. He wished to return to the United States and while some of his Zionist colleagues pressed him to emigrate, his refusal to do so was definite.

Weizmann's impatience with the Americans did not affect Ben and they worked well together at San Remo on the terms of the mandate which was finally given to Great Britain.

Julius Simon, who observed the events firsthand, wrote of Ben and the mandate:

He worked hard on the final wording of the Mandate and succeeded in embodying in it the first part of the "Savoy Hotel" formula and the recognition of the Zionist Organization as the "Jewish Agency" for the purpose of advising and cooperating with the administration in Palestine in . . . "matters as may effect the establishment of the Jewish National Home." He also secured in the body of the Mandate the inclusion of the provision that "The administration of Palestine . . . shall facilitate Jewish immigration . . . and shall encourage . . . close settlement by Jews on the land," and "arrange with the Jewish Agency . . . to construct or operate . . . any public works, services and utilities and develop any of the natural resources of the country."

Ben's contribution was indispensable, in Simon's view, though "the lion's share" of the credit belonged to Weizmann. The terms of the mandate still had to go to the League of Nations for approval.*

* The Council of the League of Nations did approve the mandate on June 24, 1922. On December 3, 1924, a Palestine Convention between the United States and Great Britain was signed in which the United States formally recognized and accepted the mandate.

An Associated Press story, datelined San Remo, gave Ben's appraisal of the political results of the conference:

"Zionism as a political movement has ended," said Mr. Cohen today. "With the creation of a national Jewish home, its work now is the development of Palestine and the bringing there of Jewish immigrants from Eastern Europe. The development will be largely agricultural. Palestine now has a population of 700,000. In the time of David it had 2,000,000. It can really support two or three times 700,000 . . .
"The plans of the Zionists are that we shall work with the hands rather than with the brain, as the Jews have been doing for the most part in other portions of the world. It will be an interesting social experiment. It will not be socialistic, but I think it may be called social . . ."[12]

Ben dispatched a long statement to Brandeis that ended:

On the whole I do not believe that we should feel dissatisfied. The situation has not been free from many difficulties, and the fact that Britain went considerably out of the beaten path of Allied procedure to insist on the declaration coming into the Turkish Treaty should be a source of considerable satisfaction to all of us.

There was lavish praise from America for Ben's contribution to the successful outcome. "You had the brunt of the work. I hope you'll feel that you had the reward, too, in having been at San Remo yesterday & having participated in full in bringing about the result," Judge Mack wrote him. Simon, who was in the United States where he had been summoned by Brandeis, wrote sympathetically, "You have a hard time behind you, but now the worst is over. Everybody is very happy here save me, although I fully realize the difference between the San Remo decision and now. I anticipate however very difficult conditions of work now because the Treaty does not contain anything more than the old declaration." Simon's pessimism was also fed by the shallowness of the Zionist roots in America that he had discovered. Except for the group of brilliant leaders around Brandeis, Mack, and Frankfurter, the organization had little hold on rank-and-file Jews and none at all on the affluent American Jews who were opposed to Zionism.

"Brandeis told the Executive Committee," Mack wrote in a follow-up letter, "Mr. Ben Cohen who has been invaluable to us—none of you having had detailed knowledge of what he has done, can form a conception of how valuable and indispensable he has been to us . . ." The plaudits made Ben impatient. He was unhappy over the inability of world Zionism to provide the means "to give our initial start in Palestine a sound and healthy foundation. And, of course, as you doubtless know, it is utterly impossible, in any circumstances, for me to remain here for more than two or three months longer."

He was equally firm with Judge Mack, whose letter of congratulations he found

somewhat undeserved and out of place. It has been only a twist of circumstances that has placed me here at the pivot of things and it has not been given to me to do anything worthy of appreciation and gratitude.

I am deeply concerned about the future organization of our forces. The San Remo decision is a great challenge to us, and few outside the inner circle realise how enormous our tasks are and how grave are our responsibilities. I do hope that Mrs. Mack's health will be such that you can come this summer, because I feel that so much depends upon the work of the summer. The constructive, directive forces must be organised and the effective coordination of effort secured; time will brook no further delay. You, who can read between the lines, know that I write this not as an empty and futile polemic. I am anxious to see a Congress this summer, because I fear tradition and authority will otherwise stand in the way of the carrying out of our plans and needlessly delay our constructive endeavors for months . . .

You can hardly imagine how anxious I am to see all of you. The last few weeks are in some respects the most trying of all. But time must run through the roughest hours.

The nexus of the Zionist political problem, as the first postwar world Zionist conference approached, was to assure the cooperation of Weizmann and Brandeis on a program of practical political work in Palestine. That was the way Ben, Julius, de Lieme, and Singer saw it. Simon returned to London on the same boat that brought Brandeis and the American delegation to the conference. On the way over he, de Haas, and other members of the delegation urged Brandeis to leave the bench and become the leader of world Zionism in meeting the Palestine challenge. Frankfurter alone demurred. It was Brandeis's duty to the American liberal cause, as the only Jew to be appointed to the Supreme Court, he insisted, "to stay at his present post." Simon did not believe the issue had been settled in the justice's mind and when he reached London, "I went straight to Weizmann who asked me: 'What message do you bring from America?' I said: 'Chaim, you have rendered an immortal service to the cause of Zionism. Now I ask you to crown your work by offering leadership to Brandeis.' " Weizmann did not respond but later, when Simon told the story to Frankfurter, the latter commented, "You could not have said anything worse."[13]

Brandeis was elected chairman of the London conference. He promptly disenchanted the oration-minded Europeans by the brevity of his opening statement. The conference should get down to business, he enjoined it. "Is this the great American leader?" the Europeans, accustomed to impassioned oratory, which many of them identified with deeds, asked themselves. Disillusionment gave way to resentment when word spread that Brandeis was writing off the veteran European leaders. They had played a historic role in bringing the Zionist cause thus far, but most of them, as Simon understood Brandeis's position, he considered "the propagandists of Zionism. What the movement now needed were builders." So Simon recalled the opening events.

Brandeis approached Lord Reading, who had been viceroy of India and was then chief justice. Lloyd George had said publicly: "The two men who, during the war, rendered the most outstanding services to the British Government were Jews. One was Lord Reading and the other Weizmann."[14] Out of Brandeis's talks with Lord Reading came the "Reading Plan."

Ben's notes for Paul Freund recalled what happened: "Brandeis was bitterly opposed to the diversion of funds raised for Palestine settlement for activities not essential to such settlement or for activities outside of Palestine. To carry out his ideas, Brandeis discussed with Dr. Weizmann, Mr. Sokolow and with Lord Reading a plan to have the [London] conference authorize a small executive with plenary powers over Zionist settlement in Palestine for a three-year term. A draft of this plan in reasonable detail was then agreed upon between Brandeis and Lord Reading."[15]

The small executive would have consisted of Weizmann and Sokolow "because of their relations with the mandatory power and because of the confidence that a large part of the Jews throughout the world had in them. The other members would be men of great business capacity. Sir Alfred Mond and Mr. James de Rothschild, both Zionists, though not active in the organization were, with the aid of Lord Reading, to secure one or two British Jewish industrialists to serve with them. Bernard Flexner, an American lawyer with extensive business experience, was also to be a member."

In Simon's account of the rise and fall of the Reading Plan, he adds an important note. Reading said to Brandeis: " 'You are acquainted with the conditions in Anglo-Saxon countries, so we, the British, can agree that the Zionists on the Executive form the majority, if you will be the fourth Zionist member.' Brandeis was willing."

Ben's notes for Freund went on: "At first Dr. Weizmann was greatly attracted by the plan and the new strength it would bring to the organization. But when he found his old colleagues from Eastern Europe were offended by their exclusion from the proposed Palestine Executive, he felt the tug of divided loyalties, and without notice to Brandeis, called on Mond and de Rothschild, expressed misgivings about the plan and suggested a substitute which Brandeis considered entirely inadequate and which caused Mond and de Rothschild, disturbed by the prospect of internal strife, to withdraw.

"Brandeis's confidence in Weizmann was shattered by Weizmann's undermining his plan without prior notice to him, and he forthwith decided that he would accept no responsibility for the work of the World Organization."

Simon described the rupture more melodramatically. Simon had already gone to bed when an excited Frankfurter and Cohen knocked at his door and told him of Weizmann's meeting with Mond and de Rothschild and urged him to hurry to the conference. "When I arrived there, all was over. The 'Reading Plan' was dead." Simon begged Weizmann the next day to make an effort to mend the damage. "But Brandeis was unapproachable. He said: 'Dr. Weizmann, you are not a man with whom I can work.' "

Ben did not hold Brandeis blameless. He agreed that it was necessary to bring in "fresh blood and business ability" and that the plan worked out with Lord Reading was feasible but he saw Weizmann's difficulties:

Weizmann was eager to secure and retain the cooperation of American Jewry under Brandeis' leadership. He probably shared more of Brandeis' ideas than most of his Eastern European colleagues and probably did give Brandeis the impression he was going along with his plan. But if Brandeis had not been so deeply absorbed in his own plan, he might have been more conscious of the inner conflict within Weizmann in sponsoring a plan which would have called upon his old comrades in arms from Eastern Europe to turn over the increasingly important management of the organization to a small group of Western Jews loosely affiliated with, or newcomers to, the Zionist movement. It is possible that Weizmann, sensing that Mond and de Rothschild might be more sensitive to the dilemma than Brandeis, called the meeting in the hope that they could help him find a way out of the dilemma.[16]

Despite the break between Brandeis and Weizmann, the former's influence at the London conference continued strong, and at the suggestion of the American delegation Simon and de Lieme, practical idealists, were added to the Zionist executive with the understanding they would head up Zionist work in Palestine. The two went to Maidenhead on the Thames where Brandeis was resting to discuss the principles that should guide their work. Brandeis turned up with Ben and they went over a proposed budget. Brandeis questioned "a high subvention," as Simon put it, for Palestine's school system. The limited Zionist funds should go primarily to finance immigration and settlement, he said. "He spoke of the early American settlers," wrote Simon, and the problems they surmounted in educating their children and concluded, "We must develop in Palestine the spirit of Anglo-Saxon manhood." Simon and de Lieme had been elected to the executive because they enjoyed the confidence of the Americans, but even they were startled by the analogy. "The Europeans never forgot it," Ben told Mack's biographer. "Brandeis was in a sense, to them, an Anglo-Saxon *friend,* not a warm and committed Jew. That does not mean Brandeis was not warm and committed within himself. But the Europeans could never reach that inner Brandeis."

In any case there was a great difference between the way that American Jews like Brandeis—and Ben—looked at Palestine and Jews like Weizmann who settled there. When the issue was between two mistresses, science and Zionism, Weizmann felt compelled to give priority to the latter. Brandeis refused to leave the court. As he had explained to a caucus of the American delegation at the 1920 conference:

. . . I represented, independently of being on the Bench, in a certain sense the Liberals, Progressives, that hope in American life, I feel and have felt . . .

If he left the bench it would bolster the belief

that a man cannot be a Zionist and a good citizen of his country because there was Brandeis, who was supposed to be one of the most American of Americans, who left his court and his country at the time that many will believe to be, the greatest need.

Dedicated and loyal as Ben was to his assignment, a large part of him had withdrawn. He was part of the inner circle yet never sought to be a popular leader. In all the missions that the London office sent to Palestine Ben never was a member. He pressed insistently to be freed to return to the United States. America was his homeland, not Palestine. That is why he resisted going there, even on a mission. He was prevailed upon to stay and tidy up the work on the mandate and the frontiers, but Bernard Flexner, who was in London, came away, as he advised Judge Mack on his return to the United States,

with the very deep conviction that Cohen should be brought home and that a failure to do this might result disastrously. When I urged Cohen, while L.D.B. was still in London, to remain I had no idea how unhappy in mind he was. Otherwise I should have urged that he return either with L.D.B. or with me. I feel the matter so deeply that I think it has a prior claim on us.[17]

Brandeis saw Flexner's note and immediately asked Mack to urge Ben to "come at once for preparatory work here. He must be protected from nervous prostration and should not be allowed to delay a day unnecessarily." Ben did not wholly welcome Mack's request that he return to work on the preparations for the Cleveland convention of the American Zionists:

The only question so far as I can see is whether or not it is not my duty, however painful, to stay on a while yet. It is true that in my present state I am unable to do any real work. And I suppose it was probably the realisation of this which prompted your act of kindness to me to suggest that I return. Still a few weeks more does not matter from my point of view. And perhaps, particularly if Dr. Weizmann goes to America in the early part of November, I ought, if only because of my knowledge of the past, to stay and see the mandate and boundary through, even to the bitter end. Then I am not certain, with de Lieme and Simon both in Palestine, whether my mere presence might not serve some useful purpose, the internal political situation being such a delicate one. But I will think it over and talk with Simon, de Lieme, and Bob [Szold, who was to join the Palestine Reorganization Commission] when he arrives.[18]

He was especially anxious not to add to the problems of Simon, de Lieme, Szold, and Paul Singer. Ben had taken over the duties of acting treasurer. A steady stream of cables and letters from the four who were in Palestine begged for money, not for themselves but for work that had to go forward. Some were bantering letters but that made it even more of a frustration not to be able to respond. Simon had made them all dress for dinner, Singer wrote, "except of course de Lieme, who came in his usual brown suit and khaki shirt, and treated us as his four secretaries with great effect. He develops an excellent humor and enormous appetite. With Szold he gets on splendidly." "Don't let things depress you," another letter cautioned. Ben informed Julius Simon in Jerusalem what he would not have told the others. "He [Dr. Weizmann] was in a very disagreeable mood and said he would not stand for being made a figurehead by the present executive." Julius sent a despairing "private" note to Ben. "Looking at the whole situation it seems practically hopeless. Nobody can do a thing without wasting endless money. And all that money . . . goes to Arabs, who put it into real estate (or else it goes out of the country). Only a small proportion of our expenditures benefits Jews here . . .

"One important thing. Seriously you must send us money. We have nothing now . . ."

Three days later, "We absolutely need at once all the money you can possibly collect . . . Do not think I have lost my head and have become a Palestinian in the bad sense of the word."

The Reorganization Commission was under attack for its insistence on businesslike methods, Simon informed him. The people in Jerusalem believed the commission "is carrying out with preconceived ideas the orders from Washington." But Palestine invigorated Simon and he tried to persuade Ben it would lift his spirits too:

I am well balanced in my mind. Is it this wonderful climate of Palestine; this exhilarating air, this permanent sunshine still now at the end of November which make our people what Schopenhauer calls recklessly optimistic?

I am sorry, dear Ben, that you are not with us to try whether this effect could not even be reached on your melancholic heart. I am so sorry that you have to work under difficult conditions.[19]

The commission returned to London with hardheaded recommendations on budget and administration. The Zionist Executive refused to accept its report. Simon and de Lieme, to underscore its importance, resigned from the executive. The executive in the United States, instead of backing them up, sought to patch matters. Ben was outraged. He tendered his own resignation from the United States Executive: "Your decision in all judgment grave blow effective regeneration movement and a repudiation of all for which we struggled."

A long letter explained his action. It was a grave mistake, he thought, for the American Executive to hold aloof from the crisis precipitated by the resignations of de Lieme and Simon and "to maintain an attitude of benevolent neutrality . . . I do not touch upon what I may personally feel was our duty to Mr. Simon and Mr. de Lieme in this matter." It was not a geographical issue—America versus Europe—but of the standards by which the Palestine homeland was to be rebuilt.

I think we can fearlessly uphold our own standards without embroiling ourselves in any personal issue with Dr. Weizmann. If not, then the issue must be faced . . . At any rate, you know from my past letters how firm and unshakeable a stand I think it is our duty to take. There is little need to repeat my views. There are times when the olive branch is good, and times when the flaming sword is better. There have been times when I feared that the difficulties of leadership have not been sufficiently appreciated by you. Now I fear that there may be a too conciliatory spirit shown, although, of course, Dr. Weizmann at least is entitled to our sympathy and respect at all times. So much I cannot say for the others . . .

The period of Ben's intense involvement with Zionism was at an end. He returned to the United States in the early spring of 1921.

He was welcomed home with enthusiasm. Felix dashed off one of his "love" epistles:

My affectionate welcome, Dear Ben. I *am* glad you are here. Soon you will see your labors in their true perspective. Even now you must know the deep gratitude we all feel. Soon more—Now only my welcome.

Brandeis's welcome, because he was not easily given to flattery, was striking:

April 3, 1921

My dear Ben,

Welcome home. You have rendered service worthy of the cause. Ably and with rare devotion. Nobly and in a spirit which we like to think is American. There has been an entire forgetfulness of self—indeed a constant underevaluation of your own achievement which has been important.

You have been steadfast. With patience, persistence and tact you have [word indecipherable, perhaps "performed" or "carried out"] under the most trying conditions, the task assigned; and by your skill have contributed largely to the success achieved . . .

I realize how much in your years abroad have been painful to you. I rejoice that those years have been so creditable to you. And I am glad to think—to know—that they have been years of large growth. Of this your letters have afforded abundant evidence.

With every fond wish[20]

A few months later when the Cleveland convention of the American Zionists refused to uphold Brandeis's position, Ben, along with the other members of the Brandeis group, severed any formal relationship with the Zionist organization.

"It was Brandeis' view," wrote Ben in his Freund memorandum, "that the American Zionists who were providing most of the funds had a responsibility to the donors to see that the funds were prudently administered for the purposes for which it was represented they would be used and that until there was an improvement in administration by the World Organization, the American Organization should apply the funds raised but through companies, boards or officials controlled by it." Or, as he succinctly put it in describing Frankfurter's withdrawal, he "withdrew from the Zionist organization in 1921 when the Mack-Brandeis group withdrew owing to the rejection of their demand for fiscal autonomy for the American Zionist Organization."

The Brandeis group, including the twenty seven-year-old Ben, ceased to be active in the Zionist movement. But as Ben wrote about Brandeis, so it was true of him: Brandeis's withdrawal from Zionist officialdom "did not betoken any lessening of his interest in Zionism or any slackening of his efforts in support of the economic upbuilding of the Jewish homeland in

Palestine . . . He inspired the organization of the Palestine Cooperative Company which later became the Palestine Economic Corporation to work in the investment field on projects capable of becoming self-supporting . . ."

Simon, after his and de Lieme's defeat at the Carlsbad Congress, came to the United States and at Brandeis's invitation, supported by Ben, accepted the leadership of the Palestine Cooperative Company.

Inevitably Ben felt badly toward his erstwhile Zionist comrades. He used such terms as "disintegration," in talking about himself, and judging from de Lieme's reply must have written him saying his personal crisis had begun in London. The Dutch leader who had settled in Palestine suggested Ben stop such self-flagellation:

I think it is an over-appreciation of yourself to think that I would see your disintegration before your leaving Europe. It is only that you came to a complete and fuller knowledge of your own self. You make discoveries and think that with these discoveries begins your disintegration. You are hopelessly immodest. What you think a new process was always so. I saw it the first time I met you with your friend Rosenblatt disputing land-policy in Picadilly.

Ben, with the sobering practical experience of the difficulties of social and economic engineering, especially from afar, even on as small a scale as in the early Palestine settlements, turned to the American scene.

IV

Ben Cohen
in the Twenties

Ben's friendships on his return from London in 1921 revolved around Judge Mack. Ben looked to the judge as a second father, spending much of his time "informally and without compensation" helping him to write his opinions, a labor of love that he rendered easily. He shared an apartment with Louis Harris, a former Frankfurter student whom he had come to know during the war. At Judge Mack's both encountered Jane Krohn— vivacious and dark-haired. She had come from Cincinnati to study at the Damrosch School of Music. Her family had given her a letter to Judge Mack, an old family friend; "Judgie," she called him. The eighteen-year-old girl interested the shy Ben but Lou soon preempted the field and in 1924 Jane and Lou married. "My family were reform Jews. I had never before met a Russian Jew, I'm scared about not being up to your friends," she told Lou. "I wasn't a student; I was a musician. He took a two months leave of absence from the family business and the first place we went to see was Palestine."[1]

Another close friend was Max Lowenthal, also a former law clerk of Judge Mack. Ben's first remunerative job on his return was as counsel to Lowenthal, who had been appointed receiver of a large company. At the same time he studied to be admitted to the New York bar. "I'm glad that nuisance is out of the way," Frankfurter wrote Ben on his admission in 1923:

I've been thinking much over your next professional step. What kind of thing do you want to do? A "big office" connection, or business (!) or—what? My own sense of your especial field calls for some connection that would leave you with a little free time for the writing of a book by which you would become as well heeded (?) . . . Subject?—any one of a dozen.

So—please tell me how your mind is moving—in what direction?[2]

To make some money he took over Lowenthal's receivership when his friend left on a honeymoon. He spent two years on it but his dreams, like those of Frankfurter, not to mention Brandeis, were not of making money. They revolved around the uses of law and government to humanize the free enterprise system. In particular, law-oriented progressives, of whom Ben considered himself one, were concerned with the minimum wages and hours cases for women and efforts to ban child labor and other pioneer efforts to humanize the working place. A later president called them and associated safeguards of wages and working conditions the "safety net" that not even he, a conservative Republican would tamper with, but in the 1920s they were bitterly opposed by his Republican predecessors under an ethic of hands-off-the-marketplace and rugged individualism.

That, too, was the America of the 1920s to which Ben had returned. Not long after he began to practice law, the Supreme Court dealt a major blow to the hopes of liberals to reform the marketplace. In April 1923 the Court in a landmark decision written by Justice Sutherland, *Adkins v. Children's Hospital,* ruled unconstitutional the District of Columbia's minimum wage statute. The Court under Chief Justice Taft, except for "Holmes and Brandeis dissenting," was in midcareer of a reactionery phase in which it implacably upheld an ultraconservative interpretation of the rights of property, "freedom of contract," and due process.

Frankfurter in 1916 had taken over from Brandeis the representation of the National Consumers League before the Supreme Court in its defense of minimum wages and maximum hours for women. Almost from the time Brandeis was elevated to the bench in 1916, he undertook to help financially "dear Felix," whom he regarded as "half brother half son" and through whom he hoped to stay in touch with the progressive cause. Felix had replaced him as chief counsel in the maximum hours and minimum wage cases and was one of his standbys in the Zionist leadership. Neither the Consumers League nor the Zionists paid Felix. He was indifferent to money and Brandeis appreciated this. Felix, in fact, had first heard the "people's lawyer" in 1905 at the Harvard Ethical Society when he argued the case for "The Opportunity in the Law" to work for the people rather than for rich corporations.

In November 1916 Brandeis had sent Felix a check for $250 to cover his expenses—travel, phones, secretarial help—"in public matters undertaken at my request." Frankfurter returned the check, but Brandeis persisted, "I ought to feel free to make suggestions to you although they involve some incidental expenses." Frankfurter consented to his establishment of a fund to defray the expenses incidental to their "joint endeavors for the public good." At first Brandeis placed $1,000 annually in this special account, raised it after a few years to $1,500, and later to $3,500. Frankfurter's salary at Harvard during these years ranged between $6,000 and $10,000.

"I represented, independently of being on the Bench," Brandeis had told the American Zionist delegation who wanted him to take over the Zionist presidency and step off the bench, "in a certain sense the Liberals, the Progressives, that hope in American life . . ." He never gave up this iden- tification with liberal hopes. But he was always highly sensitive to the conflict-of-interests issue. He and his wife avoided Washington entertain- ments, partly to avoid the chance of entanglements with the influence peddlars. Clearly he did not believe, as Paul Freund, one of his law secre- taries has pointed out, that the arrangement with Frankfurter involved him in conflicts of interest.

In 1923 the wages and hours issue came before the Court again over a challenge to the District of Columbia's minimum wage statute. The case *Adkins v. Children's Hospital* was argued once more by Frankfurter. This time he was helped by Molly Dewson, who would be instrumental in advancing women's roles in politics during the New Deal years. The "Brandeis brief" that she helped Frankfurter prepare consisted of volumi- nous data about the operation of minimum wage laws in several of the states and in Europe. "We are in the last agonies of sending to the printer today the last pages of copy for a brief of 1,000 pages," Florence Kelley, head of the league, wrote a friend. "You know what the last day for the printer means! We have two special proof readers, two extra stenographers and Merry Hell in general! Mary Dewson has taken the veil and cannot be spoken to until February 5th . . . Even Felix up in Cambridge is jumping high jumps daily."[3]

In a devastating decision written by Justice Sutherland the Court over- threw the minimum wage statute by a vote of 5 to 3. Even Chief Justice Taft joined the dissenters. Brandeis did not vote because his daughter Elizabeth was secretary of the District of Columbia wage board. "The whole thing we thought we gained in 1912 is now thrown overboard and we are just where we were," a rueful Frankfurter wrote Learned Hand.[4] The decision set the liberal agenda for the next fifteen years, in fact until the Court upheld the Fair Labor Standards Act written by Cohen.

The thrust of the Sutherland ruling was against the minimum wage that was set without a causal relationship of that wage to the business, contract, or work the employee had been engaged to perform. A statute that required an employer to pay a "fair" wage would be "understandable," the justice wrote. Ben was persuaded such a statute could be written. The Consumers League organized a conference to discuss where the advocates of a minimum wage went from the Sutherland decision. Frankfurter argued that the problem was to educate the members of the Court "and we are here to see what we are going to do about it." The fight for minimum wage legislation through state statutes should go on, he urged. But the doughty Florence Kelley, head of the league, dissented. "As to my impatience with further tinkering with legislation," she wrote Felix, "what have I done but tinker for 40 years?"[5]

While Florence Kelley and her allies went ahead with the constitutional amendment, Felix turned to Ben to draft a model state statute. "If possible I should like to see your draft of a new Min. Wage Law by May 7th based on the old D. of C. [Law] but with these additions," he wrote Ben. Guided by Frankfurter, the problem now became Ben's.

"Mrs. Kelley is a very hard customer," Frankfurter warned Ben, "as those of us who have been working with her for years well know. The thing to bear in mind is that she has given her life to causes before you and I were born, which at the end of her whole life are largely dust and ashes."[6] He had written to Mrs. Kelley "as stiffly as I know," but Ben was to be patient. Ben conferred with "the ladies," as he referred to them. Drafting a statute was the kind of work he liked to do. Arguing with "the ladies" was something else. He thought he had won their agreement to reworking the statute, but the women preferred a frontal attack to the statutory route.

By autumn Ben's first attempt at drafting a minimum wage statute was finished. "Send it on," Felix said, and he would put it up to "the ladies."

Felix also drew Ben into the efforts to find a way around the Court's decisions of 1918 and 1922 that had overturned federal statutes designed to curb the labor of children under 14.[7] Although the efforts to end child labor either through the regulation of interstate commerce or, when that was struck down, through taxation had failed, Ben thought a statute might be drafted that would "distinguish" the early decisions from a new effort. Frankfurter agreed with him. But the redoubtable Frances Kelley "didn't want to have any further backing and filling with the Supreme Court" on the issue of child labor, Ben recalled. Despite his and Frankfurter's advice to the contrary, "she wanted a Constitutional amendment." The latter was introduced. Frankfurter and Cohen predicted the amendment route "would take much time and could not be obtained, as indeed it wasn't."[8] The amendment failed in the states, even in progressive ones like Massachusetts and New York, where the Catholic opposition doomed it.

This experience would be remembered by Felix and Ben in the great confrontation with the Supreme Court in the thirties.

There is no record how Ben voted in the 1924 election which pitted Republican incumbent Calvin Coolidge against conservative Democrat John W. Davis and Senator Robert La Follette who headed a Farmer-Labor list. Frankfurter supported the La Follette-Wheeler third party ticket. The latter attracted the legions of social reformers and progressives, and it reflected the century's movement, despite Harding-Coolidge normalcy and a conservative Supreme Court, toward a more just society.

"The Fourteenth Amendment does not enact Mr. Herbert Spencer's Social Statics," Justice Holmes had declared in a notable dissent. But even more than Holmes, Brandeis was the influential figure on the bench. Asked about Brandeis's influence through Felix Frankfurter on the younger generation of Harvard Law School men, Erwin Griswold, editor of the *Harvard Law Review* in the 1920s and later solicitor general and head of the law school, recalled, "The whole attitude of the school was supportive of the Holmes-Brandeis outlook. The student body would have voted nine-to-one in favor of the [Brandeis] position. That was the Harvard Law School line."[9]

Like Frankfurter, Ben was one of the instruments of that position. Nevertheless, the triumph of Harding-Coolidge normalcy left him with the problem of what to do. He approached his old chief at the War Shipping Board, Edward B. Burling of Covington Burling and Rublee for help. He was just past thirty, eager to stretch his talents as a lawyer in the public arena, but full of self-doubt. "Now to your letter," Burling replied:

In general I think I agree with your opinion about yourself. I do think that you are characterized by an extraordinary analytical faculty. If somebody else presents a thing you can dissolve it into its component parts to an amazing degree. I also think you have strongly developed a generalizing faculty. You like to establish principles. You then apply them rather remorselessly. . . .[10]

But he doubted that an executive or administrative post fitted his talents. Ben was one of those "intellectual youths" in whom "purely mental activity runs ahead of practical application of their thinking. Most of them later on learn to make their thinking practically effective." Ben could do so if he were willing to punish himself sufficiently, but, "I always thought that you had amazing possibilities for work on corporate finance. I don't see why you haven't taken it up."

Burling's suggestion of "corporate finance" struck an answering chord. Ben turned to Wall Street not to make "a killing" but, as Jerome Frank who had preceded him at the University of Chicago later put it, to earn "a competence." After finishing with the receivership that had become his via Max Lowenthal, "I became interested in the Securities Market," he told an interviewer. Whether intentionally or unintentionally he gave himself "the education necessary to deal with the Securities Act and the Stock Exchange Act and the Holding Company Act," he said of the New Deal statutes that he later helped frame.

By his own admission, he was "moderately" successful in the market.[11] He invested lucratively in Chrysler Corporation stock, among others, and when a Chrysler automobile came down the street in those years he gave a proprietary chuckle. He became known as a "lawyer's lawyer" and, said Jerome Frank, made money enough "from fees and investments sufficient to support himself modestly for the balance of his life."[12]

But all was "marking time between public work."[13] An intensely private man, shy to the point of reclusiveness, he yearned, nevertheless, for the public side. He was an idealist but no idealogue, and if the great barrier the Supreme Court had erected before the onrush of the democratic tide was to be breached, it would and should be, he believed by education and persuasion. He was a "consensus" man in the great tradition that was being molded by Holmes, Brandeis, and Frankfurter, and in 1928 he was back at the job of working with "the ladies" to draft a state "fair wage" bill and a child labor bill that might get by the Court.

"Dear Felix," Ben wrote in 1928, "I am sending you a couple of copies of the revised draft of the Child Labor Bill, although I am not entirely satisfied with it." The details of the provisions that Ben contrived are less important than the subtlety and meticulousness of his effort to find language that would "distinguish" the new effort from the provisions that had been stricken down.

In New York a Consumers League minimum wage bill had been introduced by State Senator Brereton. "Power to report on conditions generally," Ben cautioned Molly Dewson, "is a little different from the right to name—some would call it blackmail—specific firms not adhering to the fair wage."

Fortified with Frankfurter's agreement, Ben wrote Molly, a command-ing lady whom James Farley later called "the general," some firm advice seasoned with gallantries.

I assume you spread your bristles for my benefit, because you know how much I like you when you bristle.

I take that what we are all after is a fair wage law that will accomplish the objectives which the Consumers League has been pursuing for many years, and at the same time will stand the largest likelihood of satisfying the Court . . . In other words, as a practical woman, I am sure you will want to meet the prejudices, let's call them such, of the Courts, or, at least of the Supreme Court as that Court is likely to be constituted in the years immediately ahead.

To this end, I am sending you a redraft of the Brereton bill. I cannot for the life of me see why this should embarrass in the slightest the work you have done with all the forces that are needed to push such a bill to enactment. Certainly neither Roosevelt* nor any legislatures, either Democrats or Republicans, women's organi-zations or the press, will object to making the bill more constitution-proof. It is my deliberate judgment that the draft of the bill which I now enclose will enable you to accomplish everything you could possible accomplish even if you wrote your own ticket in your own language, and yet puts the thing in much more effective shape for judicial approval.[14]

Molly in her answering letter suggested the possibility that the mini-mum wage law of Massachusetts which had not thus far been challenged in the Supreme Court be smuggled into New York State's labor practices through existing labor laws without further legislation. Ben demurred:

. . . Your scheme is very astute. I am afraid it is too astute. . . .

So be a good girl and of good cheer. You have never thought well of lawyers and have only regarded them as a necessary evil. Continue so to regard us, and take it as my deliberate and reflective judgment that the additions which I have indicated in the Brereton Act merely effectuate your purposes and carry out what you want carried out. After all, we now know, at least people like you and me, that not even the Bible was divinely inspired. Why should Senate Bill 923 be regarded as divinely inspired and not subject to improvement?

* A month earlier, November 1928, Franklin D. Roosevelt had returned to politics being elected Governor of New York by 25,564 in a general Democratic defeat in which Al Smith, the candidate for president, had lost even New York to Herbert Hoover by 103,481 votes. Eleanor Roosevelt, who had headed up the women's work in the Smith campaign, had telephoned Molly Dewson at her summer house in Maine to go out to the Midwest to iron out some disputes. Molly had performed ably and afterward, at the request of the campaign organization, had stayed through the campaign. The forces that made the Roosevelt era were gathering. Frankfurter from Cambridge had congratulated "Dear Franklin" because he up-held the same "standards of government as had Al Smith." He also urged Roosevelt on his way from Warm Springs to stop in Washington for a talk with Mr. Justice Brandeis. Roose-velt, wishing to avoid the appearance of bidding for national leadership, urged that Brandeis stop to see him in New York on his way to Boston and also that Frankfurter "run down" from Cambridge for "a good long talk."

Ben's gentle raillery reflected a newfound self-confidence, particularly in intellectual matters that contrasted with his usual diffidence. The Frankfurter-Cohen approach to the minimum wage was to couple the concept of a "minimum" wage, which Sutherland in 1923 had outlawed, with a "fair" wage, which he had indirectly sanctioned. At Ben's suggestion Frankfurter wrote Molly but she found the lawyer's reasoning too byzantine.

Of course I am mollified by your flattery as any true woman should be.

BUT . . .

We are all sick of that word minimum. It is a mean, hateful word. Its day has waned. If you cannot yield it because of the subleties of the law you must find us a synonym.[15]

The two men respected Molly. She had played a principal part in preparing the "Brandeis-brief" that Frankfurter presented to the Court in *Adkins v. Children's Hospital* and in 1928 at Eleanor Roosevelt's instigation she was in the process of persuading Governor-elect Roosevelt to appoint Frances Perkins as his industrial commissioner.

"Dear Mary Dewson," Frankfurter patiently answered:

1. Sutherland didn't mean that any law which provides for the regulation of "fair" compensation would be sustained. One can say quite dogmatically that quite the contrary would be the ruling of the Court these days. One can only hope that legislation assuring "a fair equivalent for services" would be sanctioned by the Supreme Court in those situations where "liberty of contract" would be deemed insufficient to secure a fair equivalent . . .

2. As to a minimum, the idea is to allow the law to intervene at the levels of requirement or necessity and to exclude the suggestion that fancy standards and higher individual differentiations may be authorized by the law. Perhaps the word "fair" stuck in front of standards will accomplish the same thing as minimum, if that is really an offensive term to you.

I repeat that if you can get the law by the Court with these terms that are hateful to you, and you have a sensible administration of it, you can get all you want out of the law. And if you haven't a sensible and courageous administration of it, you won't get what you want anyhow.

All of which is humbly and respectfully and hopefully submitted.

Your disobedient but devoted servant.

It was the springtide of Hoover prosperity and materialism. Progressive social legislation was stalled by the comforting and widespread notion that soon there would be two chickens in every pot, as the new President, Herbert Hoover, put it.

Frankfurter tried to help Ben to get some form of governmental work. After the stock market debacle in the fall of 1929 he desisted for a while, because "I didn't feel I ought to bother you with anything," but he now [December 10, 1929] sent Ben a copy of a letter he had just sent to urge Ben's appointment as legal adviser on Indian Affairs.

. . . If you are able to secure Cohen for your purposes, you ought to feel that a special gift of God has come your way. He is by long odds one of the acutest and deepest-cutting minds in the legal profession. He came to us from the Chicago Law School, at the head of his class . . . He ranks as one of the handful of conspicuous men who have been with us since I have been in this School—1914. He has the rare capacity of bending knowledge and learning to practical ends, together with an extraordinary shrewdness in seeing the difficulties that will turn up and taking measures for their avoidance . . .[16]

The position was offered to Ben, but it fell a victim to appointment politics and Ben's independent ways.

Ben's home during the later twenties was a bachelor apartment at the Hotel Winthrop at Lexington Avenue and forty-seventh Street. He did not like to live luxuriously. He responded to letters in detail but in longhand or on his own typewriter. It was a Spartan existence. Books, a few close friends and their children were his staples of life, as was tennis in which he played a steady but crafty game. Women interested him and he developed close relationships with several, but marriage eluded him.

On his return from London later in 1921 he had carried with him a letter from his close friend at the Zionist offices, Julius Simon, to the latter's brother John:

I must ask you a great favor and must lay a heavy task on your shoulders. It means nothing less than to inform my brother John that our dear Johanna [Julius's wife] is no more with us. She died suddenly—last night.[17]

John Simon had come to the United States at the beginning of the war and had built up a substantial export business in which the absent Julius was a partner. The two brothers had a falling out in which Ben advised Julius, who also had settled in the United States with his three children after Johanna's death, to undertake "a segregation of assets." John blamed Ben. The purpose, John later claimed, was to defraud him. He also accused Ben of seducing his wife who in 1929, after psychiatric treatment in Germany, encouraged by her doctor there, obtained a divorce. What Ben's relationship with the divorced Molly—whether confidant, lover, disinterested friend—is not clear, but at the end of the twenties he was still a bachelor, still seeking a woman to share his life with him, still seen in avuncular rather than libertine terms. He ended a letter to Frankfurter in

1928 on child labor legislation with the cryptic sentence, "Hell is heaven compared to life."

In 1921 he had joined the Brandeis-Frankfurter-Mack-Szold group in its break with the Zionist organization but his admiration for Chaim Weizmann remained and he continued to be affected by the plight of the Jews and to consider Palestine as a homeland for those who wanted to go there.[18]

Serious Arab attacks on the Jewish settlements broke out in 1929. They drew Felix and Ben back into Zionist activity. The attacks were fanned by the Grand Mufti. The British were frightened. The Labour Party had just come into power in London and the Fabian Sidney Webb, now Lord Passfield, an anti-Zionist, was colonial secretary. He was responsible for British implementation of the Palestine mandate. Passfield drafted a white paper that departed from Britain's historic policy of encouraging a Jewish national home in Palestine. It provoked an international outcry that in the British Parliament was led by Lord Balfour and Winston Churchill who had been colonial secretary in the early twenties. *Foreign Affairs,* the magazine of the United States foreign policy elite, asked Frankfurter to write an article, "The Palestine Situation Restated."[19] As often happened, Frankfurter asked Cohen to draft it.

"From the beginning there was Arab resistance to the Mandate," Ben recalled in 1970, "and the Palestine problem was rooted in Britain's failure to meet the Arabs not by helping them move forward but by trying to hold the Jewish settlers back, limit the areas of colonization."

"The cardinal vice of the Passfield document," wrote Frankfurter-Cohen in *Foreign Affairs,* "is that it conveys, certainly to the innocent reader, the impression that the Jews' coming has been the Arab's woe. That is precisely the untruth by which a small body of economically powerful Arabs are exploiting the religious feeling of Arab masses whom they themselves oppress." The article paid the authors' respects to Lord Passfield. "In common with all students of social problems, I owe a deep debt to Sidney Webb for his contributions to history and social theory."*

Neither Ben nor Felix had reason, until Britain renounced its mandate in 1937, to abandon the entreaty that ended their paper:

---

* Ben was harsher on Webb in 1970. Passfield "was unfriendly towards the Jewish development" and his White Paper cut down "seriously on the Jewish rights and their right to settle and expand their settlements . . . Possibly some of the conflict was inevitable, but I thought if instead of trying to restrict Jewish activities, they had opened a larger area for both peoples, possibly a more peaceful if not more happy solution might have been found."

When the Mandatory—and more particularly its Administration in Palestine—abandons the negative role of umpire and assumes tasks of the Mandate, its problems will be immeasurably simplified. The two obligations it has undertaken—securing the establishment of a Jewish National Home and safeguarding the rights of the non-Jewish communities—will be revealed as not only reconcilable but in essence complementary.

Ben was not a practicing Jew. He did not visit Palestine until the 1950s. "Jew was I born, Christian reared, and Pagan shall I die," he wrote his confidante Jane Harris.[20]

. . . If Christianity in general and Catholicism in particular by holding forth the prospect of great bliss in the hereafter, has made the unbearable burdens of the world bearable for masses of suffering humanity, perhaps it should be extolled as the faith of the faiths and the truth of truths. But if others find that solace in Anthroposophy or in Christian Science or in Marxian socialism or even in Freudianism, perhaps a philosophy of pluralism may admit them all as the divine truth. But I wonder whether much of this devotion to faith is more than a flight from reality—comforting, maybe; but solving nothing.

Like children we want to believe that there is a ready answer, an easy solution to our problem, if our all-knowing Father would only tell us. *Faute de mieux,* we call it faith, truth, spirit, essence, quintessence.

But I question whether this quest of the spirit has more meaning than the quest of *materia bona.* The spirit-seeker is apt to live in a world of his own, but is it really the world—with all its beauties and meannesses, with its joys and its disappointments, its achievements and its failures? And the world of the materialist is probably more empty even than that of the spirit. To the materialist *Notre Dame* is but stone and mortar, *Mona Lisa* but canvas smeared with pigments, Brahms but a medley of noises.

The long letter breathed the stoic's thoughtful acceptance of the world's "disappointments" and his recognition that the existence of "others and things beyond our control" entailed deprivation.

At the end of the twenties the depression-induced collapse of wage standards refueled Consumers League efforts to pass minimum wage legislation in the states. It again turned to Frankfurter and Cohen to update their standard minimum wage bill. Ben met with "the ladies." They now included Frances Perkins, the New York state industrial commissioner, and her assistant Frieda Miller, Molly Dewson, who in addition to working for Roosevelt's nomination as Democratic candidate for president was secretary of the National Consumers League, and Josephine Goldmark, Brandeis's sister-in-law.

The women had gotten it into their heads, Ben wrote Frankfurter, that "the educational processes of the wage boards [proposed in his bill] work too slowly."[21] Ben disagreed but did not wish "to appear always to be asserting that my views as to what is administratively sound is constitutionally necessary. (apologies to Freund)* . . . (but) I do feel that it is extremely important that the act should be so drawn that it appears to afford the machinery for the self-government of the industry, and not the imposition of even just and careful fiats of the labor department." He urged Frankfurter to come down strongly in favor of the powers of the wage board vis-à-vis the commissioner and urged a gradualistic approach in dealing with the courts. We "should make our friends feel that if you are expected to defend the act, a difficult task at best, they should not attempt unnecessary innovations at this stage—that the important thing is to get the camel's head under the constitutional tent and when that has been done it is time to begin to curry and comb the camel."[22]

Ben tried in a new draft to meet all of Elizabeth Brandeis's criticisms except those rooted in her unwillingness "to accept the idea of fair value as a ticket of admission into the constitutional tent. You do not like the British and Australian wage boards, but I cannot help but feel that they are preferable to no wage machinery at all. And I do feel that if once we get the courts to consent to some control over the wage part of the worker's contract, we will progress quicker than if we insist on the whole loaf or more and will even learn something in the process."

But the national dimensions of the Great Depression and Governor Roosevelt's readiness as candidate for president to try nationwide remedies in his approach to the disaster superseded the state-by-state approach. As the 1932 presidential election, which pitted Hoover against Roosevelt, reached an end, Frankfurter, who was moving ever closer to the Democratic nominee, drew Ben into several complex legal chores in addition to his work on the standard minimum wage bill.[23]

These new tasks did not deflect Frankfurter and Cohen from the decade-long effort to get state minimum wage legislation. They still saw the Supreme Court's veto on progressive legislation as the fundamental obstacle. They still sought for ways to get around the Court's blockade. They still searched for mechanisms by which to establish and enforce fair labor standards. All was preparation for the New Deal battles ahead.

Frankfurter cautioned the Consumers League against any assumption that a Supreme Court majority might be in a mood to overturn the *Adkins* ruling of 1923:†

---

* Professor Ernest Freund had been his teacher at the University of Chicago Law School.
† See pp. 37–38.

I know there's not a little talk current that in view of the more liberalizing tendencies partly manifested in the Supreme Court, that a direct attempt should be made to secure an over-ruling of the *Adkins* case. That seems to me hopeless strategy. I do not think the Court has so clearly departed from its earlier ruling—or the state of mind that produced it—to warrant us in daring the gods. The result, I am sure, would be a reaffirmation of the *Adkins* case.

Frankfurter praised Ben for his draftsmanship of the new minimum wage statute:

Your minimum wage draft came in this morning's mail. I have examined it with pleasure and return it. It is organizationally well conceived and executed. I congratulate you on your draftsmanship—the skillful use of phrasing where skillful use of words is important. You know well how to skate over Sutherland's ice. I have a high appreciation of your draftsmanship because I know the reefs and shoals around which you were steering . . .

You are a great comfort.

A five-way correspondence ensued.[24] It involved Elizabeth Brandeis in Wisconsin, Molly Dewson in New York, Josephine Goldmark, Cohen, and Frankfurter. The latter gave "the ladies" some hardheaded advice on the position of the Court:

Supreme Court decisions are not of our making. They may unmake us. And it seems to me foolish beyond words to be cavalier about them and to be hopeful that a changed Court or changed times will make for a very liberal outlook on the part of the Court, and more particularly does it seem foolish to me beyond measure to build on expectations of a *bouleversement* from the majority of nine. I can assure you that there is no right to any such hope under the leadership of Hughes, let alone the others. Therefore the essential thing in regard to minimum wage legislation is to get some kind of law sustained, which will start a new line of decisions on which we can build. That kind of development, that mode of departing from the mischievous past is, as I need hardly tell you, the mode by which effective modifications of past mischievous decision, and especially of a mischievous line of decisions, have been achieved. And so I think the draftsman of a proposed law ought not to add more burdens than there will be at best for those that have the responsibility to defend legislation before the Supreme Court nor more burdens than are indispensable for those members of the Court who will seek to distinguish the *Adkins* case from the new proposal.

The ladies wanted to withdraw the power of the wage boards stipulated in the Cohen draft to fix the rates for miners, learners, and apprentices and for piece rates and to vest them in a commissioner, Frankfurter's letter continued:

Yes, I know the restlessness of an eager and effective administrator like Molly Dewson, and I suspect even you have been maybe a little impatient of the slow tempo of the Wage Board. But after all there is always a question of loss against loss and gain against gain. The trouble with the wage boards has not been the machinery . . . but the type of energy and direction that is at the top in the administration of our industrial laws. *That's* the place to throw the weight for improvement.

He thought the authority conferred on the wage boards in Ben's draft very important—

. . . perhaps more important than can possibly appear to those who have not the feel about what helps and what hurts before the Supreme Court, possessed by those whose business it is to watch the Supreme Court's doings as does a doctor that of the temperature of a pet patient.

Felix sent a copy of this letter to Ben:

Please have patience with the ladies, trying though they may be. After all, their objectives are your objectives and their disinterestedness is complete. The rest ought to be ironed out through patience and skill in making them see things or in rephrasing.

Frankfurter's letters did not wholly satisfy Cohen. "It is difficult to be put in a position of 'enfant terrible' and stubbornly hang out against the whole lot of you. But that is just my position . . . If we are trying to frame a 'fair value of service' law to meet with any degree of plausibility Sutherland's view and are not merely betting on the Supreme Court reversing itself, prudence if not necessity dictates drafting the act so as to impress the court that a genuine effort is being made to have regard to the value of the services rendered."

"Some of the ladies," Ben went on, "particularly Elizabeth [Brandeis] do not believe in the fair wage theory and naturally everything that one tries to put in the act to make it plausible to the court meets with their objection . . . Let the ladies decide whether they prefer their law with the sanction of publicity only or our law with the sanction of penalties. I do not think they have a fair change to get both."

Frankfurter retreated before Cohen's remonstrance and wrote Elizabeth: ". . . I had assumed you understood that Ben Cohen and I are working in constant communication and that his purposes are my purposes . . ."

Elizabeth had sent her draft bill to her aunt Josephine [Goldmark] who supported her niece and thought Felix and Ben did too, but Ben was adamant:

After careful reflection I must, I am really sorry to say, adhere to my original view that the permissive power of the wage board to differentiate employments will strengthen the bill from a constitutional point of view. If we wish with any plausibility to follow Sutherland's theory of fair value, we must make a *show* of trying to appraise the value of the service rendered . . .

Finally, Felix from Cambridge was able to announce victory. "[Steve] Raushenbush of Pennsylvania told me today that Elizabeth had told him to drop her law and take ours, reserving, however, all her intellectual protests." A week and a half later Ben sent Molly Dewson an explanatory statement to go along with the Standard Minimum Wage Law. "It represents the composite efforts of Mr. Frankfurter and myself." The four-page statement began:

The Law has been drafted by counsel of the National Consumers League as an honest and painstaking effort to meet the constitutional objection of the majority of the Supreme Court to the minimum wage law held invalid in *Adkins v. Children's Hospital*, 261 U.S. 525. While counsel and their advisers have striven to make the bill as workable and effective as possible, they have sought not to let any preconceived ideas of theirs stand in the way of meeting the views of the court.

The controversy had not been a schoolman's debate over texts. It foreshadowed the Frankfurter-Cohen approach to many of the issues involved in a national wages and hours bill of the New Deal years. And beyond the substantive merits of the Frankfurter-Cohen approach the exchanges showed Cohen's mettle, not only in the face of the disagreements of the "ladies" but Frankfurter's too.

By 1933, however, the national dimensions of the disaster that had befallen the American people as well as the plans that were beginning to crystallize among Roosevelt's advisers as Inauguration Day neared shifted the legislative focus from state to nation, from statutes that were carefully tailored to get by the Supreme Court to emergency action:

"Dear Ben," Frankfurter dashed off a longhand note:

In all probability I shall be seeing Gov. Lehman some day next week with Frances Perkins. So please at once get on paper all your ideas
1. in support of Bill as you've drawn it;
2. in reply to claims of interstate competition and, therefore, need for national or interstate action;
3. how we can coerce or persuade common action among competing states as to minimum wage standards.

Impatience tinged Ben's reply. Frances Perkins already knew all there was to be known about the need for a minimum wage bill. The memorandum he and Felix had just drawn up for the Consumers League defended the "Standard" bill's constitutionality. The problem of one state undercutting another was "very real and very difficult," but he feared that "the inadequacy of state regulation is too likely to be common ground on which those opposed to all legislation and those wishing ideal standards will result in no action and a consequent victory for laisser-faire. I therefore believe that those who believe national action necessary ought nonetheless firmly support state action as a leverage for national action . . . Unless plans for national action are very carefully worked out, they may prove to be a snare and an illusion. Certainly at this stage they cannot be allowed to atrophy state effort . . ."

He was not arguing against national action, he emphasized, providing such action represented a "carefully formulated plan," and he voiced the philosophy of Mr. Justice Brandeis:

I am pleading against discarding small and useful experimentation in the states. I am pleading for shoes for our soldiers in place of a beautiful and expensive banner, just as we pleaded in vain with the Consumers League eight years ago to fasten their energies on a fair wage statute and not let their struggle for a constitutional amendment impair the chances of lesser gains within their reach.

If a feasible plan for national action evolved he would be the last to oppose it, but, "The constitutional difficulties are very great, and if they are [to be] met the scope of the action must be very carefully defined." He feared, moreover, that the surrender of all labor legislation and control to the government at Washington might lead to difficulties almost as great as those attending prohibition. "In prohibition we were proceeding in the right direction in strengthening Webb-Kenyon legislation and then we lost all our gains by an ill-advised attempt at national prohibition," he reminded Felix.

In connection with the prohibition analogy you are aware that I believe that the analogy of the Webb-Kenyon legislation can be carried over to the field of child labor and perhaps to other labor standards including minimum wage and thereby permitting a state under proper safeguards to prohibit the importation of goods produced in substandard states. Congress has already passed legislation dealing with convict labor on this principle. I do not believe the legislation becomes effective until 1934, but it is an important development to watch and bear in mind. It might lead in time to the overruling of the first child labor case.

There was another overriding consideration. Recovery had to precede reform. People had to have jobs before they were worried about the standards on the job.

I don't want to be a defeatist, but I fear that there is little hope for building labor standards as such until we provide work and achieve some recovery and stability. Now the groundwork should be laid to fight for our standards when recovery of a sort sets in, but employment must first be provided through other channels before we can effectively throw up our breastworks and begin an aggressive fight for labor standards. We need not say this, but we should not fool ourselves.

Despite Cohen's fears, the shock of economic paralysis, the closing of the banks, the breadlines, the insane spectacle of idle men and idle machines, the farm foreclosures, and Roosevelt's confident call for "action and action now" disposed men and women to consider labor standards as well as jobs. Lucy Randolph Mason of Virginia who had become general secretary of the National Consumers League, succeeding Molly Dewson, reported to the league's convention in June 1933.

The sudden revival and success of minimum wage laws is probably the most significant event of 1933 in state legislation. . . . The passage of the New York minimum wage law in March marked the turn of the tide and within a short time New Hampshire, New Jersey, Connecticut and Ohio passed the same bill with minor changes, while across the continent Utah enacted a law similar to that of California. The standard minimum wage bill passed the House in Pennsylvania only to die in the Senate, while a similar bill is now before the Legislature in Illinois.

The New York bill which had been passed in March was essentially that drafted by Cohen and revised slightly by Frankfurter. It blazed the trail. A newly elected President Roosevelt wired the governors of the industrial states to urge them to support a similar bill.

Roosevelt had drafted Frances Perkins as his Secretary of Labor and she presented the New York bill to the House Labor Committee explaining that she had lifted from it provisions for a suggested minimum wage amendment to the Black and Connery thirty-hours-a-week bills then before Congress. Cohen had been correct in his prediction that the drive for state minimum wage laws would serve as a lever for national action. Lucy Mason ended her speech, "The employment standards features of the National Industrial Recovery Act should be a positive help in securing permanent state legislation, while, at least temporarily, the fear of competition from other states with lower standards is removed."

Cohen and Frankfurter also were right in doubting there would be any immediate "bouleversement" in the Supreme Court. Hence their care in framing the "Standard" act. There was an emergency but they saw beyond it. The Court was conservative, reactionary, call it what one will. Nevertheless, it was there. Skillful working and draftsmanship might get around the "reefs and shoals" and above all patience.

In the light of the history of the New Deal years, specific prescriptions for particular social and economic injustices and inefficiencies did not separate men and women as much as their approach to the Supreme Court and the formidable barrier the rulings of its conservative majority had thrown up in the way of progress.

But Washington was the place to be and soon Frankfurter brought Ben there.

V

"Tommy the Cork" – Beginnings

Unlike Cohen, who learned the operations of Wall Street sufficiently to protect himself in the stock market's collapse, another former student of Frankfurter's, Thomas G. Corcoran, did not. Six years younger than Ben, after outstanding work in the Pawtucket High School, Brown University, and Harvard Law School, including a unique legal baptism of a clerkship with Justice Oliver Wendell Holmes, he had gone to work for the Wall Street firm of Cotton Franklin. He wanted to "make a million dollars." That quest, like Ben's in the twenties, taught him the bedrock complexities of business finance.

He was an engaging youth, ready with a smile, a quip, a bit of wisdom. Young and old found life more interesting in his company—the young wanted him as friend, the old as adopted son. He was the eldest son of an eldest son of an eldest son and among the Irish that conferred a special status that carried with it a sense of responsibility not only for himself but for his parents and his younger brothers, David and Howard.

His mother, Mary O'Keefe, in his words was "a statuesque girl who played the piano as nimbly as a swallow flies," and had "a raven's memory and an eagle's will."[1] Her seafaring family had emigrated from the coast of County Cork in 1800. Her father, a tall man, made a tidy fortune from a three-masted schooner which he built himself and sailed for thirty-two years. Tom's middle name, Gardiner, came from his mother's favorite brother and that was how the family addressed him. His mother and her family were lace-curtain Irish. "They were as self-consciously close to broadcloth aristocracy as Irish-Catholic stock ever got in old New England." His mother's family were Republicans as was she and conscious of a gentility that distinguished them from the "shanty" Irish. Tom's uncle Gardiner wrote him in the thirties:

Your esteemed friend, James Michael Curley, turned me down yesterday and appointed a cheap Irish man in Fall River in my place. I thought you would like to know it. God be with the day when all the damned Shanty Irish are out of public life in this cultivated old Commonwealth—back to the ditches and jails where they belong.[2]

Tom's father, Patrick, in contrast to his wife, was five feet two and, unusual for an Irishman, a teetotaler. He was a second-generation Irishman, his family having emigrated from Tipperary just after the Civil War. Unlike his wife, he was a Democrat and, unlike her, loved politics. He was elected to the Rhode Island legislature but lost a race for mayor of Pawtucket to another Irish politician, "presumably," said Tom, "because he was a Prohibitionist." His wife put her foot down and insisted that he get out of politics. Even though his mother insisted that "I was his [(her father's)] real heir," Tom was what he called an "ancestral Democrat."

Patrick shared his wife's musical interests, played the violin, joined her in duets, and later all the boys joined them in the evenings around the piano. Tom became adept at the piano and accordion, and his father's stock of Irish songs and sea chanties became his.

Another trait that Tom inherited from his father was boundless energy. Not yet in his teens, the elder Corcoran became a newsboy while going to school. His news route he turned into a delivery service that employed other boys. With the proceeds he put himself through Brown University and Boston Law School and by the time Tom followed him to Brown had become the town's lawyer.

Pawtucket, said Tom, was a New England mill town that was "fired with the vigor of a hundred thousand immigrants," mostly Irish. Because his father did not drink and his mother did not "laugh out loud or gossip with the neighbors," the Corcorans in other Irish eyes seemed somewhat snooty, "alien," Tom put it. They lived across the street from a parochial school, but all three Corcoran boys went to public school. They were proud, however, of being Irish. Tom's memories of his early years were full of references to his Irishness. "I was one of the first Irishmen to rise in Harvard Law," he wrote of his time there. And when in 1926 Justice Frankfurter sent him to clerk for Justice Holmes and he climbed the Capitol's steps to the Supreme Court, the thought that flashed through his mind was that no Irish Catholic had entered "these precincts before."

Tom excelled in high school. He was its "prize scholar" and its debating champion, played football, had the leading role in *Charley's Aunt* and, portent of events to come, was nominated by "a little Jewish kid" to challenge and win the presidency of the senior class away from the fraternity candidate.

How could he not succeed, he thought as he went on to Brown, "blessed with an agile brain, inspired by a father who never knew fatigue and by an ambitious mother, I grew up knowing I must succeed . . ." His father had founded one of the first Catholic college fraternities at Brown, but he asked Tom not to join. "Anti-Catholic prejudice had eased enough on campus so that Catholics needn't advertise their difference." Neither did he wish Tom to join one of the non-Catholic clubs because that would seem disloyal to their Irish roots. Tom's record at Brown was even more striking than that at Pawtucket. His feeling about his Irishness was not unlike that of Ben's about his Jewishness as were his talents as a debater, and above all his intellectual gifts. He was elected to Phi Beta Kappa in his junior year and was the recipient of a handful of prizes for scholarly achievement. Unlike the shy Ben, however, he played football and for four years was a member of the Sock and Buskin Dramatic Society. This showed a pleased readiness to perform in the spotlight that foreshadowed the marriage of his own ambition with Franklin D. Roosevelt's discovery of his many talents as a deputy.

His favorite courses in college were debate and argumentation. "Whatever you may have thought of the course," he wrote his "argumentation" professor, William T. Hastings, "that and the debating training I received under George Hurley were the most precious things I took away from college . . . They gave me a set of mind—an ability to use language as a utilitarian tool—which has been my chief asset ever since."[3] He wrote that in 1938. In 1921 when he was graduated and was class valedictorian, he wavered between literature and law, and the year he stayed on in order to get a master's degree, he took additional work in Greek and Latin. He was a classicist.

Undergraduate summers were spent working for the Appalachian Mountain Club in New Hampshire. He needed to earn the money to supplement his scholarships. He guided hikers, blazed trails, prepared and operated camps and, in love with the mountains and woods, became an early environmentalist. He was always learning. At Brown his roommate in University Hall, Walter Brown, a shortwave aficionado, taught him its workings as well as Morse code. In New Hampshire's green fastnesses he became a good friend of an old lumberjack who tutored him in the ways of forest, camp, and trail. Those outdoor summers made him "strong as an ox."

He was also an ascetic about women, called himself a "Christer and Puritan." "Mummy had given me an abiding discomfort about women. Don't become a male spider," she cautioned him, referring to that insect's ability to entangle its prey in its silken strands. Women liked Tom. He had beaten the fraternities in the senior class election with the help of the vote of the girls. But he was a self-described "workaholic" and in 1922 when he entered Harvard Law School in Cambridge, "I was the complete scholar. All I did was study."

To the world he presented a buoyant puckish face but privately he suffered the usual terrors of the beginner. In the thirties he asked a Harvard professor to watch out for a first-year student whom he described as frightened, "as first-year students will always be so long as Harvard Law School Pedagoguery remains so high hat."[4] One reads almost with disbelief the observation of Professor Felix Frankfurter, not only the school's outstanding legal mind but an astute observer of human character, "He is struggling very hard with the burden of inferiority imposed on him because of his Irish Catholicism by his experiences at Brown, in Providence and in Boston."[5] Frankfurter would have known how Tom felt. Tom called him "beloved adviser of the young," and the scintillating Jewish professor and loquacious young Irishman formed a mutual admiration society. He concentrated on his books and avoided social life, Tom said, out of "the fear of being shunned. I do recall Professor Williston's, the Brahmin authority on contracts, comment 'I've just read a most remarkable paper by a man with the most unpromising name of Corcoran.' "

As at Brown, he quickly climbed to the top of the class at law school, and during his three years there was either first or second. He was chosen Notes Editor of the *Harvard Law Review* in his second year. He won the four-hundred-dollar Sears Prize awarded to the most brilliant third-year man and was graduated cum laude. The school conferred no other distinction on its graduates. He stayed on in the fall of 1925 as one of nine doctoral candidates to "be groomed for the august Harvard Law School faculty." He had won acceptance ("intellectually at least,"), this most personable of Irishmen said of his four years in Cambridge. "That was enough for the time being."[6]

He had acquired habits of discipline and mastering materials that made him a worker not just a rhetorician. ". . . [G]o to Harvard," he told a prospective student, a decade later, "no matter what the sacrifice may be, if you want to get into law with an assurance that there's no end to the ladder. It's tough but it's worth it . . ."[7] It was not by chance that the law school was furnishing "a good portion of the leaders for all sides of today's issues," he said in the heyday of the New Deal.

One summer while at school, "Felix," as Tom had come to call him, sent him to his law school classmate, Emory Bruckner, then United States Attorney for the Southern District. Bruckner was preparing to prosecute Harry M. Daugherty, the former Attorney General who had been indicted for conspiracy to defraud the United States in his handling of alien property in Harding's cabinet. He was to be tried before Judge Julian W. Mack. Although Tom's job was only that of research, "it was," said Tom, "practical legal work." Frankfurter also had given him a letter to Louis Harris. Tom did not remember the occasion when they met at a party in Lou Harris's home, but Ben did.[8]

Without Felix none of this would have happened. "He was such an admiration of mine, and our tutorial relationship was so close, that if he'd told me to clerk for the Lord of Lappland, I might have said "Yes sir and may I ask you to recommend a ????? . . ." Here Tom who was voicing this sentiment in the late 1970s broke off for he no longer wished to acknowledge this affection.

On graduation from the school he received a two-thousand-dollar research scholarship and assisted Frankfurter in his Administrative Law course. He was co-author with Frankfurter of an article, "Petty Offenses and the Constitutional Guaranty of Trial by Jury," and also fulfilled the thesis requirement for his doctorate.[9] It was the era of Prohibition and the federal courts were inundated with cases involving bootleggers. To avoid overburdening the courts "plea bargaining" had become the rule. Tom's researches revealed that in Colonial America judges of primary jurisdiction had decided many lesser criminal offenses without a jury. "According to precedent, a police court magistrate might try a bootlegger. I published these findings in the *Law Review* with Frankfurter as a nominal co-author. The conferral of his imprimatur marked me as his protégé." The precedent for trial without jury was there, Corcoran and Frankfurter concluded, but that did not save Congress or the Supreme Court "from the necessity of judgment in giving past history present application." "[A]n admirable bit of work," the dean of the law school, Roscoe Pound, commented to Frankfurter, ". . . the kind of paper that has made the *Harvard Law Review* the first legal periodical in the country."[10]

It was Frankfurter again who sent Tom to Justice Holmes. It is difficult to say which distinguished jurist was the more important in Tom's life, Frankfurter or Holmes, because Tom, and Ben, in their later years carefully minimized Frankfurter's impact on them. At law school he listened to Felix. Tom's father wanted his son to join him as a partner in his Pawtucket firm. "Is it better to be the first man in Illyria," he asked, "or second man in Rome?" Though his father was the shaping influence on Tom's life, the young man's appetite for adventure and new experience, the attraction of Holmes and the influence of Frankfurter prevailed.

Frankfurter had been sending law school men to clerk for Holmes since 1915, and for Brandeis, after the latter had been appointed to the Court. So in September 1926 Thomas Gardiner Corcoran, aged twenty-six, arrived in Washington. More than fifty years later it still appeared to him "one of the most magical places in the world." As one of Holmes's law clerks he joined a select company. The tall jurist, white-haired with a cavalryman's mustache, though eighty-two and slightly stooped, still was a craggy figure who bounded up the stairs two at a time, a Yankee of commanding intellect who, said Francis Biddle, his clerk in 1908, wanted his secretaries to "deal with 'certiorari,' balance his check book, and listen to his tall talk." He was the Court's stylist as well as philosopher who "twisted the tail of the cosmos" with sentences of "phosphorescence," as Judge Cardozo, no mean stylist himself, put it. Young Corcoran who had a knack for making sentences resonate could not have wished for a more inspiring mentor. Holmes had a memorist in Tom who savored and stored up his sparkling epigrams. He liked the energetic youngster, called him "Sonny," and encouraged him "to offer viewpoints that contrasted with his own." When Brandeis later asked Holmes what he thought of Tom, he replied, "quite adequate and quite noisy."

His arrival at the "Eye" Street house in which the Holmeses lived, two blocks from the White House, was a memorable event in his life. An Irish maid ushered him into the parlor where Mrs. Holmes, the former Fanny Bowditch Dixwell, the Boston belle who had turned down William James in order to marry "Wendell," greeted him. She was eighty-three, stood five feet tall, wore her gray hair in a bun, and was cultivated and a conversationalist in her own right.

They had made it a point to learn about Tom, she began. What did he want to know about them—aside from the legal stuff? He "should know something more important. We are Unitarians. Do you know what a Unitarian is?"

"A person who had separated from the Congregationalists," ventured Tom.

"You make it so complicated," she returned. "Let me make it simple. In Boston one has to be something and Unitarian is the least you can be."

With that she led him upstairs to Holmes's study which overlooked the garden. "Wendell, this is the young man come down from Harvard to succeed Mr. Denby. He already knew all about Unitarians."

She no longer went out at night and one of Tom's jobs would be to accompany the justice on the few occasions he still did. Here was a woman of quality, Tom immediately perceived, and understood why she had once presided over Washington's most civilized drawing room. She was the first woman after his mother, he wrote in the draft of his autobiography, whom he admired and with whom he felt easy.

Most of Tom's legal work, the justice told him, would be to deal with "certiorari," the requests that a case decided by a lower court be reviewed in the Supreme Court. Each petition was to be condensed into one page and written in longhand. The justice himself wrote his opinions in longhand, which Tom later discovered to be a fine ornamental script, and allowed no typewriter in his jurisdiction. He was a voracious reader, but with age his eyes were beginning to tire and one of Tom's duties was to read to him. The titles he read would be entered in a large black Commonplace Book that Holmes had kept since 1881 in which he had entered 3,475 titles he had read. It was a volume, incidentally, that at his death in 1935 his executors, on his order, might have destroyed except that Tom who was at his bedside smuggled it out of the house and sent it by courier to the library of the Harvard Law School.

Tom kept Holmes's checkbook which had to be reconciled to the penny and accompanied him to the bank at the end of each quarter where he learned how to cut the coupons on his bonds. The reading assignments he gave Tom each evening ranged through the classics, but first they read from the Old Testament to see what they could learn of "How the higher levels of human conduct—civilization—had evolved through the process of law."

He managed in that year as Holmes's secretary to read every essay the justice ever had published and every opinion he had written. But the bite and charm of the justice's intellectual impact, the heart of the "Holmes university," as Tom called it, were in the tutorials on their daily walks. On one of them they followed a railroad spur to the end. " 'Salute, boy,' he ordered facing the spot . . . I complied, then asked, 'May I ask, sir, what have I saluted?' 'The true terminus of something,' he said. 'There are few of these in the world.' "

The justice saw the universe as "a jumping spontaneity taking irrational pleasure in moments of apparent rational sequence." That fitted the justice's view of the law as stated in the classic volume, *The Common Law,* one which Tom often quoted:

The life of the law has not been logic—it has been experience. The felt necessities of the time, the prevalent mood or political theories, intuitions of public policy, avowed or unconscious, even the prejudices which judges share with the fellowmen, have a great deal more to do than their syllogisms in determining the rules by which men shall be governed.

Tom absorbed the justice's teachings on the fundamental character of chance and change in human affairs. Holmes often referred to Eliza's escape across the ice-choked Ohio River in *Uncle Tom's Cabin.* "A person's constant goal must be to reach the next cake of ice," he expounded. Although chance and change ruled the universe, Holmes also said, "a man's character is made up of the things he can't help." Tom remembered that too.

By the end of the Court's term Tom had decided, with the justice's approval, he said, that his next cake of ice would be with a law firm on Wall Street, not teaching as he had expected at the law school. "I'm not surprised by your decision re: teaching," Frankfurter wrote him. "Marion [his wife] says that at any time you want to earn your living with your pen or typewriter, i.e., your literary product, you can!! . . . I'd give a deal for a jaw with you."[11] The professor was an expounder, not a listener, and it was a measure of Tom's vigorous mind that he wanted to talk with him.

Both the justice and his wife had become very fond of Tom and they asked him to accompany them to Beverley Farms for the summer.[12] It was the year when the *Sacco-Venzetti* case reached a climax and Tom remembered "interviewing reporters and shooing off cameramen," when the lawyers representing the condemned men made a last-minute appeal to the justice. Tom lived that summer in a nearby boardinghouse. He knew how deeply involved Frankfurter and his wife had become in the fate of the two Italians. When he arrived the day after the justice had turned down a last-minute appeal by the defense, he inquired, "May I ask you, sir, why you didn't stay the execution?" That led, said Tom, to a long conversation about the nature of the law. The state authorities had followed due process, even had taken the unusual step of establishing a special commission with the power of extrajudicial review. There were no constitutional grounds for federal intervention and whatever his personal feelings he did not have a judicial reason to postpone the execution.

"But has justice been done?" Tom demurred, the question suggesting doubt.

"Don't be foolish, boy. We practice law, not justice. There is no such thing as objective 'justice' which is a subjective matter. A man might feel justified in stealing a loaf of bread to fill his belly; the baker might think it most just for the thief's hands to be cut off, as in Victor Hugo's *Les Miserables.* The image of justice changes with the beholder's viewpoint, prejudice or social affiliation. But for society to function, the set of rules agreed on by the body politic must be observed—the law must be carried out." "Brandeis is my authority for saying," Frankfurter wrote FDR in 1935, "that of all his secretaries Tom was the dearest to Holmes."[13]

At the end of the summer of 1927, Tom left the justice to work for Cotton Franklin, a small but distinguished Wall Street law firm. Joseph Cotton, a Republican, had been one of the directors of the United States Shipping Board in the war and Herbert Hoover, who was elected president in 1928 to succeed Calvin Coolidge, appointed him Under Secretary of State. The firm's Democrat was George Franklin, who had been General Counsel for the War Finance Corporation. It was a prestigious firm and though Tom was only, as he himself stated, a "clerk," within six months he had become, as he wrote Dean Landis, a Frankfurter protégé who had remained at the law school, *"the* expert devisor of schemes to cheat the cheater." At Cotton Franklin he learned the securities business from bottom to top, how new issues were underwritten, how the stock exchange operated, and how to read the small print in holding company arrangements. He put in eighteen-hour days doing the paperwork and carrying on the negotiations connected with corporate organization and capital investment, "the life blood," he said, "of every industrial free society."[14]

He started on Wall Street when the bull market of the twenties was celebrating its greatest victories. Coolidge was intoning that "the business of America was business," and the businessman, wrote Stuart Chase, the economist, had "replaced the statesman, the priest, the philosopher as the creator of standards of ethics and behavior."[15]

Tom, too, was intent on making his own million. He lived at the St. George Hotel in Brooklyn and walked across the great bridge to his office every day. He was a worker, often staying at his desk all night. The theater had little interest for him, the arts even less. Every new issue meant a prospectus to be written. "P.d.q.," he learned, stood for "pretty damned quick."[16] Cotton taught all his young men how to make money in the law, said Tom. "It wasn't just a matter of earning high fees, but of being permitted by investment bankers to invest in the stocks they reserved for themselves before an offering public issue."

He had misgivings about this new life, he confessed to Holmes at the beginning of 1928, and felt "unsettled."[17] "[T]he longer I feel about for my place among my contemporaries the more I realize the pricelessness of the education you and Mrs. Holmes gave me." But "p.d.q." also might have characterized his hopes of quickly making a million on Wall Street and getting out. Only about a million and a half Americans held enough stock to have an account with a broker, but that was enough to abet the thought that "everyone's in the market." Although playing the market was a national craze, not the prerogative of any racial or cultural group, the whole Corcoran family was involved and Tom's letters were filled with references to what was going on on the Street—how he had made "twelve points" in this stock, "thirty percent" in that company. He was gambling for the whole family. "I got a little worried this afternoon when I hadn't heard that you had received the fifty Warrants for Fourth National which I sent you for Howie," he wrote his mother, and added, "I've been as disappointed in National Investors Corporation during the last week as you have. We expected it to go up on publication of the quarterly report of the subsidiaries . . ."[18]

The Crash is usually dated from Black Thursday and Black Tuesday, October 24 and 29. Though the market continued to go down, Tom brushed that off as "simply another periodic downturn." "Come seven, come eleven—I've got to make a pile and get out this year," he wrote at the beginning of 1930. A Honolulu law firm, "the best in the Island," wanted him to join it, but he said no. "It's hopelessly out of the question for me to come out just now. I've lost a stock market fortune in box car figures and as a sheer matter of pride I'm going to make it back before anything else. And that, Mavourneen, may be a year and it may be forever."

A letter to the justice confessed how unhinging the Crash had really been.

I know that when, during terrible last fall of a fortune lost much greater than ever I dared tell you, my heart was all the way to the ground and I was terribly tempted to drop profession, debts and everything and run—the Justice whom I could not fail was not the great judge but the kind father who chuckled so gently over my "wild" periwinkle and took me to see tulip trees and the waves breaking over

Misery. I might have pulled out on a mere judge . . . I couldn't pull out on that nice old feller.[19]

"I will be perfectly frank," he wrote his mother who was his family confederate in his Wall Street operations, "if I had my million dollars, I certainly would go." He was unable to stay away from the ticker, but as the market plunged, the only way to escape being dragged down was to get out of it. Tom failed to do so.

"The market's going up and things are a lot better," he advised his brother David who was in the export business and stationed in Tokyo. "We'll be rich yet."[20] In midsummer he was still hopeful. Business in the office was quiet. "There is no financing, there are no plans for mergers, but there are very few bankruptcies and none of the usual receiverships of corporations approaching distress. Undoubtedly this country will get out first . . ."

Instead the Depression deepened and became the "Great Depression." "Poor Dad," his mother wrote him, "he was at his wit's end where to turn. He was going to see if they would give him any more on his insurance. He did not want to say anything to you as he thought you were in the same boat. How did you get by?" She sent more bad news—of friends who bought at what they thought was the bottom of the market. "Good night!? see where it is now."

Tom's pleasure in stock speculation was subordinate to a belief that life should be lived adventurously—"nothing ever was gained by staying safe at home" was one of his guiding principles. He paid homage to the risk takers. At the same time he was a man of responsibility, answerable in his Wall Street years to his family and his Cotton Franklin chiefs. Whatever he undertook to do he did with all his might. If David in Japan wanted to know what the prospects might be if he came back to the United States— whether in business or diplomacy—Tom went to Washington, talked to his friends on the Street, and sent his brother a single-spaced, multipaged report of the sort he later would prepare for Roosevelt.

His letters to "Dear Kiddo," Howard, at Harvard Law School were crammed with the preachings of an inspired didact.[21] "Send me down a Law School catalogue if you have it. I want to see how many bad courses I can load on you for next year." When Howard balked at some of the tougher courses, Tom urged him on.

He advised Howie on the books to read:

In Constitutional I'd read right away if I could get a jump on the thing—Max Farrand's little book on the history of the bloomin' document. It's a remarkable thing to note the differences in the flexible unsacred way the Constitution was looked at by the men who wrote it, and the utter rigidity with which a certain class of judges at least—and this includes a majority of the Supreme Court—regard it today.

At the end of the school year he had an old hand's advice on how Howard should prepare for examinations: "I used to figure on going over every set of notes three times—twice before exams began and once in the interval between the specific exams on each subject." He made himself responsible for Kiddo's summer jobs and also arranged for their holiday aspects. He paid half of Howard's tuition. "I hate to say anything," his mother advised him, "but I really think you are giving the Kiddo too much money. The Kiddo is all right BUT if he has the 'green' the green will go."

His emotional life was still centered in his family. "I do insist that at least Dad go with me for a week or ten days to the mountains," he wrote his mother. "Let's not argue whether you are going or not—you are just going and that's all there is to it . . . Now don't snivel about expenses."[22]

A son's solicitude went on, as it would throughout the lives of his parents: "A million schemes in my head—all predicated upon the recent feeble rise in the market—but one of them is this grand scheme for the combined 'ejjication' of you and Dad and Howie. Suppose you take two weeks—or even three—vacation to Canada. Howie will drive you. He always wanted to see Niagara Falls. Get a map in front of you . . ."

Although these were months when he "reeked" of the market, there was always time for the justice. "Please send one large red rose to Mr. Justice Holmes for me for Christmas," he wired a Washington florist. His letters and conversation usually crackled with bonhomie and good feeling, but he exploded with fury over President Hoover's failure to honor Holmes when Taft stepped down as Chief Justice in 1930. "Dear Children," he wrote David and his wife in Tokyo:

I've just come back from a trip to Washington. Had lunch alone with the old man —found him in a rather desolate frame of mind. I know of nothing more pathetic than the way in which he told me that he hadn't wanted the Chief Justiceship, but that nevertheless they hadn't offered it to him. It's pretty damned tough when you get to be ninety years old, and when you have served on a bench twenty-five years and been a Judge sixty years, when you have sat under two other Chief Justices appointed over your head, when you have been throughout the world the acknowledged legal leader and greatest judge of your generation, and yet a skunky little twerp in the White House hasn't grace enough to make the gesture of offering you the Chief Justiceship when he knows you will have to refuse it because of your age, or at least hold it for only for a day or two in order that your name may go down as having been Chief Justice of the United States. And what I think of this House of David Charles Evans Hughes, who sat beside the old man on the bench for years— who knew that he could have made a deal by which he could have gotten back on the bench as an ordinary Justice with assurances that if Holmes declined or died Hughes would be elevated to the Chief Justiceship—that he didn't plainly tell Hoover that he was willing enough for the sake of giving this old man this honor for a little time at least to take a subordinate place. But after all Holmes will make no speeches and has earned no particular gratitude for votes, and some of the hidebound conservatives might get mad if you gave an old liberal the tinsel accolade of a little fame. That's the kind of lousy thing, however, that's going on every day.[23]

Tom was no ideologue but he had respect for the legal profession, valued competence and brains, and his anger erupted again as he thought of Hoover's nomination of a Southerner, Parker of North Carolina, to the Court:

There is a real Senate fight on about it, and I hope it stinks to high heaven. As old Holmes said, the two men who should go on that bench are Learned Hand, of the Federal Circuit Court of Appeals of New York, and Cardozo, the Chief Judge of the New York Court of Appeals. But in order that the dumb South may be kept in line to deliver some more votes for friend Herbey's re-election, the Supreme Court can be filled up with a lot of dumb-bells . . .

Tom became the dynamo among the justice's former law clerks in the preparations to celebrate his ninetieth birthday. Alger Hiss had clerked for the justice the year before and Tom, who was trying to induce him to join Cotton Franklin, consulted him on the arrangements. Hiss thought it a mistake for all the secretaries to descend upon the ninety-year old justice. He favored flowers accompanied by a parchment round-robin "composed by yourself and signed by all the band . . ."

Tom did not agree with Hiss. "I have always had a lot more respect for the ability of his constitution to stand excitement than have most people. Did he ever tell you about the excursion in which I took him over half a dozen fences to reach some blood root?"[24] Moreover Tom knew that he was "desperately lonely, as old men however great do become lonely, for the demonstrated unselfish affection of younger people who he is sure think him 'a swell feller.' So I'd be all for a Last Supper with the Disciples —rather than the unperturbed contemplation of flowers and sheepskin." He had spent the weekend looking over Holmes's speeches and essays. "I think the most appropriate 'inscription' can be taken from some part of the following paragraph of his lecture way back in 1886 to Harvard undergraduates on 'The Profession of Law':

No result is easy which is worth having . . . No man has earned the right to intellectual ambition until he has learned to lay his course by a star which he has never seen.—to dig by the divining rod for springs which he may never reach . . . Only when you have worked alone,—when you have felt around you a black gulf of solitude more isolating than that which surrounds the dying sun, and in hope and despair have trusted to your own unshaken will,—then only will you have achieved. [Thus, only you can gain the secret isolated joy of the thinker, who knows that, a hundred years after he is dead and forgotten, men who never heard of him will be moving to the measure of his thought] . . .

Tom put in the brackets what he thought the best part. Years later when he introduced Ben to a meeting of New Dealers in 1977, he invoked the metaphor of men moving to his thought in a salute to his old friend. In rapid-fire order he then suggested other possibilities from Holmes's writings and speeches:

"We cannot live our dreams . . ."
"A man can live greatly in the law as elsewhere . . ."
Another possible inscription from "The Use of Law Schools":
The mark of a master is, the facts which before lay scattered in an inorganic mass, when he shoots through them the magnetic current of his thought, leap into an organic order, and live and bear fruit.

He tried other lines from Holmes's speeches but of all these suggestions, his letter ended, "I'm all for the 'secret isolated joy of the thinker.' "

Two months later he described the justice's birthday in a letter to "Dear Chilluns" in Tokyo:

I went down with all the rest of the secretaries to call on old Holmes. We had lunch together—on a Sunday afternoon—before calling on him. The Master of Ceremonies was the Governor of the Federal Reserve Bank of New York—George Harrison . . . They were a very funny crew. All the older ones were fairly rich—although in almost every instance married it—and they all had a queer philosophical eccentricity about them. As Bart Leach, who sat next to me, remarked—"His blight is on them all." The poor old man was so embarrassed trying to talk to everyone at once—and with difficulty trying to remember some of those who dated back twenty-five years—that he was almost laughable. Poor old bird, he certainly is alone now—and the present secretary is entirely too serious a young man to be able to do much successful hand-holding.[25]

The celebration of the justice's ninetieth birthday became a celebration of the role of law in American civilization. The Harvard, Yale, and Columbia Law Reviews organized a radio broadcast of tributes to the justice and were surprised when he agreed to make a response. His brief words over the equipment that was installed in his house for the occasion showed he had lost none of his mastery of the language even though the medium was new.*

In this symposium my place is only to sit in silence. To express one's feelings as the end draws near is too intimate a task. But I may mention one thought that comes to me as a listener-in. The riders in a race do not stop short when they reach the goal. There is a little finishing canter before coming to a standstill. There is time to hear the kind voices of friends and to say to oneself—The work is done. But just as one says that, the answer comes: The race is over but the work never is done, while the power to work remains. The canter that brings you to a standstill need not be only coming to rest. It cannot be while you still live. For to live is to function. That is all there is in living. And so I end with a line from a Latin poet, who uttered the message more than fifteen hundred years ago—Death plucks my ear and says "Live—I am coming—"

Tom's anger at President Hoover for his failure to honor Holmes when Taft stepped down as Chief Justice fed a more general revulsion to the chief executive that grew out of Hoover's inability to give the nation leadership as the Depression turned into a great national disaster. It was a "sort of mental paralysis," he wrote his brother in Tokyo, "which has grown on him with the strain of criticism." He did not hold the President wholly responsible and his analysis of the Republican Party's blame for not providing the President with able deputies and second-line troops foreshadowed his future role in helping Roosevelt to staff the New Deal.

Poor old Hoover is getting hell right and left—chiefly from the people who were his most rabid supporters two years ago. Of course he didn't do much that was expected of him and he has been utterly afraid to lead anything. But nobody gave him a whale of a lot of help in the councils of his own party. After all, you can't have a great leader accomplish anything unless there are an awful lot of leaders almost as good who are willing to be the vice presidents in charge of departments. I think it's a failure of a party much more than it is the failure of a man. But inasmuch as this distress was economically almost inevitable with the turn of the business cycle, I'm damned glad the democrats didn't get into power two years ago. Certainly the distress would have been attributed not to the normal swing of the economic cycle, but to the democrats as democrats. And the possibility of a really well-balanced two party system of government would have become hopeless until this generation died and forgot about the democrats.

Tom had cheerfully taken over from another Harvard Law School colleague at Cotton Franklin the placement of Harvard Law School graduates with New York law firms. As part of his duties he went up to Cambridge to talk to the third-year class. ". . . [T]he impression that Tom Corcoran gave," recalled one of them in later years, "was that getting a job with a

* A photocopy of his beautifully scripted lines were in Tom's papers.

New York firm was simply a means of putting yourself in a position of making millions speculating in the market." The onset of the depression changed that. Never be head of an employment bureau for law school alumni "during a period of depression," he advised a friend in September 1930. "I have applicants backed up to Chambers Street and nowhere to put them . . ." At the end of the year he was writing his mother: "I may be up in the middle of the week on my way to tell the boys at Harvard not to come to New York this year and bother me."[26]

Even as the Depression deepened he was still able to place *Law Review* men, except for the Jewish boys. He had always had difficulties with placing them. He had nothing "worthy of a *Law Review* man, he wrote from Washington early in 1932.

Frankly I have always found that when a Jewish boy can't be placed in any other way in New York something could always be done through Judge Mack. I solved my last tough Jewish Law Review problem in just this way . . .

He did his best for Harvard Jewish graduates, even though among the prejudices he brought with him from Pawtucket and his Irish background was a depreciatory sense of Jews as "kikes." They were useful in politics, as he had found when a Jewish boy in Pawtucket, Jake Mogilever, had nominated him to run for class president. The man who had sent him to clerk for Justice Holmes was Frankfurter. Few places stood higher in his firmament than did the Harvard Law School, yet when Felix sought to involve him in his solicitude for the law school's Jewish job applicants:

Felix had the infernal crust to send down to me some bird who is writing a book on discrimination against Jews and wants me to be a star witness about the way they are knocked around New York law offices. I spent half the week trying to duck him.[27]

Was the glass half-empty or half-full? Politics and law, he learned, were shared enterprises which shrank racial walls and antipathies.

Still, Felix was his "beloved adviser of the young" and when he set to work to locate a job for his brother Howard it was to Felix that Tom turned. "I went down to Washington last week with my young hopeful in tow," he wrote the professor, and Frankfurter's name was "a veritable 'Open Sesame' and I'm very grateful to you for your help. If I can't get the kid what I want I'll simply send him to the Tyrol to ski." He called on Holmes and Brandeis and was startled by the moralist's view of the Depression that Brandeis sounded:

I took the child along on my visit to Justices Brandeis and Holmes and for at least these two prophets of jurisprudence he had a mighty respect. Brandeis told me that he hoped the depression would continue for another ten years to complete the spiritual regeneration of the American people. I replied that I thought it was a swell idea, but I hoped he would permit the market to rise just far enough to let me out and then he could regenerate the rest of the populace to his heart's content.

Tom was abandoning hopes of a rise in the market. The world of finance and investment had turned somber.

In Washington Tom had realized anew that it provided "the only atmosphere I ever have enjoyed anyway." He was getting ready to jump to the next cake of ice.

At the end of his five years with Cotton Franklin, he was no critic of the free market economy even though he had gone bust after the crash. He had learned how the market operated in reality, but he accepted the view of the causes of the Depression that prevailed on Wall Street. Good times must alternate with the bad. Business cycles were part of the natural landscape. Had the Democrats been in power in 1929–32, they would have been saddled with the responsibility for the great disaster. His anger at Hoover for failure to lead implied, however, there were actions to be taken. Holmes was a stoic but another guide, Frankfurter was a reformer. Tom though buoyant and an activist like Frankfurter, clashed in outlook with the "do-nothing" views of the true believers on Wall Street who asserted nothing was to be done but to allow nature to take its course. Nevertheless, he did not conclude, as Franklin D. Roosevelt under the tutelage of his first group of brain trusters—Raymond Moley, Adolf Berle, Rexford Tugwell—was beginning to, that at the heart of the nation's troubles were maldistribution, planlessness, and inequality.

VI

——————⊃ʄʇ⊂——————

Reconstruction Finance Corporation

It was appropriate that Tom should go to Washington in March 1932 to work for the Reconstruction Finance Corporation. He was a fair-minded man, of superior intelligence, and with more than the usual quota of life force. Although a Democrat he was neither reformer nor progressive. His mild criticism of Hoover was for his failure to act, and passivity, in Hoover's case, was policy. In his eyes the cycle of boom and bust were fated. To hunker down and wait for market forces to bring about revival was statesmanship. This was conventional wisdom in the financial community and Tom shared it. He did not contend, as he would have later, that different policies might have averted or, at least, cushioned the disaster. In 1929 when the deputy attorney general, John Lord O'Brien, tried to get him to come to Washington to join the antitrust division of the Justice Department, he turned him down for good Wall Street reasons. He was making too much money to leave New York and shrugged off the crash as "simply another periodic market downturn."

Joseph Cotton, Cotton Franklin's senior partner and Tom's guide at the firm, had gone to work for the Hoover administration as Under Secretary of State. It was he who had nudged O'Brien to make the Washington job offer. Tom was courting his daughter, a relationship that the elder Cotton approved, but his daughter turned Tom down, saying he spent too much time on his work and "didn't pay her the attention she deserved."[1]

Ever the activist, by 1931–32 Tom clamored for the government to do something in the face of the nation's growing economic paralysis. Hoover's establishment of the Reconstruction Finance Corporation (RFC) seemed a step in the right direction. Modeled on the War Finance Corporation of World War I, it was set up to make loans to banks, railroads, insurance companies, farm mortgage associations, municipalities—any business too big for all but the government. The RFC reflected Hoover's "trickle down" theory that aid to the economy, if administered at all, should be injected at the top of the pyramid; nevertheless, in pumping federal money into a stagnant economy it also reflected a departure from free market economics.

Hoover established the RFC in January 1932 on the urging of Eugene Meyer, a progressive Republican and a governor of the Federal Reserve Board, whom he made chairman of the new agency. Meyer phoned George Franklin to ask that he join him again as he had during the war as chief counsel. Tom heard the firm's leading partner beg off and promptly volunteered his services. Franklin approved, mentioned it to Meyer who consulted his good friend Frankfurter, and then appointed Tom to the agency's legal staff. So in March 1932 at the age of thirty-one, the ebullient Tom, whose energies no single job description would ever confine, returned to Washington and his revered Justice Holmes.

He left a gloomy Wall Street. "Whenever I walk into a New York or Chicago law office," a Harvard Law School classmate who practiced in Boston wrote him, "I feel as if I were entering a funeral home. Everybody walks around sadly and speaks with a hushed voice and with a *de mortuis* air. Doubtless the *corpus* is Coolidge-Hoover prosperity."[2] There was an added, more compelling reason why Tom welcomed the new assignment. Cotton Franklin had reduced his salary. That was clear from Tom's father's letter on the occasion:

. . . Yes, they thought they had you in a rut from which you could not escape but they did not know that T.C. could not be kept in a rut if he saw fit to jump out of it . . . When they foolishly cut your salary after all that you had done for them they might have had vision enough to see that your morale would be somewhat shaken and that you would seize a good opportunity to leave them.

The elder Corcoran knew his son's proclivity for recruitment and placement and cautioned him against denuding Cotton Franklin's staff: "It might appear that you were trying to disrupt the organization. Then again it might not suit your Board at Washington to have all your assistants come from the same office."

Tom had given his father an exaggerated notion of the scope and authority of his new job. Chairman Meyer felt obliged in his *Reminiscences* to note that "legally he did a lot of hard work under direction and did it well," but as if in answer to Tom's big talk, he explained, "I never had any notion of appointing him to be an adviser on major policy in the RFC . . . he had nothing to do with who should or should not get loans."[3] Nevertheless, Tom was a hustler, and his father cautioned him to take it easy: "A great opportunity, but do not rush it. Don't give your superiors bad habits and too great expectations by doing three men's work at the start."

Frankfurter, the mentor in whom Tom most confided at the time, gave him similar advice:

I can see you burning up with eagerness and hoping to swallow your universe all in one bite . . . In other words, don't be disappointed if at the end of a few months you will again feel fallible and finite. Thank your master, or yourself, that you found one Holmes and one Joe Cotton all in one lifetime. And don't be too greedy to encounter any more of such rarities.[4]

A postscript in longhand enjoined the younger man, "Write me occasionally." It was not meant casually. A few weeks later Frankfurter wrote more impatiently, "Why don't I hear from you at all? I know you are busy as hell, but what of it?"

On arrival in Washington Tom found that Meyer was putting together the "finest combination" of bank examiners, railroad experts, and public administrators he was ever to see. His immediate superior on the legal staff was a Harvard classmate, Republican Francis Plimpton. Tom enjoyed the RFC work but, extremely competitive, did not relish having a classmate over him. His years on Wall Street had fitted him for the regulative aspects of his job. The "green goods business," as the securities market called the raising and disbursing of capital, was duck soup for him. He resented Plimpton but he admired, as he later wrote, "the tremendously strong" executive leadership of Governor Meyer and was considered a "Meyer man" at the agency.[5]

A Congress impatient with Hoover's reluctance to act more vigorously as the Depression worsened in July amended the RFC statute by the "Emergency Relief and Construction Act." This more than doubled the borrowing power of the RFC and authorized it to make loans to states and territories for purposes of relief. "I judge by the news reports that the R.F.C. is growing bigger and [word indecipherable] all the time," his father wrote. "May we once again suggest that you do not monopolize the work." But work was precisely what Tom prized. He welcomed Frankfurter's commission to serve as his eyes and ears in Washington, and when Meyer sought suggestions from Frankfurter for four or five lawyers, he sent the letter on to Tom and was himself on the lookout for lawyers who might be useful to the RFC "for the special problems that will come your way under the new powers regarding municipalities." "FF," as he signed himself, added a grace note about his and Marion's visit to the "old gentleman," Justice Holmes, at Beverley Farm. "He actually read us some favorite verse. And about you we had a romantic orgy."[6] Frankfurter evoked confidences and Tom enjoyed the disciple's status. He gave the childless Felix what he most craved, lengthy and chatty letters. They had to be in longhand. "It's hard to write. I have no secretary I trust and I don't dare dictate." A long undated letter that summer on the clash of new ideas with old at the agency was spiced with political gossip:

I've read your correspondence with Ballantine.* What a sucker he was even to get into a paper argument with you. He's very very tired and desperate—the multitude gasped when he turned the Harvard Law School luncheon the other day into a chance to campaign for Hoover. Only a very tired man who had lost his sense of proportion could have done it. All the Administration is tired—desperately sore at the criticism they can't answer. I wonder if they'll just fold up and quit after November 8—and let the wheel go. Or I wonder if they'll be big enough to say to Roosevelt—"It's your party—take the wheel now and we'll just act as necessary dummies." A lame duck executive just now.[7]

The board doubted self-liquidating loans were workable. Although they were what Congress wanted, the field of such loans had been sucked dry by the banks. Tom himself had made loans for municipal power plants his specialty and was having "a delightful helluva time trying to make the board face the issue." The landladies of Greeley, Colorado, he went on gaily, were opposing new dormitories at the University of Colorado, the National Association of Real Estate Boards were "chiselling away" at the slum reconstruction idea. "Everybody's using all kinds of political pressure to trade us out of our pants . . . There's only one way out—tax hard and build big federal projects." Alternatively, and perhaps the most important thing the board could do, Corcoran summed up, was to sit down and draft "special recommendations for a special session of Congress."

A second letter that summer to Frankfurter crackled with speculation why Meyer had resigned as head of the corporation, taking along the director closest to him:

* Arthur Ballantine, Assistant Secretary of the Treasury.

I don't think Meyer was the kind to leave the helm of his own ship at such a crucial time—and Bestor (his only man on the Board) was in swell fettle and didn't need to be taken off. If Meyer didn't want to get off he could have had the Board increased and shown up only from time to time.

In place of Meyer and Bestor, Hoover appointed Democrat Attlee Pomerene as chairman and Republican Charles A. Miller as president. "They just can't do this job," Corcoran jibed. Power would gravitate to another director, Jesse Jones of Texas, he was sure, who would "now cash in on the barrel head for Texas and how." It was bad enough to have "a pair of pee-wee directors," but Hoover in addition had turned loose on the agency "the Army engineers—who'll do a job like Mr. General MacArthur (who's getting hell right and left now that the town's had time to think!")*

Morale at the agency had disintegrated and Corcoran viewed himself as one of "the sacrificial goats to start the organization of the self-liquidating business. I don't know what to do—whether to stick it out . . ." A furious statement of political allegiances ended this letter. "Goddam—I hate Hoover. I hate Garner† and everything out of Texas. I'm an Al Smither, hate McAdoo and don't know what to feel about Roosevelt! What's a feller to do?"

* General MacArthur as commander-in-chief had expelled the bonus expeditionary force from its encampment in Anacostia Flats, the federal troops using tear gas.
† John Nance Garner, Speaker of the House, in the shaping of the July legislation had acquired an undeserved reputation at the RFC for wild-eyed radicalism. He had become the vice presidential nominee in the deal engineered by the Roosevelt forces that gave Roosevelt the two-thirds majority he needed to get the nomination. William G. McAdoo, Wilson's son-in-law, member of his cabinet, presidential aspirant in the ill-fated 1924 Democratic Convention, had helped to engineer the deal.

VII

$$\rightarrow\!\!\!>\!\!\{\}\!\!\{\}\!\!<\!\!\!\leftarrow$$

The Brains Trust

"I shall roll up my sleeves, make America over," a youthful verse by the Brains Truster Rexford G. Tugwell read. Handsome, reflective, companionable, he had studied economics at the Wharton School under the radical Scott Nearing and the original economic thinker Simon Patten, and he had read deeply in the works of another American "original," Thorstein Veblen. He had learned the most from Patten who was a "twister of the tail of the cosmos" and taught the intellectually eager Tugwell always to look "for uniformities, laws, explanations of the inner forces moving behind the facade of events."[1]

Young Tugwell was no socialist but a militant progressive and in 1912 the only picture he pasted into his freshman journal was of the elder Senator La Follette. Theodore Roosevelt, who seized the progressive banner from a faltering La Follette seemed to Tugwell a political adventurer and opportunist and he cast his first presidential vote for Woodrow Wilson. Tugwell had gone on to obtain his Ph.D. and in the twenties as a young economist at Columbia had become a highly regarded scholar in a field most of whose practitioners were not known, as Tugwell was, for distinction of prose or original turn of mind. Moreover, brought up in rural New York, the son of a fruit farmer, he had made a specialty of agriculture whose decade-long plight made it a major concern of aspirants for the presidency, and he had done a study on the subject for Al Smith in 1928.

Therefore, when Raymond Moley, a professor of public law at Columbia who had been doing chores for Governor Roosevelt since 1928 in the field of his specialty, criminal justice, was asked in March 1932 to pull together some intellectuals who might help Roosevelt's bid for the presidency, Tugwell was one of the colleagues to whom he turned. He sounded him out and found him to be, as he later wrote, an "exhilarating companion" whose "conversation picked you up and made your mind race along." Two of Roosevelt's intimates of longer standing than Moley, his law partner "Doc" O'Connor and Samuel I. Rosenman, the governor's counsel, then catechized the youthful expert on his views about the raging Depression, its origins and remedies. "He's a pretty profound fellow," O'Connor observed and Rosenman agreed, and with the imprimatur of all three Tugwell was introduced to the governor.[2]

A second Columbia professor recruited by Moley was Adolph A. Berle, thirty-six years old (Tugwell was forty). In 1932 Berle was a junior law professor and on the eve of publishing, together with Gardner C. Means, a classic study of the separation of ownership and management, *The Modern Corporation and Private Property.* The book also showed that nearly 50 percent of American industry was owned and operated by two hundred large corporations—or "6,000 men." The Marxists toted John Strachey's *The Coming Struggle for Power,* the mainstreamers studied their Berle and Means.

Berle, the son of a Congregational minister, had been an infant prodigy. At Harvard Law School which he attended when he was eighteen, he declined to join in the incense burning that, he says, Frankfurter required of his favorites. For a while he worked in Louis Brandeis's law firm in Boston and at the age of twenty-three (in khaki) was detailed in Paris to serve the United States delegation to the Versailles Conference. He was one of the "Jeunesse Radicales" who protested and withdrew from the mission in disgust with the peace treaty. When he returned to the United States, he practiced law, for three years lived at Lillian Wald's Henry Street Settlement, and ended up at Columbia Law School, an expert in finance and jurisprudence. He was an elegant young man and many considered him arrogant and self-centered. He had a razor-sharp mind and a pen that was flecked with vitriol.

The chief member of the original Brains Trust, the oldest of the trio, was Raymond Moley, forty-five, a pipe-smoking professor who emerged as the dominant intellectual influence during Roosevelt's bid for the presidency and in the first years of his administration. He was well built, handsome, self-assured. His earliest political hero had been William Jennings Bryan whose 1896 campaign against McKinley was the first in which, although only ten years old, Moley was "intensely interested." At sixteen he became a follower of Henry George and Tom Johnson, the reform mayor of Cleveland. Later Woodrow Wilson was his hero and he decided to try to follow Wilson's professorial route into politics and did graduate work at Columbia under Charles A. Beard. After spells as a teacher in an Ohio high school and Western Reserve University, he became director of the Cleveland Foundation. He then went to Columbia University where he specialized in studies of the police, prosecution, and the courts. That brought him in touch with Louis Howe and after helping Roosevelt's gubernatorial campaign in 1928 he served on Roosevelt's Commission of the Administration of Justice in New York State. In 1932 Roosevelt turned to him to assemble the Brains Trust and on April 25, when Roosevelt was packing at 49 East Sixty-fifth Street for Warm Springs, Georgia, he told Moley to have the Brains Trust go ahead in his absence and send the stuff down to him. "And you put in whatever you want to and pull the whole thing together so it makes sense politically. Which makes you chairman, I guess, of my privy council."

Moley's ascendancy did not go unnoticed by another generator of Roosevelt's ideas, Felix Frankfurter up in Cambridge. Moley and Frankfurter had had a stormy history.[3] When Moley directed the Cleveland Foundation in the early 1920s, he had invited Frankfurter to participate in its crime survey. The studies they produced were highly regarded, but they resulted in an explosion of bad feeling between Frankfurter and Moley. "At every chance Moley tried at once to 'knock' the Cleveland Survey and to claim credit for it as a pioneer job," Frankfurter complained in 1924. "I've never known such braying from a third-rater. He is unfit for the society of scholars." Moley reciprocated such sentiments but seven years later he took the initiative in offering an olive branch to Frankfurter. He had heard only part of Frankfurter's address in Boston on crime surveys, he wrote, and because of the need to catch a train had not had the time to tell him personally how well he thought of it. It had also led him to think about his troubled relations with Frankfurter and on his return home he had written a letter in which he acknowledged "quite clearly the juvenile character of much of what I had said to you and of you. It is with a sense of relief that I am able to renounce it and indulge the hope that you will believe me entirely sincere."

Moley wrote this in December 1930 after Roosevelt's reelection as governor with a majority that immediately made him the front-runner for the 1932 Democratic presidential nomination. But he did not get around to mailing it for six months. Frankfurter's reply dwelt on their shared hopes in the Roosevelt presidential candidacy. "Yes, there is a chance of translating a good many of our hopes and dreams into reality," Frankfurter wrote him on January 4, 1932. "Circumstances, the pressure of necessity, combined with the eager outlook towards a more humane society on the part of the new leader, give the promise for the effective promotion of our common aims."

In one of the first sessions of the Brains Trust at the Governor's Mansion in Albany, Tugwell picked up the news that Frankfurter had visited the governor. It was considered a significant item by Moley and Berle as well as himself. None of them liked it. All three were to write extensively about the Brains Trust period and all were to place their resistance to Frankfurter's influence on the grounds of principle. That was to be expected from academics, and principle certainly entered into their hostility, but beneath it darker forces lurked; there was also the traditional rivalry of the courtiers for the ear of the prince.

Two schools of progressive thought competed for Roosevelt's soul, according to Tugwell, who has advanced this thesis most strongly. There was the old Wilsonian-Brandeis tradition which believed that the only antidote to the power of the corporations was to break them up. Its hallmark was the phrase made famous by Brandeis, "the curse of bigness" and competition and the marketplace were the ways to assure economic vigor. The other school, Tugwell's own, to a lesser extent Berle's and least of all Moley's, accepted concentration as a fact of industrial life and that bigness had to be controlled by planning and direction in the public interest that was represented by government. That was the way to cope with the waste, the suffering and instability which had come to a head in the Great Depression and were among the results of an uncontrolled free market.

The clash between these two schools of thought, Frankfurter contended in his later years, had been exaggerated and mythologized. All of them had confronted the brutal facts of massive unemployment, widespread bankruptcy, farm foreclosures, the paralysis of the normal mechanisms of credit, the list was endless, and all of them had searched for the key to recovery and reform, but none of them had had a coherent and systematic program, Frankfurter maintained.

The portrayal of opposed schools of progressive thought contending for Roosevelt's soul, moreover, slighted Roosevelt's own part and role. When John Kieran, the reporter for the New York *Times*, labeled the group that assembled at the Mansion as the "Brains Trust," Roosevelt, who knew that under certain conditions voters have little use either for "trusts" or "brains," quipped, according to Berle, "He had no Brains Trust, but

trusted in brains." Roosevelt, the most eclectic of seekers for solutions
when confronted with a problem, had a talent for picking the brains of
those around him. But *he* did the picking, personally appraising the mettle
of the men he assembled about him, his "privy council," and was a participant in most of the meetings of the group whether it met at Albany or
Hyde Park.

He said many significant things in his speeches on the road to the nomination, but the most characteristic may have been in his address at Oglethorpe University:

> The country needs and, unless I mistake its temper, the country demands bold,
> persistent experimentation. It is common sense to take a method and try it; if it
> fails, admit it frankly and try another. But above all, try something. The millions
> who are in want will not stand by silently forever while the things to satisfy their
> needs are within easy reach.[4]

The genesis of the Oglethorpe speech itself showed Roosevelt's eclecti-
cism in the selection of advisers and the use of speech material. It was
drafted by Ernest K. Lindley who had been covering him for the New
York *Herald Tribune* and was soon to publish perceptive books about
Roosevelt.* Lindley sometimes sat in with the Brains Trusters but he was
not one of them.[5]

Roosevelt selected the strands that went into the tapestry that came to
be called the New Deal. He had his own techniques for getting from people
what might help him govern and one of those techniques was not to discourage the jealousies and rivalries among those around him. As Tugwell
noted about Moley, "Still, he would have liked more control of the approaches to the man we were trying to help. In his own way, and for a
different purpose, Ray was as jealous as Louis Howe or Henry Morgenthau. He was annoyed, sometimes to the point of fury, when he discovered
that an important study we had been assigned to make had been let out to
someone else as well . . ." Sometimes, continued Tugwell, "Ray could
hardly control his temper until we were alone."

Berle as well as Moley jealously guarded their influence with the governor. All three resisted Frankfurter's efforts to get into the Brains Trust.
Tugwell's many books, some of the best on Roosevelt, proclaimed the
thesis of the clash between the Brains Trust and the Brandeis-Frankfurter
school. Berle's diary entry for August 5, 1932, throbbed with this antagonism:

* *The Roosevelt Revolution—First Phase* in 1933 and *The Progressive Roosevelt* in 1932.

Last night there met at the Governor's Raymond Moley, Samuel I. Rosenman, Rexford G. Tugwell, General Johnson (of Baruch's outfit), Max Lowenthal and myself, Lowenthal came in because Felix Frankfurter wanted to bring him in on the proceedings; this over Moley's objections, with which all of us concurred.[6]

Lowenthal was a protégé of Frankfurter's, had clerked for Judge Mack, was an intimate of Ben Cohen's. Although he was secretive to the point of obsession, he was also politically and legally astute. His interests were not unlike Berle's—railroad reorganization, bankruptcy, and finance. He had just finished a stint as director of the Wickersham Commission that had been established by Hoover to inquire into the breakdown of enforcement of the Prohibition amendment. He had relied heavily on Frankfurter. The latter was not a member of the commission but Lowenthal wrote him almost daily. The Brains Trust the night Lowenthal was there went over a draft speech prepared by Hugh Johnson. Berle's entry continues:

Lowenthal, after raising a number of objections, wanted to delete anything about inflation of the currency. He put this on strategic grounds, but my impression was that his real motive was something else. Either he was anxious for inflation (reflecting the views of the Amalgamated Clothing Workers Union, or some other similar group), or he had been in touch with some of the Jewish financiers, possibly Eugene Meyer of the Federal Reserve Board. But he may merely have been endeavoring to make an impression. We were under the disadvantage of having to debate the question with him present . . .

We none of us quite trusted Lowenthal, who is a typical liberal on the make, with some sincerity, some good ideas, considerable ability, and no loyalty—except to F.F. and that particular little group that revolves around him.

A Berle memorandum to Roosevelt a few days later on "The Policy Regarding the Inflation of the Currency" omitted any reference to Jewish bankers but zeroed in on the Frankfurter group: "Mr. Lowenthal's remarks at Albany, coupled with Professor Felix Frankfurter's letter to me of August 8, sufficiently indicate that the so-called 'liberal' group propose to argue the inflationist policy without openly saying so. Perhaps this is unjust; they may merely desire to keep this an open line."

In time Berle himself came to favor a mild inflation but his animus toward Frankfurter is clear. How much of it did Moley share? None of them admitted it, but everyone was eager to be near the throne. Berle and Tugwell were correct in suggesting that Moley, like themselves, was unhappy over Frankfurter's influence with Roosevelt, and Frankfurter in a letter to Brandeis in 1934 indicated that his cultivation of Moley was "another case of working with the tools we have." But whatever the reservations on each side, the two worked together, a collaboration that was pursued the more aggressively by Frankfurter. That was his nature.[7]

Moreover, away in Cambridge, he was the outsider and always in danger that to be out of sight meant to be out of mind. Roosevelt consulted him, but it was not the regular systematic consultation of the candidate with his "privy council." For the "little group," as Berle derisively dubbed the circle around Frankfurter, a relationship with Moley was the next best thing. Frankfurter's mentor remained the Olympian figure of Justice Brandeis with whom he exchanged handwritten letters on national and international policy several times a week. Between Brandeis and Tugwell there was an unmistakable clash in views about the economy, but their programs did not conflict as much as address themselves to different difficulties in the economy.

In the critical months of Roosevelt's march toward nomination and election, Brandeis's notes to Frankfurter were far-ranging. He speaks favorably of John Maynard Keynes, "an extraordinary economic mind." This was one of the earliest references in Roosevelt circles to the British economist who, before the decade of the thirties was over, came to supersede Veblen, Patten, and Marx in New Deal thinking.

Brandeis kept close tabs on the progress of the campaign.[8] "I have promised to talk to Bob La Follette about taxation during the coming recess," he advised Frankfurter. "Will we have his tax bill draft and memo by that time?" The government's taxing power always appeared to him a constitutionally legitimate way for it to shape economic policy but not all taxes recommended themselves to his sense of justice and fairness. "I have just talked with Senator Costigan who is eager to do his utmost against the Sales Tax." Herbert Hoover's recipe for combating the Depression outraged him. "Herbert Hoover has gone stark mad on economy and balancing the budget; and the shameless, stupid stampede of the Democrats makes the situation alarming." Felix should do something about it. "It is pretty late to start a counter-movement—but couldn't something be done —like the 1,000 Economists' protest against the tariff? The Economists ought to act to save their honor." The Brains Trusters, including Tugwell, had no reason to quarrel with any of these views had they known about them.

"Roosevelt's nomination is a comfort," the justice wrote from Chatham on the Cape. He wanted Frankfurter to tell him all he could about the governor. "Hope you had a fruitful visit with Governor Roosevelt," he wrote the professor in what was a reminder that he wanted to hear, and indeed, a few days later he told Felix, "That is a very encouraging report on Roosevelt." A subsequent note told Felix that "Roosevelt has gained through the Columbus Speech and his handling of the Walker hearings." The latter was viewed by progressives as a test of Roosevelt's abilities as a leader. Roosevelt had taken over from Judge Seabury the handling of his charges against Mayor Walker, the idol of Tammany, and after several days in the witness box Walker had resigned, relieving Roosevelt of the necessity of removing him from office.

Many now were working on Roosevelt's speeches, but Moley served as the clearinghouse for all the drafts. The Columbus speech mentioned by Brandeis sounded several Roosevelt campaign themes. They included his concern over a concentration of economic power that placed two thirds of American industry in the hands of a few hundred corporations. The candidate was equally exercised about a merging of financial controls that accompanied the concentration of ownership and to offset it he called for a truth-in-securities act, federal regulation of the stock exchanges, even of holding companies, and the separation of investment from commercial banking. If such legislation were enacted, financial control of the economy would shift from Wall Street to Washington. No wonder the justice approved. "I suppose H.H. will develop further tomorrow his policy of 'to those who have shall be given,' " the same memo jibed.[9]

"Tom Cochrane [sic] was in yesterday," with "interesting picture of R.F.C.," Brandeis informed Frankfurter at the end of September. Corcoran was trying to persuade the RFC to promote loans to industry for self-liquidating projects. The justice and the professor were interested in plans by which idle workers might be matched with idle and obsolescent plants and both set to work again. "You are doubtless familiar with Frank Graham's proposals regarding unemployment," Frankfurter wrote Moley, advising him of the Princeton professor's suggestion of a barter-scrip system that would put idle men to work in idle plants. As the election neared a climax, America's capacity to produce had fallen to 50 percent.

It did not matter much what Roosevelt said. Popular dissatisfaction with Hoover's policies of awaiting a "natural" recovery had taken on the proportions of a tidal wave. At the end of September Brandeis reported cheerfully to Frankfurter that "all our Washington friends believe H.H. is doomed," and three weeks later, "I shall be glad to have a session with FDR [and you] on Sunday, November 20th." The election over, a contented Brandeis wrote "FF," "The job has been thoroughly done. Now comes FDR's real task. He must sketch out his policy and put it over in Congress as W.W. did—and he must begin the work of educating the country as soon as possible."

There was little in Brandeis's letters during the campaign that even a Tugwell could disagree with. Nor, wrote Frankfurter, in a sharp demurral from a later generation's thesis of the clash in views between Moley-Tugwell and Brandeis-Frankfurter, had he himself seen "completely eye to eye with Brandeis on some economic matters."[10] There were many differences among them, including that between the accepters of bigness in industry and finance and its critics, but as time passed and events cast a sobering light on planners and collectivists as well as free marketeers, the more careful advocates of a slow experimentalism, as represented by Brandeis-Frankfurter, in a democratic society's rearrangements, have become vindicated.

Most progressives in the Roosevelt camp agreed that the root cause of the Great Depression was underconsumption and the need was to redistribute purchasing power to enable consumers to purchase all the goods the capitalist system was able to produce. Raymond Moley in April had caught this theme as the heart of Roosevelt's meaning to the country in a suggestion to the governor when he was preparing his first nationwide radio appeal on behalf of his candidacy. "He was trying to reach the underdog and I scraped from my memory an old phrase 'The Forgotten Man,' which has haunted me for years," Moley later wrote to his sister. "These unhappy times," Roosevelt said, "call for the building of plans . . . like those of 1917 that build from the bottom up and not from the top down, that put their faith once more in the forgotten man at the bottom of the economic pyramid."

Al Smith, already a candidate, and the leader of a stop-Roosevelt movement, until then had been considered the champion of the masses. Now he lashed out at Roosevelt for stirring up class against class. "I will take off my coat and fight to the end any candidate who persists in a demogogic appeal to the masses of the working people of this country to destroy themselves," he declared. The conservatives cheered. Unwittingly they had handed Roosevelt the issue of issues in the 1932 campaign. Al Smith's attack on Roosevelt's "Forgotten Man" speech, Brandeis wrote Frankfurter, shows he is "lost totally."[11]

Most victims of the raging Depression and most progressives were united on the need for federal action to bring about a redistribution of income. They urged large-scale public works and relief, heavier taxes on corporations and the wealthy, regulation of public utilities, banking and securities exchange reforms. All these recommendations were contained in a basic Moley memorandum to Roosevelt, May 19, 1932, on campaign themes. "There was no need for Moley and Frankfurter to quarrel," wrote

Elliott A. Rosen, Moley's most intimate collaborator on the latter's *The First New Deal,* "and they never did."[12]

There was, however, a difference in approach to remedies for the Depression between Tugwell and Berle on one side and Brandeis and Frankfurter on the other. The first saw the key to recovery and reform in "planning" in which government would have a role, and in the liberation of the industrialists from many of the restrictions of the antitrust laws. The Frankfurter group, with the towering figure of Brandeis in the background, distrusted central planning and were preoccupied with remedies that were constitutionally workable. All through the twenties Frankfurter and Cohen, picking up from Brandeis, had sought formulations on minimum wages, maximum hours, child labor that would get by the taboos of the Supreme Court majority. He wanted what was administratively desirable to be constitutionally permissible, Cohen had observed to Frankfurter.

That the two groups had little of the opposed programmatic sharpness that Tugwell later ascribed to them was further illustrated by Frankfurter's radio speech on behalf of Governor Roosevelt in the closing days of the campaign. He was for Roosevelt, he said, because his deeds as governor "all give proof that as President he will endeavor to translate into action that philosophy of government so ably expressed in his speech before the Commonwealth Club of San Francisco and in his address on social justice in Detroit."[13]

The Commonwealth Club speech, drafted by Berle, spoke of "the process of concentration" in the course of which American economic life had come to be "dominated by some six hundred-odd corporations who controlled two-thirds of American industry,"[14] and Roosevelt warned that the country was "steering a steady course toward economic oligarchy, if we are not already there."

The remedy lay in redistribution. The day of the "great promoter or financial Titan" was over. There were the soberer tasks of the administration of resources, "of meeting the problem of underconsumption, of adjusting production to consumption, of distributing wealth and products more equitably, of adapting existing economic organizations to the service of the people."

The Commonwealth speech advocated an enlarged role for government. The power of the "unethical competitor, the reckless promoter, the Ishmael or Insull" who pushed industry "back to a state of anarchy" might have to be curbed by government, and "Government should assume the function of economic regulation" but "only as a last resort."

Such departures from Adam Smith's free market philosophy did not bother Frankfurter. Otherwise he would not have singled out the Commonwealth speech as an approved guide to Roosevelt's intentions. Perhaps if he had known that Berle [and his wife, Beatrice] had been the authors of the first and basic draft, he might have paused.

Frankfurter's own basic philosophy was set forth in a letter to an old friend, Walter Lippmann. It reflected a readiness to go down the path to reform coupled with prudence. He wrote:

Mine being a pragmatic temperament, all my scepticism and discontent with the present order and tendencies have not carried me over to a new scheme of society, whether socialism or communism. Or, perhaps, ten years in government, and as many more of intensive study of its problems, have made me also sceptical of any full-blown new scheme and left me most conscious of the extraordinary difficulties of the problems of the Great Society.[15]

He supported Roosevelt, Lippmann informed Frankfurter, but he worried that he was too political:

The other fear I have is that he is such an amiable and impressionable man, so eager to please and I think so little grounded in his own convictions that almost everything depends on the character of his advisers.

"What a weaseling mind he has," Lippmann at the same time was writing another correspondent about Frankfurter. Occasionally Frankfurter wondered, and it was a sign of how strongly the Great Depression was beating away at settled intellectual convictions, whether Edmund Wilson who was then getting ready to vote for the Communist presidential candidate, William Z. Foster, might be getting "at the root of things—more trenchantly and fearlessly" than he did. Nevertheless he did not "embrace, and indeed distrusted, a full-blown, 'rational' countersystem." Experience had taught him that at bottom "greed is the witch" and to distrust the nostrums of those who for ten years had been running the nation's affairs. With regard to all proposals he insisted on "adequate opportunity for deliberation, even during an emergency." Wrong measures might lead to a revolutionary situation, brought on by a vast impoverishment in the face of an increased concentration and control of wealth by a few.

. . . And if that be so, those of us who, by temperament or habit of conviction, believe that we do not have to make a sudden and drastic break with the past but by gradual, successive, although large, modifications may slowly evolve out of this profit-mad society, may find all our hopes and strivings indeed reduced to a house of cards.

It is important to take cognizance of this basic Frankfurter affirmation. Not only did his protégés, deputies, foster sons, call them what you will,

Corcoran, Cohen, Landis, Lowenthal, Lilienthal, Acheson, Wyzanski, and so on, share his gradualism but it was the rock to which his friendship with Roosevelt was anchored. It is easy to overemphasize Frankfurter's employment of flattery. It drenched his letters to Roosevelt and extended to everyone who might be of use, but that self-seeking trait need not obscure the lightning-quick intelligence and tact that caused Roosevelt later to turn to Frankfurter and his "hot dogs" to supersede the first Brains Trusters as Roosevelt's advisers.

Still, at the end of the 1932 campaign, Moley and the Brains Trust were the closest to the President-elect and Frankfurter recognized that if he and his "boys," as well as the prophetlike Brandeis who stood back of them, were to get into the charmed circle, Moley was the man to cultivate.

VIII

The Interregnum Before Roosevelt Took Office

In 1932 bills had been introduced into the Senate and House to amend the Bankruptcy Law of 1898 to provide a better system for the voluntary reorganization of companies, especially railroads, that were in deep financial trouble. Historians spoke of a "cataclysm in transportation" where in four years forty-five thousand miles of railway had gone into the bankruptcy courts and into the hands of receivers and trustees. Roosevelt in a campaign address on railroads in Salt Lake City (September 17, 1932), which he entitled "The Railroad Mesh Is the Warp on Which Our Economic Web Is Largely Fashioned," had proposed "a thorough overhauling of the Federal Laws regarding railroad receiverships," and it should include a provision "by which the interests of security holders and creditors shall be more thoroughly protected at all points against irresponsible or self-interested reorganization managers."[1]

Berle was the member of the Brains Trust who dealt with railroads. Both Berle and Frankfurter had been approached for help, the former by Representative Fiorello H. La Guardia and by Hoover's solicitor general, Thomas D. Thacher, the latter by Commissioner Joseph B. Eastman, an independent-minded member of the Interstate Commerce Commission

(ICC), as well as by Thacher, who had been an assistant U.S. attorney under Henry L. Stimson along with Frankfurter back in 1910.

As the campaign had drawn to an end, a newly revised bankruptcy bill, the Senate version introduced by Senator Hastings of Delaware, was brought to Frankfurter by Commissioner Eastman. Frankfurter thought so highly of Eastman that during the campaign he had urged Roosevelt to show him his railroad speech before he delivered it.[2]

What did Felix think of the revised bill and if he did not approve what should be substituted, Eastman asked him, adding, "I find it a very difficult question because there is a great deal of law involved upon which I am imperfectly informed at the present time."[3]

"Of course we ought to do a bang-up job for him," Frankfurter wrote Cohen. "Of course Max [Lowenthal] is the fellow to do it, and also of course Max is by the laws of nature such a one-case man that certainly at this distance I will not be able to wean him from his work.

"So I turn to you and charge you with the public duty of putting your own ideas on paper for me and also extracting what help you can from Max.

"Please be good enough to get at this at once."

Ben did consult with Max. The latter was resolutely putting the finishing touches on *The Investor Pays,* a case history of the receivership of the Chicago, Milwaukee and St. Paul Railway Co., "the greatest in American history," he called it. He did, however, make time to help both Ben and Felix.

Ben's twelve-page, typed critique of the Hastings bill and its accompanying letter stressed a central point: "Whether it be the commission [the Interstate Commerce Commission] or the court that approves the [reorganization] Plan, neither of them will be able to act effectively if the formulation of the Plan is left in the hands of the old gang." The "gang" referred to the bankers and lawyers who had been found to fatten themselves on the bankruptcy proceedings of railroads whose mismanagement they had done nothing to prevent; in many cases, even had abetted.[4]

Ben had not seen "the Berle bill, altho Max has. I gather from Max's memo that it really is not adequate," he wrote. The nub of Ben's criticism of the Hastings bill was that a "public agency" should "frame or have an effective voice in the framing of the plan before it reaches the [Interstate Commerce] Commission or the courts." Ben was also fearful that haste and "emergency" would result in giving majority creditors great powers "without rigid safeguards and effective public supervision and control of reorganizations." The issue of democratic accountability went to the heart of the entrepreneurial system and Ben believed strongly that "controlling groups cannot regard reorganizations as a matter of their own private concern." His memorandum was drafted to ensure that "the great and necessary powers of reorganization committees" not "remain in large measure outside of the realm of any effective legal or social control."

"Soon I shall send you a slight revision of your altogether admirable memorandum on the *Hastings Bill*," Frankfurter commented early in January, after he and Marion had spent a night with Roosevelt during the Christmas holidays:

It's a fine job and an astonishingly quick performance. I envy you its accomplishment. All sorts of pressure is being brought to push that bill under the disguise of an emergency. Between ourselves—strictly so—the best lick I have put in on the matter is to talk to Roosevelt about it and persuade him to urge on the Congressional leaders when he sees them Thursday, not to be taken in by the emergency cry and to protest against it vigorously . . .⁵

At this point Frankfurter got in touch with Moley about the bankruptcy bill. The two men had drawn closer but bankruptcy was Berle's bailiwick. Unfortunately Berle and Frankfurter "and his group," as Berle usually identified them, did not work together well. "Dear Governor," Berle wrote Roosevelt,

Raymond will tell you of Felix Frankfurter's telephone call last night regarding the Railway Reorganization (Bankruptcy) Act.

Typically, F.F. comes in at the last minute with many ideas, some very good, none of which he could get into legislative shape in less than a year or get by this Congress; and would like to do nothing unless he can get everything he wants; but will take no responsibility for getting anything done. And he talks of opposing what has been done, using the usual bunch—which explains why in his long and interesting career his opposition has been brilliant, but his ideas have never been brought to fruition—except over his protest.

Col. [T.E.] Lawrence in his "Revolt in the Desert" observed that the men who were best at raising a revolution were usually the world's worst at translating it into a government.

Yours truly, in a mean state of mind, with considerable admiration of F.F.'s public career and an intense personal desire to see him shot.⁶

Whatever Moley's gut feelings about Frankfurter may have been as a rival for Roosevelt's confidence, they worked together as a matter of mutual convenience, although Moley, with a touch of envy, marveled at "Frankfurter's incredible capacity to influence affairs." After speaking with Berle, Frankfurter forwarded to Moley his correspondence with ICC Commissioner Eastman and Solicitor General Thacher.⁷ "At the heart" of the issue of federal control over railroad reorganizations, his covering note said, was that "the formulation and control over any plan of reorganization should be in the hands of a governmental organ sufficiently sophisticated and sufficiently powerful to protect the national public interest as well as the interest of minorities, of those who are outside of the financially dominant circles . . ."

Occasionally, Frankfurter's back needed stiffening. Two days earlier Ben, after consulting with Max Lowenthal, had wired him:

AMENDMENT WHOLLY INADEQUATE COVER OUR OBJECTIONS APPROVAL COURT OR COMMISSION INEFFECTIVE WHEN TRUSTEESHIP AND FORMULATION PLAN NOT CENTERED IN EFFECTIVE PUBLIC AGENCY . . .[8]

"We are waiting before preparing our report on S. 4921," Eastman advised Frankfurter, speaking for the Interstate Commerce Commission, "until we have further advice from Dr. Berle." He was going to New York "and can see your friend Lowenthal on Thursday." Spurred on by Ben and Max, Frankfurter wired La Guardia who was piloting the bill through the House:

. . . POWER SHOULD NOT BE ALLOWED TO INSIDERS OR THOSE WHO IN THE PAST HAVE FINANCIALLY MISMANAGED RAILROADS . . . SUCH POWER OF FORMULATION SHOULD BE VESTED IN THE INTERSTATE COMMERCE COMMISSION . . . IT MAKES ALL THE DIFFERENCE IN THE WORLD WHETHER REORGANIZATION BEGINS OR ENDS WITH THE COMMISSION . . . IT IS BETTER TO LEAVE THE SITUATION AS IT IS THAN TO STILL FURTHER STRENGTHEN PRACTICAL CONTROL NOW RESTING WITH INSIDERS PUBLIC INTEREST AT STAKE IS TOO GREAT TO JUSTIFY THIS BEING PUSHED THROUGH AS AN EMERGENCY MATTER.[9]

To Berle's argument that Congress was in no mood to give the ICC the additional money it would need in order to initiate and control reorganization plans, Frankfurter answered that "no one can really tell how Congress would respond to a great public need."[10] And even if Congress did not appropriate, the additional expenses could be charged to the receiverships. A five-page letter along these lines went to a leader of the progressives in the Senate, Robert M. La Follette of Wisconsin. But Eastman now advised him, "I do not believe that it would be possible to get through at the present Congress any legislation going as fundamentally into the reorganization matter as you think is desirable."[11] He thought there were enough advantages in the Hastings and La Guardia bills as amended to go forward with them.

Frankfurter sent copies of this letter to Ben and Max. The latter replied first:

It's all a question of what's [the] best trade you can make, and is this good enough? Will it pass? If it passes, is it worth while? If it does not pass, will it weaken your hand for a good bill in the next session to yield now?

I gather Eastman is somewhat committed now.

Hastings et al are going to be tugged by Swain [lawyer for "the old gang"] et al. Should Eastman and LaG. et al be tugged also by you and others? . . . I fear LaG., Eastman, etc. will be chiselled down by this amendment and that. . . .

Have given Ben Eastman's letter.

Ben's letter was gentler, better attuned to political possibilities. He reaffirmed Lowenthal's points, emphasizing again, "The ICC should be the receiver or trustee and the administrative work should be centered in a special division of the ICC created for this purpose in charge of the Director of Reorganizations," and he still felt the legislation was being "hastened through a little too quickly." But he also found "satisfaction in seeing the visible hand of Eastman in the bill and evidence of some understanding that was absent in the earlier work of some of the supposedly liberal ghosts." However, he saw other pitfalls. While "Eastman has made some beginning towards the proper recognition of public control of the reorganization in the case of railroads, the Hastings bill remains in nearly its virgin form as far as ordinary corporate reorganizations go." More consideration should be given this aspect of amending the bankruptcy act, "but politics is not logical."

Frankfurter made last-minute efforts to strengthen the bill. IT IS INDISPENSABLE THAT POWER OF INITIATING REORGANIZATION PLAN SHOULD REST WITH COMMISSION, he wired La Follette.[12] He was concerned lest the amended bill WOULD LEGALIZE THE MISDEEDS AND ABUSES OF BANKER CONTROL OF REORGANIZATIONS, he wired Thacher. He was sharp with Eastman. "I should be less than candid with you if I did not tell you my surprise over your evident concurrence in a railroad reorganization measure which is so far short of what I understood you deemed desirable."

La Follette replied the next day.

I fear that perhaps you may be disappointed in the position which I took on the bankruptcy legislation . . . Upon consultation with Eastman, LaGuardia and others, I finally came to the conclusion that the most effective service I could render in the premises was to attempt to strengthen the control given the Interstate Commerce Commission in the Hastings amendment on railroads, and to accomplish the defeat of his amendment concerning corporations . . .

Eastman sent Frankfurter a five-page letter on why the bill "will improve present reorganization procedure very materially . . . I have no confidence whatever that the new Congress would be able to adopt such a reorganization measure as you have in mind without very considerable delay, if it could adopt one at all." He thought the debate in Congress "and its criticism of receivership procedure . . . will in itself have a very salutary influence on the courts . . . Obviously new machinery would not in itself do the job. The success of such a special court or department would depend upon the men selected for the purpose, and the selection of just the right sort of men would be very difficult."

In the House debate on his bill La Guardia acknowledged its weaknesses and acknowledged the case that had been made by Frankfurter and his friends for strengthening the bill; nevertheless, he voted for it as it stood.

There are not any of the so-called managers of the railroads that are in favor of this bill . . . Within the next few days several railroads—it is now no secret—will be in the hands of receivers. This is your choice. Are you going to leave the management of the reorganization and receivership of these railroads in the hands of the gang that has ruined the railroads, or are you going to take them out of the hands of that gang—and I am going to name them in a few minutes—and put such control and supervision in the hands of a Government agency, the Interstate Commerce Commission?

Up to date, Mr. Speaker, the reorganization of these railroads has been under the absolute control of J.P. Morgan and Kuhn, Loeb & Co. and their henchmen, Mitchell, Whitney, Swayne and Sutherland, and like ilk . . .[13]

La Guardia was comforted that "the bill now provides that trustees must be appointed from a panel of trustees selected by the Interstate Commerce Commission." But he acknowledged that the bill did not go far enough. "I would like to see the entire reorganization taken from the courts and placed in the Interstate Commerce Commission."

Writing afterward in the *Harvard Law Review,* Lowenthal was skeptical about the approved railroad reorganization act. He noted Senator George Norris's—the Nebraska progressive—statement in the Senate that ". . . by proper practice the judges of the Federal courts, if they in real good faith exercised their judgment under the law as it stands now, could put an end to 95 percent of all these abuses."[14] Lowenthal ended his article with the hope that a new Congress might go "to the root of the matter and achieve a thorough-going reform." By the end of March, Ben's and Max's fears were justified. The Missouri Pacific Railroad with a direct trackage of nearly seven thousand miles went bankrupt and the federal judge in St. Louis to whom the railroad applied for reorganization, instead of appointing independent trustees as he was authorized to do under the new act, left the operation of the Missouri Pacific "to its present Alleghenydominated management," according to *The Nation,* and the magazine added, "The new deal for railroad reorganizations has started badly."

Significant as the chores were that Ben performed for Frankfurter, he still sought a niche where the formulation of public policy was a recognized part of his assignment. Frankfurter tried to place him with the Reconstruction Finance Corporation whose head, at the time, was Eugene Meyer.[15] Ben had also been suggested to Meyer by Judge Mack, and the banker told Frankfurter, "I am going to see Brandeis tomorrow." In a reference perhaps to Ben's lack of Republican credentials, Meyer cautioned Frankfurter, "The solution is a little more complicated from an organization point of view than I had time to explain to you . . ." A month later he reported that the RFC's general counsel, Morton Bogue, a Republican, had talked with Ben, "but Cohen doesn't seem to be interested in the kind of work we are doing. He is more interested in the legal principles than in a great administrative grind."

The same, incidentally, was said about Frankfurter when a few months later, President-elect Roosevelt asked Senator Thomas Walsh to be his Attorney General. Would he accept Frankfurter as his Solicitor General, Walsh was asked. "He did not want somebody in there," Walsh is said to have replied, "who will lose cases in the grand manner." Subsequently, after Walsh's death, Frankfurter was offered the solicitor generalship but turned it down. Ostensibly he did so because of the priority that teaching at Cambridge had with him. There are suggestions, however, that he hoped he might receive another appointment, presumably of Attorney General where his contact with Roosevelt and opportunities to shape policy would be greater than those he already had.[16]

Moley was having even greater difficulty than Frankfurter was in settling on his role in the incoming administration. Finally, on Roosevelt's urging, he accepted appointment as Assistant Secretary of State. It was free of statutory duties, Roosevelt assured him. "You could work in your own way, giving me confidential assistance."[17]

But the absence of statutory duties was precisely the vagueness about the assignment that worried Frankfurter who was now friendly enough with Moley to write him about such problems. Did Frankfurter, a subtle man, hope that Moley, who was helping Roosevelt assemble his cabinet, would see this as an additional answer why Felix was resolutely turning down the solicitor general job.

Dear Ray:
Your tasks at best will not be easy in the days and months ahead, and you are, therefore, entitled to have your status left in no equivocation and to have it as

clearly defined as the nature of your duties will demand. That means publicly and candidly declared. Of course F.D.R. is fine and sensible and generous about all these matters, but others are involved, and as time passes men's sense of good feeling and disinterestedness become frayed and fatigued. That's a situation easy to guard against at the outset, and it is to the public interest that it be guarded against, not the least to the interest of the new President himself . . .

Yours as always,

Absorbing though such matters were, especially to the participants, all were engulfed by the magnitude of the economic calamity that afflicted the United States as Roosevelt prepared to assume office. Ben's last letter to Felix about the bankruptcy bill dwelt on it. Its startling remark about John Maynard Keynes indicates that the clash of ideas among key New Dealers as Roosevelt came to the fore was not limited to the disagreement between orthodox progressives and collectivists portrayed by Tugwell.

This great country of ours surely has hit on evil days, and where and when it will end Zeus alone knows. If one could only do something constructive about it. If only we could use the hideous disclosures about the Mitchells and their ilk to make this a bearable place to live in.* But it seems that Paul must pay for Peter's sins. I still believe in the efficacy of human effort despite my mistrust in man. If you by some sort of magic bring Keynes and F.D.R. into an effective union (if you know what I mean), I would sleep better at nights.[18]

Almost at the same time, Tom was urging one of his brothers to read Keynes's newly published *Essays on Persuasion,* "the only economist who makes sense about the world economy."

Ben's reference to Keynes was no accident. He and Felix had known the economist since the peace conference days. Keynes served on a Zionist financial committee set up in London in 1919 to advise on Palestinian matters. Ben also served on that committee. In the late thirties Keynes became an intellectual colossus of the New Deal world.[19] "Young economists by the hundreds rallied to his banner," recalled Nobelist Paul Samuelson on the economist's centenary. "I know I was one of them." Another young Keynesian, John Kenneth Galbraith, credited his ideas with bringing "Marxism in the advanced countries to a complete halt." Neither Samuelson nor Galbraith arrived in Washington until the end of the thirties, but Cohen's enthusiastic reference to the economist indicates his influence at an earlier stage. Indeed, almost all leading economists during the

---

* Four days before this letter was written, Senator Fletcher of Florida, the newly designated Democratic chairman of the Senate Committee on Banking and Currency, with a new hard-hitting chief counsel, Ferdinand Pecora, had begun public hearings on the National City Bank. Newspapers flared with headlines of tax evasions and the mishandling of "other people's money." By the week's end, Charles E. Mitchell, the bank's distinguished president, resigned. More along similar lines was to come.

Great Depression held views on the contracyclical timing of public works, deficit spending, and pump priming that later came to be associated with Keynesianism.[20]

"It was true," wrote Tugwell, that Roosevelt "behaved in what later came to be called the Keynesian manner," but he arrived at such notions before he ever heard of Keynes, due to "an intellectual climate created not by Keynes alone but by many others who were considering the same problem."

Ben's letter was predictive. A year later Frankfurter was instrumental while he was at Oxford in getting Keynes to write his famous "Open Letter to President Roosevelt." In it Keynes urged "adaptations and enlargements of your existing policies," in particular, "a large volume of Loan expenditures under Government auspices," and "the maintenance of cheap and abundant credit. I lay overwhelming emphasis on the increase of national purchasing power resulting from government expenditures which is finance by loans."

Other Keynesian ideas attracted the Frankfurter group. A Berle memorandum notes that "F.F. and his friends have been arguing for a managed currency along the lines of Keynes." A managed currency that included going off the gold standard was adopted by Roosevelt. Another characteristic of Keynes's thought was acceptance of government intervention. Keynes favored elements of planning provided they left intact free choice of occupations, the right to make profits, and the allocation of resources in response to the price incentive, namely, capitalism. Such ideas reflected the affinity between Keynes and the Frankfurter group. "It did not overthrow the system but saved it," observed Galbraith of Keynesianism. The same can be said of Moley, Tugwell, and Berle as well as of Brandeis and Frankfurter. They did not seek to overthrow but to salvage a free economy.

Of the handful of initiatives launched by a passive Hoover, the Reconstruction Finance Corporation held out the greatest promise. There, as we have seen, one of Frankfurter's ablest protégés, Tom Corcoran, was at work.

Although Corcoran in 1932 was unsure about Roosevelt, Frankfurter, who had supported Smith in 1928, was one of Roosevelt's most ardent champions. He had rendered him yeoman service in inducing a resentful Smith to support the Roosevelt-Garner ticket vigorously. On October 27, almost the eve of the election, Smith spoke at a rally in Boston. "Al Smith at his Golden Best," Frankfurter said.[21]

Tom's lengthy letter to Frankfurter the Saturday after election began with a salvo of praise for Felix for his work with Smith. "You don't need my little congratulations on the mighty victory you engineered (I heard from Morris Ernst about your ride from Providence to Boston with Al Smith, etc.) Gosh didn't you do a job."[22]

Tom had doubts about Roosevelt, but Hoover's passivity had disgusted him. "I know the results of the election must have pleased you greatly," his father wrote him.

Tom's Saturday letter to Frankfurter, the lengthiest of the longhand missives he ever sent him, dealt mostly with the impact of that victory on the work of the RFC and on the personal dilemmas it created for him. The Hoover people in the RFC had tabled all loan declinations during the campaign period lest refusals hurt the President.

Historians sympathetic to Hoover have singled out the RFC as a prime example of Hoover's intellectual flexibility and anticipation of many of the New Deal's policies of federal intervention to stimulate revival. But Tom's disdain of the Hoover "contingent's" hostility to self-liquidating loans underlined the harsh limits, when looked at closely, to Hoover's interventionist policies. Hands-off-the-marketplace and private ownership remained his guiding principles. Tom's letter was particularly scornful of the RFC board's gentle handling of Seattle's application for a loan to build a municipal power plant. Even the Democrats on the board were against it, he noted, on the ground of "no competition with private enterprise." This charge of the possible displacement of private enterprise would be made against the New Deal and against Tom personally as he became one of its chief spokesmen on the Hill.

Much of Tom's letter to FF dealt with his hostility to the board's Republicans' use of the months before Roosevelt's inauguration to elevate his law school classmate, Francis Plimpton, to be the next general counsel.

Corcoran hated the thought that Plimpton might get the appointment. The other men considered him arrogant and "cordially resented" him, he asserted. But if Francis was to be G[eneral] C[ounsel], "I'd be needed so much to help him . . . I'd have to be 'loyal' and carry on under a bushel for the good of the organization."

Although he called himself a "Meyerite," Corcoran's own views on how to bring about recovery were in flux from those of the bankers toward the liberals. Meyer opposed expansion of the RFC's making direct loans to business. He had persuaded Hoover that RFC loans to the bankers would encourage them to increase their loans to business and industry. But the banks took the RFC loans and held on to their reserves in order to maintain liquidity. Credit was still frozen.

Corcoran did not go as far as the congressional liberals who like La

Guardia considered the RFC "a millionaire's dole . . . a reward for speculation and unscrupulous bond pluggers."[23] But his openness, as this letter showed, to "self-liquidating" loans, including loans to municipalities for electric light and power plants, was a drastic departure from Wall Street's and Meyer's hesitation to see federal money pumped into the paralyzed economy. Tom does not refer to Keynes in his letters at the time, but he was on the expansionist road recommended by the Keynesians. A year later a group of young British economists, led by Roy Harrod, a Keynesian, sent a message to Roosevelt via Frankfurter who was then at Oxford that was specifically critical of the RFC's lending policies:

We do not believe that loans to corporations by such bodies as the Reconstruction Finance Corporation even if financed by "inflationary money" necessarily tend to quicken activity. The test here is whether they are used to finance the output of new capital goods. If they are merely used to enable corporations to liquefy their assets they may have little or no effect in reviving activity.[24]

Corcoran's postelection letter to Frankfurter continued with an outburst of insecurity. When his racial pride was involved there was a deep sensitivity even if it was rarely revealed:

It's funny—before 1928 I would have fallen for that "loyalty" business—and like damfool Irishmen generally gleefully have followed the drums and flags of my calculating Nordic masters . . .

I'm not jealous because I realize I have no chance myself—though I have recruited & organized the office and know more about it than all the rest put together. My friends are gone. I'm on the wrong side of the fence at least until March 4, and the Democratic Directors remember me as a henchman of the hated Meyer . . .

What should he do? He listed for Frankfurter the alternatives to staying on:

If I quit (a) I'll be called a sorehead; (b) I'll have to go back to C&F and I don't want to go back there for a long time—until I can have some independent position and not be eternally controlled by a clientele I thoroughly despise.

I dunno! It may be better to quit—it's hard to learn much more than politics down here with this gang—and a new gang is five long months away (and if Couch and Jones are any indication I'm not sure the new gang will be much better!).

Any Beatrice Fairfax advice to give me?

The letter ended more cheerfully:

Saw Justice Cardozo, Morris Ernst, Gardner Jackson last week—and read to the Boss three nights. Cardozo is simply grand. I hope I can see him often. The Boss and I are reading Kenneth Graham again—"The Golden Age," "Dream Days,"

"The Wind in the Willows:" they prod him to remember his water wheel in the brook, the childhood farm at Pittsfield, his first circus. Grand!

"My best to the Lady," he ended. "May she be Mrs. Attorney General!"

The flourish with which he finished jumps out at one. It reflected gossip that FF might be picked for Roosevelt's cabinet. Had Tom divined that the professor hoped lightning might strike? The letter in any case exhilarated Frankfurter who responded with a fulsome note:

If I were the ruler of the universe—or merely the ruler of a fraction of it that are these United States—I would see to it that we had the benefit of your powers in ample measure, merely on the strength of the qualities which your latest reveals.

And no one knows better than I how generous of you it is to write with your own fist such a long chatty letter. But the substance of the business can't be dealt with by correspondence, and I personally—I mean by my own ego—would not only be comforted but relieved if we had a chance to talk things over before you make any decision . . .[25]

Frankfurter was concerned with his own as well as Tom's place under Roosevelt. He was on the periphery of the new administration but moving in closer. He and Marion were to spend a night soon with Roosevelt in Albany. A talk with Tom whose gift for keeping in touch with much of what was going on in Washington, he well knew, would be invaluable.

Tom also consulted Brandeis. That austere moralist wrote Frankfurter that he believed Corcoran should remain at the RFC. "He may be an important influence after the Democrats enter with control." Brandeis, together with Holmes, whom Tom saw regularly, not only were the great judicial dissenters but stood at the forefront of American liberalism. At Brandeis's request Frankfurter had arranged for him to see Roosevelt at the end of November on the latter's trip to Warm Springs. Afterward the justice reported to Frankfurter, "Yesterday had 15–20 minute satisfactory interview with F.D.R. at which he did most of the talking. Roosevelt seems well versed about the fundamental facts of the situation. Declared his administration must be liberal and that (he) expected to lose part of his conservative supporters—I told him 'I hope so.' That he must realign . . . part of the forces in each party."

Brandeis's views counted with Corcoran, and though he was an independent soul, the justice's attitude, as well as FF's, influenced his own outlook.

Tom did go to see Felix, as he reported to Dear Kiddo, his brother Howard. The latter after graduation from Harvard Law School was spending a year in Europe. Tom, in the usual didactic way he advised the young, counseled Howard on how to make his year in Europe count for the most.

Felix had given him "a letter to get you into the famous banking house of Warburg & Co. in Hamburg for a while." He also spent some time in New York visiting Cotton Franklin, to which he feared he might have to return and gloomily professed to his brother, "the town is blue as hell. Nothing but piddling to do and too many to do it." There were, however, bright spots. Even though the Depression was at its lowest point, he was able to report that at RFC "I'm getting a raise—to about $9,000 net after cuts. We can afford to travel." And Stanley Reed's appointment as general counsel, instead of Plimpton, further reconciled him to staying at the agency.

But the strength of Tom's negative views of Roosevelt in the period between the latter's election and his inauguration on March 4 continued to fuel his reluctance to stay on in the capital. When Roosevelt refused to join Hoover in stopgap measures to stem the banking crisis, Tom, reflecting the conventional wisdom of the financial community, was "angry and dismayed. Roosevelt seemed a villainous fool to me"; only later did he realize Roosevelt's wisdom in refusing to share responsibility while he still lacked power. "He had to be sworn in before he could govern. If he could acquire more latitude for action—more power—by letting the roller coaster slide further down the hill, he would do just that."

Notwithstanding such hesitations about Roosevelt, he and another former Frankfurter student at the RFC, Harold Rosenwald, sent "Dear FF" a twenty-page, single-spaced memo on what should be done to reorganize the agency. "If I were King," began Corcoran, who seems to have written the letter, ("and a King of a new dynasty, not burdened with respect for old mistakes").[26] Frankfurter sent the voluminous document to Raymond Moley. It came "from some of the very best brains I know, who have been in intimate touch with the inside workings of the RFC and represent the knowledge and views of men whose social and economic direction I know and trust implicitly."

There is no indication whether the memo shaped Roosevelt's policy in any way, but it sheds considerable light on Corcoran's own point of view at the beginning of an era in which he was to play a significant part. He favored centralization of control and administration, "eliminate the bipartisan board and make the Corporation frankly an Administration organization," and subordinate "the internal operating organization . . . to one headed by a simple operating executive . . ." The corporation's powers should be used "to force reorganization in the banking, urban real estate, irrigation project and railroad fields."

Such advice was similar to the views of the Brains Trust, all of whose members considered the establishment of the RFC a positive step and who agreed with Berle's basic memorandum of May 1932 to broaden the concept of the RFC to increase its authority over recipients of its loans and greatly to enlarge its loan-making resources. Corcoran and "Rosey," as Tom referred to Rosenwald, who co-authored the memorandum with him, had doubts about a measure introduced into the Senate by Wagner of New York that would have placed government relief "loans" in the hands of "social service workers rather than 'businessmen.' " The RFC could do "a more economical job" but "let the Children's Bureau have the relief loans —their hearts are nearer the problem—and if their costs are a little higher, there will be emotional compensations." This rather patronizing view was supplemented by flat approval of the Wagner bill's elimination of the requirement "that loans to public bodies for construction purposes be self-liquidating."

The recommendations were audacious but only in terms of the RFC's restraint and timidity under Hoover. Even more daring was the further recommendation in regard to the RFC's supervisory role. Its "chief function should be that of economic adviser for the whole administration." Corcoran, in effect, advocated what later came to be called "a mixed economy" of private, public, and cooperative types of ownership in which government used the commanding heights afforded by its funding powers to direct the economy.

An added fillip showed the influence Brandeis's thinking had over the authors of the draft. They advanced the idea of private corporations being given the right to borrow for self-liquidating projects to replace obsolete industrial plants, "if it is politically impossible to authorize an adequate program of huge expenditures on federal public works like Justice Brandeis's plan for afforestation and stream control."

It was Holmes, finally, who, according to Tom decided him to remain in Washington. Roosevelt's inaugural speech on March 4, which is a benchmark among such presidential utterances, left him cold. "I found his words vague, unspecific to a fault."

A curious dilemma confronted him at the time. He solved it in a half-and-half manner, symbolic perhaps of his conflicted political allegiances. Through the RFC he was privy to inside information on the worsening situation of the banks as they rushed to declare "holidays." He knew Roosevelt had to close them all. Should he leave his own savings, small though they were, in the bank? He fretted about the ethics "of a savvy insider withdrawing his nest egg." On March 3 he took out half and left half to fate.

He spoke of his misgivings about FDR to Holmes and the old man replied—how much was fact and how much Tom's embellishment will never be known—

"Franklin is just like his cousin Theodore. He has a second class intellect but a first class temperament." And that, he believed, was precisely what the nation needed in its time of crisis. Holmes suggested I might do my country and myself a service in staying on to fight a war as threatening to the nation's survival as the one he'd waged to save the Union three score years before.

So I stayed, in part because I idolized Holmes, in part because there was work to do. Work was my addiction, my passion.[27]

IX

The New Dealers Assemble

On a drizzly March 2 evening the Roosevelt special train rolled into Union Station. The President-elect and his family piled into automobiles to be driven to the Mayflower Hotel. Washington by 1933 was in midcourse between the slow-moving town Roosevelt had left in 1920 and the puissant imperial city it was to become.[1]

Streetcars still clanged along main line Pennsylvania Avenue that connected the White House and the Capitol dome. Taxis in the downtown zone cost twenty cents. Shabbiness alternated with the huge, horizontal stone structures of Commerce, Labor, the Interstate Commerce Commission, and a rigidly observed color line separated four hundred and fifty thousand whites from one hundred and fifty thousand blacks. It was a Southern city. The New Dealers, including Moley and Tugwell, who had come down with the President-elect scattered to the town's hotels—the Willard, the Hay-Adams, the Carlton, the Powhatan—to reassemble immediately to continue anxious conferences about the banking crisis. At the Mayflower Mrs. Roosevelt emerged to walk her black Scottie. Unemployed college alumni in caps and gowns could parade from the local YWCA, as they would do a few days later, to the little street between the White House and the State, War, and Navy Building, and without permit or advance notification be received and heard by the President's secretary. Downtown Washington still was human.

Inauguration Day was gray and cheerless which mirrored the mood of the departing Republicans, but nothing dampened the spirits of Roosevelt and his New Dealers. Several statements framed the challenge that confronted them that day. One was the inaugural speech itself, perhaps the most effective inaugural address in American history in view of the transformation Roosevelt's ringing promise of "action and action now" triggered in the national mood. The second was the bipartisan welcome that saluted Roosevelt's pledge in which the nation's leaders promised to "cast aside politics and group and sectional interest" in support of "prompt and decisive action . . . to prevent economic collapse."

But the statement that really captured the moment and mood was Eleanor Roosevelt's on her return from the capitol to her friend Lorena Hickok whom she had left at the White House, "One had the feeling of going it blindly because we're in a tremendous stream and none of us know where we're going to land."

The men at the core of the new administration, especially the Brains Trusters, did not arrive with a preconceived plan of salvation, but they were profoundly alive to the need to take advantage of the sudden upsurge of hope. "Such a wave of approval for F.D.R. swept the country—so long disgusted with governmental inaction," wrote Tugwell who had been named Assistant Secretary of Agriculture under Henry A. Wallace, "that it seemed best to Wallace and myself to press for immediate farm legislation. To this F.D.R. agreed."[2]

The need to strike while the iron was hot helped energize the people around Roosevelt. Cooler heads among New Dealers, especially Roosevelt's Felix Frankfurter, sent up cautionary signals. Walter Lippmann, old friend, rival for the same policy-making constituency, and occasional opponent of Frankfurter, applauded Roosevelt's readiness to use the presidency to combat economic paralysis.[3] If Congress failed to act, the President had warned in his inaugural, he would ask for "broad executive powers to wage a war against the emergency, as great as the powers that would be given to me if we were in fact invaded by a foreign foe." Lippmann agreed. "That it will be necessary for the President to obtain the extraordinary powers he referred to in his Inaugural Address can scarcely be questioned any longer . . ." The columnist concluded that "the concentration of authority in the hands of the President is the heart of the situation."

Frankfurter chided him. He had seen several administrations at close hand. "Government is not alien to me . . . there are times for emergency action . . ." Then his caveat. "But all this is a very different thing from educating the public into the psychology of dictatorship. I know your phrase has been concentration of authority, but the result is the same. We have not, and ought not to have, government by Presidential decree . . ." He struck a Brandeisian note. "After all, the Lord doesn't create people sufficiently capacious in wisdom and detachment—no matter how disinterested—to run these vast organisms, whether of government or of finance, without ample opportunity for the corrective judgment of the deliberative process." He did not object, he explained, to the Congress's relationship to Roosevelt. The actions of Congress at the special session summoned by the President "offend none of my prejudices regarding . . . the appropriate role of Congress in our scheme of things."[4]

Frankfurter was a protagonist of the American system of checks and balances into which framework any proposals for recovery and reform should fit. Amid even the emergency pressures of a collapsing economic system and the high regard in which he held Roosevelt, this solicitude for the countervailing power of Congress on the courts as against the presidency remained a characteristic of the thought of Frankfurter and his disciples. It mirrored Brandeis's struggle against bigness and the irresponsible use by bankers and financiers of "other peoples' money." It was an emphasis different from other schools of thought, especially Tugwell's.

The cooperative mood between President and Congress would pass. Within a year Wall Street and the nation's conservatives regained their nerve and led by Al Smith, one of the signatories of the letter to Roosevelt that urged him to act, denounced him for dictatorial ambitions, a cry that became a staple of Republican propaganda. For the first "hundred days," however, with the executive in the forefront and President and Congress like-minded on what needed to be done, they produced a legislative record that has become a benchmark of democracy's capacity to act.

The Brains Trust dissolved with Roosevelt's election, but the new president's need for brains was greater than ever. "There is no room for brains trust or kitchen cabinets in the American scheme of government," Berle later wrote.[5] But at the time he was conflicted as to whether to stay or go, as were Moley and Tugwell. "Pulling out from the government now may be declining a place in history, he told his wife, Beatrice. "A few hours later he went to the U.S. Treasury and has been there ever since," her diary noted. Nominally a special assistant to the chairman of the RFC, Jesse Jones, Berle worked on railroad and banking legislation. "Ought I to go into the government," Tugwell asks in his diary. At the end of January he had put it differently to Moley, "I told him not to ask for any job for me. I said, however, that I would always be glad to do what I could in any emergency, and that I might be most useful that way."[6]

After Moley's journey to Warm Springs, he "came back with word that Berle, Taussig and I were to be offered posts in the new administration: Taussig, Tariff Commission; Berle, Federal Trade Commission; and myself Assistant Secretary of Commerce. But Berle and Taussig declined, so Moley said I could have my pick of the three." Tugwell mused, "I shall think it over for a while. Professor into national responsibility is too great a transformation to be taken lightly." In the middle of February Berle had seemed to Tugwell to be weakening and he thought that by March 4 the whole group would turn up in Washington. As for himself, "I seem to have capitulated." As he explains in *Roosevelt's Revolution,* he went to talk with the President-elect at his East Sixty-fifth Street house on his return from Warm Springs. "I was simply instructed. I was to take my assignment as an Assistant Secretary. The farmers had to be got back in business. I could not get out of it now . . . We had talked a good deal. Now the time to act was coming."[7]

Moley, like Tugwell and Berle, had decided to return to Columbia. In fact he had slotted himself for a full schedule of courses and was negotiating several writing projects when Roosevelt persuaded him to become Assistant Secretary of State. Tugwell had cautioned him "not to go further in his present anomalous role." Frankfurter sounded a similar warning. "He has much work, many responsibilities, and no authority," Tugwell continued in his diary. "F.D.R. is certainly not treating him—or me, for that matter—fairly in requiring so much of us without clear delegation."[8] After two weeks in Roosevelt's Washington, Moley still was determined to go home but when he so informed the President, the latter asked in reply who would ride herd on the legislative program, who would help with the messages, and the like, and ended, "don't forget you're enlisted for a while more, anyhow. And at the rate we've been going, a lot of things can happen to make you change your mind."

Roosevelt's ringing inaugural was followed by a triumph in the banking crisis in which he first closed all the banks and then permitted the sound institutions to reopen. By the middle of March he had stilled forever the cries of those who had depicted him as weak and irresolute. He had begun to dominate the era. Although the alphabetical agencies and the New Dealers that began to overflow Washington gave Roosevelt's administration a special savor, he was in charge, even when it meant going against the advice of two counsellors, as it did in the banking crisis, one of whom he revered, the other with whom he relished swapping ideas—Brandeis and Tugwell.

From the Wilson administration on there had been a steady flow of letters and memoranda between the justice and FF in which the former sought to shape national policy. He was a man of powerful views and in FF he had a subtle and energetic collaborator. In 1933 Frankfurter pressed the justice and his views on Roosevelt and Moley.

"Brandeis had invented the New Freedom for Wilson and had helped him to formulate a spate of Progressive legislation," Tugwell wrote in a review of *Roosevelt and Frankfurter,* the correspondence of the two men. "Frankfurter saw a new opportunity to carry on in the same way with Roosevelt. There is reason to believe that Brandeis, now a Supreme Court justice, encouraged him in this and was, indeed, the younger man's encourager."[9]

On the eve of Roosevelt's assumption of office, the justice's bulletins to Frankfurter breathed fire against big business:

5. I am still troubled about Big Finance (as Max L[owenthal] seems to be).
6. And sooner or later, F.D.R. will have to deal with heavier taxes on the right. My respectable *wise* ones here seem as much afraid of putting an end to the super-rich as they are to putting an end to superbig corporations.[10]

As the banks shut down Brandeis had a radical prescription for keeping banking facilities available. "What it [the Government] should have done," he advised Frankfurter the day before Roosevelt's inaugural, "was to open wide the Postal Savings & take itself the risk of lending to worthy banks—making them, in effect, its agents to lend to worthy businesses. Then there would have been little hoarding."

Another advocate of the use of the postal savings system in the banking crisis had been Tugwell. He and Brandeis disagreed on the subject of "bigness" but two weeks before inauguration Tugwell noted in his diary that "everything is really going to pieces in Wall Street" and that Louis Howe was telling FDR "how the bankers were all hysterical"; then Tugwell added, "We discussed for some time various means of getting currency out for business purposes if all the banks should close, which now seems possible. I suggested the post offices and a liquidating corporation for closed banks with the power to issue script."[11]

But the last thing Roosevelt wanted to do in the banking crisis was to resort to unorthodoxies such as diversion of the nation's banking business to the Postal Savings System. That might accentuate the national sense of panic and bewilderment and the runs on the banks that remained open.

His remedies were conventional but he carried them out decisively, "swift and staccato action," said Moley, attributing the phrase to William Woodin, the Secretary of the Treasury. He issued a proclamation that declared a bank holiday, basing himself on a 1917 Trading with the Enemy Act that he had Tugwell research. He summoned Congress into special session and presented it with an emergency banking bill that permitted the government to reopen the banks it ascertained to be sound, "and other such banks as rapidly, as possible." The statute passed the House by acclamation in a voice vote in forty minutes. In the Senate there was some debate and seven "no" votes, but it was over in less than eight hours and at 8:37 P.M. the President signed it. All of it was done, the responsibility accepted, observers noted, with a radiant smile in contrast to Hoover's dourness. Roosevelt then went on the radio, eight days after his inauguration, and in his first Fireside Chat, to which most Americans who had radio sets listened, explained the steps he had taken to rehabilitate the banks and to assure his listeners "that it is safer to keep your money in a reopened bank than under the mattress."

Roosevelt's handling of the bank crisis coming after his bold inaugural address helped change the mood of the nation. Frankfurter in Cambridge applauded, but he was far away and wanted to be involved. He sent one of his most loyal and knowledgeable lieutenants, Max Lowenthal, to Washington on a scouting expedition. Max's assets included expertise on finance and banking. He had good political contacts on the Republican side, having served as director of Hoover's Wickersham Commission, as well as with the Democrats. He was astute. For several days from March 13 on he sent daily handwritten letters to Frankfurter.

There were dangers, he reported, among them, "Thinking, as did H.H. [Hoover], that things will get better, or proceeding rather too much on hope. This may not be true of FDR or Moley, but the men making much of these banking decisions, are the men who, tho able have worked in this fashion . . ."[12] Lowenthal's real hope of finding out what was going on rested with Moley. Unfortunately he had been called in great haste to the White House and from then on had been at the Treasury. He finally had breakfast with Moley who "persuaded Treasury [headed by Woodin] needs personnel, that Wall Street is there. He faces need of dealing with Woodin tactfully in getting his men in. He thinks of Richberg as acceptable. I said would Richberg take it. He said he must. I said why not make it easier, get emergency assistants in, one to Sec'y., one to under-Sec'y., one to comptroller."

This concern of Frankfurter's, as reflected in Lowenthal's suggestion, to colonize the Treasury might be viewed as a grasp for power, as indeed all the strivings of the people with brains around Roosevelt can be portrayed, but it also reflected the desire to have pragmatic liberalism represented in Roosevelt's government. Though Moley in his books would portray the New Dealers who continued to support Roosevelt after he ceased to do so as antibusiness in their orientation, he too, at least during the hundred days, was suspicious of "Wall Street" men, as Lowenthal's letters indicate. But the line between liberal and radical and what was politically acceptable was difficult to draw. "Moley said Tugwell is running too fast . . . and he has put Marvin Jones [the Texas chairman of the House Agriculture Committee] in there to hold Tugwell down."

Another Frankfurter loyalist, Tommy Corcoran, whom Frankfurter had sent to Lowenthal in 1926 to help research federal courts and receiverships, was in touch with Lowenthal now to help him deepen Frankfurter's beachhead in the New Deal. "What a phenomenon Tom Corcoran is," wrote Lowenthal, "and a help . . ."

Moley was a busy man during the hundred days, perhaps second to Roosevelt, the busiest in Washington. Lowenthal found that his assistant Celeste Jedel was quite ready to talk with him and seemed sympathetic. Tall, brown-haired, good-looking, she had graduated in 1931 from Barnard where she had been an honor student of Moley. She had, said Moley, "an extraordinarily brilliant mind," and the scholar Elliot A. Rosen who assisted Moley in the writing of his second New Deal book believes that the "so-called Moley diary . . . was actually written by Celeste."[13]

From then on the Frankfurter group stayed in close touch with Celeste Jedel.

"I told Miss Jedel what to watch for," Lowenthal wrote Frankfurter, "what to guide Moley's mind and stuff she can do, I think, to read memos I may send in, that I was going back to N.Y. . . . Very nice talk . . . Miss Jedel was present yesterday when Richberg was in Moley's office and warned Moley that the bank bill has done nothing for basic troubles in unemployment."

"On March 16th," wrote Moley, "the A.A.A. [Agricultural Adjustment Administration] bill and message were sent down to Congress, and for ninety-two days thereafter bills and messages were tossed into the Congressional hopper as fast as they could be prepared."[14] Said one-time critic Lippmann, "The great achievement of the past ten days has been the renewal of the people's confidence in themselves and in their institutions. They believe they have a leader whom they can follow. They believe they have a government which can act."

From the onset of the Great Depression Hoover had contended the key to recovery was "confidence." It became clear after March 4, and it is cruel to have to say so, a key to a return of confidence was his departure from the White House. On top of that, the vigor of Roosevelt's leadership electrified the country. Suddenly Washington became the place to be. Young men and women, especially lawyers, flocked to the capital. In many cases they were drawn there by sheer economic necessity. There were jobs, especially for lawyers, in the new agencies, when there were few at home, especially if one was Jewish, and at salaries twice and three times what jobs offered at home.

There were jobs by the hundreds, and jobs, in particular, for the brightest from the *Law Reviews.* And of all the recruiters Frankfurter was turned to most often. Indeed, as the memoirs of the times have become available, his ability, abetted by Corcoran, to place former students, is awesome.

Frances Perkins, the Secretary of Labor, the first woman cabinet member in American history, and a worker of long standing for social causes, went to Roosevelt's office to talk about a solicitor for her department.[15] Frankfurter happened to be there. He had already advised the secretary against employing Lee Pressman, even though brilliant and a former student. Did he have any suggestions, Roosevelt asked. Frankfurter told a story about a youthful Charles Wyzanski in Boston. Though the only Jew in the Yankee law firm of Ropes and Gray, he had, out of conviction, asked to be excused from writing a brief contending that a Massachusetts variant of the Norris-La Guardia anti-yellow dog contract bill would be held unconstitutional. "This sounds like the right fellow," said FDR to Perkins. A few days later, back at Brattle Street in Cambridge, Frankfurter called Wyzanski, "Will you take the solicitorship of the Department of Labor if it is offered you?" Wyzanski in mid-March "still" thought "FDR was quite a guy. So I said of course I would." Perkins promptly summoned him to the capital. She liked the twenty-six-year-old youngster and took him to the White House. The purpose of the meeting was to discuss a proposed five-billion-dollar public works bill which had been drafted by Miss Perkins and later became Title II of the NIRA. At the end of the long session, Perkins took Wyzanski up to the President. "Mr. President, this is the fellow I want." The youthful Wyzanski felt honor-bound to tell the President he had voted for Hoover. "I don't care," replied Roosevelt. "What I want you to do is to have on my desk tomorrow a draft of the bill carrying out the ideas that you have heard discussed."

"The first thing I did when I got out, Wyzanski continued, "was to ring Tom Corcoran . . . I knew Tom because I had met him through Jim

Landis at the Tally-Ho restaurant. I said, 'This is the kind of thing you know all about. How do you draw up such a business?' " Tom instructed Wyzanski, and "The next morning I had on the President's desk the draft of a bill of what was I think in substance very much like the bill that was passed."

Frankfurter had given Wyzanski an "A" at the law school, but Wyzanski in his oral history takes care to say that he was "no favorite of Felix's then, or, if the truth be told, really at any stage," nor was he "an admirer." Nevertheless, when in his first weeks as solicitor, young Wyzanski was overcome by the magnitude of his job and told Miss Perkins he wanted to resign, she got hold of Felix on the phone and he called Wyzanski and advised him to be patient. He stayed. Perkins liked him and talked with him about her problems, personal as well as political. "She liked to work with people who had what she used to call [a] 'Yiddish kopf'—Jewish head."

Another progressive in the cabinet, the Secretary of the Interior Harold Ickes, was a peppery Bull Mooser and lawyer from Chicago. He had appointed Nathan R. Margold as his solicitor. Margold had taught Wyzanski criminal law at Harvard Law School. He chose him, said Ickes, after advising with Frankfurter and Justice Brandeis. The thirty-three-year-old Margold, noted Ickes, was "one of the most brilliant men ever turned out by the Harvard Law School."

Jerome Frank, another "Yiddish kopf," although he had little to do with Jewish activities, also was brought to New Deal Washington's attention by Frankfurter.[16] Frank was a brainy product of the University of Chicago and its law school. He had met Frankfurter in 1930 and after Roosevelt's election wrote him, "I know you know Roosevelt very well. I want to get out of this Wall Street racket, anyhow. This crisis seems to be the equivalent of a war and I'd like to join up for the duration." "If you get a curious offer," Frankfurter advised him a week later, "don't reject it without considerable reflection." Soon afterward Frank's phone rang. "This is Tugwell, Assistant Secretary of Agriculture." Tugwell did not know Frank; nevertheless, Frankfurter's suggestion was good enough. "We want you to come down here and be the solicitor for the Department of Agriculture," Tugwell advised him. He did have a "bowing acquaintance" with agriculture, Frank informed Tugwell, because of his work during World War I with Joseph Cotton. The latter then was running the stockyards for Hoover's Food Administration. Frank's law partners thought him crazy to abandon money-making, but public service seemed preferable.

Frankfurter mentioned Frank to Roosevelt who had approved, but

James Farley, the Postmaster General and chief patronage dispenser, wanted the job for someone else. "Come on down here, anyhow," Tugwell urged Frank. "We'd much rather have you run the new Agricultural Adjustment Administration [AAA]." That interested him more, said Frank, "because the other would seem rather routine."

George Peek was the administrator of the new Triple A. He had been a prominent farm leader, a sponsor of McNary-Haugenism whose basic idea was to relieve agricultural distress by dumping farm surpluses abroad. He was not sympathetic to the basic crop reduction idea of the Triple A and he opposed the selection of Frank as his general counsel. But Frank hit it off with Wallace and Tugwell and the first week in Washington, before their families arrived, the three lived together. "We would talk about everything in the world."

While Frank waited around for the Triple A to be enacted, Harry Hopkins, the fast-moving administrator of Federal Relief, asked him for cocktails. Hopkins, forty-three-years old, a graduate of Grinnell College in Iowa, was tall, lean, single-minded, and plainspoken. A longtime worker for social reform, he gave up a $13,500 salary in New York to administer federal relief at a salary of $8,500. His offices, too, became the center of ideas and administrative drive.

"I want you to be my lawyer," Hopkins said. "I understand you're the kind of lawyer I want. You're not too goddamned technical."

"I said, 'I don't know about that. I'd like to help you.' "

"You let Jerry alone," Tugwell, who was there, advised the purposeful Hopkins. "He's our lawyer."

"Look, Harry," interrupted Frank. You don't want a fuss-budget lawyer. So if you have some problems, I'll come around once a week." He did so for several years. He took to Harry. "He intuitively went to the heart of a practical problem. Ickes was so afraid that somebody might steal a penny that he stopped the whole show in order to avoid it. Hopkins thought it more important to get 90 percent out even if 10 percent was wasted. He did it with great courage and a knowledge he might get into trouble . . . here was something like a war and by God he had to do something."

There was more to the delay in Frank's appointment than awaiting passage of the Triple A. In Wallace's presence in Roosevelt's office, Peek had complained "that I was a city lawyer and a Jew. My appointment wouldn't sit well with the farmers. Wallace was very apologetic, but said, 'Well, there it is, Jerry.' "

That angered Frank and he complained to Tugwell, a good friend and sympathetic soul. Tugwell appealed to Roosevelt who said firmly Frank would be appointed general counsel. Peek's real antagonism, Frank later decided, reflected a fear that Frank would be hostile to him. "Now, look, I want you to understand," Peek warned him on the day of his appointment, "that Wallace hasn't anything to do with this show."

Frank worked for Peek and performed chores for Wallace, but his real admiration at Agriculture was for Tugwell, an "interesting, cultivated man, capable of thinking for himself . . . eager to do something about the whole depression problem." Tugwell reciprocated such sentiments. "He was," Tugwell wrote of Frank, "in one way or another a most formative influence on shaping the NRA and the AAA—as well as many other measures. He was indefatigable in his argument, he was a thorough workman, and he was extremely persuasive. It was not long before I felt that I had multiplied my own effectiveness many times by merely having him as my second."[17]

"Overnight," said Bess Furman, the Associated Press reporter assigned to cover Eleanor Roosevelt, Washington was abloom with the alphabetical agencies created to meet a drumfire of concrete necessities. They attracted a new type of public servant. Tugwell sensed the attractions of power that was wielded on behalf of the public well-being. He had wavered between a job at Agriculture or Commerce. To serve public purposes, he decided, seemed to him the key to the good life. He spent a day with Wallace canvassing the problems that might come up in Agriculture:

We talked about the past neglect of the function of control in the general interest— how the Departments regard themselves, not as public agencies so much as special agents for the interests they represent. There is needed a new view of Commerce and Agriculture, for instance, as representatives in special fields of the public, rather than representatives to the public of businessmen and farmers. Given such a reversal of views, it would be possible to proceed toward entirely new policies in which a larger conception would be dominant. The interest of the public is in an agriculture suited to national needs; agriculture exists for the country; the country does not exist to support farmers. These ideas of mine Wallace agreed to wholly.[18]

"I was not there as a reformer with a program," said Wyzanski,[19] but even men like Wyzanski who considered themselves conservatives "were a level of employees that Washington hadn't previously seen . . . there was an ideal element in most of us." The young lawyers and economists saw one another at lunch, supper, and at parties. Washington teemed with young men and some women who were struggling with the nation's problems. "Even more intimately than at the Harvard Law School," Wyzanski found, "the young men in the government in the 1933 to 1935 era ate, slept, and constantly talked the topics of their jobs, so that there was constant communication among these people, an enthusiasm, an energy, an awareness of fresh problems and a feeling that one really counted and that what one did was very important."

One place that the most promising of the New Dealers met was at the teas of Justice Brandeis. To be a young lawyer, economist, or administrator in Roosevelt's Washington and to be invited to tea at the Brandeis apartment on California Street was not quite the equivalent of an invitation in Britain to Buckingham Palace, for the emblems of sovereignty belonged to the White House. Moreover brains and expertise rather than rank, family, or wealth qualified one for a call from the justice's law clerk. Nevertheless, they were memorable occasions for all those who were asked to come. Teas, like all the justice's domestic arrangements, were Spartan affairs. "All they'd get would be a cup of tea and a sort of ginger snap," said James Landis whom Frankfurter had sent down to the justice as his law clerk in 1925, "one of the best years I ever spent in my life."[20]

The great moment for Brandeis's tea guests came when they were brought to the justice. "Within three minutes of talking with the Justice, they would be expressing their inmost desires," said Landis. "He spent a good deal of time listening to and advising people with regard to, not personal problems . . . but problems with regard to ideals that they should pursue, what career they should pursue." It was his law clerk's function, whether at tea or dinner, to get everybody out. "If I didn't do that Mrs. Brandeis would give me hell," Landis recalled.

"In the 1920s an ambitious young man headed for Wall Street," wrote R. S. McElvaine in *The Great Depression*.[21] "During the New Deal, though, he went into government." And it was the young New Dealers who gave the new administration a touch of excitement.

X

—————⟫†⟪—————

The NRA–An Effort
to Control Business

"Roosevelt's first efforts had a collectivist character," Tugwell wrote in his review of *Roosevelt and Frankfurter*,[1] and he singled out the Agricultural Adjustment Administration and the National Recovery Administration (NRA) to make his point. In the same review, which was written in 1970, he observed, "Curiously, in these episodes Frankfurter as can be seen in the letters made no forthright comment." Frankfurter did comment, but the letters were not published in the volume Tugwell had under review, and Tugwell may not have been aware of them. Nevertheless, it is true that Brandeis was hostile to the two ventures. His distrust of "bigness" shaped his judgment of the two agencies. Tugwell in his "Notes from a New Deal Diary," that he kept contemporaneous with the events of the Hundred Days and that he deposited with the Roosevelt Library, describes a call that he and Henry Wallace, the Secretary of Agriculture, whom he then was serving as assistant secretary, made on Brandeis.

Most of our talk concerned industrial philosophy; he arguing that bigness is always badness, I maintaining that bigness needed only direction, submission to discipline.[2]

There undoubtedly was this difference in approach to national economic policy between Brandeis and Tugwell. Moley and Berle shared Tugwell's views on concentration and control of industry, although to a lesser degree. Nor is it clear to what extent Tugwell advanced collectivist considerations in the drafting of the recovery bill. His diary which does deal with his role in the early drafts is silent on the subject. As for Frankfurter, whatever his doubts about the National Industrial Recovery Act (NIRA) on constitutional grounds, and these, we will see, were major, he was ready to lend his best efforts to help it succeed, urging it to avoid tests on constitutionality while the statute was tried, amended, and modified in the course of administration.

A few statistics demonstrate the challenge that confronted Roosevelt and his associates by the industrial scene and set their agenda. Idle men and factories dwarfed those in use. Industrial production had fallen more than 50 percent, new construction had all but vanished, the unemployed were numbered at fourteen million. The industrial machine that had dazzled the world and provided millions of working men and women with the highest standards of living in history had collapsed.

How to reverse the shrinkage that had taken place since 1929? Was there a key to recovery? "We disagree on the domestic means to recovery," Tugwell wrote in his diary about discussions with a business economist whom he considered wise and sympathetic, "he believing it must come through expansion of equipment industries and I believing it can best be begun by reconstructing purchasing power."[3] The emphasis on purchasing power with its egalitarian thrust distinguished the conservative from the liberal supporters of Roosevelt and the New Deal. Aggregate mass purchasing power in the United States since 1929 had declined more than 50 percent. There was no division between the Brandeis-Frankfurter people and the Moley-Tugwell-Berle group on that. Nor were they divided on the need for a massive public works spending program.

In February Frankfurter had telegraphed Moley who was with the President-elect in Warm Springs. He should see Brandeis . . . HE IS MOST ANXIOUS TO HAVE TALK WITH YOU ABOUT A PUBLIC WORKS PROGRAM WHICH SEEMS TO HIM—AND I TAKE TO YOU—INDISPENSABLE FOR ACHIEVING RECOVERY.[4] Two months later he voiced fears to Moley that "the policy of a large-scale public works is not moving ahead as fast as it should for recovery. I cannot help wondering whether the old Treasury influences hostile to a constructive spending program are still operating."

The conservatives in the government were led by Lewis Douglas, the director of the Budget. He had been an able but right-wing congressman from Arizona who advocated balanced budgets, a sales tax, and measures that would win the confidence of businessmen. Douglas argued powerfully for his restrictionist budget and was fleetingly persuasive with Roosevelt. Tugwell describes a conversation with a leader of the Senate Progressives, young Robert M. La Follette, the son of the 1924 Farmer-Labor candidate for president:

Bob La Follette is much worried for fear our expansionist program will not follow quickly enough the conservatory steps which have been, or are about to be undertaken—closing the weak banks, consolidating railways, exposing crooked bankers and the like. I am of that feeling myself. Moley and I talked about it yesterday and he said he thought Woodin would finally see a way. I hope so, though I think the way is clear—government expenditure, and we must do it.[5]

Hoover had vetoed the public works bill that was pushed through Congress by the Democrats, and Roosevelt hesitated. New Deal thinking turned to other ways of industrial priming. Long before Roosevelt had come into office, Frankfurter had advised Moley to examine the proposals of a Princeton professor of international economics, Frank Graham. He had worked out a scheme for government subsidies to enable privately owned companies to reactivate the idle plants. Both had looked at Graham's proposals but had filed them among the many schemes for industrial recovery that were coming in, a few of them to surface later in a Tugwell scheme for government leasing of idle plants.

Right after Roosevelt's election a Berle memorandum on legislative priorities listed farm relief based on a "domestic allotment plan" as the top item and industrial stabilization as number two—"Necessarily this involves at least a limited set of exceptions to the Anti-Trust Act."[6] Soon after his inauguration Roosevelt asked Moley to collate the various plans for industrial recovery. This was not out of the blue. In February when Tugwell thought he might be named Assistant Secretary of Commerce, he and Moley talked with Henry I. Harriman, the president of the chamber of commerce. Moley stayed for only an hour of the morning's talk which went on through lunch.

I was especially interested to feel him [Harriman] out concerning the relations of government to business. Unless something can be done to bring business closer under general government direction and to change over from the old anti-trust law repressions to recognition and control of present trends and scale, I certainly would not be interested in becoming Assistant Secretary of Commerce.[7]

Shortly afterward Tugwell spent a day with Henry Wallace. The latter had liked his book, *The Industrial Discipline,* and was enthusiastic about applying some of its ideas to agriculture. Tugwell had finally agreed to become Assistant Secretary of Agriculture rather than Commerce and helped draft the Triple A bill which, with farmer participation, was a planned government effort to raise farmers' income through a system of acreage restrictions and benefit payments.

Urban-based senators under the leadership of Senator Robert F. Wagner of New York broke with precedent and voted for the Triple A even though it meant a higher cost of living in the cities. Passage of the Triple A intensified questions about industrial recovery.[8] What should the government do about that? The basic Brandeis formula, as noted, was public works. Moley was a skeptic privately. In response to Frankfurter's repeated urgings he had seen the justice on March 8, an interview that he recalled because of the hardness of the chair in which he had squirmed. The justice had urged his broad public works program be financed by closure of the loopholes in the federal tax laws. Moley appeared sympathetic, but his real view was "public works of such magnitude could not possibly be useful in meeting an emergency." And to finance them by plugging tax loopholes was "frivolous to the point of absurdity."[9]

A public works program to trigger a recovery was, nevertheless, the prescription of many, including Senate progressives like Costigan, La Follette, Bronson Cutting, as well as Wagner. All might be called premature Keynesians, and in retrospect economists agree the chief fault with their prescription was its meagerness. While deficit spending would be seen in the future as the key contracyclical measure in a period of depression, in 1933 few recognized it as a form of national planning and New Dealers looked for another key. Ideas to revive industry were being hatched in many Washington offices, one place being Senator Wagner's. By 1933 the senator by way of Tammany and Boss Murphy had become a pivotal legislator on the side of the underdog. Much of the New Deal legislation was given to him to pilot through the Senate, several of them items he had championed in the Hoover years.

When a bill was to be drafted, it went to a slim, youngish man in his office, his administrative aide, Simon Rifkind.[10] He was a product of Columbia Law School and had been with the senator since 1925. The senator had set Rifkind to work in 1931 on the conflict between antitrust laws and industrial recovery. The senator was familiar with plans to end industrial instability and cutthroat competition promoted by industrialists like Swope and Harriman as well as by labor leaders like Sidney Hillman and John L. Lewis.

What triggered action by the administration and Wagner was passage in the Senate on April 4 of a bill introduced by Hugo Black of Alabama, a populist, to spread work by shortening hours—the thirty-hour bill. It was endorsed by Labor and the American Legion and such was the pressure for it that although it was opposed by Roosevelt even Wagner supported it. Roosevelt considered the measure unconstitutional, emphasized its rigidities, and, if it were enacted, feared it would result in more plant closings rather than the opposite.

The effect of Senate passage, which presaged similar action in the House, was to persuade the White House the only way to head off the thirty-hour bill was to bring in its own industrial recovery plan. Roosevelt prodded Moley. Three days later (April 14) the *Times* columnist Arthur Krock reported a government plan for the mobilization of private industry coupled with a public works program. The leak nettled Roosevelt and evidently had come from Wagner who had lunched with Krock. But presidents cannot afford to get angry with pivotal senators and Wagner was central to the enactment of a substitute for the Black bill. A week later Roosevelt asked him to prepare a bill and the senator assembled a group of bankers, industrialists, economists, and lawyers. "I had the yellow pad on the NIRA," said Rifkind.

A lot more was going on. Tugwell wrote in his diary:

We missed a trick during the banking crisis by not setting up a national bank. We can miss another trick now by going in for currency inflation instead of expansion. The government really ought to take over immediately large blocks of paralyzed industries. At the very least, it ought to take them on lease. There is a feeling of confidence in the country and great affection for FDR but this is ephemeral and unemployment is still increasing. Activity must be revived and expanded and fiscal policy must support and further the movement.[11]

There was a rise in the stock and commodity markets:

Prices have increased some 10%. But the bottom will drop out of this unless something solid is furnished in the way of support. This ought to be a public works program and the leasing or taking over of the industries now working at 15% to 205% of capacity.

He, too, was at work on a roundup of various plans for the stimulation of private industry. Jerome Frank and Louis Bean, the Department of

Agriculture's statistician, and Bobby Straus, the son of Isidore Straus, one of Roosevelt's major financial backers, were at work with him. He then added, "[General Hugh] Johnson is also working on something."

There were many centers of intellectual fertilization in New Deal Washington and the inception of the NIRA was a good example of how cross-fertilization worked. Rifkind had planned to go back to New York, even had given up his apartment and was off to Union Station when Wagner recalled him to work particularly on the NIRA.[12] "I knew Ben and Tom and Jerry Frank and of course, Ickes, Justice Brandeis and Felix Frankfurter," he said. "I was always invited to Brandeis's teas. He was the greatest suction pump I ever met. I remember talking to Brandeis about other bills, but not about the NIRA." Then there were the parties. They were "a continuous thing. I went to them with other clerks of senators and justices." An alert young man or woman picked up a great deal at such affairs and never more so than when the NIRA was brewing. The Tugwell group made contact with the "Wagner-La Follette group," as Tugwell described it, "and reconciled their views."[13]

Another center of gestation was in the office of John Dickinson. He was bald-headed and big-chested. He had studied with Frankfurter and was a lawyer and Assistant Secretary of Commerce. An able man, he was given to profundities that caused some to label him "the Pope," but the Tugwell group worked with him, usually Jerry Frank. The latter was accompanied by a Tugwell protégé from Columbia, the portly Leon Keyserling. Lawyer and economist, Keyserling was at home in the New Deal and when Rifkind in June persuaded Wagner to allow him to return to New York, Leon became the senator's administrative aide. After a couple of meetings the Tugwell group merged with the Dickinson drafters. For two weeks they worked every night. "Their idea," recalled Frank, "was for a small number of codes related to major industries. The idea that mattress makers, barbershops and the like would have codes—no one thought of that."[14]

They had not reckoned with Hugh Johnson. A different kind of New Dealer, this former cavalryman was a colorful wordsmith, as the Brains Trust had discovered when his mentor Bernard Baruch had persuaded Roosevelt and Moley to include him in its operations. Ray Moley now ran into the colorful general in the lobby of the Carlton Hotel. He had just returned from a South Carolina hunting trip with Baruch. Moley was still trying to figure out how to ride herd on the various groups that were at work on an industrial recovery bill. Until then Johnson had only had a peripheral relationship to these efforts. Moley begged him to come to his office, "You're familiar with the only comparable thing that's ever been done—the work of the War Industries Board."

He found an office for Johnson in the old State Department building near his own. Johnson took off his coat and necktie and went to work. He was a hard worker and in a few days had a draft.

The general, unlike the young lawyers and economists who were converging on Washington, writing the new laws and staffing the new agencies, was a West Point graduate—in the same class as General MacArthur. He was heavyset and gravelly voiced, and an inexhaustable flow of expletive-mixed language masked a core of sensitivity and sentimentality.

Tugwell's diary reflected the liberals' ambivalence about the general: "I had got used to thinking of him as Baruch's man rather than an independent personality, not doubting, of course, the strength of character and real brilliance, which are obvious. I think his tendency to be gruff in personal relations will be a handicap and his occasional drunken sprees will not help any . . ."[15]

Soon Dickinson and Frank were summoned to the White House with their draft. "Now watch this man," Frank, who had known Johnson, cautioned Dickinson. "He's very smart and has terrific interest."[16]

Frank as a Chicago lawyer in the twenties had been involved with the reorganization of the Moline Plow Company after Baruch had brought Johnson into this very large enterprise as vice president and general manager. He liked the general who "put all his muscle into his words" but feared his ignorance of constitutional law. The general, said Frank, thought he was a lawyer but he had only studied law for a few weeks. At the White House meeting Johnson and Dickinson wrangled over their respective drafts. Roosevelt's mandate to the two groups was to "go away and agree. Wagner, Dickinson, Frances Perkins, Johnson and I fought over the thing in Lou Douglas' office for some time." They were "blotted out," commented Frank. The drafting job ended in Johnson's hands. Dickinson was "a keen thinker," Tugwell agreed, but "he was downright nasty to Johnson. But the general had his revenge when a few days later it leaked out he was to run the whole show."

Frank, although friendly with Johnson, tried to get Wagner who had been at the meeting with the President to intercede against this transfer of total responsibility to Johnson, but the senator demurred: "I'm in the legislative branch. That's for the executive." Secretary Wallace sought to

reassure the uneasy Frank. Wallace understood Felix Frankfurter was going to be Johnson's counsel. "Too good to be true," thought Frank. He
called Frankfurter. "No, no, no. I've turned down all kinds of jobs, besides
which I'm going to Oxford for a year," Frankfurter told him, adding, "But
it's all right because Donald Richberg is here with me now and he's going
to be the counsel."

That news cheered Frank and presumably Tugwell and Wallace.
Richberg, a Chicagoan, was an old Bull Mooser and former law partner of
Ickes. He had many ties with labor and liberals, having managed the La
Follette campaign in 1924, served as counsel to the Railway Brotherhood,
and played an important role in the enactment of the Norris-La Guardia
Anti-Injunction Act. Roosevelt liked him and Moley had brought him in
to work with Johnson in connection, particularly, with labor interests in
the pending bill.

The feature of the pending legislation that chiefly recommended it to
labor and liberals was its inclusion of labor's right to bargain collectively
(Section 7a), as well as provisions that outlawed child labor and sweatshop
conditions, objectives the progressives had sought since the beginning of
the century.

"Of course the Act hasn't yet passed," Tugwell recorded on May 30.
"The National Manufacturers Association has gone off the reservation and
are calling their whole membership to Washington to fight it—because of
the labor provisions—but I believe it will pass in substantially its present
form with the President's prestige behind it."[17] Labor took such threats
seriously. They suspected Johnson of leaning toward this effort to eliminate Section 7a and sent an SOS to Frank. He went to Wagner. The senator
was blunt to the drafters: "No 7a, no NRA." Johnson, said Frank, had
been called "a sheep in wolf's clothing." He capitulated to the progressives.

The chief doubts about the draft related to its constitutionality and
nowhere were they greater than among the young lawyers who looked to
Frankfurter for leadership. The questions about constitutionality centered
upon the reach of the "interstate commerce" clause, and the provision in
which Congress delegated to the President powers to write codes with the
force of law. "I researched that for the Senator," said Rifkind, "and concluded the Supreme Court had never declared a bill unconstitutional because of delegation. We hoped it would pass muster."[18]

Frank was one of the doubters of the validity of the codes. He thought it "shocking" that no constitutional lawyer had scrutinized the code-making process. The codes could have been made constitutional, he felt, "except that Johnson paid no attention to the problem that is bound to face us in the courts with regard to interstate commerce."[19]

The same concern was voiced by Wyzanski in a letter to Frankfurter.[20] The Supreme Court had drawn a line that separated interstate from intrastate commerce, and he feared that the inclusion of small business in the code-making provisions would cross that line. Three days later he voiced another constitutional concern to Frankfurter. The code-making process went "so far beyond the bounds of constitutionality that it would be useless" to test it in the courts. "It seems to me that those parts of Section 3 which allow an industry itself or the President on his own initiative to set up a code of fair competition are entirely too broad."

As if to underscore his doubts, Wyzanski asked rhetorically about the code-making powers given the President: "Where there are no limits set by the legislature can the power to issue regulations go this far?—As I have already written you, if Sec. 4b is good law, I wasted a year taking T.R. Powell's course." Powell was the Harvard Law School's witty and redoubted professor of constitutional law.

As the NIRA reached the stage of legislative decision, Frankfurter had been turned to increasingly by Frances Perkins and her department. They feared Johnson and were concerned also for the Labor Department's own say in NRA decisions that related to labor.

A secret memorandum to Frankfurter from Grace Abbott, the venerated head of the Children's Bureau in the Department of Labor, emphasized that it was not sufficient merely to provide that the secretary approve what the administrator does.[21] Perkins should have the authority and responsibility "to *initiate* and conduct negotiations on *all* proposals with reference to labor in the development of the industrial codes." This was not a grab for power but the determination of women long experienced in the battle for minimum wage laws and in the negotiation of wage agreements to safeguard labor's interests by specific inclusion in the bill of the Labor Department's authority. "Progressives and labor are supporting this measure," wrote Miss Abbott, who asserted parenthetically that Frances Perkins did not know that she was so advising Frankfurter, "because they believe that President Roosevelt can be trusted through the Secretary of Labor to see that the workers are given a square deal, which means an opportunity for collective agreement."

Frankfurter agreed with her letter except for its remarks about Johnson whom Miss Abbott had been told was "very difficult to work with, had no understanding of labor problems and would expect to be a dictator." Frankfurter thought the general would be "responsive" to the kind of considerations raised by Miss Abbott. Moreover, "the inclusion of Donald Richberg as general counsel goes a long way to introduce the interests committed to the Secretary of Labor at the policy-making stages of what will be done under the Act, if the present set-up prevails."[22] He agreed that Frances Perkins should share in the initiating and conduct of negotiations that involved labor and should have "a permanent delegate—a full-time representative" in the code-making process—someone like Leo Wolman, a professor of industrial economics at Columbia University who had worked with Perkins in Albany. "For Johnson is, as you know," Frankfurter's letter to Abbott went on, "what is called a man of action and is making at least—or rather will have made—a lot of psychological commitments long before the Bill becomes an Act. *Now* is the time for Frances Perkins to get Leo Wolman into the tent as her spokesman."

At the same time, Frankfurter advised Wagner of the need to add a provision to the NIRA draft—"a specific law giving the Secretary of Labor real authority in the initiation and conduct of negotiations on all proposals affecting labor in the development of the codes." The draft act was not so revised, but the general wanted labor with him and did designate Wolman as chairman of the Labor Advisory Committee. At the suggestion of William Green, the not-too-dynamic president of the American Federation of Labor, he appointed Green's chief associate, Edward F. McGrady, as his assistant administrator for labor matters. Perkins was not enthusiastic about McGrady, regarded him as a union wheelhorse, and had vetoed Farley's recommendation of him as Assistant Secretary of Labor, but as she watched him at the NRA she changed her mind and ended up making him her assistant secretary. Wolman did not have the plenary powers in labor matters that had been urged by Frankfurter, but between the Columbia intellectual and the tough-minded labor negotiator, not to mention Senator Wagner, who became chairman of the National Labor Board (NLB) set up by Johnson to adjudicate the flock of labor disputes that arose under Section 7A, labor's interests were safeguarded.[23]

As the bill neared passage, people wanted to know Frankfurter's views about it. He drafted a four-page memorandum that he entitled "The Recovery Bill and Wage Standards."[24] The chief merit of the proposed act as he saw it rested in what it would do to raise those standards. He sent copies to Wagner, Perkins, and Richberg. The voice he used in the memorandum reflected his own image of himself. He spoke as a liberal to liberals. The memorandum by implication drew the line between the business supporters of the bill who saw it primarily as a way to rationalize industrial competition by suspension of the antitrust laws and the liberal-labor supporters who were so because of their faith that Roosevelt would use the NRA to increase mass purchasing power.

He did not view the suspension of the antitrust laws as any panacea. The purpose of the Recovery Bill, he wrote, should not be "a vain effort to stabilize business on the basis of a constantly shrinking demand" but the increase of effective demand for goods and services. Businessmen concerned with a reduction of inventories might seek a way out in "restriction on production and maintenance or increase of price," but the end result of such an approach would be a decline in employment and consumption.

Easing Sherman Act restraints might bring "some stability for the benefit of the relatively strong," but Frankfurter doubted any substantial gain for the public; indeed, he had seen "little or no convincing proof that the Sherman Act has either caused or intensified the depression" and believed that "the cartel system in Europe has proved more disastrous than the Sherman Law in America."

But theory aside, Frankfurter went on, he believed in an "initial effort to make our economic machine function . . . I personally put more stress on a public works program of large proportions than any other because that will unquestionably put men to work. But if industry can be helped by giving businessmen the feeling that the worst is over, that industry is under reasonable control, that prices are likely to rise rather than fall, and that schemes that have been held back should be pushed before costs increase, no *a priori* theory need stand in the way. On this premise and on this premise alone, the NIRA may be accepted by the liberals." The pragmatist was prepared to sit on his doubts, provided that the business system was not "controlled for the benefit of businessmen alone . . . If supply is to be kept in adjustment, so must demand. The labor clauses at once assume a commanding importance as a part of any industrial code."

Industrial stabilization was achievable at the price of "an America that may become habituated to the standards of living of India or Peru." But industry could be made profitable and standards of living reach unheard of levels if mass purchasing power was increased. "Consequently every industrial code must protect the consumer by insisting that price should be so adjusted to volume that the benefits of mass production may not be lost to the consuming public and by insisting that the benefits of conscious control of industry should be shared with the workers." The objective in business control, or codification, was "the price should come down and the volume of business rise" and not "the price should be maintained and the volume restricted."

Low wages might be justified in an undeveloped country, Frankfurter went on, or in a debtor country where capital was badly needed and high interest rates had to be paid to entice capital investment. But in a highly developed country like the United States "the price paid for capital ought to be very low." Here Frankfurter invoked Keynes, the only economist mentioned in his memorandum. "Mr. Keynes prophesies that with the return of confidence and a proper balance of international payments, interest rates in the western world should surely fall. That being true, the important desideratum is an encouragement to an all-round high standard of living and a relatively shorter working day that will permit men's lives to be devoted to other things than money-making."

There followed a plea that the codes limit labor's hours to thirty-six a week as the norm "and wages must be kept at a level that will give maximum purchasing power to the workers." The pre-Depression wage level was to be taken as a minimum and "wage cuts should be regarded as market destroyers." The principle of wage fixing was relatively simple, but he recognized that "their actual adjustment may involve thousands of complicated schedules." The working out of such schedules required the participation of the organizations of the workers. Not paternalism or feudal wisdom—"the problems can be met only by the good faith, acceptance and encouragement of industrial democracy."

On June 16, the day the historic special session of Congress adjourned, Roosevelt signed the NIRA with its provisions for government recognition of trade associations, their exemption from antitrust compulsions, and the labor provisions, especially Section 7A. "History will probably record the NIRA as the most important and far-reaching legislation ever enacted by the American Congress," Roosevelt said.

For several months General Johnson, a consummate showman, occupied the center of the NRA and often the national stage as he combined patriotism with threats of boycotts of nonconformers in his drive to persuade industry to sign codes. His chief weapon was the blanket code (the

President's Re-employment Agreement [PRA]) under which an industry, pending the adoption of a regular code, was invited to sign an agreement to observe minimum wage and maximum hour standards, to abolish child labor, and to refrain from unnecessary price increases. In an inspired gesture, the general rewarded compliance with the emblem of the Blue Eagle, the Navaho Indian Thunderbird. "We Do Our Part," the emblem read. A recovery mood swept America. There were posters and massive parades everywhere. "In fact, 2,300,000 employers signed the President's Re-employment Agreement," wrote the chief statistician of the NRA's research division, "with the result that 16,000,000 workers out of a possible 25,000,000 to be covered by codes were placed under agreements within two months after the Act was signed."[25]

But fears did not vanish, especially among progressives, that the business community relieved of antitrust restrictions, would limit production and fix prices while pressing for self-regulation free from government controls.

"We talked among ourselves, Frank and I and our progressive friends," Tugwell later wrote of his attitude as 1933 ended, "in curiously reminiscent terms of chances missed, of mistakes made, and of failures. Our lost opportunity would not be retrieved now short of another crisis."[26]

Elegiac moods were not a characteristic of the irrepressible Frankfurter. His NRA worries were of another sort. He voiced them at a luncheon that New Deal lawyers, most of them young, all of them admirers, tendered him before his departure at the end of September for a year at Oxford. As Jerome Frank recalled:

Frankfurter made a speech on how important it was not to go too fast and that when you were dealing with new statutes, it was very important to have a body of administrative practice before you get them into court because the Supreme Court thought that was very important. Brandeis later told me that he had helped develop this doctrine of the administrative interpretation as affecting the meaning of statutes because federal statutes were so badly drafted [and] the only way you could get any meaning into them was to have them administratively interpreted. Frankfurter doubtless knew Brandeis's perspective, so he said, "Go slow on this. Don't get your cases up, either as to interpretation or constitutionality until you've got this body of law."

Everybody thought Frankfurter was the voice of Jove. I wasn't a "hot dog," as I hadn't studied under him, but we were good friends. I got up and said, "Well, Professor Frankfurter, that's all very nice, but what are you going to do if you're brought into court and somebody sues you? That's happening to my agency [the

Triple A] right now. I can't delay it until [unless?] I just want to capitulate and let judgments be entered." He was kind of nettled and had no answer.[27]

Frankfurter again urged a go-slow attitude in a letter to Wyzanski from Oxford. "Some of our friends seem to be spoiling too eagerly for a legal row," he wrote in the wake of the Weirton Steel Company's defiance of the rulings of the National Labor Board. "I'd feared what you made plain— namely, that it's a bad case to use as a test suit."[28]

Wyzanski had his hands full monitoring General Johnson's actions.[29] Perkins had given him the job of holding the general down and keeping him within limits. Johnson "very properly resented having a 27-year-old boy buzzing around and interfering with him." Perkins was one of the few administration people Johnson trusted. But her concerns about the general were shared by others, notably Roosevelt. In June when he had signed the NIRA bill he had surprised the general by turning over the administration of the huge public works title of the bill to Ickes to administer. The President may have had other motives besides uneasiness about Johnson's abilities. To keep power divided among his subordinates was a governing principle. The general had purpled as he heard the President's decision. He would refuse to administer Title I, he thought.

Roosevelt sensed the general's inner fury and whispered to Perkins to "keep him sweet." Perkins persuaded the general to accept a ride in her car and ordered her chauffeur to keep driving around Washington as she counseled him successfully against resignation. One will never know what Johnson might have done with the Public Works title, but giving it to Ickes proved a mistake. The secretary was so determined to keep the program free of graft and corruption that few projects were authorized. Only "a fraction of the NIRA appropriations for public works were allotted by the end of 1933"; indeed, commented Roos, the NRA statistician, "at the end of one-and-a-half years the PWA was able to spend at only one-half of the average rate which its progenitors had expected it to attain in the first six months."[30]

Thus the hopes of progressives that public works would give the fillip to purchasing power and business revival did not materialize.

Nor did many New Dealers know how much time they had in which to bring about recovery. At the end of the Hundred Days a buoyant and optimistic Roosevelt with his sons as crew skippered the *Amberjack* Down East and the image of relaxed self-confidence that he projected was shared by much of the country. But a minority—not only Communists—was sure the system was doomed. In her reminiscences Frances Perkins tells how she ran into a long-faced Berle in April.[31] "It's too late," he announced, "time has run out." None of the projects launched by the President and Congress "will make any difference in the great upheavals going on." "Oh, nonsense, Mr. Berle," the serious-minded secretary replied, unsure of whether her leg was being pulled, "you've no idea how much more human beings can endure, particularly if they see a ray of hope."

Berle persisted. "Miss Perkins," he said as they parted, "the date of the trouble is June 15th. It won't go beyond June 15th. Something will happen." He advised her to get her family out of the city.

"The 15th of June came and passed . . . Nothing happened," she pointed out to Berle when she ran into him again. "It is the 15th of August," he now said. "Don't be around here and don't allow your children to be around New York, Washington or any other big city."

But Perkins says she had ceased to care what Berle predicted. She never told the President of Berle's doom-and-gloom forecasts. "Roosevelt was a happy soul and he didn't want lugubrious end-of-the-worlders around him," she said.

And the New Dealers, while they constantly pressed forward, were infected with the President's hopefulness. As Ben Cohen said almost half a century later, "We were the lucky ones. For us it was a time when to be alive was joy and to be young was very Heaven."

XI

The Three Musketeers

In early April Moley sent an SOS to Frankfurter in Cambridge. He needed help in drafting a bill. FDR wanted action on a truth-in-securities statute. Not only had he promised such action in his campaign and inaugural address but a shocked nation daily was reading headlines from the Pecora Committee hearings about Wall Street's abuses—an appalling tale of banker evasion, misuse of other people's money, deceptive practices. A House report stated that "during the post-war decade some fifty billions of new securities were floated in the United States. Fully half . . . have proved to be worthless."[1] The President who had pledged to drive the money changers from the temple insisted on securities and exchange regulations as part of his "must" legislation.

Moley had put old Samuel Untermeyer to work on such a bill. In 1912 Untermeyer had been active in the famous Pujo investigation of the "Money Trust," and now came up, during the interregnum, with a plan to place stock exchange regulatory machinery in the Post Office Department. That suggestion, said Moley, reflected an effort to strengthen such a measure's chance of acceptance by the courts, but, he added, it was wholly impractical. At the same time, the President had asked Huston Thompson, also an old-time Wilsonian progressive and a former chairman of the Federal Trade Commission, to prepare a securities bill. He produced a draft based on ideas borrowed from Brandeis that was, said Moley "a hopeless and unintelligible confection." Nonetheless, it was introduced in both House and Senate. Snorted John T. Flynn, harsh critic of Wall Street,

"There is hardly a stock abuse which ran wild during the last dozen years which would have been curbed if this bill had been on the statute books." And when Brandeis later was asked about Thompson, he replied he had "every quality that makes a great lawyer, except one . . . brains."

The Thompson "confection" seemed usable to the Senate but in the House, Sam Rayburn of Texas, the canny chairman of the House Committee on Interstate and Foreign Commerce, considered it unworkable and a committee hearing on it was a debacle.

That was the situation when Moley called Frankfurter. Moley was to reserve rooms for him and two associates at the Carlton Hotel, Frankfurter promptly told him. Thursday evening he and James Landis, Harvard's first professor of litigation, boarded the Federal Express. In Washington the next day they were joined by Benjamin V. Cohen.[2]

Landis and Cohen had never before met. They were both men of high intelligence. Both had gone through college (Cohen through Chicago, Landis through Princeton) with A's in every subject except one. Both had attracted Frankfurter's eye at Harvard Law School. In 1918 he had joined in sending Cohen to Europe to work on the Balfour Declaration, and in 1924 he had sent Landis, six years Cohen's junior, to clerk for Brandeis. Cohen was tall, dark-haired, lean, and quiet-mannered. Landis was five feet seven, sandy-haired, muscular, and aggressive. Cohen was introduced to Landis as a specialist in corporate finance and reorganization who had made a small fortune on Wall Street. They were joined by another Frankfurter loyalist and experienced Wall Street hand, Tom Corcoran, who by now was knowledgeable in Washington's ways. Among the three Cohen was the stranger.

Frankfurter immediately went off to see Moley.[3] The latter took him first to see the President and then to Rayburn who told him he had to have the draft of a bill on Monday. Frankfurter gave this news to the three and again disappeared.

Cohen, Landis, and Corcoran soon repaired to Corcoran's apartment which was only half a block away from the Carlton. "Ben Cohen's prime contribution was that he was very familiar with the disclosure provisions of the British Companies Act," said Landis. They agreed that act should serve as their model. The British Act also avoided the question of the government's passing on the soundness of newly issued securities and that was in accord with Roosevelt's wishes.

The three worked through the weekend in a marathon session that allowed little sleep. Corcoran brought in two stenographers from the RFC. One of them was pretty Peggy Dowd. She had been assigned to Corcoran from the secretarial pool at the agency when no one else would work for the "slave driver," as the girls called him. "You're Irish too, maybe you can handle him," she was told. She had a good memory, was able to match Corcoran's whirlwind pace, and could handle his temperamental style of working. "It was a strange team," said Landis of Corcoran and Cohen. "Corcoran ebullient, moving easily with the new forces in the Administration; Cohen reserved and almost shy; but both brilliant and indefatigable workers."[4] Landis was equally tireless, equally intelligent, and somewhat saturnine. Landis and Corcoran had known each other since law school days. But neither had met Cohen before. Frankfurter soon called them "The Three Musketeers." Sunday evening Frankfurter returned and the three presented him with a draft. He read it and agreed to present it to the Rayburn committee the next day. The drafters were uneasy. All admired Frankfurter but wondered whether even he would be able to digest the complicated draft. "Our disturbance was unnecessary," Landis later wrote.[5]

Monday they first breakfasted with Thompson whom they appeased by telling him their drafts were "simply perfecting amendments" to his bill. A few hours later Frankfurter made a "masterly" presentation of the bill and at the end of the afternoon the Rayburn group adopted it as their working paper. Rayburn asked Cohen and Landis to remain as consultants. Frankfurter, telling Landis he would handle his classes, returned to Cambridge.

The drafting work was now transferred to the basement office of the House's chief legislative draftsmen, Middleton Beaman and his assistant, Allan H. Perley. They were experienced but "hard" taskmasters, said Landis. At night they were joined by Corcoran who had done a day's work at the RFC and whose job he later said was to "drink coffee laced with sugar," memorize the ceiling patterns, and to keep the peace between Landis and Cohen. He also shared their worries about "sinister Wall Street plotting" because Beaman would not allow a line to be drafted until he had talked through what they had in mind—a two days' delay.

It was sometimes touch and go between Landis, who had a tendency to "blow off" and take over, and the shyer but equally firm Cohen, who, though gentler in demeanor, knew from firsthand experience how Wall Street attorneys operated to emasculate statutes. His no-nonsense view of the distinguished denizens of Wall Street was shared by Corcoran. Cohen insisted that stock registration requirements be set forth in a detailed schedule in the body of the bill. Landis feared such an inclusion might jeopardize the statute and urged that they leave the detailed schedule to the regulators. Cohen had had enough. He called Frankfurter. He was pulling out of the project, he announced. Frankfurter backed Cohen's view on the schedule and prevailed on him to stay on the job. A relieved note to Corcoran afterward:

You must have done—as I assumed you did—a marvelous job with Jim and Ben. For Ben writes me,

"Things were a little trying for a while but I guess we will pull through all right. Tom is a prince and someday will be a king."[6]

Frankfurter, who advised Moley about the situation between Cohen and Landis, said of the latter, "in his intensity [he] has not been wholly wise in his relations with Ben." Later Landis acknowledged that "the schedule had the guts of the bill in it."[7]

Landis's apprehension about the inclusion of the detailed schedule in the body of the bill was never tested. Beaman came up with the idea to shift the list to the end of the bill as an attached section. The legislators would exhaust themselves on the early sections of the draft and never get to the last part, he predicted. He proved right.

The Huston Thompson version was in the process of adoption by the Senate. The three had Frankfurter telegraph Moley his objections to the Senate bill, which were also theirs. Frankfurter warned that the Senate bill WAS IN ESSENTIAL ASPECTS . . . PARTLY INNOCUOUS AND PARTLY UN-CONSTITUTIONAL. The telegram ended, IT IS REALLY VITAL AVOID PROG-RESS IN SENATE BILL UNTIL HOUSE GETS AND PASSES ITS BILL STOP AM AWARE OF EXIGENCIES THAT PRESS ON PRESIDENT'S TIME BUT URGE STRONGLY HIS INTERVENTION TO PREVENT JAM AND JEOPARDY OF HIS SECURITIES REGULATIONS PROPOSALS.[8]

As work on the House draft progressed, Corcoran, although not involved in the drafting, fell naturally into the role of promoting the various drafts with other agencies in the government, Treasury, Federal Reserve Board, the Comptroller of the Currency's office. As explicator and promoter of complicated material he demonstrated an unusual talent for persuasion. "We have drawn upon him for help in the redrafting of the Bill, and he is conversant with all its details," Frankfurter wrote Rayburn. "I know he is at your disposal . . ."[9]

Rayburn did not take up this offer. Frankfurter constantly sought to push Corcoran into a more strategic job than the one he held at the RFC. He recommended Corcoran to Moley as his assistant.[10] "I had a long talk with Corcoran yesterday morning and this morning," Moley wrote him a few weeks before Moley attended the London Economic Conference. "I hope you can pull off the Corcoran arrangement, or rather that FDR will," Frankfurter wrote again in mid-June. "I think the way to do it is for him to do it. It really is, if I may say so, an excellent adjustment in your absence."

Moley found Corcoran, whom he described as a young man sometimes uncomfortably deferential, with "slyly superior eyes above the puckering nose."[11] He seemed to Moley resourceful, quick-witted, and eager to work, but Moley already had decided to leave the government so had no need for an assistant. Perhaps, too, he was wary of Frankfurter.

For almost a month, said Landis, "Ben and I lived together in the Carlton Hotel all during that period of time, and we slept with the bill, we worked continuously on it."[12] In the morning when they left for the House building they sometimes encountered J. P. Morgan in the elevator. The banker had been subpoenaed by Pecora. Together with his associates, he had taken over the floor above Landis and Cohen at the Carlton. Wall Street was rife with questions about what Landis and Cohen were up to, but not a word was exchanged.

Banker opposition, nevertheless, represented another threat to the bill. Ben had been warned. Frankfurter had sent him and Tom an exchange of letters with Eustace Seligman, a senior partner at Sullivan & Cromwell. "Do you honestly believe that the losses suffered by the investors who purchased securities," Seligman asked Frankfurter, "were due, other than to a wholly negligible extent, to misrepresentation or concealment in circulars?" Seligman's "naïveté," amused Frankfurter. It reflected "the partial experience of representing special interests." He queried whether Seligman had seen the *Herald Tribune*'s praise of the House bill as a "conscientious, carefully conceived and painstakingly executed attempt" to correct past abuses.[13]

The bankers and their lawyers conveyed their worries to Moley. "I was conscious at the time that he [Moley] had some fear that we might be overzealous . . ." said Ben.[14] Through Moley the banking community insisted that a copy of the draft be sent them, and their lawyers then asked Rayburn for a hearing. Rayburn reluctantly agreed but only on the condition that Cohen and Landis be present.

On a Saturday morning John Foster Dulles, A. I. Henderson, and Arthur H. Dean, representing Wall Street's most distinguished law firms, appeared to testify. At Frankfurter's suggestion Cohen had sent Rayburn a memo that listed the connections of the formidable trio with the issuances of securities that had collapsed. Landis who had little firsthand experience with Wall Street was apprehensive about the encounter. But Dulles, who spearheaded the attack, had not done his homework and did not appreciate in his testimony the differences between the Thompson bill in the Senate and the Landis-Cohen version in the House. Landis and Cohen were relieved, Rayburn angered, especially, as he later told Landis in obscenity-laced words, at Dulles's allegations that Rayburn was promoting legislation that would undermine our financial system. The system should live up to its pretensions, Rayburn had replied. That's all the House was trying to assure.[15]

Cohen had also cautioned Rayburn about the ability of the lawyers to filibuster: "Mr. Frankfurter was of the opinion that it would be fruitless and time-wasting to attempt to discuss with the attorneys for the bankers, all their detailed criticisms."[16] Rayburn adjourned the hearings at midday and had Landis and Cohen spend "a long, hot afternoon," with Henderson and Dean and as a result they made some technical changes in their draft.

Landis returned to Cambridge and was not present on May 2 when Sam Rayburn, unsmiling as usual, presented the bill to the House. With Cohen at his side for the six-hour debate, he gained unanimous approval. "Everything went on schedule," Cohen wrote Landis. "When it was over, Rayburn remarked that he didn't know whether the bill passed so readily because it was so darned good or so damned incomprehensible."[17]

In the Senate, meanwhile, an elderly and "very decent human being," Duncan Fletcher of Florida, shepherded through the Thompson bill, "a terribly poorly drafted piece of legislation," as Landis described it.[18] The two drafts went to conference. Cohen and Landis were present as experts on the House draft. The first and decisive issue was which draft to work from. Rayburn who presided showed his astuteness as a parliamentarian when he ruled that a 5-to-5 motion to start with the Senate draft made by Fletcher at Rayburn's courteous invitation meant that it was lost and the House bill was in effect adopted. On May 27 both houses approved the conference report and Roosevelt signed the "Truth in Securities" Act with a speech prepared for him by Frankfurter: "If this country is to flourish, capital must be invested in enterprise. But those who seek to draw upon other people's money must be wholly candid."[19] And that militant critic of Wall Street, John T. Flynn, in his *New Republic* column, "Other People's Money," softened his earlier harshness: "There can be no question that the Rayburn Security Bill passed by the House marks an immense improvement over the first securities bill introduced in the Senate."

But the statute faced new hazards. The investment community had argued that it represented "unreasonable interference with honest borrowers," and a campaign got under way to choke off the normal flow of investment through misinterpretation of the new bill's provisions. Nevertheless, as Cohen told an interviewer in 1970, "it is still on the books and still being administered."

As the investment community hostility mounted, Cohen and Corcoran drafted material in defense of it. "The Securities Bill stuff is just along the lines I had hoped it would be," Frankfurter wrote Cohen. He suggested some additions—the relation of the American Act to the British Companies Act—"where the American Act is stiffer, and where it is more tender." They should be ready, he went on, to meet "the bleating that one hears so extensively that the Act curbs the legitimate investment business because no conscientious man can really undertake to make himself responsible for many of the facts as to which representations must be made."

In addition they had to be prepared to make changes. This realization that compromise was inevitable and desirable in democratic politics was another characteristic of the approach of Frankfurter and his loyalists. "I am afraid it is a little unfortunate for us that the Act passed as nearly as it was drafted," Cohen commented to Landis. "That gives us too much of a parental interest in the darned thing."

"We must, of course, recognize," Frankfurter advised Cohen, "that all important legislation is an organic evolution, e.g., the English Companies Act, our own Interstate Commerce Acts, etc. Therefore the new Securities Act must be deemed not an end but a beginning, in the unfolding of which all relevant experience should from time to time be absorbed."

Frankfurter's "organic evolution" approach to legislation guided his thinking about NRA and the Hundred Days legislation in toto. As Congress adjourned, there was an exchange between Moley and Frankfurter. "Looking back," wrote Frankfurter, "this session is a record of great achievement and of extraordinarily adroit political management. And not many people know as well as I how very considerable [a] share you have had in its management, the wise foresight and the truly liberal convictions by which the results were achieved." Moley appreciated the "kind things" Frankfurter had written. "All we know is that we stayed on our feet and kept pushing ahead." Frankfurter had been helpful. "The fight is just starting, however, and we must be eternally watchful."[20]

XII

⟶►◄⟵

"The Marines Land on Wall Street"

The second half of 1933 saw further erosion in the ranks and influence of the Brains Trust, also called "the first New Dealers." Berle, except for special jobs and letters to "Dear Ceasar," as he addressed Roosevelt, left the Administration after the Inauguration. Moley's departure was both spectacular and demeaning. Roosevelt's "bombshell" message to the London Economic Conference, rejecting a stabilization draft in the composition of which Moley, presumably speaking for the President, was a main mover, had undermined Moley in full view of the whole world. "He can hardly have looked at Moley after that," said Tugwell, the surviving member of the original Brains Trust and for a few months Roosevelt's closest adviser, "without some feeling that he had ill used a faithful helper."[1]

The episode has been fully explored from the point of view of its participants and policies. When Roosevelt read his "bombshell" message to six members of his cabinet who had come to lunch with him on the *Indianapolis,* Ickes, who emerged as one of the most militant and consistent New Dealers, wrote approvingly in his diary, for himself and the others there, "He has established a strictly American position . . ."[2]

Keynes applauded Roosevelt's refusal to accept the gold standard in preference to nationally managed currencies. And Frankfurter wrote Roosevelt, "I have felt for some years that Keynes is the best economic bet, and so I was delighted with his enthusiastic support of your forthright rejection of that London formula . . ."[3]

Brandeis, Frankfurter, and their group followed the London events closely and with considerable sympathy for the hapless Moley. "It was fine to have you here and to get a glimpse of Marion," the justice wrote Frankfurter from Chatham:

1. Inflation, going off gold and stabilization are matters as to which men may reasonably differ; and on which the same individual, be he statesman or economist, may change his own mind . . . But Keynes notwithstanding the tone and circumstance of F's July 3 allocution to the world conference are in all very disquieting as a symptom. It may be a manifestation of the disintegrative effect of absolute power on mind and character. And, in that connection, disregard of the "brain trust" may be the reason.

Remember—we have no Congress until Jan. 3/4.[4]

"Moley phoned me yesterday from Hyde Park to say he had a very satisfactory talk with F.D. Pineapple is out the window," Frankfurter informed the Justice.[5] "Pineapple" was a code word referring to a Louis Howe suggestion that Moley undertake a mission to Hawaii as a way of taking the story of Moley's treatment off the front pages. The Frankfurter memorandum continued:

2. F.D. enthusiastic about new weekly, with R.M. editor—Vincent Astor had talked with F.D. [his neighbor] the day before;

3. R.M.'s personal relations to continue . . . Only time will tell how F.D.-R.M. relations will work out. R.M. seemed happier about it than at any time—surer of it—since his return.

Moley's departure, taking Celeste Jedel with him, to publish *Today* did not wholly displease Roosevelt. As I have noted, keeping power divided among his subordinates in such a way that all served his purposes rather than he theirs was a technique of governing. Moley, for his first meeting with Roosevelt after his return from London, had written a note to himself, "Don't seem to be offended by anything that happened." Roosevelt, however, had made no reference to what had taken place except to remark, in Moley's paraphrase, that it was "too bad, we couldn't have foreseen that I'd be greeted as the 'savior' of the conference."[6]

The ever-watchful Brandeis was not happy about the Vincent Astor weekly and confided to Frankfurter that he hoped it wouldn't come off:

Indeed I think the Vincent Astor influence a bad influence. Without either party being conscious of it—I guess that association is responsible in large part for F.D. disinclination to tackle heavy estate taxes.

But Moley, he acknowledged later, seemed happy to be released and "looks like a new man." The surviving Tugwell now became Wall Street's target. As he wrote later:

I gradually emerged into notoriety as he [Moley] faded from public sight; and that was mostly because of the manufactured publicity attacking the proposed revision of the Food and Drug Act . . . By the fall of 1933, my every move was watched and recorded, and my opinions were matters of curiosity.

With Tugwell in the spotlight, others in the New Deal like Frankfurter and the Three Musketeers were let alone, although not entirely. The bankers and their lawyers, unhappy with the federal government's first modest effort to regulate the capital market, launched a major assault on the Securities Act. They made its civil liability provisions their battle cry, contending they were to blame for the market's doldrums. Brandeis did not believe that two billion, as the bankers' propaganda claimed, "or any appreciable amount of new securities" were being held back by the Securities Act.[7] Not that it would have bothered the justice if they were. "My own guess is that nothing can be more wholesome in finance than *not* issuing securities for private enterprises now. What we need is that banks shall lend to businessmen of ability and enterprise." But Wall Street's campaign was not limited to the Securities Act.[8] "There will be much to talk over Friday," Brandeis alerted Frankfurter before their last talk prior to the latter's sailing. "The industrial interests and the bankers and the Republican chiefs seem to be rallying for the onslaught. F.D. will have to watch his steps."[9]

Frankfurter passed this warning on to Roosevelt.[10] The forces of opposition—business, financial, and political—were stirring. "Ready to become overt as soon as they think they dare encounter the unparalleled tide of favor now running in your direction." He had heard of "a bankers' strike" to force Congress either to repeal or modify the Securities Act. A former student, Archibald MacLeish, told him in connection with an article he was writing for *Fortune* that "the big rich fellows in New York" despite their public display of the Blue Eagle were awaiting the opportune moment "publicly to oppose the New Deal."

At the same time that the bankers and the Republican Party were preparing an assault on the New Deal, the issue that preoccupied the New Dealers was whether recovery had really been set in motion. Early in July the stock market had suffered its greatest decline since the 1929 crash. Pecora whose hearings had gone on during the summer was certain that decline was related to his announcement of a widened inquiry that would include the workings of the stock exchange.

The Frankfurter group now was getting firsthand knowledge of what was going on in the Pecora Committee via Max Lowenthal who had gone to work for it. "Are you going to get a vacation, and when?" Lowenthal asked Corcoran after getting Corcoran's news about his efforts to influence appointments to the Federal Trade Commission which had been given the job of administering the Securities Act. Workaholism had become synonymous with New Dealism. Tugwell seemed so tired to Roosevelt that summer that he ordered the proud man, "Go and see what's happening. See what they think of us," as a way of getting him to take a holiday. "Remember, there'll be a govt. for you to run after you get your holiday, too," Lowenthal admonished Corcoran.

Corcoran was having the time of his life trying, with Frankfurter's assistance, to beef up the Federal Trade Commission. It had already appointed Jim Landis and Ben Cohen as temporary experts to help its securities division get going. His larger purpose was to clear out the old gang and get new people in. "Ray Moley is a little nervous about taking on any suggestions of this kind at the present time—also an unfortunate fact." But Frankfurter was a willing confederate, probably instigator.

"I have wired the Skipper as follows," Frankfurter informed Corcoran, " 'Landis has unique equipment for fair effective administration Securities Act during crucial months.' . . . If Jim holds on for the next seven or eight months, that's plenty," Frankfurter wrote him, "but of course you won't put this line of argument to Jim, who has too many fears and doubts for the understanding of such a situation. But you can put it to Ray [Moley] in strict confidence, who can then put it to the Skipper."[11]

The message came to Corcoran from the boat that was taking Felix and Marion to England. He wrote to many people while there, but Corcoran was his chief surrogate. He had failed to get Moley in the spring to take Tom on. Now he wrote Missy Le Hand, the president's secretary:

I venture to give this note to a very dear friend of mine, Thomas G. Corcoran, and at present, an assistant to the Secretary of the Treasury. He is a most valuable public servant and one of the most indefatigable workers for the success of this administration. From time to time he may come to you about matters, and I commend him to you warmly. He is a person of entire dependability.[12]

A Frankfurter longhand postscript to a letter to Corcoran indicated greater success in the placement of others: "That was a grand wire—to have bagged Jim & M[atthews] is more than I had hoped. I feared M. would escape you. It's *your* triumph—no doubt about it & I rejoice." In the body of Felix's letter he had asked, "Are you managing to see L.D.B. about once a week?"

Dean Acheson, a former Brandeis law clerk, tall, mustachioed, urbane, with a first-rate mind, had been appointed Under Secretary of the Treasury in the late spring. Secretary Woodin's frailty had made Acheson in effect Acting Secretary. He asked Corcoran to come over to Treasury as liaison with the Reconstruction Finance Corporation. Corcoran brought with him four young lawyers—his "team."

Dean's relations with me are very confidential and of the best, although he constantly gives me the impression without saying so in so many words that he doesn't understand and is a little afraid of my extracurricular activities "running the rest of the Government."[13]

Among these collateral activities was not to allow Ben Cohen to succumb to his loneliness and leave Washington, to temper Landis's brashness, and to organize a firebreak to banker efforts to nullify the Securities Act. Ben's letters to Jane Harris that summer reflected a reluctance to be away from New York City and a few friends like Judge Mack and the Harrises. It was no wonder that Frankfurter worried.

"All the way from Washington I travelled to see you," Ben reproached Jane, "and never a word you send to me. Is that right? And now you go away from New York—far, far away. Is that right?"[14] Jane, a talented musician, on doctor's advice was directed to get away from family and everyone. Try for equanimity and serenity, Ben advised her in words that could have been meant for himself.

It does not lie wholly within our power to change our surroundings and all the difficult problems of health, wealth, and people, near and far, but within rather wide limits we can govern the universe of our own ideas and our mental attitudes towards ourselves and towards others.

He was not pleased with his own situation:

I am not particularly happy with my work in Washington, altho it keeps me quite busy. I try to handle both Public Works and Securities at the same time and accomplish nothing at either. I am living in a house out on 2901 Woodland Drive with your friend Col. Henry Waite, Henry T. Hunt, a Colonel Clark and a Major Fleming. Just think of an old bachelor like me in such staid and provincial company. All except myself go to bed early, and all including poor me arise at seven in the morning with the birds. There are many drinks at dinner, although my double job does not permit me to get home for dinner often. Dinner is too slow a ceremony for a nervous, restless person like me.

At the end of the summer when Jane returned to New York he apologized for not coming to take her to the movies, a ritual that they shared frequently. "I have been working hard. I don't like it. And what's the use. The bankers try by hook and crook to bring our poor securities act into disrepute. And that is the reward for one's effort. It is better to bask in the sun, while the birds sing."

A few weeks later he lamented that "Felix is trying to shanghai me into the power situation and hold me in Washington over the winter. I don't want to stay, but he puts it on personal [grounds] . . . But I am afraid I will have to do it anyway. I don't know what to do about the apartment [in New York] but I hate to give it up. It's the only home I have."

"No one misses your presence here as much as I," Ben's first letter to Felix on the letterhead of the Public Works Administration (PWA) read.[15] He favored a speedier effusion of federal money but was opposed to "the doling out of funds indiscriminately to states and municipalities for worthless projects" and agreed with Lewis Mumford in the *New Republic* that a permanent public works program could be "irreparably damaged if our first venture results in the dotting of the country from coast to coast with monstrous and ill-planned monuments." He realized speed was of the essence for the unemployed and favored "a winter program of expenditures on railroad rehabilitation and a federal housing program planned for the spring." The key to ending the slump was to stimulate industrial activity and the way to do that was "a quick and comprehensive Public Works program," the solution of Keynes.

On another front, Ben reported that the "Securities Act seems to have emerged triumphant from what appeared to be a losing fight." The appointments of Landis and Matthews as Federal Trade commissioners, in part due to Corcoran's major lobbying effort, had created "a bulwark that it will not be easy for the bankers to tear down." But "the right hand knoweth not what the left hand doeth," he lamented in regard to Roosevelt's simultaneous appointment of a conservative-laden committee to study the regulation of the stock exchange. Berle was its only member who would fight for "proper regulation," and Berle was "pretty badly hoodwinked in the railroad bankruptcy legislation."

He did not want to stay in Washington, his letter ended. With Jim and Matthews on the Federal Trade Commission (FTC), there was no need for him to stay on securities matters, and with the appointment of a stock exchange committee he was of little use there. One member of the committee, Arthur Dean, of Sullivan and Cromwell, "at least will agree with me if you do not. At Public Works I am, as you know, without any real influence on fundamental policies and I have no hankering for the general run of administrative work, however important it may be in itself. I hope, therefore, that you will not be chagrined if you learn that I have returned to New York. I shall stay on for a few weeks, but unless there is a perceptible change, I prefer to regain my freedom."

That he should watch over Ben had been one of Felix's many final injunctions to Tom and most of Brandeis's messages to Felix reported on Ben's disposition. "B.V.C. in—seems content." "B.V.C. seems a bit more stable and happier."[16] Tom had been working at such a pace, Ben reported to Felix, that he has had to "go off on a more or less enforced vacation. But Tom is able to cope with any job."

Corcoran found working with Ben congenial. The two complemented each other—Cohen's thoughtfulness and draftsmanship providing solutions that Tom was able to sell to policymakers in the agencies and on the Hill, his cheer, musicality, and sheer playfulness compensating for Ben's quietness and reserve. Tom wanted to have his RFC Treasury team living with him and his secretary, Peggy, who also had become fond of the melancholy bachelor, suggested that Ben share a house he might find for himself and his New Deal companions.

Leila Pinchot, activist wife of the progressive Republican governor of Pennsylvania, wanted Tom to rent her mansionlike establishment on Dupont Circle. However, hints from Brandeis and others that a lease might carry with it political entanglements scared him off. He decided not "to get too far mixed up with them." He located a redbrick house in Georgetown which he did lease.

"I am delighted, exceedingly, that Ben is to live with you," Frankfurter wrote. "Tell me about the arrangements."[17]

"Ben moved in with me last night," he replied. "Seven of us*—Ben, Stuart Guthrie, Ed Burke, Frank Watson, Dick Guggenheim and myself have taken the old Rousseau house in Georgetown as a community proposition. I think Ben will be a lot happier with us and I'm carefully working Elizabeth Sanford [an aide to Sprague] who was fed up with nothing to do with Sprague, into other work so she'll remain here to help keep him . . . He has seen the Justice since his wire to you and has agreed to stay."

Ben's relations with Jim Landis exploded anew. One of Landis's tasks at the Federal Trade Commission assigned to him by Roosevelt was to monitor changes in the Securities Act, if any were to be made when Congress reassembled in January. The business community's campaign to modify

* Corcoran's transcribed letter at the Library of Congress enumerates only six.

the Securities Act was in full swing and among the chores Frankfurter gave Corcoran was to build an intellectual backfire against that drive. Frankfurter worried that an article in the October *Foreign Affairs* by John Foster Dulles would fool people who might see him as a prestigious former member of the Reparations Commission and the Supreme Economic Council and not as a member of the Wall Street law firm Sullivan & Cromwell "and thus inevitably one of the personal beneficiaries of the old abuses in flotations [of securities] and the loser in any new system of social control thereof." Four people might write an answer. Herbert Feis of the State Department who "would have to be educated of course by the Three Musketeers—Cohen, Corcoran and Landis . . . Ben could, of course, write a knock-out reply." If the three thought Frankfurter should do so, he was prepared to sign an article they wrote "subject to my editorial revision." A fourth suggestion was that Elizabeth Sanford "might draft the piece and persuade him [Sprague] to write it."

Cohen decided the *Fortune* piece was not "worth the answering." Moley at *Today* was hesitant. He "isn't very good these days, Corcoran informed Frankfurter, "and is much more concerned with playing safe and not getting his neck stuck out and vindicating himself than with really slugging away at a liberal program . . ."[18] But *Today* did publish a piece by Rayburn that they wrote. Ben was "tied up in knots in the Public Works Administration and he doesn't take kindly to the idea of working with Jim anyway." Frankfurter dashed off a compact unsigned piece for *The Economist* in which he spoke of the "so-called bankers' strike" against new flotations.

The key answer by Bernard Flexner was written for *The Atlantic.*[19] He was an investment lawyer with Halsey-Stuart, highly respected in the business community, and a friend of Frankfurter and Cohen since Balfour Declaration days. He described the well-organized campaign by Wall Street law firms to abolish the Act "under guise of amendment." In *Fortune* Archibald MacLeish noted that the Securities Act "has not held up any new financing because there isn't any to hold up" and pointed out the parallel with the lack of British financing at the present time. Corcoran wrote Frankfurter, "I went up to see MacLeish [a former Frankfurter student as well as poet] . . . found him glorious to talk to."[20] People enjoyed doing what Corcoran wanted. He was knowledgeable, sophisticated, never asking more than they were able to undertake. The articles he inspired and that along with Ben, he helped write, appeared in publications read by opinion molders. As yet without the authority of the White House behind him, he was already a master at shaping public feeling where it counted.

Another Frankfurter assignment was to temper Landis's egotism.

He was doing his "best" with Jim, Corcoran assured his mentor in Oxford, "but he jumps around so fast that it's hard to follow him. He has a bad habit of trying to pull criticism of the Act by reasonable interpretations which in some cases emasculated." Corcoran cited a prospective Landis ruling on an offering by a Maryland insurance company. "To his everlasting credit he pulled himself out of that one in time under the combined efforts of Ben, Matthews [George, La Follette Republican whom Roosevelt had appointed to the FTC] and myself. As you say he has all the streaks of ferocity and weakness and a terrific assumption that he speaks for the whole Commission . . . He's had two talks with the President which were very pleasant but on close analysis seem to have something of a weaselly quality of many of the President's commitments."

When Ben's low-keyed warning to Frankfurter that he might return to New York brought no response, he cabled:

AM INEFFECTIVE AT PRESENT STOP AND PROFERRED FOURTH FIDDLE AT SECURITIES UNALLURING PROBABLY RETURNING END MONTH AFFECTIONATE GREETINGS = BEN V. COHEN.[21]

Frankfurter did not answer this directly but sent it on to Corcoran:

I fear me that Jim has again been awkward in handling Ben's sensitiveness . . . he doesn't seem to take into account the inevitable difficulties in having him, a very much younger man, ask Ben to take a subordinate status . . . I wish somehow or other you would manage to convey to Jim to let you handle Ben and never for him to do it directly.[22]

Whatever the misgivings of Frankfurter, Corcoran, and Cohen about Landis, Roosevelt took to him. Landis in the end had the decision on the amendments to be introduced at the 1934 session of Congress to the Securities Act.[23] "By that time the President trusted me and Sam [Rayburn] trusted me, the other members of the committee trusted me, so what I said went," he later recalled.

FDR designated Henry Bruere, a banker, to look into the charge that the Securities Act was blocking the provision of new capital funds. "A nice fellow," Frankfurter commented from Oxford to Corcoran, who to Ben's relief had been designated Bruere's legal counsel, "a great buddy of Frances Perkins. Between you and me he isn't so hot, and don't expect any miracles . . . I am reliably informed that he is as bad as any of them in thinking that the spirit of the act prevents recovery."[24] The Three Musketeers were to try to educate him and a talk with LDB on finance in general to open his eyes a little was Felix's advice.

Bruere's report to Roosevelt concluded that there were anxieties in the banking and investment community, especially because of the Act's liability provisions and that such fears were a deterrent to corporate financing. A skeptical Roosevelt sent this on to Landis pointing out that any company with "a sound program of new financing," if it was turned down by the bankers, could apply to the RFC.[25]

Landis had taken Corcoran's counsel to heart. He was keeping the file on possible amendments and discussing them with Cohen. "I think it is very important for you to be down here during the months of November and December. I wish you could arrange it."[26] In the end amendments were introduced satisfactory to both men. Landis called them "alleviating amendments," which kept the principle of disclosure but weren't too rough on people. There was a feeling in the banking community, said Cohen, that the individual liabilities were excessive "and I think the principal change that may have induced the banking community to operate more freely under it was a provision that put in an extremely short statute of limitations."

Wall Street firms were ingenious at the emasculation of state and federal statutes of control, said Flexner in his article in *The Atlantic,* and they were consequently furious with the "lawyer-proof qualities" of the Securities Act. Eustace Seligman, a senior partner at Sullivan & Cromwell, had seen Flexner's article and "as the result he has got hydrophobia," Flexner informed Tom. Nothing "unfairer" had been written, Seligman contended. Was Halsey, Stewart, the underwriting firm that used Flexner, still having anything to do with the article's author, he asked a Halsey, Stewart partner who amusedly told Flexner. Seligman's complaint was a measure of Sullivan & Cromwell's irritation, but Flexner stayed on in Wall Street, a sign that it was far from unanimous in its opposition to the Act.

"The Securities Act is safe," Tom wrote Felix. "There may be some clarification of details. I don't mind: the Act really needs some clarification."[27] They had lined up Fletcher and Rayburn against amendments. "Jim's always nervous—but we'll win (though he'll probably die of diarrhea in the process)." A postscript reported that "Ben's happier than he writes."

"[O]ur position seems very strong," Ben agreed on the eve of the return of Congress. He was more suspicious than Tom of Landis:

The concept of "A New Beginning" takes hold as Roosevelt flies to Chicago to accept the presidential nomination. (CREDIT: New York *Daily Mirror*)

The first Brain Trust with Louis Howe. Left to right: A. A. Berle, Rex Tugwell, Raymond Moley, and Louis Howe. White House, 1933. (CREDIT: Pathé News)

The Roosevelts arrive at Union Station, Washington, D.C., for the first Inaugural, March 1933. (CREDIT: FDR Library)

Mary Harriman Rumsey, head of NRA Consumers Activities (left), and Representative Isabella Greenway, at the time a progressive, with Eleanor Roosevelt. Isabella had been one of Eleanor's bridesmaids. (CREDIT: M. Breckinridge)

Frances Perkins (left) with Mary Dewson, director of the Women's Division of the Democratic National Committee. The latter had her lists of women who should be appointed to government jobs, and if Jim Farley was unresponsive, she went to her friend Eleanor Roosevelt. The Women's Division was a stronghold of New Deal liberalism. (CREDIT: UPI/Bettmann Newsphotos)

Joe Rauh (right) with Benjamin Cohen.

Ben Cohen (right) advising Senator Burton K. Wheeler and Representative Sam Rayburn. (CREDIT: Acme Newspapers)

George W. Norris gives an illustrated lecture before the Senate Banking Committee, likening Wall Street to a spider enmeshing trade and industry in its web. Norris led the fight against interlocking directorates. (CREDIT: UPI/Bettmann Newsphotos)

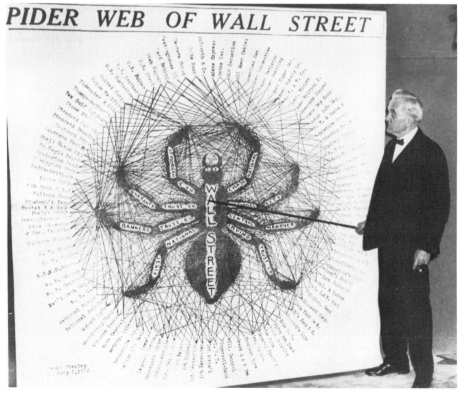

Senator Robert M. La Follette, Jr., with Henry L. Hopkins, then Relief Administrator. (CREDIT: AP/Wide World Photos)

Senator Robert F. Wagner, a New Deal stalwart in the Senate. (CREDIT: FDR Library)

Mrs. Roosevelt with Mary McLeod Bethune at the Second National Conference on Negro Youth. (CREDIT: AP/Wide World Photos)

Part of the crowd at the Lincoln Memorial that turned out in 1939 to hear Marian Anderson after the DAR denied her the use of its hall. (CREDIT: AP/Wide World Photos)

The Supreme Court before the court-packing fight. The columnist Drew Pearson dubbed them "the Nine Old Men." Standing, left to right: Justices Roberts, Butler, Stone, and Cardozo. Seated, left to right: Justices Brandeis and Van Devanter, Chief Justice Hughes, and Justices McReynolds and Sutherland. (CREDIT: AP/Wide World Photos)

The Second Inaugural, January 20, 1937. "I see one third of a nation ill-housed, ill-clad, ill-nourished." (CREDIT: UPI/Bettmann Newsphotos)

"YOU CAN'T HAVE EVERYTHING"

As New Dealers viewed the court packing fight. (© Herblock courtesy of F.D.R. Library)

I think I wrote you that when the security act amendments were first promised consideration by the skipper through Morgenthau, the skipper spoke to Jim who never gave us a full account of what happened, altho it is clear from a number of things Jim did say that the skipper got him to promise not to be a partisan or active in the fight against no amendments. All of which is quite amusing in view of the way Jim used to carry on about your not getting to the skipper frequently enough and wishing that he had a direct approach.[28]

Not only had Roosevelt dropped any effort through Morgenthau to amend the Act, but he had instructed the Dickinson committee which was preparing stock exchange regulations and which had Arthur Dean among its members to keep its hands off amending the Securities Act.

Moley's role had been ambiguous. He had published the Rayburn article in *Today,* but his editorial "advocating an N.R.A.-supervised self-government for finance, shows the influence of Averill *[sic]* [Harriman] consciously or unconsciously," Cohen wrote Frankfurter. "Of course what the boys have in mind is to have a banking committee pass on new security issues and then to be absolved from civil liability."

The fight against the Securities Act was one facet only of Wall Street's larger campaign to recapture control from the federal government over the nation's monetary and credit policies. "When I left at the tail end of September," Frankfurter wrote the President, "the lines were fast being drawn between those to whom Recovery meant Return—return to the good old days—and those for whom Recovery was Reform . . ."

As Brandeis had emphasized to Frankfurter and the latter had warned Roosevelt, the "old regime," as it gained a second wind, would place the Administration under a sustained attack.[29] The latter culminated in a flurry of resignations from the New Deal government and a headline-blazoned onslaught by Al Smith. "I am for gold dollars as against baloney dollars. I am for experience against experiment."

"You remember that before you left," Corcoran wrote Frankfurter, "you warned me that the President was toying with the idea of affecting prices by buying and selling gold."[30] Corcoran then described the autumn crisis that led up to the resignation of Acheson from the Treasury and his own efforts to prevent it. In early October, Tom had flown to New Hampshire "to climb a few hills . . . when the farm strike began and the President was casting around for some Atalanta's apple to throw in his race with the farmers and turned again to the idea of buying and selling gold without consulting the Treasury crowd until he was pretty well along on a theory advanced by Morgenthau." The latter then was head of the Farm Credit Administration and together with George Warren of Cornell, his onetime professor, had sold Roosevelt on the idea of the "commodity dollar." The theory held that by varying the gold content of the dollar, the latter's price would automatically rise or fall and thus the dollar could be so managed as to maintain a constant buying power. At the moment, it meant depreciating the dollar's value. With commodity prices again falling, the debt-harassed farmers were pressing for such inflation.

New Dealers like Tugwell, Berle, and Frankfurter ridiculed Warren's theories. Frankfurter considered them "puerile," he wrote Brandeis. But on October 22 in a fireside chat Roosevelt announced his decision to buy gold at prices to be determined daily. A memorandum by Herman Oliphant, Morgenthau's legal counsel, argued that the President had the legal power to do so even at prices above that fixed by statute. On October 25 he, Morgenthau, and Jesse Jones began to meet every morning in Roosevelt's bedroom to fix the price of gold for that day.

The opponents of the President's policy in the Treasury became "almost desperate and certainly frantic," Corcoran went on, and their strong views ended in what Acheson had described to him as a "knockdown and dragout fight" between himself and the President.[31] Tom had called Acheson from New Hampshire. He was "so excitedly mad he could hardly talk," the procedures worked out for making the gold purchases were illegal and would require him as Acting Secretary to do illegal acts, and he had told Roosevelt he wouldn't do it. Moreover, he had not been consulted in the formulation of the scheme and "he thought the Treasury and everyone in it had been humiliated. He said he had talked the whole matter over with the justice who agreed that he only could decently resign."

An anguished Corcoran sought to keep Acheson from resignation. He thought the policy issue of the legality of Roosevelt's gold purchases was secondary to Acheson's sense of being slighted. He turned to George Rublee who was vacationing in Cornish, New Hampshire, some two hundred miles away. Rublee was a distinguished lawyer, an old friend of Acheson and even an older one of Brandeis. He had served on the first Federal Trade Commission in 1914; he was an establishment person whose abilities made him valuable to both Democratic and Republican administrations.

Tom raced in an ancient Pierce Arrow, as hard to handle as a truck, in a breathless four-and-a-half-hour dash to get Rublee "to pat down Dean's feelings." On arrival he found Rublee "probably more scared" than he. They hid in Rublee's bedroom and promptly called Justice Brandeis. Frankfurter's emphatic injunction to Tom had been to stay in touch with the justice and the latter's letters to Frankfurter regularly reported on having seen Tom "Cochrane." Corcoran's telephone call breathed idolatry:

I was frightened of my own impertinence—I had never before dared call the Justice on the telephone, and even more frightened when I found he was in conference with the Chief Justice and would rather not be disturbed—and yet I insisted that I talk with him. The Justice told us that Dean had not discussed either the policy of the plan or his relations with the President with its formulation but only had come to ask him the question whether assuming that a plan such as that were illegal and Dean were asked to do anything illegal in connection with it, he should resign rather than commit an illegal act. Of course, Isaiah's [Brandeis] answer to that query was the moralistic "resign." Then, knowing that the Justice had given no advice to resign on the problem of policy which I was afraid he might have done, we called Dean at his country place in Maryland and George talking "catastrophe" if Dean should resign got him to promise that he'd do nothing on his own initiative for a couple of days until he saw how his relations with the President worked out.

Corcoran returned to Washington the first of November with the feeling that "this little boy of thirty-two had accomplished a 'Three Musketeers' day' of work. The Treasury situation was bad, 'the whole atmosphere was one of everything lost—like a bottle of ginger ale with a cork left out for a couple of weeks.' " Ben "was in the dumps and wanted to go home," Jerry Frank's Triple A organization was "hopelessly ineffective" in the farm crisis; the NRA "was another ginger ale bottle with a cork out . . . and the long threatened die-hard campaign to upset everything which you had warned was in preparation just waiting for a slip was in full cry."

Were he not such a "dumb, healthy, physically optimistic pessimist, I should almost have accepted on the spot a job George Rublee offered me of going with him to China on a financial mission for the Soongs." Despite the mood in the Treasury, they were all decided that the ailing Woodin had to go and had begun to discuss who his new successor might be:

Even Ray Moley with whom I had two hours yesterday feels that Woodin must go and there's terrific speculation as to his successor. The only two names in the field now, both of them in my opinion impossible, are Morgenthau and Jesse Jones. Everybody here is desperately looking for suggestions for a Secretary. Dean apparently is completely out. Kiplinger, with whom I labored to some purpose to cut down his criticism of Dean in Exhibit "C" is sure that Dean can neither be Secretary nor even Undersecretary because he isn't well enough known and is criticized as being too high-hat for the average man.

Corcoran was a shrewd judge of men's political ambitions:

Dean himself, says one minute that he doesn't want to be Secretary and the next minute listens to me suggest that in a vacuum he'll have to be and then admonishes me to stop "corrupting him."

The closeness of Corcoran's kind of liberalism to FDR's experimentalism—Jerry Frank was "a doctrinaire damn fool," Tom's same letter said—
was shown by Tom's pressure on Acheson to stick with Roosevelt:

First, I've given George Rublee a long song and dance on the necessity of Dean's
seeing that Franklin Roosevelt and not Lew Douglas [director of the Budget and
chief opponent of deficit spending] is President of the United States and dripped as
subtly as I could the idea that Lew might be using the enthusiastic and naive Dean
for his own purposes and that Dean must remember that he is a member of the
administration and not the partisan of an economic point of view.

Corcoran also pounded away at Moley, stressing that the dangers from
nonadministration criticisms

were nothing compared to the dangers of internal dissension among well-meaning
liberals, all of whom were anxious to help and would pull together if they were
handled the right way, and that however much the President might want to sur-
round himself with yes men, he'd have to take some of the inconvenience of letting
both sides of his well-intentioned advisers present their stories, even at the inconvenience of some having to listen to argument and being slowed up on conclusion. In
the last analysis, this crowd down here are not Prussian goose-steppers taking
orders.

He himself went along loyally with Roosevelt, he told Moley, but it was

pretty hard to keep my heart in things and defend the Administration when Isaiah
tells me as he did *in haec verba* and with really husky passion "I think they're
going completely crazy." I also pointed out to Moley the absolute necessity of the
President's checking his course with Isaiah, that practically all of the Brain Trusters, and by that I mean all of the administration group other than the politicians,
passed through Florence Courts [Brandeis's apartment] in an unending stream,
that whether they completely agree with Isaiah or not they have such a supersti-
tious awe of his prophetic quality that his disagreement and his warnings shake
their conviction and their courage and leave them fighting half-bewilderedly.

Tom did not pretend to know where things were going to come out, but
he knew one thing definitely—the Administration had to try something.
He was not bothered that he did not understand because

we've got to experiment, and of course, an experiment has no principle nor any
definite place where you know it's coming out—so following Harold Moulton's
advice [the director of the Brookings Institution] I just keep my own rifle and keep
firing. But when I come out of that half-darkened room with my ears ringing with
the warnings of that old man whose judgment I trust beyond that of anybody else
in the world, it takes all the sense of day-by-day opportunism I have to keep going
with any enthusiasm.

Ben's descriptions of the gold-trading crisis, also in letters to Frankfurter, were more analytical.[32] For him the overriding problem was to end the Great Depression, and he saw the struggle between the White House and the Treasury much more calmly than did Acheson or Brandeis.

. . . My own view is the whole dispute was a tempest in a teapot. Of course, the buying and selling of gold at variable rates is an essential part of a sound scheme of a managed currency. But it is only one of the many essential parts and at the particular moment it is of minor importance . . . England buys and sells gold in order to stabilize the exchange and no one thinks anything of it . . . It is a little unfortunate that the President has not been made to see more clearly that prices will be more directly and permanently affected by giving large credits to public works than they will be by efforts to depress the exchange value of the dollar . . .

He hoped Frankfurter would be able to get home for the Christmas holidays. "You are badly needed and the post for which I thought you were peculiarly fitted should beckon you more strongly than ever. The 'old musician' [Woodin] still nominally holds his post but real direction is needed more badly than ever. *And if you came back with Keynes, America might be a pleasanter place to live in during the next decade* [italics added]."

Frankfurter did not return but two weeks later he sent Roosevelt the views of a group of Oxford economists, led by the Keynesian Roy Harrod, who had vainly struggled "for action by their government along your expansionist lines." It said among other things, "We believe that the principal weapon in raising prices should be a great campaign of Public Works."

Corcoran's advice to Acheson to be a loyal member of Roosevelt's administration came too late. Roosevelt, increasingly irritated by Acheson's stiff-necked resistance to his gold-purchase policy, the move that Roosevelt thought was staving off an agrarian revolution, took the initiative and fired him. His "dutch" was up and he announced Acheson's resignation to the press before the Undersecretary received it. At the same time he appointed Henry Morgenthau, his longtime Dutchess County neighbor and a Roosevelt loyalist, Acting Secretary of the Treasury.

He was glad Frankfurter had not been around, Brandeis confessed to his lieutenant in mid-November.[33] Felix could not have averted Roosevelt's headstrong actions. "I am sad over the blasting of many a fair prospect. The loss will not be merely of personal prestige. Liberalism and experimentation will have received a severe setback and the reactionaries will be strengthened in their errors."

Brandeis still was sorrowing a week later. "My main grief is with the loss of FD as an instrument of advanced political action . . . The best of measures if advocated by him will be looked on with suspicion. Morgenthau's initial performance seems as bad as bad can be—wholly regardless of the unwisdom of his financial policies." And on December 7, "I continue glad you are not here. You could not help matters and might have impaired your chances of helping F.D. *et al.* hereafter."

Frankfurter, in words that echoed Cohen's of November 8, wrote Roosevelt his feeling that "the currency aspect of the situation has in fact—though not in feeling—been greatly exaggerated."[34] He recalled the discussion that he had had in Roosevelt's study when Woodin was there about gold buying: "I have felt quite clearly that you were giving that policy a tentative trial to see what it could do without committing yourself to that theory more than to any other theory, as a solvent."

At the end of the year Corcoran analyzed the Treasury events on the basis of what he had learned since his massive report to Felix of mid-November.

The Treasury mess was a drama of personalities, not of principles. Dean says he knows the President didn't like Dean the very minute they met. Dean thoroughly despised the President as a political trimmer, a skimper of problems, and an arrogant bully from the first clashes of the London Conference. He talked freely to me about it even then. And Dean can be quietly but cuttingly supercilious.

Tom blamed Lew Douglas in part for Acheson's behavior. "Then Lew, a very *poor* Machiavelli, always using Dean as his pawn in his stabilization game . . . Dean was his man in Lew's eyes, and half of the time in Dean's eyes." By the time Corcoran had returned from a holiday in the White Mountains, Acheson had wanted to quit on his own. "Everyone knew what was about—it was only a matter of time. But everyone, the Justice, Rublee, urged him to try to hang on." One day when Acheson arrived at the White House for a conference on liquor the press told him his resignation had been announced. A few minutes later the President had confirmed it and told him that "Morgenthau was boss." Tom thought it prudent for Frankfurter not to say anything more about the matter either to the President or Acheson. He recalled that Felix had pushed Acheson for solicitor-general if not under secretary and as for Acheson, "I think I told you of Dean's disappointment with your letter; he almost said that you were giving yourself an excuse for siding with the top-dog."

Dean had behaved "very wisely" after the events, Corcoran wrote. "He refused offers to lead the agitation against the President's policy," turned aside press requests for a statement, and "took L.D.B.'s advice every step of the way."[35] And historian Arthur Schlesinger later noted that he turned up, cordial and urbane, at the swearing in of his successor. "The best act of sportsmanship I've ever seen," Roosevelt told him.[36]

Acheson's departure created a problem for Corcoran personally.

My relations with Dean were ideal: My *job* didn't interfere with my *work;* he asked no questions at my running round town; he gave me a chance to recruit and help over the first bumps an exceptionally good legal division at Public Works.

A glowering Morgenthau, Tom's adjective, held him "suspect as the leader of the Achesonites." Morgenthau was "afraid of being a liberal Jew." Morgenthau was "afraid to be associated with you and L.D.B.—or have any of their disciples in influential places in the Treasury." He had sent Corcoran word that he could stay on at the Treasury "but that it embarrasses him politically if I did stay." Nor did his general counsel Oliphant want Corcoran "around in command of Paul [Freund], Dick [Guggenheim] and Frank [Watson], the best legal brains in the Treasury. He wanted to be boss himself with no competitors."

Moreover, Morgenthau considered Tom an "autonomous principality" and "too close to and on the payroll of Jesse Jones, Morgenthau's nearest rival for Secretary." Scouting around where to go, "Jesse had asked me to come back the day Dean resigned." The chairman of the Home Owners' Loan Corporation (HOLC) asked him to become his assistant. David Lilienthal, at the Tennessee Valley Authority (TVA), wanted him. "Frank Walker asked me to come coordinating with him: and Ickes really tempted me and Ben with an offer to make me Deputy Administrator of Public Works." However, "L.D.B." had pointed out that the Public Works job would take all his time, "at R.F.C. I'd still have my fingers in all financial policy." So he worked out a deal with the RFC. He "traded back" his four boys, their four secretaries, and himself "as a unit. Our salaries are the same," with physical offices for a time in the Treasury where the group would constitute "a special little brain trust unit to work on R.F.C. Legislation before Congress."

Morgenthau sent word he was "exceedingly grateful" to Tom for having made things "easy for him" and Oliphant asked to borrow the "boys from time to time: and I'm leaving three other men, whom Oliphant doesn't know are ours, planted in the Treasury, besides having an office there." So the business had ended with his being on friendly terms with all camps; moreover, "Jesse Jones is going to be the next Secretary, in two or three months," a singular misapprehension of Roosevelt's relationship with Morgenthau, not to mention Jones.

The letter ended with the news that his boys "were working on bills for all L.D.B.'s ideas, and the stock exchange regulation." Morgenthau "missed a trick in not holding on to Tom and his boys," Acheson wrote Frankfurter. "He will need all the brains he can get hold of before long . . . Those boys made a great flying squadron to tackle difficult emergency jobs as they came along."[37]

Frankfurter ended the year with his own coup. He had seen Keynes, been his guest at the Founder's Day Feast at Cambridge where there had been "seven courses of wine," and the two men had talked animatedly about the situation in the United States. "You might like to know," Frankfurter wrote Keynes, "I have had American news indicating that there will be considerable sentiment in the Senate for heavy increases in public works appropriations. The President, is, I believe, receptive. I write because I think a letter from you with your independent indications would greatly accelerate the momentum of forces now at work in the right direction— however much may have been lost already."[38] On December 16 Frankfurter sent Roosevelt a copy of Keynes's "Open Letter to the President" that was to be published in the New York *Times* on December 31. Keynes saluted Roosevelt as the trustee of the advocates of reasoned experiment within the framework of the existing social system. If Roosevelt failed, rational change will be gravely prejudiced, "leaving orthodoxy and revolution to fight it out." Unfortunately, the order of "urgencies" between Recovery and Reform had not been clearly observed, in Keynes's view. The NIRA, for example, "though its social gains have been large," was no aid to Recovery and represented a wrong ordering of priorities. The first step in recovery was "the increase of national purchasing power resulting from government expenditure which is financed by Loans and not by taxing present incomes. Nothing else counts in comparison with this." He did not underestimate the difficulty of "rapid improvisation of a vast programme on public works." Nevertheless, he urged "a large volume of Loan-expenditures under Government auspices," with preference for projects that could "mature quickly." In passing, although an advocate of a managed currency, he disparaged the "Quantity Theory of Money," the idea that there was "a mathematical relation between the price of gold and the price of other things."

"You can tell the professor," Roosevelt wrote Frankfurter, "that in regard to public works we shall spend in the next fiscal year nearly twice the amount we are spending in this fiscal year, but there is a practical limit to what the Government can borrow—especially, because the banks are offering passive resistance in most of the large centers."[39] The President had read the letter of the Oxford economists to a small meeting of his top financial people "and the comment was that the Oxonians are thinking much in our terms."

The Keynes letter pleased Cohen. It reassured him that "certain applications of his [Keynes] ideas to the American scene were not unjustified."[40]

If Corcoran's letter to Frankfurter at year's end sounded a "little cocky," it should not be so, Tom said.[41] "I have no delusions that any of us are more than rabbits dodging the lightning." He had toasted in the New Year's with Justice Holmes with "a nice brandy. He was in fine form. We talked of you and how soon we could hope you'd return! Both of us hope soon!"

XIII

———— ><•<———

Frankfurter's "Happy Hot Dogs"

Among FF's former students who considered him a guide and friend, the most mysterious was Max Lowenthal. He was the oldest of the inner circle, having worked with Frankfurter at the War Labor Board in the Great War. His literary chores completed in 1933 on *The Investor Pays,* he was promptly grabbed by Ferdinand Pecora, the scrappy chief counsel of the Senate inquiry into Wall Street's abuses. Lowenthal was a good friend of Landis and Corcoran and an intimate of Cohen whom he had preceded as Judge Mack's law clerk. His connections on the Hill and on Wall Street, his sense of a lawyer's responsibilities to the public, his political savvy, made his reports to Frankfurter a major source of information and judgment.

A month after Felix's departure for Oxford, a clipped Lowenthal paragraph etched a picture of Brandeis:

Saw L.D.B. Tuesday, the first time this fall. Stopped my going several times, and only left me when Acheson arrived to talk to him about something. Eager, when I came to end of a subject, "What else!"[1]

A few weeks earlier Max had reported to Felix about the first meeting of the Dickinson Committee, appointed by Roosevelt to prepare stock exchange regulations, with a personnel that Wall Street found reassuring:

1. [Arthur] Dean of Sullivan & Cromwell.

2. Your, our, the people's Assistant Secretary of Commerce—last year special counsel hired by Sullivan & C to defend Sugar Institute.

3. Stanley, Jim Farley's agent at the Department of Justice.

4. Berle.

"I'm attending to it," Max ended cryptically.

A teasing note was tacked on. Another Pecora aide, the militant critic of Wall Street, "[John T.] Flynn, Pecora and I making plans at Club Michal while dancers, singers and jazz band tell us about life. You know about life? Ask Marion." He could twit the professor. There were few, apart from his wife, Marion, and Harold Laski, who did so. "And did you know that Max is really a great humorist," Felix wrote Tom. "Well, he sent me a description of the Hon. John Dickinson that Dorothy Parker couldn't improve upon."[2]

Pecora did not have time for the inquiry that autumn. He had been drafted by Edward J. Flynn, the Bronx political leader who was trying to keep City Hall for the Democrats by entering Joseph V. McKee, something of a reformer, against John (?) O'Brien, the bumbling candidate of a discredited Tammany, and La Guardia, the independent Republican who was running ahead in the polls. Pecora was on McKee's ticket. He had been promised the U.S. Attorney's office if defeated, said Max.[3] "I told P., his answer not so clear." In the Pecora hearings Senator Couzens of Michigan, a former partner of Henry Ford, an independent Republican, was a standby of the reformers on Pecora's staff. "At lunch today," reported Max, "Couzens said to Pecora: 'I don't like to see you keeping company with people like McKee.'"

Pecora's absence was felt. The Senate committee heard testimony from Albert Wiggins, the retired president of the Chase National Bank. Wiggins, said Max, was "a very shrewd witness." He did not fight the interrogators:

Q. Did you kill your wife?

A. Yes.

Q. Did you drown your children?

A. Yes.

Q. Are you a bastard?

A. Yes.

"Pecora very tired," Max's next letter reported, "not so good just now. But the material [in the Chase investigation] is good, it can't help getting across."[4] Wiggins had been impressive because he was neither arrogant nor affected a pose of holier-than-thou respectability. Nevertheless, Chase under his regime had been guilty of the same practices—huge salaries, the financing of stock market pools, "insiders" profit rigging, manipulating the bank's own stock, which had outraged the country. One example of his stewardship etched itself in the public mind. He had been a member of a "bankers consortium" set up after the 1929 crash to stabilize the market. But to the Pecora Committee he admitted that at the same time he had been selling short over forty thousand shares of Chase stock, shares whose price Chase through a pooling operation helped keep high, precisely the kind of manipulation that had contributed to the collapse. And to cap it all, he acknowledged that on the profit of four million dollars that he made from this operation, he paid no income tax.

"So soft, so quiet, so at his ease," Lowenthal described him on the stand. "Sometimes a half smile . . . conciliatory, not truckling, honestly just there to answer questions, no trimming. He's good."

The headlines, however, intensified the pressure for stock exchange regulation. "Wiggin, of course, saved the skin of the Committee for a long time," Corcoran wrote Frankfurter.[5] He feared that with Pecora on the McKee ticket in New York the investigation would peter out. "Max was so frightened that he had me line up [Senator] Costigan . . . and through Gardner Jackson we lined up [Senator] Norbeck and some others." Lowenthal saw other advantages in the inquiry. It "keeps Wall Street from fighting back on other things as vigorously as it otherwise might."

The continued headlines of shady banker practices made inevitable an effort to correct them. What form that would take partly depended on the report of the Dickinson Committee. Its appointment had angered Lowenthal who saw it as an effort to undercut the Pecora group. Nor was he cheered by Jim Landis's addition to the committee. "Jim Landis, Ben told me today, phoned Dickinson, saying he, Jim (as a Federal Trade Commissioner) wanted to be on the Committee on Stock Exchange," Max wrote Felix.[6] "Dickinson?" asked an incredulous Max. "When Corcoran told me of the idea two weeks ago, I warned that Jim should not do it, except as a guard against any work by that committee and that his presence would make less vulnerable a committee which could not do a good job."

Wall Street had begun to look askance at Landis, Corcoran, and Cohen just because the Securities Act was proving to be "lawyer-proof." That, however, was what recommended the three to the senators who wanted to protect the public. Such was the burden of Frankfurter's advice from afar to Senator Couzens.[7] "I should like to take the liberty of advancing a consideration brought out by the Securities Act of 1933," Frankfurter wrote him at the end of the year. "It was drawn with the help of four unusually capable lawyers," he said in a reference to the Three Musketeers and probably Lowenthal. The Act was meticulously drafted. "Financial lawyers have not yet been able to devise means of puncturing it . . ." On matters such as stock exchange regulation, he believed, "financial lawyers can retard or defeat the purposes of Congress unless these lawyers are matched at their own game, in advance by use of lawyers equally astute in the public interest and as ready to devote their time to the public cause as are Wall Street attorneys to the cause of Wall Street interests."

It was Lowenthal, privy as he was to Pecora's thinking, who in the fall of 1933 asked Ben and therefore Tom to prepare a bill to regulate the stock exchanges. Both men were busy, Tom in relocating himself and his team of young lawyers after Acheson left the Treasury, Ben with chores for Ickes on Public Works.

Ben found the work difficult. "Not being an administrator," he confided to Felix, "it is quite a nervous strain and sometimes I fear I may break under it."[8] He wanted to "find time to work on the stock exchange bill," as well as keep track of the moves to amend the Securities Act. "It is all so difficult in view of [my] inability to articulate, accentuated as it is when I'm tired and under pressure. I would never have got over the real justification of the Securities Act if it had not been for Tom's pen, force, pertinacity, and understanding."

Both Tom and Ben, reported Landis cheerily to Felix, were in their customary way working hard and effectively, but "Tom is very much disturbed by the present Treasury situation and what will happen is still doubtful, except for the fact that wherever he lands he will land on his feet."[9]

Landis, as busy as the other two, was off on a policy of his own working with the Dickinson Committee during the day and with the Pecora group and Tom and Ben at night. Like Max, Ben was skeptical of the business-dominated Dickinson group. He predicted it would "delay rather than encourage proper regulation."[10]

He watched Landis warily. The Musketeers no longer were three.

Tom made his safe landing. Acheson, trying to unwind outside of the government, reported to Felix that "Tom with my other Treasury boys have gone back to the R.F.C."[11]

The major job at the beginning of 1934 was to draft stock exchange legislation. The definitive word to go ahead came from Moley. Although busy at *Today,* Roosevelt had called him in December to ask that he get stock exchange legislation moving. He did so "somewhat reluctantly," implying a distrust of the general Administration line of reform before recovery, but that was written in 1939 after his break with Roosevelt.[12] He had filled in the President on the "abilities and limitations" of Cohen and Corcoran, and then had called them in to ask them to go to work, accepting the President's request that he direct the fight for the Act, an assignment that he performed by telephone and on trips to Washington.

In January Tom and Ben began to work on a draft prepared by two young men, Telford Taylor and I. N. P. Stokes, neither long out of law school. Stokes was assigned to the job by Landis, who had chosen him as his confidential assistant, from Harvard Law School. Taylor after graduation from Harvard Law School in 1932 had clerked for Judge Augustus Hand on Frankfurter's recommendation, and then at the age of twenty-three followed many of his classmates to Washington, where salaries were higher and things were happening of which he wanted to be a part. At the Department of Interior he was a lawyer in Solicitor Margold's effort to infuse new blood in the department's legal operations. He joined a bachelor ménage on Eighteenth Street along with other Harvard Law School men, Tom Eliot, Alex Hawes, and Francis Shea. As a student he had done a note for the *Law Review* on commodities exchanges and when Jim, Tom, Ben, and Max looked around for some "junior assistants" on the exchange act, they set Taylor and Stokes to work on ideas they put forward. "I kept on working at Interior," recalled Taylor of the preparatory work, "and weekends and evenings worked with Tom and Ben," who at the end of 1933 became the main figures in drafting the act.[13]

Toward the end of January the Dickinson report was finished. "The other day I signed the Stock Exchange Report," Landis wrote Frankfurter, "coming from a committee consisting of John Dickinson, Berle, [Arthur] Dean, Richardson and myself. Dean signed it, even though I think he thought he was decapitating himself. It's a pretty good report even though we all know very little about the subject."[14]

Should he return to Harvard Law School next year? he asked Felix. "From a personal standpoint I look forward to an interview with the skipper with pleasure, knowing that there will be an exchange of views. I always looked forward to an interview with the Dean [Pound, who had objected to giving him a leave of absence], with dread, and I never even had one with Lowell."

Felix, aware of Landis's ambitiousness, and having been cautioned by Tom on the subject, answered warily that one should follow "a dominant impulse," and Landis clearly wanted to stay in Washington. To Tom, Felix wrote derisively: "Jim is a scream—he wants to stay on in Washington, but, as Marion said 'he wants you to hold his hand in making the decision, fix it at Cambridge . . .' Funny lad."[15]

Landis had settled his family in Alexandria just outside of Washington, but he, too, was a fiend for work and often spent nights on a cot in his FTC office. Landis's biographer describes him as busy during the day with the "business accommodationists" on the Dickinson Committee and at night with the "determined reformers" on Pecora's staff.[16] Lowenthal counseled him against signing the Dickinson report unless it was basically revised,[17] "but evidently it was not his idea of strategy." Landis's conscience may have troubled him. On a weekend visit to Cambridge "under the mellow influence of cocktails," he said he had been trying to keep the Dickinson Committee busy while Corcoran and Cohen drafted their version of the bill.

"There were at least two meetings on the initial draft," recalled Taylor, where there was "very sharp controversy" between Jim and Tom.[18] The latter advocated more drastic powers and standards than did Landis. Having had a year of administrative responsibility, said Taylor, Landis had "become rather more cautious and aware of the obstacles in getting things changed than Tom. They had a very large set-to at least twice in which the soothing voice of the eventual compromising language was devised by Ben."

Dickinson did not offer a bill but proposed the federal licensing of exchanges under the supervision of a "Federal Stock Exchange Authority" on which a member of the stock exchange would sit, a business self-government device that was proving ineffective in the NRA code authorities. Instead of outlawing pools, short selling, wash sales, and other "insider" devices that had been exposed in the Pecora hearings, it advised against "placing of this complex and important machinery in a strait jacket."

In the argument between Landis and Lowenthal over the former's signing the Dickinson report and not deferring to the Corcoran and Cohen draft, Landis evidently had sought to weaken the credibility of their independence of Wall Street charging that Ben and Tom "had a longer connection with Wall Street than Dickinson." Untrue and irrelevant, Lowenthal had rejoined, adding, as he noted in a letter to Frankfurter, "Congressional Committee chairmen obviously felt Tom and Ben safe, D not, since the chairmen used T & B and carefully refrained from using D." The reformers' gloom was equaled by Wall Street's jubilation over the Dickinson report.

Early in February Pecora and Landis were summoned to the White House. It was morning, FDR was still in bed. The two men filled him in.

Privately Landis was mildly critical of Pecora. He was a great investigator but not a "creative artist . . . We built on his work" which he, personally, was unable to translate into legislative form.[19] Such reservations, however, Landis kept to himself. Roosevelt asked them questions they thought quite intelligent and then said, "All right, go ahead" and introduce the bill.

"This really was a fight," recalled Landis, comparing it with the quiet moves of a few Wall Street lawyers to modify the Securities Act draft. Richard Whitney, the president of the New York Stock Exchange, came down to Washington and took over a whole floor at the Willard Hotel to guide it.

Frankfurter in Oxford had many sources of information on the fight—Landis, Corcoran, Cohen, Lowenthal, and, of course, Brandeis. "Tom Cochrane is doing grand service," the latter wrote at the end of January, still misspelling the younger man's name, "and everyone loves him—quite naturally."[20] Felix had doubtlessly heard from Tom, a later report noted, about "Jim's weakness," and finally on February 11, "F.D. did well on his message on Stock Exchange legislation and Tom C. says Ben Cohen did a superb job on bill drafting. He generally is most enthusiastic about B.V.C."

The bill was introduced in the Senate and House and Tom appealed to Felix for help:

BENS EXCHANGE BILL WELL RECEIVED BY PRESS BUT INDICATIONS TERRIFIC FIGHT IN WHICH SKIPPERS POSITION DOUBTFUL TO REMOVE EXCHANGES FROM ADMINISTRATIVE JURISDICTION OF FEDERAL TRADE COMMISSION PER BILL TO NEW COMMISSION DOMINATED BY EXCHANGE MEMBERS STOP URGE ALL POSSIBLE HELP THIS POINT PARTICULARLY SOON AS POSSIBLE AND THE SUGGESTION TO SKIPPER OF BEN FOR FEDERAL TRADE COMMISSION=

TOM[21]

Felix wanted to see the text of the bill. He hesitated to ask for Ben's appointment to the RFC. "Is it possible to have [Senator] Costigan suggest Ben [to] Skipper and invite my opinion?"[22] But he did write Roosevelt the same day to congratulate him on his exchange regulation message and the bill that accompanied it:

The restriction of the Exchange to its legitimate functions in our social economy has been long overdue. There has been more than ample time for self-regulation, and self-regulation they have shown is not in them. Your message and the proposed legislation ought to stop the naive talk that continues to go the rounds that the Administration should now concern itself only with "recovery" and postpone "reform" until later. What an unreal alternative that is! One is reminded of Macaulay's remark in answer to the objection that the British Reform Act of 1832 would undermine the British Constitution. "You must reform," said Macaulay, "in order to preserve." It is equally true that we must reform in order to recover an adequate way of life for the mass of our people. Of course such has been the basis of your whole program, and it is amusing how much idle chatter still goes on about "recovery" versus "reform."

The issue of whether recovery had priority over reform was not just "idle chatter." Moley had misgivings about the Securities Act because it weakened business confidence in the Roosevelt administration. Roosevelt's appointment of the Dickinson Committee indicated that he, too, was sensitive to that consideration, and there was Keynes in his letter to Roosevelt arguing that "even wise and necessary Reform may, in some respects, impede and complicate Recovery,"[23] particularly in upsetting the confidence of the business world.

But on the other side, apart from the national pressure for reform generated by the Pecora investigation, there was Roosevelt's conviction that a large part of Wall Street was on strike against him. Berle had told him in December, "Yesterday, Mr. Lewis Strauss (of Kuhn, Loeb & Co.) . . . came into the office. He said there had been a tacit understanding among the security houses that no issues would be floated for the time being, pending revision of the Securities Act, and possibly a stabilization of money."[24] "That talk you had with him confirmed my guess," replied Roosevelt, and publicly bent to the pressure, urging Congress to clarify the Act. "The President has no faith in the New York crowd," Tom decided, he "knows that fundamentally they are his most dangerous enemies—but needs some counter to their everlasting pressure."

The most radical view of banker incorrigibility came from Brandeis. There is no evidence, however, that he ever stated it to Roosevelt. "I wish he [FDR] had gone forward long ago with heavy taxation on the rich—reduction of big corporation powers and lessening dependence on banks and bankers," he wrote Felix.[25] "No policy can be safe which leaves the big fellows with the powers they still have. His advisers have infantile faith in regulation. The only safety lies in disarming the enemy." Roosevelt "erred fundamentally," he followed up, "in failing as O.W.H. [Holmes] would say 'to strike at the jugular.' He has restored the big boys' confidence and powers—instead of destroying them when they were at his feet."

The Stock Exchange bill was easier in the obligations it imposed on the securities industry than was the Securities Act, said Cohen. But Wall Street's opposition was fiercer. The Securities Act had dealt with new securities, this one with all securities. Pecora had prepared for the hearings on exchange practices by having his staff prepare a questionnaire to circulate among stock exchange members in regard to pools, short selling, and the like. The eminently respectable Richard D. Whitney (educated at Groton and Harvard), president of the exchange who was later to be jailed for embezzling securities entrusted to him, refused to distribute them: "You gentlemen are making a great mistake. The Exchange is a perfect institution." Pecora circumvented the rebuff by sending the questionnaire directly to the exchange's 1,375 members. Whitney's hauteur, however, reflected Wall Street's recovery of morale. "They felt quite broken when the New Deal first started," Ben recalled, "and they were gaining a little greater strength and confidence in themselves the following year."[26]

Wall Street was resigned to regulation, but it wanted to regulate itself. The administration bill supported self-policing, supplemented, however, by regulation by government officials. The first draft imposed high margin requirements, outlawed pools, wash sales, and short selling, and separated broker and trader functions. Frankfurter enthusiastically endorsed the draft when he finally had the text. "That is an astonishingly careful and acute piece of draftsmanship," he wrote Roosevelt.[27] "The Bill reveals real mastery of the intricacies of the Exchange and addresses itself with knowledge to them." He was impressed with the "fine press" the bill had had, he said echoing Corcoran's cable. "One word from Franklin D. Roosevelt and the dramatic first bill would have been passed with a whoop," wrote John T. Flynn, whose distrust of Roosevelt matched his distrust of Wall Street. But Roosevelt after the initial thrust that his message gave the bill's introduction kept hands off.

Wall Street unloosed a storm of propaganda. Whitney, in personal charge of the campaign to defeat the bill, together with his troops and allies, occupied a floor of the Willard Hotel. "We really knew who came in and who went out of that floor," said Landis, describing the friendly reporters and young volunteers who kept watch on "Whitney and his crowd."[28]

Fletcher's Senate Banking and Currency Committee took the lead in hearings on the bill. Corcoran and Cohen had expected Pecora to present their draft to the full committee. Then they heard that Roland Redmond, a fellow Grotonian of the president's, his Hudson River neighbor, and the stock exchange's counsel, had, at Whitney's request, been invited to sit at the committee table and question witnesses on a par with Pecora, the committee's counsel, who sat at the other end.

Between the two interlocutors as the hearings opened sat the first witness for the bill, thirty-four-year-old Corcoran. Cohen and Pecora had told him he had to take on the job of confronting Redmond. "You've been on

Wall Street and you come from a great firm on Wall Street."[29] So for a day and a half Corcoran explained the draft paragraph by paragraph. At Cotton Franklin it was part of the firm's doctrine, said Corcoran, that it "could beat any GD firm on Wall Street," and in the audience that first day was his old boss George Franklin who in 1932 had sent him to Washington. "And when it was all over, I had licked the shit out of him, Roland Redmond who had thought he was so GD smart that he didn't need to read the GD bill." A Republican senator from New Jersey, Frelinghuysen, blurted out, "Well, I don't like this bill," to which Corcoran sweetly replied, "Of course you don't Mr. Frelinghuysen, you're a stock broker." The place exploded, some at his impertinence, others at his daring. Everyone complained, George Franklin told him afterward, that Cotton Franklin had not taught him manners, "but you're magnificent" and someday he would be taking over Cotton Franklin.

Whitney, who sat behind Corcoran, when it came time to speak voiced his great displeasure with the draft. He summed up his objections:

I do not believe that the liberalism of today . . . requires the Federal government to operate our exchanges, to control our credit, and to regulate our corporations . . . I think this bill is almost a full brother to the prohibition law. This matter involves human nature. You can't stop a man from taking a drink by passing a law prohibiting it. And any attempt to regulate by statute and in minute detail the operation of the security markets is just as impossible of accomplishment.[30]

Many years later, in 1970, Cohen commented on the pleas of the stock exchange people to be allowed to govern themselves:

But if we had only legislation with the consent of the governed, in situations like this when you're trying to protect the broad public against the so-called governed, you would have no legislation. That indeed is why among those who are the subjects of the regulation, the idea of self-regulation is an extremely popular idea.

"Tom C is having a grand fight on the Stock Exchange Bill," Brandeis reported to Frankfurter, and supplemented that a week later, "Mrs. Burling reports George Rublee who attended the Stock Exchange hearings (professionally) as saying that Tom C. was an amazingly good witness." And reflecting an anxiety that the inner group around Brandeis and Frankfurter shared, he noted, "Tom C. says Jim Landis is behaving very well." From afar Frankfurter added his note to the swelling chorus of praise and wrote a friend in the United States: "You will have noticed what an effective fellow Tom Corcoran has been in the Stock Exchange hearings. L.D.B. and Max write me that Tom made a monkey of the counsel for the Exchange and testified with gaiety and power."[31]

In the House of Representatives the bill was handled by Sam Rayburn. He "remains the strong man that he was," Landis advised Frankfurter, and urged he write the Texan.[32] "With a less able chairman of the House Committee, I doubt just where we would be." Rayburn was more than an astute politician and parliamentarian. He and Landis had become "quite close friends . . . He was quite a pleasant host. He had a small apartment not far from Dupont Circle, and almost every month I'd go up there Sunday nights. He might have 20 or 30 people up there, mostly from the House and the Senate." The House paid attention to him. The bullet-headed, blunt-spoken legislator pushed the bill in the teeth of the Whitney-led opposition that constituted "the biggest and boldest, the richest and most ruthless lobby Congress ever had known." To Landis also it seemed

the Stock Exchange Bill is receiving a terrific beating. All the corporate wealth of the country has gone onto the attack and carried it all the way up to the White House. I think F.D. will stand firm on the essentials, however . . .

Corcoran testified before Rayburn's committee as he had before Fletcher's. New Dealers, the public, and the White House were impressed. His star was on the rise. Not even John Dickinson's testimony that the bill's high margin requirements would have a deflationary effect "dramatically opposed to President Roosevelt's policy of maintaining values," though it was damaging, nullified the impact of Corcoran's advocacy. HAVE STUDIED BILL, Dickinson cabled Frankfurter, AND REGARD MANY PROVISIONS AS ATROCIOUS DESTRUCTIVE AND IMPOSSIBLE STOP SOME OF YOUR FRIENDS HAVE PURSUED VERY DOUBLE DEALING COURSES WITH ME. Frankfurter disclaimed any knowledge about the progress of the bill, "but [I] naturally feel that public interest should preclude differences among men who presumably care about same things."[33]

Dickinson was "self-deceiving as to his own liberalism," Max assured Felix. Max guessed that he felt Landis had "double-crossed him" and he was "greatly piqued that he was not consulted on the drafting of the bill (not knowing that Fletcher would not have permitted it)."

Cohen and Corcoran discovered, as the bills progressed through House and Senate, that their toughest problem was not with the public hearings but to overcome objections made within the Administration. They emanated from Treasury, Commerce, and the Federal Reserve Board with each of which the stock exchange had its contacts, recalled Cohen:

. . . and so one would have a criticism of certain features of the Act and there seemed to be some effort to delay the proceedings and some of these criticisms I think they thought it would take us a few weeks to answer and to come back with a new bill but we adopted the practice of meeting any criticism they made within a day or two by working most of the night.[34]

Often this involved secret meetings with people on Wall Street who were on their side, said Cohen, but they had to move carefully. Indeed had one of the Pecora Committee workers, John T. Flynn, who approved of Ben, known of his confidential talks with some people on the Street, "he would have disapproved," said Cohen mildly. "The Federal Reserve Board came in with the purpose of trying to stop us. Instead we showed we knew what we were doing."

This, too, was an essential characteristic of Corcoran's and Cohen's service to the Administration. They were magnificently attuned to what was politically possible and always realized that whatever power they had emanated from Fletcher and Rayburn and above all the President, who gave them their marching orders.

At the advice of Moley, Rayburn, Fletcher, and Pecora, critics were met and mollified and the bills moved forward. The most severe attack was leveled at the rigidity of the margin requirements. Here a New Deal ally appeared suddenly from within the Federal Reserve Board. Winfield Riefler was thirty-eight, tall, blond, a top statistician at the Federal Reserve Board, liberal in a non-ideological way. He so impressed Corcoran and Cohen's youthful aide, Telford Taylor, that he resolved that after the stock exchange bill fight was over he would add a Ph.D. in economics to his legal degree so that he might be able to work with him. Riefler came up with a formula under which the Federal Reserve Board might be able to set margin rates. To Corcoran and Cohen it seemed "ingenious and we fought for it hard."

But the stock exchange representatives objected to the Riefler formula. Said Cohen:

On the one hand they criticized the Act as giving too much discretion to an administrative body. Then when it came to these detailed objections, the most serious was on the margins, and the only answer they had was to give greater discretion to the administrative body.[35]

For two weeks Corcoran and Cohen, at Moley's request, met with officials of Treasury, Reserve, and Commerce to revise their bill, especially in regard to margin requirements, easing liability provisions, and the absolute separation of broker and dealer functions.

At the end of March, Moley congratulated Frankfurter. "The boys did a magnificent job of drafting and since the process of amending has been underway, they have been tactful and skillful in handling the obvious necessity of yielding certain unimportant aspects in the interests of holding to the essentials."[36] It was again time, Roosevelt judged, to give the bill a push. He wrote Fletcher and Rayburn that the country could not "afford to have it [the bill] weakened in any shape, manner or form."

"The day-to-day grind is pretty exhausting on all of us," Moley's letter to Frankfurter continued, "and we need, above all things more soldiers in the public interest. Tom, Ben and Jim are doing well, but they need more leadership. The little I can give here is not enough."

The revised bill did not allay Wall Street's uproar. Whitney called it "destructive." Pecora answered him in *The Wall Street Journal,* "If all of Mr. Whitney's objections were met, there would be no bill at all." In April the revised bills reached the floor of both houses. The Senate version had an amendment by crusty Carter Glass of Virginia. It eliminated fixed margin requirements and established a separate Securities and Exchange Commission (SEC) to administer the Act instead of giving it to the Federal Trade Commission. To cries that this was what Wall Street wanted, Glass insisted that "Mr. Whitney's ideas and mine are as different as night and day" and that his chief concern was to protect the integrity of the Federal Reserve Board, his legislative baby. He did not want it "mixed up with stock market gambling."

In Ben Cohen's view, the pressure for a separate commission came from Wall Street:

. . . although we all recognized it had a great deal to commend it, we fought against it because experience had indicated that commissions in time tend to be dominated by those they regulate and . . . a commission that had other tasks than stock exchange tasks and security tasks might be less the prisoner of the financial community.[37]

On the House floor Corcoran and Cohen for the first time were subjected to full-scale Red-baiting. The bill, said Representative Fred Britten (R-Ill.) was the handiwork of "the scarlet fever boys down in the little red house in Georgetown," elevating the redbrick house that Tom and Ben shared with a few other New Dealers into a cross between a sinister Smolny, plotting revolution, and a house of ill fame where an accordion-playing Corcoran led the revels. The two were, continued Britten, Frankfurter's "cheerleaders." Even at that moment, he noted to Cohen's embarrassment, Cohen was sitting next to Rayburn on the floor of the House. Cohen, a modest man who disliked the spotlight, quickly left the chamber as Britten in mock apology professed to be "sorry I caused all this because

I truly believe that no one on the floor understands this legislation as does the logical Mr. Cohen."[38]

Britten then addressed himself to Landis who, he asserted, "probably had more to do with the writing of all these various bills than any other individual" and added that "Judge Landis has no sympathy whatever with stock exchanges."* The Frankfurter group had "kidnapped" the exchange bill and used it "to Russianize everything worthwhile under the unqualified and unprepared Federal Trade Commission."

The House bill passed 280 to 84, the Senate by an equally lopsided majority of 62 to 13. Their chief difference was the administering agencies. Landis, Cohen, and Corcoran still were not reconciled to a separate commission. They were afraid, said Landis, "a second commission would be pretty well stacked."[39] They had two new members on the FTC, George Mathews and Judge Healy, in addition to Landis. "So we had control of the FTC at the time. When I say 'we,' I mean our group. And we were afraid of this second commission."

After further trading, a conference approved a new five-member SEC but placed margin requirements under the Federal Reserve Board. Landis was unhappy that the FTC had been superseded by a new commission, but Cohen and Corcoran gradually abandoned their hostility to a separate body and concentrated instead on the identity of the five commissioners whom Roosevelt would name. Although John T. Flynn lamented the weakening of the original draft which in his view had been a "tremendously effective measure,"[40] Corcoran and Cohen, more realistic, thought the toughness of the initial version enabled them to get a final bill that gave the new commission the powers it would need to assert federal authority over the security markets. And even the acerbic Flynn began his article in *Harper's* that by the time the article appeared in print, "The marines will have landed on Wall Street. The place will be annexed to the United States." The new law did not do away with exchanges, he went on. "But the organization must be registered with the Commission. It must yield up full information about itself." The commission had two potent weapons. "One is the power of scrutiny . . . The other power resides in the Commission's right to compel the exchange, after hearing to change almost any of its rules."

"Ray Moley, Pecora, Sam Rayburn, and Garner have been magnificent," Tom had advised Felix when the bills finally reached the floor of Congress. "Otherwise we kids have taken the beating alone . . . That

---

* Britten evidently confused James Landis with baseball commissioner Judge Kenesaw Mountain Landis.

we're getting the kind of bill we expect in the teeth of the kind of opposition we have to meet . . . is to me a miracle."[41]

Felix's praise was more than usually lavish. Tom had been "superb" in his ability to give "so philosophic" a picture of the contest in Washington while he was at the very center of it.

It was a deliberate stratagem of Cohen and Corcoran, Moley later wrote, to get one House to adopt a tough draft and then use it for trading purposes with the other. "When you want one loaf of bread," he cited Corcoran as saying, "you've got to ask for two." This may not have been the conscious intent of Corcoran and Cohen at the beginning, but as a result of their experiences with securities legislation they learned.[42]

Tom emerged from the battle a national figure. Both he and Ben had sought to stay out of the limelight, lest they invite being shot at, so the sudden fame was a mixed blessing. More important, however, Corcoran became the acknowledged leader of the young liberals in Washington. And since he was always generous with his praise of Ben, the two were linked in the public eye. Many people had worked on the bill, Tom explained to a hostile House interrogator, "but I do not pretend to know as much about it, or be as competent as Mr. Cohen, who sits by my side, and who took charge of the actual details of drawing up the measure."*

Ben's praise of Tom was equally fulsome. "Poor Tom has had to bear much more than his fair share of the battle because of his sheer ability as well as his brilliant fluency and superb advocacy. I have left him to bear the brunt of the attack," he wrote Felix.[44] So the opposition had gone after Tom rather than Ben, he went on. Because of Tom's strength and cheer, few realized that he was at times "a bit disheartened and discouraged." It had been a "strange fight" for Ben, who "like a man being chased from behind with a pitchfork I have had to keep up." He singled out Moley for praise. He had been "most helpful with the Skipper. And Ray has shown real courage in the stock market fight."

There was a final encomium from Felix. Passage of the Act was "an extraordinary achievement of a small handful of men," the more so since it would be

the salvage of those very institutions for which the blind men of Wall Street profess to speak but which in their greed, had they a free hand, they would be speedily destroying.

* "The actual writing throughout was done by Mr. Cohen," wrote John T. Flynn flatly, "an abler example of legislative drafting has never made way into our statute books."[43]

As for Corcoran and Cohen, they "in particular have shown knowledge and good humor and good sense that constitutes the kind of high endeavor of which the Grand Old Man, Holmes, is such a superb living example . . . It makes me very proud indeed of your friendship." And Sam Rayburn told his biographer, "Taken together these two fellows made the brightest man I ever saw. They never insisted on their own views. When I told them what I wanted, they started to work to put it into legislation. They wrote it in such a way as to make it stick."[45]

Corcoran's efforts on behalf of the SEC bill, Cohen told columnist Joseph Alsop, gave him "a certain status among the younger men whom he had recruited to Washington."[46] Suddenly the Frankfurter group was courted by the Tugwell people. There was rough going in sight for "the whole Jerry Frank-Tugwell crowd," Corcoran predicted to Frankfurter, "for whom we're afraid there's a showdown ahead not too far away. Tugwell and Berle have been trying very hard lately to tie our crowd into a general Brain Trust unity on the basis of some compromise in name which will be their philosophy in fact. We've ducked . . ."

It was after his work on the stock exchange legislation, Corcoran believed, "that the word went back to the White House that by God I could handle myself . . . I became known in the White House as a guy who could go down and be a front-line fighter. Roosevelt liked that kind of guy and little by little, I was the guy who handled all the tough ones on the Hill."[47]

XIV

———⟶⊱⊰⟵———

Competition
for Roosevelt's Ear

Rayburn, Fletcher, Pecora, Corcoran, and Cohen stood in a semicircle behind the President as he signed the Securities and Exchange Act. Landis was out of town.

"Ferd, now that I have signed this bill and it has become law, what kind of a law will it be?" the President asked.[1]

"It will be a good or a bad bill, Mr. President, depending upon the men who administer it," replied Pecora. The same note was sounded by John T. Flynn. "The whole matter now rests in the hands of the Commission, and the President must be held responsible for the kind of administration that is given this act," he ended his *Harper's* article.[2]

Corcoran and Cohen both were alive to the question of who the watchdogs were going to be even as they drafted a description of their duties. In February Corcoran had nudged Frankfurter to get Roosevelt to appoint Cohen as federal trade commissioner. That had not gotten anywhere but in May Corcoran felt surer of the appointments. So he advised Felix. The "Skipper" had "secretly smiled" on a ticket of Landis, Cohen, Mathews, Healy, and "your friend Joe K. in Boston . . . the last is particularly 'deep well,' comes straight from the Skipper through Ray."

Eight names were on the list Moley gave Roosevelt.[3] It was led by

Joseph P. Kennedy, Roosevelt supporter and Wall Street speculator whom Roosevelt had told Moley he wanted to be its chairman. The list included Pecora and Landis both of whom also wanted to be chairman. Another name was Ben Cohen. Moley's recommendation of Cohen was cordial, "as able as Landis and more experienced," even "his personality would gain friends as people grew to know him." Tom was Ben's most energetic advocate, particularly after he had heard from Moley that the President feared an anti-Semitic reaction to Cohen's appointment. Frankfurter had sensed this might happen and in May had advised Tom to organize a letter-writing campaign addressed to the President.[4] "I don't have to tell you that the leading Jewish bankers and leading Jewish Wall Street lawyers feel about Ben Cohen's influence and the myths of my own influence in the administration precisely as their non-Jewish colleagues in finance and at the bar."

Administration of the new act, Frankfurter counseled Roosevelt, would require greater resourcefulness, firmness, and fairness than had the older regulatory commissions. The new body's effectiveness "will depend largely upon the understanding of the possibilities under the statute by those charged with its administration . . . Nothing less is involved than to keep Wall Street in its place . . ." Frankfurter mentioned no names and while Ben fitted the specifications, if it was Frankfurter's purpose to turn Roosevelt's mind in that direction it did not work.

The Jewish opposition to Cohen did not speak for "the great mass of Jews," Judge Mack wrote for himself and Bernard Flexner.[5] Ben's opponents, he assured Roosevelt, non-Jewish as well as Jewish, were actuated by private interests rather than the public good, nor were they concerned with the success of Roosevelt's administration.

In later years Ben insisted he was not interested in the appointment, but at the time he was writing his "Jane dearest" to explain why he could not see her. "But Tom has been laboring so hard in support of his 'lost candidate' that I could not feel I could let him down . . ."[6] By the time he sent off this letter, however, he was resigned to not being on Roosevelt's list.

It does not look as if I will be named to the commission—too much politics even among the New Dealers. I imagine I could have the General Counselship if I wanted it. But I think I shall come home for a while. I am a bit offended—"brogus" I think they say in your language.

A subsequent letter to Jane explained, "F.D.R. told Ickes one day he had virtually decided to put me on the Commission and the next day he did not."

Roosevelt announced his list on July 1. It did not include Ben, and, according to Moley, the Kennedy name did not sit well with Tom. He had exploded with indignation when the list was announced and then remarked, "Oh well, we've got four out of five anyhow." What did he mean by that? Moley flung back at him, and Corcoran said, "Four are for us and one is for business."[7]

Moley sharpened up such stories after his break with Roosevelt and movement to the right, but whatever truth there was to this story, and undoubtedly there was some, nevertheless, Corcoran and Cohen had the support of a segment of Wall Street with whose representatives they conferred regularly. Moreover, from the beginning of May Corcoran had known about Roosevelt's decision to have Kennedy on the commission.

As Ben indicated, after he was passed over for the commission, despite his reluctance, efforts were made to have Kennedy appoint him as general counsel. On July 12, Roosevelt's appointments secretary, Marvin McIntyre, telegraphed the President, KENNEDY ASKING ADVICE. COHEN SLATED FOR GENERAL COUNSEL HIS BOARD. KENNEDY WILLING TO GO ALONG BUT YOU KNOW QUESTION INVOLVED. LOUIS [HOWE] AND I FELT YOU SHOULD BE CONSULTED. WILL YOU ADVISE IMMEDIATELY. KENNEDY WILLING TO TAKE RESPONSIBILITY EITHER WAY.[8]

"I won't make any definite decision until I have had a chance to talk with him," Ben wrote Jane about the return of Felix from England. "But I shall probably say adieu to Washington by Aug 1st." Kennedy was willing to accept Cohen but he preferred Judge John Burns of Massachusetts. Burns, a classmate of Tom's at Harvard Law School, was the youngest judge to sit on the Superior Court. Tom liked him, and briefly there was talk about the commission having two chief counsels, but Frankfurter warned that would not work. Landis shifted his position to favor Burns on the grounds that the chairman should have his own man.

"Cohen?" responded Landis to an interlocutor at Columbia.

"Well, he's a very quiet individual—shy, great ability. He would never intrude upon anything, but he would respond to a request that was made of him. He did want one job which he didn't get, and that was originally when the SEC was formed, he wanted the position of general counsel. Kennedy didn't want him—not that he didn't want him, but he wanted Burns. My theory was the chairman was entitled to have his own counsel . . . Certainly Burns was a competent individual. So Cohen didn't get that, and I think he was quite disappointed over that. In a sense he was entitled to it from the standpoint of fairness. Well, he was something like Achilles in his tent for a short while after that. But he was too big a guy to continue to sulk."

Ben was bitter over Landis's role, as he wrote Jane[9] from the RMS *Olympic* on which he was traveling to England:

Then there was the backing and filling over the counselship. I could have had that if I wanted it, but the plots and counterplots were disgusting to me. I made conditions so that there would be no mistaking my position, and my friend Landis, who I always knew was a snake in the grass, showed his fangs. And so I am [I] think lucky to be out of it. Felix in his usual compromising way is trying to hold me in the picture, but my mind is made up. *J'ai fini.* I am going to London professedly on Palestinian matters but the real reason is that I want to get away, I shall have to return to Washington for a few weeks, but I am coming back to New York. I am not sure what I shall do, but I shall probably practice some sort of law, even though I won't like it. I'm through being a brain-truster.[10]

No one said anything about it, but it would have been unlike Roosevelt, facing as he did the 1934 off-year congressional elections, if he did not take into account Ben's emergence—even though on a lesser scale than a Tugwell or a Frankfurter—as an alleged manipulator of the President, and Jewish at that. In December of the previous year, Tom had reported to Felix in Oxford, "The Frankfurter-Brandeis-bloc-Harvard-Jews talk is much to the fore . . ." The chief target then had been Tugwell who as "Unofficial Observer" [Jay Franklin Carter] predicted in *The New Dealers* "has been the main target of the Big Business batteries (if Tugwell goes, Harry Hopkins will be next . . .)"[11]

The attack on Tugwell had been led by historian and *Herald Tribune* columnist Mark Sullivan, who wrote his Tugwell columns after visiting former president Hoover in Palo Alto. The ferocity of Sullivan's attacks had brought Heywood Broun to Washington to take a closer look at the man said to be undermining the government. Frankfurter was sent one of Broun's ensuing columns. Broun's words were nimble but laced with acid. He teased the "goblin editor" as he called Sullivan:

It now seems that Professor Tugwell is not playing a lone hand in his effort to Sovietize America while Sullivan sleeps. Some of the blame falls on the head of Professor Felix Frankfurter, who has recommended several young men who have received appointments under the Administration. "Nearly all of them are graduates of Harvard Law School," adds Mark Sullivan ominously.

New Dealers might laugh among themselves about such right-wing caricatures, but they knew they spelled danger, that there was a large public open to simplistic parables about professorial and radical conspiracies. A touch of anti-Semitism did not diminish the audience for such cartoons.

In February Mark Sullivan had written of the Stock Exchange Bill as an effort by a group of young radicals to move America toward collectivism against the will of the President. This was the line, too, of James H. Rand, Jr., of the Remington Rand Corporation and the head of the Committee for the Nation, a group of businessmen and farmers that Moley called "Bryanism Reincarnated." Testifying before the Rayburn Committee on the Stock Exchange Bill, Rand claimed the bill was meant to push the nation toward communism. To prove his point he read from a manuscript from Dr. William A. Wirt, superintendent of Schools of Gary, Indiana, and member of the Rand Committee. Wirt's manuscript described how in the summer of 1933 an unidentified "brain truster" had told him of a "group of theoretically trained young men, sincere but inexperienced" who were leading the country down "the road to Communism." When Wirt had asked this brain truster what about the President in this move toward state control, he was told, "We believe that we can keep Mr. Roosevelt there until we are ready to supplant him with a Stalin. We all think that Mr. Roosevelt is only the Kerensky of this revolution."[12]

The headlines read, even in the New York *Times,* BRAIN TRUST AC-CUSED/ROOSEVELT TERMED A KERENSKY. Representative Arthur Bullwinkle called for an investigation and hearings were held by a select House committee. No brain trusters, it turned out, were present at the 1933 dinner so graphically described by Wirt. The Kerensky remark had been made by the Tass correspondent who was there. And the other participants in the dinner portrayed Wirt as a windbag who held the floor almost continuously "discoursing on money." "Pish and Piffle," *Time* captioned its story.

The knowledgeable scoffed at the insubstantiality of the story but a residue remained of this effort to portray a weak president who was being manipulated by professors and radicals. "Frankfurter's Hot Dog Boys," Paul Mallon, another conservative columnist, characterized Tom and his associates in the Washington *Star.* Writing to Felix about the Select Committee hearings, Tom said that "stock exchange publicists (Eddie Bernays —Ivy Lee)" were responsible for injecting Felix into the Wirt story.[13] There had been "a very evident but unsuccessful attempt to make the press believe that the famous dinner had been held in our house." "What will come of it no one knows," Tugwell wrote in his diary. "If there is genuine strength in the present reaction, we may be thrown overboard."

In Oxford, Felix was worried enough by the Wirt-Rand developments to write the President:

No one knows better than you the need and the difficulties of political education. To talk too often lessens the impact: not to talk enough creates a vacuum in the public mind, into which flow all too easily the kind of childish imbecilities and shrewdly promoted fears illustrated by the incredible Wirt-Rand statements. I venture to say, however, that particularly in these restless days, in which foolishness and fanaticism and self-interest are exploited by professional poisoners of the public mind, by the Ivy Lees and the Bernays, it becomes even more important than it was in the days of T.R. and Woodrow Wilson for the President to do what you are able to do with such effectiveness, namely, to give guidance to the public in order to rally them to the general interest.[14]

The opponents of the Exchange Bill and the New Deal sensed they had struck pay dirt with the public reaction to the Wirt-Rand charges. Representative Fred Britten (R-Ill.) gave out a story that "in the Republican cloakroom of the House it is freely admitted that the Fletcher-Rayburn bills were written by . . ." and he mentioned the names of Pecora, Landis, Corcoran, and Cohen whom he described as "all disciples of the Felix Frankfurter School of Radical Thought." Then on April 20 on the floor of the House he painted a lurid picture of "the little red house in Georgetown where are held the meetings which promote the communistic legislation we all talk about in the cloakrooms. It is the little red house in Georgetown where every night of the week from ten to eighteen young men of radical minds meet, so-called 'young students;' they call them 'Frankfurter's hot dogs.'" He likened the Georgetown house with the little green house in the twenties where President Harding's cronies had met and carved up the public pelf. A LITTLE RED HOUSE CAUSES GREAT UPROAR, the Washington *Post* headlined its story.[15]

Moley assigned a reporter to visit the house for *Today.* There he found Tom Corcoran and six others engaged in a singing session. Instead of "marching legs and upraised palms" there were "active brains and hearts." It was a movement "not of shirts but houses . . . dangerous to Mr. Britten's kind of politics."[16] What Britten caricatured, Corcoran's old boss, Eugene Meyer as publisher of the Washington *Post,* decried in more civil terms. He criticized the "young intellectuals who are apparently directing the policy of this administration for their inexperience, their experimentation and the self-righteousness." The Stock Exchange Bill pointed toward "State Control of Industry." As for Republican "nonsense" about Frankfurter and his young lawyers, Moley recalled impishly in *Today* that when he had asked the Harvard professor for the most "enlightened student of banking," he had recommended Eugene Meyer.

In May just before leaving for the United States, Felix sent his "Dear Little Boys" a joshing letter about their alleged Svengali influence over the

White House. They had been having such "a good time" that even "the newspapers write about it:"

. . . And those must be marvelous revels by night in a little red house they tell me about. . . . And what darling children you must be to have wormed your way not only into the heart but even the mind and will of the President of the United States, so that he says what you tell him to say and he does what you tell him to do . . .

They were not to let the attention they were getting go to their heads, but he knew they were

such hard-headed little youngsters that there isn't the slightest danger of all this public acclaim of your juvenile games and performances either spoiling you or making life as it gets duller when you grow up seem too dull when compared with your gay childhood . . .[17]

The last weeks of June became a "waiting for Felix" time. Brandeis, the impatient foster-father, had sought to persuade Felix to advance his date of departure from Oxford because matters were in such a mess in Washington. He had taken to referring to the NRA and the AAA as FDR's "Künstucke," a German word meaning sleight-of-hand marvels. His views were no secret to Roosevelt, not because Frankfurter reported them—he did not —but Berle had. "Mr. Justice Brandeis . . . I think requires some attention," Berle alerted Roosevelt.[18] The justice had expressed himself to Jerome Frank

asking to see me and Rexford Tugwell. His idea was that we were steadily creating organisms of big business which were growing in power, wiping out the middle class, eliminating small business and putting themselves in a place in which they rather than the government were controlling the nation's destinies. He added that he had gone along with the legislation up to now; but unless he could see some reversal of the big business trend, he was disposed to hold the government control legislation unconstitutional from now on. I think also that he regretted not having had a chance to talk to you about it. He, of course, wants drastic taxation of big business units, accompanied by leaving small business, via the NRA, strictly alone.

"As to our friend of the highest court, I expect to have a good long talk with him within the next few days," Roosevelt assured Berle.[19]

"In my opinion you should come here as soon as your duties in Oxford permit," Brandeis wrote Frankfurter on May 11. "Your statement: 'I see no purpose in getting involved in Washington matters during the summer, FDR will in any event be away etc.' rests, I think, on a failure to sense the situation."[20] Even if Roosevelt were away, there remained "the serious fundamental question," his letter ended, what can and should be the program "the Keynote—of the [1934] campaign and the program for the 1935 legislation . . ." Despite the minatory signals from the justice, Roosevelt's schedule did not allow for a talk until just before the justice left Washington. Roosevelt was a stubborn man and the justice had to fit into his scheme of priorities, a psychic map that he kept secret from everyone.

Frankfurter, too, was not to be hurried. Conscious perhaps of the readiness of those around him to exaggerate his influence with the President, a tendency that he was not disposed to discourage or deflate, he avoided situations that might reveal powerlessness and stuck to his schedule. In May he expedited a meeting between Roosevelt and Keynes during the latter's visit to the United States, a visit that Roosevelt was as eager to have as Keynes was to make, a measure of the British economist's growing interest for the President. "J.M. Keynes in a letter just received—writes me," Frankfurter informed the President, " 'I had an hour's tête-à-tête with the President which was fascinating and illuminating.' " And the President replied, "I had a grand talk with Keynes and liked him immensely." Roosevelt also informed Felix, "I had a most satisfactory talk with Justice Brandeis before he left. He has and is a great soul."[21]

A good part of the Roosevelt-Brandeis talk dealt with social insurance. The forceful views of the justice on the subject did not wholly comport with Roosevelt's, as a long letter from Tom and Ben to Felix just before he sailed for home reported. That letter described the situation in Washington to which the professor was returning.[22] Apart from social insurance, which Roosevelt in a message to the adjourning Congress had projected as one of the big issues for the next session, the silence of the Corcoran-Cohen missive on other substantive issues,* its concentration on the status of Moley, Tugwell, and Frank, revealed the competition among these individuals for the ear of the President and the intellectual leadership of the New Deal.

The letter signed by Tom and Ben probably was written by the former:

> Room 1115, 1825 H Street, N.W.
> Washington, D.C.
> June 18, 1934

Dear F.F.:

1. It's very difficult to map out just what you'd expect to do on getting home. The Skipper—knows when you're coming back—will sail from Annapolis sometime late in June, probably the 26th, for a trip to Hawaii, back to the West Coast and then across country to Washington. He'll be gone "approximately thirty days", i.e. until at least August 1st, probably until August 15th. He might, of course,

---

* There were, needless to say, many such substantive issues—clarification and strengthening of Section 7(A), the collective bargaining section of the NIRA; where Harry Hopkins's relief efforts were going after the Civil Works Administration (CWA) ended; issues of constitutional legitimacy and enforcement that beset the NRA and AAA.

invite you to meet him in Seattle before he makes any speeches on the way home. Ray is writing the speeches. Or in the many other ways you know of making contact, you may be able to have an immediate influence on any planning made known to the public during the period before the return to Washington.

2. The most important consideration, however, is that (no matter whether you are in touch during the vacation) before the Skipper's return you have adequate time and be sufficiently re-orientated in this peculiar atmosphere to be able to advise concretely. Much has gone over the dam since you went away and affairs have proceeded pretty far toward concrete forks in the road. The Tugwell crowd has been pushed by its enemies—and its own loose talk—away over to the left. Ray is vacillating considerably toward the right. Isaiah is militant and impatient in the middle. You'll need, we should think, considerable detailed knowledge of what has gone on just to listen understandingly.

3. A most important concrete way in which you can help tremendously prior to the return is as an adviser or possibly a member of an informal group being formed to work out the social insurance plan talked about in the last message. So far as we know, Ben and I are to be in that group—and possibly Paul Raushenbush. But there will also be Gerard Swope, Raskob and a lot more of that stripe, besides possibly some of the Epstein crowd who will be thoroughly and impractically wild. (They did their bit toward the shelving of Isaiah's unemployment insurance bill at this session as too tame). So much turns on the performance of that group, now that the plan yet to be formulated is a political issue, that it's hard to over-estimate its importance and the necessity that the Skipper be warned against making sweeping premature commitments in the course of his trip which may prejudice the working out of a sound scheme.

4. With Ray's help we managed to have the President call in Isaiah on Isaiah's last day here, to discuss the social insurance message before it became public (although it had already been put in final form and had gone to Congress). They had an hour and a quarter of uninterrupted discussion during which they branched off into other things. Isaiah did not like the scheme in the Skipper's mind because it left administration completely in the Federal Government as opposed to the States. The Skipper gave the impression that there was nothing as yet cut and dried about the scheme and that it was all in the making. Our last information on the subject was from Ray Moley who told us that an informal committee was to be formed and that I would be secretary, "legman", and coordinator of the committee. I talked to him about your being on the committee and he thought it was a very good idea to take in. (I don't yet know whether he did or what the Skipper's reaction was).

I should say, therefore, that you would wisely plan to be able to participate on a really important scale in the formulation of the insurance program when you return and anticipate a couple of weeks of going over details of other programs with some of the crowd down here.

5. You might also wisely begin a heavy campaign of perking up relations with Ray and Jerry Frank. The enclosed clipping about Ray is partly right and partly over-done. He is really important and you're going to find yourself strangely straddled between Isaiah on one side who wants to ride ahead hard with his full program, completely contemptuous of political obstacles—and Ray on the other side,

who is afraid of Isaiah's belligerence, quite through with the agony and sweat of reforming, and wearily eager to settle down to a false security of sweet reasonableness. If you have followed Ray's editorials lately, you have some feel of where he's going. He also made the mistake this month of becoming receiver of the Hotel St. Regis representing Astor in a business way. And he's been possibly a little too close to Barney. He seems too willing to depend upon private contributions from Barney to finance this social insurance preliminary and to finance the continuance of the Pecora investigation rather than fight Jimmy Byrnes for an appropriation. He's also, for instance, taking a little to bawling us out for making things hard for him and pushing him to go to bat on matters connected with the Stock Exchange Commission and the Securities Act. Part of this I think is due to the fact that he's tired. Part is due to an over-concern with the politics of the Fall elections. I do think you had better begin to contact him pretty assiduously ahead of your return to make sure that you'll be in the old position of being able to do a really good job on him when you return.

The personal relations of Ray and ourselves with the Jerry Frank group are also very unfortunate right now. Ray attacked Jerry in "Today". Jerry blames us—particularly me—because we're so close to Ray. Gardner Jackson drunk hasn't helped. Jerry and ourselves have smoothed things over. Jerry and Ray haven't. If that can be smoothed out only you can do it. You'll have to assume that Jerry is still somewhat suspicious of us and will be suspicious of you, although very anxious to have you as an ally because he fully realizes the inherent weakness of his and Rex's position. Possibly you had better begin precontacting him also. There are many strained relationships under the surface of things not frankly admitted that only you have a sufficiently universal esteem to harmonize.

6. Your Stock Exchange congratulations are premature—wait until we see the make-up of the Commission.

Our best to the Lady.

So, so glad you're coming home.

Yours,
Tom
Ben

Frankfurter's chief personal concern on his return, apart from catching up with the news about FDR via Moley, was to position Tom and Ben most advantageously in terms of the advancement of the New Deal. "When Tom Corcoran is with us," the justice wrote him from Chatham, "I assume you will want Ben Cohen and Max Lowenthal. Arrange with Tom as to that as you see fit."[23]

"1. Moley was here a whole day & much ground was covered," Felix apprised the justice. "I followed your clue of catching up with the past, behind the scenes, as to events & personalities & had him spend hours taking me into all the highways & by-ways of F.D.'s movements . . . & their personal relations." Frankfurter knew the justice's concern that social insurance should be launched slowly with an emphasis on state administration, using Wisconsin's unemployment insurance law as a model.

"2. As to social insurance, I thought I ought to go slow & not begin with a direct attack on Moley's assumptions, but gradually indoctrinate him with difficulties & doubts, the importance of going slowly & avoiding premature commitment & getting somebody like Ben Cohen put in charge. I think there is a good chance of having Frances Perkins on the right side of working out program as *her* program & she is, as you know, Chairman of FD's Com—"

Frances Perkins had her own ideas, and as chairman of the cabinet committee on economic security she named Professor Edwin E. Witte of the University of Wisconsin as executive director of the committee's staff, and Arthur J. Altmeyer, also of Wisconsin, as chairman of a technical board. Both had been involved in the Wisconsin plan and were therefore favorably disposed toward Brandeis's ideas of state experimentation and administration.

Frankfurter and his supporters still sought to get on the inside of the preparatory work. Corcoran wrote Wyzanski, who was on vacation, to urge Ben's appointment as general counsel, and while nothing happened as a result of the letter—Thomas Eliot was named general counsel—the letter showed how Ben was viewed by those closest to him:

Dear Charley:
Judge Mack, Felix and myself have all wired Ben Cohen to sail back on the Majestic on the 8th as he had originally planned. When I talked with Felix at Cornish he told me that your people would be very anxious to make Ben General Counsel to the Social Insurance Group. I note that you agree with me that there is no one who is even second to Ben for that position—and from that position he can also give a big lift to the Railroad Retirement case.

Felix suggests that Ben being the kind of blushing violet he is it would be very wise to try to have the appointment go through before Ben comes back on the ground and has an opportunity to be shy about it. I've talked with Ray Moley who has agreed to do all he can to help get it through but he doesn't see but that the prime moving has to come from your boss.

Even on vacation, can't you start the machinery on this?[24]

Despite Frankfurter's efforts, seconded by Moley and Corcoran, he was kept at arm's length from the social security development, and so was Ben Cohen. Although the latter at the end of July had announced to Jane that he was through with being a brain truster, Felix on Ben's return from England in the middle of August was very persuasive, as Ben had feared, and a fragment of a letter to Jane reports that "Washington is as bad as ever. Felix sees F.D. on Wednesday and unless he has something very unexpected to report, I expect to come home soon . . ."

The social security job fell through. But Roosevelt had other jobs for Corcoran and Cohen, as he told Frankfurter. There was tax legislation to be drafted and utility magnates who were pyramiding vast utility empires to be brought under public control. It was all part of Roosevelt's efforts to build a democratic society free of the "appetite for great wealth and great power," as his 1935 message to Congress, which he wrote with Frankfurter's help among others, would say.

Another consequence of Frankfurter's call on the President, to which Ben referred in his letter to Jane,[25] was that he and Tom journeyed up to Hyde Park to be looked over by the President. What he saw he seems to have liked because both men moved closer to the White House. Ickes gave Ben a formal berth by appointing him general counsel of the National Power Policy Committee (NPPC). Its duty was to examine the nation's power resources and needs and recommend legislation and also to prepare a utility holding company bill. Its offices on Eighteenth Street were to become Ben's home during the New Deal years. Tom had his daytime office at the RFC, but he also had an office with Ben, and he and Peggy Dowd repaired there at the end of the day. So too did the bright young men whom Frankfurter sent to them. The office became a mecca for officials in the government who needed sympathetic advice.

Ben, in particular, was sought out by New Dealers who needed solutions. Jerome Frank, bedeviled with problems at the Triple A, ran afoul of Corcoran. "I learned that Tom Corcoran was spreading news around that I was a radical, trying to nationalize everything, and so on. I believe that this was because at that time at any rate Tommy was an ardent Brandeisian and was therefore opposed to anybody who had that kind of philosophy . . . I got hold of Ben Cohen, after trying to get Corcoran and not being able to. I said, 'Ben, you tell that man Corcoran of yours that I want to have a good talk with him.'" He did.[26]

Ben explained the milder reactions of people to him than to Tom, "since I usually am a little less assertive, people think I perhaps am more considerate, if not more conservative, which may not always be the case." Landis, whose run-ins with Ben I have mentioned in this book, nonetheless found him "an extremely sweet person." He never saw Ben lose his temper or speak harshly of anyone, "very firm in his convictions. He's not going to change his convictions in order to try and generate a little friendship."

Tom saw Ben a little differently, as he colorfully expressed it to an interlocutor in the first draft of his unpublished autobiography. He was talking about Peggy Dowd at the Carlton suite where Ben and Jim had worked on the securities legislation in 1933.

Ben and Jim, both brilliant men were both equally highstrung. They would work each other into emotional frenzies over such esoteric differences of legal opinion that I could grasp the issues just well enough to arbitrate between them. But Peggy's beauty and charm disarmed more than one seemingly impossible contretemps between my colleagues.[27]

Roosevelt liked him, Tom thought, because he "was a front [-line] fighter . . . Now, Ben, I very carefully protected him. I want to say this too. I very early learned to protect myself by having Ben as my partner . . . Ben hated conflict. Ben can't handle conflict . . . Ben blows up and gets excited and Ben has a private pipeline to God too, just between you and me." When Tom spoke of someone having "a pipeline to God," he was referring to convictions that were unbudgeable. Tom had few such convictions and while he was considered a leader of the New Dealers, that was a tribute to his ability to get things done rather than to the firmness of his beliefs.

As Landis saw the two of them, "They both appreciated each other and they both worked together, complemented each other in their work. Ben, for example, wouldn't be any good at selling, but Corcoran was good at that. Ben is an innovator and a creator, rather than Corcoran, but Corcoran peddled his goods very ably."[28]

By the autumn of 1934 Landis had begun to drift away from Frankfurter. As a member of the Securities and Exchange Commission he was a godsend to Joseph Kennedy, its first chairman. Kennedy learned from him and that was a satisfaction. With Frankfurter the teacher-pupil relationship worked in reverse and Landis had outgrown the stage of discipleship. Moreover, Kennedy tapped channels of wealth and party power that appealed to Landis and were a mystery to Frankfurter.

Although Tom and Ben stayed in touch with Jim, they had long ceased to be the "Three Musketeers." An article in *Fortune* "The Legend of Landis," pleased him with its acknowledgment of his legal brilliance but annoyed him with its emphasis on Frankfurter's role in his career.[29] Then the press opened up on Landis. Drew Pearson in *Merry-Go-Round* dredged up the story of Ben's exclusion from SEC because of anti-Semitism, adding to the story (of which Landis suspected Pecora as the source) the explosive charge that Ben's exclusion had been used by Landis to establish his own authority over the commission. "Ben must understand," Pearson had Landis saying, "that he will be an employee of the commission and will take orders from me." The "great liberal" and "one-time enemy of Wall Street" now was complaining that the Street was not getting "a fair break," said Pearson.

Felix was quickly apprised of these developments by Ben.

I suppose you saw the article in yesterday's Merry-Go-Round about Jim. I cannot find out the exact occasion or the source of the article, although I hear that three or four men, principally newspapermen are clubbed together to get him. Poor fellow! He was extremely angry at first and suggested Ferd and threatened to make a scene in the Commission. I gather that he spoke to Joe and Joe handled him extremely well, sternly but sympathetically, like a father. Yesterday Tom and I had lunch with him and he was pretty badly broken up. Today he said he felt better but was extremely contrite and he went so far as to say it probably was a good thing that it happened as it had, brought him to his senses. I don't know just what the best way of handling the matter is but I do think it opens the possibility of the Commission's really getting down and working fairly harmoniously together. If peace can be established with Joe's drive, Johnny's savoir faire, Ferd's honesty and good will, and Jim's understanding, not necessarily of the technical detail, but of our general approach both in the Securities Act and the Stock Exchange Act it should really be possible to get something done. Have you any suggestions?

Felix, sensitive as always, seems to have been aware of Landis's resentment over press references to him as one of Felix's "Happy Hot Dogs." Nevertheless he wrote him cordially,

I assume that you are not allowing brickbats to get under your skin, any more than you will have allowed bouquets, whether of natural or artificial flowers, to go to your head. You and I have often reflected on the extent to which concern over one's place in the press is the most frequent road to ruin of public men, the enemy alike of private serenity and wise public action.

Other matters preoccupied Frankfurter that autumn. He had many heroes but Brandeis was the peer among them. Isaiah had his faults, but still among the public eminences that thronged Washington, he towered. Suddenly out of the blue, General Johnson, who was in the process of being eased out of the NRA, unintentionally delivered a blow that startled and angered all the friends of the justice. Johnson did not go gently into retirement and Roosevelt to make things easier for him was cushioning his withdrawal by making him sponsor of a reorganization plan. "During the whole intense experience," Johnson said in one of his speeches on NRA reorganization, "I have been in constant touch with the old Counsellor, Judge Louis Dembitz Brandeis."

Not surprisingly, the anti-New Deal press seized upon this statement to suggest a "breach of faith and duty" and called upon the justice to excuse himself from passing on laws and procedures upon whose constitutionality he would be called upon to judge.

"It must have been more than 'liquor,' " Brandeis wrote Frankfurter. "What he said of me was not only an indiscretion but a lie . . . If F.D. does not shut up the Gen'l completely—or at least remove him—he, too, will feel the embarrassment."[30]

"Hugh Johnson's outburst about his alleged relations with Brandeis," Frankfurter wrote Roosevelt, who was away from Washington, "have created a very serious situation about which I think we had better have talk." Brandeis sent Frankfurter a detailed account of his contacts with the general. He had first come to see Brandeis in May 1933 when he came in unannounced tagging along with someone whom Brandeis was scheduled to see. Johnson began to discuss the proposed NRA legislation "and I told him frankly that the proposed measure was a bad one and my reasons, including the impossibility of enforcement, the dangers to the small industries, the inefficiency of the big unit, be it governmental or private." Later Johnson had telephoned him at Chatham to express his pleasure in the conclusion of the clothing industry code and the role of the International Ladies Garment Workers and Morris Hillquit in it. There were two other brief encounters in the fall of 1933.

Finally, he came in in early May '34, a crushed man. I told him again that the task was impossible, etc. and that he should liquidate as soon as possible. I was much touched by the brief talk. I felt that he had showed manliness in coming to me, who had predicted failure . . .

A contrite Johnson, and with the help of Frankfurter, drafted a statement of regret and clarification. "Of course I never discussed any question of law or any other controversial matters which could possibly come before Justice Brandeis in his official capacity. He would not permit it and I never would embarrass him by any such action . . ."

The justice meanwhile had told Paul Freund, a former law clerk and Frankfurter student, "to say to you [Frankfurter] that I am strongly of the opinion that neither F.D. nor the General should say a word . . . Anything the General would say now would be sure to do harm. On the other hand if the General's resignation which you say will be tendered soon and accepted—were tendered and accepted now, it will help some. The rest must be left to time . . ."

The general's statement was not released. He did resign a few days later. There was temporary embarrassment for the justice. The New York *Herald Tribune,* the chief organ of Eastern Republicanism, joined the Chicago

Tribune in calling on him to abstain from any Supreme Court case involving the NRA. Such editorials and a possible attempt to disqualify him, he wrote, were "not agreeable to contemplate, but the incident must be regarded as a casualty—like that of being run into by a drunken autoist—or shot by a lunatic."

Brandeis did explain the facts of his relationship with Johnson to Chief Justice Hughes and Associate Justice Willis Van Devanter, one of the more conservative justices. No question of judicial ethics was raised. Brandeis did not abate his extrajudicial activities—his teas and talks with people who sought his counsel. Why should he? He did more actively what every justice did to keep himself informed of vital issues and to discuss social and economic questions with friends. The situation was filled with ironies. He was an apostle of the competitive system and the free market economy and he was opposed to the NRA and in lesser measure the Triple A. He conformed to no stereotypes. The anti-New Deal press went after him on the issue of judicial ethics, hoping to weaken one of the pillars of the New Deal. Meanwhile in the Court he was a vigorous opponent of the aggrandizement of power whether by president or corporate owner.

Paul Freund, in the Solicitor General's office after clerking for the justice, reported to Frankfurter that in the Department of Justice's arguments in the oil cases,

L.D.B. was chiefly concerned, on the constitutional side, with delegation under 9(c), which permits the President to declare acts a crime without making findings. Several of the others—Van D. most vigorously—were evidently with him on this. The hearing was really concerned with the fundamentals of representative and responsible government, not with the ills of the oil industry.[31]

Brandeis was an authentic democrat, as much concerned with what a later generation called "the imperial presidency," as he was with the abuses of corporate power. When Freund, fresh from Harvard Law School, began to clerk for Brandeis in November 1932, he wrote Frankfurter:

I wonder how many people on coming away from meeting him, have had the feeling that they did "see Shelley plain," and that he did "stop and speak" to them. For me the experience comes not once but daily, and yet it always brings me exhilaration.

Even in Depression Washington the personal lifestyle of the Brandeises was a rarity. They lived simply, refused to permit anyone to entertain them, an austerity that dovetailed with the justice's concern not to compromise his judicial objectivity.

By the beginning of September, Roosevelt was persuaded that the bibulous Johnson had to go, "but he is so tenderhearted," lamented Ickes, "that he has not been able to say the final word."[32] So Ickes wrote, before the Johnson indiscretion about Brandeis. The latter clinched matters for Roosevelt. The midterm elections were less than six weeks away, not a moment in which to remove cabinet-level officers, but delay was no longer possible. Ickes, Hopkins, Richberg, and (in Perkins's absence) Wyzanski were summoned to the White House. Roosevelt told them Brandeis had complained to him. The President turned to Johnson's sponsor Bernard Baruch and used him, in Wyzanski's words, "to pry from Johnson his resignation." "I am glad the resignation was so promptly accepted," wrote Brandeis to Frankfurter.[33]

The attack on Brandeis cut athwart Frankfurter's efforts to place Tom at the vital center of the Roosevelt administration. He had made a major effort at the end of July to have Moley use Tom as his contact with the White House:

Tom is here—through tomorrow & we went over many matters for him & his boys. He is amazingly wise & of a devotion most rare.
2. The Solicitor General has asked him to come to him as an assistant, full-time exclusively, to write briefs & argue before the U.S. Supreme Court. My own judgment is for [an]other role for Tom. I've tried to make Moley see [the] importance of his continued & systematic participation in Aion [Administration] as F.D.'s adviser rendered possible by having Tom made with F.D.'s approval, as Moley's resident Washington representative, continuing nominally at R.F.C. that would enable him to use his boys & immunize him against certain obvious dangers.
What say you to Solicitor General's offer & Tom's best usefulness?

Tom turned down the Solicitor General's offer. An effort to make him director of the Budget upon the resignation of Lewis Douglas was stopped by Henry Morgenthau, the Secretary of the Treasury. As the Secretary reported in his diary, when the President asked him what he thought of the proposal, he had instantly replied, "absolutely out of the question that Cochrane [sic] was an intellectual crook . . . I would not trust Cochrane [sic] as far as I could see him."[34] Inelegant, but Roosevelt agreed to Morgenthau's recommendation of Daniel Bell for the position.

Excluded though Tom was from Treasury as director of the Budget, he realized the White House intended to use him and Ben in its legislative battles in the coming session. Although Ben on October 18 [1934] wrote Jane, "Nothing new here, much activity and little progress," that was before the midterm elections. They brought in 9 new Democratic senators and in the House the number of Democrats rose from 313 to 322, a ratification of Roosevelt's leadership that led William Allen White to declare Roosevelt had "been all but crowned by the people."

The smashing victory immediately posed the question to Roosevelt of what he would use the victory for. A work program for the unemployed? Social insurance? Further curbs on the abuses of the corporate managers? Harry Hopkins was at work on the first. Frances Perkins on the second, where incidentally, she had been advised by Justice Stone to whom she had confided some of the constitutional hazards that her social insurance draughtsmen were confronting, "The taxing power of the Federal Government, my dear, the taxing power is sufficient for everything you want and need."

And at 1810 H Street where Ben was ensconced in Interior offices as legal counsel of the National Power Policy Committee, his first assignment was to draft a report on the Public Utility Holding Company (PUHCA) and the principles that should guide legislation intended to simplify and rationalize the holding company's size, management, and initiative. At the same time he and Tom received additional assignments relating to corporate control from FDR via Felix Frankfurter.[35]

Young Telford Taylor, his work for Jim, Tom, and Ben on the SEC concluded, left the Department of Interior, where he considered the work was too dull, to work for Frank Shea who was number two to Jerry Frank in the Triple A's legal division. Taylor lived with Shea and others in a "bachelor ménage" on Eighteenth Street near Dupont Circle. Around the corner Paul Freund lived in another such ménage. All did stints, when they finished their regular work, for Corcoran and Cohen. Taylor was at work on a bill to eliminate "tramp" corporations. These corporations did their business in New York but were chartered in states like Delaware that had lax incorporation laws.

"Herewith a preliminary draft of the tax on corporate self-dealings," Freund wrote Frankfurter, "together with a somewhat revised draft of the tramp corporations tax. Tel Taylor and I plan to discuss both with Ben tomorrow. Neither one is in any sense a finished job, as we need hardly point out."[36]

The immediate upshot of this work was embodied in a Roosevelt memorandum.

January 16, 1935

MEMORANDUM FOR THE SECRETARY OF THE TREASURY

Sometime ago I asked Mr. Frankfurter to study the three subjects to which these proposed bills relate and to let me have a tentative draft of legislation. The enclosed represent much effort and careful study.

I am inclinde *[sic]* to think that you should give serious consideration to their introduction. Will you have them checked and speak to me about them?

F. D. R.[37]

Thus began 1935 and the approach of Corcoran and Cohen, and with them their mentor, Frankfurter, to the very center of New Deal power.

XV

The "Death Sentence"

After Moley's departure from the Administration, journalists and politicians considered Rex Tugwell Roosevelt's number one privy councillor. Some New Dealers such as Gardner "Pat" Jackson, an associate at Agriculture, thought him standoffish, "self-contained, aloof, always immaculately groomed . . . calculating in almost every move and word, seeming to demand and need worship . . ."[1]

Roosevelt perceived him differently. He wanted him at his side. That had been the case at Hyde Park over the Labor Day weekend. Tugwell was again a major participant in the preliminary conferences at Warm Springs at Thanksgiving where Roosevelt fashioned his "must" list for the Seventy-fourth Congress. The attraction between the two was reciprocal. Tugwell was as aware as Frankfurter of the opportunities that had been missed a year earlier for major reforms—even when the two professors did not wholly agree on what those reforms should be. But both were "loyalists," and as Tugwell swam, dined, and joshed with a relaxed Roosevelt in the Warm Springs surroundings, his diary notes reflected the fascination of many who served the President, even those who felt he was not going far enough:

I can't believe that he completely opens his mind to many others as he has to me these past days. It is a finely organized mind, too. I have always been aware of his great purposes and his practical ingenuity. I have never been able to see so clearly as I do now a kind of dogged determination to work out dreams in practice. He is convinced that he has to transform the country physically and morally in his time and do it without a great change in government structure or in domestic processes. Maybe he can. I'm willing to do my bit.

That was Roosevelt's impact on even the proudest and most discriminating of his people. Tugwell was tempted to return to the independent life of the university and scholarship, but he had learned a truth that World War I had taught Keynes. The latter had spent some time during his visit to the United States in May 1934 with Calvin Hoover, a Duke University economist and friend of Tugwell. "There is nothing to this economic advising business," Keynes told Calvin Hoover when the latter explained the Brains Trust concept to him, "a politician can never listen to you for more than an hour and that most rarely. It is impossible to teach economics in occasional ten-minute earfuls. If you want to have any real effect on events you must take an operating job."[2]

Tugwell had come to a similar conclusion. *Ideas in Action* was what Max Lerner aptly called his book about the New Dealers. But the activist in politics, when committed to ideas and values, is apt to have only a brief period of authority. Men like Tugwell, the privy councillors, attractive though they might be, were without power bases and therefore expendable. Tugwell was discovering that even Wallace, who had made him Under Secretary of Agriculture, allowed him to be excluded from vital departmental discussions by the spokesmen for the farm interests. "I just had a sob letter all written to you and Grace Falke [his secretary whom he later married] said I couldn't send it," he wrote in longhand to Jerry Frank, at the time his closest governmental associate. "All I was looking for was sympathy and since I couldn't get it here [the Department of Agriculture] I felt pretty sure you would come across. All true. I'm not too happy but when have I been . . . ?"[3] Despite his nearness to Roosevelt and his involvement in the President's plans for the next Congress, Tugwell, aware of the pressures that had gathered against him, sensed that his days at the top of the greasy pole might be numbered.

Among the subjects canvased at Warm Springs was holding companies legislation. Roosevelt was intent on it. Together with the Banking Act, the Securities Act of 1933, and the SEC of 1934, Wall Street's power would be, if not broken, seriously diminished.

While not the magic key to recovery, the securities and banking legislation did for the investment world and corporate financing what they were unable to do for themselves—eliminate fraudulent dealing and entrenched abuses and set up a governmental watchdog against their recurrence. When lawyers and financiers once complained of the alleged radicalism of

Frankfurter, a major consultant to Roosevelt on these matters, his colleague Thomas Reed Powell of the law school exclaimed in his witty way, "Hell! that damn fool is wearing out his heart trying to make capitalism live up to its pretensions."[4]

Roosevelt by 1932 saw the holding company and its control of three fourths of the entire operating utility industry as prime examples of "overconcentrated economic power" and "absentee management." For a brief moment he coupled its elimination with the development of several regional power authorities, but, evidently on the principle that one fight at a time was enough, fell silent about new dams except for the Boulder which was scheduled for completion in 1935 and required no new legislative action.

Corcoran believed Roosevelt, in addition to trying to save the capitalist system from the capitalists, had another motive, and that was to dry up traditional sources of Republican financing, and in the South, where the holding company was a mainstay of the mossback Democratic legislators, end the latter's stranglehold on Congress.[5]

The members of the National Power Policy Committee were summoned to Warm Springs to confer with the President. David Lilienthal of the TVA was there, as were Basil Manly and Frank McNinch of the Federal Power Commission (FPC), and Morris Llewellyn Cooke, liberal, patrician, long-time student of utilities and advocate of rural electrification. Healy and Cohen were not and their omission was unexplained. They sat around and talked until midnight. Roosevelt was interested in cheap power and rural electrification. His visit to the TVA en route to Warm Springs had stimulated him. The five-hour discussion produced two decisions. "Lilienthal was told to move out with a new, enlarged directorate for the Electric Home and Farm Authority [EHFA]," recorded Tugwell.[6] This involved Tom Corcoran who also was not there, but second only to Lilienthal, EHFA was his baby. It had been funded by the RFC. Corcoran sat on its board of directors. He had done the paperwork on the corporation which extended credit to farmers at very low interest, enabling them to purchase electrical home equipment—electric lighting, toasters, washers, dryers—one of the New Deal measures that transformed rural America.

The second decision related to holding companies. "As for regulation of holding companies as against their elimination, he [FDR] came out flatly for their elimination and directed that legislation be prepared for taxing them out of existence," Tugwell noted. New Dealers were divided between those who favored governmental regulation in the public interest versus other methods of control such as taxation. Brandeis had little faith in regulation, believing that the interests regulated invariably infiltrated and took over the regulatory commissions.

The discussion ranged over "the regulation versus government competition methods," commented Tugwell. "It was agreed that both ought to be done."[7] The taxation route had many advocates among the New Dealers. "I think it's the most powerful way of getting at these things," Frankfurter told Morgenthau. "I don't think there's any doubt but that [a tax on intercorporate dividends] is the most effective way of dealing with the [holding company] problem."[8] He counseled Roosevelt along these lines. "They cannot be eliminated over night, and therefore the policy would seem to be temporary stiff regulation and taxation, with the defined objective of elimination." He advised William O. Douglas, a professor at the Yale Law School, that taxation was the way to frustrate the ability of the financial world to undermine regulation, "Tax 'em, my boy, tax 'em, and otherwise reduce the opportunities for bludgeoning that interrelation and concentration of money interests make possible." Berle's letter to Cohen also suggested taxation: "A simple method of providing for elimination would be a progressive increase in taxation upwards in case you do not feel like brutally cutting off the existence of the holding company."[9]

Tugwell at Warm Springs wanted to move faster on setting up regional power authorities:

I wish we were going ahead with other Authorities faster than we are. The President is already preparing for it and has a regional set-up for the whole country in mind; how fast he will move into it, I am not clear, nor, I think, is he . . . This is not the sort of thing which worries FDR. He has an extraordinary ability to leave things in flux and to prevent their taking concrete and final shape before the time is ripe.[10]

FDR's hint at Tupelo that the TVA was only the forerunner of other regional power authorities already had alerted Wall Street and helped unite holding company opponents of the President's rumored move to eliminate them. Frank McNinch, the chairman of the Federal Power Commission, a Hoover appointee, was one of those upset by Roosevelt's insistence on elimination.

Lilienthal described him as getting "gloomier and gloomier" for he preferred regulation. "But there wasn't any question about what the President wanted," Lilienthal paraphrased the President's view.[11] An argument could be made for investment companies that held the securities of utilities in their portfolios, and an argument for management services by a holding company on a cost basis, but "a holding company which exists for the control of operating companies was against the public interest," recorded Lilienthal, "and since it couldn't be regulated, should be abolished."

The President directed Treasury to work on tax methods by which to eliminate the holding company. And in his usual way he had other agencies at work on drafts of a holding company bill. The chief drafters, however, were not there. Since September, Ben Cohen, under the direction of Robert Healy who represented the SEC on the NPCC, had been at work on such a draft.

Healy was a crusty Vermont judge, a Republican, who had been appointed general counsel of the Federal Trade Commission by Calvin Coolidge. He had directed the massive FTC study of the holding company. Roosevelt had made him one of the five SEC commissioners, in which capacity he had feuded with fellow commissioner Landis on the SEC's relationship with Wall Street. In a reversal of roles Healy pressed for a tough attitude toward the banking and investment community, and Landis, the former law clerk of Brandeis and protégé of Frankfurter, sought to build bridges with that community, by the encouragement of a high degree of self-regulation.

When Healy was named by Ickes to head a subcommittee of the NPPC to deal with public utility holding companies, he asked for Ben Cohen, "I don't know whether we could get him. I have great respect for the ability of Ben Cohen drafting bills that will stand the test." Ickes undertook to ask Ben. ". . . I think he will be more intrigued by this than by anything," commented an old hand at fighting the "power trust," Morris Cooke, also a member of the NPPC. He gave Ben a list of utility executives he should consult. October and November had been spent by Cohen canvasing the industry's leaders on meaningful federal regulation. But the industry did not want the federal government butting in. It took shelter behind state regulation. One executive whom Healy and Cohen found more hospitable to the notion of federal regulation was Wendell Willkie, the energetic and articulate head of Commonwealth and Southern.

By the end of November, when Roosevelt was having his meetings at Warm Springs, Ben had submitted a draft to Healy. It favored strict regulation, not elimination of the holding company, and called for registration with the SEC, the filing of comprehensive financial statements, uniform accounting practices, the prohibition of upstream loans, service contracts between a holding company and its subsidiaries on a mutual or cost basis. Above all, the draft provided for structural simplification, that is, the divestment of subsidiaries that had no economic relationship to other companies in the system. "Federal regulation," Cohen emphasized, showing again his subtlety as a draftsman, "need not absorb state regulation. Properly conceived, it is rather a necessary step in making state regulation effective."

Despite Cohen's absence from Warm Springs, and with Healy's blessing, he spent December, together with Corcoran and some help from Landis, on repeated revisions of the draft. As reports spread in the business community of the legislation that was being prepared, the Edison Electric Institute (EEI), the voice of the utility industry, prepared to challenge in Congress and the courts Roosevelt's strategy of starting "little TVAs" all around the country, as well as his efforts to curb the holding company. It produced a ferocious battle in Congress and a prolonged struggle in the courts.

Although the President, keeping his options open, had set the FTC, the FPC, the Treasury, and the Attorney General's Office to work on drafts and seemed to have forgotten about the NPPC's involvement, it was Ben's draft that became the central one. By the end of December it approached completion. The public had a stake in geographic and economically integrated operating systems, Cohen maintained. The continued existence of holding companies that furthered such integration was implicit in Cohen's approach. His draft did not outlaw the holding company but regulated it, Cohen explained to Ickes, in order "to provide a mechanism through which, over a period of time, existing holding company structures may be simplified, and their field limited to spheres where their economic advantages may be demonstrable." He had no wish to fragment large economic units because they were large, his memorandum to Ickes went on, but "in too many instances the holding company has not brought the American public the advantages claimed for it, but has been an instrument through which undue economic power has been concentrated in the hands of a few powerful groups."[12] As comments came in from members of the NPPC, Cohen and Corcoran, old hands at writing airtight legislation directed at the securities market, reworked the Cohen draft.

Roosevelt delivered his State of the Union Message to the new Congress on January 4. Unemployment was still the nation's number one problem and he proposed to shift the government's assistance from relief to "emergency public employment." He also promised to send up recommendations on social security, slum clearance and housing, rural electrification, reforestation, soil erosion and reclamation. The program would do more to transform America than the Hundred Days. Holding companies were referred to briefly. He intended to end their "evils," he said simply.[13]

Ben's draft was almost complete. Congress, as well as the President, had to be considered, Ben cautioned the members of the NPPC. "I think it is always helpful if Congress feels that the particular bill is their bill and not the bill of the executive." Ickes was urged to take the bill to the President and let him decide the procedure.

On January 21 there was a final conference at the White House on the various drafts. This time Cohen and Corcoran were present. "What happened was that the Skipper ordered an overnight redraft of the holding company bill—and you know what that means," Tom wrote Pecora to explain their absence on the twenty-first from his swearing in as a New York Supreme Court justice.[14]

Morgenthau, attended by Herman Oliphant and Robert Jackson, who then worked for the Treasury, was there, as well as Homer Cummings, Donald Richberg, who had succeeded Hugh Johnson at the NIRA, Ickes, and McNinch and Manly for the FPC. Roosevelt leaned to the Treasury bill drafted by Oliphant and Jackson. That proposed to tax the holding companies out of existence. Strict federal regulation was politically more feasible, Cohen and Corcoran argued, and Ickes supported them. They persuaded the President who swung to the Cohen draft but directed the insertion of a "death sentence" provision that eliminated all holding companies within five years. Also he wanted the bill to include a bill of particulars that listed the abuses of the holding companies.

"F.D. is really hot on holding cos. and for drastic action," Frankfurter advised Brandeis.[15]

A meeting with Wendell Willkie did not soften FDR's views. Harvey Couch, a Southern Democrat who had been a member of the RFC under Hoover, was now head of the Alabama Power and Light Company. Through Louis Howe, he arranged a meeting between Roosevelt and several utility magnates including Willkie. Couch, said Lilienthal, a participant who recorded the episode in his diaries, was "suave and soothing,"[16] but he could see that Willkie was getting "hotter and hotter" as the President spoke. Willkie's wrath finally overflowed and he took his glasses out of a breast pocket and without a "Mr. President" began to "bark" at him —the word was Lilienthal's. He was pleased to have the President experience at firsthand what it was to cope with this "reasonable fellow." As Willkie pointed his glasses at the President, the latter's chin jutted out and his replies became less conciliatory. Finally Willkie asked, "Do I understand then that any further efforts to avoid the breakup of utility holding companies are futile?" FDR gave him one look and replied, "It is futile."[17]

That ended the Couch mediation and set the stage for the sharpest engagement of the Seventy-fifth Congress between the Roosevelt administration and Wall Street. "Who was that fellow," Roosevelt asked Lilienthal some weeks later, ". . . who leaned over and shook his glasses at me?"* Later, Moley was to maintain that the "death sentence" provision was put into the bill for trading purposes. This was, indeed, a favorite Corcoran-Cohen strategem, but they did not have the "death sentence" in their own draft of the holding company bill, nor did Cohen believe Roosevelt had any such thought in mind. Inclusion of the "death sentence" was not accomplished easily by Cohen. Judge Healy "is not quite prepared to recommend the abolition of the holding company," he explained to Ickes. But the President's authority was final and the bill in the end read as he desired.

It was introduced February 6 by Wheeler in the Senate [S.1725] and Rayburn in the House [H.R.5423]. But unlike the campaign for the Securities Act in 1933 and the Securities and Exchange Act in 1934, Rayburn's House Committee lagged behind the Senate. Corcoran thought Rayburn was "afraid of the bill," and though he began hearings on it a week after its introduction, he finished taking testimony only in mid-April and did not file a report to the House until June 22.

Wheeler thought the President wanted Rayburn to take the lead, but Rayburn "couldn't seem to get started," perhaps, thought Wheeler, because he was "a little tepid about the so-called 'death sentence.' "

There may have been more to Roosevelt's desire to have Rayburn take the lead than his success with previous pieces of administration legislation. He did not trust Wheeler. The Montanan was a reckless, two-fisted fighter. Nicknamed "Burton the Bronc," he had run for Vice President in 1924 on the La Follette ticket, was a progressive, and one of the Senate's "greats." He had been an early supporter of Roosevelt for the nomination and at the Chicago Convention where he had helped not only to corral the West, but to encourage the final shift of ballots that gave Roosevelt the two thirds that he needed for nomination. He was also intensely ambitious. When Senator Thomas J. Walsh, the senior senator from Montana, investigator of the Teapot Dome scandal, died before he could assume the office of Attorney General to which Roosevelt had named him, Wheeler resented Roosevelt's failure to offer him the post. His witty wife's acid remarks about Roosevelt got back to the White House and the President referred to her as "Lady Macbeth."

* Roosevelt's memory about not having met Willkie before was in error, perhaps intentionally. On December 13 he had met Willkie, according to Steve Neal in *Dark Horse*. "I am glad to meet you, Mr. Willkie. I am one of your customers," the President said. "We give good service, don't we?" Willkie replied genially and to his wife telegraphed, CHARM GREATLY EXAGGERATED. I DID NOT TELL HIM WHAT YOU THINK OF HIM.

A dinner party on February 1 at Tugwell's house would have figured in Roosevelt's uneasiness about pushing Wheeler. Present were the United States Ambassador to Berlin, William F. Dodd, Jerome Frank, and Paul Appleby of the Department of Agriculture, the journalist John Franklin Carter, and Tugwell. A startled Dodd's *Diary* described the evening.

A certain well-known senator was one of the guests. From the very beginning, this senator attacked Roosevelt. He was angry with Roosevelt because he had not backed [Sen. Bronson] Cutting, a former supporter of Roosevelt. He was also disgruntled because Roosevelt had not agreed with the Progressive group on huge appropriations which would have led to national bankruptcy. He claimed that he and Huey Long, the pirate of Louisiana, had caused Roosevelt's nomination in 1932. The attitudes of this man were amazing. He talks like a National Socialist . . . He advocated German domination of all Europe, our domination of the Americas, and Japanese domination of the Far East . . . Most of the people at the dinner agreed with this big business idea of three great world powers dominating smaller peoples like the Poles and the Dutch . . .

I left with a sense of surprise, wondering whether they really meant what they advocated. But the Senator must have been sincere when he said he had persuaded Long to vote against the World Court idea about which Long knew nothing . . .[18]

There was a confirmatory account of the dinner in Tugwell's papers, a memorandum by John Franklin Carter. Under the pseudonym of "Unofficial Observer," he had written the widely read *The New Dealers:*

Wheeler—generally supported by the others present—contended that it was precisely for this reason [that our function on the World Court would be to preserve the European *status quo*] that the World Court had been rejected, that it was *not* our function to prevent the unification of Europe under Germany or any other power and that the *status quo* was responsible for the very situation, including Hitlerism, which now threatened war.[19]

After Dodd left, Tugwell observed that "Dodd was still suffering from a bad attack of Woodrow Wilson. The ominous thing, however, was that the President seems to be in general agreement with Dodd's thesis and regards himself as compelled to build a billion dollars worth of warships which will be obsolete in ten years."

Wheeler's isolationism and his hand in the defeat, a few days earlier, of the Administration's World Court adherence resolution in themselves would have made Roosevelt wary of Wheeler's intentions. The conversation about politics after Dodd left even more so. "Wheeler defended Huey Long as the best means of getting rid of the reactionary Southern Senators," the Carter memorandum continued,

Wheeler said that Roosevelt was definitely slipping throughout the country. The 1932 vote was a vote against Hoover; the 1934 was a "For God's sake do something—vote," and now Roosevelt was playing with the conservatives because he felt that he couldn't rely on the liberals. Roosevelt had missed his chance in 1933 and could not recapture it. Wheeler said that a third party in 1936 was a definite probability, with Long, La Follette, Olsen, Father Coughlin and Upton Sinclair taking the lead, and that this party would give Roosevelt a very close run for his money. (This bears out my opinion.)

"The other interesting thing about last night's conversation," commented Tugwell in his *Diary,*

was the disillusionment of a progressive like Wheeler. He has lost all faith in FDR. He complains of wobbling, of his catering to business, of unfriendly acts toward his logical supporters like Cutting and of general administration failure to strike out boldly for economic reforms. He spoke confidently of a third party in 1936, organizing all these left-wing people: Long, Coughlin, Sinclair, Olsen, etc. I'd believe it more likely if they had much in common in their programs and weren't such demagogic individualists.

Tugwell did not record what he told the President about the evening, but Dodd who dined at the White House a few days later, did tell him without naming the senator. Roosevelt immediately guessed correctly.

The President went on: Long plans to be a candidate of the Hitler type for the presidency in 1936. He thinks he will have a hundred votes in the Democratic convention. Then he will set up as an independent with Southern and mid-western Progressives, Senator X—and others. Then he hopes to defeat the Democratic party and put in a reactionary Republican. That would bring the country to such a state by 1940 that Long thinks he would be made a dictator. There are in fact some Southerners looking that way, and some Progressives are drifting that way. But Cutting of New Mexico wants the presidency too . . . an ominous situation.[20]

Roosevelt perceived that progressivism was the antidote both to right and left. His budget of "must" legislation for the Seventy-fourth Congress showed his strategy of disarming potential opponents by making the system work for all. But he also had a keen tactical sense of how to secure the presidential power against claimants who shared his ideals. So that his wish to have Rayburn rather than Wheeler take the lead was not without guile.

The utility lobby's campaign was the most massive encountered by the Administration. From shareholder to meterman, utility companies all over the land, and particularly in the South, mobilized to defeat the bill. Its "death sentence" clause, they argued, would chiefly victimize the "widows and orphans" among the shareholders. "When you hop on the power trusts, you are standing on the very arches of the Republican party," Will

Rogers had said in 1928. It remained true. "I have watched the use of investors' money," Roosevelt said in a message to Congress, that had been drafted by Cohen to accompany the NPPC's report, "to make the investor believe that the efforts of Government to protect him are designed to defraud him. I have seen much of the propaganda prepared against such legislation—even down to mimeographed sheets of instructions for propaganda to exploit the most far-fetched and fallacious fears."[21] He was "unimpressed." The bill "will not destroy a penny of actual value of those operating properties which holding companies now control and which holding company securities represent in so far as they have any value."

The Administration did not have to make a case against the holding companies. They had made it against themselves, most dramatically in the flight in 1932 to Greece of the head of the largest holding company of all, Samuel Insull, leaving behind him thousands of investors with worthless stock certificates. His pyramided empire was one of thirteen holding company systems that controlled three fourths of the entire utility industry. Wheeler's hearing would show in 1935 that another colossus, the Associated Gas and Electric Company, by pyramiding holding companies ten corporations deep, "had given holders of $300,000 of securities at the top, control over nearly one billion dollars in assets." "I hope Burt will not forget to deal with Associated Gas . . . on the floor," Frankfurter advised Cohen, "and that he will have that big chart about the company as suggested by FDR.

"I am against private socialism of concentrated private power," said Roosevelt transmitting the NPPC report, "as thoroughly as I am against governmental socialism. The one is as equally dangerous as the other; and destruction of private socialism is utterly essential to avoid governmental socialism."[22]

The theme of "private socialism" had been sounded two and a half months earlier by Moley in a lead editorial in *Today* on the holding company.[23] The editorial delighted Cohen. He wired Celeste Jedel, Moley's brilliant black-haired assistant (whom, if her relatives are correct, Ben courted) to send him at least twenty-five tear sheets which he sent around to key members of Congress and the press.

"Bigness" itself was an issue posed by the holding company, but it did not figure much in the minds of Cohen and Corcoran—and of Frankfurter. Brandeis in December had published *The Curse of Bigness* which expressed an intransigent skepticism of experimentation on a national rather than state scale and argued the difficulty of getting men and women into the public service competent to manage large governmental enterprises.

His letters to Frankfurter delightedly reported the book's weekly sales. Even Owen D. Young, the industrialist, no opponent of bigness, confessed to the Senate Banking and Currency Committee at the hearings on the collapse of the Insull utility empire, "Mr. Insull himself was ultimately unable to understand the structure."

Was the bigness of business in itself undesirable? Roosevelt was asked at a news conference by a reporter who was aware of the divisions among the New Dealers. "I should say yes," replied Roosevelt. Top corporation executives could not be sufficiently acquainted with the detailed operations of their own businesses. The interlocking companies represented by the holding company device permitted the control of the nation's industrial machine to gravitate into a few hands. "We are a great deal better off if we can disseminate both the control and the actual industrial setup as a whole."

Yet Roosevelt's message to Congress that accompanied the NPPC report carefully discriminated between holding companies "used simply as a means of financial control" and holding companies "which can prove to the SEC that their existence is necessary for the achievement of the public ends which the private utility companies are supposed to serve." The challenge was not simply to "bigness" but to "bigness" that undermined the public interest and was unmanageable.

Both Rayburn's hearings and Wheeler's documented the three most common abuses of the holding company: (1) the writing up of values—that is, loading the rate base to make higher electricity rates possible; (2) upstream loans in which the operating companies financed their holding companies instead of the other way around; and (3) the "milking" of the operating companies through the "management" and other fees charged by the parent holding companies.[24] Cohen and Corcoran's apprehensions about Rayburn's difficulties were slow to develop. Before 1933 he had been considered among the most conservative members of the House, but he had faced down Wall Street in the fight for the Securities Act in 1933 and the SEC in 1934. He started out bravely in the House hearings, taking on the most redoubtable spokesman for the utilities, Wendell L. Willkie, the president of Commonwealth and Southern. Willkie was articulate, intelligent, and had "the well-organized bulkiness of a healthy bear." A tough fighter, he was also sufficiently hospitable to reform of the holding companies to come to be characterized by his colleagues as "the Jesus Christ of the industry." In his lead-off appearance before the House Committee he skilfully made the case for a compromise so that "the honest holding companies should not be punished for the sins of their less scrupulous brethren." He wanted a "reasonable" public utility law, he asserted; his real target was the "death sentence" section.[25]

In a lengthy statement the next day Rayburn tore into the alleged eagerness of the holding companies to accept federal regulation as "largely lip service." There was "no realistic and far-sighted way to handle the relation of these private empires to the people than by their ultimate elimination," Rayburn insisted. He paid Willkie an ambiguous compliment, "I very much admire Mr. Willkie's force and ability but I would certainly not want to be on any Federal Commission trying to regulate Mr. Willkie until his power had been trimmed down to managable proportions." Since the operating companies in Willkie's system had been formed before the creation of Commonwealth and Southern, he was in "a poor position" to argue, as he had, the indispensability of the credit support of a holding company.

Rayburn's sharpness took Willkie aback. ". . . the next time you fellows prepare a statement for the chairman replying to any of us," he wrote Cohen, "do not make it so personal. Personal statements lead to personal replies, all of which in my judgment serve no good end either way." Cohen replied mildly. He did not think he should claim "credit" for the chairman's statement. It was not intended personally. The "shafts" were directed at policy. Cohen hoped "after the one pleasant talk with you, and for that matter still hope," since Willkie realized cleaning up the holding company situation was "pretty important for the industry itself," that Willkie would help to build a sound structure.

Whether or not Rayburn's remarks were meant personally was unimportant, Willkie came back. "The newspapers interpreted it as such . . . I think I am as fundamentally liberal in my social and economic outlook as you are . . . My philosophy teaches me that nothing is quite so tyrannical as an independent government commission or bureau with wide discretionary powers."

"I have read and reread your letter of March 20th," Cohen replied patiently. "I really wish that you could free yourself from the emotional commitments of the immediate struggle." He did not believe in a "benevolent paternalism" by public authorities, which Willkie had argued was fostered by this government's policy. He enclosed a copy of Moley's editorial on "Private Socialism." He was ready to discuss the point he had raised about the rights of different classes of security holders in any reorganization as well as any other in the bill "in general or in detail with you, because, as I have said, I think you can be extremely helpful. I take no stock in the reports that come from New York that you are an irreconcilable."

Such exchanges took place behind the scenes. In public the holding companies' campaign masterminded by some of Wall Street's most eminent law and public relations firms went forward hotly. ". . . I'm having a sweet time putting through a bill to reorganize public utility holding companies," Tom cheerfully informed his brother David. "Am in the papers again as a 'dangerous radical' but don't believe all the things you hear about me."[26] He was to watch his step, Tom's father cautioned him, and told him of a conversation he overheard in a local restaurant that indicated a desire on the part of some Park Avenue types to invite him to dinner and get him "good and drunk" in the hope of putting him in an embarrassing position. "We mention this incident to put you on your guard (as you probably are now) against Greeks bearing gifts, avoid them as much as possible."

By the end of March it was clear the bill was in trouble, "in the middle of a 'storm area,' " Secretary of Commerce Roper alerted Roosevelt's appointments secretary, Marvin McIntyre. The President should delay the measure and await a change in the climate. A similar warning came to Cohen from Professor James C. Bonbright of Columbia, a supporter of the bill. He advised Cohen, who had consulted him in the bill's drafting, that Wall Street was confident it would either defeat or defang the measure.[27] Cohen demurred. "Wall Street opinion at about this time last year was that the Stock Exchange Bill would be defeated or emasculated. My own judgment is that their opinion on the Holding Company Bill is about as right as was their opinion of the Stock Exchange Bill."

Despite Rayburn's mettlesome start, the intense utilities' barrage against the bill which was reflected in resistance from his own committee slowed him down. The hearings dragged on. Corcoran and Cohen turned to Wheeler who had introduced the bill into the Senate the same day that Rayburn did in the House. They pleaded with him to take the lead. He had "a first-class mind," said Corcoran, and "an intuitive understanding of his colleagues." Whatever Roosevelt's misgivings about his political ambitions and international views, he was a fighter with whom Corcoran and Cohen found it a pleasure to work. "When he was with you, you had nothing to fear," wrote Corcoran. ". . . Gentle Ben Cohen and I had that feeling when he let us sit beside him the days hearings began on the Holding Company Bill." "So I scheduled hearings," wrote Wheeler. It turned out to be the "most difficult assignment I have ever had."[28]

The bill was hard to understand and harder to explain. "How the hell can I make a speech about it?" Senator Borah of Idaho complained to Wheeler. "There isn't anyone on the floor who understands it but you." Every night for a week, Wheeler explained, "I had been tutored at my home by Corcoran and Cohen, who had done a masterful job of drafting it. During the Senate debate I had Cohen sit next to me in case highly technical questions arose."

The utility executives arrived with their charts, maps, and concerted arguments in favor of regulation, preferably by the states, rather than elimination. "Corcoran would prompt Wheeler or some other Committeeman to ask a disconcerting question" of the witness, so timed, the utilities people complained, that reporters hastily left the hearings to file their stories before an adequate rebuttal could be made.[29] Cohen was as astute as any lawyer the utilities people hired, and Corcoran's news sense was as keen as any high-powered public relations talent arrayed against the bill.

On April 18 the committee, remembering Corcoran's performance on the Stock Exchange Bill, placed him on the stand to explain the intricacies of the holding company. Corcoran bore down heavily on the Moley theme of "private socialism." Was the main purpose of the bill "to get rid of the concentration of wealth?" Republican Senator Hastings asked him. "It is not the concentration of wealth. It is the concentration of power over other people's money," Corcoran answered. He sought to reassure shareholders who feared that Section 11, the "death sentence" provision, would result in the enforced liquidation of securities in a demoralized market. He patiently explained how holding companies were to be eliminated, "without taking the skin off the back of every investor in the country."

All during the Senate hearings Willkie sounded out Cohen, Corcoran, and Wheeler, and vice versa, but the "death sentence" section prevented a compromise. "You were so damn busy during the afternoon hearings running up those pink slips with questions on them that I had the notion to propose to the Committee that they have another 'pink slip repealer,' " Willkie drily noted to Ben at the end of April. He wanted "a chat with you and Mr. Corcoran, if I may."[30]

The talk if it was held was fruitless, even though elements on both sides were disposed toward a compromise. While the "death sentence" was the sticking point, there were other complaints. "I feel pretty certain that Mr. Willkie is aware of the defects in his proposal," (relating to service contracts) Cohen wrote to Bonbright, "and that his proposal was dictated simply by a desire not to create a divided front. The utilities have adopted the attitude of trying to take as much time as they possibly can to delay the bill."[31]

Mail inundated Congress. It was directed at the waverers in particular. "Ben and I miss you terribly in this public utilities fight," Corcoran wrote Judge Pecora. "I always thought I did appreciate, but I'm learning it was impossible to appreciate how much you did in the fight on the stock exchange bill last year."[32] The President relied on Corcoran to pilot the bill through the congressional shoals. He had assisting him on the Hill, Emil Hurja of the Democratic National Committee, and two of the young men who were coming down from Harvard Law School and beginning to crowd his and Ben's offices—James Rowe of Montana, Holmes's last clerk, and Joseph Cotten, Jr. Together with Cohen who had with him Joseph Rauh and Henry Herman they drafted speeches, prepared testimony, plotted strategy. Rauh, tall, quizzical, and independent, had been sent by Frankfurter to clerk for Cardozo. The latter decided to hold on to the clerk he had for another year, so Rauh went to work for Cohen. He had recently married and the hours at Ben's office were such that he later would say his first son was conceived on a couch there.

All were crackerjack lawyers and the constitutionality of the New Deal had become a paramount issue after the Supreme Court early in 1935 struck down the first New Deal bill in the so-called hot oil cases. Wheeler asked Ben and Tom to prepare a memo for the members of the Senate committee on the constitutionality of their bill. Their eight-page handiwork asserted that the government had the power to act on the basis of the right that the Constitution vested in Congress to regulate interstate commerce and the mails and on the basis of the "due process" clause.

But it was clear from statements of the industry, especially after the Schechter decision on May 27 that overthrew the NRA, that the bill would be hotly contested in the courts. The House committee because of internal opposition to the "death sentence" marked time all spring. At one point, without consulting Roosevelt, Rayburn agreed to a suggestion by Winthrop Aldrich of the Chase National Bank to meet with him, Willkie, and two other holding company executives to try to devise a bill acceptable to the utilities and to the House committee. The meetings lasted over a week and came up with a document that would have spared most of the large holding companies the agonies of reorganization. Neither Wheeler, nor Corcoran or Cohen, learned of the negotiations "until Rayburn and Splawn [counsel to the Rayburn Committee and an expert on holding companies] got into hot water," Cohen later wrote Frankfurter.[33] Cohen did not doubt that his and Corcoran's exclusion from the conference was requested by the utilities. "Wheeler neither was invited to these conferences," Cohen's letter continued, "nor told about them. Later attempts were made to draw Wheeler into a conference, but the attempts were dropped when he suggested to the go-between who was trying to arrange the conference that he talk to me."

Rayburn ended his negotiations with Aldrich. When Roosevelt heard "the embarrassing and equivocal position," the words were Cohen's, "into which Sam and Walter were maneuvered by the utilities," he demanded they insist on the bill without modification.

Wheeler's committee approved the bill 13 to 1 and on May 29 a two-week debate started in the Senate. Wheeler had Cohen sit beside him on the floor as he defended the bill. The key vote was on an amendment of Senator Dieterich, an Illinois Democrat, to delete the "death sentence."

Corcoran and Hurja were working the Senate, and Corcoran later wrote of this episode. "I have never seen such massed power of special interest against us."[34] Even though the President through Wheeler had sent a special message urging the "death sentence," they were six votes shy of the majority needed to defeat Dieterich. Ben was on the floor helping Wheeler interpret the eighty-page statute. "I was very glad," Corcoran said, that Ben was occupied, "I am sure that Ben would never have approved" of the strategy he and Hurja used to swing the six. Hurja reasoned and Tom agreed that if there was a defection from Dieterich at the very beginning of the roll call, the suspicion would quickly spread that the President had bought somebody off and that other defections had been arranged by the White House. Potential defectors would then fear they were "in a losing fight with the President. The problem was to move the first vote and the first vote was Adams." Hurja offered to talk to Adams and find out what he wanted from the White House. "I said, Emil, I have no authority to do anything, but if you will find out what he wants, I'll take my chances." Hurja learned that Adams, who was from Colorado, "would like to have the Mining office of the SEC put in Denver." Corcoran had no authority to make such a promise, but "relying on the over-estimate of the Congress, as well as of others of my powers to speak for the President, I said, Emil, you go down and tell him that he has my word and my guarantee that the President will order the SEC, under that supposedly independent SEC, to put that office in Denver, Colorado."

That did the trick. "The vote came up and to the amazement and dismay of the cabal . . . Adams voted for the President." There was an immediate murmuring as the vote went on and enough of the six questionable votes shifted "to give us the death sentence by one vote."

"Ben Cohen and Tom Corcoran have spoken with the warmest appreciation of your generosity and graciousness with which you have treated them throughout this fight," Frankfurter, who was keeping close watch on the progress of the bill, and spending a good deal of time at the White House, wrote Wheeler.[35]

It was now up to the House where Rayburn had lost control. Senator Thomas D. Schall, the blind senator from Minnesota, had given the Administration a foretaste of what was to come. He called the bill "the Corcoran-Cohen Act of 1935 for the creation of a Federal utility dictatorship . . . If the House attempts to swallow all the Corcoran-Cohen bill . . . it will have acute indigestion which may result fatally in the elections of 1936."[36] Schall's rantings might be discounted but the talk of "dictatorship" and the unconstitutional delegation of powers, the attacks on Corcoran and Cohen, as "two bright young men brought down from New York to teach Congress 'how to shoot,' " as the leader of the Democratic opposition in the House, George Huddleston of Alabama, put it, were staples of the onslaught on the bill. Arthur Krock, a pillar of the New York *Times,* attributed Roosevelt's stubbornness on the "death sentence" to his need for the support of the Western progressives in 1936. That group, he added, was "hot for the killing and he must stand by them to the end."[37]

Krock may have been right. David K. Niles, head of the Ford Forum in Boston and a mover among progressives, had suggested to Frankfurter who had forwarded the idea to Roosevelt, that "a frank talking-things over" between the President and impatient progressives and liberals would reassure them. The session had been held in mid-May and afterward Frankfurter wrote the President:

1. There is no doubt about the high success of the Tuesday night session. I have heard from all the senators, except Norris and Hiram Johnson, and they were all truly happy. According to Bob La Follette, "it was the best, the frankest, the most encouraging talk we have ever had with the President. I know that Burt felt that way about it for I went home with him. I told Burt that hereafter if there is anything on his chest he should get it off to the President directly, that he no longer has any excuse for private grousing, now that the President has told him he could get in touch with him through Miss LeHand. The President was fair, and frank, and I felt greatly encouraged that he is going to go into the stride of his old aggressive leadership." There was real warmth and enthusiasm in Bob as I talked to him, and I know that your assertion that "the time had come" heartened and invigorated them . . .[38]

Soon after Krock's critical column appeared, he turned up at Joseph Kennedy's estate, Marwood, just outside of Washington. Kennedy then was chairman of the SEC. To Krock's dismay he discovered that the President and his party were driving out for late-afternoon drinks and dinner.

There was no escape for him but to hide when Roosevelt drove up accompanied by Missy, Tom Corcoran, and John Burns, the general counsel of the SEC, and some secret service men. Against his will, Krock later wrote, he listened to the merry party as he hid away. The President picked apart such Washington personalities as Huey Long, "a physical coward," the aging Carter Glass, who "ain't what he uster be," even the Nourmahal gang, a Social Register group with whom the President went fishing. There was a movie, and "then Mr. Corcoran took out his accordion and the real merriment began. The President joined in all the songs, in a rather nice tenor-baritone, and finally he took the instrument and performed creditably for one so unfamiliar with it.

"The Holding Company Bill was discussed and Corcoran said, 'I've never been drunk in my life, but if this amendment [the death sentence] goes through tomorrow, I'm going to get stinking.' The President laughed heartily at this."[39]

The vote he referred to was in the House. Its committee, led by Huddleston, with Rayburn protesting, had voted out a bill minus Section 11. A Roosevelt ally, a freshman representative, Edward Eicher of Iowa, had moved on the floor to amend it. One of Corcoran's young legislative aides, probably James Rowe, in an unsigned memo, advised him, "The time has come to get tough . . . A whispering campaign should be started that he [the President] will have spotters in the gallery to watch all Congressmen on rising votes with roll calls . . . Protests from the people back home . . . As the time is short we must use the most convenient organized force and that is, of course—Coughlin. Wheeler could get to him—and he *must* ask for telegrams . . . they would have neutralizing force against the investors . . ."[40]

Despite Corcoran's hopes at Joe Kennedy's, the House voted against the "death sentence." The bill then passed 323 to 81. THERE IS A GOD IN ISRAEL AFTER ALL, Thomas McCarter of the Edison Electric Institute wired Philip Gadsden, the utility lobbyist who headed the Committee of Public Utility Executives. "A political defeat of the first magnitude," for the President, Krock observed. Senate and House versions then went to conference.[41]

The utility mobilization was "the most powerful, dangerous lobby . . . that has ever been created by any organization in this country," the President said just before the House vote.[42] Its power now was manifested in the so-called Brewster incident. Representative Brewster was the former Republican governor of Maine. He had survived an assault in Maine by the Power Trust, in part because he had been staunchly defended by liberal

Ernest Gruening, then editor of a leading Maine newspaper.[43] Because of Brewster's moderation, he had not been engulfed by the surprise Democratic sweep in Maine that had brought in a Democrat as governor. Frankfurter had written FDR, "As for the one Republican Congressman—Ralph Brewster—he is not likely to give the GOP much comfort. When Brewster was Governor he had me go up and address the Legislature on his power program, which in essentials was quite in accord with your own." Brewster had indicated to Wheeler and Corcoran that he was with the President in the holding company fight, promising even to deliver Maine's Republican Senator Wallace H. White. He failed to do this, but they had his promise to speak for the bill himself, including Section 11, at the right moment. He reaffirmed this promise at a meeting in Corcoran's office of House progressives. He thought he could get twenty-five Republicans to vote with him.

On July 1 Corcoran tried to reach Brewster to get him to deliver the promised speech. Brewster turned elusive, but Corcoran pursued him and when he finally tracked him down Brewster agreed to meet Corcoran in the Statuary Hall of the Capitol at one forty-five. He was bringing Ernest Gruening, he said. Brewster arrived around two to inform Corcoran he could not deliver the promised speech nor vote for the Eicher amendment. The political situation in Maine was too delicate, he pleaded. Later that afternoon he joined the majority to vote down the Eicher amendment.

Increasingly, as the showdown vote neared, the forces against the "death sentence" had focused on Corcoran and Cohen. "You do not know and I do not know," said Joseph Robinson of Kentucky "who or what is behind these men?" Who had ever before heard of Cohen and Corcoran? These brain trusters, young and without practical experience, had no mandate from the American people was the thrust of his speech.

The day after the House vote with the bill heading for conference, Brewster took the floor to charge—he had hinted to his son an "explosion" was coming in Washington:

Thomas Corcoran, Esq., coauthor with Benjamin V. Cohen, Esquire, of the bill came to me in the lobby of the Capitol, and stated to me with what he himself termed "brutal frankness" that if I should vote against the "death sentence" for public utility holding companies, he would find it necessary to stop construction on the Passamaquoddy Dam in my district.

"If Mr. Brewster can prove, or reasonably establish," wrote Krock, "the charge that any one nearly as important in the New Deal as Thomas F. [sic] Corcoran of the RFC used Quoddy as a political bait threat, what

Republicans have hoped for since the Maine campaign of 1934 will have come true."

The utility lobby had overreached itself. As the Senate-House Conference Committee deadlocked, two lobbying investigations were touched off by the Brewster charges. The first, chaired by Representative O'Connor of the Rules Committee, a conservative New York Democrat and anti-New Dealer, proved nothing and soon puttered out. It was a confrontation between the two Yankees, Corcoran and Brewster, both lawyers, the one solemn and bald-headed, the other cheerful with a head of heavy black hair. With Judge Pecora sitting beside Corcoran as a friendly counselor in two days' testimony, Corcoran established, and Ernest Gruening backed his version, that he had never threatened to stop construction on Quoddy, which, he said he had no power to do. He had told Brewster, however, that if he walked out on his freely offered promise, his credibility was finished with the Administration:

If, as you say, you are not a free man politically and must take power company support into your calculations, then you'll understand perfectly that from now on you can't expect me to trust you to protect "Quoddy" or trust your assurances that we'll get that Maine Power Authority out of the Maine Legislature.

Rodney Dutcher, in his column which was syndicated nationally by the NEA, wrote of Brewster's testimony, "Brewster Indicts Self," and summed it up:

After Brewster explained that he had been "ready to sacrifice anything, perhaps even my reputation to get Quoddy going in my district," the record shows:
Congressman Cox of Georgia: "Do you feel your conduct has been such as to afford a reasonable basis for your associates thinking you practiced deception on them?"
Mr. Brewster: "I do." (Adding that he had been convinced Quoddy would be endangered by what he considered the probability that Corcoran would "put the screws on me.")
Mr. Cox: "Do you not feel that is a terrible indictment which you have laid against yourself?"
Mr. Brewster: "I do."
"Mrs. Brewster," said the Maine congressman, "joined in the surprise which everyone else has expressed at my vote, and expressed, I think, also some little regret."

The congratulations showered on Corcoran, the sweetest being FDR's spare "stout fellah." Corcoran appreciated that and wrote to the President:

There are certain necessary liabilities without fault in the world—and I should have understood if they attached to subordinates who get into messes.
I don't know how I came out before the O'Connor Committee today—or how I

will come out before it in the end. But I do feel that I may have convinced that Committee this morning, that however few effective guns I may carry, I'm a man of war flying one flag—and that Mr. Brewster is just a shady privateer with forged letters of marque from both sides!

"Brewster today gave a new version," Frankfurter informed Roosevelt. "In effect, he testified that he was ready to destroy his own reputation (and incidentally, that of others) for dear old 'Quoddy!' But he also admitted talking to the power people in Maine! Tommy comes out of it all beautifully."

The House lost interest in an inquiry that its sponsors hoped would expose oppressive White House pressures on behalf of the "death sentence." A fuse had been lit, however, and the Senate had launched its own inquiry, this one headed by an "arch foe" of the utilities, Senator Hugo Black. Its revelations of utility lobby tactics turned what looked like certain defeat after the House vote into an Administration victory.

Day after day that summer, relentlessly, the Senate inquiry exposed the elaborate front that had been organized and funded by the utilities to fight the bill. The strings were pulled by the Edison Electric Institute. It had organized a Committee of Public Utility Executives which in turn set up still another front, the American Federation of Utility Investors which sent out literature to every shareholder, all with monies supplied in the end by the consumers of the utilities. Sullivan and Cromwell and Simpson, Thatcher and Bartlett supplied the legal counsel and Ivy Lee and Company public relations advice.

Such was the organization. The nation also learned how the thousands of telegrams that had inundated congressional offices were produced. It was "Elmer," the elusive Western Union messenger, whose testimony when he was finally brought to heel convulsed the nation and torpedoed a campaign that cost the utilities nine hundred thousand dollars. Elmer testified how he had picked the names at random from the city directories and signed them to telegrams, including bogus wires to Senator Driscoll of Pennsylvania, at three cents a signature. The companies did not improve their standing when they claimed to investigators that the originals had been destroyed.

Many years later Corcoran, in a letter that thanked President Lyndon B. Johnson for inviting Corcoran to a birthday party that he gave Justice Black, wrote: "By Hugo's investigation of Elmer, the messenger boy, he really turned the tide of almost certain defeat for Roosevelt on that critical finishing blow to Roosevelt's financial enemies."[44]

The Conference Committee played out the final act of the "death sentence" drama against the backdrop of the Black Committee exposures. "The atmosphere was super-charged," a Cohen letter to Frankfurter recalled the following spring, "with charges that the Congressmen were being used as rubber stamps . . . that no one knew or understood anything about the bill but a couple of young men—hot heads—with no political or practical experience. Every effort was . . . put forth to sow the seeds of suspicion and distrust between the Senate and the House. Tales were carried back and forth to make the leaders of each committee feel that the leader of the other was trying to double-cross him, every petty jealousy was played upon."[45]

Rayburn was one of the House representatives, but its real leader was Representative George Huddleston, an opponent of the "death sentence." Wheeler had asked Ben to accompany him to the conference committee room. Huddleston who had attacked Ben and Tom on the floor of the House, playing on the themes of anti-intellectualism and antisocialism, insisted on Ben's exclusion as well as that of Dozier De Vane of the Federal Power Commission. They had to be satisfied with seats in the anteroom.

FDR asked Frankfurter to take a look at the deadlocked situation. The issue, Frankfurter's resultant memorandum said, was between Huddleston who, "with two Republicans in his pocket," was "irreconciliable and wants to water down even the House bill's recognition of one system as a norm" and the Senate conferees who had offered "a substantial concession . . . permitting a holding company to control more than one operating system provided that the operating units are in the same locality, small in size and incapable of separate economical operations."

The Senate should not surrender to Huddleston, Frankfurter advised. "There is everything to gain and nothing to lose in keeping the bill in conference until January. On their return home members may learn, as Senator Barkley [D-Ky.] and some Congressmen have learned, that the sentiment of their constituents is in favor of your holding company policy."

With Roosevelt letting it be known that he was prepared to keep the bill in conference, Alben Barkley was selected, because he was less controversial than Wheeler, to offer a final compromise to the House conferees. It directed the SEC to permit holding companies to control more than one integrated utility system if additional systems were unable to stand alone economically and were not so large and scattered as to impair the advantage of localized management, efficient operation, and effective regulation.

Roosevelt agreed to the compromise unwillingly. "Felix sounds just like John W. Davis," he cracked.[46] On August 20 the bill, with the Barkley compromise, was approved by Congress, the House voting for it 219 to 142. Four days later the President signed the bill giving one of the pens to Corcoran who with Cohen stood in the group behind him.

The harsh battle had additional meanings.

It was a further step in the shift of control of the national economy from Wall Street to Washington so as to enable a modern political state to tame private economic power in the public interest.

It was another phase in Roosevelt's overall national power policy. In 1934 he had authorized the creation by executive order of an Electric Home and Farm Authority, funded by the RFC, to help consumers purchase electrical appliances in the TVA area. In May, out of funds from the giant relief bill, he had established the Rural Electrification Administration (REA) and appointed Morris Llewellyn Cooke its administrator. On August 1, 1935, he scrawled, "No objection FDR," on a letter signed by Morris L. Cooke, G. R. Cooksey, and Corcoran, concurred in by Lilienthal, which urged a nationwide expansion of the EHFA operations.

The bitter battle to enact the bill, said Corcoran, was a prelude to the 1936 campaign.[47] Both he and Ben would have important roles in that campaign, for another of the results of the flawless way they had handled their assignments in 1935 was to place them in the front rank of New Deal advisers. Corcoran was officially now an "assistant to the President," and where Tom served, Ben soon followed.

The battle that had been won in Congress went to the courts. In September Corcoran and Cohen were appointed "special assistants to the Attorney General for the Holding Company Act," and on September 27 the American States Public Service Company (ASPSC) filed suit in the Maryland District Court. It was an evidence of the long and tortuous road still ahead that in November Federal District Judge William Coleman declared the Public Utility Holding Company Act "invalid in its entirety." Other companies filed their challenges. "I'm up to my ears as a lawyer writing briefs and arguing motions on utility cases," Corcoran wrote a friend. It was Ben's decision, however, to have the SEC file suit against the Electric Bond and Share Company for refusal to register, as the Act required. The "Barco case" was to become the pivotal one.

XVI

—————⫸⟡⟡⫷—————

Tugwellians
vs. Happy Hot Dogs

In September 1935 Moley's magazine *Today* proclaimed on its cover:

THE ROOSEVELT PROGRAM MOVES TOWARD COMPLETION IN THE MOST REMARK-
ABLE SESSION IN THE HISTORY OF REPRESENTATIVE GOVERNMENT IN AMERICA[1]

Moley listed the accomplishments of the first session of the Seventy-
fourth Congress.

The banking bill which recast the Federal Reserve System,
The Public Utility Holding Company Act,
Public works and relief, including "the most stupendous appropriation ever
  made in a time of peace,"
The Wagner Labor Relations Act,
The Guffey Act to stabilize the coal industry,
The tax bill—a "somewhat drastic revision of our tax policy,"
Significant changes in the AAA,
The Social Security Bill.[2]

Although Moley applauded the changes, he had for over a year been
advocating "a breathing spell" for industry and finance. The very success
of liberalism at the polls, he had argued in November 1934, gave New
Deal leaders "even greater powers to exercise self-restraint." He did not
oppose, in fact, encouraged, the 1935 burst of measures, but the time had

come for the leaders of the New Deal, he wrote in the summer of 1935, "to rest on their oars." Finally in early September, as Congress recessed, his editorial welcomed Roosevelt's proclamation of a "breathing spell to industry." His was one view of the New Deal.

Others, although they loyally supported the President, felt that much remained to be done. Of the original Brains Trust, the "bigness boys," "Unofficial Observer" dubbed them—Moley, Berle, and Tugwell—the latter was the only survivor in the administration and he was downcast. "None of the Administration's major measures had been enacted after two months of Congressional debate," he wrote in his diary.

. . . not because the Administration's policies were unprogressive or because the Progressive votes were in the minority, but because certain Liberals and Progressives announced that the Administration did not go far enough and preferred to wreck its measures for the benefit and with the support of the reactionaries, rather than follow the rule of politics, which is to obtain as much of the desirable as possible, and to remember that half a loaf—in this case three-quarters of a loaf—is better than no bread at all.[3]

"We must let the President play out his hand," Tugwell ended his diaristic jeremiad against progressives, including himself.

Earlier Berle, busy in New York City, had sounded out Roosevelt about a reconstitution of the Brains Trust.[4] Both Hull and Moley had asked him "to join in forming (or reforming) the old 'Brains Trust,' " he wrote "Dear Caesar," "except that R.M. would eliminate Charles Taussig and Rex Tugwell. Plainly this thing could be done if at all, only (a) by your direction, and (b) reporting through a cabinet member."

Roosevelt did not take the hint. His use of Brains Trusters, especially academics, had been a reassurance to the country in 1931 and 1932. Yet even then personal predilection as well as awareness of how quickly the public mind could turn hostile to the "long hairs" caused him to move warily. He had been urged, he told Homer Cummings, the Connecticut lawyer and Wilsonian, when he appointed him Attorney General, to set up a cabinet of "so-called 'best minds!' "[5] Cummings agreed that an "aggregation of prima donnas" would disrupt cabinet proceedings . . . "only one best mind was needed and that was the head of the whole show." Brains were more needed than ever, but they had to adapt themselves to Roosevelt's political necessities and commanding personality. And that made them suspect with reactionaries as well as progressives in Congress and the press. "As time wears on," Tugwell bitterly noted in his diary, "it becomes clearer that the progressives in the Administration . . . are increasingly isolated and exposed to reactionary vilification . . ."

Tugwell had been in to see him, Ickes noted in his diary.

He told me that he was definitely through in the Department of Agriculture. He criticized the recent dismissal and resignation of certain liberals in the AAA as a sellout.[6]

Tugwell had promptly resigned to the President, Ickes went on, but Roosevelt had asked him to stay "at least for the time being," and to talk things over with Henry Wallace. He had and Wallace had assured him of his continued esteem, "but with the understanding that he would have nothing to do with AAA." Tugwell told Ickes he would not stay on such terms:

Tugwell is of the opinion that this Administration has done all that it can be expected to do in the way of social advance. He thinks too that the President is slipping and that the big business interests have him stopped.

Tugwell's mood was colored by Wallace's agreement to the ouster of Jerome Frank as legal counsel of the AAA and many of the men and women who worked with him. In a gallery of talented people Frank was an extraordinary lawyer and philosopher, voluble and voluminous, and one of Tugwell's closest collaborators. He had brought together in the AAA's legal department some of the best brains in the country. They had several characteristics in common. Many had been recommended by Frankfurter. Was it only flattery when Felix wrote from the *Britannia* to congratulate Frank on the "unusually able lot of youngsters" he had assembled in the AAA's legal division? "As the American shore recedes, I take comfort in the fact that there are more intelligent and more purposeful and more disinterested men in the service of the government than there has been for at least a decade."[7]

"I found that Frankfurter . . . pretty much recommended men without regard to their idealogies but primarily from the point of view of their competence as legal technicians," Frank recalled. "My recollection is almost certain that either directly or indirectly from Corcoran or directly from Frankfurter—certainly with Frankfurter's recommendation—Hiss was recommended to me." There were Protestants and Catholics in his office. In addition to Hiss, a top deputy was Frank Shea who lived in the same house with another of Frank's lawyers, Telford Taylor, and Thomas Blaisdell, a former student of Tugwell's who had brought him into the AAA and was, according to some, "the most respected economic mind" in the department, and Gardner Jackson, a jovial Washington newspaperman who had been involved in the Sacco-Vanzetti defense and was a friend of Brandeis and Frankfurter [8] Some were Jewish, several even secret Communists. "This is my Polish corridor," Frank said cheerily.

History has subsequently dwelt on the Communists on Frank's staff but at the time they were not perceived as such nor did they work in a systematic, organized way. "Pat" Jackson, a sophisticated anti-Communist recalled that Lee Pressman, the strongest of the Communist group, along with Nathan Witt, another Frankfurter recommendation, had urged him to "get into the show and help remake the world." But Pressman did not have "any overall plan, other than a very pronounced focus on the dispossessed of our country in agriculture, and elsewhere . . ." As for Hiss, he was in Jackson's view, a "cold fish" who "was never there when we had our powwows."

Frank's testimony on the Communist issue did not disagree with Jackson's. "The person I would least suspect would be Hiss," he said. "I don't think he's got the guts, besides . . . Alger always had a kind of upstage manner socially." Lee Pressman was another matter. Pressman had been quite close to Jerry, a lawyer at the same New York firm. Frank had helped build him up and considered him "probably the best lawyer I've ever met."

"Pressman confirmed that he fell for this," that is, becoming a member of the Communist Party. "He said that Abt and he had. He said the cell of which he was a member in 1934 in the Department of Agriculture did not contain Hiss. Whittaker Chambers said it did. Pressman said before the congressional committee that if Hiss was a member, he didn't know it. Hiss wasn't a part of his group at any rate . . . What motive did he have for absolving Hiss? He didn't say Hiss wasn't one. He just said, 'Chambers' story isn't true.' "

By definition the Communists were missionaries and crusaders, but there was little to distinguish them in the early New Deal years, as the testimony of Frank and Jackson illustrates, from the general run of liberals and reformers in the New Deal agencies, including Frank's.

A more telling issue against Frank, and therefore against Tugwell with whom Frank was associated, was his being Jewish. When Wallace had asked him to be general counsel of the department, George Peek, a representative of the traditional big farming interests, particularly the processors, who was slated to be administrator of the AAA, complained in Wallace's presence, recalled Frank, that "I was a city lawyer and a Jew—my appointment wouldn't sit well with farmers." Frank learned the real reason for Peek's hostility on the day of his appointment as general counsel of the AAA when Peek called him in and instructed him, "Now, look, I want you to understand that Wallace hasn't anything to do with this show." In those days Frank dismissed his being a Jew with the quip, "One of the virtues of having Jews in the government is that they can't get the Presidential bee in their bonnet." But there was a paradox in a group of Harvard-trained, city-bred lawyers, many of them Jewish, writing marketing agreements that were not part of their experience, and many of the "agrarians" in the department resented it. Lee Pressman attended a meeting to draw up a macaroni code and asked what the macaroni code would do for the macaroni growers.

Frank sought not to be influenced by his own being Jewish in the selection of lawyers for his large agency, which came to number 130 lawyers. Yet he had to draw the line.[9] Frank Shea kept coming to him with lawyers he wanted, recalled Frank. One day he brought three names—Schachner, Muravchik, and Timberg. "I said, 'Goddam it, Frank, I've got to be careful. You've got too many Jews in here now. The people will begin to say that I'm just selecting Jews.'

" 'You're a damned anti-Semite,' Shea said and raised hell."

Peek had been at loggerheads with Wallace from the time Roosevelt appointed him. Wallace had not been happy with that selection. Together with Tugwell and Frank, Wallace saw crop reduction as the primary weapon to combat the farm depression. For Peek, the marketing agreements were primary. Adlai Stevenson, then a young lawyer with the AAA, wrote his wife, ". . . in essence we're really creating gigantic trusts in all the food industries." As the break between Wallace and Peek approached, "Peek was beginning to talk about too many Jews around here." Frank was not sure Peek was anti-Semitic, but he was willing to use it as a weapon. "This was, of course, the kind of thing that was appealing to farm groups."

Peek resigned and Chester Davis, a man of considerable charm and graciousness who headed one of the agencies within the AAA, was promoted to administrator. For a while everything went well between the administrator and the reformers, who were to be found chiefly in Jerome Frank's office. But Davis resented Jerry's friend Tugwell. He called Tugwell a theoretician and impractical. He disliked his intervention in AAA matters. He disliked even more Tugwell's relationship with Wallace and most of all with Roosevelt—"his relationship with Roosevelt was a thorn in the flesh of all of them, except Wallace," said Frank.[10] To keep Davis's goodwill, Frank decided to avoid contact with Wallace, socially as well as professionally. But the issues between Davis and Frank were fundamental.

"The issue was increasingly the consumer versus the processors put in more subtle ways," recalled Frank. Was the Agricultural Adjustment Act "a Republican statute?" he and Paul Appleby, a liberal administrator and Wallace aide from the University of Syracuse, asked the secretary, adding, "All the benefits of it are going to the big landowners, insurance companies. The little farmers are not getting much out of it. The share tenants and croppers are getting nothing out of it. What kind of statute is this?" Wallace just said, "Oh, for heaven's sake, can't you fellows let me alone?"

Trustification had been Brandeis's worry all along. When the AAA was pending in Congress, the justice had initiated a talk with Pat Jackson, "worried as thunder about it—predicted that the result would be an increase in tenancy, absentee ownership and corporate farming."[11] Sharecroppers would be pushed off the land and turned into hired seasonal laborers. He asked Pat to pass his concerns to Tugwell and Frank.

The AAA still had to pass the court and constitutionality hurdle, and Brandeis was much on the minds of Frank and presumably Tugwell. In the summer of 1934 Thurman Arnold of the Yale Law School came to Washington at Jerry's invitation to help with the milk-licensing cases in which the milk industry insisted that it was not subject to federal price and rate regulation. Arnold was one of the most knowledgeable men about the antitrust laws. Their prohibitions against production restrictions and price agreements had been set aside by the milkshed-marketing agreements and the licensing provisions that underpinned them. Frank was uneasy about them.

"We weren't allowed to conduct our own litigation," said Frank.[12] He had to go through the Department of Justice and its lawyers, Frank claimed, were not very good in those days. But he was allowed to have someone sit in for him as a consultant. Arnold did so and in the outdoor dining room of the Cosmos Club said to Frank, "I've got it all fixed with them. They'll let me take this case if I want to. We'll get a case right up to the Supreme Court."

"I said, 'Well, goddam it, I don't want this case up to the Supreme Court.' "

"You're like Frankfurter."

Before Felix had gone abroad to Oxford he had met with Jerry and Harold Stephens of Justice and all had agreed that "resort to the Courts would be the last and not the first measure" of enforcement of the AAA's marketing agreements.

"No, I'm not like Frankfurter," Jerry countered. "I'm perfectly willing to go up, but goddam it we're wrong in these cases. Our constitutional procedure is all bad. We'll get a hiding if this goes to the Supreme Court. I don't want it to go up."

"You're a coward," Arnold replied indignantly. But emboldened by early district court decisions that upheld the constitutionality of the AAA, Jerry and his lawyers began to think about a Supreme Court test. Uneasy about Brandeis, he dispatched two of his assistants, Lee Pressman and Howard Bachrach, to Cambridge to probe Brandeis's friend Thomas Reed Powell on litigation strategy. Powell wrote Frankfurter about the visit.

Lee is much concerned about the particular form in which litigation arising out of the A.A.A. will get before the Court. He says that Brandeis is very strongly opposed to much of what is going on because it is making for control by the big fellows and suppression of the little fellows.[13]

Powell cautioned the two lawyers not to base their litigation strategy on a guess about how Brandeis might vote. They should warn their boss, Jerry Frank, not to read too much into Brandeis's Delphic comments made over tea. He was glad, Frankfurter wrote Powell, that he had reinforced his own recommendation that they avoid litigation. Felix intimated that Jerry and his staff were unduly influenced by the law clerks of some of the justices "who tittle-tattle too much on what comes to them in their confidential relations."

Jerry knew that in the end he would have to go to the Supreme Court or would be brought there—whether on the licensing issue or another.[14] In the late summer of 1934 he asked Pat Jackson to find out whether Brandeis would see them in Chatham on Cape Cod. Three of them journeyed up to the Cape, Frank, Jackson, and Tom Blaisdell. They were mainly concerned with the milk program, Jackson recalled. They wanted Brandeis's blessing and all afternoon talked away in his spare study, adjourning every once in a while to go out and look at the sea. Brandeis encouraged them in their approach, or so Jackson thought. "Contrary to his early beliefs," he told them, "he thought there were certain natural monopolies that had to be very rigidly controlled by government. Among them was steel." On their departure Frank and Blaisdell, recorded Jackson, "felt very much encouraged that we would not be knocked out in whatever was going on in Triple-A, if Brandeis's attitude were to prevail, which subsequent events proved to be a wrong interpretation actually."

Frank and most of his colleagues would no longer be in the Triple A when the question of its constitutionality reached the top court. The rupture at the Triple A arose over the cotton contract and the fate of the share-tenants and sharecroppers under it. The contract had been worded to lessen the chance that in cutting down cotton acreage the victims would be the tenants and sharecroppers. Hiss had been responsible for the wording of the relevant section, as he was for an opinion against corporate-owned cotton plantations in Arkansas. That was the state of Joseph Robinson, the Democratic leader in the Senate, and one of its senior solons. The Hiss opinion threatened to stop benefit payments if tenant removals did not cease. The sharecropper's plight became a major concern of the liberals in the AAA. Outside the government the tenant farmer gained a national champion in Norman Thomas. According to the 1930 census there were over a million and a half sharecroppers, 937,000 white, 671,000 black. Between 1929 and 1933 their cash income had fallen from $735 to $216 a year. In the beginning the issue under the cotton contract had been whether rental checks should be sent jointly to owners and tenants. The traditional Southern attitude was voiced by Senator "Cotton Ed" Smith of South Carolina who strode unannounced into Hiss's office. "You're going to send money to my niggers, instead of me?" he asked and announced, "I'll take care of them." He ought to address his question to higher officials, Hiss informed him. In the end, however, the checks were made out to the planters and the legal department took the view that it lacked authority to settle differences between landlord and tenant regarding the division of rental monies for the land taker out of production.

But the allocation of rental monies soon was overshadowed by the problem of tenant displacement. Frank and his people realized that crop reduction, whatever its benefits, was incompatible with improvement of tenant conditions. Davis was not unsympathetic but did not want to clash with the planters and their congressional allies. Even as Frank and his lawyers fought within the AAA for a contract provision and policy statement that defended tenant rights against displacement, the issue was forced. Norman Thomas spoke to hundreds of sharecroppers in Tyronza, Arkansas, and flayed the Department of Agriculture for ignoring the rights of the tenants. He helped them form a Southern Tenant Farmers Union (STFU) which took the unprecedented step of uniting blacks and whites. "Norman Thomas has been attacking us rather bitterly on this score in the South," Wallace informed Marvin McIntyre of the White House staff, "and the communist brethren are looking toward this particular field as a rich one to cultivate." Tugwell, himself a major target of the Red-baiters, perhaps for that reason regarded the sharecropper agitation as a nuisance. "Eastern urban radicals led by Norman Thomas," he described them in his diary, and added harshly that they were essentially agitators who did not want grievances removed.[15]

As the STFU enrolled tenants by the thousands, the planters retaliated with harassment and evictions. The liberals in the legal division wanted the AAA to enter the case on the side of the tenants. Frank decided to send down to Arkansas a woman lawyer, regarded as a conservative in the office, to check the complaints in Tyronza. HAVE HEARD ONE LONG STORY HUMAN GREED, Mary Myers wired Frank, CROPPERS MUCH HIGHER CLASS THEN I EXPECTED AND ALL PATHETICALLY PLEASED GOVERNMENT HAS SENT SOMEONE TO LISTEN TO THEM.

The planters sensed the trend of Myers's thinking and the American Cotton Cooperative Association (ACCA) warned Wallace that a pro-tenant policy would scare the South and cause thousands of friends of crop control legislation to reverse their support. Up to then the liberals in the AAA had assumed they were carrying out Wallace's wishes. Gardner Jackson even managed to arrange a meeting between Wallace and the STFU leaders at which the secretary promised "full consideration" of their appeal to the AAA to intervene on the side of the tenants.[16]

Here Chester Davis put his foot down. He asked Wallace to meet him in his hideout where, according to Wallace's diary, he accused the liberal group of intrigue and cited Frank's opinion that it was legally incumbent on contract signers to keep the same tenants on the land. "He thought that Jerome Frank was definitely endeavoring by means of the slippery legal interpretation to put him on the spot," Wallace recorded. The secretary minimized Davis's allegations of a conspiracy. "I do recognize, of course, that Paul and Jerome and Rex Tugwell and others of the extreme liberal group want to see things brought to pass faster than Chester does. I can see how in endeavoring to push things along they might do things that would seem to Chester like double-dealing."[17]

The next day Davis received the legal section's official opinion that the contract required a landlord-producer to keep his tenants. Davis went to Wallace's office. Frank must be fired. "He feels that he could clear up the situation if he could get rid of Jerome Frank, Lee Pressman, and F.M. Shea . . ." Wallace reluctantly agreed. Davis called Frank in. "I want your resignation." "I said, 'This is rather abrupt. Do you mind if I talk to Henry first?' "

"No, go ahead."

Frank got to see Wallace only late in the day.

"Henry, Charles has made this surprising statement," Frank said. Wallace's reply was no surprise to Frank, who had heard similar views from him before. "Jerome, the time has come when for the time being I've got to work with the farm leaders. You're identified with opposition to them in these matters and so I've got to change my policy." He had a right to ask him to go, Jerry replied.[18] He had wanted to resign and asked for a little time. Wallace agreed and left but, said Frank, did not come back. The next day Wallace and Davis held a joint press conference and announced Frank's firing and that of several others. They were a bunch of "*New Republic* liberals," Wallace explained.

Wallace felt badly. When the people in Frank's office and that of the Consumers Counsel, which had also been included in the "purge," as it came to be known, asked to see him, he agreed to see two of them and Frank and Hiss went. According to the version Gardner Jackson heard afterward, Wallace had come from behind his desk, hand outstretched, tears in his eyes, pleading he had to do it. "Why didn't you tell us?" Jackson reported Frank as replying. "We might have differed, but we would have understood the necessities that you felt."[19]

Tugwell was in Key West, Florida, taking a look at the federal rehabilitation of that old city and meeting "a number of artists and writers who winter there," when he heard from Grace Falk, his confidential assistant, that Jerry "had been forced out suddenly." Davis's pretext had been the Hiss legal opinion, "O.K.'d by Jerome interpreting the cotton contract to mean that landlords had to keep the same tenants for the life of the contract." But that was not the real reason, wrote Tugwell. "I could see that it was part of Davis's studied plan to rid the Department of all liberals and to give the reactionary farm leaders full control of policy, this meaning, of course, full satisfaction to all the processors with whom we have dealings since most of the farm leaders are owned body and soul by the processors."

He hurried home, breakfasted with Jerry, "The whole thing seemed to him planned to take advantage of my absence. . . . I went and talked to Harry Hopkins who was outraged, to Louis Howe who was sympathetic, to HAW who was red-faced and ashamed, and to the President. My first impulse was to resign . . ." The angry entry ended: "I made up my mind that (1) Jerome must have justice, (2) that my position must be recognized, and (3) that the ownership of the Department by the processors must be prevented."[20]

Wallace briefly considered making Jerry assistant solicitor of the Department of Agriculture, but Davis refused to stay if Frank was anywhere in the department. Tugwell identified with Frank and brushed aside Wallace's statement that Davis felt friendly toward the under secretary. "I told him that our economic views diverged sharply, that there was certain to be a clash and that when it happened I knew he would certainly support Davis."

A few days later he told the same things to the President and offered to resign. Roosevelt prevailed upon him to stay but began to discuss with him and Hopkins a new agency that would group the resettlement, rehabilitation, and land-planning activities of the government and that Tugwell might head. "Jerome Frank is fixed in the RFC in charge of railroad reorganization," he recorded sadly on February 24. "Lee Pressman is in FERA, Shea in SEC, etc. So all those cleared out of A.A.A. in which the papers called a 'purge' are now as well fixed as ever. But it leaves A.A.A. committed to the farm leaders' policy of cooperation with the processors and so makes my position pretty impossible." FDR took him to Hyde Park for five days at the end of that upsetting month. "I have been thinking and planning the Resettlement set-up," he noted in his diary.[21]

As Tugwell's position in the Administration weakened, for that was the effect, despite Roosevelt's solicitude for him, of the "purge" and his reduced influence at Agriculture, the Frankfurter group prospered. Corcoran had alerted Frankfurter on the eve of his return from Oxford that relations with Tugwell and Frank were strained and "only you have a sufficiently universal esteem to harmonize" them. Later Corcoran and Frank became good friends but the clash in 1934–35 mirrored the shift in fortunes of contending groups within the New Deal. In May 1934, Moley had attacked AAA lawyers in *Today.* They "talk too much in public and private." They should stick to their jobs and "leave social theory, patronizing references to 'folkways' and 'experimentalism' to less responsible outsiders . . . If I may make clear to some of the self-styled 'intellectuals' of the Administration what some regular Democrats are saying about them, they talk too much and work too little."

That brought a nine-page retort from the combative Frank.[22] Moley's attack on him, said Frank, was also an assault on Frank's good friend Tugwell. Frank dismissed Moley's intimation that he did not pay attention to more "prosaic duties" and noted that he had had "exactly five days of continued rest" since his arrival in Washington in March 1933. He denied Moley's imputation of condescension in his use of the terms "folkways" and "experimentation" and ended with the postscript, "By the way, I'm not 'young' and I'm not a 'self-styled intellectual.' I have just submitted this letter to Rex for approval. He thinks it highly desirable that I send it."

Moley claimed his statement had been general, not aimed at Jerry, although Jerry's use of "folkways" did have a note of condescension, he insisted. Frank, who rarely allowed a controversy to rest, noted the attacks on him and Rex by Hamilton Fish and other congressional conservatives. He implied that Moley's criticism had added fuel to those who misrepresented them because of their resistance to the large processors. But he finally conceded that if he had to make the offending speech again, "I would not use the word 'folkways.' "

In the course of these exchanges Frank had appealed to Frankfurter in Oxford to "call off his boys." Although no such letter is to be found in Frankfurter's or Frank's papers, nor Frankfurter's alleged reply that he was unable to do anything at that long a distance, Frank's oral history allegations of such an exchange were consistent with Tom's warning to Frankfurter in Oxford of demoralization among New Dealers.

A letter to Felix in Oxford in April 1934, written by Tom but signed "Tom & Ben," hinted at the feuds among the New Dealers and cautioned Felix that the "skipper's personal machine . . . has broken down."[23] Equally alarming, "Administration has broken down in the three big divisions of the program that were most ballyhooed—P.W.W., A.A.A., and N.R.A.—and the impossibility of administering A.A.A. and N.R.A. which Isaiah foretold over a year ago are now yawning open . . ." There was a Nazi-inspired drive "on so-called radicals" which has become "particularly virulent against you. There has always been a whispering of your influence in the Administration . . ." And basic to an emerging sense of disorganization among the New Dealers was "the utter lack of a central thread of philosophy through all the twistings of expediency." They needed Felix's "directional help" in order to get to the midterm elections in November and secure "another commitment from the electorate . . . Please remind the skipper that every fundamental change, like the Stock Exchange bill, needs electioneering like a Congressional campaign . . ."

Jerry Frank, unable to get Corcoran on the phone, turned to Cohen, whom he had preceded at the University of Chicago, making even better grades, and who shared his affection for Judge Mack, to arrange a meeting. When he and Corcoran finally got together they had "a fight" such as Frank had never had "with anybody in my life . . ." The issues were not wholly clear from Frank's account. "It became known and was obvious," recorded Frank in his oral history, "that both Tugwell and I believed that greater centralization of government was essential and that the New Deal necessarily involved that. There were many problems that couldn't be solved except on a national level."[24] But as Frank conceded ironically, that was not the issue in Corcoran's attacks as Frank was "black and blue from these battles where I was battling for the anti-trust laws, feeling obliged to in these marketing agreements, [and] I learned that Tom Corcoran was spreading news around that I was a radical, trying to nationalize everything, and so on. I believe this was because at that time, at any rate,

Tommy was an ardent Brandeisian and was therefore opposed to anybody who had that kind of philosophy."

Early in Frank's extensive correspondence with Frankfurter the latter had declined to enter the argument between "localism vs. centralization." Frankfurter asserted, "That's a long story in which you and I might not come out the same door. I have an almost crushing sense of the difficulties involved in governing a continent, and that kind of a prejudice bears heavily on what it is that I should want to have continent-wide in its control."[25] Of course, "continent-wide" regulation was precisely what the NRA and AAA had undertaken and Frankfurter's attitude had been, despite the skepticism that he shared with Brandeis, not to oppose either frontally but to help reshape them under the impact of events.

Another warning against setting up black-and-white categories in appraising the conflict between the Brandeis-Frankfurter and Tugwell-Frank groups was the presence of Gardner Jackson at Agriculture. He was as devoted a follower of Frank as of Brandeis. Pat admired Jerry more than any other person in the New Deal. "Jerome was the guy that impressed me, with his very warm, outgoing personality, and his passion to create a better social arrangement for the dispossessed of the country."[26]

Jackson roamed the Hill where he was well liked, ". . . friends of mine in Congress began to tell me that we were being badly undercut by Tommy Corcoran and his operations on the Hill where he was pushing and successfully pushing the 'death sentence' holding company bill . . ." In his promotion of that aspect of the New Deal legislation he encountered arguments that that was altogether too advanced, too radical in its concept. "He would counter by saying that it wasn't radical at all, that the Congressman or Senator with whom he was talking ought to look into what the fellows in Triple A were up to, that that was the real radical nest down there, that they were trying really to overturn our whole economy."

Frank and Corcoran later became close friends. It was Corcoran whom Roosevelt assigned the job of finding another place for Frank. Tom spoke to Stanley Reed at RFC and Reed made him special counsel on railroad reorganization, Frank's old specialty. Nevertheless, Jerry continued to believe that Tom's "propaganda" on the Hill made it easier for Davis to institute the purge, "because he helped create the opinion that I was very radical. Actually my radicalism in Davis's terms was that I was supporting the anti-trust laws. So you got the paradox of the trust-buster boys trying to knife me because I was trying to do what they wanted to do, although I wasn't too wholehearted about it as a generalization."

Frankfurter tried to keep the controversy between Corcoran and Frank at arm's length. "I do not know what your differences with Tom Corcoran are all about," he wrote Frank. "While I esteem Tom very highly I'm accustomed to make up my own mind—and to determine my own friendships." Frank thanked him for this cordial assurance. Then the purge had come and Corcoran helped him find another berth with the Administration. But Frank was dubious about staying on in Washington and asked advice of Frankfurter. "Bluntly, I know not what Rex has in mind for you," Felix counseled, "but I share strongly your doubts about the worth of your continuance in Washington. The Administration has plainly reached a new stage. From now on it must be to a large extent trench warfare. I don't think your temperament and your interests are peculiarly suited to participation in that kind of enterprise."

Frank left the government to join the New York firm of Greenbaum, Wolff and Ernst, but he continued to seek vindication of his New Deal activities in Frankfurter's eyes. The Moley charge that he condescended had rankled. "Yes, I know you want to win particular cases," Frankfurter wrote him. "But I also know that you are a damned romantic intellectual who finds it not wholly easy in view of your brilliance and wide reading to use language that will make the Sutherlands of this world feel that you are their kind of fellow. Please note than I do not say McReynoldses."[27]

Frank read this as confirmation of Frankfurter's "adversely critical attitude" and so wrote him. Frankfurter protested his admiration and affection but then went on to criticize him anew. He had heard of some of Frank's conversations with people "that seem to me to illustrate that gratuitous candor is sometimes a greater driving force with you than art." Frank offered to send him some of his briefs to show that he could argue a case in conventional terms. Frankfurter turned the screw of criticism a little tighter.

Of course I shall read the briefs you sent me at the very first opportunity. Of course I shall continue to think that you are wrong in thinking, as I believe you think, that most of the law is the bunk, but that you dish up the bunk because other people like to feed on it. All of which has nothing to do with your skill as an artist in making the judges believe that you like the fare which you serve them.

Finally, in lieu of a talk, which Frankfurter would have preferred, he wrote him a four-page letter relying, he said, on "the tough fibre of our friendship" to tell Jerry some home truths.

I couldn't help recalling, as I read your letter with its intimations of your absolute correctness and carefulness of speech, your implacable pursuit of a Coolidge-like discretion, and perchance never an irresponsible utterance even after a few highballs—or perhaps I am wrong in thinking that you ever had highballs. . . . It is ridiculous for you to say that your tongue is always held very closely in check and that you never said anything to friends which by the time it got to the Packers and others came into the possession not of friends, but of enemies, not of people who shared your social dreams, but profited by their frustration. I say that it is ridiculous for you to deny that you ever talked freely, because that is the very texture of your temperament, and because intimates to whom you said things, that the Packers and others used against you, told me directly that you said them.

. . . .

And what you, and a number of people in Washington had not realized from the beginning, is that public life is warfare, that it is always permeated by people who are in Holmes's phrase, fired with a zeal to pervert, that the luxury of letting one's mind roam through one's tongue is a luxury that can't be indulged in, and that there are a lot of things that can be and should be done but shouldn't be talked about.

He ended with a protest against the "personal bickerings" among liberals:

I have sometimes wondered why conservatives can hang together so well. Is it their general lethargy of mind compared with the greater liveliness of independence and inquiry on the part of those who do not think that this is the best of all possible worlds? Or is it that the latter are recruited to no small degree from among exhibitionists and prima donnas?

Although he begged Frank not to "fly off in personal defensives" he was not surprised when his reproaches produced a six-page single-spaced surrebutter which highlighted Jerry's grievances against Corcoran. Davis had used Moley, Jerry wrote, "and there Tom's activities had helped, for he had helped make Moley inimical to me," and when Ben finally had persuaded Tom to talk with Jerry "he didn't deny that he had to do with Moley's attack . . . he did much to give credence to the fact that I was an extreme left-winger who was boring from within; that he contributed to Moley's attack on me as an irresponsible extremist—(an attack inspired by Moley's desire to get at Rex) . . ."[28] Tom had, indeed, "come to the front after the purge. And he and I are now working splendidly together wherever our paths cross." The letter ended in a plaintive postscript, "What's the use, I ask myself, "of trying at this late date, to convince Felix? His estimate of me was forming in this matter when I was out of touch with him and Tom was not."

Frank enclosed a clipping that Felix's sister Stella had sent him from the *Herald Tribune*. The front-page story described General Hugh S. Johnson's article in *The Saturday Evening Post* that called Professor Felix Frankfurter "the most influential single individual in the United States" through his personal influence on Roosevelt and through "one of the cleverest infiltrations (of purposeful officials) in the history of our government."[29] The "happy hot dogs," as he christened the infiltrators, sought to "bore from within," a phrase, as Johnson knew, usually applied to the tactics of the Communists. While "Tugwellians" and "happy hot dogs" both minimized the notion that Frankfurter had now come out on top, and both joined ranks to criticize Davis's purge, the article alleged that "the leaders of the Frankfurter clan" had used the Gardner Jacksons and the Jerome Franks of the AAA purge "as horrible examples of 'radicalism' " in order to consolidate their position "with the essentially conservative leaders on Capitol Hill."

There had been an almost qualitative jump in the influence at the White House of Frankfurter and his "boys." It was signaled by the cooption of Corcoran for Roosevelt's personal staff. Frankfurter was instrumental in this, as was "Missy" LeHand. The latter, of Irish heritage and from Massachusetts, championed the young man whose puckishness, intelligence, and derring-do she appreciated. With Louis Howe increasingly an invalid, she knew better than anyone except Eleanor Roosevelt her boss's need for companionship as well as staff assistance. She knew, too, the jealousies around Roosevelt.

Frankfurter paved the way. He had been "shocked," he wrote Roosevelt, "at the way in which fat reports are submitted to you without any précis, without any intellectual traffic directions. Equally intolerable is it that you should not have at your disposal the kind of preliminary sifting of legislative proposals and bills that you had when you were Governor of New York."[30] Frankfurter had someone "strangely enough, ready to hand," with the requisite qualities of discretion, analytical ability, a stylist, a shrewd judge of personalities, and "a very good lawyer . . . I mean Tom Corcoran." Once Tom did take off his hands "a thousand and one chores," he will ask why he had been so long without the necessary help. "The truth is that you have inherited a one-horse-shay method of running the country which simply will not do for the needs of a streamlined society."

Sometime in the early spring of 1935, in the midst of the holding company fight, Corcoran was appointed "anonymous administrative assistant," as he described himself, with the special job of liaison "with friendly Senators on the Hill."

And the first thing I know, I am called in through Missy's office and she goes in and introduces me to him and says this is the fellow that Frankfurter thinks would be a good assistant to you in view of the fact that the load in the Congress is now something incredibly different than it ever was before.[31]

Charles West, a former Democratic representative from Ohio, was in the Oval Office when Missy ushered Tom in. Roosevelt said, "Now, Charlie, you handle the House. And he said to me, Tommy, you handle the Senate."

Through Missy, I was given the privilege of using the White House telephone exchange for important calls . . . an incredible tool . . . My position as a Presidential lobbyist on the Hill was most unofficial (and depended on the continued good will of Mr. [Jesse] Jones). I was only an RFC lawyer, and Assistant Attorney General. But when I phoned someone, being able to say I was calling from the White House, or having a White House operator put me through—gave me a certain cachet . . . I was careful never to abuse that privilege . . .

I was also discreetly warned by Missy to understand that I had to be very careful not to step on the toes of people who had come to Washington with Roosevelt after long years of service. Some had worked with him as long ago as the Wilson Administration . . . And as in any administration, many of the entourage were very jealous. For that reason, it was arranged that each morning I would reach Missy's office through a lower passage in the West Wing which led to a private staircase. I'd tell her what I learned the day before, then wait to see if the President wanted to see me, or simply go about my business for the day. If Roosevelt needed to talk with me personally, Missy's office opened directly into his, and she showed me in. In that way, I avoided crossing paths with any of Roosevelt's old guard and kept the jealousies down to a manageable level. I never had a White House job or office . . . I had office-hours access to the West Wing but I never attended any formal White House functions . . . Participating in the operations of this masterful governor, I wanted nothing except the excitement of "being part of great things" as Holmes put it, "by being part of great men."

"Dear Missy," Frankfurter wrote her, "I am gratified, as you probably suspect, at the arrangements made by the President for annexing for his immediate help the resourceful talents of Tom. I know this arrangement was essentially due to you, and I have no doubt that events will prove that in bringing it to pass you have rendered another great service to the President and Administration."[32]

Where Tom went, Ben soon followed:

We finally worked out an arrangement by which I was allowed to bring Ben Cohen into the White House itself. Into the conferences—into the speechwriting . . . I simply showed up in the office one day with Missy and told Missy this was my friend Ben that I was living with and he was the best lawyer I ever knew and that I thought that not only myself should have the assistance of him, but the President should have from time to time and sooner or later, without any official business at all, Ben himself, as a second political assistant to the President and from there we graduated into speechwriting and from there it graduated into politics.[33]

Felix kept control of his "boys." At the end of the 1935 summer when he practically lived at the White House and devised the compromise formula that broke the "death-sentence" deadlock in the Senate-House conference committee, a vacancy arose on the Securities and Exchange Commission. That agency now had under its administrative aegis the Securities Law, the Securities and Exchange Act, and the Public Utilities Holding Company Act. Frankfurter advised Roosevelt against the appointment of either Ben or Tom:

1. May I suggest that you tell Ben and Tom, when you have them in, that while Ben is doubtless the best man qualified to administer the three laws—looking forward to a Holding Company Act—which he largely drew, nevertheless, some men are needed for staff rather than line service and you will continue to need the team, Ben and Tom, for staff work. That is the reason Tom has not been utilized for other important posts.

2. If you think well of it, it would help to tell Ben that you have had a frank talk with me about the matter and that I felt very clearly that membership on the Commission was not the best use of Ben's abilities.

3. It would be well to ask the boys for names of people really qualified for the vacancy . . .[34]

This was hardly the recommendation one would have expected from the man who in the interregnum before Roosevelt's accession to the presidency strongly advised Moley, then Roosevelt's chief privy councillor, to have the President regularize his status. Service as a "minister-without-portfolio" had its glories and excitements, but exposed Moley to the vagaries of public opinion and kept him dependent completely upon Roosevelt's disposition, Frankfurter had argued. It was strange that two years later Felix did not acknowledge to himself the need of Corcoran and Cohen for similar recognition. Or did he? Was he aware, and afraid, that in the degree to which they received official status they became less available to him? Frankfurter had become not only Roosevelt's chief adviser, but the chief irregular in that untidy Administration. Presidents needed such "irregulars," especially one as immobilized as Roosevelt, but it was also true that Frankfurter prospered in his relatively remote Cambridge aerie because of the presence on the scene of his "boys."

XVII

Price Was the Key
and the Key Jammed

At the end of June 1934 two New Deal loyalists, Frances Perkins, the sobersided, social-minded Secretary of Labor, and Mary Harriman Rumsey, the progressive head of the Consumers Advisory Committee of the NRA, elder sister of Averell Harriman whom she was converting into a Democrat, told Leon Henderson they were to see FDR and asked him for an "aide memoire on NRA."[1]

"I sat down at the typewriter and wrote this," noted Henderson on a seven-page typed memorandum, "and did not make a correction." The forty-year-old Henderson was then director of Research of the NRA. General Hugh Johnson, whose days at the agency were numbered, had appointed him after a celebrated encounter with representatives of consumer organizations that had been organized by Mrs. Rumsey in reply to Johnson's gruff demand to be shown a consumer. At the angry meeting inspired by consumer outrage at the escalation of prices resulting from the codes, Henderson, not a man to be bullied, stood up and outshouted the general on the subject of prices, whereupon Johnson, in one of those conciliatory gestures that showed he was not wholly a man of the right, appointed the young economist director of NRA research.

In that position Henderson was emerging as one of the most militant of the New Dealers. The congressional authorization of the NRA had to be renewed in 1935. That, plus the growing unpopularity in the country of the Blue Eagle as well as Johnson's impending departure, caused the New Dealers to ask the question as to how industrial policy should be reshaped.

"The NRA record is highly creditable as to organization," wrote Henderson, "increases in real wages (steel wages for 34 hours per week are almost equal to 1929's 55 hours in terms of purchasing power for those employed), profit margins, increases in net worth, and restoration of business confidence."

The "real persistent" problem was unemployment—and the NRA had few weapons with which it might affect it, except for increased productivity. That meant codes had to be revised, reasoned Henderson, and prices reduced as the basis for volume production. A national price policy was needed, Henderson emphasized, and that required a knowledge of how prices might be used as a mechanism for achieving a desired result such as the reduction of the number of unemployed.

This was the view of many progressives in the New Deal. They shared Henderson's view that in the writing of codes industry had been interested only in the prevention of downward spirals of prices. But if government was going to interfere with the forces of bargaining, in order to limit such spirals, Henderson's memo asked, "why should not profits, salaries, and maximum prices be limited by the same authority?" If an industry wanted the government to stabilize its prices, it should submit "to considerable supervision and yield certain advantages to consumers. At present, emergency prices are looked upon as industrial rights."

New Dealers had varying degrees of faith in the NRA's ability to handle the wage-price interaction, but they were agreed that the NRA under General Johnson had turned the codes into a form of industrial self-government. "If the business features of the codes are defective," wrote Cohen in a review of banker James P. Warburg's onslaught on the New Deal in *It's Up to Us,* "it is largely the responsibility of business itself. The deficiencies of the codes are the deficiencies of self-government in business, not the deficiencies of the New Deal."[2] Cohen's chief emphasis in the review was to eschew ideology and embrace experimentalism. That is what made work for Roosevelt so congenial. "The New Deal's approach of reason guided by experience," he wrote, "will bring us further than any fixed or rigid conception of economic law." He deplored Warburg's reproaches, Cohen called them "obsessions," that government "cannot be flexibly intelligent" when the entire philosophy of the New Deal assumed that "democratic government can be and must be just that . . ."

Tugwell had played a major part in the establishment of the NRA, viewing it as a "control-coordinating mechanism," but he was among the first to acknowledge in the summer of 1934 that its failure to exercise this function had been one of its "strategic mistakes" and that at the center of this failure had been the price issue. With this in mind he had asked Gardiner Means to analyze the price problem in relationship to "Industrial Policy Making" and the reorganization of the NRA. Means's report, which Tugwell sent to the President September 8, 1934, was an authentic addition to economic analysis. Together with *The Modern Corporation and Private Property,* which he coauthored with Adolph Berle and which had become "a part of the accepted image of the modern economy," it established him among the New Deal's original economic thinkers. Tugwell had brought him down from Columbia Law School in the summer of 1933. That first summer he had shared a house with the old reformer and chief of the Consumers Counsel office, Fred Howe, and with Tom Blaisdell until his wife, Helen Ware, a professor at Vassar, arrived to work in the Consumers section of the NRA under Mary Rumsey. He had been attached to Wallace's office, occupying a desk alongside Mordecai Ezekiel and Louis Bean. His specific job was to analyze economic problems outside but related to agriculture. He and his wife had become stalwarts in the New Deal.

Means's price study demonstrated statistically that the "reality" of what he called "administered prices" had destroyed the role of the market as an overall coordinator of the forces of production and distribution so as to assure the optimum use of resources. Means showed how administered prices differed from market prices. "A market price is one which is made in the market as the result of interaction of buyer and seller. The prices of wheat and cotton are market prices as are many other agricultural products." An administered price, on the other hand, was set by administrative action. "Thus, when the General Motors management sets its wholesale price for a particular model and holds that price for six months or a year the price is an administered price."

Acceptance of the reality of administered prices necessitated a choice, said Means, between two alternative methods of controlling them: "atomization" of large corporate units with the resulting loss of production efficiencies, or, supplementation of the market mechanism with governmental intervention that involved new techniques of control.

Tugwell sent this analysis to Roosevelt with a plea that he "take time to study [it] carefully."[3] Means's report dovetailed not only with an emerging realization in the Administration of the relationship of money volume to price, that is, monetary policy, but it suggested two lines of action in the pending reorganization of the NRA. "If together with currency action," Tugwell advised Roosevelt, "we could (1) proceed under anti-trust laws against unauthorized price fixers, and (2) have a series of authorizations for government control of monopolies (businesses capable of fixing their own prices) we should be on the right track."

The Means analysis made the rounds among the New Dealers, especially the economists. Rumors of its existence swept Capitol Hill and Senator Borah, erstwhile Republican progressive and enemy of trusts, in the belief that it was being withheld from Congress, persuaded the Senate to ask for its publication as a Senate document.

The publication intensified the heated discussions. Jerry Frank, preoccupied though he was by the purge, wrote Means two lengthy letters of dissent.[4] The price problem "was one of central importance in our economy," Frank agreed, but he quarreled with Means's assertion that "the market breakdown is not a matter of monopoly (as the courts have interpreted the term) . . ." Rigid prices and production control arrangements, Frank argued, did indicate collusion, difficult as it was to obtain evidence to that effect. "Why do you think so many industries were so eager to procure code provisions authorizing price fixing in one way or another? Obviously, in many cases, because those codes made legal the practises which they had theretofore surreptitiously practiced."

Frank noted that Justice Brandeis

would either break up monopolies indicated by rigid prices or regulate them. His own decided preference is to limit the number of regulated monopolies and break up most of the large enterprises. I do not happen to agree with him that most of the monopolies should be broken up, because I think that many of them have evolved efficiencies which would be lost if they were pulverized.

Frank brushed aside Means's suggestion that tripartite boards of business, labor, and consumers should handle the setting of prices. The present controllers of the rigid price industries, he claimed, would be "delighted" with such a proposal. "For they know that with a three-part board, they will eventually control at least two of the three parts when the price problem arises."

Although Frank considered himself an assentor to, if not believer in, "bigness" in contrast to Brandeis's emphasis on the breakup of concentrations of economic power, the views of both sides fluctuated in their acceptance of some measure of both monopoly and antitrust regulation. "Neither you nor I," Frankfurter wrote Moley after passage of the holding company bill, "are doctrinaires either about the curse of bigness or the blessings of littleness. Like most things that matter in the world, it's a question of more or less, of degree, of when is big too big, and when is little too little. In any event, what we need most is luminous, authentic experience."[5] Everyone was groping for the key that might bring recovery and end unemployment.

Frank had missed the essential point of his analysis, Means replied, namely, that "competition never worked as classical economists thought it would, if only monopoly were absent and competitive conditions were maintained." Frank with his powers of almost total recall, promptly came back with quotations from the classical economists who, he insisted, had anticipated Means's discovery. But his main point, said Frank after this bravura display of learning, was his fear that an "indiscriminate" resort to trust-busting might "deprive us of the sound benefits of bigness in some industries" and, in any case it would be difficult to enforce. As for Means's proposal to create tripartite supervisory authorities which would be "something like code authorities," they had been tried, were "a mere piece of machinery," and should be subordinate to the formulation of policies.

Frank did not spell out the policies he had in mind. They were less important perhaps than the process of trial and error that characterized the New Dealers. They were committed to no single theory in their effort to improve standards of living. What set them off from earlier efforts to navigate the road from Depression to recovery was a recognition of the role of government in such efforts. Roosevelt turned his back, wrote Means, "on the classical wisdom. This is the fundamental reform which he made. He rejected the theory that the modern free enterprise system would automatically tend to maintain full employment. He rejected the theory that the unemployed were responsible for their own unemployment, and he rejected the theory that incomes reached through the market system tended to reflect the individual's contribution to production."[6]

Means described this basic shift in government policy in 1960 in an address to Carleton College, the old home of Thorstein Veblen. Less widely shared by New Dealers in the thirties was his further point that Roosevelt's "most basic single reform was that of the monetary system and the establishment of monetary management by government." The gold standard was abandoned and the domestic economy liberated thereby from a rigid relation to the world economy.

Three laws—the Securities Act in 1933, the Securities Exchange Act in 1934, and the Public Utility Holding Company Act in 1935—which Cohen, Corcoran, and Landis had toiled over—had brought about what one lawyer-scholar called the "transformation" of Wall Street's handling of corporate finance.[7] The shift of monetary management from Wall Street to Washington was further accomplished by the Banking Act of 1935. It transferred power over open-market operations from New York to Washington and thus "made monetary management a practical instrument of government."

Tugwell, an enthusiastic evangelist of the Means analysis of the effects of administered prices and the need to do something about them, gave a copy to Marriner Eccles. He had helped bring the Utah banker, an advocate of compensatory spending (although he had never met or read Keynes), into the Administration. Eccles showed no interest in the Means report. That disappointed Tugwell, who behind the scenes was pushing vigorously for modifications of the NRA that would salvage that organization and give the government some say in the movement of prices. He had explained to Averell Harriman, Tugwell noted in his diary,

. . . my feeling that the problem of prices is the one which NRA must at all costs concentrate on and find the solution for. So long as some prices are rigid and some rather flexible, there will continue to be a disparity of purchasing power which will prevent recovery and make difficulty even after recovery comes. Gardiner Means has just completed a very significant study of this question which I recommended that Harriman read.[8]

But the emergence of Eccles indirectly reflected a withdrawal of faith in the feasibility and prospects of the NRA as a planning mechanism. Eyes were beginning to glaze over, Tugwell noted in his diary, when he talked of the planning aspects of the NRA.

There were deep differences, Tugwell believed, "between those of us who thought that industrial relationships and public policy with respect to them needed to have firm public management and those who thought that some fiscal or budgetary management was sufficient."[9] The "spenders," as he called them, wanted a compensated budget and by 1935 the Roosevelt administration could be said to have agreed. "It was still an almost secret addiction," testified Tugwell. "But the President I think was by then convinced and the theory had the momentum of a movement." Keynes's arrogance, he noted, however, had irritated Roosevelt. "He was pretty condescending to Americans," Tugwell remarked, but whatever Roosevelt's feelings about the Englishman, he had influenced the President.

When he [the President] talked with me about Keynes he was inclined to take the line that he had confirmed the New Deal policies but had not added anything. I myself thought he had probably told the President a few useful truths about the gold-buying policy. And I was inclined to feel that Keynes had more success than the rest of us in rounding out for the President the policy as a whole and fitting the parts together. Up to that time I think the President had accepted relief and public works as humanitarian necessities but had not come around to the theory of budgetary management as a major influence on the economy. After Keynes's visit I fancied we heard a good deal less about economy and a balanced budget.

The shift in theory was personalized in the resignation of Lewis Douglas as director of the Budget and the growth in influence of Eccles. Within the Roosevelt administration Douglas was the chief apostle of rigid economies, a balanced budget, and winning the confidence of the business community. "He was always wrong," commented Tugwell a little sourly, for he himself had become the chief target of the Roosevelt-haters, "he represented discredited policies without apology; he hated the New Deal and he affiliated happily with the most reactionary Republicans" for all of which he was awarded the most "honorific" posts. But as events in 1933–34 demonstrated the unreality and wrongness of his solutions, Roosevelt accepted his resignation.

When Roosevelt in October 1935 told Ickes and Hopkins on board the USS *Houston* about Douglas's departure from the Administration, he mimicked the former budget director.[10] He had asked Douglas to defer his resignation in view of the impending 1934 congressional elections. Douglas had refused and, Roosevelt cheerily added, that "notwithstanding the resignation" the election had gone overwhelmingly Democratic.

Into the breach made by Douglas's departure marched not only Keynes as mediated by such advocates as Tugwell and Frankfurter and his followers, but also Eccles and his concept of a deliberately unbalanced budget. The Mormon banker had first been called to Tugwell's attention by Stuart Chase, an iconoclastic and popular writer. Eccles had visited Washington in February 1933, when he lunched with Tugwell in a drugstore booth and set forth his spending views. A few months later Tugwell asked him to return. This time Tugwell took him to meet Wallace and Ezekiel at a meeting interrupted by ringing telephones and insistent secretaries. Eccles, a man who brimmed self-confidence, suggested dinner at his hotel where they might talk quietly and uninterruptedly. Tugwell called later and asked to bring some other guests. They were Harry Hopkins and Jerome Frank.[11]

The New Deal would have many ups and downs in mood but that 1933 autumn the first economic reversal had hit the Administration after the heady success of the "Hundred Days." Recovery, it dawned on the New Dealers, was not about to be achieved as easily as had been hoped. Eccles remembered a conversation at Warm Springs in 1938 during the 1937–38 recession. The President, he recalled, was at his "jovial best," when Mrs. Roosevelt said, "I suppose people will call this 'the second Roosevelt Depression.' "

The President sat upright in his chair. "No, dear," he corrected her, "the first Roosevelt Depression."

"It's the second one," Mrs. Roosevelt insisted.

"With an edge to his voice, the President replied, "The first!"

"But, Franklin," Mrs. Roosevelt said, "aren't you forgetting the Depression in the fall of 1933 after you tried to balance the budget and after the NIRA codes went into effect?"

The President looked to Eccles for help, but since Mrs. Roosevelt's views coincided with the banker's, and he was not the courtier type, he kept his silence.

The policy of deficit financing expounded by Eccles at the Shoreham Hotel dinner recommended itself to his listeners. It refreshed them to hear such views expressed by a successful banker and industrialist. Another Mormon, George Dern, the Secretary of War, took Eccles to see Acheson who was then Under Secretary of the Treasury. The next day Tugwell went with him to call on Ickes. It was all part of an effort, Tugwell later explained, to get him into the Administration. When he could, Tugwell urged him on the President:

I was disappointed when the post went to Henry Morgenthau after Woodin's death. The Morgenthau appointment meant that the Treasury was to be a purely Presidential reserve and so was good in that way. But I had my heart set on Eccles.[12]

Tugwell, however, persuaded Morgenthau to consider Eccles as a possible colleague at Treasury, and in February 1934 Morgenthau named him as a special aide to deal with monetary and credit matters.

As such, Eccles after a talk with Winfield Riefler, the resourceful economist at the Federal Reserve Board and secretary of a cabinet-level committee to devise a housing program, undertook to represent Treasury on that group. Eccles, a hard-nosed banker, helped shift the task force's approach from what he called "social-service-worker thinking," in which public housing and government-financed slum clearance had priority, to a housing program that addressed itself to middle-class needs, in particular through a government guarantee of mortgages and encourage small-home construction. The resultant Federal Housing Act included a provision for a Federal National Mortgage Association—"Fannie Mae"—that was funded by the Reconstruction Finance Corporation. The terms of the guarantee were the work of Frank Watson, one of Tom Corcoran's young lawyers at the RFC who lived at the "Little Red House" with Tom and Ben, and Riefler—the latter had come up, it will be remembered, with the "margin" formula in the framing of the Federal Securities Act.

The housing task force was one of the channels by which Eccles's ideas on deficit spending gained currency among the New Dealers. Eccles's chief argument in the housing task force in favor of a housing program was that government should seek to generate "a maximum degree of private spending through a minimum amount of public spending."[13]

In *Today,* although its editor, Moley, was opposed to deficit spending, Cohen in his review of Warburg's anti-New Deal book, quietly supported the concept. Public works expenditures and unbalanced budgets did not represent waste, he argued. When private enterprise was "timid" in the matter of capital expenditures, "and private capital more so, what real waste is there in the government's giving a stimulus to the interchange of work and services, particularly if that stimulus is likely, if applied in sufficient volume, to stimulate private enterprise and private work?" He did not mention Keynes but Keynesianism was in the air as Eccles was discovering, even though he had not read his books nor met the man.

The Utah banker was an eloquent advocate of Keynesian views, "a better talker than listener," Tugwell later commented a little tartly. At the time, however, he championed Eccles who soon came to have a major impact on United States financial policy. Tugwell had wanted him as Secretary of the Treasury, but when that did not work out "to have him made Governor of the Federal Reserve was next best. We at least had in a post of importance one who understood the compensated budget." That was a great gain even though the banker was indifferent to Tugwell's theory of "conjuncture," that is, that government had to manage prices if equilibrium was to be achieved in the economy.

Morgenthau also had recommended Eccles's appointment as governor of the Federal Reserve Board. Roosevelt and the banker hit it off, agreeing to end the power of the twelve largely autonomous Federal Reserve banks, especially New York's. On November 4, the Roosevelt mandate renewed and strengthened in the off-year congressional elections, Eccles came to a meeting with Roosevelt fortified with the memorandum that led to the Banking Act of 1935. It was the work of Lauchlin Currie, a young Harvard economist who would increasingly figure in the debates among the New Deal thinkers and who was then at the Treasury, a member, said Eccles, of a "Freshman Brain Trust." The memorandum began:

If the monetary mechanism is to be used as an instrument for the promotion of business stability, conscious control and management are essential.

Without that control, experience showed that

the supply of money tends to contract when the rate of spending declines. Thus during the depression the supply of money instead of expanding to moderate the effect of decreased rates of spending contracted, and so intensified the depression. This is one part of the economy in which automatic adjustments tend to have an intensifying rather than a moderating effect.[14]

Unless the Federal Reserve Board acquired the power over open-market operations, it would continue to be unable to determine the volume of money and credit. The memorandum then outlined remedial steps, including the all-important one of vesting the power over open-market operations in the Federal Reserve Board in Washington. For two hours the banker presented the contents of the paper to Roosevelt. His attention "never wavered," says Eccles. "Now and then an electrifying question would shoot out from him." The remedies proposed conformed with Roosevelt's own determination to make Washington not Wall Street the directing authority in the world of money and credit.

"Marriner, that's quite an action program you want," said Roosevelt. He slapped his hands down on the desk in a gesture of acceptance. "It will be a knock-down and drag-out fight to get it through. But we might as well undertake it now as at any other time." A few days later he announced Eccles's appointment as governor of the Federal Reserve Board.[15] The White House press release carefully noted the nominee was a Westerner, a banker and businessman who had been successful even in the years of the Depression. Eccles moved over from Treasury to the Federal Reserve Board and brought with him Lauchlin Currie whom he appointed as assistant director of Research and Studies.

In 1913 Congress had established the Federal Reserve Board thinking it had created the means by which the nation's monetary policy would be subject to government regulation and thereby be guided by the public interest. The Federal Reserve Act was sound in objective, said Roosevelt in 1935, but deficient in means. In February bills that embraced the changes Eccles wanted were introduced in Congress. Most of the financial world opposed them. They argued as usual that they were not needed. Moreover, to weaken the power of the regional Federal Reserve banks would lend the system to political domination by the President. Whatever was needed should be studied further.

Not all economic ills would be cured by monetary policy alone, Eccles explained in his testimony before the Senate Banking and Currency Committee. "I realize that without a properly managed plan of government expenditures and without a system of taxation conducive to a more equitable distribution of income, monetary control is not capable of preventing booms and depressions. But the volume and cost of money had their importance, were the peculiar responsibility of the Federal Reserve System, and it should have machinery to facilitate its exercise of that function."[16] Despite the opposition of the Senate patriarch, Carter Glass of Virginia, ironically the author of the initial act in 1913, the changes passed handily and a new power was born in Washington. Its use would be fitful, its independence of both Congress and the President would be periodically challenged, but the power was there.

The one occasion monetary control was exercised in the thirties proved in hindsight to have been badly timed. "The increase of member bank reserve requirements in the spring of 1937 was a mistake," wrote Professor Leslie Chandler, himself a director of the Philadelphia Reserve Bank, and it helped bring on, as we shall see, the 1937–38 recession.[17]

In the spring of 1935 Eccles's advocacy of compensatory spending seemed to New Dealers more relevant to triggering a recovery than did monetarism. In the Thanksgiving Day 1934 discussions at Warm Springs, Tugwell had noted the President's disposition to shift from direct relief of the unemployed to "a works program which will give employment instead of charity."[18] At Hyde Park over Labor Day he and Harry Hopkins had reinforced the President's inclination in that direction. In the autumn, while Tugwell had been in Europe, Hopkins, Ickes, and Morgenthau had worked up a plan of implementation:

I was very much interested, therefore, to sit with Harry and three of his assistants last night while they put final touches on their proposal for a works scheme. I found at Warm Springs that the only questions the President had in his mind were (1) whether sufficient works could be got underway so that relief might be got rid of in from six to eight months and (2) what proportion of them could be self-liquidating so that the financial scheme we had in mind could be used.

Roosevelt advisers fought sharply among themselves over whether "the works program should pay the prevailing wage, as labor in particular demanded." "I have the gravest doubts about fixing work wages at lower than prevailing rates," Tugwell worried, "but Eccles seems determined on it."

Busy as Eccles was with the Banking Act, he entered a strong plea for the giant $4.5 billion works program that Roosevelt urged in his State of the Union message. Its approval by Congress made the overhaul of the Federal Reserve System even more urgent. Otherwise, private bankers in the regional Reserve banks might be able to block the program by stalling Federal Reserve funding operations. The new Act would prevent that.

There were other hazards to passage of the works bill and its $4.5 billion appropriation, "a staggering sum," as Moley called it in *Today*. "Morgenthau is really opposed, I think, and finds objections but no suggestions," wrote Tugwell. "Ickes and Hopkins are so worried about who is to do the job that they can hardly think of the job itself." The relaxed Warm Springs atmosphere, however, (and this may have been in Roosevelt's mind), eased the clashes. "I played some poker and some golf," said Tugwell, "having not done either for years and years. It was amusing to see Betsy Roosevelt trim the Secretary of the Treasury, the Administrator of Public Works, and the Relief Administrator all at once. She took about $15 away from them."

Progress on the works bill cut athwart an argument among the New Dealers over the new social security legislation. The conflict pitted the Brandeis group against Hopkins and Tugwell. The latter noted in his diary:

The Brandeis group would like everything turned over to the states; the others would like more power left in the Federal government. The President is pretty well committed to the Brandeis point of view and I have had several arguments with him about it, particularly with respect to the kind of tax which it is proposed to impose. The payroll tax seems to me very little better than a sales tax which the President has always opposed. I told him so. I also argued that without a Federal subsidy there would be very little real control by the Federal government. Harry and I argued about this with him for nearly two hours the other day and I doubt whether we made very much impression. I did, however, get from Lubin* several relevant arguments to support the Federal subsidy point of view and sent them over to the President privately.

Tugwell's disagreements with the prevalent line of thought on social security were basic. He argued for a national system of unemployment insurance paid out of income taxes as well as for a system of health insurance.

. . . but the Frankfurter and Brandeis influence on him has just been too strong. They will hold to the principle that the forty-eight states should be used as economic laboratories and they therefore want the Federal government to do as little as possible, overlooking what seems to me to be the great difficulty that with the national spread of big business nothing but a national system would offer adequate protection and sufficient standards.

* Isidor Lubin, commissioner of Labor Statistics in the Department of Labor, a leading New Dealer.

Tugwell thought he and Hopkins agreed, but Edwin E. Witte, the Wisconsin man whom Frances Perkins had selected as executive director of the preparatory committee, later told Tugwell that Hopkins had fallen in line and accepted the preparatory commission's bill. Tugwell and Jerry Frank continued to object, especially to the proposed cooperative federal-state system of unemployment insurance, desiring a national system instead. Wallace, however, overruled them, and Tugwell, as Hopkins had earlier, accepted the decision. "There comes a time in such cases when it is time to stop arguing," commented Tugwell.[19] Both he and Hopkins "wanted a social security system much worse than we wanted our own bill. And when the time came we stopped arguing." Tugwell and Hopkins both regarded the giant works program as "the real effort toward security," and unemployment insurance "a very minor part indeed of the whole problem of work protection in a capitalist system." He did not mention old-age pensions.

Tugwell's sixth sense about when to stop arguing was one of the traits that commended him to Roosevelt. However, he continued to question the ultimate feasibility of a works program that deferred to business sensibilities. "I doubt very much whether, if the government is to keep entirely out of the traditional field of private business, scope enough can be found for employment which will escape criticism on the ground that it is essentially useless."

Tugwell was an adventurous, resourceful thinker, perhaps the outstanding one around Roosevelt, and nowhere more so than in his constant worry about what to do with the ten million who remained without jobs. He chided Roosevelt for sharing a little the conventional moral notion that "people who are unemployed are in a sense bad." It was a continuing discussion between them, not so much of a work ethic in which both believed but of the goals of work.

I told him that I thought his attitude on this had always been wrong and that his insistence upon putting men to work ought not to be so great but that he ought rather to turn it into the channel of advocating public work of a sort in which the profit motive and individual incentive would play no part.

Technological advance had brought the United States to a point where even with the reestablishment of production that gave Americans a high standard of living,

we should still nave perhaps five million unemployed. The problem is to divert sufficient income to their support or to the support of useful civilizing works which will give us some more amenities of life but in which nobody could see any profit.

Roosevelt objected strenuously to Tugwell's "aspersion" on his attempts to put men to work.

He said that we ought to do a lot of this public work by hand methods. He had just been talking to Mayor La Guardia about using more hand labor and less machinery. I told him that that reminded me of a story I had heard of two unemployed men who were watching a steam shovel. One said to the other, "If they did not have those damn machines, we would have a job." The other said, "Yes, and if they did it with spoons a lot more people would have jobs." The President said I was just trying to be clever and reduce the thing to an absurdity, but I had evidently made my point, because he was much disturbed about it.

He had reduced the theory to an absurdity, Tugwell agreed, but he wanted to make the point that there was no limit to the amount of work that could be done to improve the community. "There is only a limit to the amount of work which may be done in making suitable goods which people will buy or can buy. Therefore it is entirely legitimate to create work in the sense that you do public improvements which the business system will not undertake . . ."

The big bill passed. "Of course, the worst handicap under this program will be the old difficulty of finding work to do which does not compete with private industries in ways which will bring terrible pressures and reactions against us as we try to work," mused Tugwell. Second only to Hopkins, the job of finding such projects was his—Roosevelt by executive order made him administrator of the Resettlement Administration. It was funded out of the work relief bill.[20]

With the work bill passed and social security on the point of approval by Congress, Roosevelt prepared to speak to the country in his first 1935 Fireside Chat. Moley came down to work with Tugwell on the speech. "We did not succeed in changing the speech as much as we would have liked," recorded Tugwell, "and I thought it was one of his poorest speeches . . ."[21] Whatever its shortcomings, it did incorporate Tugwell's belief that social security was a protection for the future, whereas the immediate necessities of the unemployed were faced in "the most comprehensive work plan in the history of the Nation."

There was a significant omission in the Fireside Chat. It did not refer to compensatory spending. Despite Eccles's advocacy, it was, as Tugwell suggested, "a secret addiction." Moley's distaste for the theory may explain why. He had written in *Today* on the eve of the work bill's passage:

It should be repeated over and over in every business conference that the Keynes theory of pump-priming so far as the recovery effort is concerned is dead. The time has passed for a trial of it.

Part of Moley's hostility no doubt was political, designed to disarm the conservatives who indicated they were ready to make the spending issue a major impeachment of Roosevelt in the 1936 campaign. But a part was also due to Moley's acceptance of the business point of view that its confidence was only to be recaptured by an end to public spending and an indication by the President of a wish to balance the budget as rapidly as possible. Roosevelt's State of the Union message before Congress had promised to make 1935 "a genuine period of good feeling," but as Moley noted with some mordancy, the year was to prove "a period of growing bitterness, of gradual insistence by the President upon the passage of such a gorge of indigestible measures that the New Deal itself was completely transformed."

This judgment, which appeared in 1939 in *After Seven Years,* measured Moley's own shift in values. It contrasted with Moley's almost lyrical approval in *Today* of Roosevelt's leadership in the 1935 session under the caption "Congress Keeps the Faith."

Tugwell, whose values did not shift, breakfasted with Moley after Congress approved the $4.5 billion work bill and wrote happily, "A considerable change seems to be coming over Washington after the confusion and hesitancy of the last few weeks. Everyone seems to have taken new courage now that the work relief set-up has been determined."[22]

Passage of the work relief bill had intensified the rivalry between Ickes and Hopkins over their share in its administration. He ought not to resign, Corcoran had advised Ickes, who was upset over reports of the allocation of responsibilities in the pending bill.[23] "He said I was the last hope of the progressives in the Administration." Tom was helping the secretary in other ways. In April his revered Justice Holmes had died. Tom drafted the five-minute tribute that Ickes delivered over the Columbia radio network. When Ickes gave a dinner for the "progressive crowd," Tom and Ben were there, Tom with his accordion. Above all, Tom, and by implication Ben, sided with Ickes in his struggle with Hopkins. "Everyone seems to agree that Hopkins is deliberately planning to discredit and undermine PWA so that he will have the expenditure of all of the four billion dollars," Ickes recorded in his diary after Tom had come to him. The principals were called to Hyde Park to discuss a reallocation of funds in the big appropriation. "Hopkins has finally convinced him," wrote Ickes desperately, "that the goal ought to be to put men to work, regardless of what they were being put to work at, and if there is no legitimate work, to put them to work notwithstanding."

Moley might try to reassure the business community that the giant work relief appropriation signified no genuflection in the direction of Keynesian pump priming, but that was precisely what, in addition to its humanitarian aspect, it portended.

In 1985 Nobelist Paul A. Samuelson, one of "the men who brought Keynesian ideas to Americans," as Galbraith put it, with "his pioneering textbook" *Economics,* brought out a twelfth edition of that work which he co-authored with Professor William D. Nordhaus.[24] At its first appearance in 1948 Galbraith had correctly predicted "the next generation of Americans would learn its economics from this work." There was little questioning of its influence. The latest edition sought to strike a balance between monetarism and Keynesianism, and it concluded, "Money definitely matters. In their early enthusiasm about the role of fiscal policy, many Keynesians unjustifiably downgraded the role of money. However, strict monetarism swings the pendulum too far in the opposite direction. Other things than money matter." Keynesians were "too confident about the predictability of the economy," and some of them "were nonchalant about inflation—just as some monetarists badly underestimated the social and economic costs required to wring inflation out of the economy."

Monetary and fiscal policy as instruments of management became more important as ways "of reconciling price stability, maximum product and minimum unemployment," wrote Galbraith, as wage and price controls moved "out of bounds."

They came opportunely in 1935 for in the spring months NRA received its quietus from the Supreme Court. Tugwell lunched with the President on the White House porch in early May. Conversation started out on the subject of a European war and Tugwell discovered "that the President feels about it as I do that European war is likely to happen within a few years . . ."[25] The date May 8, 1935, indicated how early in his administration Roosevelt grasped the likelihood of war in Europe and how little this comprehension had to do with domestic political considerations.

The two men also talked about a Supreme Court decision that had ruled the Railway Pension Act unconstitutional on grounds of too large a delegation of power. "We both agreed [it] will probably mean that the Court will declare the NRA Act unconstitutional in the pending case." Tugwell seemed reconciled to its demise. He had long abandoned his original hope the NRA might serve as the central coordinating and planning mechanism in America's industrial economy. If the Court did invalidate it, "I pointed out that we have a campaign issue for the President's campaign which is really ready-made."

But it was not the Court alone that stood in the way of Tugwell's dream of a government management and planning mechanism.

Certainly I have detected traces of polite boredom and mild impatience when I have continued to urge my own view that under intelligent State control it should be possible to introduce a planned flexibility into the congestion and rigidity of our outdated economic system. Yet this polite, shall I call it sales-resistance, on the part of some of my colleagues is nothing compared to the water-tight mentality of some of the progressives I know. The Progressive theme song is, "I'll tell you about *my* panacea but you won't tell me about *your* panacea."

XVIII

———————————

The
Eclipse of Tugwell

"We shall have to ask for a Constitutional amendment to get a mandate on it and it seems to me that a better campaign issue could not be devised."[1] So wrote Tugwell in his diary a few weeks before the Supreme Court undid the NRA. He had talked with the President and both men were resigned to an adverse decision. By then almost all the New Dealers realized that the NRA through its codes had become a captive of industry and, though many supporters of Frankfurter as well as of Tugwell still hoped to salvage it by reforms, the possibility of an adverse Supreme Court ruling no longer seemed the disaster it once did.

Conservative Democrats will fall away, Tugwell anticipated, as a result of a drive for a constitutional amendment; "still if we are to extend what we have called the New Deal, there seems to be no way out of a constitutional amendment which would prevent a reactionary court from stopping our further progress."

Frankfurter and his people had a better understanding than did Tugwell of the nature of the judicial process and system. They feared the amendment route and tried to delay a showdown with the Court through some of Corcoran's friends who were in the high command of the legal division of the NRA, in particular Blackwell "Blacky" Smith, whom Tom had helped persuade to leave Cotton Franklin for the NRA.[2]

In the spring of 1935 Frankfurter and Corcoran still believed the NRA could be administratively "reformed," and if not challenged in the courts could work itself out of trouble. But a federal district court in the South sustained just such a challenge to the NRA's code-making authority. It ruled that it involved an unconstitutional delegation of congressional power to an executive agency. Tom did not consider it "an important jurisdiction or an important case," but it worried the NRA high command. Uncontested, the ruling might encourage more challenges of code enforcement. The NRA decided it had to carry a favorable case up to the Supreme Court. It picked a countercase to the *Belcher* ruling, one in which the respected Judge Learned Hand of the Second Circuit Court of Appeals had upheld the government, *United States v. Schechter Poultry Corporation,* the "sick chicken case" as it came to be known.[3] Corcoran backed by Frankfurter tried to delay the appeal. But Blacky and the NRA leaders were adamant. The people in the NRA were "entitled to make some mistakes for themselves," Blackwell Smith protested to Tom. "I think now that the decision has been made to go up on the *Schechter* case, the whole gang ought to put their shoulders to the wheel and try to make a success of it. This includes trying to warm up the Oracle [Felix Frankfurter] to the proposition that he should not be unhelpful to a major project when actually under way."[4]

None of this moved Frankfurter. He had come to distrust Donald Richberg who had taken control of the NRA after Hugh Johnson's resignation. Frankfurter thought Richberg, despite his labor credentials, had abandoned his New Deal views, he told Ickes, and become "a real danger" to the Administration.[5] Roosevelt was away from Washington on a fishing trip in the Caribbean, but Richberg wired and asked that he approve taking the *Schechter* case to the Supreme Court. Roosevelt scrawled on the radiogram, TELL RICHBERG TALK WITH CUMMINGS ABOUT EXPEDITING NRA CASE.

Blacky's arguments that a decision had been taken did not deter Corcoran any more than they did Frankfurter. "I believed that this was the wrong case to bring before the Court . . . He [Frankfurter] privately warned me that it was the wrong one to do battle over" and "flatly predicted the Court would rule against the government if this case came before it . . . Frankfurter didn't tell me—and I was too prudent to ask—why he believed what he did. Perhaps Brandeis had told him . . ."[6]

Tom, who was a nominal assistant to the Attorney General in connection with cases growing out of challenges to the Public Utility Holding Company Bill, sent his own wire to Roosevelt:

F.F. CALLED. HAS LEARNED VERY VERY CONFIDENTIALLY CUMMINGS UNDER URGING OF RICHBERG TO SILENCE CRITICISM OF *Belcher* dismissal and pursuant to wire from you intends announcing to press this afternoon that government will immediately expedite to Supreme Court NRA case from Second Circuit in New York involving Poultry Code. F.F. suggests most impolitic and dangerous to yield to antagonistic press clamor* now because fundamental situation on Court not changed. Further suggests you wire Cummings not to take hasty action and hold situation on NRA appeals in abeyance until you return. Suggest at that time thorough discussion in presence of all concerned.

Roosevelt, according to Cummings, respected the Attorney General's "almost uncanny judgment as to what cases to press and what cases to postpone."[7] Nevertheless, after Corcoran's alert, he had fired off a message to the Attorney General, the President told Corcoran, to hold up the appeal but it had arrived too late. Corcoran did not know what had happened. Cummings resented Frankfurter's being a "super attorney general," he believed. That was a factor. Moreover, Cummings had once considered Frankfurter a rival for the job. Though Cummings never brought up the matter of Corcoran's going over his head, Tom sensed from then on a studied aloofness in his attitude. "Gentlemen tend to ignore insubordinate subordinates if they can't fire them outright."

It was no surprise, therefore, that a month after Corcoran's wire to Roosevelt, Roosevelt and Tugwell should have assumed the *Schechter* case would bring on a constitutional crisis. Roosevelt's hunch about the fate of the NRA had also been fed by the hostile questions in the arguments that preceded decision the justices had put to Stanley Reed, the Solicitor General, and Donald Richberg, the head of the NRA, who had joined him to argue the case. The questions boded ill on three main points:

whether the purchase, sale and slaughter of kosher poultry in the New York City market represented articles in interstate commerce and subject therefore to Congress's power to regulate such commerce;
were the hours and wages of the *schochtim* (slaughterers) an aspect of interstate or intrastate commerce (and subject therefore only to state regulation);
whether Congress has the right to delegate that authority to the Executive?

The Court handed down its rulings on May 27—"Black Monday" as it came to be called. First it unanimously held that Roosevelt had exceeded

* The American Liberty League and the National Association of Manufacturers, backed by allies in the Senate and press, were denouncing the government's unwillingness, implicit in its successful move to have the *Belcher* case dismissed, to test the constitutionality of the Act.

his authority over the regulatory agencies in his removal of William E. Humphreys, a contumacious Republican member of the Federal Trade Commission. Then Justice Brandeis read a unanimous opinion that overthrew the New Deal's Frazier-Lemke Act which sought to protect farmers against mortgage foreclosures. And, most important, it ruled unanimously against the government in the *Schechter* case. This decision was read by Chief Justice Hughes, a bearded jurist of majestic mien. New Dealer Paul Freund, a lawyer for the government and former Brandeis clerk, recalled the moment when Hughes paused and stated, "Defendants do not sell poultry in interstate commerce." Freund remembered how "Richberg literally slumped in his chair; he seemed crushed." Hughes dismissed the government's invocation of a World War I analogy to the Depression as an unprecedented emergency that justified extraordinary remedies. "Extraordinary conditions do not create or enlarge constitutional power," he declared.

The government had been aware that its assumption that Congress had the right to delegate even limited legislative authority to the Executive which in turn gave it to the code-making groups was the weakest point in its argument.[8] "Unfortunately, you were quite correct in your anticipation that 'delegation' was the 'hot spot' of the argument," Frankfurter had cautioned Reed as the government prepared its case.[9] It could not be seriously contended, ruled Hughes, that "Congress could delegate its legislative authority to trade or industrial associations or groups so as to empower them to enact the laws they deem to be wise and beneficient for the rehabilitation and expansion of their trade or industries." And, having held that the poultry-slaughtering business was not a part of interstate commerce, it followed that the regulation of wages and hours in that business could not be justified by an appeal to the rights of Congress under the commerce clause.

Cohen and Corcoran sat in the old Senate chamber where the Court met and heard the chief justice's words of doom. Unlike Richberg, they were ready for them. "But we'd expected a split decision; this one was unanimous," recalled Corcoran.[10] That depressed them and when a message came, after the justices filed out, that they should meet Justice Brandeis in the robing room, any pleasure at being summoned to the inner sanctum, as Corcoran thought of it, was overtaken by a sense of foreboding. Both venerated Brandeis and were quite willing to consider themselves his "little soldiers," as he sometimes called them. "If Holmes had the visage of an eagle," Tom thought, "Brandeis appeared a condor—a tall, long-limbed creature with a fleshless beak of a nose and glaring eyes."[11] He was not a handsome man. "He didn't need to be because his intellect was blinding to a kid like me."

That day as he and Ben entered the robing room and the justice stood with his arms aloft to have his gown removed, he looked to Tom like "an avenging angel."

The Justice was visibly excited and deeply agitated. "You have heard," he gasped, "our three decisions. They change everything. The Court was unanimous. Hughes delivered the NRA opinion; Sutherland the Humphreys opinion; and I the Frazier-Lemke opinion. You must phone Felix and have him down in the morning to talk to the President. You must see that Felix understands the situation and explains it to the President. You must also explain it to the men Felix brought into the Government. They must understand that these three decisions change everything. The President has been living in a fool's paradise."

"But, Sir," Tom interposed, "I understand that the Court's remarks on interstate commerce may seriously impair the holding company legislation."

"I am not familiar with the various pieces of legislation," replied the Justice, "but I should not be surprised if everything would have to be redrafted. The President has been living in a fool's paradise. The Court unanimously has held that these broad powers cannot be exercised over matters within the States. All the powers of the States cannot be centralized in the Federal Government. The Federal Commissions exercise quasi-legislative and quasi-judicial powers. We have over-ruled much of what was said in the Meyers Case, and restricted the decisions to purely executive officers—officers performing ministerial acts which the President himself might perform if he had the time.

"Make sure that Felix is here in the morning to advise the President. The matter is of the highest importance. Everything that you (the administration) have been doing must be changed. Everything must be considered most carefully in light of these decisions by an unanimous Court."

Tom's account of the justice's message was more colorful:

"Without a preamble, he said, 'You go back and tell your President that this Court has told him it is not going to permit the centralization of power in big industrial leaders from the federal government which his advisors are imposing upon this country. He is overcentralizing this country with his planning and you are to tell him so because I have told you so. Furthermore, as far as you yourself are concerned—and you know my affection for you—I warn you to send back to the states all those bright young men you have brought to Washington. It is in the states where they are needed and it is in the government of the states where they belong.' "

Felix took the train to Washington. Before repairing to the White House he met with Ben and Tom. On the typescript of Ben's notes of the session with Brandeis, Felix wrote, "Given to me by B.V.C. in Washington on Tuesday, May 28, 1935."

"Today was a bad day for the Government in the Supreme Court," Cummings, who had overridden Frankfurter's advice to delay, wrote in his diary.[12] In the *Schechter* case it had gone "the whole distance and knocked out the codes and even went to the point of indicating that even if it had been passed by Congress itself and no question of delegation had been involved, nevertheless, it would have been unconstitutional and void . . . If this decision stands and is not met in some way, it is going to be impossible for the Government to devise any system which will effectively deal with the disorganized industries of the country . . ." Everyone was talking about a constitutional amendment, Cummings concluded, "or other methods of endeavoring to prevent the Supreme Court from thwarting the purposes of the people, as expressed through their representatives."

Cummings studied the rulings all afternoon and at five-thirty was summoned to the White House where he joined Richberg and Reed in a two-hour conference with the President. The disaster no longer seemed so awful. "Personally I cannot help but feel that, while in a certain sense they are a set-back for America," the Attorney General noted, "they are a God-send for the Administration." Much of the criticism of the NRA had been justified, he felt. "Now that the NRA has been practically destroyed, we shall hear more about the value of the things destroyed." When he went over to the White House at nine the next evening, Frankfurter was with the President "and we three talked for about an hour and a half."

Tugwell, although busy with the establishment of the Resettlement Administration, kept in touch with the President's reaction to the Court's ruling on the NRA. He had spent an evening with Ray Moley the previous week. "We also talked at breakfast the next morning and I outlined to him my notion that the campaign in 1936 ought to be run on the issue of a constitutional amendment." Moley was interested, although Tugwell predicted that "the Frankfurter-Brandeis group will not want any extension of federal power and will oppose any amendment which permits it."[13]

The Supreme Court's decision was "a good deal worse" than Tugwell had anticipated. And when he saw the President he was in a fighting mood and felt exactly as Tugwell did "that we faced a great crisis which must be met head on."

The stock market had plunged after the decision and the President was besieged "by all the people who were fighting NRA before to save them from industrial chaos." The President had to draw the issue clearly, Tugwell emphasized, patch up the NRA, and affirm his intention to seek a constitutional amendment in the campaign and settle the question once and for all:

Certain it is that the wings of the Supreme Court must definitely be clipped. They cannot tell the Executive how to manage the country in crises of this kind. What I am afraid of is that powers will be so dispersed that no crisis can be met and we will fall into a kind of chaos . . . We are all of course disappointed at the unanimity of the decision. We thought that people like Cardozo and Brandeis, or perhaps not Brandeis but at least Cardozo and Stone would go along with us, making economic rather than legal tests of the situation . . .

Tugwell and Hopkins went to see the President. "He seems to think we can tackle the question [of industrial management] by way of labor and conditions of work which seems to me to be starting at entirely the wrong end." The President disagreed with Tugwell's strategy of amending the Constitution; so did Hopkins. The influence of Frankfurter had prevailed, Tugwell believed. The President was indifferent to any overall mechanism of control and regulation, though he was interested in the possibility of designating one commodity after the other as public utilities and subject, therefore, to regulation. Tugwell doubted the Supreme Court would permit that.

While we were talking Felix Frankfurter came in and I had some little private talk with him. He admitted that we needed a constitutional amendment but thought that we had to have some more adverse Supreme Court decision before we get to it, on very much more popular issues. I pointed out to him how fundamental the decisions were and he admitted all that, but felt that this was not the time to tackle or to begin discussion on a constitutional amendment. The opinion of everyone seems to be against me on this and I am afraid the New Deal is going to lie down and take this political decision as the final direction in which we must go for the next year until we get some more decisions which make a constitutional amendment seem obvious to the whole country . . .

By Friday of that hectic week, the thirty-first, the President had mastered the legal complexities sufficiently to expound them nationwide and in a two-hour session with reporters took the country to school on the meaning of the Court's rulings. He began by reading from the telegrams sent by businessmen who had appealed to him to do something to rescue them from the decision's consequences. As for the decision itself, it was "more important than any decision probably since the Dred Scott case." He dealt with the Court's refusal to acknowledge that the 1933 emergency made any difference on how Congress sought to cope with the crisis. Yet a great deal of the 1917 wartime legislation, he noted, "was far more violative of the strict interpretation of the Constitution than any legislation that was passed in 1933," and had not been challenged.[14]

The Court did indicate, Roosevelt noted, that the delegation of legislative power might be overcome in a rewritten act. Its interpretation of the interstate commerce clause, however, which limited its application "to goods in transit and nothing else," was a reading of that clause fit for "the horse and buggy age" when the Constitution was written and not for present-day civilization.

We are interdependent—we are tied in together, and the hope has been that we could, through a period of years, interpret the interstate commerce clause of the Constitution in the light of these new things that have come to the country.

Did the Court's narrow interpretation of the commerce clause "mean that the United States Government had no control over any national economic problem?" he asked rhetorically. He underscored the central issue. "Is the United States going to decide, are the people of this Country going to decide, that their Federal Government shall in the future have no right under any implied power or any Court-approved power to enter into a solution of a national economic problem, but that the national economic problem must be decided only by the States or move on to national solutions of economic and social problems that were national in scope?" The Supreme Court's decision had faced the country with "the biggest question" outside of the time of war, "and, as I say, it may take five or ten years to decide it."

Was there any way to decide the question, an alert reporter asked, without a constitutional amendment? "Oh yes, I think so," the President said firmly. But how could it be done, the reporter came back, except by amendment? "No, we haven't gotten to that yet," the President ended the session.

Several correspondents, reported the Washington representative of *Today,* called the President's "horse-and-buggy" press conference, "the most remarkable they ever attended," but its impact on the country was disappointing.

From the press conference the President went into a Cabinet meeting. Afterward Ickes wrote, ". . . we have to meet this issue or abandon any effort to better the social and economic conditions of the people . . . I shall welcome an opportunity to write and speak on this issue." One of Ickes's aides went to see Brandeis at the justice's request. He brought back word that the justice thought "the President is making a great mistake in taking the position he has on this issue. I do not agree with this point of view."

Tugwell also received a report on the justice's view. It came from young Milo Perkins, a liberal Texan who had gone to work for Wallace. For fifteen minutes the justice had held forth fervently on the "horrors of bigness and the sanctity of littleness in *all* fields of human activity." The placement of men in jobs that called for superhuman abilities ruined people and their power to think creatively. He advised Perkins to go back to Texas, "to the country, where the real movement to reshape America would originate." Perkins did not doubt Brandeis's commitment to greater happiness for the average man. "Here is a grand old man who really feels that he is helping people," but whose mind narrows when his "pet convictions" take over. "He is determined to break up federal power," Tugwell wrote in his diary on reading Perkins's memorandum.

Brandeis's advice to the Administration via several intermediaries not to get into a head-on clash with the Court's narrow interpretation of the commerce clause did not stop the New Dealers. "The decision means one thing," wrote Moley.[15] The Administration had to seek its welfare and regulatory objectives through a Constitutional amendment "and not through a distortion of the words 'interstate commerce' or any other words that have been used to enable legislation for one purpose to be enacted under a clause of the Constitution clearly intended to cover something else." He followed up the next week with an editorial, "Let the election of 1936 be a great and solemn referendum" on the issue of an amendment to extend federal power. The phrase "great and solemn referendum" had last been used by Woodrow Wilson in the ill-fated effort to overturn the Senate's rejection of the League of Nations, Walter Lippmann reminded him, and called Moley's proposal "A Way to Commit Suicide."[16] He challenged Moley to put his proposed amendment in words. That was a "rhetorical strategem," replied Moley. The Court had been right in the *Schechter* case to hold the NRA unconstitutional as the Constitution then read. So it had to be amended. Lippmann, he insisted, was opposed to a constitutional amendment because he was opposed to federal efforts to regulate economic life. But he did not try to formulate his amendment in words.

Moley's vulnerability was his narrow interpretation of the commerce clause, Lippmann came back. He assumed "the commerce clause is a perfectly precise grant of power. I do not think it is or ever has been." The *Schechter* opinion should not be read as meaning "the end of growth in constitutional power." He cited Thomas Reed Powell's view in *Fortune* that Congress was now compelled to return to a "slower, more considered, more particularistic legislative approach." The Administration, noted Lippmann, was having trouble in fixing a wage for unemployed relief workers. How much more gargantuan was the job of trying to use federal compulsion to do so with the nation's wages, hours, prices, and production?

Walter Lippmann immediately saw the significance of the NRA's demise for New Deal efforts to master the Depression. "If anything has been demonstrated in this depression which can be relied upon as a guide to policy, it is that reflation—not planning, not regimentation, and not laissez-faire—is the remedy." The great advantage of fiscal policy was that it "effects only the general purchasing power of the nation, and can be administered without detailed intervention in each man's affairs." Nor did Lippmann consider the NRA's end a tragedy. "The power to fix the wages paid for killing chickens is negligible and would be totally unnecessary and would not even be desired, if the great power to stabilize the total purchasing power of the nation were properly used." Moley stood his ground. He preferred "a very careful amendment," he declared in an editorial, "The Constitution as an Issue." But despite the views of Moley and Tugwell in favor of making the pending election a referendum on the Constitution, Roosevelt, although determined to end the Supreme Court's blockade of positive, popular government, had not decided on the route he would travel. "The President avoided very carefully in Cabinet meeting talking about the Constitution at all," Tugwell recorded June 5, "and he really let nobody know where he was going and I don't suppose there are three of us in Washington who do know. I know because of my rather intimate talks with him that what he is hoping is that the true situation will sink into the consciousness of the country so he will be able to get a constitutional amendment within a few years."

Others in Washington saw the problem of how to handle the Court's blockade a little differently from Tugwell. In November a district judge in Baltimore at the instance of the utility companies had ruled the Public Utility Holding Company Act unconstitutional while in Louisville a district judge upheld another New Deal measure, the Guffey Coal Act. All of which, said Cummings at a Cabinet meeting, reminded him "of what Mr. Justice Hughes said when he was Governor of New York, namely, that 'we live under a Constitutional Government, but the Constitution is what the Judges say it is.'"[17] It was not far from that conception of the Court's powers to the notion that the simplest way to go was to change the composition and tenure of the judges by statutory action. That, indeed, was where Cummings was heading.

Ickes lunched with the President in November.[18] "We fell to discussing the attitude of the Supreme Court on New Deal legislation, and I asked the President whether any one of the present Justices was going to retire and give him a chance to appoint some liberals. He said he did not think so, and he went on to say that Justice Brandeis, as he got older, was losing sight of fundamentals. I asked him what Frankfurter thought of Brandeis's changed attitude and he said that he was broken-hearted over it and did not like to discuss it."

At that time Roosevelt was exploring the possibility of a constitutional amendment that would give Congress the power to overrule a judicial veto. While "the matter could not be discussed now," that is, before the 1936 elections, reported Ickes, the President saw the Court's challenge as analogous to that confronted by Lloyd George who had threatened to create several hundred new peers, enough to outvote the existing House of Lords, if it continued to refuse his bill on Irish autonomy which had been passed by the House of Commons.

As 1935 drew to a close and a presidential election year impended, the political situation had changed. Huey Long, the potential third-party candidate whom Roosevelt feared most, had been assassinated in Louisiana. When James Farley met the President in Charleston at the end of a deep-sea fishing trip on the USS *Houston,* he told Ickes, who along with Hopkins had accompanied the President, that if Long had lived he would have polled some six million votes.[19] "I always laughed Huey off, but I did not feel that way about him. He was good for that many votes."

Huey's removal from the political scene diminished the thunder from the left. So did the huge relief appropriation as well as the inauguration of the Social Security system with the appointment of Gil Winant, a progressive New England governor, as director. Roosevelt with a successful legislative program behind him proclaimed "a breathing spell." This delighted Moley, but Tugwell, the sole survivor in the Administration of "the bigness boys," as "Unofficial Observer" [John 'Jay Franklin' Carter] called them, was unhappy.

On the evening of the Gridiron Dinner in mid-December, Tugwell held a small dinner of progressives at his house. To it he invited Phil and Bob La Follette, Floyd Olson, the governor of Minnesota, Representative Maury Maverick, a Texas liberal, Mayor La Guardia of New York City, A. A. Berle, Jerry Frank, and James Landis.[20] "It has no purpose," his invitation read, "except to pose the question: What are we going to do with the permanently unemployed? Not that we can answer it, or do much about it if we could, but we can at least discuss the situation."

But events were overtaking Tugwell and his solution. Ickes had wanted Tugwell as his under secretary when he left Agriculture but at the end of November Ickes noted in his diary, "There seems to be a pretty general feeling that Rex Tugwell will soon be out of the Government. He has been under terrific attack lately on account of a speech he made in Los Angeles, excerpts of which did not look as if he had been wise."[21] The speech on "The Progressive Task Today and Tomorrow" intensified a conservative clamor for the dismissal of "Comrade" Tugwell, as the Hearst editorialists put it. As the 1936 campaign began Tugwell faded from the White House scene. Farley advised Roosevelt that Tugwell should stay out of sight. "We had no defenders," said Tugwell of the conservative attacks on the Resettlement Administration and himself in the campaign, "and we were told to keep quiet ourselves."

"The lines are slowly drawing here," wrote Berle to H. G. Wells on receipt of his little book *The Shape of Things to Come,* "for a political-intellectual conflict exceeding in bitterness that which revolved around Wilson after Versailles."[22] Berle sympathized with Tugwell's efforts to tame "bigness" to public purposes. The success of the large corporation on the production side was indisputable—it "can be a good servant," he said. But the opposite school, the "atomizers" was in the ascendant, so Tugwell, who in Berle's view "yearned for quiet," resigned. Berle considered this parting with Roosevelt "inevitable. A statesman, or if you choose, a politician, necessarily practices the art of the possible during his term of office. When compelled to leave aside great and social visions with which he agrees, and with them their chief advocates, the politician is neither deserting a friend nor betraying a principle. He is merely practicing his profession, as he is bound to do . . . Roosevelt knew and appreciated Tugwell's quality. He also knew that Tugwell's ideas were not generally held, let along likely to attract votes either at the ballot box or in Congress."

Tugwell, a man of class and intellect quietly resigned. His elimination brought no satisfaction to Cohen and Corcoran. "When Tugwell left," Ben said to Tom, "we're in danger now," meaning, he explained to an interviewer, "there was no one to the left of us to take the heat."[23]

More fundamentally, Tugwell's resignation meant that in the clash of ideas among the New Dealers, Tugwell's notions of a planned capitalist economy were overtaken by Keynesianism. And in the vanguard of those Keynesians who were not economists were Corcoran, Cohen, and their mentor Frankfurter. A profile of Cohen was prepared in February 1935 at the offices of *Today*—Celeste Jedel may have had a hand in it—and sent to Corcoran for revision. He edited it carefully. But the article never appeared.[24] The explanation, perhaps, was in the article which declared, "Mr. Cohen is not well known, and does not care to be."

The well-informed piece linked Ben's Zionist experiences in London in the establishment of a Jewish National Home in Palestine with his work in the New Deal.

The enthusiasm stirred in the Jewish people by the Balfour declaration and the Palestine Mandate resulted in intense advocacy of idealistic proposals for planning on a grandiose scale. One of Mr. Cohen's tasks was to listen to all such plans and sift out and work through the practicality of those which held any common-sense promise. It was a job of maneuver and compromise of conflicting ideas. His associates have heard him say that the Palestine macrocosm offered him a prototype for almost every individual and every proposal he has met in the vastly larger scene of present-day Washington.

A sense of reality convinced him of the impracticality of planning too closely the detailed future of even a small and homogeneous country. While believing in safeguards against exploitation and erratic speculative movements, he came to have little sympathy for those who try to force the economic activities of a whole people into fixed grooves.

In considering the many proposals for the colonization of Palestine, Ben, said the article, felt their advocates should be free to go ahead "but only at their own risk, and with their own funds."

This is much his cautious attitude toward planning proposals for the American economy. His intimates know him to be deeply sympathetic toward new ideas and a believer in continual experimentation. But while recognizing the broadening social and economic influence of government he is too much of an individualist, too conservative in one sense and too much of an experimentalist in another, to want to see the economic life of any community completely tied up with, and at the risk of the man-made judgments of any omnipotent organization, whether public or private.

If his political beliefs could be reduced to a single sentence it would be: he is equally fearful of both a super-state and of a private socialism of super industry.

The article ended: "He is a friend of the British economist John Maynard Keynes, leans toward the Keynesian spending theory and generally comes as close to the old-fashioned pre-depression liberalism of the elder La Follette as you can get these days."

Tugwell also had cut his political teeth as a La Follette progressive, pasting the senator's photograph in his freshman album and preferring him to Theodore Roosevelt. While the economic perceptions of Cohen and Corcoran diverged from those of Tugwell, especially on issues of collectivism and planning, Tugwell sometimes called it the "composed order," they were united in the realization that a key, perhaps *the* key, to recovery was an upsurge in consumer purchasing power.

At the end of Tugwell's diary entry after the Court upset the NRA, he wrote: ". . . the issue is drawn very clearly, it seems to me, between lawyers and those who take an economic view of the situation."[25]

But the dichotomy was not at all that clear. Frankfurter's "hot dogs," whom some of the newspapers also lithographed in pink, had moved into the foreground and they indeed were lawyers, but like Brandeis, they understood economics as well as politics and were uniquely equipped to help Roosevelt in the great constitutional crisis that now had burst upon the country.

XIX

The 1936 Mandate

The 1936 presidential campaign was the first in which Corcoran and Cohen were involved in a major way. It was the first Roosevelt campaign also without Louis Howe, the wizened Gray Eminence who lay dying in the White House. His intimate knowledge of the regular party organization matched Roosevelt's and had helped keep the tempestuous amalgam of regulars and New Dealers together in the first term. Until Harry Hopkins moved into the White House in 1940 no one tried to fill Howe's place but Corcoran's White House assignments became more frequent including liaison with and assistance to Moley with Roosevelt's speeches. At one time Howe and Moley had been rivals for pride of place among Roosevelt's counselors but Moley's departure from the Administration after the London Economic Conference had eased Howe's jealousies. "Once out of government," said Cohen, "even though he [Moley] came down weekly, it was difficult for the continuity of his work with Roosevelt to be maintained."[1]

"Franklin's on his own now," the fading Howe told a visitor in regard to the impending election. The President "would have to run his own campaign," Steve Early told Ickes.[2] The latter considered that "too much of a load for him to carry . . ." but Roosevelt, an old hand at party politics, welcomed the added responsibilities of election strategist as well as implementer. The 1936 campaign became peculiarly his.

Despite the urgings of Moley and Tugwell, Roosevelt was counseled on the constitutional issue chiefly by Frankfurter, avoided making the election a referendum on a constitutional amendment. Moley attributed the breakup between the President and himself, which came to a head in the first six months of 1936, to differences over how to approach the campaign, including the opposition's attacks on the President for dictatorial aspirations and a readiness to subvert the Court and the Constitution. Moley judged Roosevelt's approach not as political strategy but as a sign of Roosevelt's growing megalomania. Was it the President's plan, Moley asked himself, to get "a blank check from the American people—a mandate, not to the party, or a party platform, but to himself?"[3] Why had he abandoned Moley's advice that business be given a "breathing spell?" Why did he welcome the hatred of business and the press? When he used the word "leadership" did he really mean "the maintenance of his own ascendancy" with which he identified the cause of progressivism?

Such questions, according to Moley, welled up in him beginning with the draft that he prepared for Roosevelt's annual message to Congress. Roosevelt requested, "A fighting speech." "He got it," said Moley who "alternately loathed and excused himself" for writing it. In that January 3 message Roosevelt summed up the past thirty-four months of his administration. "We have returned the control of the Federal Government to the city of Washington."[4] The "new instruments of public power," in the hands of "a people's Government," were "wholesome and proper," but wielded by an "economic autocracy," he warned, would "provide shackles for the liberties of the people."

In accordance with Roosevelt's strategy, the speech said nothing about the Constitution or the Court. On January 6, however, in the *United States v. Butler* case, the Court overturned the AAA. This time the Court was not unanimous. An adverse opinion had been expected by Roosevelt and his legal advisers, but the violence of the majority's views, as read by Justice Owen Roberts, startled them. Corcoran recalled that in the hearings that preceded decision, Justice McReynolds, whom Corcoran considered "the nastiest of the President's critics," took the lead and "so viciously abused" Solicitor General Stanley Reed who defended the AAA that Corcoran's "old friend . . . almost physically was compelled to stop his argument." Congress did not, under the Constitution, asserted Roberts, have the power to impose processing taxes.[5]

Justice Harlan Fiske Stone, writing also for Brandeis and Cardozo, in dissenting, raised the central issue—the Court should not impose its own political and economic views on the nation. "Courts are not the only agency of government that must be assumed to have the capacity to govern," and the Executive and Congress were within their rights under the

Constitution to assert that "the power to spend and tax includes the power to relieve a nationwide economic maladjustment by gifts of money."[6]

Two days later the President addressed the Jackson Day dinner. Although he identified the "basic issue" before the nation as the "retention of popular government," he was silent about the Court's implicit attack on it in its AAA ruling, a lack of comment that was noticed and which he defended by an unwillingness to rush to judge two of the "most momentous opinions, the majority opinion and the minority opinion, that have ever been rendered," by the Supreme Court.[7] There was more to his silence than a desire not to seem impatient.

"Please resist all—say nothing," Steve Early, his press secretary, implored him, mindful of the disappointing reaction to his "horse and buggy" session with the press.[8] Avoid confrontation had been Brandeis's advice after the NRA decision. Roosevelt's faith in the jurist had begun to waver but others said the same. Roosevelt loyalists like Frank Walker begged him to assure the country that he accepted the decisions of the Supreme Court as a matter of orderly government, however disagreeable such decisions were. Within Roosevelt's cabinet, opinion was divided. Ickes, its most militantly, progressive member, was strong for a head-on clash with the Court. Frances Perkins, equally progressive, if more benign in demeanor, in Ickes's scornful words, thought "that we ought to pussy-foot on the Supreme Court issues" and then added slurringly, even for a diarist of the thirties, "that was to be expected of a woman."

Behind the scenes feelings ran high. "They know not what they do, these bunnies of the Court," Frankfurter in Cambridge wrote Landis who had succeeded Joe Kennedy as head of the SEC.[9] But after the *Colgate v. Harvey* decision, "the most indefensible decision on any court in my lifetime," the Court no longer held surprises for Frankfurter. There the Court majority, just before the AAA ruling, had overturned a Vermont taxation bill, invoking the Constitution's "immunities and privileges" clause in order to set itself up, said Stone in his dissent, as a "superlegislature." "We are intellectually outraged here," wrote Thomas Reed Powell, the constitutional scholar at Harvard. "Henry Hart [professor at Harvard Law School and former Brandeis law clerk] told me," said Frankfurter's letter to Landis, "that he found me much more calm and philosophic than Tom Powell on reading the AAA opinion . . . It is a great comfort, however, that Stone has put in memorable language the ultimate issue regarding the Court's responsibility and behavior."

"The President told me," noted the Attorney General in his diary, "that Mr. Frankfurter remarked that the Supreme Court seemed to be taking 'slow poison,' and I reminded him that Mr. Hughes said, in his book some years ago, that the Court had chiefly suffered from self-inflicted wounds."[10] At the White House Judicial Reception, the President said loudly to Stone so that Roberts might hear him, "I am glad that you taught me law," in a reference to his studies at Columbia Law School after Harvard. Although Stone had drawn the issue that underlay "the real Constitutional struggle," as Cummings termed it, the President this time kept a studied silence.

Roosevelt ought to seek substitute legislation for the outlawed NRA and AAA, advised Frankfurter, without "any concession to the rightness of the majority opinion," but not stoke up "legal controversy with the majority." Instead, Frankfurter urged "quiet" education of the public mind to the significance of the two opinions.[11] Roosevelt needed no urging to use the presidency as a "bully pulpit," Theodore Roosevelt's phrase that FDR also invoked. Few leaders had shown an equal mastery of the synchronization of public education with governmental action.

The real significance of his preference for the advice that Frankfurter, abetted by Corcoran and Cohen, was giving him in the constitutional crisis, over that being proferred by Moley, rested in the differing recommendations on how to meet that crisis in the election campaign. "Go slowly and you will carry the Court with you" was the advice of Frankfurter and his friends.[12] Incrementalism, trial and error, and patience marked their approach. Against Administration voices that urged immediate confrontation with the Court in bringing cases to trial, Frankfurter and his youthful allies urged caution. A lower court in Kentucky denied the government the right to condemn property for a low-cost housing project. The President, backed by Ickes, wanted to go ahead and seek a ruling in the Supreme Court. The government should seek to have the case dismissed, Corcoran and Cohen urged Ickes. Otherwise the government would lose, they predicted, and the adverse ruling would not help to build up the body of opinion against the Court they were seeking.

The government had made a major mistake in choosing to let the NRA which "unpopular, badly administered and under revision in Congress itself," wrote Corcoran, "come before the Court ahead of the AAA. I am convinced that up until the time of the NRA, the reactionary Justices were not sure of how far they dared to go, or how broadly they dared to talk."[13] If instead of the NRA, the AAA, "popular with the public, well-administered and deemed worthy of defense by a savage minority on the Court itself, had come up first," it might have been killed, but not "in the sweeping terms they later used." However, the country's "roar of approval" for the ending of the NRA "nerved" the Court's reactionaries for "the succession of outrageous murders they perpetrated later on."

The Constitution would grow in time, the attitude and personnel of the Court could be changed. Such was the advice Frankfurter, Corcoran, and Cohen were giving Roosevelt. Ben wrote a speech for Senator Wheeler to give on the floor of the Senate that winter. The Court should be mindful, it said, "that the country will not submit to denial of powers that the Constitution conferred on Government." Great abuses invited great changes. "If the Court does not mend its ways, it will be faced with changes it does not like." Wheeler never got to deliver the speech, nor did Cohen's proposal for an act of Congress ever surface. This would have stated that "if at any time a majority of the Court should be composed of members over seventy, the President would appoint such additional judges as may be necessary to give the Court a majority of members under seventy."[14]

The President had his own approach to clipping the Court's wings through congressional action, as he explained to Ickes. This would give Congress the right to override Court vetoes of congressional statutes. But first he wanted the Court to impeach itself in the eyes of the public by a "clean sweep of all New Deal legislation." Not "enough people" had as yet been touched by the Court's adverse rulings "to make a sufficient feeling on a Supreme Court issue."

Where the Supreme Court led, the lower courts followed. "At no time in the country's history," wrote Frankfurter and Adrian S. Fisher in the *Harvard Law Review,* "was there a more voluminous outpouring of judicial rulings in restraint of rights of Congress than the body of decisions in which the lower courts, in varying degrees, invalidated every measure deemed appropriate by Congress for grappling with the great depression."[15]

David Lilienthal reflected the despairing mood of the New Dealers in the face of the judicial usurpation of power. When in February the Court in *Ashwander v. Tennessee Valley Authority* ruled the TVA did have the power to construct a dam for purposes of national defense and to contract with the Alabama Power Company for the sale of "surplus power," Lilienthal sighed with relief. "I had completely resigned myself to a bad decision, only holding out hope that we would have some crumb of comfort in that unlike AAA and NRA we would not be swept completely out to sea, bag and baggage."[16] But two months later Justice Sutherland, writing for the majority, rebuked the SEC for allegedly star chamber investigatory procedures. In May it severely diminished the government's ability to regulate the coal industry, overturning the Guffey-Snyder Coal Act. Then in the final case of the term by a vote of 5 to 4 it ruled unconstitutional New York State's minimum wage law. That statute had been drafted by Cohen and Frankfurter to get around the prohibitions on national minimum wage action that had been imposed by the Court in its 1923 *Adkins* ruling.

"We finished the term of Court yesterday. I think in many ways one of the most disastrous in history," wrote Justice Stone.[17] Roosevelt departed from his silence on the issues of Court and Constitution just enough to comment:

It seems to be fairly clear, as a result of this decision and former decisions, using this question of minimum wage as an example of that "no-man's land" where no Government—State or Federal—can function is being more clearly defined. A State cannot do it, and the Federal Government cannot do it. I think from the layman's point of view, that is the easiest way of putting it and about all we can say on it.[18]

The President, however, refused to be drawn out on the issue of how the situation might be met. "I think that is about all there is to say on it." Many methods for dealing with the constitutional crisis were being proposed to him. More than forty proposals had been introduced in Congress. Some dealt with the size of the Court, others proposed an increase in the number of votes needed to rule legislation unconstitutional, still others focused on retirement plans for aged justices.[19]

The Administration's selection of any one plan might have multiplied division and confusion. Silence drew the issue more effectively than speeches. Roosevelt's opposition did it for him. January 1936 was the heyday of the American Liberty League. Its most illustrious recruit was former Governor Alfred E. Smith who before an audience at the Hotel Mayflower on January 25 that, the New York *Times* reported, "represented either through principals or attorneys, a large portion of the capitalist wealth of this country," compared the New Deal to socialism and hinted he might be "taking a walk." Edward I. Roddan, former White House correspondent for the International News Service and now an employee of the Democratic National Committee, conferred with Roosevelt and effectively stamped the League as a "Millionaires' Union." But as for the President directly, "I am keeping very quiet in regard to Al Smith . . ." By the end of February, Moley editorialized in *Today* that the Republican Party was disenchanted with the league. "All that the Liberty League has done (and this applies particularly to the Al Smith dinner) has been to stamp upon the opposition to Roosevelt the label of big money and big business."

The headlines went to Al Smith and his wealthy backers. More discerning observers did not consider their attack the "real struggle." The old Wilsonian progressive and publicist, Norman Hapgood, sent Roosevelt a Lippmann column to the effect that the basic cleavage in the Democratic Party was not between the Al Smith crowd and the New Deal but between the antimonopoly philosophy and the collectivist approach. Hapgood agreed. He saw two philosophies within the New Deal, "both wishing to curb the power of the plutocracy . . ." Hapgood recalled a dinner of New Dealers in early New Deal days where Tugwell had said, "I do not see why your crowd and ours cannot work together," and then had added, "but not Brandeis."

Roosevelt disagreed with Hapgood.[20] He disliked the frame of mind that talked of "your group" and "my group" among liberals. Where most theorists saw polarities and irreconcilable schools of thought, he saw compromises to be arranged, opponents to be reconciled, supporters to be held. In regard to monopolies, Roosevelt wrote Hapgood, "Brandeis is one thousand percent right in principle but in certain fields there must be a guiding or restraining hand of government because of the very nature of the specific field." "Too many cooks," wrote "Unofficial Observer," Jay Franklin Carter, in *Today.* He characterized the struggle among the New Dealers as between the "Bigness Boys" and the "Little Ones." It was "ludicrous" for "witch-sniffing Tories" to group Tugwell and Corcoran as brothers under the skin. "The two theories have only one thing in common; a socially responsible determination to wrest the major control of the American economy from the big financiers." And that essentially was Roosevelt's theme in the approaching election.

The attack on the Roosevelt administration by right-wing Republicans and the American Liberty League as a socialist plot to transform the federal government into a personal dictatorship was "pure political moonshine," wrote Berle, who kept in close touch with the Administration.

"Nationwide thinking, nationwide planning and nationwide action are the three great essentials to prevent nationwide crises," Roosevelt stressed at the end of April at the Thomas Jefferson Dinner,[21] but he did not say how he proposed to meet the refusal of a Court majority to allow such action by the executive and the legislature. "What we do seek is a greater purchasing power and a reasonably stable and constant price level . . ." the speech went on, but he again declined to go into methods.

To the disaffected Moley such generalizations were added proof that Roosevelt was still "trying to reconcile the idea of industrial self-rule under government supervision," which Moley favored, "with the big-business-is-bad-business philosophy." The Jefferson Day speech on economic objectives, in Moley's opinion, "turned out, unfortunately, not to be fish, flesh, or fowl."[22] Thus Roosevelt's pragmatism, his unwillingness to become the prisoner of any one school of thought, which in the view of a New Dealer like Ben Cohen was a commendable approach to public affairs where the answers often could be seen only "darkly," was for Moley an indictment.

Privately, New Dealers were asking themselves hard questions after the death of the NRA. They were embodied in a ninety-page memorandum, written by Leon Henderson, a bulky, bellicose man and first-rate economist, on "the present status of competition." His analysis was based upon his experience as economic adviser of the National Recovery Administration. It was written at the request of Senator Robert J. Bulkley, chairman of the Senate Committee on Manufacturers, and circulated, as was much of Henderson's work, to top New Dealers like Cohen and Tom Blaisdell.

An examination of the "operating characteristics" of American industry, wrote Henderson, immediately posed the central problem of "what is the status of competition?"[23] Concentration of economic power in industry had increased; administered prices had contributed to the rigidity of prices and the curtailment of production; other nations had accepted some measure of "controlled competition." Further inquiry, which he recommended, would shed light on such questions as whether the American economy was "self-adjusting"; can capacity operation be attained under present conditions; how serious was the threat of fascism through economic dictatorship; what techniques and policies "will best promote maximum production at moderate prices with full employment?"

The memorandum foreshadowed the turn in New Deal thinking from Tugwell's emphasis on planning and collectivism to anti-trust, or, as Brandeis had once called it, "regulated competition," but the issue did not surface in the campaign, except that Corcoran arranged to have Henderson involved in the presidential election on a full-time basis. The Democratic National Committee's appointment of him as economic adviser was a significant step forward in the empowerment of "genuine economists in government decision making."

Was Moley right in wanting Roosevelt to go to the electorate in 1936 with some form of amendment to the Constitution addressed to the judicial blockade and with an economic program in which he opted between trustbusters and collectivists, and thus get a "mandate" for his answers? Such questions are not wholly answerable. Presidential candidates often campaign on platforms of seemingly firm promises, only to abandon them when confronted by national necessities in office. Roosevelt, the experimentalist, faced a different problem. He genuinely did not know the answers. The Court had to be curbed; that was clear. How he should do it was less so, except to try to shape his reelection in a way that in voting for him the voters would say they wanted the situation to be met. The competitive system of private enterprise could function better but he was not ready to commit himself to any one way of doing it except to have the voters make it clear through his reelection that they wanted corporate power made responsive to the public interest. His silences as well as declarations shaped the agenda for the 1936 campaign.

At Little Rock, Arkansas, just before the nominating conventions, he skirmished with the "constitutionalists" as his opponents dubbed themselves.[24] They were pressing him to propose an amendment. His speech there suggested the possibilities for federal action within the terms of the Constitution as written. He spoke of the Louisiana Purchase which had been negotiated by direction of President Jefferson through the U.S. Minister to France, Robert L. Livingston, a kinsman. Jefferson had

the courage, the backbone, to act for the benefit of the United States without the full and unanimous approval of every member of the legal profession. Indeed, he was told by some of his closest advisers and friends that the Constitution of the United States contained no clause specifically authorizing him to purchase or acquire additional territory; and he was told that because specific authorization did not exist under that great Charter of Government, none could be exercised. Jefferson replied that there were certain qualities of sovereignty which could not be separated from the Federal Government, if such a Federal Government was to endure; and furthermore he told them that if he delayed, the Emperor of the French might change his mind and the great territory west of the Mississippi River would be lost forever to American expansion. He and Robert R. Livingston and James Madison put the treaty through; and the next Congress appropriated the money to pay for it; and, my friends, nobody carried the case to the Supreme Court.

Roosevelt then moved on to Texas to celebrate the centenary of its independence from Mexico where he again sounded the themes of nation-mindedness, the need of people to see beyond the borders of their own states, of consumers and producers to recognize their interdependence, and of the need for national action to control malefactors who sought refuge within state lines.

In early 1936, Moley, increasingly at odds with Roosevelt and the New Deal, welcomed the news of the addition to Roosevelt's basic speech-writing team that had consisted of himself, Judge Rosenman, and Corcoran, of Stanley High. The latter was brought in by Steve Early, perhaps as a counterweight to Corcoran of whom he was jealous. At least so Tom thought. The forty-one-year-old High was well-connected in Protestant circles, having been a secretary of the Methodist Board of Foreign Missions. He also had been an editor of a Prohibition daily and had worked for Hoover in the 1932 campaign. But New Dealers did not make a fetish of party regularity and found him a likable and effective coiner of phrases. "I held no brief for Corcoran as against High," wrote Moley. "Possibly they would make a good team. My one concern was to inch out of my responsibilities without a fuss." As the convention approached, Roosevelt as he had in the past turned to Moley for help with the speeches. But their sessions together now often resulted in arguments, including a "nightmarish" wrangle, as Moley later described it, on the decks of the *Potomac* one May weekend.[25] Finally when Corcoran came to Moley for help on Roosevelt's acceptance speech, he said no. The refusal stunned Corcoran. The President's approach to the campaign differed from his own, Moley explained. "Go along, anyhow," Corcoran pleaded. He could slip his own notes of moderation into Roosevelt's texts. But as Moley was discovering, and that was the root of his clashes with the President, he was allowed to write the music only if it fitted the themes set by the President. But for Corcoran, an underling, he had pious words of admonition. A speechwriter's function was "to serve Roosevelt's ideas . . . you're a clerk, not a statesman." He had spoken impulsively, an abashed Corcoran said, and Moley agreed to look over what Corcoran had written, even dictate a few suggestions. "Rough notes for suggestions for acceptance speech by Corcoran and Professor Moley," the resulting nine-page draft said.

Despite his brushes with Moley, Roosevelt asked him and Judge Rosenman to come down to Washington to help with the various writing chores at the time of the Democratic Convention in Philadelphia. A cordial President greeted Moley.[26] "I want the speech to be only fifteen minutes long," he said. Moley inwardly smiled as he thought of the lengthy draft Corcoran had shown him at the Mayflower. He did not know that Roosevelt also had set Rosenman and High to work on a first draft. Moley and Corcoran left the White House, returned to the Mayflower, wrote several pages and then came back to the White House for dinner. The others who were in the small family dining room were Missy, High, and Rosenman. "High twitted Moley on his rich friends," said an informed account of the dinner, and the "President took up the chaffing." Moley grew furious, Roosevelt angry, the others embarrassed. It was the only time, wrote Rosenman, "I saw the President forget himself as a gentleman." As Moley and Corcoran walked back from the White House to the Mayflower, Moley ruefully commented on the fate of those who served kings. When it suited Charles I's purpose in his fight with Parliament to sign the death warrant of his loyal servitor, the Earl of Stafford, who had carried out his autocratic orders, he did so. "That's what happens with Kings—they exact complete loyalty from you but they never can afford to give you complete loyalty, personal loyalty in return—all promises of kings are presumptive and all of us and you have seen it tonight, Tommy, all of us are presumptively liquidable." Although when the two met the next morning, the tension had abated, the breach would prove to have been final.

Roosevelt handed the Moley-Corcoran draft that was conciliatory and moderate to Rosenman and High to weave together with their version which, said Rosenman, was "militant and bare-fisted."

Roosevelt put more "fire" in it, Moley later wrote, "eliminating a long passage on cooperation [with business] and inserting in its place a diatribe about 'economic royalists,' 'new economic dynasties thirsting for power,' 'economic tyranny.' " How much was Rosenman and High, how much Roosevelt is unclear, but it was what Roosevelt wanted. The verbiage left Moley "wholly unmoved." But what seemed to Moley fustian was the guiding concept of Roosevelt's campaign. Moley's old partner in the Brains Trust, A. A. Berle summed up the essence of the Roosevelt revolution in a 1964 review of a book on Tugwell which, in the language of the lawyer and scholar, made the same point Roosevelt was making in the 1936 campaign:

The New Deal did intend to make so-called "private enterprise" and the property involved in it ultimately responsive to the decisions of a democratically elected political state . . . The New Deal and its intellectuals also considered that private property . . . had not, and intended that it should not have, constitutionally (let alone divinely) guaranteed privileges of economic decision making beyond the control of democratic political decision and without responsibility for social result.[27]

The platform adopted at Philadelphia bore the President's stamp as deeply as did his acceptance speech. Since early June Cohen and Corcoran had been helping with it. And as June arrived, Frankfurter sent his version of four thousand words to Roosevelt. A noteworthy feature of his draft was its silence on the amendment issue in accordance with his view "no amendment—what we need is that the Constitution be properly interpreted."

Senator Wagner who was to be chairman of the Convention Resolutions Committee also took a hand. He was being helped by his former legislative aide, Simon Rifkind. Tom brought Felix a first Wagner draft as it came "from Rifkind's hands." Usually diplomatic, Frankfurter exploded. It was "wishy-washy, uninspiring mush . . . This draft has no inspiration, no generalized philosophy, no call to arms."[28]

Roosevelt carefully marked up the Frankfurter draft but he knew what he wanted. He had Wagner come in. Missy was there as were Rosenman, High, Ambassador Bullitt, and Assistant Attorney General Dickinson. He asked for a shorter, simpler document, one that began as the Declaration of Independence had. "We hold these truths to be self-evident . . ." He handed over a sheaf of drafts and suggestions to High and Rosenman to do the job. They worked all night and Roosevelt liked the result. He read it to Donald Richberg who pulled out of his pocket a statement on the Supreme Court. It pledged the party to seek a "clarifying amendment" in the event pressing problems could not be solved within the Constitution. When Corcoran and Cohen heard about this addition from Moley with whom they were having dinner, they sought, unsuccessfully, to have it changed.

Roosevelt tried the draft out on his Cabinet. "His idea is," recorded Ickes, "that instead of having the conventional platform containing planks on every subject under the sun, a short declaration of principle, not to exceed 2,000 words, be adopted. There is a swing to his draft."[29] Hopkins was even more enthusiastic. The platform was "certain to be regarded as one of America's greatest political documents," he wrote Wagner. Roosevelt had it framed to hang on his wall.

Roosevelt's short acceptance speech focused on "the small group [that] had concentrated into their own hands an almost complete control over other people's property, other people's money, other people's labor—other people's lives . . ." They were "economic royalists"—the phrase was High's—who constituted a "new despotism." "The royalists of the economic order have conceded that political freedom was the business of Government, but they have maintained that economic slavery was nobody's business. They granted that the Government could protect its citizens in their right to vote but they denied that the Government could do anything to protect the citizen in his right to work and his right to live." The 1929 collapse had shown up this new despotism for what it was, the 1932 election had been a mandate to end its power, and "under that mandate it is being ended."

Sam Beer, a young Rhodes scholar fresh out of Balliol, had come to Corcoran via Frankfurter and Harold Laski.[30] How Roosevelt loved the phrase "economic royalists" and how he "rolled it off in great style," he recalled. The vivid metaphor caught and fused the concept of those who controlled great wealth in the twentieth century with those who exercised royal authority in the eighteenth. That was the controlling image that Roosevelt was trying to project onto the election and Philadelphia was a fitting place to give it national currency and it matched the convention's mood. The acceptance speech that he heard as a young man, wrote Beer forty-three years later, when he was a distinguished professor at Harvard, "faithfully reflected the moving half-formed purpose of the New Deal to create a new balance of economic power."

Franklin Field where Roosevelt delivered it was jammed with a hundred thousand roaring, applauding listeners. The huge crowd fell silent as Roosevelt launched into his peroration. "Governments can err. Presidents do make mistakes but the immortal Dante tells us that divine justice weights the sins of the cold-blooded and the sins of the warm-hearted in different scales." Corcoran's father hearing it over the radio detected Tom's Dante studies in that quotation. And he was right. Roosevelt's final words were another Corcoran inspiration. He had read somewhere in Walter Lippmann the phrase "appointment with destiny." That would not do. The opposition might throw it back as "appointment with the dentist." So Tom suggested "rendezvous with destiny." That too bothered the speech-writing team because it recalled Rupert Brooke's "rendezvous with death at some appointed barricade." But Ray Moley argued for it. Moley had "a fine Irish feeling for words," said Tom, and the consensus of the group was to put the phrase in the speech "with all its risks."

"The greatest political speech I have ever heard," wrote Ickes. Roosevelt has stated "the fundamental issue . . . whether we are to have real freedom for the mass of the people, not only political but economic, or whether we are to be governed by a small group of economic overlords.[31]

"I would have to support him even if he should fire me," concluded Ickes, who had recently threatened to resign over differences with Hopkins and Wallace.

Tom and Ben were at Franklin Field. They were becoming mainstays of Roosevelt's campaign organization. They wrote speeches for others in the Administration besides Roosevelt. These ranged from Aubrey Williams, the militant head of the National Youth Administration (NYA), to Joseph Kennedy, the financier, and John Cudahy, who was our ambassador to Poland. Corcoran had "warmth and wit and a keen and exuberant mind," noted Rosenman who saw a good deal of him and Ben in the campaign.[32] "Ben was more resourceful, a more careful and astute lawyer and a more philosophical thinker—but shy and reserved and constantly in the background." Each was devoted to the other and would "claim that the other was the more important member of the team." Ben stayed away from sessions at the White House and preferred to work in his office, but Tom was everywhere "ready to do almost anything to advance the program."

One of Tom's assignments was to pick up a check from John L. Lewis. Neither Roosevelt nor the leader of the miners thought it prudent for him to appear at the White House. So Roosevelt asked Tom to go to his head-quarters and fetch the check, which, said Tom, was for $465,000.[33]

When old Roosevelt hands like Judge Rosenman wanted to know what the younger New Dealers were thinking, or if the campaign train needed a memo on some specific issue, they turned to the two. They understood Roosevelt's approach. He did not want to be the prisoner of any one school of thought or any single co-worker, Ben realized. He liked to have people around him with different ideas "so that he could see how their ideas worked, what groups were attracted and would support them and what ideas were impractical from the point of view of political support."

Tom's study of Roosevelt emphasized other qualities, his enormous vitality, "carefree courage, the ebullience of his spirits. The President liked him, Tom thought, because he, too, had style and he was a "good editor," who gave shape to the flow of contributions, from Cabinet members and others, that came in for each speech. Moreover, he edited Roosevelt's drafts for their literary flavor, gave them, Ben said, "a lilt." Holmes had taught him that the secret of spoken style was "sound . . . particularly when the sound was to be delivered in Roosevelt's exquisite tenor." A pharmacist's mate would swab Roosevelt's nasal passages before each broadcast. "So far as the sound of his voice was concerned, Roosevelt looked upon a speech with the same care that a prima donna would take care of her voice before a singing appearance."

Corcoran enjoyed the exciting experience of being at the center of the creation of power. He relished the speechwriting and he even enjoyed raising money. He and Ben were "backup men" at the "base camp." Their chief job was to feed the campaign train which usually meant Sam Rosenman who traveled with the President. "There was constant communication between the train and Ben and myself" and their job was to prepare speech material to fit the particular circumstances of a particular whistle-stop.

There were others at the base camp—notably Stanley High with whom, according to some accounts, Tom was soon at loggerheads—but in addition, there were young men and women, mostly lawyers, but also some economists and political scientists who became part of the speech and research operation. Sam Beer was at work on a handbook that showed how the charge of bolshevism had been raised against previous reform efforts in American history, reforms that later became part of the American way. The material became urgent in the face of the opposition's increasing resort to the Communist smear tactic. Hearst was a particular sinner, all of his newspapers carrying front-page, double-width column messages from him, such as:

Wherefore let me say that I have not stated at any time whether the President willingly or unwillingly received the support of the Karl Marx Socialists, the Frankfurter radicals, Communists and anarchists, the Tugwell Bolsheviks and the Richberg revolutionists which constitute the bulk of his following.
I have simply said and shown that he does receive the support of these enemies of the American system of Government, and that he has done his best to deserve the support of all such disturbing and destructive elements.[34]

It is doubtful those attacks had much impact, but Tom's shop could not be sure and answers were prepared. Others besides Beer were at work on lists of hostile questions that were asked about Administration policies and personnel. Elizabeth Wheeler, a strong researcher as well as a senator's daughter, compiled one of these. James Rowe, who had been Justice Holmes's last secretary, another. Tom sent them over to Gerard D. Reilly, an assistant solicitor at the Department of Labor, to assemble the answers from the various departments and agencies. Others worked for Ben, especially Joseph Rauh, who was waiting to clerk for Justice Cardozo.

Roosevelt spent the July weeks after the convention sailing Down East with three of his sons as crew. Then there were "non-political" appearances, first to inspect the inundated flood areas in the East and later that summer on "a journey of husbandry" to the drought-ravaged Great Plains states. "Husbandry was a lovely word," said Tom who had contributed it —"He had been taking care of the nation's affairs like a shepherd tending his flock."[35]

The Labor Day weekend the speech-writing team was at Hyde Park. Judge Rosenman and High had their wives there, and Tom brought Peggy Dowd. They blocked out the major speeches that had to be prepared. Roosevelt decided to invite up Moley and, to avoid hurting his feelings at the sight of all the speech writing going on without his participation, had Mrs. Roosevelt lodge the others over at Val-Kill, two miles east of the Hudson River house. The reconciliation did not come off. Roosevelt liberals were losing their interest in Moley. Tom wrote Felix lamenting Moley's editorial "glorification" of General Franco and his Foreign Legionnaires. "I know what I think Celeste [Jedel] ought to do."[36] "Poor, dear Ray," Felix scribbled in return. "Landon is a gift," he added, as the Republic candidate proved to be neither a crowd stirrer nor a political strategist.

The immediate reason for the speech writer's presence at Hyde Park that Labor Day weekend was a Fireside Chat that Roosevelt delivered on the eve of Labor Day. Its first part stressed the indispensable help the federal government was giving to the drought areas that he had just visited. Federal assistance included emergency work projects for farmers as well as production loans that led into a defense of government spending for industrial employment. "Pump priming," and "compensatory spending" were not mentioned but were the essence of the last part of the speech which had been Tom's responsibility. "Government orders were the backlog of heavy industry; Government wages turned over and over again to make consumer purchasing power and to sustain every merchant in the community . . . Government spending has saved," Roosevelt said. Tom had talked with Felix about that section of the speech. Then Henry Morgenthau, the Secretary of the Treasury had called. He hoped Tom would not rip up the section of the speech he had contributed. The Secretary suggested Tom accompany him after breakfast to the Treasury building. "I guarantee to keep him ill at ease with exquisite courtesy all the way from N Street to the Treasury," Tom wrote Felix. "How my 'Sir' will purr! And would you prefer his left or his right kidney?"

Tom cleared with Missy on this speech.[37] He had spoken with Morgenthau, he informed her, and was seeing Herbert Gaston of the Treasury that night to see "if we can rework the Employment Service material" to "hitch-on" to the report on the drought area "and lighten it up for the end of a long radio speech. I hope I'm not superarrogating!" The next day he sent Missy, "Herewith a complete new draft, as worked out jointly with Gaston." A penciled note on top of the speech said that the "unemployment position" had been drafted by Treasury and "cleared by the labor leaders, Lewis, Green and McGrady." The draft "peters out at the end," Tom's note to Missy concluded. "It's 4 a.m. and my perorator ain't working very well."

Roosevelt delivered his first formal campaign speech at the end of September to the Democratic State Convention in Syracuse, New York, where he denounced the "many false issues," the "red herrings," the opposition was raising, in particular the effort to make "Communism an issue in the campaign."[38] To this he not only gave the lie but, declared, "I have not sought, I do not seek, I repudiate the support of the Communists," and sounding the Macaulay theme of enlightened British conservatism, "Reform if you would preserve," underscored what his administration had done to reduce the "widespread economic maladjustment" which gave rise to communism. In twenty-three "campaign" addresses after Syracuse, and more than forty informal, whistle-stop remarks, he dwelt on his accomplishments and elucidated his objectives, never mentioning Court or Constitution nor the feuds between NRA collectivists and Brandeisian trustbusters, Keynesian spenders and the budget balancers. He carried out what Frankfurter in June had agreed should be his purpose, to charge the emotions of the American people "with the conviction that you are the only dependable instrument for pushing forward their hopes and justifying their confidence."

Chicago was one of those "tidal waves of humanity" scenes as Senate Majority Leader Joseph Robinson described the campaign outpourings. It had special meaning for Tom, for Roosevelt decided he should join the train for the major speech on the economy that was to be given in Chicago. The speech contrasted the previous Administration's inaction with Roosevelt's "deliberate acceptance of Government responsibility to save business" but warned of concentration of the "less than two hundred huge corporations" that controlled half of the nation's industrial wealth. "The struggle against private monopoly is a struggle for, and not against, American business . . ." Roosevelt did not say what he intended to do against monopolies, but so pitched his speech that the voters in voting for him would be endorsing a continuance of that struggle. It was, wrote Rosenman, the best speech on the western campaign swing.[39]

For Tom to be on the Presidential Special was to be close to heaven. "I was allowed to sit in the car from which the President would appear on the rear platform" at each whistle-stop and confer with the local leader as well as speak briefly. When the last such leader had gotten off the train and they settled down to go over the text of the Chicago speech, Roosevelt asked him, "Tommy, did you learn anything about politics today?" One thing had puzzled him, Tom replied. He was certain that every local leader left the train "with the idea that if you are elected, he would become an assistant secretary of Agriculture." Had he really promised? an amused President replied. Roosevelt had not made a "precise promise" but every leader had left with the impression that he was going to be.

"And he said, 'Yes; I had hoped that would happen.' "

But what would he do?—Tom did not mean to be impertinent—"How do you make a decision after you're elected, to whom would you keep what they thought was a promise and you knew perfectly well was not a promise?"

"And he laughed and said; 'That's the difference between being a campaigner and a President and furthermore, it's one of the problems of the Presidency.' "

"And I said, 'Well, how do you resolve it?' "

"He said, 'You give the job to the fellow who will make the most trouble if he doesn't get it.' "[40]

Roosevelt in Chicago put into political rhetoric what the New Deal economists were thinking. Confident of Roosevelt's victory as well as the economic upturn, some of them met at the home of Reserve Board chairman Eccles. Isadore Lubin, Frances Perkins's commissioner of Labor Statistics, who had heard Roosevelt's acceptance speech in the company of Corcoran and Cohen worried lest "the present upturn of the business cycle will have worked itself out by 1940, and we would be faced with another depression."

The nation was "midway on the road to full recovery and it appeared that pump priming had been a success," Lauchlin Currie, who was at the meeting, wrote in a memorandum at the Federal Reserve Board.[41]

The Republicans in the last-minute desperation that afflicts most campaigns inspired a "pay envelope" drive in which many employers warned their workers they might never get back their Social Security contributions. An angry Roosevelt told his speech-writing group, which at the end of the campaign still consisted of Rosenman, Corcoran, Cohen, and High, to take off their gloves for his windup speech at Madison Square Garden. They gave him what he wanted including a few phrases that brought the roaring crowd to its feet:

Never before in all our history have these forces been so united against one candidate as they stand today. They are unanimous in their hate for me—and I welcome their hatred.

I should like to have it said of my first Administration that in it the forces of selfishness and lust for power met their match. I should like to have it said of my second Administration that in it these forces have met their master.

Tom left the Madison Square Garden meeting in the company of Emil Hurja of the Democratic National Committee. Hurja asked, "Tommy, is that your line—next term they'll find their master?"

"No, that's Stanley High's . . . the so-called punch-line man."

"Well I have a hunch that punch is going to hurt the President more than it is going to help him. I accept the President's judgment as the best we have but for myself, I wish he hadn't felt he had to say that."[42]

Tom, Sam, and Stanley were at Hyde Park on election night to hear the returns. Corcoran played the accordion. That had become a staple of Roosevelt entertainments. As Roosevelt sat at the dining room table keeping tally, the returns flooded in. Toward midnight Roosevelt's Hyde Park neighbors, red flares in their hands, a band at their head, paraded down the driveway and Roosevelt and his family went out to greet them. Two grandchildren watched from windows above.

His landslide was the largest in American history, 27,476,673 to Landon's 16,679,583.

"What a responsibility for one man to carry," Eleanor Roosevelt wrote in "My Day," and then in a letter from Kansas City, for, with the election over she was off on one of her lecture swings, she wrote FDR, "You should hear the messages that come to us everywhere, by letter, by wire, by telephone! You could be a king or a dictator and they'd fight for you! Lucky you have no ambitions!"[43]

Corcoran's prominence in the campaign, and insiders realized that also meant Cohen's, with the disappearance of Moley and Tugwell, elevated the two into the leadership of the three to four hundred New Dealers who, in effect, constituted a liberal party within a party. Whatever discipline this group accepted was the spontaneous agreement of a shared point of view but the only organization they had came from the leadership of Corcoran and Cohen whose preeminence they recognized.

"The unofficial party whip of the New Deal," wrote Lauchlin Currie, "was Tom Corcoran," and "insofar as the New Deal had an intellectual coordinator and keeper of its conscience, it was Ben Cohen."[44]

"For four years—from 1936 to 1940," wrote Rosenman, "I would say that they were as intimate and important a part of the Administration as any Cabinet officer or Presidential adviser—and much more so than most of them."

XX

———————⟫ʗ ʗ⟪———————

The New Chief Advisers

Roosevelt's use of other peoples' minds, wrote Stanley High shortly after Roosevelt's landslide victory in the 1936 elections, is what makes the role of presidential adviser to him of unusual importance. High should have known. The evangelist turned politician had been a congenial collaborator as well as pungent phrasemaker. He had his flaws, though, among them gabbiness about White House goings-on and about his part in writing Roosevelt's speeches. He was a man of malleable sentiments who had worked for the Republicans in 1932 and would do so again in 1940 and 1944. Nonetheless, he was a sharp observer and he made use of the vantage point on Roosevelt's speech-writing team in 1936 to report on the President and the people close to him in a series of articles in *The Saturday Evening Post* that were incorporated in a book that appeared in the autumn of 1937, Roosevelt—and Then?[1]

"The role of chief adviser is undoubtedly held at present by Thomas Corcoran, 'Tommy the Cork,' " High wrote breezily. "It might be more accurate to say that it is held jointly by Tom and his even more anonymous associate Ben Cohen. The two of them constitute a shadowy, fantastic team entirely unique, I should say, in the annals of American politics." High found Tom "scintillating," but without Ben "he would be much less useful." It was Roosevelt's use of brains, however, that intrigued High. Most of the members of the 1932 Brains Trust had scattered. "But there will always be a Brain Trust as long as Mr. Roosevelt is President. The personnel shifts and changes. At present its chief members are Tom Corcoran and Ben Cohen. Six months hence Corcoran and Cohen may have moved on or out. But if they do, a new combination is sure to move in."

A few weeks after the 1936 elections underscored the country's approval of Roosevelt's leadership, Corcoran saw the President about his, and by implication, Ben's future with the Administration. Roosevelt wanted to thank him for his work in that campaign and to enlist him for the next four years. Tom, never modest about his accomplishments, sent an ebullient account of that work to his brother Howie, "Dear Stout Fellah:"

> . . . Peggy and I were in the thick of it right up to the last minute. We had a kind of headquarters with the Progressive Committee at the Roosevelt Hotel in New York where we liaisoned between the Progressives and the Democrats and the new American Labor Party. We worked on all the Presidential speeches and most of the time not spent in New York was spent at the White House. We got out 300,000 copies of a new version of that book I showed you entitled "Brass Tacks" and we managed a $95,000 radio program of twenty-two speeches for the Progressives and the Non-Partisan Labor League. We promoted a March-of-Time movie on the President and the White House and we ghosted for Governor Winant, Jesse Jones and Joe Kennedy and ran an economics information bureau for the Democratic National Committee.
>
> It was all lots of fun . . .[2]

Roosevelt did not want to lose him. Nor did Tom want to lose his access to the President and the White House. He left several accounts of the meeting with the President. They reveal a conflicted personality which the President with his overpowering charm and the pressure of national needs had little trouble in shaping to his purposes.

On one level of consciousness Tom wanted to get out. He had a standing offer from the Cotton Franklin law firm to return. He genuinely loved the law. A return to Wall Street would enable him to resume pursuit of that first million dollars the 1929 crash had ended. He pretended to himself he did not like the political game. But there were other considerations. The first was Peggy Dowd. Tom's mother had died in 1936 and she had discouraged Tom's thoughts of marrying the beautiful and tireless Peggy, your "warm over french fried potatoes of a secretary," she had called her. With his mother dead, the determination to marry Peggy became stronger than ever. "Subsconsciously, I didn't want to lose my secretary, Peggy

Dowd, whom I would later marry." Tom knew she "wouldn't fit in a New York law office and I knew she wouldn't go."[3]

It also meant at that time leaving Ben. "I would have had trouble at that stage getting Ben as the first Jew into the Cotton Franklin operation if Ben would go."

"The President talked steadily for one hour," Henry Morgenthau, Jr., the Secretary of the Treasury, reported in his diary. "He asked me to think over whether Ben Cohen would be better in the Attorney General's office or in the Securities Exchange Commission. Without knowing the man, I felt he would be much less conspicuous with the Attorney General."[4] Less conspicuous? Clearly anti-Semitism still was a limiting factor on the use of a Cohen. Shielded by a Corcoran his abilities could be used. Ben understood that. So did Tom.

"Who ever could tell no to the President," Tom remarked of the post-election talk with him.[5] He had spoken earnestly about his desire to get back to real law—either the United States Attorney's job in New York, or Cotton Franklin, or even the solicitor generalship, if it should open up. "I'm afraid if I don't get back to law soon, I'll forget how to appear in court."

"Well, can't you at least find a way to finish the Minimum Wage Bill?" the President pleaded. "I need you and Ben."

Corcoran varied his account of this meeting with the President. In one version he has a "specific promise" from Roosevelt to help him become U.S. Attorney in New York or to appoint him solicitor general. In another he sweetens the memory of his agreement to continue to work with Senator Hugo Black on the Wages and Hours Bill with a reference to Justice Holmes who had died in 1935. He wanted to finish the bill "because it has in it the child[6] labor provisions, which I promised Justice Holmes, who wrote the dissenting opinion in Hammer and Dagenhart (1918)* that I would sometimes try to get done to vindicate him."

Tom gave still another, perhaps controlling, reason for staying on. "I was thrilled with what he told me was his program for the next four years. It included finishing the Minimum Wage Bill, what is now called the Fair Labor Standards Act, and in addition, getting through a reorganization bill of the Executive Departments, the extension of the Tennessee Valley principle to all rivers that could benefit by it." In addition, he and Ben had on their agenda once the Wages and Hours Bill passed, an effort "to ratio-

---

* *Hammer v. Dagenhart* (1918), a landmark Supreme Court decision that ruled the federal law which prohibited interstate transportation of the products of child labor to be unconstitutional because it exceeded the scope of the federal commerce power.

nalize the 26 statutes which constituted what was known as the anti-trust law." He and Ben wanted to "agglomerate" the twenty-seven [he used both figures] different laws that constituted the so-called anti-trust law, "from its beginnings in the Sherman Act up to the latest Robinson Patman Act." He knew from his personal experience on the other side when he had been with Cotton Franklin how the complexities of these laws were used "to obfuscate, to make the anti-trust problem a futility in substance if a gold mine for the legal profession."

"At any rate, after the conference with the President, I was back with Hugo and Ben up to our knees in the Senate Wage and Hour Bill."[7]

One subject Roosevelt did not broach, and neither did Corcoran. What was to be done about the Supreme Court's estoppel of the government's efforts to cope with the needs of the times—in effect constituting itself a "super-legislature?" Roosevelt had shaped the election into a plebiscite on the New Deal and his leadership. Quite reasonably he read the overwhelming returns as a mandate to continue. But he had not stated, and Frankfurter, Corcoran, and Cohen had supported him in this, how he proposed to get around the Court's efforts to undermine the New Deal. Nor did he indicate in his talk with Corcoran how it figured on his agenda for the second term.

Nevertheless, it was much on his and everyone's mind. Many of the measures that had made the 1935 session of Congress so conspicuous a record of legislative achievement that it was called "the second New Deal" —the Social Security Act, the National Labor Relations Act (NLRA), the Public Utilities Holding Company Act—were even then working their way up to the Supreme Court.

The fate of the Public Utilities Act was a particular concern of Corcoran and Cohen and a sense of responsibility for shepherding it through the courts was a powerful reason to stay on in Washington. In November 1935, a rabid anti-New Deal district judge in Baltimore had held the PUHCA "void in its entirety." In rapid succession fifty separate lawsuits were filed by the utilities in thirteen different federal courts to enjoin enforcement of the Act. Three hundred and seventy-five firms sought a declaration of exemption from the Act. The SEC which was responsible for the administration of the Act convened the government's top lawyers. They included in addition to Corcoran and Cohen, who had been appointed special assistants to the Justice Department in connection with the Act, Landis and Burns of the SEC, Robert Jackson, assistant general counsel of the Treasury, and James Lawrence Fly, general solicitor of the TVA.

Cohen laid down the basic strategy. He was no litigator but in Rauh's view he outlitigated corporate America's best. "Ben was the greatest lawyer (I include Supreme Court justices)," said Rauh, "I ever met and the Holding Company litigation is a main support of that view." Cohen proposed the SEC pick its own test case, and singled out the refusal of the Electric Bond and Share Company, the nation's second largest utility system, to register as the one to challenge. Within minutes of receiving the information of Electric Bond's formal refusal to register, Landis, the chairman of the SEC, called New York to begin proceedings in Judge Mack's court. By doing so, the government narrowed the issue down to Electric Bond's refusal to comply with the registration requirement of the Act. Cohen made a rare courtroom appearance before Judge Mack, whose clerk he once had been, to urge him to dismiss Electric Bond's countercomplaint and to limit the case to a consideration of the sections which included the registration provision.

Even John Foster Dulles, who was advising the utilities, a Wall Street friend reported to Ben who passed it on to Felix, considered the government's strategy "remarkably astute" and credited Ben, whom he described as a "very bright young man" but a "misguided idealist" for it. The report delighted Felix. Even though he considered that Dulles's "moral pretensions were a form of technicality," he had "never doubted his discernment." He passed the morsel on to Roosevelt. This elicited congratulations from FDR to Ben on the "grand job you did in the Burco case. To have beaten John W. Davis must have given you a real thrill—I know it gave me one."[8] The *"Burco* case" represented the counterstrategy of the utilities to the SEC's suit against Electric Bond and Share. The government's brief in it had been presented by the solicitor general but it had been the work of Ben and Tom. The Supreme Court had rejected the request of Burco, Inc. that it decide on the constitutionality of the PUHCA. The way was still clear for the Electric Bond case brought by the SEC.

A note from Roosevelt was a sweet accolade, but it was the work that Ben enjoyed. Even as the utility companies fought the Act in the courts, they sought to modify it legislatively, a political move that was led by Wendell Willkie, the head of Commonwealth and Southern, with whom Ben had developed a friendly and mutually respectful relationship.[9] When Willkie sought to interest Frankfurter in his efforts to amend the Act, much of the Harvard professor's replies was drafted by Cohen.

The legal scholar and historian Joel Seligman has noted how deeply Roosevelt was involved with the fate of the PUHCA and cited a New York *Times* story in July 1937, that when it came to naming a successor to Justice Van Devanter, the first of the Court's "quartet of Tories" to step down, seven of the men under consideration, according to Washington speculation, had been involved with either enactment or defense of the Act.[10]

Ben continued to maintain that he preferred to return to New York, still kept his apartment and books there, still sought escape every weekend from his lonely existence as a bachelor. New York was where Jane Harris and Celeste Jedel were. Nevertheless law and politics and public service fascinated him. Washington was the place to be, his loneliness assuaged by Tom and the young men and women who gathered around them. He and Tom now were not only among the chief presidential advisers but the leaders of the several hundred men and women, mostly young, who were the New Dealers.

The term "New Deal" itself was undergoing a sea change. When Roosevelt in accepting the nomination for the presidency in July 1932 had pledged himself to "a New Deal for the American people," it had signified the activist, interventionist, experimental, do-something approach to government that a democratic administration would follow in contrast to the laissez-faire, hands-off-the-economy tenets of the Hoover administration. The burst of executive and legislative activity that marked Roosevelt's first term in office had confirmed this concept of the New Deal. The New Dealers were the men and women who helped Roosevelt set up and administer the new agencies and laws. In great measure these laws were emergency responses to the needs bared by the devastating Great Depression. The agendas of many movements and thinkers fed the process of trial and error over which Roosevelt buoyantly presided. By the end of 1936, however, the issues confronting government had changed. They were, in the first place, to deepen a recovery whose signs were everywhere. To reduce unemployment even further, and to have the programs in place to prevent another depression, or if not prevent, if a disaster proved to be a natural one like a hurricane, to handle it with the public interest foremost. The second major issue that confronted Roosevelt and the New Deal was the constitutional one—whether the Supreme Court would allow the government the powers to solve through Congress the nation's problems. "The challenge of a third of a nation, ill-clad, ill-housed, ill-nourished, was still with us," Roosevelt said at his second inaugural address, "and we seemed to be without the necessary weapons to meet the challenge."[11]

In Roosevelt's second term the New Dealers became more sharply defined as the "party within a party" that carried forward Roosevelt's purposes. They had no organization, no chain of command, no hierarchy, but they were a felt presence.

"Whose Party Is It?" a Stanley High article in *The Saturday Evening Post,* asked at the beginning of February. The article was not without malice because the gossipy High had it in for Corcoran and knew that baring the friction between regulars and New Dealers touched a raw nerve in Roosevelt's ability to lead the party. Party realignment, said High, was among Roosevelt's aims in his second term, even if it meant sloughing off the Solid South conservatives as well as other old-line Democrats. Ickes, no mean demolition man himself, thought the piece "dynamite," and an unusual White House statement issued afterward the Secretary judged to be "a devastating repudiation that will undoubtedly destroy his [High's] prestige as a supposed member of the inner White House circle."

Jerome Frank's wife, the poet Florence Kiper Frank, penned a "Capital Dialogue" for FPA's Conning Tower.[12] It reflected the growing split that the "party within a party" concept produced. Its first verse read:

> Said Corcoran to Farley
> "There's no use getting snarly.
> There's no use getting hot and tense
> Concerning the spheres of influence."
> "My boys expect their recompense,"
> Said Farley to The Cork.

It was signed with a pseudonym because Jerome Frank, himself exiled from Washington in this feud, deemed it prudent not to have his wife publish it under her own name.

As Roosevelt began his new term, the New Dealers had become its most striking aspect second only to the President. And at their head marched Corcoran and Cohen. "Long live the Corcorans and Cohens," wrote a GM executive from faraway India to Tom's brother: "For if Edward has his Simpson why should we begrudge our first citizen—his Corcoran and Cohen?"[13] An irrepressible Tom ranged the city attentive to the New Dealers in the many agencies, their chief "coagulator," as columnists Joseph Alsop and Robert Kintner described him. "In any weather," said Tom of his high noon hours in the New Deal:

My day began at the RFC across the street from the old War, Navy, State Department Building [now the Executive Office Building]. I'd read the papers, make a few phone calls and by mid-morning as a matter of course, take a short walk. I crossed 18th Street, skirted the Executive Office building and entered the basement of the White House west wing. A long hall led to an interior stair near Missy LeHand's desk outside the Oval Office. She'd give me my orders for the day, or often wave me through the side door to see the President, . . .[14]

Ben, meanwhile, his disheveled suit flaked with cigarette ash, sat at his desk at the National Power Policy Committee offices, dealing out wisdom in his quavery falsetto. "Talking it over with Ben," had become routine with the New Deal's chief thinkers. Henderson, Herman Oliphant at Treasury, and Lubin at Labor always had done so. Robert Jackson, a personable young attorney from upstate New York, had become an intimate. Lauchlin Currie at the Federal Reserve was another New Deal standby. William O. Douglas had left the Yale Law School where he was an outstanding authority on corporate finance to work in the SEC, and his friendship with Corcoran and Cohen would help him toward the chairmanship of the SEC which had become a New Deal stronghold and to the Supreme Court.

They argued endlessly among themselves. "Ben, Jewish, made up with people much faster than Tom, Irish," recalled Rauh, who served them both. "Tom once told me how he had backed Ben in a fight with Leon only to have Ben make up with him and leave Tom in the fight." But all united behind Roosevelt.

One of the younger men who had worked in the campaign, a Boston lawyer, William S. Youngman, Jr., whom Tom afterward helped place in the solicitor general's office, reflected the New Dealers purposeful mood after Roosevelt's stunning victory:

I hope that some of the members of the Supreme Court are digesting the election returns and that you may be able to line up the tremendous majority in Congress for further progressive legislation.[15]

XXI

Roosevelt's Court Reform Plan

The New Dealers, especially the lawyers, many of them Frankfurter's "hot dogs," indeed, the professor himself, had little to do with the planning and writing of Roosevelt's Court-packing plan, that is, with the statute, the presidential message that accompanied it, and the Attorney General's supporting data. All burst upon a surprised nation on February 5—as Roosevelt meant them to do.

In one sense the "happy hot dogs" were guiltless; in another they were peculiarly responsible, as Raymond Moley, who had gone into the opposition, pointed out.

It was they, essentially Frankfurter, Corcoran, and Cohen, who had maintained throughout the campaign that not the Constitution but the Court majority was to blame for the Court's effort to undo the New Deal through a perverted assertion of judicial supremacy. This contention, as well as its corollary, of the need to avoid the amendment route, paved the way for the Attorney General's recommendation to Roosevelt, which he embraced, of the plan to add one justice up to six for every justice who did not retire after the age of seventy.

In the spring of 1936 Cohen had pondered a modified form of court enlargement which Tom and he had tried to sell Senator Wheeler. They included it in a draft speech that cautioned the high bench that great abuses invited drastic remedies. They considered the Montana senator a friend, a courageous liberal who had fought the public utilities battle with them, and knew him to be as unhappy as they over the Court's ultraconservatism. Wheeler had declined to deliver that speech and later let them know that he thought to raise the court issue in a campaign year would be a disservice to the President. A kindred proposal in 1924 by the elder La Follette when Wheeler had been his running mate had had a devastating backlash. Tom and Ben had not quarreled with this advice. Ben continued to insist, however, there was much to be said for the proposal.[1]

In late November 1936 the solicitor general Stanley Reed had asked Tom and Ben for a memorandum on the Court situation and followed up in December with a request that they draw up some specific amendments "in case of need." Ben sent the result of his labors to Frankfurter, a little doubtfully:

After working hard to show that it is impossible to draw such amendments, I have found it hard to sit down and draft them myself. But I am sending you the result of my labors. You can act as *advocatus diaboli.*[2]

The formula that he preferred said: "If at any time a majority of the Court should be composed of members over seventy, the President should appoint such additional judges as may be necessary to give the Court a majority of members under seventy." Ben's proposal, Corcoran noted later, did not permanently increase the size of the Court, for it would return to nine as justices over seventy dropped out.[3] The proposal evidently was shown to the President. He disregarded it. "Amendments had to clear Cummings' office and Ben got nowhere," commented Tom.

Tom and Ben knew something was afoot after the election about the Court situation. Nevertheless, they too, were surprised when they finally learned of the Court-packing plan. They did so just before it was sent up to Congress and under circumstances that precluded their making any substantive suggestions, especially on the plan's claim that the Court was behind its docket, a claim they knew was incorrect.

Cummings was determined to keep them out, an exclusion concurred on by Roosevelt. The Attorney General, a graduate of Yale, had been a National Committeeman from Connecticut, a leader in the party establishment, and a member of the FRBC* club. He was a competent lawyer but not in the class of Frankfurter, Corcoran, and Cohen. He resented them and resisted their encroachments on his terrain. Roosevelt knew this. He

* For Roosevelt Before Chicago.

did not discourage jealousies among his subordinates. They enabled him to keep control of the large egos that usually accompany political ambition.

On January 30, his birthday, while Eleanor Roosevelt entertained the movie stars at luncheon in the State Dining Room, a fateful four-hour conference took place in the Oval Room upstairs where Roosevelt gave the final go-ahead to the Cummings plan. Afterward Judge Rosenman, whom Roosevelt had called down from New York to help with the message, asked whether he might consult Tom Corcoran. Yes, Roosevelt answered, but keep him out of any conferences and don't tell Cummings.

Roosevelt was sensitive to the feelings of the party establishment. After his historic victory in the 1936 campaign, he was sure, as were most politicians, that passage of his legislative recommendations was foreordained. Nevertheless, he did not disregard normal political precautions. That meant keeping Corcoran and Cohen out, also Frankfurter, and having Cummings take the lead. Some consultation was necessary, however, and on January 24, Cummings wrote in his diary:

I *think* it was this day that the President told me he had a talk with Lewis [John L.] on the plan and the latter agreed to support it and thought it better than the amendment plan.
The President also told me he had tried it on Tommy Corcoran and the latter agreed it would work. He also told me he had informed Ogburn [AF of L Counsel] and the latter was immediately favorable.[4]

What does this entry mean? Neither Corcoran nor Cohen mention any such conversation with the President. And if it took place, did it happen under circumstances that foreclosed suggestions? Robert Jackson, New Dealer and assistant attorney general, states flatly that Cummings later told him, "Corcoran and Cohen didn't know anything about it."

The same Cummings entry reported that "F.D.R. wrote Frankfurter and told him he had a Court plan but could not reveal it . . ." Roosevelt did write Frankfurter, although the letter said nothing about having a Court plan. "Very confidentially, I may give you an awful shock in about two weeks. Even if you do not agree, suspend final judgment and I will tell you the story."[5] To which Frankfurter replied three days later, "Are you trying to find out how well I can sit on top of Vesuvius by giving me notice that 'an awful shock' is in store for me 'in about two weeks?' " That was the eighteenth. Felix and his wife, Marion, came to Washington for the second inaugural address. In Washington he was bound to talk with his "boys" if not with Roosevelt. So he too must have known something was brewing.

What Corcoran and Cohen knew or suspected, they usually communicated to Frankfurter. As Joe Rauh, who then was clerking for Cardozo after a year of working for Corcoran and Cohen, said, "They were pretty important guys but when Felix walked in the door there wasn't any question who was boss."[6] They not only looked to Frankfurter for leadership but they knew he wanted to be on the Supreme Court. Roosevelt did too. The question was one of openings and timing. A major grievance against "the nine old men," as they had been dubbed somewhat inaccurately by Drew Pearson, was the unwillingness of the oldest to retire and give Roosevelt a chance to name people to the Court.

After Roosevelt's reelection, however, vacancies were assumed to be inevitable and Washington legal circles speculated about candidates. Frankfurter was one of them, as Ben Cohen reported to Harold Laski, the friend of Frankfurter as well as Holmes, and a leader of the British Labour Party. Ben wrote two days after Roosevelt's Court proposals were introduced and the President's supporters, whatever their misgivings about the plan, assumed its passage was certain:

Dear Harold:
We are living through stirring days here, fighting to make the Supreme Court reign under rather than over the Constitution.
History will judge the President's proposals by their works, and their works will depend on the quality of the new appointees. I don't know any one more suited than Felix for the difficult and important tasks of adapting constitutional doctrines to present-day conditions while still preserving their value as a symbol of the orderly continuity of our national life. There is a subtly instigated movement over here to create the impression that Felix is too radical to win confirmation and that the President would defeat his own purposes by taking on the fight. This movement is inspired not by the President's friends but by his opponents who want to stop Felix's appointment at the source because they fear they cannot stop his confirmation. But the movement has made headway and is encouraged by those who are pressing the claims of other judicial aspirants.
Tom Corcoran tells me that you had a talk with the President some time ago and he expressed to you his desire to put Felix on the Court. Do you not think that it might be helpful if you wrote a note to the President commending the courageous statesmanship of his proposals but warning him of the forces which will be at work to devitalize and discredit his proposals after their acceptance by pressing the claims for judicial preferment of second-rate aspirants over men like Felix who will bring real vision and statecraft to the Court? The perspective and disinterestedness of distance should add weight to your advice.[7]

Roosevelt knew that Frankfurter wanted to be named to the bench. That, as well as Cummings's jealousy, and his own concern not to rub the

Old Guard Democrats the wrong way, were probably in his mind when he kept Frankfurter out of the secret.

The night before Roosevelt announced the plan, a group recruited from the inner circle of the White House went to dinner at the James Roosevelts. The latter had become one of his father's secretaries and the little party consisted of Missy, Grace, Tom and Peggy, and Sam Rosenman. "I've got the Boss' O.K. to go down and tell him [Justice Brandeis] in confidence what's coming," Tom informed Sam. "He sure won't like it." Two years later Corcoran gave Harry Hopkins a more graphic account of the Brandeis episode. From the time Tom learned from Rosenman what was in the message he had tried to see the President in order to warn him that its statements on the crowding of the Supreme Court's calendar were wrong, he told Hopkins:

I did get in to see him the morning the message went to the Hill—I urged him to talk to Brandeis in advance, hoping to soften the blow on him—The President told me to see him at once—I crashed the sacred robing room—he walked with me in the hall while the balance of the Court filed by not knowing of the bombshell that was awaiting them. Brandeis asked me to thank the President for letting him know but said he was unalterably opposed to the President's action and that he was making a great mistake.[8]

Brandeis's hostility to the plan, Tom knew, would upset Roosevelt. He stayed clear of the White House to delay giving the President the news. Ben, meanwhile, had gone to New York City; arriving in Penn Station he picked up a paper and read about the President's press conference and the plan's introduction. He turned around, got on a train, and went back to Washington in order to be with Tom.* The two men decided that despite their disagreement with the message's emphasis on an overburdened judiciary, the die was cast and they would loyally support the President. That was the attitude of most New Dealers. Youthful Paul Freund whom Frankfurter had sent as a clerk to Brandeis was part of the solicitor general's small staff. He had argued and won the *Ashwander* case in which the Court to everyone's surprise sustained the TVA. Freund lived in one of the houses in Georgetown that was a hotbed of new-fledged legal talent. "When the Court plan was announced, we were all shocked . . . All of us felt that the Supreme Court was a real obstacle, but that wasn't the way to get rid of the obstacle." Yet "extraordinary and incredible" as the plan might otherwise seem, it "can only be understood in the context of the Supreme Court's behavior up to 1937."[9]

* Bob Jackson, on route to Washington, also learned about the plan from a newspaper he picked up in the Philadelphia station.

It was that behavior on which Frankfurter focused when asked by FDR for help.

He took a cue Ben gave him:

Dramatically and artistically you did "shock" me. But beyond that—well, the momentum of a long series of decisions not defensible in the realm of reason nor justified by settled principles of constitutional interpretation had convinced me, as they had convinced you, that means had to be found to save the Constitution from the Court and the Court from itself . . .[10]

Another consideration, Ben had suggested to Felix in writing to Roosevelt, was "obviously you have been confronted with many different views of what had to be done, and some action was required." "There was no perfect easy way out," Frankfurter's letter to Roosevelt continued. "Risks had to be taken . . ." This formulation over which he agonized contained "a little implication," Ben said, "that perhaps he did not agree with the action taken." Paul Freund put it more strongly. "I think he [Frankfurter] would, if forced to, have voted against the plan because it went counter to all his instincts about separation of powers and independence of the judiciary."[11]

Encouraged by Felix's response, the President after an account of the "elimination" process by which he had chosen the Cummings plan, asked, "Do you want to help me?"[12] If the answer was yes, would he send him an elaboration of what he had written? He would go over the matter with Tom and write him again, Frankfurter assured him. He did so three days later with some "notes" on how the Court had "distorted the policy of judicial review into a revision of legislative policy . . ."

The opponents of the plan, meanwhile, had made it plain that passage of the bill foreshadowed a bitter struggle. Few believed that Roosevelt could be thwarted, but the press was almost unanimous in condemnation. So were the bar associations. And most ominous was the terse statement by the chairman of the House Judiciary Committee, Hatton Sumners of Texas, "Boys, here's where I cash in my chips."

A strategy board began to meet daily at the White House. It consisted of Corcoran and Ed Keenan, an aide of Cummings, Assistant Attorney General Robert Jackson, Charles West, the White House's liaison with the House, and Charles Michelson and Edward Roddan of the Democratic National Committee. In addition James Roosevelt sat in for his father and Tom also spoke for Ben. Tom instead of being on the fringes of the bill's progress quickly became the chief agent on the Hill of the President's wishes. Soon the office that he shared with Ben became, if not the headquarters, the most energetic center of work for the bill. Basic memoranda were written, mostly by Ben, that set forth the constitutional situation and the arguments for the bill. A list of witnesses who might appear before the Senate Judiciary Committee—law school deans, professors, historians—was carefully composed. Speeches were written for others to deliver.

Authorities on the law and the Constitution like Charles Beard and Stuart Chase, Deans Lloyd Garrison of Wisconsin and Leon Green of Northwestern, Bob Jackson and Thurman Arnold testified at the Senate hearings, made speeches elsewhere, or supplied material for speeches made by others. "They say you took John W. [Davis] for a merry ride," Corcoran thanked Professor Edward S. Corwin of Princeton for his "fighting speech in Boston." "I enjoyed the occasion, and only hope I didn't injure the cause," the distinguished constitutional scholar replied modestly. Tom and Ben were the catalysts. They had a speech-writing team headed by Milton Katz.[13] They coopted him for the job despite his dislike of the bill's approach. Jim Rowe and Weiner assisted Katz. "We shall need speeches on the general subjects described below . . ." Tom would notify them about the coming week's work. "We can't locate the quotation attributed to Voltaire; 'Lawyers are the conservators of ancient barbarism,' " an answering Katz memo said. "However, we have gotten a fairly good substitute from Erasmus, who refers to lawyers as 'that most learned species of profoundly ignorant men.' " Katz was a good friend of Ben's and Tom's. They thought he had the best mind among the younger men in Washington. He had worked at the RFC, the NRA, the SEC, and though he protested that the Court-packing bill was "lunacy," he was willing to write speeches that did not praise the plan but criticized the Court for a breach of trust.

The bill was in trouble. Tom's report to Roosevelt after its introduction on the attitude of Brandeis was an omen. Roosevelt had been surprised and pensive. "I had hoped he would be with us . . . I don't think he understands." He wanted Tom to go down to the Senate and find out where Tom's friend Wheeler was going to be in the fight, also Senators La Follette and Maloney, a young Catholic from Connecticut.

Tom's encounter with his friend Wheeler was tempestuous.[14] After it he saw the struggle against judicial supremacy in another light. He discovered that underlying the issues of Court and Constitution was the question of how much power Roosevelt was going to have vis-à-vis the Senate after his landslide election,* and the New Dealers identified their hopes for further

---

* There are several versions of this talk and of Wheeler's attitude. They differ in several respects. One is in Corcoran's unpublished notes for an autobiography. Burt Wheeler's version is in *Yankee from the West.* A third is in Charles Michelson, *The Ghost Talks.*

reforms with that power. Whatever Roosevelt's wariness of the senator, Tom and Ben liked the pugnacious Montanan for the magnificent way he had championed the Holding Company Act, so the talk started out amiably. Tom began with "the pitch" that if the Court plan should go through he hoped Roosevelt would appoint Wheeler to the Court "and make up for not appointing him Attorney General." This last was a sore point with the senator who felt Roosevelt should have chosen him after the sudden death of another Montanan, Senator Tom Walsh, the attorney-general-designate, instead of Cummings.

Wheeler does not say this. Rather, he describes Tom's offer as one of Roosevelt's inviting him to sit in on the naming of new justices. "You want to see a liberal Court, don't you?"

"Of course," Wheeler replied, but did not budge in his opposition to the bill, and, as he talked, worked himself into "one of his passionate furies," according to Tom. Finally he burst out at the hapless Tom, "Do you remember Huey Long?" When Tom replied he had known the Louisiana senator, Wheeler recalled that Roosevelt had gained the nomination in Chicago only because of Huey and that Huey had been for Roosevelt because of Burt Wheeler.

"Did you see what Roosevelt did to Huey?" Wheeler shouted.

"You don't think Roosevelt had him killed?" Tom finally managed to say.

Wheeler did not answer except to repeat, "I say did you see what he did to Huey? Now I've been watching Roosevelt for a long time. Once he was only one of us who made him. Now he means to make himself the boss of us all."

Then he continued in words heavy with portent and hate. "Well he's made the mistake we've been waiting for for a long time—and this is our chance to cut him down to size."

"But, Burt, the Court," protested Tom.

"Your Court plan doesn't matter: he's after us."

Desperately Tom tried to ease the situation. "I can't believe you mean what you say." In any case, he went on, with Roosevelt's power "something was going to pass."

A flabbergasted Tom returned to the White House. Historical analogies ran through his head as he faced the disagreeable prospect of again bringing "bad news to the Persian king . . . So now the Kingdom was at stake. It wasn't the Court issue—the barons were at Runnymede. At the very beginning of Roosevelt's second term his own friends who had made him were now determined to destroy him. Women's jealousy was a peanut compared to male envy. They would make him a lame duck with all the work there was to do."

Tom saw the President alone to tell him about the conversation. "I flopped my job. I only give you words. I did not take them down but they're burned in my brain."

Roosevelt listened, was silent, then, "Huey—my God—they don't believe—"

"I don't know." Wheeler had never quite said Roosevelt had a part in the assassination. "Burt is a terribly passionate man—that's his strength . . . I can only tell you what the Senator said. But clearly from now on this is not a legislative fight about the Court: this is a barons' revolt against you and I'm afraid you'll have to fight it that way. But everything can become different. Can't you send for Burt right now? It's got to be you yourself, not me."

"Have you talked to La Follette?"

"Not yet, sir."

"To Maloney?"

"No."

"Try right now. I'll think about Burt."

Roosevelt did invite Wheeler to dinner. He did so through Charley Michelson, an old friend of Wheeler's and a supporter of James Farley, the chairman of the Democratic National Committee. Michelson disliked Corcoran as an interloper.[15] For that reason, perhaps, he denies that he invited Wheeler, but Wheeler says flatly that Michelson conveyed the message that the President wanted him to have dinner with him to discuss the Court issue.

" 'Charley,' I said, 'I've just given out a statement opposing the packing of the Court, so the President ought to save the plate for someone who persuades more easily.' "

"I have a whole scenario to present to you," Cohen told an interviewer in 1974 in regard to the Court-packing plan.[16] He began to talk of Chief Justice Hughes, the Jove-like figure who presided over the Court in bearded majesty in the thirties, and of the oldest member of the Court, Justice Brandeis who like his faithful collaborator Felix, called Tom and Ben his "boys" and was a figure of reverence with most New Dealers.

I didn't know until Freund's article in the *Harvard Law Review* which brought out that Van Devanter wrote Brandeis and Hughes that he ought to resign because he couldn't any longer write his opinions, that both Brandeis and Hughes urged him to stay on and therefore bore a heavy responsibility for denying FDR appointments to the Court that would have reflected the new approach.

Freund's article quoted telling letters to and from Van Devanter. "My dear Van," wrote Brandeis, "I am sorry you are ill, take very good care of yourself. The Court never needed you more. L.D.B." A few months earlier Van Devanter, who was one of the "Four Horsemen," as the tight Tory bloc was often called, wrote his sister,

. . . After the term closed Justice Brandeis particularly asked an opportunity to have a talk with me. In the course of the talk he said he wished specially to urge that I should not think of retiring; that he did not wish to see any change on the Court just now, and quite apart from that wished me to continue on the Court . . .[17]

The same article revealed that the chief justice, although he acknowledged Van Devanter's "pen paralysis" in the matter of opinion writing, appreciated the justice for his statements at conference, which if taken down with a little editing would have served as opinions, as well as for his "perspicacity and common sense."

Said Ben: "If Hughes and Brandeis had not tried to keep Van Devanter on the Court there would have been a vacancy and that would have led to the appointment of someone who would have gone along with the majority and with [Justice] Roberts indicating that he was going in a different direction, the Court would have evolved without statute or amendment."[18]

That had been the basic position in the face of the judicial blockade of the New Deal, of Felix as well as Brandeis, of Tom and himself. "That opinions on the Court would change showed up in a number of cases where a lack of votes had held up rulings. It would have been better to bide one's time until views changed. The Frankfurter-Brandeis view was 'go slowly and you will carry the Court with you.' That also was my view. The Constitution will grow in time."[19]

"Brandeis," the interviewer exclaimed. "Why?"

"Brandeis felt fairly friendly towards FDR when he first came in but he was appalled by the NRA and AAA. Also he was beginning to fail. When old people fail they never recognize it. Indeed it works the other way. They do foolish things to prove to themselves they are as good as ever."

Senator Wheeler, an old friend of the justice's, was slated to initiate the opposition case to the Court-packing bill before the Senate Judiciary Committee when he received word from his daughter Elizabeth that the justice would welcome a visit from the senator. She had worked for Ben and Tom in the campaign and the invitation had been transmitted by Mrs. Brandeis who had come ostensibly to visit Elizabeth's newborn baby. Wheeler immediately went to California Street to urge that the justice and chief justice appear at the Senate hearings. Brandeis refused nor would he advise the chief justice to [attend], but if Wheeler called the chief justice "he'll give you a letter."

Wheeler had clashed with Hughes and was reluctant to telephone him. Brandeis thereupon called the number himself and placed the receiver in the senator's hands. Hughes invited him to come right over. When did Wheeler want the letter? Hughes asked him. It was Saturday and he needed it for Monday morning. Hughes told him to come by the next afternoon. He did so and the chief justice handed him an envelope with the words, "The baby is born." The next morning in a crowded Senate caucus room Wheeler finished his testimony by pulling out of his breast pocket Hughes's letter. It had been approved by Brandeis and Van Devanter and demolished the docket contention of the Court plan. Its impact was immediate and devastating, and it proved to be one of the decisive elements in the Senate Judiciary Committee's 10 to 8 vote two months later to report the bill unfavorably.

Even before the Hughes-Brandeis-Van Devanter letter Roosevelt realized he had made a major tactical error in presenting the bill as an effort to enhance the Court's efficiency rather than to overcome the ultraconservative views of the Court's majority. "I made one major mistake when I first presented the plan," Roosevelt wrote in a rare admission of a blunder. "I did not place enough emphasis upon the real mischief—the kind of decisions which, as a studied and continued policy, had been coming down from the Supreme Court. I soon corrected that mistake," he said in a reference to his speech at the Democratic Victory Dinner, and then five days later in a Fireside Chat, stated, "If We Would Make Democracy Succeed, I Say We Must Act—NOW!"[20]

Both documents had been worked on by Tom, Ben, and Bob Jackson, who in the course of the Court battle were becoming "a trio." In addition Frankfurter made a major contribution. The real theme of the Victory Speech had been suggested by chance by Stuart Chase. He had sent a letter to the *Times,* a copy of which he sent to Roosevelt, stating that the real issue was the social legislation that the courts had overruled, and asking, "What would you do if you were the President of the United States, following a mandate such as that delivered in the last election" that people wanted action now?

Roosevelt liked the letter so much he sent a copy to Frankfurter, asking, "What would happen, for example, if I were to go on the air and talk to Americans along the lines of Chase's article to the *Times?*"[21] Frankfurter concurred heartily and Chase was delighted for the *Times* had not used his letter. "This is to thank you for your telegram and for your kind permission to use your ideas," Tom wrote Chase. "I hope they were used in a way worthy of their brilliance."

Despite Roosevelt's shift of emphasis, the Hughes-Brandeis-Van Devanter letter, Wheeler's effective leadership of the Senate opposition to the Court-packing bill, and the hostility of the bar associations shook its chances of passage, but the finishing blow was administered by the Court's change of direction. Unexpectedly, the dissenters became the majority and key New Deal measures were sustained.

The first reversal occurred in a 5 to 4 ruling that upheld a State of Washington minimum wage statute similar in terms to the New York State law it had ruled unconstitutional less than a year earlier. The swing vote was that of Justice Roberts. He scandalized the legal profession by giving no reason for his change. Two weeks later the Court found the Wagner Act constitutional.

Joe Rauh was clerking for Justice Cardozo at the time of the Court's reversals. The justice whom Rauh considered "a saintlike human being" was a bachelor. His law clerk became his son and confidant:

I remember when he came back after the Wagner Act had been upheld in the *Jones v. Laughlin* case. He said, "Oh, Mr. Rauh, you won't believe what happened. Roberts and Hughes switched without even saying why they were switching." He referred to the fact that in the *Carter Coal* case the year before the Court had ruled out a law very similar to the Wagner Act. Everyone knew why. It was because Roosevelt's court-packing plan had the Court scared stiff. I still remember the wonderment with which Cardozo said, "You know, judges ought to explain their actions. They have a right to change, but they oughtn't to pretend they're not changing."[22]

"After today," Frankfurter telegraphed the President in words heavy with sarcasm, "I feel like finding some honest profession to enter."[23] From Cambridge Ben heard from Professor Calvert Magruder who had been chosen by Frankfurter as Brandeis's first law clerk and who had had a major part in the drafting of the Wagner Act:

I hope you are not as gloomy and depressed as Felix seems to be about the great constitutional decisions last Monday. I had supposed the decisions were due to the sweet reasonableness of the statute, its careful draftsmanship . . . I am told this had nothing to do with it, and that the case was decided by the skulduggery of F.D.R. and his wrecking crew . . .

At almost the same time Ben wrote Magruder to congratulate him on the decisions.

While the decisions have been ascribed to many things and many people, I haven't heard anyone ascribe them to faulty draftsmanship. You really deserve great credit for the painstaking and unobtrusive way you labored on the Act in the dark days before collective bargaining became respectable.[24]

"Our letters apparently passed in the post," Ben wrote him the next day:

I am highly elated with the Wagner decisions. Under the lash of sinister influences the Supreme Court may yet become a truly great Court, and its opinions, if we ignore some excusably face-saving palaver, may ultimately acquire some sanctity from the force of reason. *Adkins* is blasted. *Carter* is retreating in rout, and *Hammer v. Dagenhart* is the next citadel to be stormed.

But we must be on our guard and not be lulled into a false sense of security as we were by the *Nebbia* decision . . .

The case of *Nebbia v. New York,* had encouraged liberals to hope the Court would go along with the New Deal measures, drawing particular encouragement from the statement of Justice Roberts. "[T]his court from the early days affirmed that the power to promote the general welfare is inherent in government."[25]

Not long after the Wagner Act ruling the Court reinforced its reversal of position and upheld the Social Security Act. In this case, the chief justice assigned the writing of the majority opinion to Justice Cardozo who, in Rauh's view, was "without doubt the most liberal" member of the Court.[26] Cardozo opposed the Court plan but in a "rather calm and understated way . . . Cardozo liked the New Deal; he really believed in it." Then on May 16, as if to underscore that the Court indeed was changing, Justice Van Devanter notified the President of his intention to resign.

The astonishment of the New Dealers at the turn of events is reflected in Ben's letter to the dean of Northwestern University Law School, Leon Green:

I was sorry that I did not get the opportunity of seeing you after you testified before the Senate Judiciary Committee. I wanted to congratulate you on your valor under fire.

It is difficult to know whether we should laugh or cry about the denouement. After all we started to get a more liberal interpretation of the Constitution and a more liberal Court. In order to give us a more liberal interpretation the old Court has turned a triple somersault. To give us a more liberal Court, the process of retirement has commenced. One aged justice who could not keep up with the times has retired. The opponents of the Court proposals assure us that another aged conservative justice will depart as soon as firing ceases. It would have taken four new justices to give us as liberal a court as we ought to have next year when Van Devanter and Sutherland are gone . . .[27]

There had been various moves to get a compromise bill all during the struggle. In March Cohen had given Corcoran a memorandum on a telephone call from Herman Oliphant at Treasury:

If sentiment gains headway for an amendment limiting the age of the Justices, he thinks that advantage might be taken of it and its effect neutralized by the following compromise proposal which would not seriously affect the substance of the original proposal:

(1) Permit the Court to drop back to nine as vacancies occur.

(2) Provide for the statute to lapse at the end of five years if prior to that time a constitutional amendment fixing the age of the justices shall have been adopted.

(3) Give some support to an appropriate amendment providing for the compulsory retirement of judges after a certain age.

I think that these suggestions at the appropriate time might be of value.[28]

In May Senator Bone, another Western liberal senator who supported the President, persuaded him to see Wheeler, and when Roosevelt agreed Bone promptly called him from the President's office. The senator grabbed a cab and came to the White House. He told the President that if he dropped the Court bill he could have two resignations on the Court. Roosevelt, according to Wheeler, showed "a flicker of interest," but in the end insisted that the bill be passed.[29]

As it became clear that the opposition had enough votes to defeat the President on the bill, the hunter's instinct to bring him down gained the upper hand.

"I hope the Congress may be able to wind up its affairs in two or three weeks," Ben wrote Jane Harris in mid-July. "I think some sort of settlement or compromise on the court plan will be reached by then, and if not they will probably agree to take it up promptly when they reconvene in October or January."

The Court fight provided one of the rare occasions when Roosevelt's sense of timing failed. While he was still feared because of his landslide vote, his pride as well as a sense of commitment to judicial reform kept him from yielding, and when he did authorize his lieutenants to seek a compromise it was too late. Even Corcoran and Cohen were opposed to compromise—"one reason being that Roosevelt had promised the next appointment to Joe Robinson [the Senate majority leader] and you could hardly see Robinson as a liberalizer of the Court." Asked whether the Court's sustaining of Social Security at the end of May had changed his time schedule, Roosevelt told a news conference ". . . we are all hopeful that in the days to come the same human point of view will prevail; but of course there are a great many things that have not been passed on yet—an enormous number of things."[30]

Shortly afterward, however, the Senate leaders who had remained loyal to him advised a retreat and he authorized Robinson to work up a substitute. Fate intervened and the senator at the beginning of July was felled by a heart attack. With his death efforts to achieve a compromise fell apart and on July 22 a triumphant opposition voted to recommit the bill. The vote was 70 to 20; five senators did not vote.

In this final act Frankfurter and his boys played little part. Of course, the whole story is not known. On April 20 Frankfurter, at Roosevelt's invitation to "slip into town unobserved," had been at the White House from five in the evening to nine-fifty the next morning "along with F.D.R. except at dinner when Mrs. Roosevelt and her secretary joined us." Afterward he had seen Tom and Ben. "I forgot to tell you and Ben that we talked about that too [changes at the TVA] in the course of the long night."[31]

What did they talk about? History is not simply what is recorded and its narrators can only guess at what happened. Frankfurter's basic position, as Cohen said, was that given time, the Court would evolve. But Cohen also had asked, as if speaking to himself, why Felix had not pointed out to the President the signs that showed changes were at work. "Perhaps because he was involved in other struggles," Cohen answered to himself.[32] To disagree with Roosevelt was difficult. C. C. Burlingham, influential in the world of law, wrote Roosevelt to urge him to accept a compromise in view of the shifts in the Court. Even that venerable Brahmin figure felt "audacious and effronterous . . ." in so writing. Frankfurter by nature was a consensus man. Not only was it his forte to find compromises in the most tangled disputes, but he found it especially difficult to disagree with men he revered—Roosevelt and Brandeis in particular.

His reaction to Brandeis's allowing Hughes to speak for him in challenging Roosevelt on the docket issue illustrated the dilemma in which he had been placed—he had to choose between loyalty to Roosevelt or the justice. He drafted a long letter to Brandeis: "I resent the C.J.'s [Chief Justice's] putting you in the front line even with your approval," but he did not mail it. He tried again after the Court's reversal on Washington State's minimum wages legislation, "one of life's bitter-sweets . . . the manner and circumstances of the over-ruling make last Monday one of the few, real black days in my life." Roberts's reversal was "a shameless, political response to the present row. If he had a decent, disclosable change of mind it would have been ordinary manliness to have avowed it in a brief memorandum."

"As for the Chief Justice—I have long written him down as a Jesuit. I deplored his letter and certainly its form . . . I am very sorry to write thus, but I am very, very sad." This letter he did mail.[33] But he still felt he owed it to Brandeis to say more. He was moved by Joe Robinson's death, he wrote the justice.

In the Court fight he showed more character and candor and restraint than, I am sorry to say, Burt Wheeler—not to speak of the cheap Burke—is showing. Wheeler's canonization of Hughes is positively indecent, considering the views I heard him express about the Court two years ago, and I deeply resent his persistent effort to identify you with the Court and to use you as a screen for hiding its grave abuses in the past.

On this he wrote in longhand:

The above I wrote in a letter to L.D.B. Perhaps unwise—but partly, the same old reason, to try to have as much content of candor in our relationship as possible partly to ease talk, if, when & as, by letting him know as tactfully as I can, as much as possible of my view.

The Court fight estranged Tom from Brandeis. Ben supported Tom, but in his usual way avoided gestures of finality, of ruptured friendships and abandonment of communication. The rift with Brandeis exacerbated their resentment to the drumfire attacks that beat down upon them as the alleged authors of the Court plan. "Bolsheviks and headless Rasputins" were among the epithets. "I just don't believe that they can build you up into a Rex scapegoat too—I'll bet you," Felix consoled his "Dear Boys."[34] The same letter asked surprisingly, "I don't take any stock in the L.D.B. retirement talk—or should I?" One would have thought that Frankfurter would have been the first, except Brandeis's wife, Alice, to have known.

Sometimes Tom and Ben were teased in verse as High Johnson did in his nationally syndicated column:

> Oh, Mr. Cohen! Oh, Mr. Cohen!
> What has happened in this Congress of our own?
> Why, Mr. Corcoran? Why, Mr. Corcoran?
> Let's not become discouraged or despair
> What with Franklin's charming touch
> And then thousand million bucks
> We can buy another mandate
> With lots of votes to spare.

That was written in good spirit but the attacks turned nasty after Wheeler's inaccurate but effective attack on the Administration's "bright young men," whom correspondents were immediately informed privately were Corcoran and Cohen as "the authors and successful vendors" of the President's plan. "There is very little I can tell you about the material we prepared for Wheeler on the Court more than a year ago," Ben replied to an inquiry from Felix,

It was sometime between February and April 1936, that Tom came to me and told me that he had had a talk with Wheeler, that Wheeler was very incensed by the decisions of the Court and wanted to make a speech in protest against these decisions. I took some of the material which we had worked up for Moley but which he had made very little use of and I reworked this material somewhat and then Tom took it, chiseled, polished and expanded it into the shape that you now see it. As you may recall, I had been playing with the idea that it was the duty of Congress to take some action to curb the arbitrariness of the Court's decisions ever since Stone made the direct assertion in the A.A.A. case that the Court was adopting a tortured construction of the Constitution.

Wheeler never said a word to me about his disagreement with anything in the material that we sent to him. Tom either handed him the material or sent it to him and if Wheeler said any word of protest to Tom it certainly did not make any impression on him because both Tom and I had assumed that the only reason he did not deliver the speech was that he never got around to it.[35]

The attacks on the two, but on Tom especially, came to a boil with a lead piece in *The Saturday Evening Post,* by its ace reporter, Alva Johnston, entitled "White House Tommy."[36] Mixing truth with half-truth and distortion, the article portrayed Tom at thirty-six as having risen "to a position of power vaguely resembling that which the Duke of Buckingham held under James I, or which Olivier the Barber held under Louis XI." This short, plump, jolly-faced man derived his power on the Hill through jobbery, patronage or the withholding of it, and the deft use of his White House connection. He was notorious for "turning on the heat" with "I'm calling from the White House" and then holding forth to a senator the "mutual advantages" that would flow from his voting right. A "good phrasemaker," he was Washington's "most active ghostwriter" and encouraged the President's "vindictiveness against opponents," especially the savage blasts against industrialists and plutocrats. He had peopled the agencies "with his *cum laude* boys," whom his enemies referred to as "Corcoran's Ogpu," and second only to Professor Frankfurter he was "the greatest employment agent in the country for youthful brains." He had no philosophy except ambition, had the earmarks of "the soldier of fortune," and was out to teach business that in Roosevelt it had "met its master," ascribing to Corcoran thereby the phrase in Roosevelt's windup Madison Square Garden speech that Tom had disliked and was actually High's handiwork. "I got another offer today in six figures," the writer quoted Tom as telling his friends, and ended his article on a note of doubt that "he will leave Washington as long as he holds the status of White House Tommy. There is no fun equal to that of experimenting on a nation."

"As soon as a fellow gets close to the throne around here," wrote a columnist for the Washington *Post*, "the whispers start and the knives come out. After Alva Johnston's 'White House Tommy' article in this week's *Saturday Evening Post*, Thomas Corcoran and Benjamin Cohen had better watch out."[37] John T. Flynn, the business columnist, said the "vicious punch" had come from the "displaced courtiers . . . from those former New Deal favorites who have lost their place in the first circle and blame Tom Corcoran for their expulsion."

Frankfurter in Cambridge realized *The Saturday Evening Post* jab had caused pain:

The thing I'm maddest about in that dirty piece is the passing pleasant remark about me. Thoreau, you will recall, said that if an innocent is jailed, the place of every decent man is also in jail. And so, I should have been on the scaffolding of meretricious "dirt" with you. For, of course, it's all of a piece—I mean this is but hired verbalizations of all the honorable prostitutes that your great labors and devotion for all that is decent in American hopes have earned. Less I cannot say— more I need not.
I know your fighting power. I also know your great gifts for letting storms pass and commanding your soul in serenity.[38]

At the end of the Court's term Corcoran had made a courtesy call on Justice Brandeis before he left for Chatham on Cape Cod. Frankfurter knew of Tom's unhappiness with the justice's role in the Court fight and used healing words:

After all, Tom, your tongue is tougher than your heart—which does credit to both your heart and tongue.
L.D.B.'s face glowed with pleasure when he told me of your visit. We are what we are—and Isaiah is what he is. Prophets are not "good fellows," you know, and age does funny things in addition.

Another letter was even more rhapsodic about Tom:

One of these days—certainly in the days of your great grandchildren, if not before —you will have become a mythological figure, like one of those supra-human real figures in Irish lore or Scotch annals or Eastern tales, that of a being who single-handed fought whole armies, was everywhere at the same time, knew not defeat, fed on hostilities, loved loyally.

The work of reconciliation went on. Ben sent Felix a copy of a letter that he had sent Brandeis. "Now the Court hostilities have abated there are certain facts you should know." Cohen described his and Corcoran's relations with Wheeler on the proposal "for a temporary increase in the size of the Court." The President had had nothing to do with it, did not know they were doing so, nor had Wheeler at any time taken exception to their suggestions. He enclosed a copy of the memorandum he had given Solicitor General Reed in January on what to do about the Court and added:

Neither Tom nor I was consulted in the formulation of the Court proposal which the President did decide to sponsor. I saw neither the President's message nor the bill which accompanied it until I read them in the newspaper. Tom likewise did not see the bill before it was released to the public. He was shown a draft of the message a day or two before it was sent to the Congress, but he was not asked or given the opportunity to make any substantive suggestions.

Once the President's proposals were made, Tom and I worked for their adoption because they appeared to us to be the only constructive proposals in the field that had a chance of adoption or of influencing the adoption of a more liberal viewpoint by the Court. The President having made his decision and announced his proposals, the practical choice was, so at least we believed, between giving support to those proposals or a do-nothing policy. Despite obviously unfortunate irrelevancies and omissions in the message transmitting the proposals and obviously unfortunate inconsistencies in the bill itself, Tom and I had no doubt as to what our choice ought to be, and we acted accordingly.

Ben should not expect too much from the justice, Frankfurter cautioned. "Your letter to L.D.B. is really perfect. Marion thinks so too. But let me warn you not to be surprised if you hear not a ripple. If he does not want to answer a letter he has a way of not even acknowledging it." But Felix was wrong. "My dear Ben," the justice replied in longhand, "I am indeed glad to have yours of July 30 with enclosures; and hope there may be a chance soon for a full talk with you and Tom not only on the past but on the future."

Felix spent that summer at Cohasset on Massachusetts Bay. He sent Ben a careful analysis of why the Court bill had been defeated and asked him to have copies made of it.

Defeat of Supreme Court legislation was due to:

(1) Oblique way in which plan was originally floated—age, overwork of justices, and congestion,—thereby
(2) giving opportunity for Hughes' letter and
(3) confusion of the public mind. Thus,
(4) intensifying terrific release of emotions that cluster around the Supreme Court as a symbol, most powerfully expressed by some liberals, but

(5) especially enlisting powerful hostility of the Catholic Church (concretely relying on decision in *Pierce v. Society of Sisters*)—wasn't it coincidence that all Catholic Senators were in opposition—and

(6) because of relaxation of pressure due to recovery, for new legislation no powerful support behind the President's proposal except Labor, and to the extent that Labor was spearhead of support it became a source of weakness, because

(7) violent aspect of C.I.O. strikes aroused another set of American emotions—"law and order" (e.g. this alienated the Vice President from the President's program) and fused with loyalty to the Court and its inviolability, which became decisive

(8) after Court's strategic retreat, in overruling minimum wage decisions and sustaining by broadest possible interpretation Social Security and Wagner Acts, cut President's grievances from under, leaving only an abstract, future issue and that not purely abstract but entangled in present sinister appearances, still more weakened

(9) by Van Devanter's resignation and widely believed talk that one or two others of the reactionaries would go.

There were, of course, minor windfalls to opposition:

(1) Farley's incredible gaucheries which offended Senators' feelings of self respect;
(2) Ashurst's incompetence and general weakness of Administration Senators on the Judiciary Committee.
(3) Sumner's speech in the House;
(4) Joe Robinson's dramatic death;
(5) Lehman's well-timed attack;
(6) Final negotiations for Administration in hands unfriendly to proposal—Garner.[39]

Frankfurter followed up this incisive analysis of the "168 days" of the Court fight with a four-page letter to "Dear Frank." He sensed that he, too, like Tom, needed encouragement.

No one in our time has illustrated more strikingly than your Prexy Eliot's dictum, "for a real fighter, after a battle has miscarried, the question is, 'when will the fighting be renewed?' " Nor does anyone know as well as you that there are various ways of fighting, and different times dictate different modes. And so I know that in the quiet recesses of your mind much strategic and tactical thinking has been going on.[40]

He urged the President to speak to the country and to set the Court battle in the context of the nation's history and his objectives—"it will dramatize why it was undertaken & how greatly, for the present at least, you attained the concrete aims that moved you."

Frankfurter enclosed some notes that he had drafted for a possible Fireside Chat. Roosevelt was grateful for Frankfurter's "grand letter . . . You are absolutely right about the radio." Roosevelt did speak on Constitution

Day. Tom had Frankfurter's notes. He and Ben made them sing. "Tom, Ben and I worked on that speech," recorded Rosenman. "The general theme of the speech was Tom's idea: that the Constitution was not a lawyer's contract, strict and inflexible, but a layman's document, appropriate to a layman's broad and flexible construction."[41]

Frankfurter wanted Roosevelt to say "for the present at least there appears to be a majority of the Court which realizes that the function of legislation belongs to the Congress and not to the Court." That note was absent from Roosevelt's speech except indirectly. "We know it takes time to adjust government to the needs of society," he said. "But modern history proves that reforms too long delayed or denied have jeopardized peace, undermined democracy and swept away civil and religious liberties."[42] More strongly than before he sounded the warning of spreading dictatorship to which he juxtaposed the contrasting principle that guided his own policy and united the New Dealers:

In our generation, a new idea has come to dominate thought about government, the idea that the resources of the nation can be made to produce a far higher standard of living for the masses of the people if only government is intelligent and energetic in giving the right direction to economic life.

Joe Robinson's unexpected death in July obliged Roosevelt to select someone else to fill Justice Van Devanter's place. The Attorney General came with his list, mostly appellate court judges. At the same time, presumably at Roosevelt's direction, Tom journeyed to Cohasset to get Frankfurter's ideas on whom he might name. Felix and Tom went over the list carefully and Felix indicated a preference for Stanley Reed, the solicitor general who would be "thoroughly at home in the procedural problems that come before the Court" but Senator Black, a skillful investigator who had piloted difficult matters through the Senate, he thought would "have to muster an immense amount of rather technical jurisdictional learning . . ." As between the two and speaking as a lawyer, "I should plump for Reed."[43] Cummings held several "elimination" sessions with the President. Roosevelt leaned to Black, Cummings noted, but was reluctant to lose the Alabaman from the Senate. Cummings returned the next day with a memo that listed the pluses and minuses of Black and Reed, only to discover the President had already notified Black that he planned to send up his nomination that day. In addition to liking Black for his support of the New Deal Roosevelt counted on Senate reluctance to refuse to confirm one of its members. It was only after the Senate voted to confirm and the Blacks had sailed for England that a newspaper broke the story of Black's membership in the Ku Klux Klan. Rumor became indisputable fact. There was a hue and cry that Black should resign. Even within the President's own circle opinion was divided. Tom who had worked with Black not only in the Court fight but on the Wages and Hours bill, took it on himself to phone Black in England to urge him to stand fast, not to answer the charges until he returned to the United States when he could do so in a radio broadcast.

He went to see Black on his return to tell him about the pressures on the President to get him to withdraw. He was sure the President would not do so, but he urged him to explain to the nation the circumstances under which he had joined Klan. "He said I know everyone in the South is waiting for the broadcast and what they are saying is let's see if old Hugo will chicken out. Well, old Hugo is not going to chicken out."

He went on the radio the next day, October 2, to speak over the three networks. The New York *Times* four-column headline the next day read:

BLACK ADMITS HE JOINED THE KLAN; THEN QUIT, THEN IGNORED UNSOLICITED CARD; CITES RECORD AS A LIBERAL IN SENATE.

"The speech was successful," wrote Tom in his autobiographical notes and Black went on to become one of "the most effective of Justices ever to sit on the Court."[44] He became one of Tom's closest friends and would take on Tom's daughter Margaret as clerk, the second such appointment of a woman in the Court's history.

Two days later Black took his seat on the Court. When he filed in, the last of the eight justices who followed the chief justice, Mrs. Black smiled at him and his face lit up. After the twenty-one-minute sitting, Mrs. Hughes and Mrs. Brandeis came up and greeted her. But Mrs. Brandeis, Alice, when Ben called on the justice a few days later, was still unreconciled both to Roosevelt as well as Black. Ben and the justice first talked about Roosevelt's "Quarantine the Aggressor" speech in Chicago the previous week.

I called on LDB Saturday. He is looking well and seems quite calm. He appeared to like the President's speech at Chicago on foreign affairs and thought that we might without militarily entangling ourselves, determine with whom we should trade and adopt an economic boycott if we liked.[45]

They also talked about Palestine and their concern with a report of the British Royal Commission that favored some form of partition between Jewish and Arab areas. The justice wanted Ben to go to London, but Ben pleaded New Deal business, especially holding company litigation which was slowly moving toward the Supreme Court as well as a regional conservation bill presented that:

He then took me out to see Alice. I mentioned the documents I had sent him, and his countenance lit him and he said he would [be] very much interested and wanted to talk them over sometime at length and then pointed to the other room, indicating that he did not want to talk before Alice.

He left the room for a little while and Alice said, "Wasn't the Black appointment unfortunate?"

I replied, "it was an unhappy incident, but no one could have ever thought about his alleged Klan activities in view of his consistently liberal record for the past eleven years."

But she said, "He should have spoken when the question was raised."

I agreed, but added that I thought it would have made no difference in view of his record.

She was not so sure about it, but agreed that the question would have been settled one way or the other.

"It is, she added, "a very unfortunate thing for the Court. I think it will continue to be a disturbing factor for a long time."

"I don't think so," I replied. "I think it will quickly be forgotten once he is sitting on the Court."

"Oh no!" she rejoined. "You see F.D.R. has made up his mind to do something about the Court and won't rest until he has his way, and every time the question of the Court comes up, the Black appointment will come up."

"I don't see what you mean," I said. "I thought the President had got pretty much what he was after so far as the Court was concerned."

"You mean the decisions," she said.

"I mean," I replied, "a liberal interpretation of the Constitution. No one could,— and no one before the Congressional Committees tried,—to justify the decisions of the Court during the year preceding the controversy."

"And," she asked in amazement, "you don't think F.D. will try to do anything with the Court?"

"Not if the Court behaves itself," I responded.

LDB is still keen on doing something about the regularity of employment and the curse of bigness. But we did not get down to details. He seemed to think that the drop in the price of cotton was to be blamed on AAA and the loss of foreign markets. But I avoided discussion on the ground that I really knew nothing about it.

The letter ended on a note that reflected his and Tom's disenchantment with the justice, a disappointment that darkened their relationship with Frankfurter as well. They began to look at him a little critically. Ben's letter to Felix continued:

A more serious matter was his deep disappointment that Tom was not with me. He mentioned Tom several times. I told him that Tom was working with the skipper and I was sorry he could not come with me. He hoped he would come soon.

When I told Tom, he closed his jaws and said, "I am not going to see him. He did not shoot straight with us last year, and it is best not to renew the relationship. The skipper is very bitter, and I think it is best that he should not think we are in touch with him [LDB]. I went to say goodbye at the end of the year as a matter of courtesy, but I don't want to go back as we can't restore the old relationship."

I don't think you should write Tom as it is a matter of considerable emotion with him. But I think you should know so that you can talk over the matter with him sometime when you are together. Even then you will have to tread lightly as Tom feels that you are tied too much emotionally with LDB. He thinks it was LDB's hold on you which stayed your hand in the court fight. And he is particularly bitter that LDB should not even consider resigning under circumstances which might ensure your appointment. Tom did not repeat these thoughts at the present time, but I know that they partially at least influence his reaction. But please don't repeat all of this to Tom.

The defeat of the Court plan was attended by rumors that Corcoran and Cohen had been "blown out of the political picture" and were on the way out, of a "complete rupture" between Roosevelt and Frankfurter, neither of which was true.

He had received a very tempting offer via Joe Kennedy, Corcoran informed his father. At the same time, the President was pressing him to stay on. The latter would be "a stepping stone," his father commented, and would carry with it "honor & glory . . . though not much money." He was sure, however, that in any new arrangement under Roosevelt, Ben and Bob Jackson would be taken care of and "you like Washington and your contacts there. Money seems to be the one thing lacking." Moreover, the President's enemies "would rejoice at your departure," and if Tom did decide in favor of the money offer, "would you not be accused of turning turtle on the liberals?"

The rumors about Frankfurter after the Court bill's defeat became a witches' brew. A friendly Washington correspondent Richard L. Stokes of the St. Louis *Post-Dispatch* reported that the friendship between Roosevelt and Frankfurter was an outstanding casualty of the Supreme Court battle. "That the chief loss is the President's, most observers would confess. Of all the New Deal prophets, Frankfurter was esteemed the wisest, sanest, and most disinterested."[46]

Tom had helped Stokes with background material for the article. "In confidence, I must tell you," Stokes wrote him after his anguished protest, "that I wrote in a section embodying without quoting you of course, your view that Professor Frankfurter was willing to go along publicly with the

Supreme Court plan." But a hard-boiled editor struck the passage out as unbelievable, "and I could not tell him the source of the information."

Frankfurter sought to soften Corcoran's anguish:

I know how sensitive you are—and how devoted, so I write to underline what I said on the phone—"take Stokes & the *St. Louis P.D.* thing off your mind." Generosities—yours to Stokes—often are outraged or miscarry & this was just one of them & the thing to do is to absorb it & close it on the book of life.

So far as F.D. is concerned I am rather distressed to have him think that in any way in which I could avoid it I could become even the unwitting instrument of criticism of him. I didn't mind being blackguarded all these years because I cared deeply about him & for the things he cares for & works. But it gives me pain & disgust to be praised by people whose purposes are not my purposes & on wholly false & manufactured grounds.

All this I should like to tell F.D. except that since March 4, 1933 I have made it a fixed rule not to add to his burdens by bothering him about anything pertaining to myself.

You are of course at liberty to tell him all this—or, if you think, he would prefer to hear it at first hand, I'd be glad to write him. I leave it all to you—unless you want to throw it back for my judgment.

The story of a "rupture" between Roosevelt and Frankfurter was made up out of whole cloth. Frankfurter had helped with the Constitution Day speech, exchanged enthusiastic notes with the President over his "Quarantine-the Aggressors" speech, and was invited to spend the night at Hyde Park at the end of October. Afterward he wrote the President, "Ben Cohen and I have been working on the three phases of tax legislation about which you and I talked and I enclose the results of our labors."[47]

A battle was lost but the war won, Roosevelt said of the Court crisis. That was true but equally true and painful were other things. Tampering with the Court was a dangerous business, as Wheeler earlier had warned and subsequently taken a main hand in demonstrating. Another result was Roosevelt's loss of power. The Republican weakness in Congress was offset by an alliance between Republicans and conservative Southern Democrats. The significance of the Court fight, wrote Corcoran in one of his autobiographical fragments, was precisely in Roosevelt's loss of the fundamental support of the South.[48] Before the Court fight Roosevelt had been at a peak of power and acclaim unknown to United States history. After the Court defeat, "he descended into a position of political impotence and antagonism incredible to him."

"For Roosevelt's advisers," and they included Tom and Ben, "the practical question was how to help him survive disaster as best possible, sure that no one else had the capacity to bring the country out of a continuing recession."

After the Court fight it was no longer possible to equate the New Deal with the Democratic ascendancy. More clearly than ever the New Deal was a movement within the political parties, Republican as well as Democratic. "I could not refuse to work," Tom wrote of the battle over the Court plan, "not to save the Court—but to ensure that Roosevelt's second term would not be 'a lame duck term' in which he could get nothing done while others cast lots to see who's going to be the next President."

He and Ben stayed on. "Tom and Ben are back of it." Those were the words quietly passed around Washington, meaning that "things were going to happen."[49]

XXII

————⟡⟡⟡————

Crisis in Economic Theory: Spenders vs. Budget Balancers

The conviction that government had to rescue the market economy after its nearly total collapse in the early thirties had united the various schools of New Deal thought in Roosevelt's first term. In sharp contrast to Herbert Hoover and the people around him, New Dealers did not believe that laissez-faire and the free play of market forces left to themselves would automatically bring recovery. It was not clear, however, until the battle with the Supreme Court majority was won that despite the defeat of the Court-packing plan itself the federal government would be allowed to shape and lead economic policy as it did foreign and military affairs. In the ashes of that defeat Roosevelt and his lawyers, however, had established government's right to promote the general welfare through economic and social legislation. The great battle had been fought, Lauchlin Currie who was then in his thirties, wrote later, "and decided in favor of those who maintained that it is the proper role and responsibility of the State to insure that the economic machine functions at more or less full capacity."[1]

Government's right to do so within the framework of the Constitution had been established. The question remained, however, as to what was the right road to recovery. That issue would be fought out in Roosevelt's second term. The advocates of a "natural" as distinct from a government-shaped recovery were still powerful. Tugwell was gone, Moley was in opposition, Berle was more and more involved in foreign affairs. It was the turn now of younger economists, the statistic-minded disciple of Thorstein Veblen and assistant of Frances Perkins, Isidor Lubin; the burly, combative, sentimental Leon Henderson who was the chief economic adviser of the Works Progress Administration (WPA); and the best economic theoretician of the lot, quiet-voiced Lauchlin Currie, whose 1935 memo on monetary policy and open-market operations Marriner Eccles, and, after him, Roosevelt, had adopted as their own.

Henderson, in the 1936 campaign had served as economic adviser to the Democratic National Committee. The establishment of such a post in itself was a recognition of the interdependence of economics and politics. Henderson had no staff and knew little about monetary policy, so he had asked Eccles at the Federal Reserve Board for help. As head of an independent agency, Eccles thought it inappropriate to engage in campaign activity, so he turned the job over to Currie. The two men hit it off and Henderson introduced Currie to key figures in the New Deal group, Corcoran and Cohen, Lubin and Jerome Frank, to William Douglas, Harry Hopkins, and Henry Wallace. Currie's economic ideas began to influence the whole inner group and he became known throughout the government as the leading advocate of "pump priming."[2]

Ranged against the pump primers were the balanced-budget men led by Secretary of the Treasury Henry Morgenthau, Jr. In Roosevelt's first term the nation had risen from almost total economic paralysis in 1933 to what was by 1937 the most sensational recovery from a depression in history.* A few economists, most notably Leon Henderson, cautioned privately and publicly that the recovery could be short-lived. Unless private investors stepped up their spending as government curtailed its outlays, they foresaw a business recession.

But the unbalanced budgets that in the view of New Dealers like Henderson, Lubin, and Currie had played a major part in the upturn during Roosevelt's first term had had Roosevelt's support largely for humanitarian and compassionate reasons. So Currie believed. Roosevelt was not yet a convert to the Keynesian concept of compensatory spending. Quite the contrary. His annual budget message at the beginning of 1937 emphasized

* Joblessness had declined from 14 million in 1935 to 5 million in early 1937.

reductions in government spending and promised a completely balanced budget by 1939.[3]

The promise of a balanced budget reflected Roosevelt's own inclination and it was fiercely encouraged by his Dutchess County neighbor, Henry Morgenthau, Jr. The Secretary of the Treasury was intransigently honest, absolutely loyal, and a good administrator. He surrounded himself with able men, including New Dealers like his legal counsel, Herman Oliphant, and his policy adviser, Harry Dexter White, but was himself neither a thinker nor abreast of economic theory. Then neither was Roosevelt. Their mutuality in this regard, given Roosevelt's masterful personality, meant that in the final analysis Roosevelt was his own Secretary of the Treasury, and that was the way he wanted it. He wanted men and women of strong views but who did his bidding in the end.

Within the government, Morgenthau, as complete recovery seemed at hand, became the chief advocate of a return to balanced budgets.[4] At the end of 1937, moreover, economic arguments were fortified by political considerations. The Court-packing fight had cut into Roosevelt's middle-class support.

Advocacy of a balanced budget, Morgenthau thought, was the way to regain middle-class confidence. Red lights were beginning to flash among the economic indicators, but Roosevelt and Morgenthau decided that the way to keep them green was to win the confidence of the business community through a balanced budget. "I'm willing to bet my job as Secretary of the Treasury that I'm right," Morgenthau told his staff. Then on October 19, 1937, the stock market plummeted and "Black Tuesday" brought murmurs of a "Roosevelt Recession." The Administration bore the responsibility for the collapse, Winthrop Aldrich of the Chase National Bank told a bankers meeting. "He blame[d] the SEC and the tax on corporation surpluses," recorded Ickes. The New Dealers thought differently. Corcoran and Cohen came in to see the secretary to urge a housing program. "With business falling off, unemployment increasing, and the public works program at an end, they regard housing as the one thing that we have left to serve as a pump primer."

"The President doesn't quite know which way to turn," Ickes noted at a Cabinet meeting at the beginning of November.[5] He had "almost jumped down his [Morgenthau's] throat," when the secretary urged Roosevelt to reassure business that he was not against it as such. Morgenthau was even more graphic in his diary about this exchange with the President. He quoted Roosevelt as saying to the Cabinet:

Last night when I went to bed, alongside my bed was the darndest letter you ever saw from Henry . . . It was just terrible. I am sick and tired of being told by the Cabinet, by Henry and by everybody else for the last two weeks what's the matter with the country and nobody suggests what I should do.

Henry Hopkins had an idea. The President instead of limiting himself to the heads of departments ought to talk directly with the boys who actually wrote their memos and hear from them what should be done. The President agreed and it was arranged that Currie, Henderson, and Lubin should see him. The meeting was set for November 8 and Currie drafted a five-page memorandum on the "causes of the recession" and recommendations that all three signed.[6]

The memorandum listed these causes as (1) "an upsurge in costs and prices," (2) the failure of consumer purchasing power "to expand sufficiently to maintain the new levels of business activity," and (3) a "decline in building" and a "decline in the government's net contribution" to buying power. It challenged the Wall Street view that the undistributed earnings tax and the capital gains tax or the government's regulatory activities "played any significant part in bringing about the decline." There would be no "natural" upturn in the near future and "the recession *could* be severe and prolonged if government does not intervene."

To increase purchasing power, the three urged a substantial rise in government purchases, more spending on relief and public works, and governmental stimulation of a residential housing program. "The objective of a balanced budget for 1939 should be retained," it said decorously as a final point. The conference with the President went on all afternoon. An unexpected participant was Paul Mazur, a Lehman Brothers partner, who was invited by James Roosevelt, his father's secretary. Mazur later gave the story out to the press, said Lubin. "We always felt that he had violated the conference."

At the meeting Lubin proposed that WPA be used as "a catalytic agent" to get more housing. Like many other progressives Lubin agreed with the purposes of the WPA to provide work relief for the jobless but felt that it was "not generative enough . . . I felt that we could tie up WPA with private investment." The inner New Deal group talked about such a linkage frequently. Lubin and Henderson owned adjoining properties down on Chesapeake Bay. Currie was often there. "We would go fishing. Not much fish but we drank to console ourselves and would get back at 4 a.m."

Currie's forte was compensatory fiscal policy which in the crisis of 1937–38 meant a resumption of government spending. He had tutored

Henderson on the subject in the 1936 campaign. In that campaign Roosevelt, although not yet a convert to unbalanced budgets, had defended government-spending programs, even enunciating a homespun version of the multiplier effect of such spending.

Henderson blamed the monopolistic practices of many mass production industries for keeping the multiplier effect from working. There is no record of what he said at the White House conference, but a few weeks later to a meeting of shirt and pajama manufacturers he charged that the biggest companies through monopolistic practices and "tilted prices extracted their winnings, then reduced their production when they felt a falling off of orders." This choice of a reduction of output instead of cutting prices, he said, meant dropping workers, the first step in lowering purchasing power. "There is something very much wrong with a free competitive system, where any one company can make profits at fifty percent of productive capacity."

Henderson had achieved a modest renown with the columnists with his early prediction of a business recession unless private investment replaced the contributions of government as it cut down its spending.

A resumption of federal spending on a grand scale was Currie's main thesis at the meeting with Roosevelt. But "little tangible" resulted from it, he felt. The inclusion of Mazur meant that Roosevelt was again presented with conflicting views among the experts.

Henderson was an effective and colorful publicist. In a speech over the facilities of the CBS network on New Year's Day on "What Has Happened to Recovery?" he ticked off the causes of the recession as he saw them. Because "prices had been rising faster and longer than wages" there was "not enough purchasing power in the hands of the mass of people to buy the full output of farms and factories." The rise in prices "was touched off" by monopolistic practices—"many an industry, like the steel industry, has pegged its prices, thrown its employees out of jobs and ploughed under potential production . . ."

There were roughly five approaches to dealing with the 1937–38 recession:

(1) The advocates of a balanced budget and economies in government.

(2) Advocates of a reconciliation with business even at the price of repeal of the undistributed profits and capital gains tax and easing up on the utilities.

(3) Reconstitution of an NRA type of planning.

(4) An attack on monopolistic practices, especially the rigged prices and restricted production of concentrated economic power.

(5) A resumption of spending.[7]

The schools overlapped. Keynes who wrote an unsolicited letter to Roosevelt at the beginning of 1938 advised a large increase in public expenditures as well as measures to regain the confidence of business. Those who attacked monopoly also favored planning. The question was what aspects of the economic process should be planned. Few New Dealers wanted to see a return of the NRA code authorities, but compensatory fiscal policy by its very terms meant directing the economy. The struggle over the various approaches to dealing with the recession was essentially, as Herbert Stein has written in *The Fiscal Revolution in America,* a struggle for the mind of FDR. That mind was disposed by upbringing and by the economics it had learned at home, at Groton, and at Harvard in favor of a balanced budget.

So at the same time that Roosevelt listened to Currie, Henderson, and Lubin, he approved Morgenthau's speech to the New York banking community in which the secretary assured it of the Administration's intention to balance the budget, a pledge that provoked snorts of disbelief from the bankers and their lawyers. Jerome Frank had just been appointed an SEC commissioner. He was at lunch with William O. Douglas, its chairman. Frank's reaction typified the scorn of most New Dealers for Morgenthau's line. "Everytime that God-damned fool announces a balanced budget, it means that Government purchasing power is being cut and that's about the only thing that's keeping things together. The trouble is," continued Frank,* "the President won't spend any money. Nobody on the outside will believe the trouble we have with him. Yet they call him a big spender. It makes me laugh."[8]

The President was of many minds about reconciliation with business. As he told Morgenthau when the secretary urged it again in the face of the recession, he had tried it repeatedly and been rebuffed. Only his departure from office would satisfy Wall Street, he believed. When the stock market crashed in October, he told associates, as Berle recorded it, that it might be "concerted action on the part of the New York financial district to discredit the Administration."[9]

Berle scoffed at this, but he wanted to help the President who consulted him in the crisis. The President persuaded him to leave La Guardia and become an assistant secretary of state. Roosevelt really needed a "chancellor," Berle thought, but mindful of Moley's fate, he realized Roosevelt would never accept such a guiding presence. Nevertheless, he decided to

---

* The conversation was recalled by another participant in the luncheon, Ernest Cuneo, lawyer and confidant of La Guardia and Corcoran.

try to reconstitute some form of Brains Trust. He, Tugwell, and Charles Taussig, a liberal industrialist who was in and out of the New Deal, undertook to pull together some leaders of business and labor, as well as themselves, to map out a program for dealing with the recession crisis.

That winter was a bleak one for New Dealers. "The President is ill, tired and obviously confused," Berle, who saw him in October, noted.[10] Roosevelt's meeting with the New Deal economists at the beginning of November had been without result and Currie thought there were moments when the President's faith in the basic New Deal policy of compensatory budgets was shaken.

Tom wrote anxiously to Frankfurter about the mood of discouragement that had swept the New Dealers.

The liberal crowd down here badly needs a center around which to rally—just so they may touch each other and feel that it is not too desperately lonely in the front line trenches.

It isn't a matter of formal meetings—those can always be held in some cafeteria. What they need is an unending series of little dinners and five o'clock drinks where they can meet in small but shifting combinations.

I've been thinking how to do it for a long time. Harry Hopkins was going to make his house a rallying place. Just now he's out for two months. The only practical solution is Ben and myself—but frankly we can't afford it with all the other drains.

Can you find me some angel or a choir of angels . . . ?[11]

Frankfurter does not seem to have replied and the idea was dropped except that Corcoran and Cohen, as Currie wrote, were regarded as the chief "coagulators" of the New Dealers.

Was Roosevelt's cup half-empty or half-full? Was it a lack of fight, as New Dealers like Ickes suspected, or part of the process of making up his mind in the face of the conflicting advice he was receiving? Morgenthau, backed by Hull and Jesse Jones, even, in Ickes's view, by Perkins and Wallace, was being urged to extend an olive branch to business. Wall Street, "bewildered and frightened" as it was by the stock market plunge, wanted as the price of an armistice, tax concessions and a balanced budget. On the other side, Eccles, Ickes, Hopkins, the younger New Dealers clamored for a resumption of spending and disputed the allegedly harmful effects of the business taxes.[12]

Some of the New Dealers held a strategy session in Bob Jackson's office. Cohen and Corcoran were there; Henderson, Lubin, and Oliphant. The special session of Congress that Roosevelt had convened on November 15 was in an anti-Roosevelt mood. The group feared the repeal of New Deal measures and to offset it pressed Jackson to go after the monopolies. But his first speeches on the subject fell flat. Corcoran and Cohen wrote one for him to deliver the day after Christmas. "They made a real stinker of it," wrote Alsop and Kintner, who had been briefed by Corcoran. The monopolists had "priced themselves out of the market, and priced themselves into a slump," Jackson thundered. That speech landed on the front pages. Corcoran and Cohen told Ickes he had to follow up, which he did with a speech about the "sixty families."

Did Jackson and Ickes reflect Roosevelt's policies? the business community anxiously asked. It had not escaped Wall Street's notice that Roosevelt's companions on a fishing trip to the Dry Tortugas a little while earlier had been Hopkins, Ickes, and Bob Jackson. It was Corcoran who told Jackson the President wanted him along. The President and his friends had spent several days fishing, playing poker, loafing, and talking. Although the President kept to himself a good deal of the time it was obvious to Ickes that he was taken with the youthful assistant attorney general. This reassured Ickes. "There is no doubt he is a real liberal," Ickes said of Jackson. "He sees what the big corporations and big business generally are doing to the country."[13] Jackson scoffed at the idea that amending the tax system will make for recovery. Roosevelt during the trip asked Jackson to prepare something for him on monopolies. Corcoran and Cohen lunched with Ickes after the trip. They already had talked with Jackson. "Tom told me that the liberals on the hill are beginning to feel lonely and discouraged."

Then had come the Jackson and Ickes speeches on concentrated wealth as leading to the recession and fascism. Suddenly the monopoly charge "caught fire and burst into conflagration!" "It Can Happen Here," Ickes's speech was entitled in a takeoff on the title of Sinclair Lewis's bestselling novel about American fascism. Although newspapers speculated, noted Ickes, that the President might declare war on the monopolies in his annual message, Ickes wondered whether he and Jackson had gone out on a limb and some conservatives indeed hoped the President would repudiate them. Ickes was relieved when the President, in his State of the Union address "after distinguishing between big business and predatory monopolistic business . . . said in a slow deliberate voice that no responsible member of the Administration had expressed any different views. "I regarded this," Ickes's diary continued, "as an endorsement of what Jackson and I had said and many of the newspapers have taken the same view." Jackson had no such anxiety. "Bob," the President told him, "I'm sick of sitting here kissing people's asses to get them to do what they ought to be volunteering for the Republic."[14]

Jackson at the moment was in the position of a Roosevelt favorite. Roosevelt had taken a shine to the assistant attorney general, whose testimony on the Supreme Court bill had overshadowed that of his chief, Homer Cummings, and who Roosevelt thought had presidential possibilities, but the President's mind was fully disclosed to no one. The somewhat muted character of his endorsement of the Ickes and Jackson speeches indicated his mind still was not made up. Indeed a good deal of the time of the New Dealers was spent in intense discussions of how to present their policies to the President. Said Currie:

For most of us the President was an aloof figure and in a discussion of a program there was always discussion as to the best channels by which an idea might be brought to the President and the best sponsorship of a project or a piece of legislation.

Corcoran was of course pivotal in such consideration: It was widely believed that he slipped in and out of the President's office frequently and had ready access to the President at all times. Tom did nothing to discourage this impression and to this day I don't really know how frequently he saw the President or how close his relations really were. When he said "The Boss wants so and so," I never questioned it.[15]

But there were other indications that Roosevelt liked his aides' attack on the "sixty families." He told Tugwell, whom he saw at the end of 1937, that he wanted to "scare these people into doing something." He had spent half a morning with some big businessmen, he cheerfully reported to his Cabinet. Alfred Sloan of General Motors and Ernest Weir, the steelman, were in the group. Prior to the Ickes-Jackson fusillade, they had refused even to come in, the President said. Afterward they were "only too glad to come" and one of them implored the President, "for God's sake call off that man Ickes." At the next Cabinet meeting Roosevelt reported a visit of the automobile manufacturers who also would not have come except for the Ickes-Jackson onslaught.[16] Another result of the Jackson-Ickes speeches was a "marked revival of spirit and aggressiveness on the part of the New Deal crowd," said Jackson.

Those speeches seemed to tilt the balance against the budget balancers but the question of compensatory spending still was unsettled in the President's mind. He had a letter from Keynes, the President told Ickes, "advising him to do some pump priming which was the proper thing to do in 1933 when the water had receded to the bottom of the well, but he doubted whether it was the thing to do now with the water within 25 or 30 percent of the top. He seems to have adopted a policy of watchful waiting so far as the economic situation is concerned. He knows that unemployment is increasing, that business is falling off, but he doesn't seem to know what he can or should do about it."[17]

In a state of indecision he sought advice everywhere, including Tugwell and Berle. Berle disliked the attack on monopolies.[18] The Jackson-Ickes speeches were "rather second-rate demagogy" even if half of their content was borrowed from *The Modern Corporation and Private Property.* "I know too much about the two hundred corporations to make a personal devil out of them. I know too much about the sixty families to think that they will amount to much. And I do not see that anything is accomplished by calling the particular group 'Bourbon.' "

With the President's encouragement Berle and Tugwell were at work on their own program for a grand truce between the Administration and business. Berle went to see Thomas Lamont. The banker was amenable to an increase in relief expenditures and an unbalanced budget provided the undistributed profits tax was repealed and capital gains modified, that peace was made with business generally, and the utilities in particular.

With this preliminary agreement in mind, the "Advisory Group," as Berle called it, met at the Century Club in New York to work up a formal recovery program. Philip Murray of the Congress of Industrial Organizations (CIO) and Lee Pressman, its counsel, and a secret Communist as he himself later testified, joined John L. Lewis for labor's viewpoint. Owen D. Young and Thomas W. Lamont were there for business as well as Taussig, Tugwell, and Berle. A modified version of the Berle-Lamont understanding was agreed to and Tugwell undertook to arrange a meeting with Roosevelt. The group met with the President on January 14 and on a suggestion of Owen D. Young, which Roosevelt accepted, agreed to recommend a list of proposals. Then the group fell apart. Someone at the White House, said Berle, had leaked the story to the press. "Mr. Berle's economic zoo," Arthur Krock called it. Resistance developed in the CIO. "It seems that the extreme left faction in the CIO want to block any agreement between Lewis, Lamont and the White House," wrote Berle. Washington buzzed with rumors. "There has been no end of a split in Washington over our maneuvers. Corcoran and Cohen think their position is threatened and have started a row." Lamont and Young were unhappy that what had been started as an initiative of goodwill was now embroiled, as they saw it, in politics.

Young was the first to withdraw. A week later Lamont. The latter had talked with the automobile people who had been in to see the President.

"They had a pleasant time, but got nowhere . . ." The "advisory council" ceased to function, although the President persuaded Berle to stay on in Washington as assistant secretary of state. There he not only dealt with foreign affairs but advised the President on economic and political matters:

I went to work last week to try to establish contact with the Left Wing. Rex Tugwell was kind enough to invite Robert Jackson to dinner. Charles [Taussig], Bob [La Follette], Rex, Jerome Frank and I hashed over the situation.

The next evening Berle was dining alone in a Washington restaurant when Ben Cohen came over. They agreed to try to work together, but little came of it. The dislike between Berle and the Frankfurter people was long-standing.

With the New Deal spending program appearing "to be in the doghouse," as Eccles put it at the beginning of 1938, Currie decided the most useful thing he could do was to examine the causes of the recession. The resulting document, although marked confidential, was mimeographed and "widely read and circulated in New Deal circles . . . It probably had as much influence as anything I wrote in the Government," Currie later said.[19]

Wall Street complained that the Roosevelt administration promoted a planned society, but Currie's analysis showed that the recession of 1937–38 was the result of an "absence of careful planning." By this he meant that the payment, despite the President's veto, of a veterans' bonus added a "fortuitous and unplanned" billion dollars to the purchasing stream and the beginning of the collection of Social Security taxes withdrew money from that stream in a similarly unplanned way. A wave of inventorying in the expectation of higher prices and costs was unplanned as was the excessive advance in building costs which had cut off a housing boom.

Currie's coherent account of the recession was not ideological. It demonstrated that "the largest single factor in the steady recovery movement was the excess of federal activity-creating expenditures over activity-decreasing receipts." The soundness of compensatory fiscal policy in a depression had been vindicated in the period from 1934 to 1936 but at the end of 1936 the orderly increase in the rate of recovery gave way to speculative forward buying and inventory stocking. At that time the size of the government contribution, which included the unplanned bonus payment, was partly responsible. Timing was of the essence in compensatory policy. "With the benefit of hindsight . . . it would have been desirable had the rate of increase in consumption slackened in the summer and early fall of

1936. This, theoretically, might have been achieved through a reduction in the net federal contribution to community expenditures."

Currie was no "spending" zealot. He also broke ranks with some liberals and radicals in pinning some responsibility for the cost-price push on labor. "Organized labor asked for a greater increase in hourly earnings than could be compensated for in a short time by increased efficiency." And the managers of industry had responded to the rise in labor costs by advancing prices more than costs. "The broad lesson or moral that emerges is that, in the solution of the problem of securing greater business stability, far more attention must be paid to the problem raised by 'administered' prices on the one hand, and trade union policy on the other, than has hitherto been considered necessary . . . In these circumstances, it appears imperative that a national policy be developed in connection with organized industry and organized labor to ensure that their policies will not wreck the possibility of securing a greater measure of economic stability."

It appears evident, concluded Currie, "that if fiscal policy is to be truly compensatory, a far greater degree of flexibility in expenditures and receipts must be possible than is now the case."

New Dealers were meeting all over Washington in "think" sessions—at Senator Robert La Follette's, Mordecai Ezekiel's, at Paul Appleby's, who was a deputy of Henry Wallace. Everyone was searching for projects that would increase the flow of public and private spending. Currie's essay cleared the air. It refuted the arguments of the budget balancers, reinforced the position of the Keynesians, and set a pattern of national economic reporting that would subsequently be reflected in the annual reports of the Council of Economic Advisers.

The President turned over the unsolicited letter from Keynes to Morgenthau. The secretary answered, ignoring its recommendations of increased spending. Despite the earlier handling of the Keynes letter, it, too, was part of the process of Roosevelt's making up his mind. "I am terrified," Keynes wrote, "lest progressive causes in all the democratic countries should suffer injury, because you have taken too lightly the risk to their prestige which would result from a failure measured in terms of immediate prosperity. There *need* be no failure."[20] Roosevelt was alive to considerations that commingled his place in history with practical solutions.

Not theory but the deepening recession ended Roosevelt's wavering between the budget balancers and compensatory spenders. The stock market had taken another "sickening dip," as Morgenthau put it when the President went to Warm Springs at the end of March. Roosevelt summoned

Harry Hopkins who was recuperating in Florida from surgery. Hopkins, in turn, asked his assistant, Aubrey Williams, and Leon Henderson to come down and be available not far from Warm Springs. The two were joined by Beardsley Ruml, the treasurer of R. H. Macy's and a longtime advocate of tax cuts as a way of stimulating the economy. The group worked up a schedule of spending projects and the rationale for them in terms of the federal contribution required to push the national income from $56 billion to $80 billion, at which point there was to be full employment. Hopkins shuttled their memos over to Roosevelt. The President approved, and when he entrained for Washington at the beginning of April, Hopkins with him, the battle had been won. The President delayed announcement of this major fiscal decision until Morgenthau, who was holidaying at Sea Island, was notified.[21]

At Atlanta, Roosevelt's train picked up Ben Cohen and Bob Jackson to work on a monopoly message. Cohen had met on this with Corcoran in Charleston, South Carolina. A Roosevelt message on monopoly and concentration would be part of a one-two New Deal punch.

Roosevelt's spending decision brought Morgenthau one of the darkest moments in his Cabinet career. He returned to Washington on April 10 and soon was closeted with Roosevelt. Hopkins and Jimmy Roosevelt were also there.[22]

"We have been traveling for this last week and have covered a lot of ground," the President informed him, "and you will have to hurry to catch up."

"Mr. President, maybe I can never catch up," Morgenthau bravely replied.

"Oh yes, you can—in a couple of hours," Roosevelt countered and began to present the program that had been worked out at Warm Springs. It had all been done, Morgenthau later told his staff, without the participation of anyone from Treasury. Hopkins had "sold" the President on spending. Morgenthau was "scared to death . . . the thing hadn't been thought through . . . They have just stampeded him during the week I was away." He was angry enough so that at a later meeting when Roosevelt outlined his program to congressional leaders Morgenthau shocked them with the statement that the deficit for 1939 would go up by $3.5 billion. "You should not have brought it up without speaking to me first," Roosevelt later coldly told him. Morgenthau told Jimmy Roosevelt to tell his father, "I will let you know whether or not I can finance it."

Morgenthau spent a sleepless night and concluded he had no choice but to resign. ". . . [I]f you insist on going through with this spending program I am seriously thinking of resigning," Morgenthau told the President the next day. But the President was an old hand at keeping his Cabinet together. He mentioned the solidarity of the British cabinet, the magnificent job Morgenthau had loyally done, and when Morgenthau complained that no one in Treasury had been consulted, Roosevelt's voice became excited and he said Morgenthau's resignation would mean destruction of the Democratic Party.

They were unable to agree and parted, but after another sleepless night Morgenthau decided that except for his father he loved no man more than Roosevelt, that the areas in which they agreed far outnumbered those in which they differed, that there were no other places where he might serve as usefully as he did in Roosevelt's administration, so he stayed. So had Ickes after he threatened to resign over Roosevelt's failure to transfer Forestry from Agriculture to Interior. So had Corcoran when impatient and exasperated over Roosevelt's failure to fight the Administration's foes vigorously enough. Even Ben Cohen, outwardly the most even-tempered of men, was known by his younger associates to kick the files in fury over a Roosevelt decision but stayed on. All stifled their rebellions for all knew that it was in service to Roosevelt and the causes he championed that they were achieving the highest moments of personal fulfillment. "We all served his purposes," another New Dealer, Eleanor Roosevelt, later wrote of her husband.

On April 13 Judge Rosenman arrived to work on the draft of the re-newed spending message that Roosevelt had brought with him from Warm Springs.[23] He had read its recommendations to the congressional leaders and then turned it over to Sam and Tom to work on the message that was to go to Congress the next day and on the Fireside Chat to be delivered the same evening. It was one in the morning when Sam and Tom gave their draft to the President. After sitting for a while with his eyes closed, a weary President sat forward and said in an exaggerated drawl, "Mah F-r-a-a-nds." And after the laughter subsided he dictated steadily for an hour —"when we let him at last go to bed," wrote Rosenman. Harry Hopkins joined the group the next morning for the finishing touches.

The new policy was announced. After an analysis of the causes of the recession of the kind the Currie essay had made familiar among New Dealers, which stated that the immediate problem was that "we suffer from a failure of consumer demand . . . How and where can and should the Government start an upward spiral?" Roosevelt recommended additional public expenditures of $2.062 billion, federal loans of $950 million, the reduction of Federal Reserve requirements, a desterilization of $1.4 billion of Treasury gold.

Roosevelt's Fireside Chat was entitled "Dictatorships Do Not Grow Out of Strong and Successful Governments, but Out of Weak and Helpless Ones," and it placed the crisis in an international context of rising totalitarianism.[24] "Democracy has disappeared in several nations not because the people of those nations disliked democracy, but because they had grown tired of seeing their children hungry while they sat helpless in the face of government confusion and government weakness through lack of leadership in government." The soundness of America's democratic institutions, he said firmly, "depends on the determination of our Government to give employment to idle men." In the rise in national income from 1932 to 1937, "government spending acted as a trigger to set off private activity." That was the purpose of the new program.

"By the end of the year," wrote Rosenman, "economic conditions began to improve markedly."

The recession eased but unemployment remained high. The Keynesians felt they knew the answer. The President's recommendations of April 14 were "a great victory for the New Deal point of view," wrote Currie, "but I did not feel that it went far enough." He urged the President to do more.

I calculated that under the new program the new government contribution would average $200 million a month in the second half of 1938 as contrasted with $100 million a month in the first half and this was not sufficient. I wrote that "there is grave danger that the principle of conducting fiscal policy to compensate for excessive variations in private spending will be discredited unless the new spending program is immediately effective." This principle is the most important contribution of the New Deal in the solution of making our capitalistic democracy work![25]

There was always the problem of how much the public was willing to sanction. The New Dealers debated endlessly as to whether he was going fast enough, but they also recognized that in the matter of timing his sense of what was possible was uncanny. He had to move warily after the defeat of the Court bill. The special session of Congress that he had convened in November 1937 ended without passage of a single bill that he had urged upon it. That included taxes. Roosevelt had consulted Frankfurter who in turn had worked with Cohen in suggesting a modification of the undistributed profits tax to help smaller corporations. However, the bill, as it emerged from conference in May 1938, ignored Roosevelt's insistence on fairness and progress in a revised system. It repealed the undistributed profits tax and eliminated the progressive ratios of the capital gains tax. The bill also contained many desirable features so Roosevelt allowed it to become law without his signature. He and the New Dealers went down fighting, but compared with the Revenue Act of 1936, the bill was a defeat.

A reorganization bill was also on his "must" list for 1938. The opposition fought it furiously, saying it was designed to enhance Roosevelt's dictatorial ambitions. Roosevelt's protests that it involved no increase in presidential power were of no avail and with Representative O'Connor, the Democratic chairman of the House Rules Committee, leading the fight against it, the bill was defeated.

Having administered this rebuff to the President, Congress in early 1939 passed a similar bill with little opposition. One of its provisions gave the President six "anonymous" assistants. The press immediately speculated Corcoran would be one of them. He was not, and, indeed, such an office would have been a comedown. But Roosevelt did select Lauchlin Currie. When his name was suggested, Roosevelt replied, "Currie? I remember him well. He can disagree with one without getting red in the face and pounding the table."[26]

He was taking Currie away from him, Roosevelt informed Eccles, in naming him assistant in charge of economic affairs. Currie's first love was economic theory, but a keen political sense guided his actions at the White House. Keynesians soon began to appear in all the agencies. Keynesian analyses invaded congressional hearings.

Roosevelt's embrace of an unbalanced budget marked the heyday of the Keynesians in New Deal Washington. Back in 1934 seven senior members of Harvard's economics department had published a deprecatory analysis of the New Deal, *The Economics of the Recovery Program.* Professor Joseph Schumpeter's cynical introductory essay with its denial of government's ability to do anything about cyclical fluctuations, set its tone. "Headed by Schumpeter," Currie later wrote, they "came out for a balanced budget and for 'weeding out the inefficient,' and in general damned the New Deal." At the time Currie had led the younger men of the department in publishing a letter to Roosevelt in praise of the New Deal. Now at the end of 1938 a group of young Harvard and Tufts economists published *An Economic Program for American Democracy* that Alan Sweezy, one of its contributors, said reflected the "self-confident, crusading spirit" of the Keynesians. WHAT IS THE TITLE OF THE BOOK YOU TOLD ME ABOUT? James Roosevelt wired his father,[27] indicating how deeply its contents had penetrated the White House.

As the White House's "first economist," Currie recruited Richard Gilbert of Harvard, one of the authors of *An Economic Program for America,* and "his group" for Harry Hopkins at Commerce, "which gave support to

Bob Nathan, long a lone outpost in hostile territory." He turned his post at the Federal Reserve Board over to Émile Després, another contributor to *An Economic Program*. He brought Kenneth Galbraith to Washington and placed Gerhard Colm, a Keynesian refugee professor, at the Bureau of the Budget. A group of former students—Walter and William Salant, Griffith Johnson, Alan Sweezy, Arthur Gayer, Malcolm Bregan, George Eddy, Albert Hart, and Martin Krost occupied key posts. The Keynesian position at Treasury grew stronger as Harry Dexter White, an old Harvard colleague with whom Currie lunched regularly, gained influence. The Keynesians developed close working relationships with Gardiner Means and Thomas Blaisdell at the National Resources Planning Board, with Mordecai Ezekiel and Louis Bean at Agriculture, Isidore Lubin at Labor, and with Jerome Frank and Leon Henderson. Currie recalled at a meeting of the American Economic Association in 1971, "We didn't sleep much but when we did, the *General Theory* kept working."[28]

XXIII

The "Safety Net" Strengthened

After Roosevelt's 1936 landslide he had appealed to Tom Corcoran, and through him to Ben Cohen, to stay on in the Administration and help him enact a fair labor standards act that would govern wages and hours and outlaw child labor. The Supreme Court's overthrow of the NIRA in 1935 had opened a breach in the government's efforts to maintain decent standards which such a measure would repair. It would also end a line of judicial interpretation that began with *Hammer v. Dagenhart* in 1918 when the Court by a 5 to 4 decision held that Congress was without the power to prohibit the shipment in interstate and foreign commerce of the products of child labor. A contrary view had been expressed by Justice Holmes writing for the Court's minority of four, but the majority view had been controlling from then on ending in the constitutional crisis of 1936–37.

It seemed plausible in the wake of Roosevelt's monumental victory in 1936 to postpone renewed federal efforts to regulate wages and hours until the Court roadblock to federal action had been removed. In January, Court reform had been seen as the gateway to fair labor standards; by May, the shoe was on the other foot. Court packing had been stalled and the Wages and Hours bill was introduced, for its own sake—it had been promised all along—but also to strengthen Roosevelt's political leverage.

Moreover, the Court in its series of reversals in the spring of 1937, especially the decisions that upheld Washington State's minimum wage law and the National Labor Relations Act, encouraged the thought that the judicial blockage of federal action was being lifted. Even the Court's personnel was changing with the retirement of Van Devanter.

Tom Corcoran, recalling his positive response to Roosevelt's appeal that he stay on to help with wages and hours, invoked the memory of the great justice for whom he had clerked. He had promised Holmes, he said, he would do what he could to reverse *Hammer v. Dagenhart*. Ben, indeed all of the New Dealers, shared Holmes's view of the wrongness of *Hammer v. Dagenhart*. Ben had spent more than a decade of his life, from the time of his return from England in 1922 up to 1933, in drafting a model state minimum wage statute meant to get around the Court's *Hammer v. Dagenhart* prohibitions. The latter had been stiffened by the Court majority's ruling in *Adkins v. Children's Hospital* (1923) further barring government efforts to set labor standards.

Roosevelt had promised to send up a fair labor standards measure and Tom, Ben, and Bob Jackson, despite their preoccupation with the Court-packing measure, had been at work on a draft. Roosevelt wanted a simple declaration, a workingman's charter, and wrote out a one-page version illustrating what he meant. The lawyer-scholars on his staff talked him out of that. Corcoran, Cohen, and Jackson argued successfully that the constitutional justification for the bill should be spelled out in its provisions. Those provisions would come under Court scrutiny and they further argued it was prudent to assume the Court would be pretty much the same as it was then constituted. So the final bill as it was introduced May 27, 1937, by Hugo L. Black in the Senate and William P. Connery in the House consisted of forty-seven printed pages.

Tom drafted the presidential message that asked for the bill. It thrilled him to insert a section from Holmes's dissent in *Hammer v. Dagenhart* and that the President should say that "although Mr. Justice Holmes spoke for a *minority* of the Supreme Court, he spoke for a *majority* of the American people."[1] The nub of the message was the need to be "guided by practical reason and not by barren formulas." The measure, if enacted, would set "rudimentary standards of decency" under an administrative board of five members to be appointed by the President with the concurrence of the Senate. The administrative board would be an assurance of flexibility in setting maximum hours and minimum wages.

The House and Senate held joint hearings on the bill that had been drafted by Cohen. "The bill had lots of 'kibitzers,' " said Rauh, "Corcoran, Jackson, Ambrose Doskov, Frankfurter, Jerry Reilly, even yours truly, but Ben was *the* draftsman." Tom had been the chief drafter of the President's message that went up to Congress with the bill. Then he wrote a speech for Senator Black to deliver over NBC. Black examined the draft and overhauled it, he advised Corcoran. "Please let us know when we can get it." The speech emphasized the new bill's differences with the NIRA, "it has nothing to do with fixing prices, with trade practices, with production controls, and with monopolies."[2] Wages and hours had enough enemies without multiplying them by efforts to deal with prices, production, and monopoly. The bill did not seek to subject industry to "a national straitjacket," Black answered a Republican attack on it along these lines. The opposition in the same breath, he noted, complained of the "large discretionary and dictatorial powers" that would be given an administrative agency. In other words, the Republican senator who had already attacked the bill over a nationwide hookup said that the bill was too tight; but if he was wrong on that, he wanted people to believe it was too loose.

A crucial leadoff witness was the assistant attorney general, Robert Jackson. His chief, Homer Cummings, did not want him to testify. "It certainly created a lot of opposition in the South," wrote Cummings in his diary, "and stiffened the resistance of the Southern Senators. Many of them actually froth at the mouth when the subject is mentioned."[3]

Despite Cummings's opposition, Jackson appeared. He had a way of asserting his will without leaving wounds. His statement on the bill's constitutionality was hailed as "a brilliant summation." Jackson paid his respects to *Hammer v. Dagenhart* and the line of judicial reasoning it had inaugurated, "this perversion of our Constitution . . . We should give the Court a chance to remove this blemish from our judicial history." In the *Washington Minimum Wage* case the Court, in the language of Chief Justice Hughes, had courageously declared, "Our conclusion is that the case of *Adkins v. Children's Hospital* should be, and it is, overruled." Jackson hoped that *Hammer v. Dagenhart* would then be laid "to a tardy and unmourned repose beside the lifelike remains of *Adkins v. Children's Hospital.*"[4]

He sketched in what he called the bill's "hopeful approaches to constitutionality" and the different judicial theories of the commerce power that the bill invoked and that had been asserted at various times by the Court itself. He called these "cushions" on which the Court could find a constitutional seat and noted the efforts that had been made to give the Court every opportunity to find for the government. "This bill does not plunge the Nation headlong into a rigid and widespread policy of regulating wages and hours. It permits the building up of a body of experience and prevents the extension of regulation faster than the capacity properly to administer is acquired."

The Secretary of Labor followed a few days later. Perkins rarely was at a loss for words; nevertheless, "I do not believe that I could add anything of value to the thorough and scholarly testimony of Mr. Jackson on the constitutional problems with which this legislation is confronted."[5] Her remarks were prepared with the help of her new solicitor, Gerard Reilly. He, too, was a Harvard Law School graduate, had known the Corcoran family in Pawtucket, and was a frequenter of Corcoran and Cohen haunts. Along with Cohen he played a major part in the bill's various drafts and redrafts as it went through the legislative process. Perkins struck one special note in her testimony: the bill should not discriminate against women. It should make certain "that the minimum wage should be established on the basis of occupation and not on the basis of sex."

The hearings went well and on July 31 Black secured a Senate vote in favor of the bill. Nevertheless, it was a low moment among New Dealers because of the defeat of the Court-packing plan. Most of them had had questions about the plan, but its rejection was a major setback to Roosevelt and with him the New Deal. Newspapers reported that Tom and Ben had resigned. Sponsors of such false reports hoped, perhaps, that reality might catch up with rumor. Ben wrote Jane, one of his few confidantes,

Despite all reports, Tom & I really have made no definite plans for the coming year. I am not sure what we will or ought to do. I'll talk things over with you when [you] are better, although I do think that it probably [is] best for both of us to stick together & that neither of us can be as effective working alone as we can be together.[6]

Ben had no problem working with Tom; still, he did not like his own guerillalike status in the government. He was a modest man but he knew that effectiveness in government was in part a function of office. And though he fled the limelight there was a part of him also that liked it. Tom and Felix worried about Ben. There was a vacancy at the SEC. Why would that not be an ideal place for Ben who had written much of the act that set it up? Felix wrote from Cohasset, Massachusetts, where he was summering:

Tom
I didn't want to go too far about Ben at SEC because I wasn't sure you could swing it. But if you can why wouldn't that be ideal from every point of view— present & future & as a demonstration of how such a job should be done. And

wouldn't it be interesting news for the [word indecipherable]?! You said that Bill D[ouglas] would be agreeable—that would be swell.

F.F.[7]

The appointment did not take place. Perhaps Ben asked Tom not to pursue it. Certainly Douglas, who respected and was fond of Ben, would have been agreeable. Perhaps the White House, namely, Roosevelt, vetoed it. The President valued Ben's services but he was conscious of the attack his administration was under because of its alleged partiality to Jews. The strength of anti-Semitism was always a factor in the thinking of politicians and the greater the menace of Hitler, who consciously used it as a weapon in his struggle against United States influence in the world, the more cautiously Roosevelt felt obliged to move. Ickes proposed Ben as an assistant Secretary of the Treasury.[8] "No," said Roosevelt. "He would be a good man," Ickes quoted the President as saying, "but he questioned the wisdom of appointing a Jew under Morgenthau."

So Ben plugged away at Wages and Hours. At the invitation of Senator Black, together with Reilly he sat in on the executive sessions of the Conference Committee. Reilly was tall, thin, sharp-eyed, a good draftsman, and a bridge between Cohen and Corcoran and his chief, Frances Perkins.[9]

Much of the resistance to the bill came from labor. Both the American Federation of Labor (AFL), headed by William Green and the CIO, whose chief was John L. Lewis, dragged their feet on the measure. In reality they were opposed but did not want to say so openly. They did not like the idea of government setting wages. "Jerry, it's bad medicine for us," a spokesman for the AFL council told him, "to give these jerks something for nothing and then they won't join the cause." "Lewis and Green objected to any governmental wage fixing," Jackson agreed.

Perkins had another problem with the legislation. Like other Cabinet members she was always on the alert to protect and augment her turf. She wanted the administration of labor standards to be lodged in her department. Cohen, Corcoran, and Jackson favored an independent agency, similar to the National Labor Relations Board and the Social Security Administration. The administrative process, they felt, would give the standards the flexibility they needed so that adjustments might take into account geographical and industrial differences. The quarrel over administration was the only "big one" between Reilly and the other New Dealers.

An important element in the under-the-surface resistance to the bill was the beginning of a breach between Roosevelt and his Postmaster General, James Farley. Although it was Farley who had brought Jackson to Washington from upstate New York, it had not escaped his notice that Jackson was being promoted by Roosevelt as a candidate for governor of New York, indeed, even was being talked about as a possibility for the presidency. But New York was Farley's bailiwick. He had his own political aspirations. He did not take kindly to the possibility of competition from this New Dealer. To thwart Wages and Hours, not openly but by foot-dragging, was to slow down Jackson.

The biggest obstacle, however, to enactment of the Wages and Hours bill was opposition from the South. Roosevelt had assumed that a campaign for Wages and Hours would reunite a party that had been badly split in the fight over the Court-packing plan. But as Cummings had realized, the opposite was true. The Southerners were against the minimum wage, Jackson felt, just as they were against labor's right to organize. "But that wouldn't be a wise platform for them to stand on. So they were for this guardian of liberty . . . the Court." The Court-packing plan had not caused the split in the party, he concluded. "I don't think the Court fight did anything but merely emphasize or bring into the open certain divisions already existing."

Even though the bill would set the standard minimum wage at 25 cents an hour, which was 15 cents less than the NRA minimum had been, still it meant a substantial wage increase in the South's industries. ". . . [A] minimum that was low," said Jackson, "looked high in some sections of the South."[10] In a sweeping Southern attack on the bill "Cotton Ed" Smith, the senator from South Carolina, achieved a certain notoriety with his declaration that "it takes only 50 cents a day to live reasonably and comfortably" in his state.[11]

With Black's prodding, the Senate had approved the bill promptly, eliciting an exultant telegram from Frankfurter:

Dear Boys
    The Senate vote on Wages & Hours—under all the circs [circumstances] is a great triumph. You've done it again.

                                                                    F.F.

In the House, however, although the bill was approved by its Labor Committee, John O'Connor, the chairman of the Rules Committee, even though he was the brother of Basil, Roosevelt's former law partner, was a pillar of the Dixiecrat coalition that had emerged to obstruct the New Deal. He refused to allow the bill to be brought to the floor and the House adjourned in the summer of 1937 without a vote. "Please don't ask me about the wages and hours bill," Ben wrote Jane Harris. "They chewed it all up with amendments and the political atmosphere is so bad that it doesn't look as if even the scrawny remains would pass."

Roosevelt again urged passage of the bill at the extraordinary session of Congress that he convened on November 15. Again the bill sailed through the House Labor Committee, now chaired by Mary Norton of New Jersey after the death of William Connery. Again it ran afoul of the Rules Committee. This time with Roosevelt's encouragement, Norton started a discharge petition which with some diligent arm-twisting attained enough signatures to bring the bill to the floor. Then the AFL balked and proposed its own substitute. Although it was defeated, the federation possessed enough leverage in the House to have the bill recommitted and the session ended.

A renewed effort was made when Congress reassembled at the beginning of 1938. Tom was unable to work with Mary Norton. He had opposed her election to the chairmanship of the Labor Committee, and he was happy to have Jerry Reilly, with Ben helping out, to work with her. "Ben would think out the problems," recalled Reilly, "and try to compromise them with his ability as a drafter. A congressman would say 'nothing doing.' The meeting would adjourn and Ben would come in with a substitute." Again the House Labor Committee approved and once again was stopped by the Rules Committee. Even a new discharge petition was stalled by a lack of signatures.[12]

A primary in Florida transformed the situation. "Remember how stymied we were to get that bill through Congress," Cohen and Corcoran later wrote Claude Pepper, "until your election broke the deadlock?" Pepper, a classmate of Tom's at Harvard Law School, was opposed for election as one of Florida's senators by a Democrat who proclaimed himself an opponent of the fair labor standards bill. Several New Dealers, led by Harry Hopkins and Tom, persuaded Pepper to embrace the bill firmly and pivot his election around it. Tom was given carte blanche at the White House to mobilize the federal machine on Pepper's behalf. With Roosevelt's backing, he raised a substantial sum of money for the senator. "Much to the surprise of the professionals," recalled Reilly, "Pepper won," and in the words of Cohen and Corcoran, made himself "the father of the Fair Labor Standards Act."[13]

As the word of his victory raced around the House it took only two hours and twenty minutes for the discharge petition to muster the needed number of signatures.

The measure passed the House on May 24, 1938, by a vote of 314 to 97 and the Conference Committee version was signed by the President on

June 25. "Everybody claimed credit for it," wrote Frances Perkins. "The AF of L said it was their bill and their contribution. The CIO claimed full credit for its passage. I cannot remember whether the President and I claimed credit but we always thought we had done it. Certainly he gave a sigh of relief as he signed it. 'That's that,' he said."[14]

The final version of the bill lodged its administration in a wages and hours division in the Department of Labor with an administrator who was appointed by the President. "As it passed," said Robert Jackson, one of those who along with Corcoran, Cohen, Isidore Lubin, and Gerard Reilly had carried laboring oars on the stormy journey, "it was a rigid, arbitrary minimum wage without the flexibility which would have been given to it by an administrative process." Nevertheless, as Jackson conceded, the bill did aid the unorganized workers.[15] With subsequent amendments and modifications it strengthened the situation of the unorganized workers at the bottom of the economic pyramid, the members of precisely that third of a nation, ill-housed, ill-clothed, ill-fed that Roosevelt in his inspired inaugural declaration had vowed to help.*

It was probably, said the factual-minded Lubin, "the most vital social legislation" in the nation's history; both in "its philosophical basis" and in the numbers it affected, "every worker in interstate commerce in the United States."

Passage of the Fair Labor Standards Act (FLSA) had other repercussions. It helped ease the sting of the initial defeat in the House of Roosevelt's reorganization bill. In that vote 108 Democrats had deserted the party. It was, said Lubin, "the worst defeat Roosevelt was ever to suffer in the House." Enactment of the FLSA showed that Roosevelt and his New Dealers still had clout.

---

* The bill set a statutory minimum of 25 cents an hour for the first year, then 30 cents an hour up to 1945 when 40 cents became the minimum. Hours were limited to forty-four the first year, forty-two the second, and then forty. In 1981 when Ronald Reagan took office, the minimum had risen to $3.35 an hour and has remained there, despite inflation and despite the traditional practice of pegging it at 50 percent of the average private hourly wage. The minimum wage has proven to be, in the eyes of many students, "the most direct, comprehensive means of increasing the earnings of the working poor."

XXIV

⸺⸺⸺◦⸹◦⸺⸺⸺

"New Deal Washington
Was Out en Masse..."

Roosevelt's battle to end the judicial blockade of New Deal legislation quite rightly occupied the headlines, but of scarcely less interest to New Dealers was the legal tussle between the holding companies and their lawyers to overthrow the Public Utilities Holding Company Act. Almost three years elapsed between the passage of the Act in 1935, the filing of the first suit challenging its constitutionality a month later, and the Supreme Court decision in March 1938 instructing the companies they had to register with the SEC as the Act required. At the center of that litigation was Ben Cohen. Not a litigator himself, he worked out the strategy, wrote many of the government's briefs and, despite his high-pitched voice and shyness, when necessary appeared in court.

The Public Utilities Holding Company bill had been ferociously fought by the companies and their lawyers in Congress. Defeated there the battle moved to the courts. The opening legal rounds were fired in the fall of 1935 and early 1936. It pitted men like John Foster Dulles and John W. Davis, the counsel of the Edison Electric Institute, who had assured their clients that the courts would rule the Act unconstitutional, on one side; on the other side, the best legal minds in the New Deal—Corcoran and Cohen, Landis and John Burns, the chairman and chief counsel of the SEC, and Robert Jackson, assistant attorney general acted for the government.

Dulles and Davis wanted a quick decision on constitutionality from a Supreme Court which was then striking down New Deal legislation right and left. Many government lawyers conferred on the counterstrategy, but it was essentially Cohen who urged that a test case in the courts be avoided as long as possible and then have that test come on a case of the government's choosing, not the utilities'.

Roosevelt, ever the politician, understood that the utilities, their bankers and lawyers, desired to bring him down. He appreciated the efforts of the government lawyers to outmaneuver longtime foes like Dulles in the battle that shifted to the courts after Wall Street failed to defeat the bill. When Dulles was quoted to him as having, within the confidence of a utility boardroom, spoken admiringly of the government's litigation strategy, he penned a rare note of congratulation to Ben.[1]

That had been in the fall of 1935, a few weeks after the measure was enacted. A bondholder of a bankrupt holding company petitioned the federal court in Baltimore to review the constitutionality of the Act. The wiliness of the suit that was brought before Judge Coleman in Baltimore lay in its exclusion of the government as a direct party of interest. This suit of a bondholder against the bankrupt company to "protect" his holdings just happened to have John W. Davis, the eminent counsel of the Edison Electric Institute, as its lawyer. Another creditor urged the same court to uphold the Act's constitutionality. His counsel happened to be a lawyer who had opposed the Act. The government's participation was restricted to a "friend of the court" appearance.

Joe Rauh, fresh out of Harvard Law School and Frankfurter's seminar in federal jurisdiction, bright, spirited, and full of progressive drive, had been sent by the professor to clerk for Justice Cardozo,[2] and Rauh in September 1935 marked time in the offices of Corcoran and Cohen. They put him to work on the PUHCA litigation and gave him his first job, which was to locate the bondholder whom Davis said he represented. Rauh found him, a Baltimore dentist. The government lawyers put him on the stand. "Do you have a lawyer here?" they asked him. "Oh yes," came the reply, "some guy named Davis." The government lawyers introduced him to Davis. Despite the collusive nature of the proceedings, Judge Coleman, rabidly anti-New Deal, ruled the Act unconstitutional and instructed the company not to comply with its registration provisions.

The utilities were jubilant. They inundated the federal courts with similar suits. "If you had asked anyone in 1935 if the Supreme Court would uphold the PUHCA, you would have been laughed at," said Rauh.

To the chagrin of the utilities, the government on Ben's advice refused to accept the challenge. Instead it looked for its own test case and found it in the refusal to register of the world's largest electric utility holding company, the Electric Bond and Share Company. When its president informed Landis, the chairman of the SEC, that it planned to initiate suit, Landis put in a call to New York City where the SEC's counsel, John Burns, Robert Jackson, Corcoran, and Cohen were ready. They beat the utility to the punch with the government's own suit before Judge Julian W. Mack.

Meanwhile the Baltimore decision by Judge Coleman in the *Burco* case, as it came to be known, was appealed to the Circuit Court of Appeals. Again the government was present only as *amicus curiae*. Corcoran appeared for the government. His brief, written by Cohen, argued that a determination of the Act's constitutionality should not be made in so collusive an action. Again the government lost. There were heated arguments in the government as to whether the government should seek review by the Supreme Court, that is, file for *certiorari*. "How can we possibly not ask for a review of a decision by the Circuit Court of Appeals that held the bill unconstitutional?" the men around Cohen challenged him. He was firm. "We want the Supreme Court not to act," he replied at that point. The utilities, confident the Court would rule for them, were eager to have the highest Court review Judge Coleman's decision. The alleged adversaries, except for the government, including John W. Davis, petitioned for *certiorari*. "Everyone in Washington thought that the Act was doomed—everyone, that is, except Cohen," Rauh later wrote.[3]

Cohen filed the government brief against the granting of *certiorari*. He had little time in which to do so. "He kept writing and rewriting it all night for three nights," said Rauh.[4] His essential argument was that the collusive, nonadversarial manner in which the suits had been brought made them improper vehicles for determining the constitutionality of so important a statute. The Court did deny *certiorari*, as indeed Dulles had privately feared (see p. 354).

The government's own test case against Electric Bond and Share moved forward. The atmosphere was quite different from that in the *Burco* case. After the briefs were filed, the chief lawyer for Bond and Share wrote Ben, ". . . you did an effective and telling job. I warmly appreciated the temperate fairness of your references to our clients . . . If only half as much give-and-take fairness and mutual respect had gone into consideration of the bill itself as have characterized the relations of counsel in our case, I am sure that the Electric Bond and Share group, at any rate, would not have contested the resulting legislation."[5]

In January 1937 Judge Mack ruled that the companies must register with the SEC. Landis, about to assume the deanship of the Harvard Law School, permitted himself a moment of public triumph. The companies with the concentrated attack on the Act had "cut their own throats," he exulted. Despite the Court's conservatism, "we have no worry about its going to the Supreme Court."[6]

A section of the utility industry led by Wendell Willkie, the head of Commonwealth and Southern, said privately it was not opposed to government regulation, only to Section 11, the "death sentence" provision of the PUHCA. This produced a lengthy exchange of letters between Willkie and Cohen. Both sought an opening for compromise; neither was sure of the intentions of the other.[7]

To Willkie's claim that he accepted government regulation and was concerned only with the "death sentence," Cohen replied drily, why then did his lawyers in court argue that the Act as a whole was inseparable and that its provisions were each severally unconstitutional. He did not argue thus out of sheer perversity, Cohen went on, but because of the time and energy he had had to spend in court on behalf of provisions "to which you and other utility officials publicly state you do not object?"

He had been told by his lawyers, Willkie came back, that his protection came "in testing the Act as a whole." Perhaps they might be able to agree on litigation "by which we can get an immediate test of Section 11."

Cohen questioned the advice Willkie had received from his counsel. "The contention of Government counsel, as you know, is directly to the contrary." He was interested only in a test of Section 11, the utility magnate insisted, and left to others "the self-hypnosis of advocacy."

This letter upset Cohen. The correspondence was going around in circles, he responded a little wearily. "I certainly have tried to guard against anything approaching what you term 'self-hypnosis of advocacy.' " Although their interchange of views seemed to Cohen to have reached a "dead end," he suggested a way out of the dilemma:

If the major holding companies should decide to register, I know of no reason why they should suspect that the [Securities and Exchange] Commission should be unwilling if the occasion arises to cooperate in a bona fide test of Section 11 based not upon a hypothetical but a genuine concrete situation.

Willkie respected Cohen's wish not to correspond further but he had hoped "we could get our views reconciled." That made Cohen contrite. He would be most happy to talk with Willkie either in New York or Washington. "I did gather the impression from our correspondence, perhaps mistakenly, that there was not much practical chance of our being able to come to grips with the situation until the Supreme Court shall have determined the validity of the registration provision."

That determination was not far away. In November the Circuit Court of Appeals upheld Judge Mack's decision against Electric Bond and Share on the right of the SEC to require registration. He hoped, Cohen wrote Willkie, that the Circuit Court decision "will strengthen your hand in obtaining the cooperation of your company and other companies in the practical administration of the Act. . . ."

Tom and Ben had kept Felix abreast of the litigation to uphold the PUHCA and of the correspondence with Willkie. But Cohen was very much his own man. As David Ginsburg, who had come down from Harvard at the same time as Joe Rauh and later clerked for Justice Douglas, said:

Felix was not brought in very much on the strategy. Ben had a certain pride in these things. He liked to work and think independently. It was Ben who ultimately determined the approach to this legislation.[8]

But Felix was kept sufficiently informed so that after the Circuit Court verdict upholding Mack he wired Ben, A DANIEL COME TO JUDGMENT. I SUPPOSE YOU DESERVE NO CREDIT SINCE THE CONSTITUTION SPEAKS SO CLEARLY. BUT I CONGRATULATE YOU NEVERTHELESS.[9]

The Electric Bond and Share case was heard by the Supreme Court in February 1938. Corcoran lunched with Ickes and afterward took him to the Court building to listen to the proceedings:

Bob Jackson was arguing when I went in and I thought he handled himself very well indeed. Then Ben Cohen followed. Ben is a "lawyer's lawyer." His argument was highly technical. He doesn't talk as easily and persuasively as Jackson but he did very well indeed, and the following day, according to Tom, he did even better.[10]

David Ginsburg dispatched a graphic account of Ben's appearance to FF. It is a New Deal cameo:

NATIONAL POWER POLICY COMMITTEE
INTERIOR BUILDING
WASHINGTON

1718 Que Street, N.W.
February 12, 1938

Dear F.F.,

Shortly before 2:00 o'clock Wednesday afternoon, Ben concluded his oral argument in the Bond and Share case. I couldn't help remembering how the attack on the Holding Company Act began on September 17, 1935 with the notice that the

American States-Lautenbach-Burco* petitions had been filed the day before in the District Court in Baltimore. Joe and I had been in Washington just one week; ten days later we attended a hearing in Baltimore that then seemed to us a little surprising, and today seems shocking and incongruous. Since then the Burco case has been stifled, the North American case won, and the Bond and Share case chosen and completed. We shall win again, I know, and to Ben must go the laurel. Many capable lawyers have contributed something to the Government's case, but every page of every brief carries Ben's imprimatur, and his strategy and his intelligence characterizes every argument. No one disputes that fact. And somehow, because it is Ben, no one wishes to dispute it.

Monday morning found Ben at the office early, dressed in striped trousers but without the cutaway coat. Somehow a cutaway looks so conspicuous, and besides it was too heavy, and he wouldn't get one today anyway, and it wasn't really necessary, and . . . the double-breasted coat would do just as well. About 10 o'clock the reply brief arrived—an unexpected, insidious, and unnecessary little business that undoubtedly disturbed us far more than it enlightened the Court. We quickly read it through, Ben muttering all the while, occasionally bursting into indignant and incoherent explanation as he strode around the room. By 11:15 the brief was digested, hysteria was at precisely the right pitch, the necessary changes had been made in the oral argument, and we began our trek to the Court with at least 75 pounds of assorted legal literature.

I still cannot understand just why it was necessary to carry with us the 3 volumes of House Hearings, the single large volume of Senate Hearings, the 6 volumes of the Splawn Report, all the Holding Company Act debates in the Congressional Record, the 8 volumes of our own record (really 16, since we took 2 sets), all the "requisite" charts, all the briefs and papers in all the lower courts, 6 sets of all the Supreme Court briefs, 12 pencils, 6 tablets, and other miscellany that was truly miscellaneous. However, it would have been capricious to object to this vigilance on Monday since we had been at least as forearmed before the District Court and the Circuit Court of Appeals. Henry Herman† and I must have appeared more than slightly litigious as we staggered up the 70,000 steps to Equal Justice and the offices of the Solicitor General.

The court room was jammed. Everyone was there from Alice Longworth to Ben's colored messenger. New Deal Washington was out en masse, the S.R.O. sign (long queues) having been posted since midmorning. Unfortunately, two other cases had been docketed to be heard before No. 636, with the result that argument on a muddled question of Oklahoma public-utility practice, and on a captious objection to a New York City tax was heard by an unexpectedly brilliant gathering. Our case was reached by 4:20 Monday afternoon. Reed very unobtrusively left the bench just as the Chief announced No. 636; Ben was so excited that he scarcely noticed the fact that only seven Justices remained.‡ A few minutes later, however,

---

* "American States-Lautenbach-Burco petitions"—American States Public Service Company petitioned the Baltimore U.S. District Court against registration on September 17, 1935. *Burco, Inc. v. Whitworth,* 297 U.S. 724 (1936). Dr. Lautenbach was the Baltimore dentist.
† Henry Herman, a lawyer, worked in Ben's office and shared an apartment with him.
‡ Stanley F. Reed had been named to the Supreme Court in early 1938 and was succeeded as solicitor general by Robert H. Jackson.

he clutched my arm and whispered frantically, "Where's Stone?" I broke into a cold sweat, but a moment later found Stone hidden behind a pile of books. We were sitting just below him. Another disqualification would have been too much.

Thacher* delivered a very effective ten-minute stump-speech, during which he achieved his usual boiled-lobster red. We returned to the office immediately after 4:30, and there reviewed the oral argument, reread the briefs, paced the floor, and ate candy. Another council of war before bed time, and home by midnight.

Tuesday morning, more taut than ever, Ben arrived before 9:00 o'clock. This time he was upset about Jackson who had seen fit, perhaps sensibly, to attend a little cabinet dinner the night before instead of preparing and reviewing his oral argument. We left the office at 11:15 and found the court room more crowded, if possible, than the day before. Ben was certain to be reached. Today Paul and Henry Hart† sat with Ben and Jackson at the front table; Henry Herman and I sat at the small table just behind ready to thumb the record on the least provocation. The General Counsel's staff of the SEC was clustered close by, with a strong utility representation just outside the bar—Willkie, Fogarty, Grosbeck, Zimmerman, Hopson and the rest.‡ Willkie shook hands with Ben and told him, confidentially, that he was there at his own expense, just to hear Ben. Tom sat on the side with Ickes.

Thacher opened, of course, in a verbal blaze of glory which this time quickly became dull and monotonous. No questions from the bench; no excitement of any kind. Just a drone of words. Only the Chief refrained from taking an occasional 40 winks. McReynolds, when awake, continued with whatever he was doing (from the reminiscent look on his face I should say he was writing his memoirs). Butler leaned forward to talk with Roberts; Roberts pointed to Tom; Butler turned to stare, and then leaned back without a smile. The Justice said not a word. Black listened intently. And all of us missed Cardozo so very much.

Thacher finished at 1:40, leaving Jackson 20 minutes before the luncheon recess. Jackson opened with the same broad factual-constitutional argument that he used in the lower courts, ignoring again the carefully prepared argument in our briefs. But somehow he was infinitely more effective than before; perhaps because the occasion was personally important; perhaps because he realized that there could be no further appeal. Almost all of the Court was closely attentive. During the recess about ten of us had luncheon together in the Solicitor General's offices, with only Mrs. Jackson and two of her friends to keep the conversation from lapsing into a continuation of the oral argument. About 3:30 there was a bustle in the court room, and striding down the center aisle came Senator Wheeler. Ben turned, smiled, beckoned, and the Senator joined Government counsel at the front table.

* Thomas D. Thacher, chief counsel for Electric Bond and Share had been a roommate of Felix Frankfurter when both were beginning attorneys for U.S. Attorney Henry L. Stimson. He had been Herbert Hoover's solicitor general.
† Paul Freund and Henry Hart had both been law clerks of Brandeis; both later served in the solicitor general's office and still later became professors at Harvard Law School.
‡ Chairman of Commonwealth and Southern.
  J. F. Fogarty, head of North American Company.
  C. E. Groesbeck, chairman of Electric Bond and Share.
  J. E. Zimmerman, chairman of Philadelphia Electric Company.
  H. C. Hopson, head of Associated Gas and Electric.

There's a rumor afoot in Washington that the Chief smiled at Wheeler and gulped twice; you may accept it as a fact, however, that he did not smile at all, and that he only gulped once. Jackson finished at 4:17 having taken only a minute or two more than his allotted hour and a half. All of us had been afraid that he might run over his time, since Ben really needed every moment of his 90 minutes. Jackson had done a good, lawyer-like job, but somehow the atmosphere set by Thacher, built on shifting emphases, half-truths, and misstatements, deliberate and inadvertant, had not been dispelled. No questions. The Court had begun to see what the case was about, but not with clarity or certainty. Jackson seemed to have reassured them that this was a proper case for the exercise of federal power, but for Ben remained the job of establishing that the Congress had not overreached itself.

Ben spoke for 17 minutes. The room was electric. He was nervous, he was not in appearance prepossessing, but he rudely awakened the Court from its customary afternoon doldrums. The Justice relaxed with an almost beatific smile on his face; Black perched himself on the edge of his chair, cupped his face in his hands and didn't move while Ben spoke; Roberts simply glowered and looked away; Stone leaned back, put his head on his chair and stared at the ceiling; the Chief's eyes began to sparkle and he sat rigidly erect. I know how melodramatic this must sound, but no one who was there can deny that all of this is true.

The remainder of the day and evening passed slowly. We dissected Thacher's argument, prepared a new opening for Wednesday and worried, and suffered, and finally went home shortly after 11:00 o'clock. Those few hours were unpleasant.

Not nearly so nervous as he had been the day before, Ben made a beautiful opening on Wednesday noon. His voice was strong and clear, and as he spoke, slowly and so convincingly, all of us leaned back, not to criticize as we had before, but simply to listen to him speak and to revel in it. He was magnificent. Ben is not an orator, but his deficiencies, if any, were forgotten in the fervor and passion of his argument. He never once looked at the Justice, nor even at Stone; lost as he was, he still remained too self-conscious for that. He addressed himself almost wholly to the Chief, with an occasional glance at Black.

He explained, and he illustrated, and he quoted; he replied specifically to Thacher's argument and gesticulated with scorn at "these defendants"; he pounded points home with his fist; he thundered of Senator Wheeler who "fathered" the bill; he slyly paid his respects to section 12 (i) and (with a glance at Black) emphasized the need for control of lobbying; and when Stone indicated in the only significant question in the entire six hours of argument that he understood and accepted the Government's position on separability, Ben grinned at the Court in that boyish way of his—and continued to pile Pelion on Ossa. Then he read the Court a lecture. "The Government no less than the defendants might secure certain definite advantages by having this Court pass upon the validity of the Act and each of its provisions. But the judiciary is not concerned with political or partisan issues as such; and to force upon it the review of legislation severed from the concreteness of vital controversy would go far to discredit the judicial process, and would throw upon the judiciary the full impact of bitter partisan and political strife. It is the merit and strength of the judicial process that it limits itself to concrete issues in genuine controversy." Even if the Court should feel disposed to go beyond registration and to sustain provisions of the Act other than sections 4(a) and 5, as did

Judge Hand in the court below, nevertheless the Government feels that such action would be exceedingly unwise. Dicta, critical or laudatory, must be avoided. "This restriction of the issues is sought by the Government not upon the basis of any technical or arbitrary rule of law or procedure. The restriction is dictated by considerations of policy and principle fundamental in our federal system of judicial review." And by way of conclusion, "The Government submits that there is no satisfactory legal basis upon which this Court can strike down these simple publicity requirements and by such action, bar the only effective approach to the solution of one of our gravest national problems."

MacLane spoke for 45 minutes and in my opinion gave the case away. He devoted his last 15 minutes to an explanation of why the defendants had argued the case as they had. The Government had selected Bond and Share for a test case, and it was their duty to seek an adjudication on as many issues as could properly be presented to the Court. Surely they could not be censured for doing only their duty. It was a pitifully obvious attempt to avoid the moral obloquy of the course they had followed.

Except for MacLane's apologia I should have predicted a 5 to 2 decision; as it is, my guess is 7 to 0 for the Government. I trust it is sheer coincidence that *Carter v. Carter Coal Co.* * was No. 636 of the October Term, 1935, and that *Securities and Exchange Comm. v. Electric Bond & Share Co.* was No. 636 of the October Term, 1937.

When I recall our multi-party telephone conversation last Sunday afternoon I recognize how much nonsense this is, but not even that can take away the satisfaction of a job well done. I'm proud of our briefs and I'm proud of Ben's argument. We've all worked hard; Henry Hart and Paul joined Ben, Henry Herman and myself after the first galleys came back—both of them were extremely helpful. Although I had met Henry Hart before, I knew him only very casually until this past month. He seems to be an exceptionally capable and charming person, unusually thoughtful, and selfless, and kind. I've learned to like him a great deal. But I'm glad it's over. During the past 12 weeks I've lost at least as many pounds, and almost all of my friends. I'm eager to get back to the warm, untroubled comfort of a nice, clean rut.

If Jackson is confirmed, and I believe that he will be, it is possible that there may be an opening for me in the SG's office. If you have time, and at your convenience, I should be grateful for your opinion.

Dave G.[11]

A friend of Tom's in Los Angeles wrote him a congratulatory note: "I understand that Ben made a fine argument in the Electric Bond and Share case, and even the 'Tories' out here are resigned to the Holding Company Act being sustained."[12] Tom was away and Peggy Dowd answered for him: "The 'Tories' may have been resigned after Ben's argument but I'll bet they were surprised at the six-to-one decision."†

---

* *Carter v. Carter Coal Co.* 298 U.S. 238 (1936). In that decision the Court had overturned the labor provisions of the Bituminous Coal Conservation Act. It said that the regulations of minimum wages, wage agreements, and collective bargaining were local matters.

† Justice McReynolds cast the negative vote, Justice Reed had not participated.

XXV

———————⟨∘⟩———————

Drafting Roosevelt for a Third Term

The "great mandate" of 1936 had dimmed by 1938 when the next presidential election moved into view.

Amos Pinchot, a Bull Moose progressive, Wilsonian, and supporter of Alf Landon in 1936, protested Roosevelt's decision to resume spending and pump priming. He saw it as a way of bribing the electorate. "What? Another blurb from Amos?" the President said on seeing the twenty-one-page missive. "Thank him and file it."[1]

Passage of the $3 billion "relief and pump-priming bill," Pinchot predicted direly, "will go far toward liquidating our two-party system of government by putting a faction of one party, dominated by one man, in control of the United States."

Pinchot's view of pump priming as the New Deal "faction's" way of buying the electorate was widespread in the opposition. That opposition was, in fact, riding high. It had defeated the President's court-reform plan, had voted down the reorganization bill and, except for the Fair Labor Standards Act and the relief bill, stalled action by the Administration. It had effectively neutralized the "great mandate" of 1936.

The setbacks stung Roosevelt and ever the activist, mindful as he always was of his cousin TR and his efforts to drive Taft from the presidency, he thought about a purge of his opponents and, so far as 1940 was concerned, began to look for candidates that would support and continue his policies.

For a moment Roosevelt thought he had found in Robert Jackson an instrument of party revitalization, which was the way the New Dealers saw the purge. So taken was he with the forty-six-year-old lawyer from Jamestown, New York, that he encouraged Jackson to make some speeches in New York and passed the word to Corcoran to help Jackson secure the nomination for governor of New York. "If you were elected governor in 1938, you would be in an excellent position to run for the Presidency in 1940," he told Jackson. "I don't intend to run."[2]

During the Court fight Corcoran had become friendly with Ernest Cuneo. A hulking man and former professional athlete, he was a lawyer and brain truster for La Guardia, familiar with New York City's rough-house politics, a phrasemaker with an instinct for feeding political stories to two of the most widely read columnists of the day, Walter Winchell and Drew Pearson. Tom designated Cuneo as Jackson's campaign manager. Tom liked Cuneo as much for his blunt ability to disagree as for his canniness at political implementation. There were frequent midnight scraps in Tom's garretlike office at the RFC where Tom, underneath the eternal green eyeshade, parried Cuneo's fierce opposition to pegging Jackson's candidacy to the Wall Street conspiracy theory. Cuneo lost that battle. He also found to his dismay that Jackson, a "terribly decent man," lacked any "instinct for the jugular." He helped write Jackson's speeches, but Jackson was not "born for roughhouse combat," he concluded, was not even sure he wanted to be President.[3]

The Jackson boom never got off the ground. At New York's Jackson Day dinner, where it took an order from Roosevelt to get Farley to put Jackson on the program, the Postmaster General blandly blanketed Jackson amid speeches by several other candidates. An appearance before a young Democratic organization in New York that was not under Farley's control and for which Jackson was briefed all of a Sunday by Corcoran, Cohen, and Morris Ernst (an astute New York lawyer who had argued and won the censorship case against James Joyce's *Ulysses)* was portrayed in the press as an anti-Farley move. Over the facilities of Town Meeting of the Air, a Jackson debate with Wendell Willkie, who was on his way toward the Republican nomination, was packed with Willkie supporters. "It sounded as if Bob were being snowed under by the thunderous waves of Willkie applause," Cuneo recalled.

The American Labor Party, then headed by David Dubinsky of the International Ladies Garment Workers Union, was unreceptive to the

Jackson candidacy. Finally, the incumbent Governor Herbert Lehman, who had said he did not wish to run for reelection, changed his mind, and that effectively ended the Jackson bid for the governorship, although he remained Corcoran's candidate for president in 1940 unless Roosevelt should run again.

Roosevelt named Jackson solicitor general. The post had always appealed to the assistant attorney general as "the highest prize that could come to a lawyer." Jackson had never gone to college or to law school, having apprenticed in a lawyer's office, so the appointment was high tribute to his legal talents. He was in Jamestown when he heard the news from Corcoran over the telephone. The President had authorized Tom to tell him. When he returned to Washington Jackson's chief, Homer Cummings, asked him whether he wanted to be solicitor general and when Jackson said yes, replied, "Well, I'm inclined to think that can be arranged." Jackson did not have the heart to tell him he already knew.

Was the Jackson candidacy Corcoran's idea? Cuneo says yes. Jackson explicitly denies it. Tom was the President's agent and carried out his wishes. Tom had won the President's confidence, Jackson felt, by his wit, intelligence, and readiness to do whatever the President asked him, but it was what the President wished him to do. "Corcoran was leg man for a man who had no legs."

Roosevelt did not need to be fired up by the New Dealers to launch the purge. The New Deal program was at stake. And beyond his commitment to that program were personal feelings of resentment over the rebuffs he had been handed by members of his own party in the Court fight in 1937 and the rejection of the reorganization bill in 1938. Eleanor Roosevelt constantly cautioned him that as president he should not be prey to such resentments, but that may have been too much to ask of anyone.

How much the purge was Roosevelt's own idea, how much it was that of his New Deal allies and subordinates is an issue on which the witnesses diverge according to their interests and biases. The New Dealers without Roosevelt were a sect, not a majority. Roosevelt's majority in the absence of party control was impotent.

Edward J. Flynn, the Bronx party chief on whom Roosevelt relied as much as he did on Farley, singled out "the advice of Thomas G. Corcoran" and the defeat of Roosevelt's Court program as the decisive factors in Roosevelt's purge decision. "I felt he could not win in the long run because the people of the states would resent his interference. . . . Again, my opinion was not followed . . . I refused to have anything to do with the activities connected with 'purging' Senators."[4]

Farley saw Roosevelt at the beginning of 1938. "The President's hate for members of the party who had opposed him in the Court fight had not cooled by the lapse of time," he later wrote.[5] The "purge" was the President's idea, he insisted. But Farley did not try to dissuade the President, taking refuge in the President's willingness to have him as party chairman to stay out of the primaries. When Vice President Garner in the late spring urged him to speak frankly to the President about his opposition to the purge, Farley begged off. "John, I just can't do that unless I resign from the Cabinet and the Democratic Committee. I don't like the purge any more than you do," he went on, "but the situation won't be helped by my breaking with the Boss."

Whatever the surface amenities between Roosevelt and Farley, Roosevelt's inner political antennae alerted him to Farley's discontents. They were rooted in Farley's own ambitions to be the Democratic nominee for president in 1940. They had surfaced in Farley's resistance to the Jackson boom at the beginning of 1938. A few months later, when Roosevelt encouraged Hopkins to enter the race for the Democratic nomination in 1940, he described Farley to Hopkins as "clearly the most dangerous" of his potential rivals for the nomination with, according to Hopkins's notes of his talk with Roosevelt, little knowledge of foreign affairs and less of the New Deal.

Farley did not acknowledge even to himself, to judge by his writings, that Roosevelt's behind-the-scenes political maneuverings stemmed from his commitment to New Deal purposes. He considered the purge a violation of a "cardinal political creed" that a president should keep out of local political matters, and Roosevelt's flouting of that creed showed he was intent on creating "a personal party." Unwilling to acknowledge his own real motives, Farley focused on Roosevelt's alleged egotism. He disparaged the New Dealers who in his view had little power of their own. If they dominated the Washington scene that was because of Roosevelt's ascendancy. And of all the New Dealers, his hostility converged on "Corcoran and his crowd . . . I know they have inspired the stories against me," he complained to Roosevelt.

Charles Michelson, the Democratic National Committee's shrewd spokesman since the Hoover days, also disliked Corcoran. "The antagonism between Farley and Corcoran," he wrote, lay in mutual jealousy. Corcoran was always trying "to horn in on the National Committee. He was, in characteristic courtier fashion, jealous of anybody else who had access to the President, though his ostensible objection to Farley was that the latter was no true New Dealer."

Precedent for the President

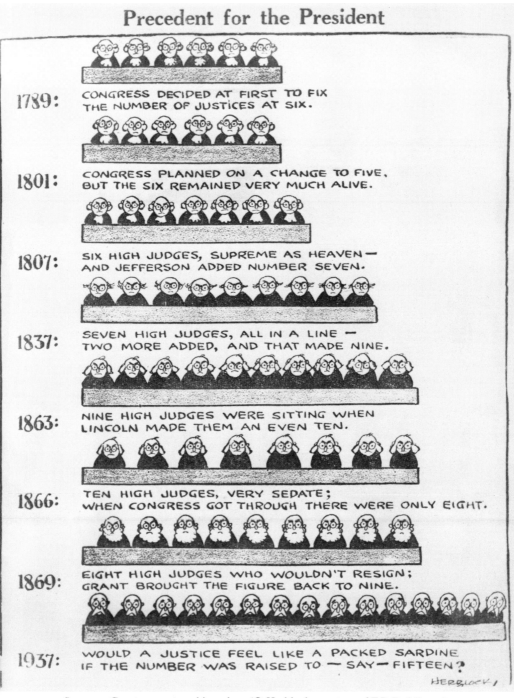

1789: CONGRESS DECIDED AT FIRST TO FIX THE NUMBER OF JUSTICES AT SIX.

1801: CONGRESS PLANNED ON A CHANGE TO FIVE, BUT THE SIX REMAINED VERY MUCH ALIVE.

1807: SIX HIGH JUDGES, SUPREME AS HEAVEN — AND JEFFERSON ADDED NUMBER SEVEN.

1837: SEVEN HIGH JUDGES, ALL IN A LINE — TWO MORE ADDED, AND THAT MADE NINE.

1863: NINE HIGH JUDGES WERE SITTING WHEN LINCOLN MADE THEM AN EVEN TEN.

1866: TEN HIGH JUDGES, VERY SEDATE; WHEN CONGRESS GOT THROUGH THERE WERE ONLY EIGHT.

1869: EIGHT HIGH JUDGES WHO WOULDN'T RESIGN; GRANT BROUGHT THE FIGURE BACK TO NINE.

1937: WOULD A JUSTICE FEEL LIKE A PACKED SARDINE IF THE NUMBER WAS RAISED TO — SAY — FIFTEEN?

HERBLOCK/

Supreme Court—court-packing plan. (© Herblock courtesy of F.D.R. Library)

Felix Frankfurter and Justice Louis D. Brandeis at the latter's summer home in Chatham, Massachusetts. (CREDIT: The Atlantic Monthly)

Roosevelt invited Robert Jackson, then Assistant Attorney General, to join him on a fishing trip in order to look him over. Others on the trip were Harry L. Hopkins and Harold Ickes (not shown). (CREDIT: FDR Library)

William O. Douglas. (CREDIT: FDR
Library)

Lee Pressman, who later acknowledged his membership in the Communist Party, follows John L.
Lewis, the CIO chieftain, into the automobile negotiations. After the "purge" at Agriculture,
Pressman became the CIO counsel. (CREDIT: AP/Wide World Photos)

Jerome Frank (left) and Leon Henderson. Both were leading New Dealers and, when this photograph was taken in April 1939, friendly rivals to succeed William O. Douglas as Chairman of the SEC. (CREDIT: AP/Wide World Photos)

A wartime photograph of John Maynard Keynes in Washington. "We didn't sleep much," said Lauchlin Currie, "but when we did, the General Theory [of Keynes] kept working."(CREDIT: AP/Wide World Photos)

Thomas C. Blaisdell, Jr., a Tugwell man. It was at Blaisdell's farm that the leading New Dealers sought to agree on a compromise formula that would unite the "planners" and the Keynesians. (CREDIT: AP/Wide World Photos)

Secretary of the Treasury Henry Morgenthau. A New Dealer, he nevertheless led the budget balancers in the 1937–38 depression. (CREDIT: AP/Wide World Photos)

Justice Frankfurter sees off Lauchlin Currie. The latter as one of Roosevelt's six "anonymous assistants" had helped make Keynesianism government policy. Here he is on his way to Chungking on a Roosevelt mission to Generalissimo Chiang Kai-shek. (CREDIT: AP/Wide World Photos)

Richard Gilbert, a young Harvard economist, as head of Harry Hopkins' group of Brain Trusters argued for a "guns and butter" policy in the earl months of the war. (CREDIT: AP/Wide World Photos)

om Corcoran and his bride, the former Margaret "Peggy" Dowd. She
as the only one who could keep up with his rapid-fire dictation and
und-the-clock working habits. (CREDIT: AP/Wide World Photos)

en and Corcoran in later years.

Members of the Board of Economic Stabilization staff at the White House. Seated: Benjamin Cohen. Standing left to right: Samuel Lubell, Donald Russell, and Edward Pritchard. (CREDIT: UPI/Bettmann Newsphotos)

Isador Lubin, Commissioner of Labor Statistics through the FDR administrations. FDR checked all statistics with Lubin, who was a Veblen protégé and a pillar of progressive strength among the New Dealers.

"White House Janizaries," General Hugh Johnson dubbed the inner New Deal group that was guiding the purge. Harry Hopkins, although he had just undergone major surgery at the Mayo Clinic, was the leader of the group. Harold Ickes was deeply involved. Others whom *Time* listed among the "Janizaries," who met at Hopkins's Georgetown house, were James Roosevelt, then serving as his father's secretary, Joseph Keenan, a Department of Justice official who had been part of the White House political staff in the Court fight and continued on, David Niles, a Boston progressive and Hopkins's chief political adviser.[6]

Corcoran and Cohen were there. Some called them the "Washington Service Station," others referred to them as the "Twins of Evil." *Time* was more detached. "The firm of Corcoran and Cohen had started out to do a job for a client—the President of the United States. If remaking the Democratic Party is part of that job, Partner Corcoran is well up to learning and playing politics tooth and nail."

Another participant listed by *Time* was Bob Jackson. "I had nothing to do with the purge," Jackson insists, "knew nothing about it, didn't advise it or assist it in any way . . . I don't know whether anybody except the President set out to do it, but it was certainly an ill-advised venture." But if Jackson had no part in the purge, the project to make him governor of New York was not unrelated. Like the purge, the Jackson boom had the purpose of party liberalization. Like the purge it affronted the party moguls led by James Farley.

New Dealers' support of Pepper in his primary in Florida had as its immediate objective to get action on the wages and hours bill. Pepper's victory was sensationally effective and encouraged Roosevelt and the New Dealers to hope that intervention in the primaries was the path to reestablishing Roosevelt's control over the party.

In June Roosevelt summoned Judge Rosenman to come down from New York and join Corcoran and Cohen in writing a Fireside Chat, after the adjournment of Congress and before he left on a trip across the continent, that would explain the purposes of the purge.[7] It was Tom who came up with the label "Copperheads" for the conservative Democrats who opposed Roosevelt's program and by which the speech became known:

Never before have we had so many Copperheads—and you will remember that it was the Copperheads who, in the days of the War Between the States, tried their best to make Lincoln and his Congress give up the fight, let the nation remain split in two and return to peace, peace, peace at any price.

Having dubbed his opponents Copperheads, Roosevelt announced his plans:

As head of the Democratic Party, however, charged with the responsibility of carrying out the definitely liberal declaration of principles set forth in the 1936 Democratic platform, I feel that I have every right to speak out in the few instances where there may be a clear issue between candidates for a Democratic nomination involving these principles, or involving a clear misuse of my name.

So Roosevelt set out on his unsuccessful cross-country crusade to purge the party. As *Time* wrote about the relationship of Roosevelt and his lieutenants in this venture: "When Senator Tydings of Maryland or Senator George snarls at 'two little Wall Street lawyers who want the power to say who shall or shall not be Senator,' they know that their quarrel is not with lawyers Corcoran and Cohen but with client Roosevelt."

By the summer of 1938, Corcoran and Cohen had become names to conjure with in New Deal Washington. *Time*'s cover for September 12, 1938, was given over to the two of them.[8] Neither had positions in the government commensurate with the jobs they did. That added an aura of mystery to the two which men's imaginations filled as they wished, some benignly, others maliciously. The subject of Corcoran's powers came up at a Roosevelt press conference just before he embarked in July on his transcontinental speech making, a trip that took him ultimately to the Cocos Islands and the Galapagos.

"Well, isn't Tommy kind of crowding you off the front page?" Roy Howard, editor of the increasingly anti-New Deal *World Telegram,* needled Roosevelt.

"What makes you ask that?" the President countered.

"It seems to me that as far as the newspapers are concerned, Tommy is stealing the show."

"Well, so far as the newspapers are concerned," the President rejoined, "you are not going to hold me responsible for that, are you?"

Roosevelt appeared to think, commented the New York *Times* reporter, that the stories that attributed unusual powers to Corcoran were an attempt to build him into a bogey man.[9]

The difficulty with Corcoran's position, said Jackson, and he could have included Cohen, was that he did not have any position. "I said to the President once, 'If you put Tommy Corcoran in a recognized job of any kind, put him in an office and put his name on the door so that people will know that is Corcoran's door, all this mystery about him will disappear. He is now a mystery man because he comes in the back door and he doesn't have any office and he cannot be found." People hated Corcoran, thought Jackson, because they hated Roosevelt.

Similar myths exaggerated Cohen's powers. In September he returned from a trip to Europe on which he had combined discussions of the Palestine Economic Foundation, on whose board he had continued to serve, and a vacation. His return on the SS *Manhattan* was surrounded, said the New York *Times,* "by a system of secrecy and protection more elaborate than any remembered in that port by customs men." Cohen carried a bulging briefcase. It did not hold official papers, he assured the press, only neckties, a toothbrush, and pajamas. "You are credited with being one of the two men—three including President Roosevelt—who run the affairs of this country, and as such an important public figure do you return with any new ideas?" he was asked. He reflected for a moment and replied, "No, nothing in the way of new ideas. I have simply been on vacation."

Someone asked him if, as a voter and a citizen, he favored a third term for Mr. Roosevelt. He replied that he was not in politics and when a reporter suggested that "a lot of people think you are," Mr. Cohen laughed and walked away.*

* Cohen had gone to England for a holiday but his real purpose, which was supported by Brandeis, Frankfurter, and Mack, was to try to persuade the British to ease their increasingly severe limitations on the entry of Jewish refugees into Palestine. Between January 1933 when Hitler came to power and the time of Ben's trip some 150,000 or 30 percent of the Jewish population had fled Germany. The fate of those who remained was much on the minds of most New Dealers, especially Cohen and the little group of former Zionists. "I sort of feel that I am on a fool's errand," Cohen wrote Jane Harris from the *Normandie.* "I am sure that there is nothing that I can really accomplish and I can't just regard this journey as a pleasure trip, somehow."[10] The British who held the mandate in Palestine under the pressure of Arab riots were in fact moving toward a total shutoff of emigration to Palestine.

There was plenty of room in Palestine to take care of all Jews who were fleeing persecution, Brandeis told Ickes, describing talks he had been having with the President on the subject.[11] Palestine was able to handle fifty thousand this year and in several years to come, he insisted.

"Last night Felix spoke to the President over the telephone about the Palestine situation," Ben wrote Missy LeHand in October, just after Munich. "The President suggested that Felix dictate to me a draft of a note which the President might send to Mr. Neville Chamberlain. The following is the draft which Felix dictated to me:

With increased pressure on the Jews in Central Europe the tasks of sheer humanity we set for ourselves at the Evian Conference have become even more difficult of fulfillment. Apart from mere numbers, Palestine is a symbol of hope to Jewry. Therefore I earnestly urge that no decision be made which would close the gates of Palestine to the Jews. Shutting the gates of Palestine to Jews would greatly embarrass efforts towards genuine appeasement because it would be interpreted as a disturbing symbol of anti-Semitism."[12]

The British did shut Palestine's gates. Roosevelt moved circumspectly. He did not like to pressure the British in view of United States reluctance to shoulder its share of international responsibilities. He was aware, moreover, of how easy it was to fuel anti-Semitism and xenophobia in the United States. He had initiated the Evian intergovernmental conference to help refugees from Nazi Germany. Its major problem was a scarcity of places where the refugees might go. The United States like other Western nations had its restrictive quotas. Roosevelt

Although in the minds of the public and the politicians Corcoran's name was inextricably associated with the purge, he kept behind the scenes and played a minor role except in its beginnings with the successful effort to keep Pepper of Florida in the Senate and at the end with the defeat of the reactionary chairman of the House Rules Committee, John J. O'Connor.

Corcoran was a political animal but he did not like politics—at least, so he told himself. He was a serious lawyer, his proudest claim his relationship with Holmes, his greatest joy working with Ben and on several occasions delivering brilliantly crafted testimony before congressional committees. He was a scholar, too, of sorts, not quite up to Ben but meticulous, accurate, and indefatigable in his briefs. As part of the service he and Ben rendered Roosevelt, not only in the writing of speeches but in the preparation of legislation, they had research teams of young men and women going night and day, assembling the legislative histories of the various issues they dealt with. These began with the first discussion in Congress of an issue such as housing, whether during the reform wave under Theodore Roosevelt or in Woodrow Wilson's progressive phase. The file on an issue also abstracted newspaper and magazine comment, even books. Together the issue files constituted a veritable history of the reform impulse in Congress.

Tom enjoyed supervising that operation as much as he did the compilation of his commonplace books of quotations to be used in the speeches that he and Ben wrote for Roosevelt and others. He was a scholar, but he also was a politician. Much as he denied it to himself, he liked working the Hill, enjoyed having congressmen guess at the reach of his power under Roosevelt, intervening to place a sympathetic lawyer in a strategic office. Even New Dealer Bill Douglas considered him Roosevelt's "hatchet man."

---

had gone beyond the quotas to permit the entry of more than ten thousand refugees on "visitors permits" but that scarcely dented the problem. Palestine was the solution. There is no record Roosevelt sent the message Ben dictated to Missy. He did press Chamberlain but it was as if he walked on eggs.

It was after the Nazi pogrom in November known as "Kristallnacht." The British were reported ready to admit a few refugees into Palestine again. At Thanksgiving Roosevelt publicly praised the rumored move in a two-sentence statement that ended, "I have no means of knowing the accuracy of this report but I hope that it is true."[13]

Frankfurter appreciated Roosevelt's domestic and diplomatic necessities. He sought to strengthen Roosevelt's intentions by overlavish praise of the Thanksgiving statement. He thanked Roosevelt for the "courageous resourcefulness with which you are making the Chamberlain Government do its duty in utilizing Palestine as the obvious first line of relief for the victims of the latest and largest Nazi barbarities."

The refugee crisis merged with that known as "Munich," in which Britain and France welched on their commitments to Czechoslovakia in order to buy from Hitler, as Chamberlain put it, "peace in our time." Most New Dealers were strongly anti-Fascist but also, when they were not isolationist as some like Jerome Frank were, relieved when war was avoided.

He was fond of people and they of him. He was witty and resourceful in the give-and-take of political trading, a process he was not reluctant to further with his accordion and svelte voice. He was enough of a scholar, however, to appreciate Ben and Ben was enough of a political activist to understand Tom. They were good partners because Tom's gregariousness offset Ben's shyness, his ready retort Ben's slower, high-pitched profundities. "Their mutual admiration is boundless," wrote *Time*. " 'If it hadn't been for Tom,' says Ben, 'I never would have been heard of.' Tom thinks Ben ought to get Cardozo's place on the Supreme Court."[14]

Bill Douglas, who had become chairman of the SEC on the departure of Landis in 1937, said of the two, "Tom was the 'first' man of the team; Ben was the thinker and draftsman *par excellence.*"[15] The SEC administered the three Acts that Ben had drafted: the Securities Act, the Securities and Exchange Act, and the Public Utilities Holding Company Act. "Each was an artistic creation with symmetry and internal proportion," Douglas said. Working with the Acts, as the SEC did, "made us realize what works of art they were."

Tom's protestations of not wanting to be political cannot be dismissed out of hand; but neither can the testimony of Farley, Flynn, and Charley Michelson be ignored, that Tom and his New Dealers were trying to encroach on the Democratic National Committee's prerogatives.

Like the Court fight, says Corcoran in his autobiographical notes, the purge attempt was sporadically managed from the Department of Justice. "I kept out of it," he claimed, "until I was finally—after failure elsewhere —pulled in to give Roosevelt a victory in his own state of New York" against O'Connor.[16]

On July 7, Roosevelt had started his western trip. The stock market was booming. Even Morgenthau agreed with Ickes the country was in for a period of better business. Corcoran told Ickes the President had swung "clear around" on public works. He "regards it as the spearhead of his recovery program."[17] But the trip proved a failure.

Every candidate, whether pro- or anti-New Deal, made it a point to be seen with FDR as his train traveled through their states. Civility had been the order of the day. Those whom he had called "Copperheads" were treated with "due courtesy," Roosevelt wrote his son James. A few, like Senator Pat McCarran of Nevada, Roosevelt treated with silence. Others, like George of Georgia and Tydings of Maryland, he had opposed vigorously. "My old friend, the senior Senator from this state," he said on the basis of material sent him by Tom, in Barnesville, Georgia, and in the senator's presence, "cannot possibly in my judgment be classified as be-longing to the liberal school of thought."

Despite FDR's immense popularity with the people, the primaries were a string of unmitigated disasters. After the summer debacle, Tom suggested to the President he try for a "Yale game" victory.[18] The President as a Harvard man knew that a Yale victory at the end of the season took the sting out of all previous losses. John J. O'Connor, the antagonistic head of the all-powerful House Rules Committee who had given them so much trouble over the Minimum Wage Bill, seemed an opportune target. More-over, he stood in the way of the election, when the time came, of Sam Rayburn as speaker. The way to do it, Tom advised the President, was to intervene in the nomination process. O'Connor, the representative of New York City's "silk-stocking" district, was sharp-tongued, intellectually arro-gant, and disliked in Tammany Hall. Perhaps something could be stirred up there. "He dared me to try it for him," Tom said of the President's reaction. He would, if Roosevelt told Farley it was the President's idea and leave Corcoran to handle it.

The President also enlisted the help of Bronx boss Ed Flynn. The latter did not like O'Connor and that helped persuade him to lend a hand, but "if Corcoran or any of his ilk had anything to do with the campaign, I would immediately withdraw."

To mobilize the President's forces, Corcoran moved into New York, living off and on in the apartment that Ben maintained at the Hotel Wind-sor in O'Connor's district. Corcoran's first job was to intercept Farley off Sandy Hook on a ship returning from Europe. Roosevelt feared Farley might issue a shipboard statement supporting O'Connor for renomination.

Tom boarded a Coast Guard patrol boat due out to the Ambrose Light where he clambered up a ladder to board the ship. He gave Farley the President's message that he wanted Jim to keep his hands off the O'Connor renomination. Farley, an unhappy but silent observer of the purge effort, complied.

Next Tom needed money. "I was a persuasive money-raiser—without strings." With the help of Leland Olds, shepherd of the St. Lawrence Seaway Project and chairman of the Federal Power Commission, Tom found his way to a "nameless operator" in Tammany who knew where the opposition to O'Connor simmered and how much money would be needed. Olds led him to friends of the President in New York who helped with the funds to fuel the organizational revolt against O'Connor's renomination. Out of this revolt, too, James Fay emerged as a candidate against O'Con-nor. As in the Pepper contest Tom mobilized federal office holders in the disputed district. On instructions from Hopkins who was with the President, he visited Morgenthau to ask him to order the IRS men in O'Connor's district to work for his defeat. That would be a "grave mistake," Morgenthau told him and he refused, as an act of friendship to the President. Corcoran, according to Morgenthau, retreated saying, "I think you are right. But I was simply the messenger boy." He settled for Morgenthau's adding three more temporary men to work against O'Connor.

Working in tandem that was not acknowledged and often hostile, Corcoran and Flynn prevailed.[19] O'Connor was beaten, Fay elected. That brought thanks from FDR. Corcoran was at the theater the night of O'Connor's downfall, hovering near a pay telephone. Halfway through the play he heard the results from his man in New York. He immediately called the President. "Tommy, . . . I have never had such a lift in my spirits in my life. I'm eternally grateful and I will never forget it."

"Tom Corcoran did a fine job," Ickes noted in his diary. "I think this victory in total effect offsets the defeats that this Administration suffered in South Carolina, Georgia and Maryland."

Most of the New Dealers were willing supporters of Roosevelt's efforts to reshape the Democratic Party into a coherent liberal instrument. The success of the purge of O'Connor, who had opposed Rayburn's election as majority leader in the House, strengthened the Texan's chances when the time came to be elected speaker, a post he ardently desired and that Corcoran, Cohen, and the New Dealers desired for him. The O'Connor defeat also gave Corcoran the chance to counsel Roosevelt that his difficulty with Congress and the Party was in his lame-duck status, and the way to counter that was to keep open the possibility he might run for a third term. Support of a lame-duck President, Tom thought, was too risky a proposition for local politicos. "No matter what its gratitude to Roosevelt the local political hierarchy could not be expected to interfere with the organizational momentum of local politics when they expected to continue for years after a lame-duck President was gone. This is when the Third Term began," Corcoran wrote. Roosevelt did not stop him.

I did not know that he had in mind to accept a third term but I did know that he understood the value of a demonstration that since he had done so many other unprecedented things in politics, that the idea must lodge in his mind as a way of maintaining his power to accomplish what he wanted to accomplish even in his second term. And so, without telling me not to do it, I began in little ways to get abroad the idea that a third term was not impossible to think about and might be desirable. If I had any preference myself for a successor to Roosevelt as a candidate, it would have been Bob Jackson first and Bill Douglas second.[20]

Cuneo, who had become Corcoran's intimate associate in political operations, described the situation in graphic "guys and dolls" language. "When the Purge failed, the President had to run again. He was at his Alamo, his Custer's last stand, and the only way out of the closing ring was violent attack. He had to be drafted and drafted he was." After the O'Connor defeat, wrote Corcoran, "I was unhappily in politics up to my neck through the Third Term election."

Both Cuneo and Corcoran in their recollections said Theodore Roosevelt's "Bull Moose" precedent weighed heavily in Roosevelt's mind. "I will not say that he ever deliberately indicated that he was interested in a third term," wrote Corcoran,

but he was very much interested—that if he did not dictate who should succeed him and continue his policies, he was not above thinking, like TR, that he would break precedent as Teddy had broken it when he bolted and ran on the Bull Moose ticket. Always, as Holmes said, he was the heir of Teddy Roosevelt.[21]

On the issue of a third term, Ickes agreed:

I brought up the question of 1940, saying to Tom frankly that I did not see that there would be any option except for the President again to be a candidate. There is no liberal leader in sight who could be nominated or elected, in my judgment. Tom feels the same as I do. He believes that if we have two years of good business, the President will be renominated and re-elected.

Despite Roosevelt's continuing popularity the purge attempt culminated in a Republican resurgence in November in which they increased their representation in the House from 88 to 170 and added eight senatorial seats. Though still a minority in both houses, the Republicans would be able in coalition with conservative Democrats to block any measure they did not like.

Out in the socially pioneering state of Wisconsin its governor, Philip La Follette, the brother of Bob, launched the Progressive Party as a national third party. Not all New Dealers stayed away, but those who went in reality were keeping an eye on its development in the interests of Roosevelt and his aides. David Niles, who was working for Hopkins, attended. So did Berle, representing La Guardia. Phil La Follette, unlike his brother Bob, was opposed to Roosevelt. He had been to Italy and Germany and the events attending the launching of his party, in particular the huge darkened stage on which he was the only figure, reminded people uncomfortably of the spectacles in Rome and Berlin. The Republican press gave the event tremendous play in the hope that a weak third party might divide the Democrats. Berle, who refused to add La Guardia's name to the list of incorporators of the new party, although he was authorized to do so, wrote:

The obvious thing to do here is to have the Administration use the third party as a potential threat to the Democrats who desert a reasonably progressive policy. Since a good many of the President's own men have been going off the reservation very freely, I believe this use might be made of it in some places.[22]

He had successfully fought off a third-party movement, Roosevelt told Cummings on the eve of his unsuccessful purge trip, "but if the conservatives had their way Phil La Follette would enter the lists as a serious contender—and might draw off enough votes to give the election to the Republicans . . ."

Roosevelt's talk with Cummings, who stood in well with the party establishment, was one of several that he had with Cabinet members and others on the eve of his transcontinental purge trip. Cummings's account of the talk showed that Roosevelt was disclosing his mind to no one and that Corcoran was as much an instrument of this broken-field running as were Cummings, Ickes, Hopkins, Jackson, Douglas, Berle, even Eleanor Roosevelt.

"We again talked of Presidential candidates," Cummings recorded in his diary,

He said the Presidency is a killing job. Jesse Jones—already ill—could not stand it one month. Garner, he said, could stand it by not attending to it. He spoke of Wallace as having his [FDR's] philosophy, but said he did not know how to make a speech . . . He said, "You [Homer S. Cummings] can do it. You make the best speeches of anyone in the Administration . . ."

Mayor La Guardia, Roosevelt went on, was little in stature but he knew how to catch the crowd. He "has something." Governor Lehman was a "dud" as a speaker. Cummings interrupted to say that Wallace was too recently a Republican to get the Democratic nomination "and the same for Ickes, only more so." "How about Jim [Farley]," Cummings asked. Roosevelt cautiously said only, "He is aiming high."

Cummings did not take too seriously the President's mild suggestion that the Attorney General should think of himself as a candidate. He wanted to resign to make some money. "Only over my dead body," protested the President in one breath, then in another began to talk about Cummings's successor as Attorney General. Bob Jackson's name immediately came up. Too many in the Cabinet from one state, the President regretted, thinking of Farley, Morgenthau, and Perkins, not to mention Hopkins who, though he asserted residence in Iowa, was regarded as a New Yorker.

Cummings stopped off at Hyde Park at the end of the summer after the purge had backfired:

I told him Mayor Kelly [Chicago] said the President would find in the end that he would have to run for President. The President said, "No, I won't." I said Mayor Kelly said, "You might feel that way about it but events will bring it about, especially as there is no other candidate in sight." He said, "We can find one." He seemed very emphatic about it.[23]

Ickes had had a similar talk with Roosevelt as early as May. As matters appeared to him, said Ickes,

he, the President, was the democratic hope of the world and that he might find himself in the position where he might have to run again in 1940. I told him I loved him too much to wish such a thing on him, but there wasn't any other leader in sight who would carry on the fight as the leader of liberalism. He said that he didn't want to be President again, that he was slowing up. I sympathized with his point of view but I wondered where we were going to find a candidate in 1940 who would measure up from a liberal point of view and who could win the Democratic nomination. He admitted the difficulty.

But as Corcoran learned, Harry Hopkins considered himself such a candidate and, equally important, thought he had a green light from the President to go for it.

Harry—lean, cadaverous, crisp-spoken—was a brilliant organizer and political analyst. He fathomed and articulated the President's wishes so well that he was close to becoming the adviser whom the President had lost in the death of Louis Howe. At the end of 1937 two thirds of his stomach had been removed at the Mayo Clinic because of cancer, but physical disability only rendered him closer to a man who himself had two withered legs. Harry was the head of the WPA and a New Dealer. Hugh Johnson considered him the "leading Janizary" around the President.

Harry tried to shield WPA operations from party machine entanglement. That did not keep him from seeing the organization as a steppingstone for his own aspirations as well as a bulwark of the New Deal. The opposition's fears, voiced by Amos Pinchot, that the WPA fed the political power of the New Deal were not without foundation. "Spend and spend, elect and elect," opposition orators ascribed to Hopkins.

Aubrey Williams, Harry's number two man at the WPA, a tempestuous, lionhearted New Dealer, blurted out the darker intentions of the organizers of the WPA at the beginning of the purge. He spoke at a conference of the Workers Alliance, an organization of the jobless that was headed by David Lasser, a New Dealer, but was dominated by the Communists. The New Deal was under attack, Williams started out: "I don't need to tell you. Just judge the folks who come to ask you for your support by the crowd they run with. Vote to keep our friends in power." That blew up a political storm. The Chicago *Tribune* called for Aubrey's resignation. Even the New Deal papers called the speech "demagogic incitement."[24]

"I could have killed myself," Williams told Hopkins. Hopkins's rebuke, if any, was mild. Hopkins had encouraged Roosevelt in his moves to reshape the party, and his speeches that summer stated the Williams thesis in less vulnerable language. He told Democrats in Boston,

Everybody knew which way we were going . . . Yet there were men . . . who tricked the voters by wearing our insignia, only to turn against us as soon as they got into office . . . Even while they hacked away at the foundations of the program with one hand they were patting the President on the back with the other, protesting to the voters that they were really good Democrats . . .

Under these circumstances what would you expect the President as the leader and spokesman of his Party to do? . . . He is merely saying . . . "If you believe in this Administration, do not send these men back . . .' Adulation has not made him arrogant, defeat has not made him timid. What we have to decide is whether . . . we want to abdicate the stronghold of Democracy or to fight for it. And I think we, too, have only begun to fight.[25]

Harry was becoming the closest of Roosevelt's counselors. Many affinities drew them together, and the strongest may have been that he understood and helped shape Roosevelt's purposes. At the end of April, Roosevelt had sent word through Missy that he wanted the WPA administrator to attend Cabinet meetings. Then came a significant conversation between Roosevelt and Hopkins about Harry as his successor. Hopkins later made notes of the talk which he interpreted as Roosevelt's having given him the "green light."

In this "extraordinary private conversation," as Sherwood described it, Roosevelt did not rule out the possibility that in the event of war he might run, but he yearned to return to Hyde Park.[26] Mrs. Roosevelt was opposed to a third term, Roosevelt said. The two men canvased the list of possible candidates. Roosevelt ruled out Hull, Wallace, McNutt, Frank Murphy, the governor of Michigan, and George Earle the governor of Pennsylvania. Hull was "too old." Another possible candidate, Ickes, was "too combative." The "most dangerous" of the candidates was Jim Farley who in the view of the two men was clearly campaigning for the job.

They then turned to Harry's assets and liabilities. Among the latter was his first marriage to a woman who was Jewish which had ended in divorce. His second, although happy, had ended in his wife's death from illness. Harry's health would be a campaign issue. While the Mayo doctors said they had eliminated the cancerous growths and that the odds were two to one against a recurrence, Roosevelt wondered how a presidential campaign might affect Harry's recovery. He himself might have been able to shed the brace on his left leg if he had not been persuaded to return to politics in 1928. But Harry had strong assets, Roosevelt felt. He would be elected and of all the names mentioned would do the best job of running the country. He would appoint Harry Secretary of Commerce so that the business community could see he did not have horns and the "social worker" image would be dissipated.

Armed with the presidential nod, one of the first men to whom Hopkins turned was Corcoran. That did not go well. Corcoran has left his account of what happened.[27] Some time toward the summer of 1938 when Tom and Harry were at Hyde Park working on a speech, Harry, looking gaunter than usual, came into Tom's room at midnight. He asked for help. A beautiful woman had jumped to her death out of a hotel window in New York. She was a wealthy widow and Long Island socialite whose name had been linked with Harry's. If Harry's name now appeared in the suicide stories, that, together with his divorce from his first Jewish wife, would end his political aspirations. Would Tom be willing to call Bernard Baruch through the White House switchboard and get Baruch to ask his friend Herbert Bayard Swope to see to it that Harry's name did not figure in the accounts of the woman's suicide? Corcoran did call Baruch. The latter called Swope and Harry's name was not in the suicide stories.

Tom's reward came the next morning. Harry thanked him and added, "Tommy, I will be the first to tell you—the President wants me to succeed him." Corcoran was surprised. Although his hopes for Jackson were ebbing, they still lingered. Moreover, he had begun to work "subterraneously," as he put it, for a third term with what he called the President's "non-dissent." But Hopkins knew that Corcoran had persuaded Ed Noble, the inventor of Life Savers and chairman of the Civil Aeronautics Board, to contribute $50,000 (then a princely sum) to the 1936 campaign and he wanted Tom to do the same for his candidacy. "He tells me he wants me and the President wants you to ask Ed Noble for $50,000 for my campaign. Will you do it?" Tom, who had his own agenda for the 1940 election, doubted, moreover, that Harry despite the potent support of the WPA organization and his abilities as a campaigner was electable, especially in view of his surgery and his divorce. "But if the President will tell me to arrange this for you, I will let down the net and try to see what I can do with Mr. Noble."

Harry demurred. "But you mustn't talk to the President about me or about money. I'm acting for the President but he doesn't want to be asked about it. You will have to do this on faith in me [and] on my own communication with you about it."

Tom refused. He had to have word directly from the President. On this unhappy note the conversation ended. Corcoran never talked with the President about it, nor did Harry ever renew the request. But from then on, says Corcoran, although there was never a hostile word between them, the friendship withered.

Later Corcoran was told that he had become Harry's whipping boy around the White House—"that little Jesuit," Harry would say. Although both were leaders among the New Dealers and cooperated on matters of policy, both were courtiers for Roosevelt's favor. The closer Roosevelt moved to Hopkins, the chillier it became for Corcoran. William O. Douglas, another leading New Dealer, the outspoken head of the SEC, said of Hopkins that he "threw sand into every competitor's machine," the same charge that Michelson had leveled at Corcoran.[28]

Sherwood in his classic *Roosevelt and Hopkins* reported the conversation between Roosevelt and Hopkins but added he had been unable independently to confirm the President's intention, as expressed in the notes Hopkins had made of the occasion. A footnote in a later edition of the book noted Grace Tully's emphatic insistence that Roosevelt could "never have conceived" of choosing Harry, a sick man and divorced, to succeed him. Corcoran does not go that far. It was conceivable, he said, the President let Harry feel he was grooming him for a successor, but for the purpose of "concealing his own plans."

As Roosevelt had promised Hopkins in their talk about the presidency, he let news filter out in the autumn that he intended to appoint Hopkins Secretary of Commerce. Cummings wrote in his diary:

The President said that the appointment of H. Hopkins gives business the jitters but they would get over it in a week or ten days and then they would like him. He would be direct and frank—and won't kid them, as Dan [Roper] had done.[29]

Ickes had followed the presidential saga through Corcoran. He liked Harry, would vote for him but just could not see him as a candidate for President. "Despite all that Tom said about Harry and 1940, he frankly admitted that he believed the President would have to run again himself."

As for the President's intention to make Harry Secretary of Commerce, Ickes recognized

that he does get along well with the economic royalists. There is something debonair and easygoing about him that makes him personally attractive, he seems to like to accept invitations to expensive homes, he loves horse racing and jokes and women and, except for his social service and relief records, he would be highly acceptable to this class.[30]

Ickes was generous enough to add that Hopkins fundamentally was "a liberal with a real concern for the underprivileged."

Another powerful New Dealer who liked Harry even though she was beginning to have some of the same doubts that Ickes expressed was Eleanor Roosevelt. But she had always been a partisan of Hopkins and predicted in "My Day," when he was slated to become Secretary of Commerce, that he would do the job well, and added, "I think he would be that way about any job he undertook." When the issue of a third term for her husband came up she made her own feelings quite clear. Her daughter Anna told Jane Ickes that when someone commented to Mrs. Roosevelt about the family's continuing to live in the White House after 1940, she replied crisply, "Well, I don't intend to."

Among the many counselors to whom the President talked about 1940 was A. A. Berle whom Roosevelt had persuaded to stay on as assistant secretary of state. The President liked to have brainy men around him as long as they were loyal and did not incur enmities that made governing impossible. Berle was such a man. An original Brains Truster, he was constantly trying to reconstitute that group. In particular he wanted Rex Tugwell to give up his job as head of La Guardia's City Planning Commission and return to Washington. Tugwell awaited only a call from Roosevelt, and it did not come. He came to see Ickes about a PWA tunnel project for New York City:

Rex says that, for his part, he thinks that none of the liberal candidates whom he would be willing to support, namely, Hopkins, Bob La Follette or myself, can be nominated, and he has come to the conclusion lately that the President will have to run again in 1940 because he alone of the trustworthy liberals can be nominated. I told him that I had come to this conclusion some time ago.[31]

A reconstituted Brains Trust would help Roosevelt solve the economic problem, Berle thought, but he also wanted reinforcement in his continuing struggle with "the Corcoran contingent," as he called it. Corcoran and Berle were always at daggers points. Corcoran may have inherited the animosity from Frankfurter whose student Berle had been, an infant prodigy who made a point of not burning incense at Frankfurter's shrine.

It was possible to be wary of Berle quite apart from Frankfurter. Berle was proud of his intellectual abilities, understandably, but to the point of arrogance. He was one of Frankfurter's best students, said Cohen,[32] but Frankfurter did not like him because "he was a little overly proud of his precociousness." Because he had never been brought into Frankfurter's "charmed circle," thought Cohen, he not only felt aggrieved but "he was a little jealous of Tom Corcoran."

"The President wants to liberalize the party," Berle noted in his diary as the President set off on his transcontinental trip:

Corcoran and his friends construe this as making a private club limited to the rather narrow academic progressivism, not too far dissociated from the class war . . . Further, they have just learned that they have no men. Both Hopkins and Jackson are out of the question . . . This leaves only Ickes . . . I took occasion to say to the President that this simply could not go on, but I am not inclined to think the President will—or can do very much to control howling Harold.

Actually, this is slowly lining up as a duel between Garner leading the conservative forces, Ickes leading the progressive forces and Cordell Hull as a moderate in the middle. I propose to hold my forces because there might be a chance for Fiorello; if not, then for a Hull-LaGuardia ticket which at least is a possible result.[33]

The Corcoran people were without power, Berle noted a week later, except for the President, but unfortunately Corcoran often was assumed to be speaking for the President by certain departments, and the President, "as far as I can discover . . . knows of this—tacitly and cynically allows it to go on . . . It is interesting to note that, outside various fields, the 'boys' have very little influence." They lacked the confidence of the country and "command no men who are available for election."

The Berle-Corcoran antagonism reflected competition for the President's ear, as well as differences of temperament. Not policy differences. Berle approved the President's decisive turn toward spending in the spring of 1938. He, too, was a Keynesian, and the memorandum on recovery that he sent the President in Warm Springs in April 1938 followed the line, he noted, "which Corcoran and Hopkins are tackling but it was reached independently."

Berle disagreed sharply with Corcoran over 1940. His candidates were La Guardia or Hull. The Corcoran people vigorously opposed Hull as well as La Guardia, Farley, and McNutt. "I spent most of Saturday with La Guardia," Berle recorded at the beginning of 1939:

The President had talked to him very frankly. He had stated first that he was not interested in a third term; that he had about come to the conclusion that the Convention would nominate a middle-of-the-road man; that he was prepared to accept Hull provided the Convention would nominate a progressive for second place. He named as men who would fill that requirement Hopkins, Jackson, La Guardia or Murphy. La Guardia thought there was no possibility of his name getting through the Convention. I told him I thought it was just as possible for him to get through as for any of the other men named. The President encouraged the progressives to say and to keep on saying they would run a third party if the result of the Convention left them no place to go.

Such was Roosevelt's thinking at the end of 1938. The New Dealers differed. No liberal could get the nomination in 1940, they conceded, except for "the Boss," and they were determined to draft him. Just before Christmas, Harry was sworn in as Secretary of Commerce. To Ickes, the only other cabinet member present, he looked "pale and thin."[34] Harry had given up the idea of an organized campaign for the presidency. He realized, he told Tom, who passed it on to Ickes, that

he was merely being used by the President as a stalking horse so far as the Presidency is concerned. He does not think that he could be nominated and said that if the President wanted to use him for that or any other purpose it was all right with him.

At the end of 1938 *The Saturday Evening Post* ran three articles on the New Dealers, "the chief hero of whom," noted Ickes,

is Tom Corcoran with Ben Cohen as second lead. The theory of those articles is that the New Dealers have succeeded the brain trusters and that the cohesive force which keeps the New Dealers together is Tom Corcoran. I am the only member of the Cabinet who is a New Dealer. Harry Hopkins is described as the person who is closest to the President and there is no doubt that this is a fact.[35]

XXVI

———————————⟢⟣———————————

The New Deal and
the Approach of War

By 1939 Roosevelt's administration was more heavily weighted than ever with New Dealers. Commerce was under Harry Hopkins. The Department of Justice was headed by a progressive Catholic, Frank Murphy of Detroit, and Robert Jackson was the solicitor general, still the Corcoran-Cohen choice for the presidential nomination if Roosevelt did not run. And, if not Jackson, they wanted William O. Douglas, the hard-hitting chief of the Securities and Exchange Commission. Social Security housed another nest of New Dealers. Two of its commissioners were Molly Dewson, an associate of Eleanor Roosevelt and the best "she-male politician" Charley Michelson had ever met, and Gil Winant, the former Republican governor of New Hampshire, a progressive of Lincolnesque mien. And among the first anonymous assistants chosen by Roosevelt after passage of the reorganization bill were two associates of Corcoran and Cohen, James Rowe and Lauchlin Currie. But numbers mattered less than policies for the New Deal represented a state of mind, not an organization.

The President struck a new note in his State of the Union message on January 4, 1939, which he wrote with the usual help of Rosenman, Corcoran, and Cohen. It was three months after Munich had failed to give the world the "peace in our time" that British Prime Minister Neville Chamberlain thought he had achieved by appeasing Hitler with the Sudeten territories. Roosevelt emphasized the nation's defenses and "methods short of war" by which to protect the democracies against international lawlessness. The New Deal was invoked not in order to propose new programs, but for reforms "as basic as armaments themselves" in the preparation of the nation's defenses. Munich and later events justified the President's shift of emphasis. It was true also he had to be mindful of his weakened political position on domestic issues. The purge had failed. He was in his second term, and though the threat of running for an unprecedented third offset his lame-duck vulnerabilities, he was unable to ignore the strength of the conservative coalition in the new Congress. What it refused to give him for relief it voted, even if grudgingly, for national defense.

More plainspoken and reflective of the mood of most New Dealers were a few words uttered by Eleanor Roosevelt on where the nation stood in its progress toward recovery and reform. She was at a dinner of the American Youth Congress, still regarded by her as an independent left-leaning coalition of youth groups. Should she tell the country the truth, she asked Berle who presided at the dinner, namely, that the nation had still to solve the fundamental problem which was economic, not political? It did not matter much, she went on, which party was in power, the problem was work. She and Berle both knew there were eleven million unemployed. The nation had only a couple of years until the next war, she predicted, and "if we do not get something started by then, we are in for trouble." Berle encouraged her to speak her mind.[1]

The Republican speaker at the dinner who preceded Mrs. Roosevelt had taxed the Administration with mollycoddling America's youth with agencies such as the National Youth Administration (NYA), the Civilian Conservation Corps (CCC), the Works Progress Administration (WPA). She believed in the NYA, in Social Security, and in other New Deal measures, Mrs. Roosevelt said in measured words of reply. "But never as fundamental answers, simply as something which has given us hope, which has given us perhaps a suggestion . . . We have bought ourselves time in which to think, that is what we have done."

"Am I just going into an impulsive handspring," asked columnist Heywood Broun who was in the audience, "or is this one of the finest short speeches ever made in our time?"[2]

Eleanor Roosevelt had been happy to exchange views with Berle before she spoke. She still was unsure of herself. Even the Brains Trust when it came to women in government patronized them. Of the first group of brain trusters, Tugwell had been closest to her in sympathies, yet regarded her as the product of a defective education. Women had made considerable gains under the New Deal. Molly Dewson, a vice chairman of the Democratic National Committee, always had her list of women candidates for government vacancies, appealing to Eleanor to intercede with the President when Farley resisted. Molly was succeeded as head of the Women's Division by another liberal, Dorothy McAllister. Women were very much a part of the New Deal constellation in Washington. But Eleanor, an old hand at pushing women's interests in politics, had few illusions. As she told Frances Perkins who came to her with her troubles at the Department of Labor, "How men hate a woman in a position of real power."[3]

Progressive as Corcoran was inclined to be during this period, his ideas on the role of women were old-fashioned and in large measure reflected his upbringing in an intensely Catholic household. His brother David considered sending his son to a small Adirondacks deep-woods camp for children, Tanager Lodge.[4] "Why," Tom asked its manager, a skiing friend, was it "coeducational . . . It bothers me somehow to have the breeds of cat mix. And my brother, the boy's father, has the same neolithic worry about that problem." The director defended his camp against what he suspected were fears that "coeducational" meant "a sissy camp." His brother had decided to send his son to a camp for small boys, Tom later informed him. It was difficult, he explained, "to convert parents who have themselves been tied up in separate boys' camps to take easily to the progressive school educational theory."

Tom admired Joseph Kennedy for the way he brought up a large brood of children. He sent his boys to secular prep schools and colleges and the girls to parochial schools. Corcoran liked that. Women, including Senator Wheeler's daughter, were among the young people Tom and Ben used as research assistants but they were a handful. Cornelia Wickenden, out of Vassar, had followed her husband, Tex Goldschmidt, of Columbia down to Washington in 1933.[5] Both were deeply involved in the New Deal's relief efforts headed by Hopkins and Aubrey Williams. They were workaholics. Washington was a small town and they knew everyone, but she had little to do with Corcoran, she said, "because Tom was very anti-female. He once boasted to somebody that he had never recommended a woman for a job above the rank of secretary."

Women in the New Deal had a special feeling for one another. Comparatively speaking there were relatively few in the government, some lawyers in the National Labor Relations Board, in the Women's Division of the Democratic National Committee, and a sprinkling like Wickenden, assistants often to such powerful figures as Tugwell, Hopkins, and Williams.

There were more women in government than ever before, but still few enough to give them a conscious pride in the women who made it in a man's world, Frances Perkins, Molly Dewson, and above all, Eleanor Roosevelt.

A reporter told the President at his news conference that people "will never forgive him" for putting Frances Willard, the feminist, in the series of outstanding Americans memorialized on stamps. "Well," the President defended himself, "I have to grant about every one hundredth request that comes from women. That's a fact. I turn down ninety-nine and have to give them something." "We are listening," piped up Ruby Black, a press conference regular who was at work on the first biography of Eleanor Roosevelt.[6] The exchange ended in laughter, but it indicated Roosevelt's limited recourse to women—enough to justify Administration claims in comparison with former presidencies to have made a quantum leap in their employment but still far short of according them equal rights. That was true for other minorities as well, notably blacks, Jews, and labor. These groups peculiarly concerned Eleanor Roosevelt. From the time of her emergence in politics and public life in the early 1920s she had pressed the case for equal rights. In 1920 women had just been given the vote and FDR, the Democratic candidate for vice president, realized that to have Eleanor on his campaign train was politically advantageous. Women's voting power had begun to count, and prodded by Eleanor he listened to the issues with which they were concerned and gave them just enough recognition to keep them with him but not so much as to scare off his antifeminist cohorts who shared the view, that was also his, that politics was the business of the male animal and should be left to him.

In 1939 the conservative coalition in Congress felt strong enough to challenge Roosevelt's recommendation for a large relief appropriation. Joblessness was still the number one challenge but Roosevelt's relief request, fortified though it was by considerations of economics as well as compassion, was slashed. "The cut went thro by one vote," Eleanor Roosevelt wrote her confidante Lorena Hickok, "& FDR heard & read it in Cabinet looking straight at Jack Garner." Roosevelt held the vice president responsible. "Cactus Jack" Garner of Texas was a man of beetling brows whose populist views in the depths of the Depression had frightened Wall Street. By 1939, however, they had given way to a conservatism that placed him at the head of the anti-New Deal, anti-Roosevelt forces in Washington. A self-made man with little patience for people on relief, he ascribed their lack of jobs to personal shiftlessness rather than systemic faults. When he heard that the unemployed might march on Washington in support of larger relief appropriations he wanted Roosevelt to call out the troops. In such a case, said Eleanor Roosevelt to whom he volunteered this prescription, she would go down and join the protesters.[7]

"The New Deal had bought time to think," an approving Berle recorded Eleanor Roosevelt's words at the Youth Congress dinner, "but the thinking had not been done." And he added, "I was really excited about this because I have been thinking so myself from the very beginning."[8]

The most ambitious effort to think through the nation's economic problems had just been begun by a joint Congress-Executive inquiry known as the Temporary National Economic Committee (TNEC). It grew out of Roosevelt's concern with monopoly's responsibility for the sluggishness of the recovery. Liberty was endangered not only by joblessness, Roosevelt's message to Congress said, but by "the growth of a private economic power that was stronger than the state itself." "Existing anti-trust laws are inadequate," his message continued.[9] He proposed a thorough study of the effects of concentration upon the decline of competition. He was not antibusiness but "it is of course necessary to operate the competitive system of free enterprise intelligently."

He wanted Congress to authorize an investigation by the executive branch of government. Congress did approve the inquiry's establishment but in its refractory mood stipulated that half its members come from Congress, the other half from the Executive. Senator Joseph O'Mahoney of Wyoming, a middle-of-the-roader in his economic views but politically safe so far as the conservatives were concerned because he had voted against the Court-packing plan, was made chairman. Congress voted the money, but it knew the ideas would have to come from the executive. Leon Henderson, "a statistician with imagination," as Krock described him, was named executive secretary.[10] "For God's sake, speak up if there is anything I can do in any way at all," Lubin implored him that winter in a letter illustrative of the close relationship among the top New Dealers. Henderson's memos had been among the first to warn of a new depression because of monopoly's policy of high prices and restricted production.

Henderson was assisted by another New Dealer Thomas Blaisdell, forty-five, who had been brought by Tugwell to Washington in 1933 from Columbia where he had taught economics. He came to the TNEC from the National Resources Committee where he had been directing the studies of its industrial committee on how changes in industrial structure might help secure the full and balanced use of the nation's resources. After the death of the NRA, where Blaisdell also had worked, whatever national planning survived took place in the National Resources Committee. The President's uncle, white-haired Frederic A. Delano, headed it. He was a former rail-road executive, and a respected financier. His benign presence shielded the group from those who equated planning with Sovietization. If one targeted a $90 billion national income—it was then running at about $70 billion and ten million unemployed—the only agency in government in a position to work out the production and consumption requirements mandated by such a budget, many New Dealers felt, was the National Resources Com-mittee.[11]

In June 1938, concomitant with Congress's authorization of the TNEC inquiry, the industrial committee of the National Resources group had held a memorable all-day meeting at Tom Blaisdell's farm in Virginia.[12] Its participants were a veritable Sanhedrin of New Dealers. Gardiner Means who also worked at the National Resources Committee was there, as were Henderson and Currie. Ezekiel and Louis Bean, "ideas men" for Henry Wallace, were present as was Harry White of Treasury. A telegram to Lubin who was in the hospital in Baltimore urged him to HURRY HOME IF YOU ARE CURED OF JOHN L. WOOZINESS, a reference to John L. Lewis's anathemas that had begun to irk the New Dealers. The wire was signed "Leon [Henderson], Ben [Cohen], Ted [Kreps, an economist], Harry [White], Lauchlin [Currie] Zeke [Ezekiel], Dave [Niles], Aubrey [Wil-liams]." Blaisdell also had invited to his farm Corwin Edwards of the Justice Department, Jerome Frank of the SEC, and Ben Cohen.

Concentration, competition, prices, compensatory spending were the day's themes, almost a précis of the TNEC hearings.

No transcript was kept but afterward Blaisdell asked the participants to send him summaries of the discussions as they appeared to each. A major topic, he wrote, had been "federal control of the rate of economic activity by flexible budget and financial policies vs. the control of production poli-cies of particular industries," that is, compensatory spending as the form of public control as against an NRA-type, industry-by-industry regulation.

Gardiner Means who had been close to Tugwell immediately sensed the great compromise that was in the making. "Both lines" of control—anti-trust activity that would enhance competition and government regulation, indeed, ownership—were needed to ensure a full and balanced use of re-sources, the conferees seemed to him to have said. The clash between two New Deals, Tugwell's "collectivism" versus a Brandeisian "atomization" that Tugwell's writings later emphasized, was seen at that reconciliation meeting as an issue of emphasis rather than exclusion. It seemed to the participants, wrote Means, that "some activity along each line of approach was essential." The two approaches "were entirely complementary" and "it would be dangerous to treat either approach as intrinsically superior to the other." Beardsley Ruml, a member of the National Resources Committee itself, thought the group's concurrence on compensatory spending was its most unusual feature. The issue that still needed clarification, he felt, was whether government spending should be oriented toward the producer or the consumer.

The government should do both, summarized Corwin D. Edwards who was advising the Attorney General on antitrust matters, to place more funds in the hands of consumers and channel funds to producers in such a way as to influence production and price policies. The issue in increasing consumer funds was "how far to unbalance the budget and of selling this fiscal policy to a doubtful electorate."

The NRA experience haunted the meeting. Those who had been connected with it—the words might have been written by Brandeis—"stressed the impossibility of a broad program of regulation because of the lack of essential knowledge, the lack of a sufficient informed and disinterested personnel, and the likelihood that . . . the regulated industries would come to dominate their regulators." Regardless of the final direction controls might take, summarized Edwards, all agreed that "the first steps necessarily would need to be more effective laws against unregulated monopoly."

A pleased participant in the discussions at Blaisdell's farm had been Mordecai Ezekiel.[13] A Sephardic Jew, this descendant of an old Virginia family was Henry Wallace's economic adviser and an articulate advocate among New Dealers both of compensatory spending and planned industrial production. An unfrightened spokesman for a planned economy, he incorporated his views in *$2500 a Year: From Security to Abundance* and in *Jobs For All,* a book that was about to appear. He saw the central challenge to the economy as emanating from technological change. "Our technical ability to invent machines and processes is outrunning our social ability to translate improved technology into higher standards of production and consumption," he told a "Town Meeting of the Air."

Lauchlin Currie had made an astute distinction at the meeting in his discussion of price flexibility, Ezekiel wrote Blaisdell, and it should not be overlooked by the New Dealers in their efforts to achieve a meeting of minds. Currie not only had emerged as the leader of the Keynesians in Washington, but the wispy, quiet-spoken economist was the most theoretically minded of the group, a theoretician who considered even his good friend Leon Henderson deficient as a conceptualizer. As Ezekiel told it, Currie had distinguished between efforts to influence prices in their "long trend aspect" and their "business cycle aspect." The objective for the long range was to ensure that prices fell as the real cost of production fell. "Only in that way can the gains of technological advance be passed on to the consumers." But it was well-nigh hopeless, Currie went on, to believe depressions "can be cured by readjustment in prices." Deflation as a cure of depression was probably "an impossible solution in modern society," Currie said, addressing himself to the balanced-budget, government economies school of thought. "Instead, other means of checking depressions, such as compensatory public fiscal policy, will have to be relied upon."

Ezekiel did not want Blaisdell to miss the point Currie had made. Wherever Ezekiel could find a platform he sounded the call for the tie-up between processes of planned industrial expansion and continued public expenditures. This linkage was at the heart of the consensus at the Blaisdell farm. Pump priming alone, Ezekiel wrote in a *New Republic* series on "After the New Deal," was not an enduring solution to the problem of unemployment. It had to be bound up with a program of planned expansion.

Currie was troubled by the proposed inquiry's stress on monopoly. He knew that Ben Cohen, whom he greatly respected, and Corcoran were at work on a revision of the antitrust laws.[14] This was an effort, said Corcoran, "to reorganize or agglomerate 27 different laws" from their beginnings in the Sherman Act to the latest Robinson Patman Act. As a young Wall Street lawyer in the late twenties, Tom had seen how the complexities of all these laws "could be used to delay, to obfuscate, to make the antitrust problem a futility in substance, if a gold mine for the legal profession." Currie did not disagree but he felt that the stress on monopoly was of little use in industrial analysis. It was not his primary field, so a few days after the Blaisdell session he brought Ben together with one of his most talented Harvard associates, Alan Sweezy. The younger man had been a guiding spirit in the drafting of *An Economic Program for American Democracy,* the little book that in 1939 became the bible of the New Dealers. Sweezy stressed the uselessness of "the simple antithesis between competition and monopoly" in analyzing most industries, and he listed the considerations that pointed to the desirability "of various types of restraint on competition." That did not mean competition should be abandoned entirely, but it had its limits which Ben might bear in mind in his work of redrafting the antitrust laws.

The distinction was not lost on Ben. It was a position he held himself. Six months after the TNEC hearings began, Henderson sent him a memorandum drafted by Corwin Edwards on "Possibilities of Agreement on

TNEC Recommendations." Ben did not like Edwards's "characterization of the breakup of excessively large units as 'atomization.' I do not know of any serious student who has suggested the atomization of any important capital goods industry, but there is quite a difference between imperfect competition among a dozen or more units and a monopoly exercised by one or two units."[15]

The TNEC began its hearings on December 1, 1938. They continued intermittently for eighteen months. The lead-off witnesses were Henderson, Lubin, and Willard Thorp of the Department of Commerce. All in all, 552 witnesses testified. The committee's massive record occupied thirty-one volumes, six supplements, and forty-three monographs. The American economy was dissected as if in a laboratory.

Raymond Moley was there to cover the hearings for *The Saturday Evening Post.* He pictured them as a titanic struggle between government and business.[16] "Business in the Woodshed" his second article was captioned, but, said Stuart Chase, another observer at the hearings, "there were no fights at all," only a dispassionate effort by business men, bankers, economists, senators, and government officials to understand what was happening.

Moley's articles measured his disaffection by 1939 from his former New Deal colleagues as much as they represented a social scientist's analysis of why there were still ten million unemployed. He even derided his old Brains Trust colleague Adolph Berle, another witness who began his testimony with the acknowledgment that he himself was a Keynesian. That was enough to sour Moley as did Berle's proposal of a system of "capital credit" banks, not a profit-making but a quasi-public enterprise authorized to lend money to government agencies for projects such as hospitals, bridges, and housing as well as to private business and in that way overcome the deficiency in demand represented by twenty billion dollars' worth of savings, that is, "idle money."

Berle had been preceded by Professor Alvin Hansen of Harvard, a leader of the Harvard Fiscal Policy Seminar. His appearance was arranged by Lauchlin Currie who, wrote James Tobin, later a Yale Nobelist in economics, transformed the TNEC hearings into a showcase for Keynesian economics. Currie from his vantage point in the White House as one of Roosevelt's "anonymous assistants" orchestrated this Keynesian phase of the hearings.

Roosevelt sent a special message that set the stage for this new phase.[17] The sessions were held in the large Corinthian-pillared Senate hearing room. "It is common knowledge that the dollars which the American people save each year are not yet finding their way back into productive enterprise in sufficient volume to keep our economic machine turning over at the rate required to bring about full employment," Roosevelt's letter said. It was the job of the TNEC to find out why so much money and savings "have remained idle in stagnant pools," he went on. The stubby Hansen, wearing the green eyeshade that had become his hallmark in the Fiscal Policy Seminar at Harvard, took the large crowd that filled the august hearing room to school on issues of capital finance and capital credit.

"I recall very well arranging for him [Alvin Hansen] to be our star witness in the TNEC hearings," recalled Currie, "rehearsing together our testimony and going over a long list of 'good' and 'bad' words prepared for the use of government witnesses by Stuart Chase. Unfortunately, somebody slipped the list to the press which had great fun with it."[18] Currie was "Mr. Inside and Hansen Mr. Outside," said Tobin. Between Hansen, whom Paul Samuelson called "the American Keynes," and Currie, a major refinement was introduced into New Deal views of compensatory spending. Hansen's analysis of investment demand challenged the assumption that a recovery primed by government investment would enable the government to withdraw. Declining population growth, disappearing economic frontiers, combined with a rising rate of saving created a lasting problem of deficient demand that could be met only by expansionary fiscal measures. It might be necessary to continue a substantial government contribution indefinitely.

Currie came to a similar conclusion. At the White House he was on the lookout for savings-offsetting federal projects. Through the columnists Joseph Alsop and Robert Kintner he floated the idea of a federal railroad equipment corporation empowered to issue its own debentures and to build rolling stock and locomotives to be rented to the rundown, nearly bankrupt railroads. Such a federal corporation would boost government expenditures by $200 million to $800 million a year. But its beneficiaries, the ailing railroads, opposed the project lest it open the way to nationalization and Jesse Jones at RFC gave it a cold shoulder.

Undeterred, Currie sold the President on a Works Financing Act of 1939 that would have enabled government systematically to offset personal and corporate savings through public expenditures on self-liquidating public works. Cohen and Corcoran drafted the $3 billion measure. Said Currie:

With the Works Financing Act of 1939 and our long discussions on a major revision of the Social Security System, Roosevelt finally acquired a firm grasp of the theory.[19]

But the evening of August 1, recorded Berle, "we suffered our first smashing defeat in the House, the defeat of the so-called 'Spending-Lending' bill (which really is a very conservative way of getting capital into action)." It was "really defeated by Harold Ickes," Berle claimed, "who wanted a straight public works administration program, which he hoped to administer." Currie differed in his analysis of the defeat of the bill which, he said, was "peculiarly his." Congressional opponents of the New Deal had effectively labeled the Works Financing Act as "the Lend-Spend Bill" and thus helped defeat what was to have been, said Currie, "our main orientation in fiscal policy."

A year after Currie went to work for Roosevelt, he presented the President with a "formidable document" on full employment. He wanted Roosevelt to be aware of "the basic economic theory" of his new, anonymous assistant:

It represents the progress to date of a line of investigation I initiated at the Reserve Board and is today being carried on by the brilliant group of young economists in Harry Hopkins' office.* The basic analysis is that of J. M. Keynes. Since Professor Hansen and I testified along these lines before the TNEC, it has become generally the New Deal economists' diagnoses of a prescription for our economic problems.

An introductory set of propositions "dogmatically" stated the Keynesian case. Contrary to the conventional view, "savings" were the villain in the unemployment scenario. "Savings not invested are not merely a waste; they are definitely harmful in bringing about a *decline* in incomes and employments, unless offset." If the unemployment problem were to be solved, "we either have to build up the combined total of savings-offsetting expenditures to around $20 billion, or cut down our national savings in relation to income (or increase consumption relative to income) . . . There is no other way out . . ."

How effective were the Keynesians? E. Cary Brown in a "Reappraisal of Fiscal Policy of the Thirties," which is widely accepted by economists today, showed statistically that the priming effect of increased federal deficits was offset by cuts in state and local outlays as well as by the increase in

---

* This referred to the group of economists assembled for Hopkins by Richard Gilbert, a Currie nominee. It was called the "Division of Industrial Economics" and its members were V. Lewis Bassie, Gerhard Cohen, Don Humphrey, Griffith Johnson, Victor Perlo, Roderick Riley, and Walter Stark.

federal and local taxes. Deficit spending, in other words, was never fully tested.[20]

The basic economic battle of the thirties was between the advocates of a "natural" recovery and those who maintained, as Currie put it, that "it is the proper role and responsibility of the State to insure that the economic machine functions at more or less full capacity." The insistence of Roosevelt and the New Dealers on that principle was for Currie "the greatest and most enduring contribution of the New Deal."

The fiscal revolution was an expression of that principle. It became national policy that in the event of a severe recession the government would take "strong expansionary budget measures." At the end of 1939 when war needs overshadowed domestic policy debates there were still about ten million unemployed. But by then, as Herbert Stein has written in his excellent account of *The Fiscal Revolution in America,* it had become accepted policy that:

(1) We would run deficits in depressions.

(2) We would not (as Hoover had) raise taxes in a depression in an attempt to balance the budget.

(3) In severe depressions we would raise expenditures—at least for relief and recovery.

(4) We no longer believed depressions were necessarily short or self-terminating.

(5) We did not think that depression deficits, even if large and prolonged, would lead to national bankruptcy.[21]

While the two chief New Deal instigators of the Keynesian revolution in Washington, Eccles and Currie, had arrived at the basic Keynesian ideas of anticyclical spending independently of the British economist's *General Theory of Employment, Interest and Money,* the latter had a major intellectual impact. "By 1940," wrote Stein, "Keynes had very largely swept the field of the younger economists." As one of them, Paul Samuelson, then a graduate student and later a Nobel laureate, wrote of himself and his contemporaries when they first encountered the *General Theory,* "Bliss was it that dawn to be alive, but to be young was very heaven."

In June 1939 the British King and Queen visited the United States. That was FDR's show. As its impresario he attended to the smallest detail of this unspoken demonstration of Ango-American solidarity. The New Dealers had a cameo role in which Mrs. Roosevelt presented many of them to the King and Queen on the south lawn of the White House. Mrs. Roosevelt wanted to bring "the Left Radical members of the Federal Government into connection with the Royal couple," sarcastically reported the semiofficial German news agency.[22]

The New Dealers were divided in their sentiments on foreign policy. Most of them were anti-Fascist, often adorning the letterheads of organizations in aid of Spanish democracy, of Chinese resistance to Japanese aggression, of the anti-Nazi boycott. When Juan Negrín, the former Spanish loyalist premier, came to Washington, Henderson organized a stag dinner for New Dealers to meet him.[23] Frankfurter came, as did Henry Wallace, Lubin, Cohen, and Corcoran. Ben and Tom talked with Constancia de la Mora, granddaughter of a famous Spanish premier and spirited information minister of the defeated government. They transmitted her appeal for Roosevelt's help to avert the massacre of thousands of republican refugees in and about Madrid. Hopkins no doubt was invited but it was a period when, although Secretary of Commerce, he was frequently sick in bed.

Anti-Fascist the New Dealers were, but in liberal circles suspicion of England under Neville Chamberlain ran high and expressed itself in a skepticism that negotiations between Britain, France, and the Soviet Union for a military alliance to resist Hitler's further aggressions could be successful. That British and French rulers wanted to push Hitler eastward was a settled conviction among anti-Fascists at the time. Tom with his Irish heritage had little love for England. But he was an intensely loyal man and to no one more than Roosevelt. He did not permit "one percent deviation," said Sam Rosenman.[24] Whatever his reservations about England, he joined Ben and Sam to work on Roosevelt's 1939 State of the Union message. Its keynote was that there were "many methods short of war but stronger and more effective than mere words, of bringing home to aggressor governments the aggregate sentiments of our people." Later that year Corcoran helped FDR draft his speech calling for repeal of the arms embargo. Nevertheless, he was anti-British, disagreed with his old mentor Frankfurter upon the issue of British aid, and felt more comfortable working on Chinese matters.

No poll of New Deal sympathizers was taken that 1939 summer when the world trembled on the brink of war, but the divided heart of one of the staunchest of them, Jerome Frank, was typical. As a member and then chairman of the SEC he felt obligated to inform FDR of his authorship of an isolationist-minded book, *Save America First.* Frank was so fervently isolationist that he asked the American League for Peace and Democracy, a Popular Front project of the Communists, to remove his name from its literature because it favored collective security.*[25]

* It did so before the Nazi-Soviet Pact at which time the League, like all Communist-dominated groups, switched its stand to a "Yanks are not coming" mode.

Just before Congress recessed in July 1939 Roosevelt invited Hull, Senator Borah, the leader of the isolationists, Garner, and others to make a final effort to get the arms embargo repealed. Borah, antimonopolist and onetime leader of the Senate insurgents, brushed off Hull with the fatuous assertion that his sources of information were better than Hull's and that they told him there would be no war. "Well, Captain, we may as well face the facts," said Garner, "You haven't got the votes and that's all there is to it." "Curiously," noted Berle at the State Department, "it is the New Dealers in the House who are making the most trouble" in repealing the arms embargo.[26]

Late in August the world learned of the Nazi-Soviet Pact. Berle had long had a presentiment that "the Russian and the German points of view are moving closer together" and predicted that they would "wind up together." By August Berle from his vantage point at the State Department where he saw all the cables concluded pessimistically it was "perfectly plain that the European crisis is fairly rushing on: that the plan is to invade and seize all of Poland, and to do so before effective allied assistance can be brought to bear."[27]

Then it happened. Roosevelt, off on a sailing cruise in the Atlantic on the USS *Tuscaloosa*, heard the news and sensed immediately it meant war; that Hitler, freed of having to fight on two fronts, would invade Poland. He returned to Washington by special train.

Ickes had mixed feelings as did many New Dealers about Russia's signature on the pact. The alliance was a great shock, but "I find it difficult to blame Russia."[28] Russian conduct seemed more culpable a week later, "and yet it is shocking that Russia should have entered into an alliance with Germany, which may mean the submerging of democratic civilization not only in Europe but in the world."

Corcoran, a Roosevelt man to his fingertips, sought the political implications for the New Deal of this teaming up of "German drive and skill with Russian materials." The pact vindicated New Deal efforts to reform the free enterprise system, he felt. "The totalitarian idea of economic organization is going to be with us now as a competitive reality" for a long time, threatening the free enterprise system—the one system "in which alone we can probably get along with any satisfaction."

Berle diagnosed the "cynical" agreement in geopolitical terms. It established a "bloc running from the Pacific clear to the Rhine," gave the Germans a free hand in Poland, the Russians in the Baltic states. "This is a picture not unlike the picture of Europe after Napoleon had made his famous Russian treaty at Tilsit." Franco's Spain, Fascist Italy, Japan in the

Far East, had been united with Hitler against Russia. Now they might "shake loose and gravitate into the West European orbit."

Though the alliance of red and black stunned liberals, such feelings were superseded for the moment by anxieties whether Britain and France would live up to their guarantees to Poland and resist Hitler's new aggression. Roosevelt invited Ickes to a Saturday night poker game at the White House. Others there were Bob Jackson, "Pa" Watson, Steve Early, Admiral McIntire. Around 11 P.M. a dispatch was handed to the President. "War will be declared by noon tomorrow," the President told them. "All of us were pleased at this prospect," wrote Ickes, "not because any of us wanted war, but because, believing it to be inevitable in the end, we thought it better for England and France to get into it as quickly as possible."

Bill Douglas was with retired Justice Brandeis the day Hitler invaded Poland. "He saw his people facing new and horrible ordeals. He paced his apartment, old and bowed, his hands behind his back, whispering, "Will England fight?" "At five o'clock this morning our telephone rang," Eleanor Roosevelt reported from Hyde Park, "and it was my husband in Washington to tell me the sad news that Germany had invaded Poland and that his planes were bombing Polish cities."

Stalin's willingness to sign a pact with Hitler was a turning point in New Dealer relationships with Communists. As Reinhold Niebuhr, the liberal theologian who was a friend of many of the New Dealers put it, "I don't believe in my country right or wrong, especially when it's not my country."

New Dealers had been content to have their names on letterheads, to serve on directing committees, so long as the objectives were ones to which they subscribed. But they were infuriated when overnight, because of Communist colonization, objectives were shifted from intervention to isolationism, from zealous support of Roosevelt for a third term to equally fervent hostility. It was a sobering educational experience.

Many New Dealers were Jews and as such were particularly sensitive to the growth in anti-Semitism that Hitler's successes stimulated. Frankfurter's Jewishness had been used against him when in 1938 Roosevelt considered naming him to the Supreme Court vacancy created by the death of Cardozo. Roosevelt wanted to name his old friend but had him in mind for the Brandeis seat when that justice retired. In 1938, however, Brandeis showed no sign of doing so and New Dealers felt Roosevelt should not take chances and nominate Frankfurter to the Cardozo seat, even though Roosevelt had promised it would go to a Westerner. Name Frankfurter to the Court, Ickes told Roosevelt, and the Court will be yours for the next fifteen years. Corcoran was his old teacher's unofficial campaign manager and every night Frankfurter called him and Cohen to find out how the campaign was progressing. Corcoran went to see George Norris, the senator from Nebraska and dean of the progressives, to urge him to call on Roosevelt on Frankfurter's behalf. Norris did so, and even though a delegation of wealthy Jews urged Roosevelt not to appoint Frankfurter, Roosevelt went ahead. Frankfurter's account of his appointment is sparing in his oral history. He says little of Tom and Ben's part, emphasizes how "surprised" he was when FDR offered him the job and his genial complaint that everywhere he went people said to him he had to appoint Felix. "Of course everywhere Roosevelt went, he bumped into people who told him he had to appoint Felix," Cohen later commented in high sardonic tone. "Tom saw to that. And as for being surprised, Tom called him every night to report on the campaign and he did it on my phone."[29] His own "guess," wrote Ickes, was that "until it was all over the President did not realize that we had ganged up on him for Frankfurter."

"I made some mumbling remarks," Felix wrote Tom and Ben about Roosevelt's call that he was sending Frankfurter's name up to the Hill, "we understood one another clearly without any words—and to you two I can now talk for only your hearts to hear."

The question of Jews in the New Deal had always dogged Frankfurter's relationship with Roosevelt. It testified to Roosevelt's openness, Frankfurter's indispensability, and the discretion of both that Frankfurter played as important a role in Washington as he did.

Ben Cohen was another target of anti-Semitism—and more than Frankfurter its victim. He rarely spoke of it, concealing its wounds in the usual stoicism with which he met life's indignities. But it affected his ability to do things in Washington. From the time of the SEC's establishment in 1934 he had been urged as one of its commissioners. The bill giving it statutory existence had been largely drafted by him. It was a job, the *American Hebrew* wrote, he would have had if anti-Semitism had not got in the way.[30]

"The coming of Felix will strengthen us immeasurably," Tom wrote his father, "and it was a long tough fight in which the old A. G. did his damnedest . . . As soon as Felix and Harry [Hopkins] and Frank [Murphy] are confirmed, I'm leaving first for my operation and then for a long vacation."[31]

Cummings had opposed Frankfurter because he thought the seat should go to a Westerner and also because he felt the Harvard professor had encroached on his relationship with Roosevelt. Frankfurter's Jewishness did not concern him but the basis of his opposition to Roosevelt's decision to name Jerome Frank to the Circuit Court of Appeals was not wholly free of anti-Semitic feelings as well as distaste for his womanizing. "He does not rate it," he told Roosevelt. He lacked "judicial training . . . The Court of Appeals is a fine court . . . It does not need the Frank type." Such a nomination will condemn the other sitting judges "to pass the rest of their days in the enforced company of Jerome Frank—you can't do it, you ought not to do it—and you wouldn't like it yourself if you were on the bench."[32]

Bill Douglas talked to Roosevelt about the Circuit Court appointment of Frank who was marking time in Washington as a member of the SEC. He came away with the impression of some powerful opposition to the appointment. Perhaps, Frank speculated, the obstacle was revealed in a statement of Corcoran's "to the effect that the President can't appoint F.F. to the Supreme Court and, at the same time, appoint me to the C.C.A."

Morris Ernst, a partner in Greenbaum, Wolff and Ernst with which Jerry had been associated, confirmed the suspicion. Murphy who had succeeded Cummings as Attorney General told Ernst that he had learned at the White House that Frankfurter's appointment "precluded the appointment of another Jew at this time, but that a successorship to Manton later, was a possibility."

Jerry talked too much, Corcoran said to him. Corcoran had to go into the hospital. Nevertheless, when he came out Frank heard from Douglas that Tom was trying to reopen his case, "but he thinks it's a forlorn hope." What should he say to others, Frank asked Corcoran:

As you doubtless know, the President said to me that he would not appoint me because, although I'd be confirmed, he believed that the appointment would augment anti-Semitism and that it would be injurious to American Jews." (1) If he failed to keep his promise because he feared that to do so would seriously augment anti-Semitism, then America is in a grave situation. For then, although his attitude is, of course, far more benevolent than Hitler's the logical consequence of his reasoning moves in the direction of incipient Nazism in America: Jews must not be active in American public life (unless perhaps they are markedly conservative and have displayed no emphatic New Deal sympathies).

If a liberal President so appraises American public opinion, then American liberalism is in danger. For, when *anti-Semitism becomes that powerful, it is not alone the Jews who are threatened but all liberal America, since anti-Semitism is, today, the sign in which the blackest kind of reaction conquers.*

All lawyers are to some extent casuists. Frank could not have failed to realize that anti-Semitism was a fact of American life, a fact that a Presi-

dent, no matter how free of such feelings himself, had to take into consideration in confronting a hostile Congress and obtain legislation such as
repeal of the arms embargo that in the interests of the nation he considered
a "must."

Cummings testified to the reality of anti-Semitism. "I suppose no group
in our national life is safe from that sort of assault," he commented after a
conversation at his house had brought home the intensification of that
prejudice in New Deal Washington.[33] New York's *Daily News* had published a column by John O'Donnell and Doris Fleeson "dealing with the
Jewish question listing a large number of people active in the New Deal
who are Jewish or of Jewish origin." Doris, said Cummings, thought it was
a terrible article to publish "and was almost ready to cry about it," but the
publisher, Captain Patterson, was adamant and the article appeared.
Whatever Cummings's feelings about Frank, he sympathized with Doris.
Captain Patterson's insistence on the column was symptomatic of a rise in
anti-Semitism that came to a head in 1941 with Charles Lindbergh's use of
it in America First's campaign against Roosevelt's policies of aid to Britain.

"Jew Deal" was a frequent epithet used by critics of the New Deal.
Roosevelt did make use of Jews. "He made use of Jewish brains," wrote
"Unofficial Observer" in his 1934 book *The New Dealers,* "exactly where
and how they should be used. He is using them not because they are
Jewish but because they are brains."[34] "Dig me up fifteen or twenty youthful Abraham Lincolns from Manhattan and the Bronx to choose from," he
told the distinguished lawyer, C. C. Burlingham in 1936.[35] "They must be
liberal from belief and not by lip service . . . They must have no social
ambition." Roosevelt was hospitable to the use of Jews; nevertheless, it was
a fact that "of his 192 judicial appointments seven went to Jews and fifty-
two went to Catholics," the remainder to Protestants. In cold figures the
percentage of Jews, compared to Protestants and Catholics, that Roosevelt
appointed to office was not particularly impressive. It was only so in contrast to the dearth of Jews in previous administrations. In 1936 Roosevelt
invited Judge Rosenman and his wife to accompany him on the campaign
train. The judge sought to beg off. "Mr. President, I don't think we ought
to be on that campaign train because that's going straight through the
Bible Belt of the WASPs, and I don't think you ought to have two Jews on
that train." Roosevelt would not hear of it. "That's no way to handle anti-
Semitism. The way to handle it is to meet it head-on," he protested. The
Rosenmans were on the train.

Roosevelt's invitation in 1937 to Frank to come back into the government was a gesture of friendliness to Jews as it was a tribute to Frank's brains. He reconfirmed the gesture in 1939 when Corcoran, acting for Roosevelt, asked Frank to accept a district judgeship. This offer Frank turned down after talking with "Felix, Bill and Ben" but he had begun to doubt his anti-Semitic argument. "I ceased long ago to bother about the AAA incident," when Wallace had purged him and many of his associates, he wrote Tom. "And the present one will be forgotten by me before long."[36]

His close friend Bill Douglas was named by the President to fill the Brandeis vacancy. That left the chairmanship of the SEC open. Douglas told him he would urge "the Skipper to designate me rather than anyone else," he informed Tom. Would he help? "I know that if you do so, my chances are most excellent." That is what happened.

The outbreak of the war diminished interest in the TNEC. The Cohen-Corcoran project to revise the antitrust laws fell by the wayside as it became clear that war imposed the necessity of coordinating production. Frank, who represented the SEC in the monopoly investigation, thought to rescue the TNEC by making it a watchdog against price gouging and profiteering. He gave Ben the draft of a letter that Roosevelt might send O'Mahoney. Jerry sparked ideas. That was why Roosevelt liked him. He accepted Frank's draft verbatim and O'Mahoney released it. His committee had the powers Roosevelt wanted it to assert, the senator believed, but he would have to discuss it with his full committee and "what it can do remains to be seen."[37] But it did not work out and Roosevelt later established a special agency.

The nature of the problem was changing with the outbreak of war in Europe. So was the status of the New Dealers.

A warning signal to the New Dealers, especially Tom and Ben, came from Hyde Park. It was shrouded in ambiguity, a trial balloon, perhaps, that Roosevelt could disavow, as he did. Tom's distress suggested he feared his days as a White House counselor might be numbered; that he, too, and Ben with him, like Moley and Tugwell before them, might be dismissed.

That summer Moley's memoir *After Seven Years* appeared with its less than flattering portrayal of Roosevelt as an intellectual lightweight and as a puppet manipulated by a wire-pulling Corcoran. "Don't worry about Moley," Tom wrote his brother Dave in Buenos Aires. "I suppose it sounds bad in print down there, but up here everybody understands. I've got his job and he's also sore because I wouldn't play stooge for him inside the White House. There's been so much swill poured on me in the last couple of years—and particularly last summer during the maneuvering for a Third Term—which sure looks good now—that the Moley stuff is only part of a lot more."[38]

But Tom knew the fate of those whom the press built into assistant presidents. They were exiled.

Eight days after Hitler invaded Poland the President was at Hyde Park "to catch up with much-needed sleep." The day before Roosevelt had declared a "limited emergency." He did so making use of a statute unrepealed from World War I. That enabled him, he told Berle, to transfer budget items and to bring the Army and Navy to full peacetime strength without alarming the country that he was preparing for war.[39] He also called a special session to lift the arms embargo. Out of a desire to stress unity and patriotism he had Early disclose his cancellation of a previous commitment to speak to the Democratic women. Early also revealed an Executive Order authorized by the Reorganization Bill in which Roosevelt reorganized his own staff and assigned specific duties to specific officials, thus banishing, Early hoped, "old much heralded and celebrated creatures of the imagination."[40]

"How about Corcoran and Cohen." the reporters asked him. They were not "creatures of the imagination," Early countered and added in words that made the weekend's headlines, "Really there never was a Brain Trust but much has been written about one—that is out the window now."

When an aggrieved Tom called Early to protest the disparaging headlines that reporters made out of these comments, Early sent Tom a transcript of his remarks showing that he had not mentioned Tom and Ben and had refused at a subsequent press conference to interpret the Executive Order "as applying to you and Ben." The explanation did not satisfy Tom who was sure Steve had the question planted "in order to take a whack at him and Ben." Steve had been jealous of Tom for a long time, noted Ickes, and his statement was "pretty brutal." Tom protested to the President who "handled this whole thing at his press conference in a way that was entirely satisfactory to Tom and Ben."

The President reconstructed what he thought had happened. The reporters with him at Hyde Park, hungry for a story over the weekend, said, "Why, here is our chance," when the Executive Order was announced. They had set up the "Corcoran-Cohen banshee" and now they could prove its existence "by killing it." Is there any change in their status? the reporters persisted. "No, just the same as it was before." He was a little uncertain what that status was, a reporter commented. "I should think you would be. A lot of other people are, too."

Tom and Ben were satisfied, according to Ickes, yet could not but wonder whether Early would have dared say what he did without some private knowledge that the President in the interests of national unity was seeking to divest himself of some politically burdensome baggage.[41]

New worries had begun to afflict the New Dealers. Bob Jackson, Corcoran, and Cohen lunched with Ickes. "All of us have been greatly concerned by the inroads into Washington of Wall Streeters and economic royalists since the war was declared," the pugnacious Ickes wrote. The four asked themselves "how far the President would go and permit others to go in abdicating in favor of big business as Wilson did at the time of the First World War." Louis Johnson, the ambitious Assistant Secretary of War, had named Edward Stettinius of U.S. Steel and Walter Gifford of AT&T to a war resources board. "Something tells me," Berle noted in his diary, "this Board is going to have the solid enmity of the so-called New Dealers." He guessed right, for Ickes was warning Roosevelt that "the liberal movement in the United States had lost all of 20 years as the result of Woodrow Wilson's turning Government over to the big interests during the last war." "Don't think I am not watching everything with an eagle eye," Roosevelt sought to reassure him.

A leading group of New Dealers gathered in Ickes's office, Cohen and Corcoran, Frank Murphy, Bob Jackson, Isador Lubin, Jerome Frank, and Lauchlin Currie. All were exercised about the efforts, particularly of Louis Johnson to bring the "fat cats" into the government. They constituted themselves a watchdog committee, pooling and clearing information through Ben and meeting from time to time.[42]

The President, whatever his personal preferences, was not a wholly free agent with respect to how the country saw him, whether as patriot or partisan, centrist or liberal. Roosevelt's political purposes, perhaps even his basic values, limited the roles he chose to enact. The outbreak of war, America's national interests, required that he move away from partisanship, strive for consensus. In time the most convinced liberals saw that. But 1940 was a presidential year and there was no abatement in the struggle for control of the Democratic Party. "Only a liberal candidate on a liberal platform can win next year," Roosevelt told Farley, who wanted the nomination himself, the summer of 1939. "I will not support anyone but a liberal. I will not support either a conservative or a straddlebug." So Roosevelt described his encounter with Farley to Ickes. Even if Roosevelt were so minded he could not dispense with his characterization as a "liberal." Had he closed the door on a third term? Ickes immediately inquired, as Roosevelt reported his talk with Farley. In the event of war all bets were off, he had advised Jim at the end of their talk.

But there were many definitions of liberalism among Roosevelt's New Deal followers. The Ickes-Corcoran "gang" were putting "a third term movement into the field of some proportions," noted Berle.[43] He was himself the proponent of a Hull-La Guardia ticket. Berle was not popular with other New Dealers. "We never regarded Moley, Tugwell and Berle as being real New Dealers," said Currie. "I knew Berle quite well as Assistant Secretary of State and he was quite conservative."

Berle reciprocated New Dealers' dislike of him. His diaries were studied with references to the "Corcoran-Ickes crowd," "gang," "the Tommy boys." Berle considered them little better than political jobbers. He saw two groups in the "intra-Administration struggle for power"—sane, efficient, moderate progressives like himself on one side, and the "Tommy boys" on the other "who, however idealistic they are, are actually as ruthless in their desire to get hold of and use power for personal ends as any group of spoilsmen or Tammany politicians."

But where did Roosevelt stand? "My sweet and cynical Caesar," Berle was candid enough to admit to himself, had just the kind of humor to countenance the rivalries among his advisers "without saying very much one way or the others."[44] As a way of keeping the reins of power in his own hands, Roosevelt did not require the rivals to be loyal to one another, only to him, mildly admonishing them to "leave the politics to me."

His privy councillors might feud with one another, but as long as they fed him ideas and loyally supported his selection of the ideas to be promoted, he was content. The supreme issue that autumn was repeal of the arms embargo. Tom and Ben wrote one draft of the President's speech to the special session of Congress that he summoned for that purpose, Roosevelt dictated another to Sam Rosenman who then worked on combining them. After dinner Hull and Berle came in with a redraft of the presidential draft. Hull, Berle, and Rosenman worked with Roosevelt on that until 11 P.M. Then Sam and Grace Tully finished a final draft at 2:30 A.M. Rosenman spent the next morning in the President's bedroom reviewing that draft page by page.[45]

"I regret that the Congress passed that Act," Roosevelt said of the 1935 neutrality law and its arms embargo provision. "I regret equally that I signed that Act." The speech ended with an assertion of his new role, one to which the New Dealers would have to accommodate.

These perilous days demand cooperation . . . without a trace of partisanship. Our acts must be guided by one single hard-headed thought—keeping America out of this war. . . .

XXVII

Whose New Deal Is It?
Tugwellism
Without Tugwell

Brainy as were the New Dealers, Roosevelt was their leader, and never more so than in the crisis of the coming of World War II. While liberals gathered in anxious conclaves to guard New Deal portals from corruption by the "fat cats," Roosevelt recognized the need and opportunity to shed the mantle of militant reform for that of reconciliation and national unity. His handling of Tugwell and Corcoran illustrated the shift. The first he would not have back in too prominent a position in his government; the second he was to let go. Both were absolutely loyal. Under any calculation of the golden rule both merited reciprocal appreciation from "the Boss," especially as Roosevelt used them to exhaustion for the mean jobs as well as the sublime. Both, however, had been so effectively defamed that the task of governing was eased by their disappearance from the scene. Roosevelt chose that course. Some considered it ingratitude. Others recognized the necessity but would not have been able to do it themselves. And still others considered the unsentimental abandonment of faithful servants as confirmation of their picture of him as a power-hungry man intent on a third term. Historians, however, have recognized that Roosevelt's shift to reconciliation and national unity was the right path to choose.

The youthful director of the Bureau of the Budget, Harold Smith, whom Roosevelt increasingly used because he was clear-eyed as well as loyal, told Robert Sherwood for his classic book *Roosevelt and Hopkins:*

The President was the only one who really understood the meaning of the term *total war* and the necessity for it. The others believed you could fight a war with one hand and carry on domestic business as usual.[1]

"Letter from Adolf Berle saying that the President would like to have me back in Washington," a mystified Tugwell noted in his diary.[2] He was working for La Guardia in New York City. The letter puzzled him because two months earlier when Hitler had invaded Poland he had reminded Ickes, who once had wanted him to be under secretary, "with the world so disturbed I might now return to Washington." He had half expected Ickes to renew the offer but when he lunched with the secretary after a holiday in Key West, instead of the under secretaryship the secretary had offered him the Division of Territories and Overseas Possessions. The nine-thousand-dollar pay it offered was substantially less than he received from New York and Tugwell felt unable to afford the cut; moreover, "there was no tenure beyond 1940," so Tugwell turned him down. He assumed Ickes had consulted the President who had not agreed to his appointment as under secretary.

Ickes indeed had consulted the President who had indicated "it might be a mistake to make Tugwell Under Secretary." But "the President thought well of offering him the Division" because Tugwell "would not be so busy that he would not have a good deal of time to devote to affairs of general interest."

When Tugwell was in Washington he also lunched with Berle *en famille* out at Woodley, once Stimson's home. It was a sunny fall day and they sat on the hillside and talked. Berle quickly came to the point. In Washington's confusion with the coming of the war, "something like the old brain trust ought to be at work." But the problems were different, Tugwell thought to himself, nor did he mention that a Brains Trust *"was* at work though we were not included." But he had his difficulties in New York with La Guardia and his chief planner, Robert Moses, so he did not demur, although he thought it queer that FDR did not approach him directly "since our relations had once been so close." But when Berle reiterated that Roosevelt did want him back, he replied that nothing would please him more provided it were in a position where he might have his say on economic policies. They agreed that the under secretaryship at Interior was not such a post.[3]

Tugwell, however, remained in New York. Presumably Berle did inquire further and discovered that the enthusiasm for Tugwell's return was limited and when finally at the beginning of 1941 he was invited back it was to head a commission on land reform that took him to Puerto Rico, lending some substance to the rumors that La Guardia had asked Roosevelt to take him off his hands.

The continued banishment of Tugwell had its ironies. The swift and overwhelming Nazi conquest of Western Europe had created a sense of alarm in the United States and public receptivity for the centrally planned, that is, government-directed production and control that Tugwell had long advocated. As the United States became "the arsenal of democracy" and amazed the world with its capacity to produce, the armed forces of the United States were equipped, as were those of America's allies, and joblessness in the U.S. ended. The deficit soared, production expanded, and, as both Keynes and Tugwell had predicted, the Depression ended. Under pressure of the war emergency economic policies converged in one of those "conjunctions" of credit, price, rationing, and targeted production that Tugwell had urged and which now materialized without him. These things happened, testified Bob Nathan, under the rubric of "mobilization" for defense.[4] The voluminous yellow-pad estimates of national income that he had developed as chief of the National Income Section of the Department of Commerce he moved to the mobilization effort. Government-directed coordination and planning of production, of which Tugwell had been a symbol and for which he had been hounded out of Washington, suddenly became respectable and urgent.

Tugwell did not return to Washington and Corcoran and Cohen from the time of the "brain-trust-out-the-window" remark felt their days as White House advisers were numbered. Reflecting on Roosevelt's actions in those crisis-driven months, Cohen many years later defended the President:

Roosevelt after 1938 was in a terribly difficult position. He was concerned to get the neutrality law revised, to increase defense expenditures, to get a draft law. A great many in Congress including New Dealers, like Wheeler, La Follette, Bone, were intransigeant isolationists. A lot of New Deal people on the fringes thought we were getting involved in a war that was not ours. Roosevelt was beginning to see that we were going to need our idle factories and men for defense rather than the New Deal.[5]

Then Cohen added, and the remark's significance was underscored by the universal respect in which his fellow New Dealers held him:

Both Tom and I were quite far from the idea that war was going to spoil our precious and delicate New Deal. Tom was encouraging lots of the New York friends like Forrestal to come to Washington.

This, however, was said in 1974. In 1940 Ben viewed the influx of dollar-a-year men less benignly. It was a period when he often kicked the office files in despair.

His rage was momentary: "I was very much concerned with the rise of Hitler from the beginning," he said. Fascist movements were on the rise in the United States. "By sheer law of imitation, if Hitler succeeded, there would be reverberations here. Felix had some of the same feeling."[6] This last was an understatement. "The latter [Frankfurter] is really not rational these days about the European situation," remarked Ickes whose own boiling point was notably low.

Cohen's clarity as to the meaning of Hitlerism for the United States, not to mention for the Jews, reconciled him more quickly than Tom to Roosevelt's opening to the right even if it meant that he and Corcoran had to get out of town. In August, even before the Hitler-Stalin Pact, Frankfurter had advised them both to get away from Washington in order to retain perspective:

Both of you need refreshment. There comes a time when all intermissions by oblivion of the immediate are essential. That time, I'm sure, has come for both of you. There is a long, long pull ahead.[7]

That was in August 1939. Later that year Felix sensed an inner conflict in Tom reflected in a restraint toward him and his wife, Marion. Perhaps it is "merely part of your general unhappiness over the world and things in Washington," he wrote. He felt they should talk it out—"you know what a great believer I am in face-to-face, man talk where I have given my heart and head."

Almost as dominant that winter in the minds of many New Dealers as America's relationship to the march of dictators was speculation about Roosevelt's intentions toward a third term. Tom talked with the President and concluded that he felt, as he reported to Ickes, that he had gone as far as he could on domestic problems:

He told Tom that someone else would have to mop up after him. He added that the solution for our economic troubles might be more developments along the lines of the TVA. Of course this would mean much more government initiative, control, and management than we have had, but my thought for a long time has been that the inevitable trend is in that direction.[8]

Eleanor Roosevelt had a similar impression of the President's views. She felt he was reconciled to a ticket headed by Hull with a young liberal as running mate. Tugwell in Washington late that winter had a "frank talk" with his old chief Henry Wallace who, remembering Tugwell's old intimacy with Roosevelt, wanted to know whether he still thought FDR would not run. Tugwell still held that view.[9] How much of a part would Corcoran play in the selection of a ticket, Wallace asked anxiously, because, noted Tugwell, "Corcoran has never liked H.A.W. I said that Corcoran had only one candidate—Jackson and that although I myself am fond of Jackson, I thought he was unacceptable politically and would be hard to designate unless F.D.R. had absolute control of the convention. It seemed to make him feel a little better."

Berle ran into Ernest Cuneo who had been a former student of his at Columbia and was close to Walter Winchell and Drew Pearson, radio columnists who together commanded a vast listening audience. Like many other New Dealers, Cuneo was promoting several tickets, although through Winchell and Pearson he was filling the air with squibs whose purpose was to draft Roosevelt for a third term. To Berle, however, he reported that the President was talking about a Hull-La Guardia ticket. "I think I can fairly claim to have been the first to think of it," Berle proudly recorded in his diary.[10]

There were other conservative contenders for the nomination in addition to Hull, notably James Farley and Vice President Garner.

The latter, a particular bête noire of Roosevelt and the New Dealers, had been mercilessly flayed before the House Labor Committee by John L. Lewis as a "poker-playing, whiskey-drinking evil old man who was trying to drive his knife into the heart of labor." "True," commented Ickes, and added ruefully, "but the fact of Lewis being the attacker would improve Garner's public standing."[11] Garner's fellow Texan, Sam Rayburn, convened a meeting of the Texas delegation to sign a statement of faith and confidence in Garner. One member of the delegation, a young congressman who had scored an upset victory by running as a Roosevelt man, refused to sign. It did not endear Lyndon Johnson to his fellow Texans but made him a rising star among New Dealers like Corcoran and Cohen.

By the spring of 1940 Garner's candidacy was collapsing as the phoney war began to turn into the real thing. "The possibility of a defeat of the Franco-British alliance must now be squarely reckoned with," Berle noted in his diary at the end of March on the basis of estimates supplied him by the Army and the Navy. On April 9 the Nazi invasion of Norway began. Berle was in Texas to address the Young Democrats. He found that Texans realized they would have to do what the President wanted them to do. The Garner candidacy was finished. His speech, said Berle, "was really a kind of requiem for the Texas conservatives . . ."[12]

The same dire events spurred the "Tommy boys." Ickes, Jackson, and Cohen conferred and decided the third-term movement should take more visible form and be headed up in Washington. They would meet weekly. Ben agreed to telephone Tom who was on a skiing honeymoon in Canada and ask him to return at once. Ben reported that he had suggested to the President that Ickes take charge of the third-term movement, but when Ickes consulted the President he said he wanted no headquarters, no manager, and if that lack of central direction made for confusion that was all right with him. Still, as with Corcoran earlier, Roosevelt did not say no when Ickes told him a group was meeting regularly for clearinghouse purposes.

The Texas and California primaries showed how much this group was doing to draft Roosevelt. Alvin Wirtz, Texas lawyer and sponsor of Lyndon Johnson, had been made under secretary of Interior, the post to which Tugwell had aspired. Wirtz was a crony of the Texas regulars who were backing Garner. He went to Texas to arrange the Garner surrender terms. "We told him," recorded Ickes—and the "we" referred to Johnson, Corcoran, and Ickes who were all on a conference call—to "hold the lines" for a bargain under which Texas would not be used in any "stop Roosevelt" movement in return for which Garner would continue to be the state's favorite son. The Garner people reconciled themselves to the inevitable as Berle had earlier sensed. Three days after the conversation with Wirtz, Roosevelt swamped Garner in the California primary by a 7 to 1 vote. Although he still kept his intentions secret, Roosevelt was jubilant and aware, recorded Ickes: "I had made some substantial contribution to the result."[13]

The British debacle in Norway was followed in early May by the German invasion of the Low Countries and France. Opposed as Berle was to the "draft" movement, nevertheless he wrote perceptively that the question of whether Mr. Roosevelt will run or not "is being settled somewhere on the banks of the Meuse River . . . circumstances are drafting him."[14]

As the clamor increased for the President to run again, Roosevelt became more secretive. He showed his hand to no one, Berle noted. In *Look* magazine Tugwell flatly predicted he would not be a candidate again. Ickes refused to believe Tugwell knew "any more about the situation than anyone else," and added that the people closest to the situation believed the President "will have to run."[15]

Ickes and Berle were right. The cataclysm in Europe crystallized Roosevelt's acceptance of the idea he would have to run. Until those events all his actions were consistent with the notion, first suggested by Corcoran, that if he were to avoid being a lame-duck President and retain any leverage with Congress and the 1940 Democratic Convention he had to keep open the possibility he might be a candidate again. His continued secrecy about his intentions were his way now of telling everyone that the party and the nation had to make plain that they were indeed drafting him. So the bewildering charade began of the leader who was being drafted having to arrange a "spontaneous" draft. Without the New Dealers this might not have been possible, but their participation had to be muted, especially that of the duo that had come to symbolize the New Deal: Corcoran and Cohen.

The day after the California primary Roosevelt convened a dinner meeting at the White House to discuss plans for the chairmanship, keynote speech, and platform at the Democratic Convention. It was to be held in Chicago in mid-July. Hopkins who had begun living in the White House, Justice Douglas, Bob Jackson, and Ickes were there, as well as Currie and Lowell Mellett of the President's secretariat, and Corcoran and Cohen. Roosevelt had begun to assert direct leadership of the election campaign even though Ickes grumbled afterward:

We ought to be organizing our forces and selecting our convention leaders. I am afraid that the President will leave the important things until the very end and that would be a mistake.[16]

What seemed to Ickes and other New Dealers to be drift was one of the most extraordinary exhibitions of mastery in American political history. Roosevelt had a strategy both with regard to the convention and more importantly toward the dire events abroad. Part of that strategy was keeping the reins of leadership in his own hands, and his chief agent in that respect was Ickes's envied rival, New Dealer Harry Hopkins.

Illness had obliged Harry to abandon presidential aspirations, even the active conduct of the Commerce Department. On May 10 at dinner at the White House his illness flared up and Roosevelt persuaded him to stay overnight. He remained there for three and a half years. For Roosevelt it was a boon to have this sympathetic and politically knowledgeable man at his side to talk over the many problems that were crowding in upon him.

Illness ruled Harry out as a contender for power in his own right. Not that he did not jealously guard access to the President, as privy councillors have done immemorially, and Corcoran dated his exile from the White House to the time of Hopkins's entrance. But Harry could no longer be built up into an assistant president.

Harry as adviser had basic traits that he shared with the President—a solid sense of first things first and the indispensability of timing in political leadership. Although by training a social worker, under Roosevelt's tutelage he soon became adept in defense and foreign policy matters.

The same shattering events—the invasion of the Low Countries and France, Chamberlain's resignation and replacement by Winston Churchill, the latter's appeal to Roosevelt for help—that were shaping Roosevelt's decision on a third term enabled him to go to the Congress and country with proposals for an unprecedented buildup of American defenses. His plea for mammoth appropriations was written not only with the help of Rosenman but also that of Corcoran and Cohen. As the grim news from Europe poured in they worked with figures provided by the Army and Navy on what the services needed. After years of neglect the generals—the admirals less so—were cautious in their requests. Roosevelt upped the figures of tanks, transport, artillery, antiaircraft, and ammunition.[17] Above all, he asked that the nation's productive capacity be stepped up to produce fifty thousand planes a year, a dizzying figure that the isolationists derided but the people applauded. Roosevelt's request for a $1.2 billion preparedness program brought him, recorded Ickes, the "finest reception" that he had had in years and 80 percent of the telegrams that came in, Roosevelt told the Cabinet, approved.

Privately some New Dealers were critical. Hopkins was still advised by the small Brains Trust he had assembled at Commerce headed by Richard Gilbert who had been recommended by Lauchlin Currie. A Gilbert memo at the time of France's collapse, "National Defense and Fiscal Policy," which circulated to the government's top economists, boldly argued the New Deal case for butter as well as guns. It taxed the Administration, meaning Roosevelt and Hopkins, with a timid approach to defense appropriations:

We may later be obliged to pull in our belts—all the more reason why today we should raise living standards as far as possible. Later we may demand unprecedented sacrifices—all the more reason why today everyone able and willing to work be given immediate opportunity to do so.[18]

The way to expand production, Gilbert went on in a Keynesian analysis, was to go for full employment which "can be financed only by borrowing." The old relief policies and consumption taxes were "completely inappropriate . . . It is not debt, but idleness—factories unbuilt, resources undeveloped—which undermines our strength, which diminishes our capacity to meet the emergencies of the future . . . Fully a third and perhaps half of our potential productive effort is being wasted through idleness."

While Roosevelt's call for a $1.2 billion preparedness program was greeted in some quarters with incredulity, Gilbert and his small group wanted the Administration to ask for more:

The regretful tone in which additional appropriations are requested is out of keeping with the march of events and the temper of the country. In the next defense message, the sums requested should be larger than those requested in the earlier message, and they should be requested boldly and with confidence. The President should tell the country that further large requests will be necessary.

Who was the better judge of public opinion, the President or they, Hopkins asked a group of youth leaders Mrs. Roosevelt had assembled in the State Dining Room. Hopkins was also addressing the New Dealers with many of whom the young people had ties and who now in moments of exasperated impatience Hopkins referred to as the "goddam New Dealers." It was just before Italy came into the war. For three hours the President, his cigarette jauntily angled, had fielded the group's questions, many of them skeptical of the President's reform purposes. The President left and Mrs. Roosevelt and Harry took over. Both passionately defended the President. Mrs. Roosevelt reminded the group the President had previously said the same things to the country that he did in his fifty-thousand-planes-a-year speech, and Congress had replied, in her words, "Oh, no; oh, no, you are dreaming, Mr. President. No, these things are not ever going to happen." And then "circumstances hit the people of the United States on the head" and "today, they are all running to him . . . And they are all saying, 'Oh, Mr. President! yes, we are ready to do it.' "[19]

The crisis had disposed people to listen to Roosevelt again and he moved with the same skill that he had shown in the 1933 crisis toward preparedness, aid to Britain, and a third term. But what would happen to the New Deal and the New Dealers? anxiously asked people like Mrs. Roosevelt, Ickes, and Jackson. Wrote Ickes:

I carried to the President a suggestion from Ben Cohen that instead of setting up something in the nature of a War Industries Board of the last war that every Cabinet officer be left free to select business advisers of his own who would work with him. This would make these business advisers subservient to the Government instead of the Government's being a tail to the businessmen's kite.[20]

Roosevelt, advised by Hopkins, had other plans. On May 28 he announced the establishment, under an unrepealed 1916 statute, of the seven-member National Defense Advisory Commission (NDAC). It superseded the National Defense Council. William Knudsen of General Motors was to handle production, Stettinius of U.S. Steel, matériel, Hillman of the Amalgamated Clothing Workers, labor matters, Chester C. Davis, agricultural production, a railroader, Ralph Budd, transportation, Dean Harriet Elliott of the University of North Carolina, consumer affairs, and Leon Henderson left the SEC to deal with price stability.

The presence of Hillman and especially of Henderson assured New Deal representation in the mobilization process. But a Fireside Chat on national defense that Roosevelt delivered two days earlier was noteworthy for, among other reasons, the absence of Corcoran and Cohen in its preparation. Roosevelt worked with Rosenman and Hopkins on it. It was a portent of things to come. New Dealers became known as "all-outers" in the preparedness effort but Roosevelt placed them in a manner that fitted the strategy he had in mind. The final moves that resulted in his draft nomination for a third term were a New Deal victory but, except for Hopkins, without central participation of the New Dealers who had led the draft campaign.

By the end of June, France under Pétain had signed an armistice with Hitler. The Continent lay prostrate. Bereft of arms and munitions, Great Britain, led by a defiant Churchill, alone refused to make peace. The new Prime Minister importuned Roosevelt for immediate help. That could be done only by the transfer by the Army and Navy of planes, PT boats, old destroyers that the generals and admirals understandably felt were needed for America's own defense. Churchill's pleas constituted one set of problems for Roosevelt. Another set of controversies revolved around the establishment of the NDAC. A third group lay in the reorganization of the Cabinet to bring in intervention-minded Republican leaders like Stimson and Knox—as he did on the eve the Republican Convention that nominated Wendell Willkie. And, as June gave way to July, the final acts of an "invitation to the draft," as Wheeler styled it, had to be managed. Repeated acts of leadership were called for and they had to be performed not only amid the swirl of awesome events but in the face of intense, often bitter, rivalries and jealousies.

In the final weeks before the Democratic Convention Roosevelt relied almost exclusively on a group of political leaders who, except for Hopkins, were stalwarts in the Democratic organization—Ed Flynn of the Bronx, Frank Walker of Montana, Mayor Ed Kelly of Chicago, Senator Byrnes of South Carolina, and Harry Hopkins. Except for the last, all were hostile to the New Dealers, viewing them as "jobholders" who clung to Roosevelt as their "meal ticket."

The New Dealers were aware of the unfriendliness of the regulars, and as they realized Roosevelt would not select Jackson or Douglas as a running mate, explored the availability of Burt Wheeler. The Montana senator was a battle-tested progressive, had fought with them for landmark legislation like the Holding Companies Act and the SEC, and, because he had led the opposition to Roosevelt's court reform and was known for his independence, commanded the confidence of a substantial conservative following. Moreover, between the time of the defeat of the Court-packing plan and the 1940 political conventions there had been, according to Wheeler, a resumption of friendly relations with FDR.[21]

So on a June evening the Wheelers were invited to dinner by Robert Kintner, the co-author with Joseph Alsop of a closely-read column in the *Herald Tribune* and of the lively little book, *The Men Around the President*. Others present at the dinner were Leon Henderson, Ben Cohen, and Edward Foley, counsel for the Treasury. Dinner over, Henderson, a cigar in his hand, pushed back his chair and fixing his gaze on Wheeler said to him, "The Convention is going to nominate you for Vice President and you are going to have to accept."

According to Wheeler, his answer was a flat no, "because the President is going to get us into this war and I won't go out and campaign and say he won't." All urged him not to close his mind to a possible vice presidential candidacy and, still according to Wheeler, intimated they were speaking with the authority of the President. According to Cohen, however, while Henderson did go pretty far in indicating he was for Wheeler and all had agreed Wheeler was the only liberal whom Jim Farley would not veto, and though Wheeler seemed eager for the nomination, "none of us purported to be in a position to offer the Senator the nomination for Vice President or anything else," and all realized that if the President should run for a third term, he would "probably be unwilling to accept Wheeler as a running mate." So Cohen wrote Frankfurter about the episode. The New Dealers viewed the Wheeler probe as exactly that, as part of an urgent quest for an alternative to the conservative candidacies that were being bruited about— Jesse Jones, Paul McNutt, Hull, Farley—a search that became more frantic as it became clear Jackson and Douglas were out.

Roosevelt's choice for a running mate settled on Henry Wallace, the Secretary of Agriculture, a New Dealer but outside the circle of Corcoran's influence. He "has never liked Wallace," commented Tugwell, and Wallace knew it.[22]

Roosevelt conferred with Ed Flynn and other leaders of the regular organization—Frank Walker, Kelly, Mayor Hague of Jersey City on the vice presidency. "After a considerable canvasing of names the President and the rest of us who consulted with him," recorded Ed Flynn, "agreed that Wallace should be chosen."[23] He was loyal and he brought Roosevelt "a certain strength among farmers." Flynn was moving into the place that had been occupied by Farley as Roosevelt's chief channel to the organization regulars. He regarded the New Dealers as amateur politicians who were resented by the actual political leaders of the country and he gave them, especially Corcoran, a wide berth—not because he deemed Corcoran an amateur but because the regulars felt he deprived them of patronage. "Not only did Congressmen resent Tommy's dictatorial issuing of order," wrote Charley Michelson, "but even more bitterly were they incensed when they found the jobs they regarded as Congressional perquisites being filled by Tommy's nominees." The same was true in the Senate. The feeling toward Corcoran was "exceedingly bitter," Wheeler informed Wallace.

Events in Europe and the Orient quickened Roosevelt's acceptance of the notion that he would have to run for a third term, but he wanted that translated into a spontaneous draft demanding that he run again. Spontaneous drafts rarely happen in politics. Had the New Dealers not taken it in hand, this one, too, might not have developed. But Roosevelt's conscience and respect for tradition required that the draft seem spontaneous, as in a way it was. Roosevelt had not allowed the New Dealers to set up a directing organization. It was only ten days before the Chicago convention that he brought the leaders of the regulars who wanted a third term together. The crucial group at the July 5 dinner at the White House consisted of the President and Hopkins, Flynn, Walker, and Kelly, and Senator James Byrnes of South Carolina.

The President began the discussion after dinner. He referred to the pressures on him to be a candidate again and his grave misgivings about such a move. He regretted that he had failed to develop anyone else who could win, but that was a fact. He doubted that Farley or Garner could do so. Should he then permit the use of his name? He asked for their advice.

Byrnes, who weeks earlier had been asked by the President to help Wagner with the platform, was privately nonplused by the little speech. He doubted its sincerity. He thought Roosevelt might have become a little frightened about the third-term issue and wanted to be "persuaded" to make the run. "The group told him it was his duty to run," wrote Byrnes blandly, suggesting it was all a charade.[24] But was it? Roosevelt needed the feeling that he was being drafted, but drafts, as I have suggested, do not happen in national politics. Unseen hands guide the process. In this particular case they belonged in the final days to the President.

Four days later Hopkins and Byrnes arrived in Chicago. "They were there to stage manage the President's nomination," wrote Wheeler sarcastically.[25] Hopkins set up at the Blackstone Hotel with a direct line to the White House. Byrnes was across the way at the Stevens. Both men spread the word that the President was available. The day after the convention opened Senator Barkley, the convention's chairman, read a message from the President stating that he had no wish to be a candidate again and releasing all delegates. A penciled version of this message in Roosevelt's handwriting was in Hopkins's pocket when he arrived there. The sentence releasing the delegates was added on instructions from Roosevelt.

A fifty-three-minute demonstration ensued. It was managed by the Kelly organization. "We want Roosevelt," bellowed a voice from a microphone in the basement. It was a case of organized spontaneity. Several cabinet members had asked Roosevelt before Chicago whom they should consult if they wanted Roosevelt's instructions on strategy. "Jimmy Byrnes," he replied. "When I saw the President Tuesday night," recorded Ickes, "I asked him whether we were to be permitted to go to Chicago without a program, without a floor leader, without knowing who was to make the nominating speech—in effect leaderless and planless. He grinned at me and said that he was 'trusting to God.' "[26]

Divine confidence was rewarded. On the first ballot the vote was Roosevelt 946, Farley 72, Garner 61, Tydings 9, Hull 5. But the double vision through which delegates saw much of the proceedings left many soured and cynical and their wrath focused on Hopkins. The President had made a mistake in sending Hopkins to Chicago as his personal representative, wrote the loyal Flynn. "Hopkins was not a political leader."[27] His handling of matters intensified the restlessness of the delegates, especially over the designation of Wallace. Eleanor Roosevelt, whose speech to the delegates had been instrumental in getting its rebellious members into a better frame of mind, spoke to Hopkins as she boarded the plane to return to Hyde Park. He brought up the mistakes he had made and she was sure he must have been given to believe he was responsible for the convention. As she entered the plane she said to Harry, "You young things don't know politics."

An undelivered speech showed Roosevelt's conflict of emotions about running for a third term. The President's personal staff had assembled in the Oval Room to listen to the balloting on the nomination for vice president. All knew of the revolt against Wallace. Trusted advisers like Hopkins, Walker, Byrnes, and Kelly had called the President to tell him the nomination was in trouble. All the conservatives in America were out to "beat Henry" was Roosevelt's reaction. He would not run with a reactionary and refused to deliver his own acceptance speech "until we see whom they nominate."

As he sat at a card table listening to the radio and playing solitaire his face grew grimmer.[28] Finally he asked Missy for a pad and pencil. As the room wondered what he was up to, he scribbled away for five pages and handed them to Judge Rosenman to smooth them over and "hurry it up." It was a statement to be issued in the event Wallace lost, declining the nomination. It did not have to be used. Wallace won. But Roosevelt's readiness to bow out indicated that the trappings of office meant little to him. What counted was the ability to lead and that was involved in the convention's acceptance of his nominee for the vice presidency.

Ben and Tom were not among the people in the Oval Room during the Wallace nomination. In the drafting of Roosevelt's acceptance speech, however, wrote Judge Rosenman, "The President relented on Tom, and he and Ben came in to help toward the end of the speech. It was the last speech that the three of us worked on together."

Some laid their banishment to the fine hand of Hopkins. Ickes, their champion, had arrived in Chicago to find Hopkins "running things to suit himself and he doesn't like to share any possible credit with anyone else." Ickes agreed he never "should have been sent" but it gave him little comfort to learn afterward from the President's physician, Admiral McIntire, that he had heard the President say to Mrs. Roosevelt, "Harry had been given no authority to make any decisions," on which bit of information Ickes commented sardonically, "Harry acted as if he had authority, and the delegates, generally, went on the assumption that he had authority."[29]

The Chicago convention did not diminish Harry's closeness to the President. Among members of the President's inner circle he was notorious for his jealousy, "intense," Justice Douglas described it, of others like Tom who were presumed to be near the President. Harry's palace politics were a factor, especially with Missy's illness, in excluding Tom from the White House. But Tom, and with him Ben, for the two were usually thought of together, also had made many enemies in the course of service to Roosevelt, especially among the regulars. The leaders of the party machine "resented the work he was doing in their field," wrote Rosenman, "they were jealous of his influence on Presidential appointments; they felt he was hurting the party by his maneuvers."[30]

As Roosevelt once had done with Tugwell, he now did with Corcoran. He got him out of Washington, sending him to New York as a vice president of the Norris-La Guardia Committee of Independent Voters for Roosevelt and Wallace. "Treasurer of the irregulars" was Corcoran's jocund description of his stealthy relationship with the New Dealers who clustered under the committee's banners in the campaign. Ed Flynn, who took over the chairmanship of the Democratic National Committee from Farley, insisted the Independents be housed elsewhere and that Corcoran in particular stay out of sight and hopefully out of mind.

"I went to the President," recorded Flynn, "and told him I did not want the New Deal amateurs to be associated with the National Committee at all in this campaign."[31] To mix regulars with New Dealers was to try and mix "oil and water . . . After some discussion the President agreed." When Flynn got wind of a direct tie line from Corcoran's desk at the Roosevelt Hotel to the White House, Corcoran, on advice, put the instrument away in a drawer. Corcoran raised money, took some part in the scheduling of speakers, wrote and funded a full-page anti-Willkie broadside, but it was all a far cry from his involvement in 1936 and 1938. His exile, moreover, reflected the secondary status to which Roosevelt had relegated the New Deal. "Today all private plans, all private lives, have been in a sense repealed by an overriding public danger," the President had said in his acceptance speech. And while that speech had stressed the military and foreign policy steps he had taken to meet the danger from abroad, it made only a lukewarm reference to the New Deal. "Yes, very much remains to be done, and I think voters want the task entrusted to those who believe that the words 'human betterment' apply to rich and poor alike."

The mildness of that commitment became evident that summer in the fights in Congress over an excess profits tax and the funding of plant amortization. Roosevelt had asked for the excess profits levy "so that a few do not gain from the sacrifices of the many," and to ensure that defense contracts did not produce a crop of "war millionaires." But Congress, reflecting the views of business, the "dollar-a-year" men, even Republicans like Stimson and Knox resisted that levy. When Morgenthau to whom the bill was entrusted asked Roosevelt whether to consult Corcoran and Cohen as he had before on tax matters, "The President for reasons I don't know, did not want to see Corcoran and Cohen. I tried my best, but he definitely did not want to see them, so I dropped it."[32]

All that summer debate raged within the higher echelons of the Administration between New Dealers on one side, the military and business on the other, over the priorities that should be assigned to considerations such as taking the profits out of war, distributing the defense burden equitably, and encouraging businessmen to convert and expand their plants for war production. Congress was also considering a draft act, and the contrast between the sacrifices being asked of America's young men and America's defense contractors particularly galled the New Dealers. It would be perfectly terrible, Justice Black told Ickes, if his eighteen-year-old son were conscripted while the corporations were allowed to make any profit they could.

Morgenthau came to Hyde Park to talk with the President about taxes only to find him ready to take any bill that Congress gave him, which, Henry told Mrs. Roosevelt, in effect meant a bill drafted by lawyers for the chambers of commerce. When the President so informed his Cabinet, Ickes wrote angrily in his diary, "On the contrary, I believe that we ought to tell the country now that the big interests are insisting on a bill that will mean a new crop of war millionaires and that the Administration does not intend to permit this even if it means new factories of our own and taking over old factories and running them ourselves."[33]

Ickes was in a fractious mood. "After all, he cannot contain all of the wisdom in the United States, nor is the New Deal his personal property to use or to throw away as he may choose."[34]

Roosevelt's major preoccupation that summer had been Churchill's plea for destroyers and other matériel. Ben Cohen, sidelined though he was as a spokesman for the New Deal forces around the President, played a quiet but decisive role in that transaction. Earlier through Ickes he had suggested a way of attaching the dollar-a-year men to the regular departments and thus avoiding the threat of a supergovernment heavily freighted toward big business. The suggestion had been ignored. Roosevelt wanted to shake up the bureaucracies and also to demonstrate to the country the olive branch that he had extended to business and finance.

Now Ben wrote directly to the President via Missy. From the time of the fall of France, Churchill had been pleading with the President for the transfer of military equipment, torpedo boats, bombers, and especially some old destroyers. After Dunkirk, with invasion imminent, the British had only sixty-eight destroyers fit for service compared with the more than three-hundred in World War I. A shipment of mosquito boats had been stopped by a Senate outcry from the isolationists and defeatists that United States forces needed them. Their opposition had been reinforced by an opinion from Attorney General Jackson ruling that the transfer could not be made. The disastrous ruling had caused Roosevelt to shelve a request for overage destroyers, especially as the Chief of Naval Operations said he needed the vessels.

Word reached Ben from Joseph Alsop the columnist, and other spirited interventionists, that both the State Department and the President had decided nothing could be done. In early June Ben had drafted a memorandum that—Bob Jackson to the contrary notwithstanding—the President had the legal authority to make the transfer. Ickes doubted it in view of Jackson's opinion. So did Tom. "The President could not now reverse himself," Ickes advised. Public opinion would be against him. The Neutrality Act would have to be amended, Ickes felt.[35]

Undaunted, Cohen's memorandum boldly stated there was "considerable leeway within the framework of existing statutes for the transfer of planes and other needed equipment to the Allies." He sent a copy to Oscar Cox, a brilliant young Yale lawyer working at the Treasury on mobilization matters until he was spotted by Harry and grabbed as a right-hand man for the various projects Roosevelt was handing him.

"A fine job," Cox wrote Ben.[36] It might cause less of a furor, he suggested, if one of the destroyers should be sunk, if the British or the Canadians had already taken title to them and if they were manned by British crews. Cohen incorporated the suggestion into his memorandum and sent it to Roosevelt. The nub of Cohen's argument was that the release of the destroyers would "strengthen rather than weaken the defense position of the United States."

The memorandum impressed Roosevelt, he advised Frank Knox, his new, interventionist Secretary of the Navy.[37] It was "worth reading" even though Congress and the new authorization bill he had just signed would not allow it. Cohen consulted Frankfurter on how to change the situation. The justice advised him to send his brief as a letter to the New York *Times* and that it should be signed by a group of citizens outside of the government. Frankfurter suggested Acheson as a signatory, also C. C. Burlingham, the grand old man of the New York bar who had opposed the court plan and so would not be considered a tool of the President, and John Foster Dulles. The latter was involved in some conflict-of-interest situation and proposed Thomas D. Thacher, who had been solicitor general under

Hoover. George Rublee, another old Wilsonian establishment type, was also enlisted.

Cohen and Acheson repaired to the library of the New York Bar Association and drafted a tightly reasoned opinion that upheld the President's right to act. It appeared as a three-and-one-half-column letter in the New York *Times*.[38] Frankfurter called Stimson afterward. They agreed it was touch and go whether international law on the rights of neutrals permitted such an action. But the President, whom Stimson also called, said the letter had encouraged him and he would discuss it with the Attorney General. To the secretary he seemed ready to push ahead.

The letter had a persuasive effect on the government. In his shy way Cohen later stated, "many people feel that that letter made enough impression on him to have him take up the problem again."[39]

Not everyone agreed with Cohen's argument. Authorities on international relations, like Professors Quincy Wright and Edwin Borchard, maintained the transfer would be unneutral and contravene the canons of international law. The draft act was being debated in Congress and the isolationists said they wanted every boat available so that the country could say to the boys, "Young man, you have every possible weapon of defense your government can give you."[40]

Burlingham sent Wright's letter to Ben, "having embarked on this voyage I rely on you to carry us through."[41] Cohen prepared a reply for Burlingham, Acheson, and, above all, the President to make. The destroyer deal, with the addition of bases, was on the road of enactment. To those who argued that international law was being flaunted, Cohen's new memo said:

The Government has always stood for the observance of the rules of international law. It shall continue to do so. But no one nation can accept as binding upon it rules of law which other nations refuse to recognize. International law rests to some degree at least upon mutuality.

International law which is not mutually observed becomes the instrument and ally of the aggressor.

"Bob Jackson," noted Ickes, "has apparently found a legal method by which the transfer can be consummated without legislation."[42]

At the beginning of September the United States and Great Britain announced the destroyers-for-bases deal, an extraordinary trade which was freighted with overtones of an American commitment to the anti-Hitler cause but which the President had piloted so skillfully during a presidential election campaign that the criticism of such arch-isolationists as

Charles Lindbergh and the editorial writers of the Chicago *Tribune* was muted, again indicating the astuteness of Roosevelt's turn to the right.

"But you know that F.D. has a campaign on his hands," Missy said when she summoned Sam Rosenman whom she had tracked down on the West Coast. Roosevelt was to address the Teamsters Union Convention in Washington on September 11. Harry Hopkins and Rosenman worked on the speech in a bedroom at Hyde Park. It was to be a New Deal talk but Corcoran and Cohen were no longer part of the speech-writing teams. Lauchlin Currie contributed to it, and the fate of his suggestion on Social Security illustrated the heavy going that confronted new New Deal proposals. It had long been the economist's contention that because of the way the old-age security program was set up "the accumulation of a fund from payroll deductions increased savings and decreased consumption" and thereby delayed recovery.* Roosevelt approved a movement away from the giant fund idea to a pay-as-you-go theory. Harry and Sam incorporated the thought in the Teamsters Union speech, but it was ignored by the press and Currie realized "the idea was dead and the moment of domestic reform past."[43] In a democracy, Currie acknowledged, "a condition of leadership is that the leader must lead in the direction the country wants to go."

The ailing Harry Hopkins finally resigned from the Cabinet and from political ambition in his own right. His resignation evoked a poignant tribute from his old rival Ickes: "No one has ever battled as consistently for the New Deal and the President, week in and week out as you have," Ickes wrote him. "You have never failed the President and the liberals in the country in a single instance that I can recall . . ."[44]

The President had telephoned Corcoran at the time of the convention. That he had initiated the call was itself a rare event. " 'Now listen, Tommy,' " he said according to Corcoran, " 'Stop this New Deal talk.' He said we're no longer interested in the New Deal, we are interested in winning the war." It was "the first time" Roosevelt had talked with him "in a very hard way." Was the President saying what he did to impress someone he had with him? Tommy wondered, a war contract guy? someone in defense?

* The Harvard and Tufts economists in their *Economic Program for American Democracy* estimated that "the reserve provision in the old-age insurance law reduced consumer incomes in 1938 by $300 million a year and from 1940 to 1945 the excess of tax collections over benefit payments will average more than $800 million a year . . . The whole attempt to build up a reserve is economically unsound and should be abandoned."

Ben and I were always concerned about what happened to Wilson. When Wilson got in the war, the new freedom stopped. Now, we weren't convinced that it had to stop. The same about the New Deal. I really believed in this thing. I really believed in the TVAs, and I really believed in the anti-trust laws, and I really believed in the reorganization of the government.[45]

Tom and Ben talked over the strange call "and we decided both of us to leave after the campaign was over." Corcoran asked Cotton Franklin, his old Wall Street firm, to take him back and along with him Ben, who would have been the first Jewish partner. "So we lived through that very fuzzy time when we really didn't know whether we were in or whether we were out."

Tugwell was in Washington at the beginning of 1941 to organize the commission set up by Ickes to enforce the five-hundred-acre law in Puerto Rico. He was eager to get out from under La Guardia in New York. He found the liberals dejected. "Much gossip about business entrenchment in the [National Defense Advisory] Commission, about favoritism, about unwillingness to take risks, etc; all the progressives seem very much out of it."[46] Ben Cohen whom he wanted as legal counsel was "almost incoherently enraged about the sellout, as he called it" and was "considering seriously setting up a private practice with Corcoran."

The New Dealers kicked and grumbled but Roosevelt's sense of priorities was right, as Cohen later conceded:

From the isolationist side, every move of Roosevelt's was a trick. He just wanted to get us into the war. But no one was sure—perhaps not he himself—how far he would go. He didn't want to go any further than he could go, that is, further than he could carry the American people. He recognized from the time of the quarantine speech that we were going to be involved and should be prepared in case we had to intervene.[47]

Unhappy as many of the New Dealers were, Roosevelt's State of the Union message reconciled them to their role as soldiers in the ranks. Vision as well as an unerring sense of priorities were involved in that address. The basic speech-writing team had become Hopkins, Rosenman, and the playwright Robert Sherwood. Berle helped with the preliminary draft, as did Cohen, but the words of vision were Roosevelt's: "We must look forward to a world based on four essential human freedoms," he dictated as Rosenman took down the enumeration that followed on a yellow pad.[48] "Listened to F.D.R.'s message on the state of the union," recorded Tugwell:

Jubilant at his statement of "war aims." I do not know that I had any influence but I do know that my letter to him of last September, which I have repeated since, suggested this. Democracy has plenty of believers behind the totalitarian lines but only a radical statement of democratic aims could consolidate the revolution incipient in their beliefs. The statement to me was very moving. Disarmament, freedom of religion and thought, and the guarantee of security—those all of us can fight for. This is better than Wilson's 14 points. And, speaking of them, I recall in those days the same reluctance to accept resort to force which I have felt in this crisis and the same relief at a definition of aims which was acceptable. But there were disappointments then.

XXVIII

———————$\Rightarrow\!\!\curvearrowright\!\!\curvearrowleft\!\!\Leftarrow$———————

Blacks and the New Deal

In November 1933 Felix Frankfurter, a longtime supporter of the National Association for the Advancement of Colored People (NAACP), sent its secretary Walter White to Tom Corcoran in Washington. "It certainly ought to smooth the path in remedying my failure to know him," White gratefully responded.[1]

White was too canny a politician, his black constituency still too tied to the Republican Party of Abraham Lincoln and distrustful of the white South's hold on the Democrats, to limit his Washington contacts to the New Dealers. But it was clear to him as it was to other black leaders that blacks, being among the poorest of the poor, stood greatly to gain from the emergency relief and recovery programs that were being started by Franklin D. Roosevelt; that the strongest advocates of Negro inclusion in such programs were the New Dealers among whom Corcoran already, at the end of 1933, was a force to be considered.

Over at the White House in the same period that White was meeting Corcoran, Eleanor Roosevelt assembled a group of black leaders, Walter White among them, to discuss the part Negroes should have in the subsistence homestead programs. The discussion of the resistance of white homesteaders at Arthurdale in West Virginia turned into a general discussion that went on until midnight of the desperate plight of the Negro in the Great Depression and whether relief from deprivation should have priority over desegregation. The consensus of the group was that Negro participation in the aid programs of the New Deal should come before desegregation, especially in the South. "We had no racial doctrine," said Will Alexander, a liberal white Southerner who worked closely with Eleanor Roosevelt on these issues, "except that we were not to discriminate in the distribution of these benefits—the care of these people . . . I frankly admit it. We accepted the pattern."[2]

That was the attitude generally of the New Dealers. Some led by Eleanor Roosevelt, Harold Ickes, the old-time Bull Mooser who had been involved with the NAACP in Chicago before he came to Washington, Aubrey Williams, the mettlesome Southerner who was deputy to Hopkins in the relief agencies, felt the issue of racial discrimination keenly and took risks in fighting it; others sought the inclusion of blacks in the relief and recovery programs; and there were still others like Frances Perkins at Labor who "dreaded" dealing with a problem that might mean confrontation with the Southerners who controlled vital legislative committees in Congress, and Henry Wallace, the New Dealer who headed Agriculture but who was, as Alexander indicated, "terribly afraid" of the racial issue.[3]

As for FDR, as he explained to White who wanted him to intervene more forcefully in support of the NAACP's main civil rights objective in the early New Deal years, the antilynching bill:

I did not choose the tools with which I must work. Southerners, by reason of the seniority rule in Congress, are chairmen or occupy strategic places on most of the Senate and House committees. If I come out for the antilynching bill now, they will block every bill I ask Congress to pass to keep America from collapsing. I just can't take the risk.[4]

That shaped the view of men like Corcoran. "There *wasn't* any race problem in the Thirties," he told Nancy J. Weiss, the Princeton scholar, in the course of her interview for her definitive book, *Farewell to the Party of Lincoln.* "When Roosevelt came in in 1933, there were many more important things to worry about than what happened to civil rights . . . We weren't concerned with civil rights because there was so much more to worry about."[5]

For Tom and his "skipper," political realities arrested an enthusiasm for equal rights that Roosevelt, a Georgian by adoption, did not feel, and that Tom, despite his Irish sensitivities, was not disposed to argue about. "Remember," he explained to the inquiring scholar, "we were in a difficult situation—we always had to have that southern [support]. All of this trimming and compromising is the price you have to pay for democratic government at all."[6]

Even in an agency like the Federal Emergency Relief Administration

(FERA), forerunner of the WPA, which was run by Hopkins, another stalwart on the issue, race was handled gingerly. Elizabeth Wickenden directed the Transients program for the agency. She was a dependable advocate of black rights but she, too, acknowledged, "We treated blacks like everyone else in doling out benefits, but we really weren't aware of their problems."[7]

Awareness was what distinguished Eleanor Roosevelt from everyone else. She refused to permit institutions or high-sounding principles to stand in the way of seeing problems as they really existed. The only way to get to know those problems was through individuals, she felt. So she became a friend as well as a colleague of Walter White and had him and his family to Val Kill, remembered his birthdays and other occasions. She did the same with Mary McLeod Bethune, daughter of a sharecropper, one of seventeen children, "as black as black can be," as one of her admiring cohorts said of her, and acknowledged by blacks in Washington as their leader. Eleanor Roosevelt had suggested her appointment to Hopkins, and the "Black Cabinet," as the small but growing group of black advisers in the agencies and departments (which Bethune assembled in 1935) called itself, accepted her leadership. The Black Cabinet's members were young, college-educated, and had sense enough to envy "Ma" Bethune's "almost mystical sense of identity with the Negro masses."[8]

In the thirties, when Mrs. Bethune checked into the hospital, there were roses every day from Eleanor Roosevelt. If there was no other place to turn, Mrs. Roosevelt always had time for her, and the day Mrs. Roosevelt greeted her at the threshold with a peck on the cheek without self-consciousness, she told her daughter Anna that she felt she had conquered another barrier of prejudice in herself.

New Dealers like Eleanor Roosevelt and Harold Ickes took risks in their stands on racial issues, less concerned with the political calculus that guided FDR and associates like Corcoran, but even the political realists were aware that the Negro vote was shifting. In advance of the 1936 elections White called to their attention that the relatively small black vote could be a determinant in seventeen pivotal states. He showed his tables to the President and he was impressed. "The skipper said he would call them to Farley's attention promptly," Max Lowenthal, who was in touch with White, informed Tom, and sent him a copy of White's analysis.[9]

Though Roosevelt and his lieutenants were aware that the shift in Negro voting patterns might be decisive in several states in 1936, it did not make them the readier to embrace the agenda of issues about which White said Negroes were most anxious. These related not only to the antilynching bill, but to documented "discriminations" in relief and public works, "particularly in southern states," the white primaries in those states, the treatment of blacks in the armed forces.

By 1936 change was evident to the perceptive in the political allegiances of the blacks. At the Democratic Convention in Philadelphia that year, for the first time in the party's history there were ten black delegates and twenty-two alternates from twelve states. The Good Neighbor League, which was set up for the progressives and independents who would not march to the National Committee's drum, had a "National Colored Committee" of forty well-known Negroes. It issued literature and sent out speakers to the black areas. Its key pamphlet was entitled "Has Roosevelt New Deal Helped the Colored Citizen?"[10]

The answer on Election Day was a resounding yes. In the landslide election in which Roosevelt amassed 60.8 percent of the vote, Harlem gave him 80 percent of its ballots, the black neighborhoods of Pittsburgh 75 percent, Philadelphia's black precincts 69 percent. Commented Frank R. Kent, the conservative political columnist, about this swing in the Negro vote, "Nothing of more far-reaching significance has happened in politics for a good many years."

But idolization of Roosevelt by the blacks, the popularity with them of such New Deal programs as the WPA, the NYA, and slum clearance, did not affect the Administration's legislative priorities. Blacks had become part of the Roosevelt coalition but Southerners still sat astride key congressional committees. Walter White discovered this when his old standby in the Senate, Robert Wagner, together with Senator Van Nuys of Indiana and Representative Gavagan reintroduced the antilynching bill. It passed the House with little help from the Administration but was stalled in the Senate by a Southern filibuster. In desperation White invoked the help of Lizzie McDuffie, Roosevelt's black maid. She transmitted White's plea that Roosevelt speak out against the filibuster. He could not, he told her gently. In a Congress which in the course of the Court-reform fight had turned hostile to him, his intervention would backfire. "Can't people read between the lines?" he appealed to her. "Mrs. Roosevelt would not be sitting in the Congressional galleries listening to the antilynch deliberations if I didn't favor the bill."

As Tom Corcoran explained to Nancy Weiss in a 1977 interview: "We had first of all the court fight and then we had the purge fight, and then we had the third term fight, and then we had Hitler and the war."[11] For a "practical person" like Roosevelt, he went on, that left "only a niche" for racial issues. "They were scared," said Bob Weaver, leader of the Black

Cabinet, as he described the attitude of Roosevelt and his staff, and he could have included most New Dealers. They regarded racial issues as "political dynamite" and their automatic response, he recalled, was "Don't touch it." So staunch a progressive as Abraham Epstein,[12] the veteran advocate of old-age security, rebuffed the efforts of the NAACP and Urban League to have agricultural and domestic workers included in the new system's protections because, he told Roy Wilkins, "the old-age security advocates were not seeking to solve the race problem and did not draw a bill with the idea in mind of speeding the solution of the race problem." That was in 1934. In Roosevelt's second administration when the boldhearted Aubrey Williams tried to enlist Roosevelt in the fight against poll taxes, the President patiently explained to him, "Politics is the art of the possible."[13] The effort to abolish the poll tax would damage the chances of other legislation. "I believe you should never undertake anything unless you have evidence that you have at least a 50-50 chance of winning."

New Dealers like Eleanor Roosevelt, Harold Ickes, and Aubrey Williams were few and no one was able to challenge Roosevelt's inescapable logic. The fight for racial justice had to go on and would go on and racial issues were not the only ones on which New Dealers had to keep a best, that was not achievable, from becoming the enemy of the good, which was. Blacks recognized this even as they fought hard for more. When Bob Weaver spoke to the 1937 NAACP convention on behalf of Roosevelt and the New Deal, he cited what it was doing for blacks that year—390,000 blacks employed on WPA projects, 20 percent of the total number of WPA jobs; 10,000 black children cared for daily in WPA nursery schools; 35,000 black students in high school and college thanks to NYA help; 5,000 black teachers teaching blacks to read and write. Ten percent of the CCC enrollees were black, PWA had built black schools in the South, and low-rent housing was arising in black areas.

Vernon Jordan, later head of the Urban League, remembered growing up in the first black public housing project. It may have been segregated, he said, but it was "clean and warm" and the blacks who moved in were "ecstatic." Carl and Louis Stokes remembered the day they and their mother moved into a Cleveland housing project as one of "pure wonder" and how extraordinary it was "to live in dependable warmth."[14]

The results showed in the outpouring of black support for Roosevelt. When Hopkins became Secretary of Commerce in 1939 he told his deputy for politics, David Niles, he wanted to appoint a Negro adviser.[15] There was a problem, Niles counseled him. The "deserving Democrats" suggested by the Democratic National Committee were rarely of the type esteemed and respected by blacks generally. A few "good appointments" of blacks would help cement black support for Roosevelt and the party but they had all be careful to select people recommended by blacks themselves. That was a new note in Administration thinking about Negro participation in the New Deal.

The vast muster of blacks, and to a lesser degree of whites, for the concert of the great contralto Marian Anderson in front of the Lincoln Memorial measured both black joy in the advances that had been made under the New Deal and their growing insistence on their rights as Americans. The Daughters of the American Revolution had denied Marian Anderson's sponsors the use of its Constitution Hall for her concert. That triggered Eleanor Roosevelt's resignation from the organization and persuaded Ickes, whose department included the Park Service, to permit the concert to be staged at the Lincoln Memorial. He did so after getting FDR's approval. Seventy-five thousand people massed at the base of the Memorial and stretched up the Mall to the Washington Monument—the first such demonstration of blacks and whites in Washington's history. "It was beautiful," said Joe Rauh who like other New Dealers was there with his wife, Ollie. The majority of blacks were poor but dressed in their "Sunday best" and their eyes shone with a sense of dedication and commitment. It was "unique, majestic, impressive," recorded Ickes who had presided. To Marian Anderson it seemed "that everyone present was a living witness to the ideals of freedom for which President Lincoln had died." And Mary Bethune almost walked on air as she came away, "My hopes for the future were brightened."[16]

Washington's days as a Southern city were numbered. But it would take time. Eleanor Roosevelt, with White's concurrence, had thought it best to stay away.

Then the war came. The black legislative agenda, like other reform proposals, receded from the Capital's attention and changed its thrust. On the day that Hitler invaded Poland, White, who wanted to see the President about new black concerns such as segregation in the armed forces and exclusion from defense jobs, was advised by Aubrey Williams not to press for an appointment.[17] The President had more pressing matters to deal with. A few months later Roosevelt appointed a National Defense Advisory Commission of six. A woman was among them and a representative of labor, but not a black. Were blacks welcome in the New Deal coalition? Some wondered. Still, a few weeks later, for the first time in the Democratic Party's history its platform, which had been crafted under

Roosevelt's guidance, had a plank addressed to black concerns. Some thought it too vague; others too extreme. The judge of where the line was to be drawn had been Roosevelt. When some young people just before the convention taxed him with not pressing harder on the Negro problem among others, he replied by invoking Abraham Lincoln. If his questioners had read the Carl Sandburg biography that had just appeared they would have known that:

Lincoln was a pretty sad man because he could not do all that he wanted to do at one time, and I think you will find examples where Lincoln had to compromise to make a few gains . . . He was a sad man because he couldn't get it all at once. And nobody can . . . Maybe you would make a much better President than I have. Maybe you will, some day. If you ever sit here, you will learn that you cannot, just by shouting from the housetops, get what you want all the time. Was he sincere or acting a role? Did he himself know?

After three hours of questions and challenges, Roosevelt had been wheeled out to take a call from the Secretary of State, leaving his questioners in the hands of Mrs. Roosevelt who had assembled them and Harry Hopkins who had begun living in the White House and was considered a friend on matters of social reform. Hopkins had been doing a slow burn over the drumfire of defiant questions that had indicated disagreement and distrust of Roosevelt's choice of priorities. "He would agree with most of the things you people agree on," he protested. But he was President and "anybody who has watched him in the last seven years knows he is a pretty good judge of public opinion and where it is." And it was a little presumptuous for his young questioners to say to him in effect, "Now I think you are making a great mistake. You do not sense what public opinion is. You could move this thing this way if you wanted to."

Mrs. Roosevelt agreed with Hopkins that evening,[18] yet there was a large difference in her attitude toward issues such as the poll tax and the like, and her husband's. He was the political broker, she the moralist. And in the campaign in 1940 morality turned out to be the best politics, at least so far as blacks were concerned. At Democratic headquarters when Negro participation was discussed there were officials who shrugged blacks off as useless for anything except labor battalions, but not when Mrs. Roosevelt was there to hear them. And it was she who during the campaign dined with the Brotherhood of Sleeping Car Porters at their annual convention and at Mrs. Bethune's request received the National Council of Negro Women at the White House. Blacks had made great gains under Roosevelt but better than almost anyone else in the Administration, including the New Dealers, she sensed the rising black anger over treatment of the

Negro in the armed forces, the symbolic importance to them of the passing over of Colonel Davis, a black, in the promotion lists, and she never was sorry to have pressure brought on Franklin by those who faced Zionward.

Black pressure during the campaign focused on the issues of black participation in the defense effort. Wendell Willkie, Roosevelt's opponent, actively courted black support including that of Walter White. At the latter's request Mrs. Roosevelt arranged a meeting between the President and a delegation of Negro leaders. "The Negro people . . . feel that they are not wanted in the armed forces of this country," A. Philip Randolph, leader of the Sleeping Car Porters, declared to the President. Roosevelt was conciliatory, promised consideration of black demands and to talk with the delegation again.

Another meeting did not take place. Stimson and Knox resisted black demands. Knox even threatened to resign. Stimson did not go that far but he opposed desegregation, noting in his diary, "The Negroes are taking advantage of this period just before election to try to get everything they can in the way of recognition from the Army." Roosevelt finally announced a policy of enlarged utilization of blacks in the armed forces but on a segregated basis.

An accompanying announcement issued by Roosevelt's press secretary Steve Early, a Southerner, said the policy came as a result of Roosevelt's meeting with the black leaders. That produced a furor in the black community. Early explained he had not meant to suggest the black group had approved the policy, but the White House knew it had blundered. Just before election it announced the promotion of Colonel Davis to brigadier general, of William H. Hastie as a civilian aide to Stimson, and another black as executive assistant to the director of Selective Service. Black allegiance to the Democrats and Roosevelt had become precarious. At least so campaign officials thought. When it was disclosed that Steve Early had kneed a Negro policeman in the groin as the presidential party raced to make the train to Washington after Roosevelt's speech at Madison Square Garden the night of October 28, alarm bells rang everywhere in Democratic precincts. How should the "unhappy" episode be handled, a worried Hopkins phoned Ickes.[19] It might lose Illinois for Roosevelt, Paul Douglas warned from there. Corcoran, working with the Norris-La Guardia Citizens Committee in New York, begged Ickes to get hold of Marian Anderson to sing under Democratic auspices and thus take some of the sting out of the episode. The contralto did sing over the air in the Democratic campaign's last roundup. By then Republican efforts to make capital out of the incident had fizzled, especially after the black policeman involved told the press, "I will vote for Mr. Roosevelt . . . It would be silly to blame the President for something he could not help."

Election Day balloting showed that Roosevelt's popularity with blacks had endured. Although he prevailed over Willkie with an overall vote of 54.7 percent as against the 60.8 percent that he had amassed against Landon, in black precincts he garnered 67 percent compared with 71 percent in 1936. His slippage among blacks was markedly less than among whites and as Walter White had predicted, "The Race is more Rooseveltian, 'especially Mrs. Rooseveltian,' then Democratic."[20]

XXXIX

Labor's Magna Carta

In a flamboyant address to the American Economic Association in 1971 that was meant to rattle the academic dovecotes, Leon Keyserling, who had been Senator Wagner's aide in the formative New Deal years, entered a sharp demurral to the "preoccupation of the academicians" with the Keynesian revolution in dealing with those years.

"With all due respect to Keynes," protested Keyserling, who knew he was flying in the face of prevalent opinion at the conference:

I have been unable to discover much reasonable evidence that the New Deal would have been greatly different if he had never lived, and if a so-called school of economics had not taken on his name.[1]

Keyserling's protest was in the form of a commentary on a leading paper, "The Keynesians and Government Policy, 1933–1939" that had just been delivered by Alan Sweezy. While at Harvard in the thirties, the latter had been one of the authors of *An Economic Program for American Democracy*. In 1971 he was professor of economics at the California Institute of Technology. He had not mentioned Keyserling. He and his colleagues did not choose to argue with him, setting forth instead the progress of the Keynesians in the thirties. Nevertheless, responsible New Dealers saw merit in Keyserling's opinion. Economists like Tom Blaisdell felt that history had slighted the role that liberal senators like Robert Wagner and Robert La Follette, Jr., had played in the New Deal. "The economy wasn't changed that much by some of the things Ben [Cohen] emphasized," said

Walter Salant, a penetrating American Keynesian and another author of *An Economic Program for American Democracy,* "compared with the things Keyserling emphasized."[2]

Privately, Keyserling was outraged by "the mythology about Ben and Tom" as creators of the major economic and social legislation of the New Deal. Greatly as he respected both men, neither had had anything to do, he insisted, with the NIRA, the AAA, the TVA, the National Labor Relations Act, the Housing Act. "I never ran into them in connection with any of this legislation, all of which except the TVA and the AAA were sponsored by Senator Wagner in whose office I worked . . ."

Keyserling's judgments about the part of Cohen and Corcoran may be disputed, but his own role in the drafting of the National Labor Relations Act was paramount. Just as his predecessor in Wagner's office, Si Rifkind "held the yellow pad" in the drafting of the NIRA, including the magical Section 7(a) words that guaranteed the right of collective bargaining, so Keyserling, a "constant arguer," portly, brilliant, a protégé of Tugwell who brought him from Columbia to Washington, held the yellow pad in the drafting of the National Labor Relations Act.

A momentous piece of New Deal legislation, it permanently altered the shape of American politics and economics. It was Senator Wagner's "baby" not Roosevelt's, and though the senator and President were allies, Section 7(A) was another illustration that the New Deal was no well-ordered hierarchy but a state of mind with important mainsprings in the Senate as well as the White House.[3] Rifkind, aided by Keyserling, drafted the celebrated words, so transformational to labor's status, that "every industrial code must provide among other things that employees shall have the right to organize and bargain collectively through representatives of their own choosing, and shall be free from the interference, restraint, or coercion of employers . . . in the designation of such representatives." When industry, which was being released from antitrust restraints, balked, Rifkind's boss, Senator Wagner, told it bluntly, "No 7(a), no bill."

And that was the way it was. In 1933 the outlook was bleak for labor. Union membership which had risen to almost five million at the end of World War I by the time of the Great Depression had sunk to under three million. With the support of the courts, industry had used "yellow dog contracts," company unions, antipicketing injunctions to weaken drastically organized labor's power. Although Roosevelt took no active part in the fight for 7(a) he, like almost all New Dealers, considered an increase in mass purchasing power a basic objective and the enhancement of labor's bargaining power a way of attaining that end.

When the NIRA was approved, the unions happily seized upon 7(a). Their organizers went to the country with a new patriotic message: "The President wants you to join."

An epidemic of strikes erupted, troops were called out in many states, and in August 1933 Roosevelt established a National Labor Board with Wagner as its chairman to adjust differences that stemmed from conflicting interpretations of 7(a). When employers hurried to the courts to challenge the National Labor Board's right to supervise union representation elections, Roosevelt stepped in with an executive order that authorized such elections. His order upheld the bitterly contested "majority rule" principle which gave the representatives chosen by a majority the right to represent all the workers in a plant. Employers disputed this reading of the NIRA. So did General Hugh Johnson and Donald Richberg, both of whom favored minority representation, and Roosevelt retreated into ambiguity on the point.[4]

Wagner undertook to clarify 7(a) and the powers of the Labor Board through congressional action. He told Keyserling to consult with Wyzanski at the Department of Labor and the lawyers at the Labor Board. The first Wagner Bill was drafted and introduced by the senator on March 1, 1934. The rights of labor had no firmer champion than Wagner. He had entered politics at about the same time as Roosevelt had. Child of a German immigrant family, he knew what it was to be poor, and he had gotten his start in politics via Tammany Hall. Later he would, with a smile, refer to Tammany as "the cradle of modern liberalism in America." Introducing his "Labor Disputes Act of 1934," Wagner pointed to the "slow progress" in a fairer distribution of purchasing power which was a basic New Deal objective and which he felt "can be remedied only when there is cooperation between employers and employees on the basis of equal bargaining."[5]

The proposed act spelled out "unfair labor practices" and took the National Labor Board out of the NRA. That pleased Frances Perkins who wanted the new board to be lodged in her department; moreover, she preferred a mediation to an enforcement approach to labor's rights. Industry, which had recovered from its 1933 loss of nerve, mobilized against the Wagner version with full-page advertisements. On the other side a burst of militant strikes engulfed many communities. Roosevelt, who again had kept hands off, stepped in with an Executive Order that set up a three-member National Labor Relations Board (NLRB) to conduct collective bargaining elections but with weaker powers than Wagner proposed to give it.

The Wagner version passed the House and in the Senate Robert La Follette, Jr., prepared to offer the Wagner bill as a substitute for a joint resolution drafted by Wyzanski and Richberg that authorized the President to set up a board for the period of one year. "This is really one of the most embarrassing moments of my whole political life," said Wagner, explaining that he had to acquiesce in Roosevelt's wishes and not pursue his own bill. Regretfully La Follette followed suit. "After all, it is the child of his brain." "We will fight for it next year," Wagner promised him.

The new board was headed by Lloyd Garrison, the liberal dean of the Wisconsin Law School.[6] Glenn Frank, the president of the university who had ambitions of his own in the Republican Party, opposed Garrison's taking the position. Why didn't he do so for the summer and get it going? Perkins pleaded. Garrison went to Washington where Perkins took him to see the President, who greeted him "gay as a lark," a cigarette jutting from his jaw, full of stories: "Well, good luck and off with you."

The five months Garrison stayed in Washington proved to be "very concentrated," he recalled in a large understatement. "We had no precedents—just a simple sentence." The big issue was whether the majority would speak for all. The unions contended that if minority unions were allowed the door would be opened to play off one against the other. "We decided for the majority view—not a closed shop but that it should represent all." General Johnson made difficulties. "He was a profane, engaging rascal. We made decisions. Even the modest sanction of taking away the Blue Eagle." He didn't want to do that, Garrison warned Johnson:

The public and especially labor have begun to lose faith not only in the power of the government to enforce 7(a) but in its intention to do so. The increasing use of the strike weapon is due, at least in part, to a feeling that it has become useless to look to the government to enforce the law.[7]

As Glenn Frank had dourly predicted, Roosevelt and Perkins did press Garrison to stay on. "I wish I could," the mild-mannered Garrison replied, "but I gave my word to Glenn Frank." "There are lots of law schools in the country," remonstrated Roosevelt who made it difficult for others to say no, "but only one country to serve." All he could get out of Garrison, however, was an agreement to stay on until he had found a successor satisfactory to him and to Perkins.

The issue of enforcement of Section 7(a) guarantees came to a head in a new draft of the Wagner Act that Keyserling prepared for the senator for the 1935 session. Though the White House was as hostile to the new Wagner Act as it had been to the old, the senator, more labor's man than

Roosevelt's, directed Keyserling to move ahead on a bill. The 1934 elections had increased Roosevelt's strength in Congress, but also labor's and it wanted a bill.

Keyserling at the time shared a house on Thirty-fourth Street with several New Deal lawyers, including Tom Emerson whose militant outlook he liked.[8] Emerson, a product of Yale Law School where he led his class, had eschewed Wall Street for civil liberties law and had been recruited for the NLRB by Garrison. Like Keyserling he had itched to involve himself in the problems of labor, for he considered the trade union movement "the major progressive force in the New Deal at the time" and the promotion of collective bargaining a service to the public interest. "Keyserling's role was *the* role," he recalled. "We worked over it in great detail and I saw him develop the whole thing."

Abetted by NLRB lawyers Keyserling forged a powerful instrument to enforce collective bargaining. He spelled out the "unfair labor practices" that would violate the statute. The draft outlawed company unions, codified the principle of majority rule and exclusive representation, and ensured the board's independent status.[9]

Confronted with the reluctance of the Justice Department under Homer Cummings to enforce NLRB findings in the courts, the lawyers of the new agency would be authorized to represent it in the courts, a provision that the Justice Department fought until Wagner warned it of a floor fight. Throughout the drafting process the issue of survivability in the courts, especially the Supreme Court, was foremost in the minds of the framers. Keyserling's strategy was to base its claims to constitutionality on the "commerce clause." He hoped the upper bench would go along with a liberal interpretation of that clause and the bill's reasoning that work stoppages damaged interstate commerce as did inequality of bargaining power and the shortfalls in consumer purchasing power that resulted therefrom.

Wagner introduced the bill on February 21, 1935. Roosevelt took a hands-off attitude which the knowledgeable read as opposition. Perkins fought to have the new agency shifted to her department. Wyzanski sought to introduce the concept of "correlative responsibilities" for labor and management. Industry fought the bill as did the Communist Party, which had not yet entered its "popular front" phase. Donald Richberg, then with the NRA, sought to dilute the majority rule stipulation and protect the company union.

But labor, its power augmented by the results of the 1934 elections, labeled the measure one of "transcending importance." The spirit of the times was militantly liberal and when it appeared, as the Senate neared a vote, that the Supreme Court would invalidate the NIRA with its provisions for collective bargaining as well as its bans on child labor and sweatshop conditions, Roosevelt pledged full support for the measure. The Senate approved it by a vote of 63 to 12 and Roosevelt signed it over the protests of Homer Cummings, who thought it of "rather doubtful constitutionality." In signing the bill Roosevelt emphasized that the new board would be an "independent quasi-judicial" agency to enforce rights defined in the bill. He gave two of the pens to William Green and Senator Wagner. "Wagner was almost alone among liberal Democrats in placing a high value on trade unions," wrote Arthur Schlesinger, "and it was Wagner who was almost single-handedly forcing a reluctant administration into a national labor policy."[10]

But would the bill survive the courts? Philip Levy, one of its drafters and Wagner's administrative aide after Keyserling, attributed the bill's fortunes in Congress to the assumption of many that the Supreme Court would hold it unconstitutional. Why, they reasoned, go on record unnecessarily?[11]

Roosevelt gave Perkins the job of finding the three members of the new board and she came up with J. Warren Madden, a University of Pittsburgh law professor and dean whom the President designated chairman; John M. Carmody, an industrial engineer who had been chairman of the National Bituminous Coal Board; and Edwin S. Smith, a holdover from the old board who was to turn out to be its most pro-labor member and probably a Communist. The pivotal position in the new setup, especially in view of the pending battle in the courts, was the general counsel. Calvert Magruder had held the post in the old board but he wanted to return to Harvard Law School. Keyserling wanted the job but Wagner's support was, in Keyserling's words, "very lukewarm. I like to believe that he wanted me to remain with him." There were other objections to Keyserling. "He had never practiced law," said Madden, "and we thought that he was too young and relatively inexperienced." The position finally went to Charles Fahy. Not a crusader but a legal technician, he was nevertheless a man of broad sympathies when it came to hiring policies. He was assistant secretary of the Interior, wanted the job, and got it.[12]

One of the young lawyers whom he inherited from the old board was Nathan Witt. Much of the recruitment of young lawyers for the new board's staff Fahy delegated to Witt whose legal expertise, cultivated interests, and modest demeanor made him an attractive figure. He was a secret Communist but in this period that affiliation infused his work for the board with a crusader's vigor. Fahy was a first-class lawyer, Witt later said, but "he was not as devoted to the Act the way I and some of the younger people were. To him it was just another career . . . He got there by accident; I got there by design."[13]

Those for whom labor was a cause and for whom working for the new agency was an intellectual and ideological fulfilment, like Tom Emerson, Witt, and to a lesser degree Keyserling, differed from those in the New Deal for whom the labor movement was as flawed, prejudice-ridden, and economically egotistic as other elements in the Roosevelt coalition, but who supported labor's right to organize and bargain collectively.

A New Dealer like Eleanor Roosevelt thought unions were necessary but not infallible. Abuses were possible, wrong decisions made. It would be bad if any one group in the Roosevelt coalition should gain a monopoly of power, she maintained. There were corrupt labor leaders and Russia was a "dreadful example" of what could happen in a worker-controlled society. The majority of New Dealers considered labor an ally but not a sacred cow. Lauchlin Currie in his analysis of the causes of the 1937 recession candidly listed the pressure of organized labor "for a greater increase in hourly earnings" as one of those causes. FDR best epitomized the conception of a public interest that transcended constituent interests, including labor's. He resisted pleas from John L. Lewis, leader of the CIO, that he intervene in the sitdown strikes on the workers' side and a few months later, in a showdown between Little Steel and the Steel Workers Organizing Committee, he again kept hands off with the words of Shakespeare, "A plague on both your houses." This brought from an angry Lewis, who had contributed almost a half million dollars to the Roosevelt 1936 campaign, the scripturally cadenced reproof: "It ill behooves one who had supped at labor's table and who has been sheltered in labor's house to curse with equal fervor and fine impartiality both labor and its adversaries when they become locked in deadly embrace."

One reason for Roosevelt's firm opposition to sitdown strikes and to automatic partisanship with labor was his belief that labor had in the Wagner Act rights that would be upheld by the National Labor Relations Board and sustained, it was hoped, in the courts.

This last, however, was a big question mark when Fahy, Emerson, and Witt contemplated the future. The Supreme Court was at the height of its rulings against New Deal statutes. Passage of the Wagner Act, like that of the Public Utility Holding Company Act, ran into a stone wall of hostility from industry, the bankers and the lawyers allied with them. The new NLRB was assailed by injunction suits in the lower courts. The newly established American Liberty League through its "Lawyers Vigilance

Committee" issued a "Report on the Constitutionality of the National Labor Relations Act" which ended, "We have no hesitancy in concluding that [the Wagner Act] is unconstitutional and that it constitutes a complete departure from our constitutional and traditional theories of government." "We knew that until the Supreme Court declared the act constitutional, it was going to be very difficult to get any kind of enforcement," said Emerson.[14]

Since they knew they were headed for the Supreme Court, the board sought test cases. David A. Morse, a Harvard Law School graduate, was dispatched to New York. "We think that you'll be able to find a case up there that may help us determine the constitutionality of the National Labor Relations Act." He did, filing a lawsuit against the Associated Press for refusal to bargain in good faith with Heywood Broun's American Newspaper Guild.

Cases were selected and action to uphold the Act moved to the offices of the solicitor general. The team that worked on those briefs, recalled Charles A. Horsky, a Montanan who reached Washington via a law degree from Harvard and a clerkship for Judge Augustus Hand, consisted of Abe Feller, a lawyer in the antitrust division, Wyzanski who had moved to the solicitor general's office, and Horsky. "Everybody I met in Washington was out to save the world," Horsky said of the day-and-night sessions they spent preparing the briefs. "When you went to a party, you didn't talk sports, you didn't talk women. You talked about the case you were on and what the problem was with the conservative Supreme Court."[15] In the NLRB cases "we would sit around and try to decide point by point what kind of positions we ought to take. Then I would spend the afternoon and usually most of the evening trying to put that on paper. Then we would meet again in the morning to look it over, and we'd tear it all apart and try to do it over again."

Horsky and the diminutive Feller were good friends. Joined by Wyzanski they often met just to talk. They were the most interesting conversationalists Horsky ever met. "We talked about everything: the Restoration, the Roman Empire, problems of South Africa, exploration of the North Pole . . . The thing I most remember about those times is the *esprit de corps,* the sense that you were doing something worthwhile, that it was important to do it the very best way you could, and that it was important to get it done on time . . . We felt that we were going to change the United States and make it a better place. And we did, damnit, we did."

The Court in its decisions against the New Deal had rejected the "general welfare" clause in the Constitution that Congress and the President had asserted to justify government's expanding powers. Would it uphold Congress's right to make laws affecting "interstate commerce"? On February 9, 1937, eleven lawyers addressed the Court. Seven, headed by John P. Davis, represented the employers, four spoke for the government: Fahy, Wyzanski, the solicitor general Stanley Reed, and Warren Madden, chairman of the NLRB.

"For weeks Abe Feller, Charles Horsky and I had written or talked six labor briefs to death (or perhaps to life)," Wyzanski wrote Frankfurter. "Any one of the three of us could without a note have told what was in those records, what the difficulties in the cases were, and how we thought they could have been resolved."[16] Justice Roberts had been "rather ominously silent," Wyzanski thought, and he regretted the sparseness of questions from the bench, but he predicted victory in at least two of the cases.

Though Keyserling considered Wyzanski no friend of the Act, Emerson who was in Court to hear the arguments, rated his performance there a *"tour de force."* And Paul Freund, the scholarly mainstay of the solicitor general's office, considered Wyzanski "the most brilliant of the advocates . . . He always spoke without notes, indeed without any books on the lectern, referring to cases from memory by volume and by page." John W. Davis, who also faced Wyzanski in the Social Security case, said of the young lawyer's presentation there, "In my palmiest days I could not have touched that argument."

More than a thousand people tried to squeeze into a sedate courtroom that held only two hundred and fifty on the April day on which the Court handed down its decision. Chief Justice Hughes read out the ruling that upheld the statute. Tom Emerson described the scene to Peter H. Irons of Princeton:[17]

It was an amazing performance. Hughes thundered out the decision with his beard wagging. You would have thought that he was deciding the most run-of-the-mill cases, that the law had always been this way, that there never had been any real dispute about it . . . as if the Constitution had always been construed this way.

Hughes adopted the views set forth in the government briefs. As he said: We are asked to shut our eyes to the plainest facts of our national life and to deal with questions of direct and indirect effects in an intellectual vacuum . . . When industries organize themselves on a national scale, making their relations to interstate commerce the dominant factor in their activities, how can it be maintained that their industrial labor relations constitute a forbidden field into which Congress may not enter when it is necessary to protect interstate commerce from the paralyzing consequences of industrial war?

After the decision Wyzanski wrote Frankfurter, "Right along I have said that the cases were won not by Mr. Wyzanski but either by Mr. Roosevelt or, if you prefer it, by Mr. Zeitgeist."[18] New Dealers were exultant. When the Wagner Act was enacted in 1935, lawyers on the staff of the old board numbered fourteen. That number swelled to a hundred as the new board swung into action. Even so stalwart a progressive as Tom Emerson, after the Court in 1936 had held the Guffey Coal Act unconstitutional, decided the National Labor Relations Act was doomed and accepted John Winant's offer to join the staff of the Social Security Board. He now rejoined the board.

"The Labor Board was the place to go if you were concerned with justice in the workplace,"[19] said Ida Klaus, a petite, dark-haired Portia who had come to Washington in 1933 at the invitation of her Columbia Law School professor Herman Oliphant. She, too, after the *Schechter* case had doubted whether it would survive in the Supreme Court. "But as soon as the Act was declared constitutional I said I wanted to go to the NLRB." Madden interviewed her and sent her to Fahy. She wanted to do litigation, she told him. "A lady trial lawyer?" Fahy said quizzically. "Yes," she replied firmly. "Well, it's possible. I do a great deal of injunction work." He sent her to Witt, then head of the Review Division. He took her on. Its job was to read the records and report the facts of the cases to the board. By the time Klaus filed her first report Witt had become assistant general counsel and Emerson, back with the board, headed the Review Division.

"There were at least ten women there," recalled Klaus. "I don't know of anyone who was turned down." But, she added dispassionately, "women got the little jobs and on promotions they didn't fare so well."

By 1939 there were two hundred lawyers with the board whose overall staff numbered eight hundred. It became the instrument that built into the very dynamics of a free market economy mechanisms that guaranteed the wider and fairer distribution of mass purchasing power that was a constant purpose of the New Dealers. During the twelve years of the Wagner Act's existence, the board conducted thirty-seven thousand elections and considered more than forty-five thousand cases of unfair labor practices. Union membership, which had been less than four million in 1935, grew to fifteen million in 1947.

Politically the trade union movement became a counterforce to industry. To Keyserling, the author of the bill, it would always seem passingly strange that none of the Brains Trusters "foresaw the extent to which the Wagner Act would weld the working people of America into a more effective fighting force on the political front for the programmatic objectives which animate the Democratic Party . . ."²⁰ "Much of the New Deal legislation was ameliorative," said Ida Klaus, "designed to lift us out of a great depression." The Wagner Act went beyond recovery from a depression. "It also effected profound changes in the balance of economic interests." It recognized conflicting interests as a fact of economic life and set up government as the stabilizer. It was enough of a change, Ida Klaus thought, to merit characterization as "a new economic order . . . a new system of government."

XXX

————————⟶⟨⟨—————————

Communists
and New Dealers

When the New Deal came to power the commingling of radicals, liberals, and progressives, of socialists, Communists, and labor activists in the face of the capitalist system's debacle was common practice. Louis Jaffe, an owlish, learned product of the Harvard Law School from which he had graduated third in a class of eight hundred, was sent in 1932 by Felix Frankfurter to clerk for Brandeis.

"We were all sorts of radicals," he said, recalling the heady days of 1933 when Nathan Witt was one of his closest friends. "The world was in a bad way and we thought the New Deal was going to make it better. We were very indoctrinated with liberal and socialist views. Great reforms were under way and labor was being recognized as a great force." Jaffe knew most of the "second-level" people in the New Deal including, he enumerated, "Hiss, Witt, Pressman and Abt." Progressive in outlook himself but no ideologue, "I was completely unaware that they were all Communists." In retrospect Jaffe mused in his old age, "I might have succumbed because I was so devoted to Nat Witt."[1]

Because of his friendship with Witt, Jaffe went first to the Triple A and then, after conservative farm interests managed to purge Jerome Frank's liberals and radicals, he followed Witt to the National Labor Relations Board. Younger than Jaffe, Witt was more committed politically to the

Left and, unknown to his friend, was on the way to becoming one of the chief underground Communists in Washington. A product of the Lower East Side, Witt had gotten to Harvard Law School on tuition money he had earned as a cab driver. There he had attracted the attention of Landis and Frankfurter. "To say that I have been extraordinarily impressed with him and his qualities during these months is not to overstate the case," the unsentimental Landis wrote to Frankfurter. "Witt is intensely independent and always critical," yet not one to say things "solely to please another person." At the same time "he is touchingly considerate of other people's aims as well as their feelings."

What was he planning to do? Frankfurter asked Witt as graduation approached. "Well, I'm going to be a labor lawyer and do civil liberties work," Witt replied. Instead of sending him to one of the many union officials Frankfurter knew, he sent him to a Wall Street law firm. "Before you get to be a labor civil liberties lawyer," he advised him, "you want to get to be a *good* lawyer, and on Wall Street you get the best possible training." A few weeks later Witt advised Frankfurter he had seen Bethuel Webster of Colonel Donovan's law firm who had given him a job. "What a beautifully solid and serene lad this is," Frankfurter scratched on the margin of Witt's letter before sending it on to Landis.[2]

Both Landis and Frankfurter were old hands at appraising the young men who went through their classes. The spell that Witt cast on them reflected the sweetness of his personality. That he should have at about this time joined the trek of bright young men and women to New Deal Washington and become a secret Communist testified to the severity of capitalist breakdown.

By self-definition Communists were a vanguard group, a "party within a party," their purpose the conquest of power on behalf of the working class, their boast that unlike the reformists, they meant business. The eminent intellectuals—Dreiser, Wilson, Dos Passos, Steffens, et al.—who supported the Communist ticket of Foster and Ford in the 1932 presidential campaign, did so, they said, because the Communist Party was "frankly revolutionary." Men like Witt, Pressman, and Abt became Communists even as they joined the New Deal because they thought traditional reformism was finished and that the Communists alone sought the "overthrow of a system which is responsible for all crises."

Although historians have discovered no "smoking gun" of a plan, masterly or otherwise, to establish a Communist espionage presence in New Deal Washington, some time in 1933–34 Harold Ware, son of the Communist leader Mother Bloor, and a dedicated Communist, took charge at the instance of the Comintern of setting up an underground Communist group in Washington. Ware was an agricultural specialist himself who had worked on collective farms in the Soviet Union as well as in Washington during the Coolidge and Hoover administrations and at the time published a farm letter with a leftist orientation. But his real authority lay in the liking people had for him. Witt, who was among his first recruits, named his child after him. Others in Ware's original nucleus were Pressman, John Abt, Henry Collins, John Kramer, and, according to Chambers, Alger Hiss.

In the pattern of amoebic fission the original group soon was split into a handful of cells of five or six, according to Hope Hale Davis who joined the Washington underground in the fall of 1934. They were bound together by Harold Ware, "our much beloved organizer" as Davis, who split with the party in 1939, described him.* In turn Ware reported to Jay Peters, one of the pseudonyms of a representative of the Communist International at Communist Party headquarters in New York City, the awesome "ninth floor," as it was referred to in Communist circles. Peters occasionally descended upon Washington, but the chief contact of the underground with Communist Party directives was through Ware. Did they feel there were too many Jews in the cells, Hope Davis was asked. "We didn't think of it that way. But one reason we were so delighted with Ware was that he was a true-blue American."³

Pressman later admitted to having been a member of the original Ware group but denied having seen Hiss in it. He called it a "Marxist study group." The cells met weekly or fortnightly. With the aid of party litera-ture that reached them through Ware they sought to apply a Marxist analysis to events, including developments in their own agencies. Dues were collected religiously and new members recruited. "The Party had two interests in Washington," Davis, who later was made a cell head leader against her will, dryly observed, "to get its people into key positions and to get documents useful to the Party." Even in the underground's earliest days there was purloining of government documents as part of a Commu-nist's "internationalist" duties. According to Chambers, however, espio-nage was not a primary aim of the underground at the outset.

The members of the underground were enjoined to the strictest rules of secrecy and discipline by Ware. The cells were kept from knowing of one another's existence and the members were directed to slough off earlier leftist associations and to stay away from outspoken liberals like Gardner

* She is writing a book on her experience as an underground Communist in the thirties.

Jackson and from mass organizations like the American League Against War and fascism. The rules of conspiracy were so strictly enforced that later when Herbert Fuchs, a Communist of several years standing, went to the National Labor Relations Board to be interviewed by Witt for a job there, he did not know Witt was a party member nor, he thought, did Witt know he was.[4] All had party names and to the hard-working members of the underground the conspiratorial element added a touch of danger that was not unglamorous. It also helped to foster a sense of brotherhood that served in their minds to confirm them in their roles as revolutionaries, not as abettors of espionage.

In 1935 Ware, who had an aficionado's weakness for fast driving, was killed in an automobile accident. Joseph Clark, then the Young Communist League organizer in Detroit, was invited to an "enlarged plenum" of the Communist Party's ruling body where Earl Browder, its leader, paid tribute to Ware. He cited his work in agriculture and his Russian experience and then added that some of the most important things that Ware did they would not be able to talk about for a long time. Several heads nodded knowingly, recalled Clark, and he assumed this was a reference to "international work" centered in Moscow.[5]

Since Communists were set off from others on the Left primarily because of their commitment to overthrow a system that was not susceptible of reform, their interest was in the struggle for power—the winning over of sympathizers, the placement and promotion of the loyal in an agency—and only secondarily in program. Nevertheless, many of the discussions in the underground, said Hope Davis, were precisely on the issue of Roosevelt's experimental, piecemeal reforms. It was a dogma of correct Marxist analysis that they could not work, and those who entertained the possibility were made to feel as if they were heretics. People were conflicted recalled Davis.[6]

In the purge of liberals and left-wingers at the Triple A, Gardner Jackson had been one of those asked to resign.[7] The evening of the purge he ran into his friend Lee Pressman, another dischargee, at the Sheraton Hotel. The always forceful Pressman startled Jackson because he was amused and cynical. What else was to be expected of a reformist government seemed to be his attitude. Two years earlier it had been Pressman who, along with Witt, had urged Jackson to join the AAA because of the chance they saw for great reforms. In the interim "reformism" had become a dirty word. After the purge Witt went to the National Labor Relations Board which was in the process of being reshaped. Pressman soon became John L. Lewis's general counsel. That Witt and Pressman were disciplined Communists was unknown to their closest non-Communist associates. In the purge at the Triple A, recalled Jackson, the word "Communist" was never used. It was the "radicals" who were being "booted out."

Even among New Dealers the distinction between Communists and radicals was not clear. At the time of the purge, Jackson went up to the Hill to talk with congressional friends only to learn that Tom Corcoran, in the process of selling the Public Utility Holding Company bill and its "death sentence" provision to congressmen who thought it was too advanced, urged the reluctant legislators to look into what the fellows at Triple A were doing—"that was the real radical nest down there, that they were trying really to overturn our whole economy." Corcoran dismissed Jackson's complaint as coming from a tippler. But Frank Watson, a housemate of Corcoran's who in fact had brought Watson to Washington from Harvard Law School, lent substance to Jackson's charge of Red-baiting. "Our group was not deeply involved in crusading," recalled Watson. "At the Agricultural Department they had a more radical view."[8]

Corcoran did feel that the "Tugwell crowd," in which he included Jerry Frank and his lawyers, "has been pushed by its enemies—and its own loose talk—away over to the left," as he alerted Frankfurter in a letter that Cohen also signed on his return from Oxford.

Tom and Ben knew from their own experience how necessary it was to guard the New Deal flanks against the right-wing charge that New Dealers were Reds. In April 1934 Representative Fred Britten (R-Ill.) had painted a lurid picture of "the little red house in Georgetown," in which they lived, that promoted "the communistic legislation we all talk about in the cloakrooms." And a month later he told the House, which was considering regulation of the stock exchange (SEC), "The real object of the bill is to Russianize everything worthwhile."[9]

The scare headlines given to Britten in 1934 and to a school superintendent's tale of a "brain trusters" plot for a social and economic revolution in which Roosevelt was slotted for the part of a Kerensky was a line of attack to which the Right increasingly rallied. Ironically it made it more difficult to bring to light the Ware group and other Communist cells that were beginning to take root in the government. And if the attack on the New Deal as communistic did not serve adequately to obscure the distinction between the two, an event in the Communist world during the summer of 1935 compounded the confusion.

The Seventh Congress of the Communist International took place in Moscow from July 25 to August 20, 1935. It reversed the self-destructive "Third Period" policies of the 1928 Sixth Congress which, on Stalin's assumption of an imminent capitalist collapse, had committed Communist parties everywhere to the establishment of a dictatorship of the proletariat, set up dual trade unions, proclaimed uncompromising hostility to socialist and social democratic parties as "social fascist." A major result of this enormous Stalinist miscalculation, even Communists realized, had been the victory of a Soviet-hating Adolf Hitler and the endangerment of the Soviet state. Moscow needed allies and to secure them convened the Seventh Congress and called for the establishment of "popular fronts." As John Gates wrote later in *The Story of an American Communist,* the Congress approved the new policy of subordinating the ultimate goals of the Communist movement to the drive against fascism . . . Communists could now support their own capitalist-democratic governments, even participate in them . . ."

The work of Communist penetration and colonization became easier although it took some time for the new directives to percolate downward. As a phase of its dual union policy the Communists in the first half of 1935 had opposed the Wagner Act. "The Wagner board to be established by this bill," their spokesman had declared at the hearings, "will be a weapon to destroy the power which the workers have gained through their economic organizations by outlawing strikes, establishing compulsory arbitration, and increasing company unions." In the struggle to pass the Wagner bill, said William Green of the AFL, "I found the forces of communism fighting shoulder to shoulder with spokesmen of American industry in an attempt to defeat it." And at the American Newspaper Guild convention a month before the Seventh Congress the delegates were urged by the Communists to fight the Wagner Bill and seek instead a constitutional amendment safeguarding labor's rights.[10]

The Seventh Congress and the period of the Popular Front (1935–39) proved to be the heyday of Communist influence in the federal government. Moscow's reversal of policy enabled Communists in the National Labor Relations Board to persuade themselves with a measure of justice that their purpose was to strengthen, not undermine, the intent of Congress in passing the Labor Disputes Act, as it was called at the time.

Herbert Fuchs, a New York lawyer who had joined the Communist Party there in 1934 because it seemed to him it "was serious" about the fight against fascism and for social justice, decided in 1936 to seek a job in Washington.[11] He found work at first with a Senate subcommittee investigating railroads, headed by Senator Wheeler, and in 1937 when the subcommittee reduced its staff he transferred to the National Labor Relations Board. His Communist contacts in Washington directed him to set up a cell there. In the period that he was the group's leader (1937–42) the group grew from an initial four to seventeen. This was in an agency that by 1939 numbered two hundred lawyers and had an overall staff of eight hundred.

Fuchs broke with the Communist Party in the 1940s and testified before the House Un-American Activities Committee (HUAC) in 1955. He was considered a "believable" witness. Fuchs's contact with higher Communist authority was Victor Perlo, a bright young economist, himself the leader of one of the cells set up by Ware. "I can see Victor Perlo now," said Hope Davis, describing the group's discussion of world events, "drawing a map of China on a child's blackboard with a different color of chalk for each province as he traced the route of the Long March being led by Chu Teh, Chou En-lai and Mao Tse-tung."[12]

Perlo was known to the Fuchs group as "Mike" and "Chief." He instructed the cell's members to be "extremely inconspicuous" in regard to their political beliefs and to stay away from the mass organizations. The undergrounders did not like that. They wanted to be active. They had become Communists out of a belief that the Party fought harder than any other group for a better world and now, as Communists, they were asked to be less active than ever. They complained to Fuchs, who felt similarly and transmitted their protests to Perlo. Perlo met with the unit and sought to override its complaints. According to Fuchs he did not succeed. Some became members of the Lawyers Guild, some joined the "Washington Committee for Democratic Action."

In addition to the collection of dues, the surveys of world events, much of the unit's discussion centered on developments in the board. "We told ourselves," Fuchs testified before HUAC, "and we were told that to be good Communists at the NLRB the better job we did for the Board and for the Government was it. That was the best thing." "Was it ever indicated," asked HUAC's Chairman Walter (D-Pa.), "that the best thing for Communism was to decide cases in such a way as to cause dissatisfaction and a class consciousness?" "I don't think that we thought that way, Mr. Walter," replied Fuchs. "I think that we thought we were doing a patriotic duty by participating in the enforcement of the Wagner Act, and we were zealous in the belief that it was a good thing."

Non-Communists and anti-Communists on the board, like Ida Klaus and David Saposs, the socialist who was director of Research, would not fault such sentiments. But until the Nazi-Soviet Pact in August 1939, when the paths of liberals and Communists again diverged, there were few who realized that behind the façade of identity of aims the Communists, even when their presence was suspected, drove for control. It took the most sophisticated among the non-Communists some time to catch on. Louis Jaffe would come to Abe Feller, one of the lawyers who had defended the Wagner Act in the Supreme Court, and Ida Klaus with his suspicions.[13] "We collected shreds of evidence," recalled Klaus, "of how these people were behaving and began to put the pieces together." Feller, a close friend of Witt's, along with his wife, Alice, dropped in at one of Witt's Friday nights. "My God!" he later told Klaus, "the whole crowd was there singing Soviet songs—Pressman, Silvermaster [Nathan Gregory Silvermaster, a Russian-born economist with the Farm Security Administration, and the leader, according to Elizabeth Bentley's testimony in 1948, of an espionage group that reported to her]. "We fled," Feller ended his account.

The total number of Communists at the Labor Board numbered fewer than twenty-five, but some were strategically positioned. Not only Witt but one of the board's three members, a New Englander, Edwin S. Smith, cooperated with them. He later became a registered agent of the Soviet Union. Smith and Witt, said Saposs, ran the board. "Oh, yes; no doubt about it. They enjoyed it."[14]

Until the Nazi-Soviet Pact, New Dealers had some sympathy for those they suspected of being Communists, partly because of the way the Right linked Communists and liberals, partly because the Communists seemed to point Zionward, and partly as a matter of civil liberties. The Communist approval of the pact angered them. In one Popular Front organization after another liberals split away. Whatever sympathy there was for the American League for Peace and Democracy, for example, faded abruptly when its board refused to condemn the pact by the lopsided vote of 14 to 1. The National Lawyers Guild, a star-studded organization, even before the pact was hit by resignations when lawyers incensed by Communist manipulation rebelled. The pact accelerated the exodus. Showdowns took place in the Youth Movement where Eleanor Roosevelt abandoned a longtime sponsorship of its leaders and activities. In the North American Committee to Aid Spanish Democracy, Leon Henderson quit its chairmanship. And over at Assistant Secretary of State Berle's house, he received the first evidence of a Communist underground in Washington that was also an espionage network. Isaac Don Levine, editor of an anti-Communist monthly, *Plain Talk,* brought a "Mr. X," Whitaker Chambers to talk with the assistant secretary:

I slowly manipulated Mr. X to a point where he had told me of some of the ramifications hereabout; and it became necessary to take a few simple measures. I expect more of this kind of thing later.[15]

Berle treated the information Chambers gave him gingerly. Although he had made four pages of notes, titled "Underground Espionage Agent," on his long session with Chambers, he did not file them with the security officers of the State Department or the military intelligence agencies, even though he served with the latter's representatives on an interdepartmental coordinating committee. He turned them over to the FBI only in 1943 after the Bureau had learned of their existence from Chambers in 1942.

Chambers had wanted to talk to the President or have Berle inform the President, but Roosevelt, the European war having just erupted, understandably was busy and Berle in a 1942 entry in his diary states, a little defensively, that he did apprise Marvin McIntyre, the President's appointments secretary. He never knew "what McIntyre reported to the President."

But he did take protective measures against Communist espionage, organizing a counterespionage network and spurring "a high state of activity in the FBI":

It is sufficiently plain that in the Communist reaches at least we are dealing with a large, thoroughly capable and thoroughly well-organized espionage system, reinforced by the ability to create certain centers of disorder through the hold on labor and other organizations. In addition there is a certain amount of political support arrived at through manipulating the soft-headed liberals.

But until after the war the perception of Communists as spies was held by very few.* Not even Berle—nor Chambers nor Bentley—knew the full extent of Communist espionage penetration of the American government. Michael Straight, as he later revealed to the intelligence agencies of the United States and British governments, had been directed in 1937 when he was a twenty-one-year-old student at Cambridge, a Communist, and an Apostle, to shed his Communist ties and return to America as the handsome, gifted, wealthy scion of a great American family that he was. The message came to him via Anthony Blunt, art historian and underground Communist and like Straight a member of the secret, elite society, the Apostles, that also numbered among its members G. E. Moore, E. M.

---

* It is not within the scope of this book to review the story of the Washington underground and the espionage networks that the country learned about in 1948. Professor Herbert L. Packard of the Stanford Law School states that his study *Ex-Communist Witnesses* (1962) covered a public record of "more than 200,000 pages of testimony contained in the transcripts of over one hundred different court trials, administrative hearings, and Congressional investigations, all relating in one way or another to the issue of Communist penetration in the United States. . . ." A second study, also initiated by the Fund for the Republic, *The Communist Controversy in Washington* by Earl Latham, was published by the Harvard University Press in 1966. An indispensable account by Allen Weinstein is *Perjury: The Hiss Chambers Case,* New York, 1978.

Forster, and J. M. Keynes. Blunt would say only that the message came from "our friends in the . . . Communist International." But in Washington where Straight settled he was soon contacted by a Michael Green, a Soviet agent, who learning that the young man had landed a job as an unpaid volunteer in the Economic Adviser's Office at the State Department suggested that if interesting documents crossed his desk he should take them home "to study."[16]

Straight did not want to be a Soviet agent in the State Department and was elated when Tom Corcoran in 1938 approached him to work for him. The pickings for Green were slim but Straight was happy with his desk in Ben Cohen's offices of the National Power Policy Committee. There he became a speech writer, sometimes working through the night with Corcoran and Cohen on the draft of a speech ultimately intended for Roosevelt. Some of his best times were the *tours d'horizons* conducted by a witty, marvelously intuitive, theorizing Corcoran, and Straight found himself drawn to the New Dealers. What Corcoran and Cohen did not know and Straight increasingly sought to keep at a distance even from his own thoughts was the latter's relationship to the Soviet agent Michael Green, a connection that continued until Green was recalled to Moscow in 1942. How was Corcoran to know when Straight's identity as a Soviet source was buried deep in Straight's interventionist and pro-New Deal attitudes that were a matter of choice as well as protective coverage during the period of the Nazi-Soviet Pact?

Nevertheless, the New Dealers did learn a great deal about some of their colleagues in the twenty-two months between the Nazi-Soviet Pact and the Nazi invasion of the Soviet Union. Tugwell speaks of the "singularly stupid behavior of American communists during the spring of 1941 . . . Strikes in important aircraft factories were inspired and the White House was picketed." Walter Salant, a Keynesian and a member of the mini-Brain Trust that Hopkins assembled under Richard Gilbert, worked cheek by jowl for two years with Vincent Perlo, a key figure in the underground. "He was quite brilliant," recalled Salant. "At 19 he had already published an article in a mathematical journal." A great problem in 1941 was how to cope with Communist-inspired activity in the country's munitions plants. "No one doubts that there are active communist influences at work in some factories of which the North American Company is one of the most important because it has large orders for aircraft," Ickes recorded. The trouble on the West Coast was so serious, said Salant, that Gilbert went out to take a look at the dispute with a view to a settlement. He came back persuaded that wage controls were as necessary as price controls, a conclusion that the others in the Gilbert group agreed with—except Perlo. "Perlo resisted that," said Salant, "and Gilbert kicked him out."[17]

A few weeks later Hitler invaded the Soviet Union and the Communist line was reversed again. "I have asked the Federal Bureau of Investigation to continue their surveillance over Communist activities here," wrote Berle:

A party line which could change from one of hostility to one of collaboration overnight could change back with equal speed. Anyhow, freedom from subversive activities (in plain English, from plotting, sabotage, political strikes and in some cases, murder) ought not to rest on the grace of a foreign government. It ought to rest on our own strength.[18]

XXXI

$\rightarrow$〔 〕$\leftarrow$

Ministers Without Portfolio

In early 1940 Tom married his darling secretary Peggy Dowd. Since 1932, when he had drawn her from a secretarial pool, "Peggykins Mavourneen" had been the only one able to keep up with Tom, and also Ben, even to three in the morning. When Tom was away from Washington his first thought was for Peggy and the letters of love mixed with didacticisms flowed back—"I approve of your flirtations . . . Hold Ben's hand—it's a nice hand . . . Emotions!" From Joe Kennedy's in Palm Beach where he had gone to recuperate, "Simply g-r-r-and—private ocean, private swimming pool, private tennis court—even a private moon." She was indispensable to Tom and he knew that she loved him; still, he liked being the gay bachelor about town and did not particularly want to get married. But in a time-honored strategem Peggy began to go out with others and Tom concluded there was nothing to be done but get married.[1]

Peggy's version was a little different. "I bore no ill will towards your mother," she told him, "but it's a long time since I knew that I was in love with you that your mother died, but I understand the Irish—you're the oldest son and the oldest son, I don't know when it began, the oldest son feels he can never marry until his mother dies so his mother will never believe that any other woman came before her."

Sophie Nack, a colleague of Peggy's, less Tom's secretary than Ben's, sent her the office news in St. Jovite, Canada, where the two were skiing. ". . . It's a fine tribute to you that you and TGC are still honeymooning. As Ben said—'What do people think—that Tom is an institution instead of a man?' "[2]

According to Tom, his two chief mentors, FF and FDR, although devoted to Peggy, felt that he should have married a woman of wealth able to fund the political career to which they thought he was naturally adapted. Marion Frankfurter had a special place in her affections for Tom. It was an accepted practice in Britain, she told him, for bright young lawyers to marry into the English gentry. According to Tom, even FDR said he could do better. Through Missy Tom asked Roosevelt to receive him and his bride. Peggy bought herself a new hat and dress for the occasion. The two waited in the family quarters for FDR to free himself of his schedule, only to learn from Hopkins, who came by, that he was not able to see them.[3]

Peggy was crushed and Tom was furious. It was the beginning of his break with Roosevelt, he later wrote. Tom gave many explanations for that break, as will appear in this chapter, but the slight to Tom and his wife that Tom alleged not only seems out of character for a man who Tom himself dubbed a "patrician Episcopalian" but was indignantly challenged by one of Tom's closest associates, Jim Rowe. Rowe, a tall Montanan, was like Tom a protégé of Frankfurter, a clerk of Holmes, later one of Tom's law partners, and one of Roosevelt's six anonymous assistants, appointed as such at Tom's urging. "The problem between Tom and the President," said Rowe when told of the snub story, "was that Tom would stand in front of the President and insist on a course of action and pound on the desk. Now, you know, no one ever pounded the desk with Roosevelt."[4]*

Whatever the truth to Tom's story, as Roosevelt prepared for his third inauguration both Tom and Ben were disaffected and talked seriously about leaving the government to set up in private law practice in New York. From the moment of marriage, moreover, Tom's thoughts reverted to making some money. [And] the birth of his first child, Margaret, at the beginning of Roosevelt's third term reinforced that desire. "I certainly don't know what I'm to do," he wrote his father, "I'm certainly not going back into the Government until I've bought the baby shoes."[5]

Congratulations flowed in from everywhere, the President and Mrs.

* His trouble with Corcoran, Lyndon Johnson said Roosevelt had told him, and this was reported to Corcoran by Rowe, was that "I [Corcoran] got credit for everything and that I wasn't above getting credit for everything he did, and for that reason he and I had differed." [Corcoran in an interview with The Lyndon Johnson Library.]

Roosevelt, Ickes and Morgenthau, the Peppers, Lyndon Johnson, the Rauhs, "Hacky" the White House telephone operator. JOY IN THE CORCO-RAN CAMP, wired his father.

A self-conscious but poignant note came from Felix:

The tragic note is at the core of human destiny, for man's lot is finitude. And so, in a strange way, at the very moment that I heard of your mystic achievement of fatherhood, I think of your childhood and thoughts of your mother seize me.

Your daughter is destined to bring you pain and gladness as you gave both to your mother. But the fulfilling experience & the irreplaceable joy that will come to you, in increasing measure, is that the very vainglory of sorrow & gladness will strike the deepest roots in you.

May the child have brought her own blessings—for her Mother, her wild and tender Dad and herself.[6]

A perceptive message came to Peggy from Jim Rowe. He knew the pressures and temptations on Tom to leave the government. "Personally I think Washington is a much better place to raise your daughter than New York," Rowe advised her. "Don't you? If so, start lobbying."[7] Jim knew from Ben as well as Tom how serious was Tom's discontent. He asked Ben to draft an appeal Roosevelt might send to Tom to stay in Washington. "From an experienced *pater familias,* welcome to the high ranks of Fatherhood!" Roosevelt wrote him,

. . . I know you are troubled about your family responsibilities. But this is the most critical year in our country's history and you simply cannot leave me now. You must know that I understand fully how much your front-line fighting has put you "on the spot", and that you can no longer contribute effectively without portfolio. As our plans unfold, National Defense will have positions of rank and responsibilities where your great talents and powers will be desperately needed.[8]

As Tom could understand, it would take some time to find the right spot but he was to stand by and await assignment. The letter ended on a note that Roosevelt knew had worked with Tom in 1933:

You have been fond of quoting Holmes as your great exemplar. Fundamentally, he was a great soldier in life, not merely on the battlefield. Ask yourself how he would have answered this call.

Tom marked time and began to make money in Washington. Once he had scorned Dean Acheson's offer to join him in private law practice just because it meant appearing before agencies he had helped to create and staff. Now he did precisely that. Momentous events were taking place. His role, despite a preference to remain in government, was that of bystander and moneymaker. His fellow New Dealers, men and women whom he had groomed, flooded into the defense agencies. They were the "all-outers." Tom's friend Leon Henderson was typical. He was one of the six starting commissioners of the National Defense Advisory Commission, an "effective and forceful leader," who built up an effective staff within the agency, said Bob Nathan, another "all-outer."[9]

Almost unnoticed, that New Deal brainchild, the TNEC, slipped out of existence. A Henderson-Lubin personal statement sought to supplement its innocuous final report.[10] It chided the committee for failure to take into account "the economic world of tomorrow which will be a very different kind of world than that which we have known in the past." The great lesson of the Depression, they maintained, had been that "private enterprise does not adjust itself quickly to violent economic dislocations, that in any major crisis of peace-time or war-time, Government leadership and Government participation are required to help get the job done and to avoid great social and economic hardship." But few any longer listened.

All during the winter of 1940–41 Tom commuted between a small apartment that he and Peggy shared with Ben in Washington, and New York, where he lived in the small apartment Ben maintained there. He had begun a lucrative private practice in which he sold his great influence with government officials, earning in the first few months, as he testified before a Senate investigating committee at the end of the year, a hundred thousand dollars. It was not illegal; still, it was less than disinterested and not what he wanted to do. He still wanted to work for the government. Above all, he still wanted the appointment Roosevelt had promised him as recently as January to the solicitor generalship. Roosevelt had first promised that position to him when he had asked him to stay on after the 1936 elections.

Peggy, moreover, pressed him to remain in Washington. So he mapped out one of the campaigns for which he was famous. In addition to presidential nomination, the appointment required Senate confirmation, as well as unofficial acquiescence by the Court before which he would be the government's chief advocate and where he was disliked by the Chief Justice. Neither set of hostilities seemed to him insurmountable. Like politicians from times immemorial he proceeded to call in his chits. Roosevelt received letters urging Tom's appointment from Mayor Kelly, House Leader McCormack, Speaker Rayburn, Senators Byrnes and Maybank and, most important, from members of the Supreme Court in whose appointment he had had a hand: Black, Reed, Douglas, and Byrnes.

No letter, however, came from Felix Frankfurter. Bad feeling had erupted between the two over the appointment of a federal administrator of the federal courts. Tom had a candidate, Stewart Guthrie who once had lived with him and Ben in the "Little Red House" on R Street. Chief Justice Hughes also had a candidate. The Court divided and the stalemate was ended only when Frankfurter worked out a compromise with the Chief Justice. Angry words were exchanged between the justice and his former student. Tom lost his temper, persuaded that Frankfurter's motive was politics within the Court, an effort to ingratiate himself with Hughes.

The outbreak of the war in Europe intensified the breach. "For several reasons," wrote Tom afterward, "I misread the importance of events in Europe during the war."[11] The country was intensely isolationist. Tom was, too, so far as Europe was concerned. The reorganization of the Continent, even by a tyrant, he felt was not the worst thing in the world. Hitler was too cunning, he thought, to declare war on the United States. But a main reason was the Irishman's immemorial hatred of the British. Frankfurter, whom Ickes described as "really not rational these days on the European situation," and who was in love with all things British, wanted Tom to use his influence with his Irish friends to end Ireland's neutrality as between Britain and Germany, in particular to open up her ports to British shipping. Hitler's air fleets were seeking to break British resistance by raids of devastation. During the grim period Marion Frankfurter took in two English children, and once when Tom turned up at her and Felix's apartment with his accordion forbade him to sing Irish songs, so strongly did she feel.

Tom did talk with his Irish friends in New York but they, mindful of the British record of repression and betrayal in Ireland, rebuffed him. So he reported to Frankfurter. The latter, aware of Tom's phenomenal abilities as a mediator, accused him of halfheartedness and, flushed with rage, reproached the friend whom he regarded as a son for behaving like Synge's *Playboy of the Western World* and murdering his father. Tom stormed out of the justice's chambers.

According to Tom, it was against this background of growing estrangement that he confronted Frankfurter with the request that he endorse him for the solicitor generalship and the justice refused.

Other reasons are suggested in a memorandum that Jim Rowe prepared for Roosevelt on the matter:

If Tom Corcoran would be a real Solicitor General, he would be the best this Administration has ever had. He would make Stanley Reed look silly. He would be considerably better than Bob Jackson, which is indeed high praise.

But the question is would he be Solicitor General or would he continue to do the things he has always done. He can't do both. Next to the Supreme Court, the position of Solicitor General is the highest legal position in the country and should have corresponding dignity and aloofness from any other pursuit.

Some time ago Felix Frankfurter asked me to come down and talk with him, and asked me frankly whether I thought you would appoint Tom as Solicitor General. I told him I had no idea but I was, frankly, doubtful.

F.F. cited me a similar case in which Lincoln wanted to appoint someone to the Supreme Court but hesitated for months because the man in question had Presidential ambitions and was not the kind to give them up. He finally exacted a promise of "no politics" and made the appointment. Two weeks later the distinguished Justice was again running for President at top speed. (Since I have forgotten his name, he evidently didn't do so well.)

So such promises are doubtful. But if you could get such an unmistakable and clear promise, there could be no greater Solicitor General. Most people have forgotten it, but Tom is a brilliant legal scholar and, what is more important in a Solicitor General, has a felicity and clarity of expression both in formal and informal talk surpassing any other lawyer I have ever heard in court.

But in Tom's present frame of mind, I don't know whether such a promise, even if made, would stick.

There is also the more obvious disadvantage—confirmation. It is a well-known fact that Tom is campaigning for the job. It is rumored that certain Senators have said there would be a bitter fight over confirmation, including an exhaustive investigation into his private law practice during the past few months. This also disturbs F.F., who does not think it would do the Court too much good to have such a public quarrel. It would certainly do you no good.[12]

Roosevelt, aware of the confirmation difficulties, at one point that spring suggested an alternative to the solicitor generalship: "Tommy, I'll give you my old job, Under-Secretary of the Navy." He called Secretary Knox who then summoned Tom. They lunched at the Carlton. "Tom," Knox entreated, "please don't take it." It would be seen as an earnest that Roosevelt did not trust Knox and that Tom had been appointed in a monitorial role. Tom did not press the matter.[13]

The issue of the solicitor generalship dragged on. Ben loyally sided with Tom. This distressed Felix who even showed Ben an unsent letter to Tom. "In view of some of the things I said last night I want you to see this letter which wrote itself after long brooding but which on further reflection I decided not to send."

Since you have not asked me, as you have other members of the Court, to urge your nomination as Solicitor General, you must have assumed that I would have had to decline to do so, painful as it would be to deny a request of yours. Your assumption is quite correct, but I am not sure that you are clear in your own mind about the reason that would have moved such a declination. I want to leave no doubt on the subject.

It has nothing to do with your silly behavior toward me since the Guthrie business. You cannot change my feeling toward you. As you must know, that feeling is more than a blend of one's feeling for a younger brother and an older son than any of my students ever aroused in me. You cannot change that feeling. The door of my devotion to you is always open. But you must be singularly unknowing of me to have ever assumed that my private affections are the measure of my public responsibility.

Nor do I think that you are wanting in the qualifications that a Solicitor General ought to possess. That you have great gifts of advocacy no one knows better than I. But the occasional argument of cases before the Court is by no means the most important part of a Solicitor General's work. Tasks that took the full working hours of Lloyd Bowen and Fred Lehmann—and I have known no lawyer, I do not exclude Brandeis, more able than those two—cannot be performed on less than full time by anyone else. If you tell me that you would make the technical functions of the Solicitor Generalship your exclusive job, I am bound to tell you that no man can promise away his temperament. You could no more promise away yours, fortified as it has been by nearly ten years of experience, than Salmon Chase could when he promised Lincoln that he would quit seeking the Presidency once he became Chief Justice.

These may be stodgy views but at any event they are not novel. It is largely because of my conception of the job of Solicitor General that I denied myself its attractions when the President asked me to become Solicitor General. The talk I had with him at that time—on March 8, 1933—is one of the very few of which I made a minute. I would like to quote from it because it tells you better than I can now why I feel as I do and why I have deemed it so unwise and unkind for some of your friends to be urging you for this job.

[FF quoted his exchange with FDR that ends: "The fact of the matter is that I could not have anything to do with the matters on which you want my help and do my job as Solicitor General. It just couldn't be done."]

For obvious reasons there are two people whom I should like to know at first hand not at second hand my attitude on this matter, and so I am sending Ben and Francis Biddle to his house, a copy of this letter.[14]

"The nation was not yet at war," Tom later recounted, "but war had been declared between Felix and me, a terrible conflict fought with a singular weapon: silence."[15] They never talked again.

The break between Felix and Tom confirmed Ben's feeling about Frankfurter. As he explained to Tom, he was "a trimmer." Frankfurter, Ben said in an interview in 1974 that he put off the record, "supported another candidate for the Solicitor Generalship when Tom bid for it. Charles Fahy got the job. He was a very fine Solicitor General. Felix supported his candidacy and that was wrong in light of his relationship to Tom. He was not required to support Tom, but he didn't have to say anything. I could understand Felix's not wanting to pressure the President, but to try to block Tom's appointment was another matter."[16]

Tom's fall from favor ushered in a difficult time for him. "Many of those whom he had befriended," recalled Ben, "refused to help because he was no longer a wielder of power."

Tom's bad times were also Ben's. Not only because his bosom friend was having difficulties but so was he. He was a lonely man, "never happy," except perhaps in work, said Jane Harris who of all his intimates knew him best. When Tom and Peggy set up housekeeping together on Garfield Street they found a place for Ben. He would become "Uncle Ben" to the children in the Corcoran family. When the first of those children, Margaret, was born in 1941 Ben realized he had to establish his own household as well as decide what he was going to do. Winant enlisted the help of Ray Moley in New York to persuade Ben to accompany him to London where he was going as ambassador. "I am glad that Winant wants Ben because all of Ben's real interest now is in England," noted Ickes, and then in a paragraph the acerbic secretary delineated the "parfit gentil knight" of the New Deal:

I will miss Ben. He is really a wonderful character. He has an unusually fine mind, and he has all the genuine kindliness that one finds oftener in Jews than in other people. I do not know of anyone in Washington who does not admire him. With his gentleness he has made a deeper and more abiding personal impression than many others who have been much more aggressive and active.[17]

When the ship on which Winant and Ben traveled docked in Plymouth, the King, as an earnest of the importance Great Britain attached to the tie with the United States, was there to greet the two envoys. Pageantry and spectacle interested Ben less than work. Although Ed Murrow cabled Frankfurter, YOUR FRIENDS WINANT AND COHEN ARE DOING EVEN BETTER THAN YOU SUSPECTED, Ben found little to do in London and by the beginning of summer was back in the United States. I DON'T FEEL THAT I MANAGED SOMEHOW TO BE OF SUFFICIENT HELP TO YOU TO WARRANT MY RETURN, he cabled the ambassador in explanation. "Terribly sorry nobody could have helped more than you did," replied Winant. The ambassador begged him to return. "He has taken your place . . . You are always wanted here."

The search for a place to live and for a job to do accentuated a midlife crisis for Ben. He was in his forties. He had long craved the companionship of marriage. Bachelorhood was his destiny, not his preference. Since his London days and his rejection by Ella Winter, those whom he wanted to marry would not have him while those who sought him, like Margery Abraham of the Zionist offices, he eluded. "She would have been too powerful for him," Jane commented.[18]

One of Ben's closest friends from Versailles days was Julius Simon, a German Zionist leader. "Here is Julius," he would announce on the phone. Ben loved him and he also seems to have loved his brother John's wife. At least so John Simon alleged when John's wife left him in the twenties and Ben was named as co-respondent in the ensuing suit.

In the mid-thirties he had briefly wooed Celeste Jedel. A slim woman, she was a Barnard graduate who had studied under Moley at Barnard, became his assistant in the early New Deal years, and continued to be his girl Friday in New York when Moley became editor of *Today*. Frankfurter, Corcoran, and Cohen had discovered that she was the best channel to Moley. "Dearest Lady-With-the-Bright-Black-Eyes," Corcoran addressed her. She was intellectual as well as attractive, a combination Ben found irresistible. According to her family, he set his cap for her but she had refused him. "How could you turn down a great man like Ben Cohen," her father exclaimed in bewilderment.

That was Ben's experience with women. His longest and deepest friendship was with Jane Harris. That was an affinity that some of his closest friends felt was more than platonic. Jane was an accomplished violinist, confident hostess, and the comely wife of one of Ben's closest friends, Louis Harris. Often during the thirties she came to Washington to be with Ben, waiting around patiently as he toiled at his drafting labors, often going to a late movie with him where he dozed off, sometimes the only sleep he had. He unburdened his soul to her and many years later, after Louis died, he proposed to her. When I in an interview asked why she, too, had rebuffed him, she burst out, "How could you marry Ben? He's brilliant but . . . ," and her voice trailed off. Pressed again, she replied reluctantly, "I could not imagine him as a lover." What had Jane meant, the author of this book asked a friend who knew and entertained them both. Jean Pennypacker in the late thirties was married to Robert Kintner and Ben was often at their house. "I don't think Ben was the kind of man that roused women's sexual curiosity," explained Jean. "Ben always said to me that if he had to do it all over again he would wish not to have graduated from Chicago at some terribly early age because he had never had the time to develop the social graces . . . He always pursued what appealed to him intellectually. I think he always felt a little hesitant with women. Not intellectually . . . I can't imagine that he ever went to a college dance or a football game. I imagine he was just in class or studying all the time." A moment later Jean added, "I think Ben really wanted to be closer to people but just didn't know how. He never took the time to learn, but certainly I know any number of women that found Ben enchanting on an intellectual level. He treated women as equals, never talked down to them. He sent them books. He sent me that slim volume by the six Harvard and Tufts professors to make more of a New Dealer out of me."[19]

There was an occasional rumor of homosexuality. Some time in the thirties Ben shared an apartment with Henry Herman, a bearlike man of kindliness and charm, a good legal craftsman but not brilliant. Ben mothered Henry who was under psychiatric treatment for homosexual tendencies. He committed suicide in 1938. He wanted, his suicide note said, to convince Ben in particular that "in working for and with him I found much happiness and not a little excitement. He gave me for a time confidence in myself . . ." Ben had been abroad when Henry killed himself and Joe Rauh met him on the train, riding from Baltimore to Washington, to tell him what had happened. Henry's brother wrote Joe, "I hope Ben didn't & isn't taking all this too seriously. I'm sure he must realize that he is directly responsible for the most pleasant and productive period in Henry's life." What do they want me to do? Ben asked when told that Tom worried about rumors of homosexuality, go down to the red-light district and get myself married?[20]

Among Ben's other discontents was a sense that the Administration did not appreciate him. While he was in England a new move began to push him for the SEC. Its chairman, Jerome Frank, finally had been named to the Circuit Court of Appeals. It could be a "great commission," Rowe advised Roosevelt. "I understand that you intend to nominate Ben Cohen. This is the one single thing that can do more for the SEC than anything else. He has the wholehearted respect of the staff more than any other previous or present Commissioner."[21]

This was high praise, considering that James Landis and William O. Douglas had once been chairmen of SEC, but the appointment was never made. Whether Ben declined because he felt he could not have a shaping influence in it on the war effort or Roosevelt felt he could not afford to fuel Hitler's anti-Semitism by the appointment of a "Ben Cohen" to a prominent place in his administration or he feared any move that might revive Supreme Court/purge animosities on the Hill or for some other reason is not clear.

When some Zionists spread the rumor that Ben was not returning to London because of differences with Winant over Palestine, Ben wrote sternly to Rabbi Stephen Wise and Robert Szold: the story was to be stopped because it was untrue. If the rumors continued "I may in my wrath forget the Sixth Commandment."[22]

But as the United States moved closer to war, Ben remained a minister without portfolio. He had returned from London, Ickes noted, "anxious that we get more materials of war to England before it is too late."[23] The absorption of many New Dealers, especially some of his and Tom's younger protégés, was precisely that: to get war supplies produced and on their way to where they were needed.

That was the concern also of Keynes who returned to this country in mid-1941 after the passage of the Lend Lease bill. "I had him to my house to meet some of the younger people," said Currie. The meeting was not successful.

He felt that we should be tightening up a bit. We couldn't have guns and butter. Many of the New Dealers still felt that we could have both.[24]

Walter Salant was one of the men whom Currie had assembled at his house to meet Keynes. He was on the staff of Richard Gilbert, the leader of the "brilliant group," as Currie described it to Roosevelt, that had moved over almost en masse from Hopkins's office at Commerce to a similar brain-trusting role with Leon Henderson at the Office of Price Administration and Civilian Supply. Here the group championed the New Dealers' thesis that the attainment and maintenance of full employment would permit both guns and butter. Gilbert had taught Salant at Harvard. Both had contributed to an *Economic Program for American Democracy,* for a time Holy Writ among New Dealers. In Salant's view Gilbert was "the outstanding unsung hero of American wartime economic policy."[25]

Keynes had told his American disciples they were too optimistic in their assertion that, the "bottleneck areas" excepted, the American economy in June 1941 still was operating far below capacity and that heavy taxation and other belt tightening would be premature. At first Keynes had thought the Americans simply did not understand his "multiplier" concept that held, as Salant put it, "a dollar of increase in expenditures would result in more than a dollar increase in demand" and therefore bring on inflation sooner than they anticipated. Soon, however, Currie, Gilbert, Salant, Humphrey, and the others had persuaded him that indeed they were familiar with his *General Theory* and were not arguing out of naïveté.

Their thinking so impressed him that a few nights later he met them again, the group now widened to include Leon Henderson, Sumner Pike, Isador Lubin, Ken Galbraith, David Ginsburg, Calvin Hoover, and J. M. Clark. Keynes, aware now he was not dealing with simpleminded people, developed at greater length his contention that special anti-inflationary measures should be taken long before the point of full use of the economy's resources was reached.

Salant was after him again the next day. This time with a long letter and tables meant to answer his fears that they, as Keynes put it, "overestimate supply and underestimate demand, and consequently underestimate the danger of inflation." Keynes still was not persuaded, so Salant tried again. The British economist softened. "I like your way of estimating the effect of the various disturbing factors," he wrote Salant. He conceded the technical competence of his young American friends and said their clashing assumptions about the "propensity to consume" would have to be left to experience to test. "Greetings to yourself, Gilbert and Humphrey," he wrote Salant on leaving Washington. "Do not think because I have been in a critical mood that I do not appreciate the value and significance of the work you are all doing . . . I have been greatly struck during my visit by the quality of the younger economists and civil servants in the Administration. I am sure that the best hope for good government in America is to be found there. . . ."

Gilbert, Humphrey, and Salant thought Keynes had not appreciated the resistance among United States industrialists to the expansion of productive capacity. "There were a lot of people—influential people in the business world," recalled Salant, "who were afraid to see a great expansion of capacity because they were looking ahead, at least that was our interpretation, to the time after the war when the expansion of capacity would have caused capacity to be excessive. This arose, for example, in connection with the cutdown in automobile production on the one hand, in order to make room for more tank production, or whether to build more factories and have both. Our line at the time was, you can have both and you should have both."

Led by the "indomitable" Gilbert, as Keynes described him, "our gang," said Salant, had "wild ideas" about how much output could be enlarged. Their projections were exceeded by the actualities after Pearl Harbor. Robert Nathan, the "shaggy" numbers man, also had moved from Commerce to Defense. There he was trying to get the military to state their requirements. "They didn't take kindly," he recalled, "to a bunch of know-nothing civilians coming in and raising questions about strategm and almost tactical issues and needs and requirements."

Nathan credited Jean Monnet, the Frenchman who later became known as "Mr. Europe," with persuading Roosevelt and Churchill to direct their service chiefs to come up with a figure of what they would need to win the war. In September Roosevelt ordered that a "Victory Program" be prepared of production requirements. Nathan was handed the job of translating this into a "feasibility study" based on America's raw materials, factories, and labor force. Gilbert helped him. Through Hopkins at the White House Gilbert persuaded Roosevelt to raise the Administration's production targets. His analyses, together with those of Nathan, who had a talent for one-sheet summaries, itself a high road to gaining Roosevelt's attention and support, okayed the job.

On January 6, 1942, Roosevelt in his annual message announced the nation's new production goals. "We must raise our sights all along the production line," he told Congress. He set 1942's targets at sixty thousand aircraft, forty-five thousand tanks and six million tons of shipping. The figures, wrote Sherwood, "were greeted with derision," a "numbers racket," hooted some officers. But the targets were met and exceeded.

A self-constituted watchdog committee of younger men had assembled for the purpose of ensuring arms goals were realized and weapons dispatched.[26] Cohen, Oscar Cox, and Bob Nathan were in it. Three recent Frankfurter clerks attended its meetings—Joe Rauh, his first law clerk, Ed Prichard, his third, and Philip Graham, over whose marriage with Katherine Meyer, daughter of the Washington *Post*'s publisher, the justice presided, his fourth. Another key participant was Wayne Coy. Originally a newspaperman, he had gone to the Philippines with McNutt where he had developed a reputation as a problem solver. Roosevelt made him director of the Office of Emergency Management to keep track of the fulfillment of defense directives.

Oscar Cox was another behind-the-scenes New Dealer hero of the burgeoning defense effort. He had kept the "yellow pad" in the writing of the Lend Lease bill under which all of the group were working. He had started out with Morgenthau at Treasury but Harry Hopkins soon preempted his services. He became in effect Hopkins's lawyer. Cox was acute, methodical, and thorough as his diaries systematically attest. They frequently refer to Cohen whom he consulted almost daily during the period the Lend Lease bill was being drafted. "He was the most remarkable bureaucrat of all," said Rauh, "a genius" at cutting red tape. Cox was named general counsel of Lend Lease, Joe his assistant, and their office also housed Ed Prichard, Phil Graham, Abe Feller, and Lloyd Cutler. The New Deal had gone to war.

In some measure all were under the influence of Frankfurter and Cohen. When Rauh first came to Washington his heroes, in addition to Roosevelt, were Frankfurter who had sent him there, Corcoran, and Cohen. "To me they were like the Trinity," said Rauh, although by 1941 Corcoran's name was less frequently mentioned.[27]

"Phil and I were looking at the top-secret monthly publications of the

Office of Production Management," recalled Rauh. "The President was making speeches about clouds of planes and we found that only one bomber had been delivered to the Air Force in August 1941." Rauh and Graham dashed off a memorandum to go from Wayne Coy to the President which Coy sent over to the White House posthaste. Back came a memo from Hopkins telling Coy not to bother the President with such matters and besides his facts were wrong.

"We almost died," said Joe. He and Phil hurried to Bob Nathan who was the statistician at the Office of Production Management and whose figures had prompted their memo. He brought out his yellow sheets. "I think I made a mistake," he finally commented. Joe and Phil blanched. "We did not produce one plane." The two rushed back to Wayne Coy and drafted a tough note for him to send to the President. Sometimes the three of them—Joe, Prich, and Phil—enlisted Frankfurter to go and talk to the President.

They could view Frankfurter critically although always with affection. When Prichard was Frankfurter's law clerk he came to Rauh with Frankfurter's draft opinion in the *Gobitis* flag-salute case. "You've got to do something to prevent this disaster" against civil liberties, he implored Joe. If he did, said Joe, he would have to explain to the justice how he had seen the draft. Could he say Prichard had shown it to him? "God, no!" said Prichard. There was nothing to be done. Ickes tells of his "utter astonishment and chagrin" at the opinion, echoing the sentiments of New Dealers generally. Justice Stone alone dissented and elicited a significant note of congratulation from Ben Cohen. Generally, Frankfurter and Cohen were thought of together.

"For Ben and Felix the war was everything," said Rauh, "and I bought it. Ben wanted to go to war, and in that sense he led Roosevelt." Cohen came in to see him, reported Ickes:

He was looking for comfort but I could give him none. He is terribly distressed about the rudderless course that our ship of state seems to be pursuing these days. Apparently Ben can think of nothing else and broods over the fate of the world as a mother does over her sick child. I do not feel any more hopeful than he does but I have gotten down to bedrock of something approaching fatalism.[28]

Letters still were dribbling in to the White House urging Corcoran's appointment as solicitor general. But Roosevelt had decided against it. "Tom now seems resigned to the fact that he is not going to get it," Rowe advised the President, but he and other of Tom's friends hoped Roosevelt would delay the naming of Charles Fahy, said Rowe, until the "vicious attacks" on Tom in the Scripps Howard papers for influence peddling abated. A week later Rowe changed his mind. The Damon and Pythias relationship between Corcoran and Cohen took an unexpected turn. With Tom's turndown, Ben, who had loyally supported him, felt free to allow friends to put forward his own name. Rowe memoed Roosevelt:

A drive is now beginning for Ben Cohen. I fear it will be the same sort of thing as the Corcoran drive and if there is any delay in the nomination it will merely serve to reopen old wounds. Furthermore whatever the press would say now about a rebuke to Tommy would be said three weeks from now anyway.[29]

Ben had returned from London resigned to the belief that he would have to leave the government. So he told Bob Kintner, a good friend, newspaper columnist, and man of action. It would be "a tragedy for the government to lose your great abilities and experience at a time when competent manpower is one of the real weaknesses," Kintner remonstrated with him.[30] Learning that Corcoran was out as solicitor general, Kintner on his own went to Wendell Willkie, whom he knew and whom he also knew to have a high regard for Ben's abilities and fairness. He asked Willkie, for whom Roosevelt had made possible a visit to besieged London, to write on Ben's behalf. It was a moment when Ben's despair had become a preoccupation of his friends.

Frankfurter implored him to put aside a sense of personal injury over not having a job in the war effort in the interests of a larger cause. It was Frankfurter at his best:

You have been very deeply in my mind, and with anguishing thoughts. No man can put himself in another man's shoes, but I'm bold enough to venture to say that while you have hosts of friends—I know no one else who has so many and such devoted friends and literally no one who is unfriendly—I yield to none in the depths and delicacy of attachment—or in the feelings of unhappiness when you are unhappy. For no one—I venture to believe—has had such continuing constancy of identification with your hopes and dreams, your sorrows and disappointment. Moreover, as I've had occasion to tell you before, I know only too well, from long and poignant experience how it feels to have the very quality and substantiality of one's work lead to treatment that—since we are all human—irks by its discriminations.

But these outward recognitions are really not the enduring things—and they never have been with you. *That* has been one of your glories—that you care for *die Sache,* the thing and not its trappings. And that is all I meant in my too brutal phone talk—that the world is aflame, the whole dignity of man is at stake, in which you and I as individuals count for nothing (nor do all the small fry that trot the stage for a few short hours), but in which, it so happens, your great gifts and genius, both intellectual and moral, count for so much. I'm sorry I could not tell you all this at Mt. Kisco—but I had not seen my brother for two years and I did not know you had run off so early.[31]

"My dear Mr. President," Willkie wrote Roosevelt:

It was said to me the other day that you are considering appointing Benjamin Cohen to the office of Solicitor General.

I am writing you this letter without either the suggestion or the knowledge of Mr. Cohen with whom I never discussed the subject.

I have known Ben since the very early days of your Administration. I have disputed with him much and disagreed with him more. I do not agree today with many of his social and economic beliefs. But I can say to you that from these disputes and differences, I have come to have a profound respect for his ability and character. No one in your Administration has represented you more disinterestedly or more zealously.

I would not recommend anyone to you for official promotion in whose appointment I had the slightest personal interest. I recommend Mr. Cohen to you only because of his merits.[32]

Willkie sent a copy of his letter to Kintner to show to Ben if he wished to. Ben exulted over that letter. It bolstered his self-esteem. Every time Joe Rauh came to his office, Joe had to read it.

He had thought about it a great deal, Roosevelt replied to Willkie. The Court would not have disapproved of Ben but Roosevelt sensed they felt ". . . he had not had enough experience in presenting cases before them," whereas the Court knew Fahy. He had argued many cases before them and they liked him.

Ben is such a straight shooter and such a modest fellow, I sincerely hope he will continue with the Government. It is really too bad that he has had so much publicity from columnists, etc.

Francis Biddle had succeeded Jackson as Attorney General after Jackson's elevation to the Court. He had urged Tommy's selection as solicitor general and when that was out had urged Ben. "That would reopen the Court fight, too," Roosevelt was reported to have said. Ickes disagreed. "Ben would be confirmed quickly and with little if any opposition. But the President isn't looking for even any slight trouble these days and he is perfectly willing to use his desire to placate Congress as an excuse for deserting his old friends."[33]

When Cohen heard of Fahy's selection, it was one of the few times Rauh saw tears in his friend's eyes. (The other was after Pearl Harbor when he showed Rauh a photograph of nisei children being herded into box cars under War Department detention orders.)

Several proposals were made to Ben. Roosevelt asked him to keep an eye on Bob Donovan's new organization, the Office of Strategic Services, to ensure it did not conflict with the Office of Facts and Figures. "I am not 'asking' you to do this! I am 'telling' you!"[34] Nothing materialized. There was a flare-up of strikes, in particular that of the coal miners led by John L. Lewis. There were other problems that affected labor's role in the defense setup and Congress rang with proposals to curb labor's rights. Rowe consulted Justices Frankfurter and Jackson and advised Roosevelt that they thought the only man capable of the "delicate draftsmanship" involved in writing new labor legislation was Ben Cohen. "F.F. also asked me to point out this has nothing to do with Ben's present pathological state and that he is not 'trying to make work' for him." Ben was sympathetic to labor and bills drafted by him would go far in quelling labor's "quite justifiable fears that Congress is trying to murder it. And, surprisingly, Ben is popular on the Hill, particularly with Sam Rayburn."

But as Ickes noted at the end of November, Ben still was marking time. Not until late 1942 when Justice Byrnes resigned his seat on the Court at Roosevelt's request to become director of the Office of Economic Stabilization, which in effect placed him in charge of home-front matters, was Ben given an assignment commensurate with his talents as counsel of the organization. Bob Jackson lunched with the secretary. Ben had remarked to Ickes that a Jackson concurring opinion had been the best of the three rulings on the unconstitutionality of a California statute:

I told Bob what Ben had said and his reply was that there was no one whose favorable opinion he would rather have. He regards Ben as having the best legal brains he has ever come in contact with. I recall that several years ago Julian Mack [judge of the CCA] told me the same about Ben. The pity is that this valuable set of brains should not be put to work by the Government on some important task. But this is the fact.[35]

Corcoran, while successfully warding off charges of influence peddling, had busied himself with China's needs. He did so at the suggestion of Currie. On Roosevelt's orders Currie had addressed himself to the dispatch of help to the Chinese government in Chungking. Currie, said Tom, told him it was Roosevelt's wish he undertake the role of expediter of Lend Lease supplies to China. Henry Morgenthau, heavily involved himself with Chinese funding efforts in the United States, resented Corcoran's entry on the China-aid scene. He warned China's ambassador Hu Shih and its finance minister, T. V. Soong, Chiang's banker brother-in-law, against the use of Corcoran as a lobbyist:

I don't like it. The President doesn't like it. I never have worked that way . . . and I am not going to work that way. As far as Treasury is concerned, I want to make myself perfectly clear, we don't have that kind of thing going on.[36]

Soong and Hu tried to clarify Corcoran's role, to picture him as in no way attempting to obtain illegal favors from the American government. They kept him on. At the end of 1941, when Pearl Harbor brought the United States into the war, Corcoran was the legal counsel for China Defense Supplies and his brother David its president. One of Tom's major concerns was to provide materials and find pilots for Claire Chennault's air operation against the Japanese, the Flying Tigers. Lauchlin Currie also was involved. "The President gave me the job of recruitment of mercenaries for the Flying Tigers," Carrie recalled. "The only pilots we could find had flown for the Spanish Loyalists."[37] Currie ran into the problem of Miss Shipley who presided over the issuance of passports at the State Department. "I had to enlist Berle's help," added Currie.

It was all patriotic work which Corcoran relished. But it added to suspicions that he was using governmental contacts to build a personal fortune. THE CORK MAKES $100,000 IN ARMS FEES IN 1941 was the headline of one of Thomas Stokes's articles on the subject in the Scripps-Howard press.[38] China defense was only one of his interests. Ickes reported how Tom had come in with Henry J. Kaiser, the liberal-minded defense contractor whom he was helping to get government aid to build a magnesium plant.[39] The government wanted the plant built, and this was Corcoran's defense, "I think the real test by which to judge the way I have acted," said Corcoran when he was called before the Truman Committee, "is not by whom I know, but whether what I have done has helped or hurt the Government's defense effort."[40]

"I want to raise my glass to Tom," Ickes, testy and incorruptible, was to say at his old friend's fiftieth birthday dinner in 1950, "for what he has been and what he can be." Ben did not follow Tom into his influence-peddling ventures, but he never was heard to criticize them. It was not until the end of 1942 that he himself became Byrnes's counsel at the Office of Economic Stabilization.

A telltale exchange took place between Tugwell and Corcoran on the eve of Pearl Harbor. The government was rife now with the planning and coordination mechanisms—Office of Production Management (OPM), Office of Price Administration and Civilian Supply (OPA&CS), Supply Priorities and Allocations Board (SPAB)—of the sort Tugwell had urged in the mid-thirties and that Corcoran in the effort to sell his own handiwork on the Hill had insinuated represented the real radicalism in the New Deal. "Among all the discouragements there are to record," said Tugwell in a reference to his vain efforts to get a significant job in Washington, "I suppose I can now write down one victory." He had picked up the ringing telephone in Charles Taussig's suite at the Carlton, thinking it was for him.

> But when I identified myself, he [Tom Corcoran] said: "Oh, Rex, I think it should be said, and said by me now, that in all those controversies we had six and seven years ago, you were right and I was wrong. If we had done then what you wanted to do, we should not be in the mess we are in." I dissolved in astonishment—the Irishman, Tommy the Cork—being generous, and of all people, to me! But he insisted and said it all over again. He even made me feel that maybe he was right. I was surer then and fought harder. But as I look back I do believe that I was essentially right. He was a harder fighter and more unscrupulous. I suppose he did hurt me enormously in underhanded ways with reporters and so on. But this was amends indeed![41]

Tugwell and Corcoran—Roosevelt did not feel he could give either one a prominent place in his administration.

The younger men were all going into service. Rauh and Phil Graham were together when they heard the news of Pearl Harbor. They promptly repaired to an Air Force recruiting office only to be chased out for lack of one qualification or another. They persisted in their enlistment efforts. Rauh received a lieutenant's commission and was ordered to the Southwest Pacific. Graham later served General Kenney in the same area. At Union Station a few friends came to say goodbye to Rauh. Ben and Tom were the first to arrive, but as soon as Felix came Tom left. The breach was never to be repaired.

Was the New Deal over? The President sought to give that impression. He portrayed himself as "Dr. Win-the-War." "The remedies that old Dr. New Deal used were for internal trouble," he told a press conference. "But at the present time, obviously the principal emphasis, the overwhelming emphasis should be on winning the war." After victory reform would again be in order, but "we don't want to confuse people by talking about it now."[42]

Eleanor Roosevelt disagreed. She replied to a question at her press conference, that she, for one, had not laid the New Deal "away in lavender." Of course the New Deal "has become rather old, rather stable and permanent, too, in many ways." But the country needed something more than "win-the-war." So the struggle continued.

Of all the New Dealers who pressed FDR to move forward Eleanor was the most insistent. But even she had to admit, as Hopkins did in 1940, and Ben Cohen would in retrospect, that Roosevelt's was the firm hand on the New Deal tiller and that while he often tacked and veered his sure sense of priorities was in quest not in despite of the American dream.

"I'm beginning to think I ought to be more patient," Eleanor wrote in the final months of the war, "for in the end FDR does seem to get pretty much what we want."

Epilogue

In June 1971 some of Tom Corcoran's friends organized a seventieth birthday celebration. The senior judge of the Federal District Court in Chicago, William Campbell, spoke. He had been Tom's channel for communications between Roosevelt and Cardinal Mundelein. Another speaker was Judge Ammi Cutter, a member of Tom's 1925 class at Harvard Law School. Justice Hugo Black came to praise Tom as did James Rowe, a law partner and political associate. A letter from former President Lyndon B. Johnson recalled how Tom at Roosevelt's direction had kept a "kindly eye on that country boy from Texas" when he arrived as a young congressman.

One associate of Tom's in New Deal days, Joseph Rauh, was not there. He still was one of Ben's most intimate friends but his relations with Tom had collapsed. Joe explained his absence:

Ben was the epitome of the public interest lawyer. Tom was the epitome of the public interest lawyer who then was working against what he had done. Tom was my hero in the Thirties. If I feel strongly on the issue it is because a great many of my New Deal friends have become rich. I don't envy them but I am not dispassionate about the New Deal lawyers who have become establishment lawyers. They might have made this a better country in the last thirty years (Interview 13 April 1984).

The main speaker at the dinner for Tom was Ben. The two men had continued to see each other in postwar Washington, once a week at luncheon at the Cosmos Club and often elsewhere. Ben chose Tom's relationship to the New Deal as his subject. It may also have been his answer to

Joe: "I think we may count the New Deal years among the best years of his life," he began:

Indeed I recall during the stock exchange bill fight, Tom's talking past midnight with a former associate in New York and recounting the activities of a single day and night. He had spent the morning explaining the bill to and being grilled by the Senate Committee. After a quick lunch, he returned to his office where a long row of distinguished counsel for various groups affected by the bill were waiting to talk with him and present amendments which in their view would make the act more workable but which in some instances would have opened loopholes through which their clients might escape. In the late afternoon and through a sandwich dinner he had met with a group of us who were checking over a redraft of the bill to be presented in the evening to an inter-department committee on which the Reserve Board, Treasury and Commerce were represented and which had been set up by FDR to make sure that we were not, as had been charged, destroying our financial system. You had to be good to get by that committee which had been briefed by the stock exchange and banking interests. But try as they did the committee could not flaw Tom's arguments. They tried, as they had tried before, to delay us by asking for a redraft, hoping that that would take us at least several days. But Tom, as he had done on previous occasions, told them that time was urgent and the redraft would be ready the next evening. We were now at 1:00 AM just finishing marking up the redraft. Peggy who knew no hours when Tom needed her would have the new draft retyped before sunrise. Our pace was too hectic for the committee and Tom felt certain they would give up the ghost at our next meeting and let us proceed.

After explaining all this with unconcealed glee to his former associate in New York, Tom concluded: "I can't tell you how exciting life is down here. Just think, we kids being able to do all this while we are still in our early Thirties. I am afraid that after this all life will be anti-climax." Being somewhat older than Tom, I muttered, "Oh Boy! You don't know how true, how painfully true it will be that after this all life will be anti-climax."

It was inevitable, continued Ben, that Tom would incur enmities.

But it angered me then and it angers me now when he gives aid and comfort to his enemies by his own loose sputterings denigrating his true motivation and his own good deeds. In the New Deal days his enemies used to take seriously his idle talk that his boys would have to make their mark before they married and had children as they would be unable to accomplish much of lasting value after they had taken on the burden of wife and children. Now his enemies pretend to take seriously his sputterings about power as if he were only concerned with power for power's sake rather than for the vindication of the humanistic values of life which he cherishes and esteems beyond their ken.

Ben recalled Tom's formidable abilities as a New Deal talent scout and recruiter and ended: "There never has been a better esprit de corps in government than that inspired by Tom in the New Deal years."[1]

Notes

References to a single event are grouped in a single note. Book titles are cited in full in their first mention in each chapter. Frequent citations have been identified throughout by the following abbreviations:

AJC OH	American Jewish Committee Oral History, New York City.
BVC	Benjamin V. Cohen
COHC	Columbia Oral History Collection, New York City.
FDRL	Franklin D. Roosevelt Library at Hyde Park, New York.
FF	Felix Frankfurter
JPL	Joseph P. Lash
LC	Library of Congress
LDB	Louis D. Brandeis
NA	National Archives
NPPC	National Power Policy Committee
RGT	Rexford G. Tugwell
TGC	Thomas G. Corcoran

After Seven Years	Raymond Moley. *After Seven Years.* New York, 1939.
FDR *PPA*	Franklin D. Roosevelt. *Public Papers and Addresses.* Edited by Samuel I. Rosenman. New York, 1938–50 (volume denoted by year).
"Memoirs"	Thomas G. Corcoran. "Rendezvous with Destiny" (unfinished autobiographical memoir, written with Philip Kooper), LC.
"Notes"	Thomas G. Corcoran (recollections dictated to help his collaborator on "Memoirs"), LC.
Roosevelt and Frankfurter	Max Fredman, ed. *Roosevelt and Frankfurter.* Boston, 1967.

Secret Diary   Harold L. Ickes. *Secret Diary.* 3 vols. New York, 1953–54.
    I. *The First Thousand Days, 1933–1936.*
   II. *The Inside Struggle, 1936–1939.*
   III. *The Lowering Clouds, 1939–44.*

Prologue

1. On the origins of the Brains Trust, see Rexford G. Tugwell, *The Brains Trust* (New York, 1969); Rexford G. Tugwell, *Roosevelt's Revolution* (New York, 1976); Raymond Moley, *After Seven Years* (New York, 1939); Adolph A. Berle, *Navigating the Rapids* (New York, 1973); and Samuel I. Rosenman, *Working with Roosevelt* (New York, 1952).

2. Unemployment figures were supplied to JPL by Robert R. Nathan and Walter Salant.

3. TGC and BVC on each other, *Time,* September 12, 1938.

4. Accounts of the New Dealers Reunion Dinner held March 4, 1977, in the New York *Times* and Washington *Post, Time, Newsweek.* Speeches were made by Marquis Childs, RGT, TGC, and BVC. Copies in Corcoran and Cohen papers, LC.

5. Arthur Schlesinger, Jr., to Fritz Mondale, in Corcoran papers, LC; and Corcoran to, LC.

6. RGT to Leon Keyserling, January 16, 1987; and Leon Keyserling to JPL, October 18, 1984.

I. *An Unusual Scholar*

1. Bernard Freund to JPL, July 2, 1984; and Frank Tick to JPL, July 25, 1984.

2. Robert Lynd and Helen Lynd, *Middletown* (New York, 1929).

3. On the Jews of Indiana, see Joseph Levine, *The American Heritage—Roots of Greatness,* published by the Indiana Jewish Historical Society, July 1977, p. 43.

4. For BVC on his sense of Jewishness as a boy, see AJC OH.

5. M. C. Schwartz, American Jewish Archives, Hebrew Union College.

6. Interview with BVC, September 20, 1982.

7. Interview with Alan D. Whitney, BVC's high school classmate, January 18, 1984.

8. Class yearbook, *The Correlator,* May 1911.

9. Interview with BVC, September 20, 1982.

10. Ibid.

11. George Eliot, *Daniel Deronda,* (New York, 1960), p. 356.

II. *Harvard and World War I*

1. Joseph P. Lash, ed., *The Diaries of Felix Frankfurter* (New York, 1975); and Michael Parrish, *Felix Frankfurter and His Times* (New York, 1982).

2. Interview with BVC, September 20, 1982.

3. Roscoe Pound to BVC, March 2, 1917, in Cohen papers, LC.

4. FF to Learned Hand, May 24, 1917, in Hand papers, LC.

5. On Brandeis's attitude toward U.S. entry into World War I, see Leonard Baker, *Brandeis and Frankfurter* (New York, 1984), p. 144.

6. Edward Burling's letter of recommendation in Cohen papers, LC.

7. Shipping Board to BVC, September 20, 1918, LC.

III. *The Zionist Experience*

1. BVC's account of how he came to be with the Zionists at the Peace Conference is in his introduction to Julius Simon's *Certain Days—Zionist Memoirs* (Jerusalem, 1971).

2. On the meeting at the Savoy, see ibid., p. 87.

3. BVC reports to LDB and Julian Mack are in the Zionist Archives and Library, Park Avenue and Sixtieth Street, New York City.

4. Alan D. Whitney to JPL, January 18, 1984.

5. On BVC and Ella Winter, see Margery Abrams to JPL, March 26, 1983; and JPL telephone conversation with Stella Frankfurter, November 4, 1983, in JPL personal papers.

6. Max Lowenthal to BVC, December 7, 1919, LC.

7. Harry Barnard, *Judge Mack* (New York, 1974), pp. 96, 254.

8. Felix Frankfurter and Walter Lippmann on being a Jew in Michael Parrish's *Felix Frankfurter and His Times,* (New York, 1982), p. 129; and BVC's notes for Paul Freund, January 11, 1969, LC, on FF's Jewishness and on the Jewish activities of LDB.

9. For BVC on Julian Mack at Paris, see Barnard, *Mack,* p. 254.

10. On Weizmann's attitude toward BVC, JPL interview with Margery Abrams, November 1983; BVC on Weizmann, interview with JPL, September 20, 1982; and Simon, *Certain Days,* pp. 79, 95, 96.

11. For BVC and the mandate, see Zionist Archives; BVC to Julian Mack, November 27, 1919; Julian Mack to BVC, October 1, 1919; BVC to Jacob de Haas, April 1920; BVC to LDB, March 12, 1920; "Zionists" cable, April 7, 1920; BVC to de Haas, April 14, 1920; FF to Chaim Weizmann, February 9, 1920; Bernard Flexner to BVC, March 5, 1920; and on BVC's role in the wording of the mandate, see Simon, *Certain Days,* pp. 88, 89, 112.

12. AP dispatch in BVC papers, LC; BVC to LDB, April 25, 1920; Chaim Weizmann, *Trial and Error* (New York, 1949), p. 260; Julian Mack to BVC, April 25, 1920; and Julius Simon to BVC, May 5, 1920.

13. Simon, *Certain Days,* p. 100.

14. Ibid.

15. BVC to Paul Freund, January 11, 1969.

16. Simon, *Certain Days,* pp. 100, 103–6; on the split between Weizmann and LDB; on the Reading Plan, Simon, *Certain Days,* p. 79; BVC on the Reading Plan in notes for Paul Freund, LC; and BVC on the attitude of European Zionists toward LBD, Barnard, *Mack,* pp. 261–62.

17. Bernard Flexner to Julian Mack, October 2, 1920; and LDB to Julian Mack, October 4, 1920.

18. BVC to Julian Mack, October 8, 1920 in Zionist Archives.

19. Julius Simon to BVC, November 24, 1920, Zionist Archives; and BVC to U.S. Zionist Executive, January 17, 1921, Zionist Archives.

20. LDB to BVC, April 3, 1921, LC.

IV. *Ben Cohen in the Twenties*

1. Interview with Jane (Mrs. Louis) Harris, November 4, 1983.

2. FF to BVC, December 17, 1923, LC.

3. Leonard Baker, *Brandeis and Frankfurter* (New York, 1984), p. 238.

4. Michael Parrish, *Felix Frankfurter and His Times* (New York, 1982), p. 165; and FF to Learned Hand, April 11, 1923, LC.

5. Baker, *Brandeis,* pp. 239–40.

6. FF to BVC, "Sunday"; and FF to BVC, June 5, 1923, LC.

7. FF to BVC, June 14, 1923; and FF to BVC, November 7, 1923, LC.

8. BVC, AJC OH.

9. Baker, *Brandeis,* pp. 240–41.

10. Edward Burling to BVC, February 20, 1925, LC.

11. BVC on Wall Street, AJC OH; and BVC to FF, May 27, 1928, LC.

12. Jerome Frank in an unpublished article on BVC, November 4, 1945, in Corcoran papers, LC.

13. BVC, AJC OH.

14. BVC to Molly Dewson, November 30, 1928, LC.

15. Molly Dewson to FF, December 9, 1928; and FF to Molly Dewson, December 10, 1928, LC.

16. FF to BVC, December 10, 1929, enclosing copy of letter to Lewis Meriam recommending BVC as adviser on Indian problems, LC; and Lewis Meriam to BVC, January 16, 1930.

17. Simon, *Certain Days—Zionist Memoirs* (Jerusalem, 1971), p. 381.

18. AJC OH.

19. Felix Frankfurter, "The Palestine Situation Restated," *Foreign Affairs* 9 (April 1931): 409–34.

20. BVC to Jane Harris, August 11, 1931, and August 22, 1931, made available to JPL by Mrs. Harris.

21. BVC to FF, January 8, 1932, LC.

22. BVC to FF, January 11, 1932, LC.

23. FF to FDR, September 10, 1932; Joseph Eastman to FF, December 16, 1932; and FF to BVC and BVC to FF, January 9, 1933, in FF papers, LC.

24. FF to Josephine Goldmark, January 10, 1933, and BVC reply, FF papers, LC; FF to Elizabeth Brandeis, January 17, 1933; BVC to FF, January 19, 1933; FF to BVC, January 27, 1933; BVC to Molly Dewson, February 6, 1933; FF to BVC, February 6, 1933; and BVC to FF, February 7, 1933, LC.

V. *"Tommy the Cork"—Beginnings*

1. "Memoirs."

2. Thomas Gardiner to TGC, Corcoran papers, LC.

3. TGC to William Hastings, December 18, 1938, Corcoran papers, LC.

4. Monica Lynne Niznick, "Thomas G. Corcoran" (Ph.D. diss., Notre Dame University, 1981), p. 60.

5. Jerrold Auerbach, "Lawyers and Social Change in the Depression Decade," in *The New Deal,* ed. John Braemas, Robert Brimmer, and David Brody (Columbus, 1975), p. 147; and "Memoirs."

6. "Memoirs."

7. TGC to Richard P. Carroll, September 24, 1938, LC; Niznick, "Corcoran," p. 12.

8. "Memoirs"; and cf. BVC version in AJC OH.

9. Felix Frankfurter and Thomas Corcoran, "Petty Offenses and the Constitutional Guaranty of Trial by Jury," *Harvard Law Review* 30 (June 1926).

10. Niznick interview with TGC, August 7, 1979; Joseph P. Lash, *From the Diaries of Felix Frankfurter* (New York, 1975), p. 36; and "Memoirs."

11. FF to TGC, February 7, 1927, LC.

12. "Memoirs."

13. FF to FDR, March 19, 1935.

14. Niznick, "Corcoran," p. 26.

15. Robert S. McElvaine, *The Great Depression* (New York, 1984), p. 16.

16. "Memoirs."

17. TGC to Oliver Wendell Holmes, March 6, 1928, Corcoran papers, LC.

18. TGC to his mother, April 10, 1930, family letters, LC; and "Memoirs."

19. TGC to "Dear Ted," March 24, 1930, LC; and TGC to Holmes, March 8, 1930, in Niznick, "Corcoran," p. 27.

20. TGC to David Corcoran, family letters, LC.

21. TGC to Howard Corcoran, August 30, 1930; September 25, 1930; May 15, 1930; and n.d., family letters, LC.

22. TGC to his mother, July 17, 1930, LC.

23. TGC to David Corcoran, April 14, 1930, LC.

24. TGC to Alger Hiss, January 29, 1931, and February 2, 1931, LC.

25. TGC to "Dear Chilluns," April 1, 1931, LC.

26. Chester Lane, COHC; TGC to Samuel Becker, September 1930; and TGC to his mother, December 6, 1930, LC.

27. TGC to Kenneth Simpson, March 10, 1932; and TGC to his mother, December 6, 1930, LC.

VI. *Reconstruction Finance Corporation*

1. "Memoirs."

2. R. Amis Cutter to TGC, November 30, 1931, LC; and Thomas P. Corcoran to TGC, February 20, 1932, LC.

3. Eugene Meyer, *Reminiscences,* vol. 2, p. 624, COHC; and Thomas P. Corcoran to TGC, February 20, 1932, LC.

4. FF to TGC, February 25, 1932, and April 23, 1932, LC.

5. TGC to FF, January 23, 1933, LC.

6. Thomas P. Corcoran to TGC, July 11, 1932; and FF to TGC, June 16, 1932, LC.

7. TGC to FF, n.d., LC.

VII. *The Brains Trust*

1. Rexford G. Tugwell, *To the Lesser Heights of Morningside* (Philadelphia, 1982), pp. 5, 43, 50.

2. *After Seven Years,* p. 15.

3. Raymond Moley to FF, December 8, 1930, Frankfurter papers, LC; FF to Raymond Moley, January 4, 1932, LC; and FF to LDB, August 4, 1934, LC microfilm.

4. FDR *PPA,* 1932, p. 646.

5. Ernest K. Lindley, *The Roosevelt Revolution—First Phase* (New York, 1933).

6. Rexford G. Tugwell, *The Brains Trust* (New York, 1968), p. 154; and Adolph A. Berle, *Navigating the Rapids* (New York, 1973), pp. 27, 54.

7. Raymond Moley, *The First New Deal* (New York, 1966), p. ix; and *After Seven Years,* p. 22.

8. LDB to FF, February 13 and 25, 1932; March 11, 1932; July 11, 1932; August 4, 1932; and August 28, 1932, LC.

9. FDR *PPA,* 1932, pp. 682–83; and LDB to FF, August 28, 1932; September 29, 1932; and October 20, 1932, LC.

10. *Roosevelt and Frankfurter,* pp. 24–25.

11. LDB to FF, October 4, 1932, LC.

12. Elliott Rosen, *Hoover, Roosevelt and the Brains Trust* (New York, 1977), p. 140.

13. *Roosevelt and Frankfurter,* p. 93.

14. FDR *PPA,* 1932, p. 751.

15. FF to Walter Lippmann, April 27, 1932, in *Roosevelt and Frankfurter,* pp. 71–72.

VIII. *The Interregnum Before Roosevelt Took Office*

1. FDR *PPA,* 1932, p. 720.

2. FF to FDR, September 10, 1932, in *Roosevelt and Frankfurter.*

3. Joseph Eastman to FF, December 16, 1932, LC.

4. BVC to FF, January 9, 1933, "Brief Comments on the New Draft of the Hastings Bill, S4921," LC.

5. FF to BVC, n.d., but comments on new draft, LC.

6. Adolph Berle to FDR, January 11, 1933, LC.

7. FF to Raymond Moley, January 11, 1933, LC.

8. BVC to FF, January 9, 1933, LC.

9. FF to Rep. Fiorello H. La Guardia, January 12, 1933, LC.

10. FF to Adolph Berle, January 13, 1933, LC.

11. Joseph Eastman to FF, January 21, 1933; Max Lowenthal to FF, January 23, 1933; and BVC to FF, January 27, 1933, LC.

12. FF to Sen. Robert La Follette, January 26, 1933; FF to Solicitor General Thacher, February 27, 1933; FF to Joseph Eastman, February 28, 1933; and Robert La Follette to FF, February 28, 1933, LC.

13. *Congressional Record,* March 1, 1933, pp. 5530, 5531.

14. Max Lowenthal, *Harvard Law Review* 47 (1933); and *The Nation,* editorial note, April 12, 1933.

15. Eugene Meyer to FF, April 10, 1932, and May 10, 1932, LC.

16. *After Seven Years,* p. 123.

17. Ibid., pp. 81, 116.

18. BVC to FF, February 25, 1933, LC.

19. John Maynard Keynes to FDR in New York *Times,* December 31, 1933; Adolph Berle on FF "group" and Keynes, *Navigating the Rapids* (New York, 1973), October 17, 1932; and London *Times* obituary on Keynes, April 22, 1946.

20. James Olson, *Herbert Hoover and the RFC* (Ames, 1977), ch. 5.

21. *Roosevelt and Frankfurter,* pp. 169, 171.

22. TGC to FF, "Saturday" letter after 1932 election, LC.

23. Congressional Record, January 11, 1932, p. 1742.

24. *Roosevelt and Frankfurter,* pp. 169, 171. Letter of FF to FDR, November 23, 1933, enclosing a letter from "an influential group of Oxford economists."

25. FF to TGC, November 16, 1932, LC.

26. TGC and Harold Rosenwald to FF, January 23, 1933; and FF to Raymond Moley, February 10, 1933, L.C.

27. TGC tells this story in "Memoirs," "Credo" section, p. 8, LC.

IX. *The New Dealers Assemble*

1. On Washington, D.C., when President-elect Roosevelt returned: Federal Writers Project in American Guide Series—WPA, *Washington* (Washington, D.C., 1937); Bess Furman (Armstrong), *Washington By-Line* (New York, 1948); and Lorena Hickok, *Reluctant First Lady* (New York, 1962).

2. RGT diary, March 31, 1933, FDRL.

3. Walter Lippmann, *Interpretations, 1933–1935* (New York, 1936), p. 27.

4. FF to Walter Lippmann, in *Roosevelt and Frankfurter*, pp. 116, 119.

5. Adolph A. Berle, *Navigating the Rapids* (New York, 1973), p. 84.

6. RGT diary, entries for December 30, 1932; January 31, 1933; and February 15, 1933, FDRL.

7. Rexford G. Tugwell, *Roosevelt's Revolution* (New York, 1976), p. 24.

8. RGT diary, January 31, 1933, FDRL; and *After Seven Years.*

9. RGT in *Political Science Quarterly* 85 (March 1970):102; and LDB to FF, November 17, 1932, LC.

10. LDB to FF, March 3, 1933, LC.

11. RGT diary, February 18, 1933, LC.

12. Max Lowenthal to FF, n.d., March 13, 1933, LC.

13. Elliott Rosen to JPL, November 18, 1984.

14. *After Seven Years,* p. 166; Walter Lippmann, March 15, 1933, in Lippmann, *Interpretations,* p. 35.

15. Charles Wyzanski, COHC, pp. 104, 149, 153, 185.

16. Jerome Frank, COHC, pp. 11, 20, 36, 74.

17. Tugwell, *Roosevelt's Revolution,* p. 116.

18. RGT diary, February 17, 1933, FDRL.

19. Charles Wyzanski, COHC, p. 198.

20. James Landis, COHC, pp. 69, 70.

21. Robert S. McElvaine, *The Great Depression* (New York, 1984), p. 141.

X. *The NRA — An Effort to Control Business*

1. RGT in *Political Science Quarterly* (March 1970):103.

2. RGT diary, April 15, 1933, FDRL.

3. Ibid., February 4, 1933, FDRL.

4. FF to Raymond Moley, February 9, 1933, and April 3, 1933, LC.

5. RGT diary, April 1, 1933, FDRL.

6. Adolph A. Berle, *Navigating the Rapids* (New York, 1973), p. 79.

7. RGT diary, February 12, 1933, FDRL.

8. Perkins diary, COHC.

9. Raymond Moley, *The First New Deal* (New York, 1966), p. 275.

10. Interview with Judge Simon Rifkind, July 28, 1983.

11. RGT diary, April 21, 1933, FDRL.

12. Interview with Judge Rifkin, April 21, 1933.

13. RGT diary, April 21, 1933, FDRL.

14. Jerome Frank, COHC.
15. RGT diary, May 30, 1933, FDRL.
16. Jerome Frank, COHC.
17. RGT diary, May 30, 1933, FDRL.
18. Interview with Rifkind.
19. Jerome Frank, COHC.
20. Charles Wyzanski to FF, May 24, 1933, LC.
21. Grace Abbott to FF, May 25, 1933, LC.
22. FF to Grace Abbott, May 30, 1933, LC.
23. FF to Sen. Robert Wagner, May 30, 1933, LC.
24. FF memorandum, "The Recovery Bill and Wage Standards," May 30, 1933, LC.
25. Charles F. Roos, *NRA: Economic Planning* (1937; reprint, New York, 1971).
26. Rexford G. Tugwell, *Roosevelt's Revolution* (New York, 1976), p. 262.
27. Jerome Frank, COHC.
28. FF to Charles Wyzanski, February 6, 1934, LC.
29. Charles Wyzanski, COHC.
30. Roos, *NRA,* p. 418.
31. Perkins diary, COHC.

XI. *The Three Musketeers*

1. Report of House of Representatives Interstate and Foreign Commerce Committee, H.R. 4314, p. 2.
2. John T. Flynn, *The New Republic,* May 1, 1933; and James Landis, COHC.
3. *From the Diaries of FF,* (New York, 1975), May 8, 1933, pp. 137–40.
4. James Landis, COHC; and FDR to the Congress, FDR *PPA,* 1933, March 29, 1933.
5. James Landis, "The Legislative History of the Securities Act," *Georgetown Law Review,* (October 1959):24–49.
6. FF to TGC, April 17, 1933, LC.
7. Donald A. Ritchie, *James M. Landis* (Cambridge, 1980), p. 47; FF to Raymond Moley, April 15, 1933; FF to BVC, April 14, 1933, LC; and Landis, "Legislative History," COHC, p. 38.
8. FF to Raymond Moley, April 28, 1933, LC.
9. FF to Sam Rayburn, April 24, 1933, LC.
10. Raymond Moley to FF, May 25, 1933; and FF to Raymond Moley, June 15, 1933, LC.
11. *After Seven Years,* p. 284.
12. James Landis, COHC.
13. Eustace Seligman and FF exchange in Cohen papers, May 1933, LC.
14. BVC, AJC OH, p. 44.
15. Landis, "Legislative History," p. 40.
16. Cohen papers, n.d., LC.
17. BVC to James Landis, May 5, 1933, LC.
18. James Landis, COHC, p. 157.
19. FDR, *PPA,* 1933, pp. 213–14; and John T. Flynn, *The New Republic,* "Other People's Money," May 31, 1933.
20. Memorandum of American Bankers Association on Securities Bill, in Cohen papers, LC; BVC, AJC OH; FF to BVC, June 13, 1933, LC; BVC to James Landis,

June 7, 1933, LC; FF to Raymond Moley, June 16, 1933; and Raymond Moley to FF, June 19, 1933, LC.

XII. *"The Marines Land on Wall Street"*

1. Rexford G. Tugwell, *In Search of Roosevelt* (Cambridge, 1972), fn. p. 285.
2. *Secret Diary,* I, p. 59.
3. FF to FDR, July 6, 1933, in *Roosevelt and Frankfurter,* pp. 147–48.
4. LDB to FF, July 8, 1933, LC.
5. FF to LDB, n.d., LC.
6. *After Seven Years,* p. 271.
7. LDB to FF, August 5, 1933, and September 28, 1933, LC.
8. Rexford G. Tugwell, *Roosevelt's Revolution* (New York, 1976), p. 201.
9. LDB to FF, August 5, 1933, and September 10, 1933, LC.
10. FF to FDR, October 1, 1933, in *Roosevelt and Frankfurter,* p. 158.
11. FF to TGC, September 26, 1933, LC.
12. FF to M. A. LeHand, September 24, 1933, LC.
13. TGC to FF, October 13, 1933, LC.
14. BVC to Jane Harris, June 28, 1933, and September 7, 1933, n.d., copy in possession of JPL.
15. BVC to FF, October 9, 1933, LC.
16. LDB to FF, September 28, 1933, and November 9, 1933; BVC to FF, October 9, 1933, LC.
17. TGC to FF, October 13, 1933; FF to TGC, September 26, 1933; and TGC to FF, October (probably November) 11, 1933, LC.
18. TGC to FF, October 13, 1933, LC.
19. Copies of articles in the *Economist,* January 6, 1934, by FF, *The Atlantic,* February 1934 by Bernard Flexner, and *Fortune* by Archibald MacLeish, Cohen papers, LC.
20. TGC to FF, October 13, 1933, LC.
21. BVC to FF, October 22, 1933, LC.
22. FF to TGC, October 22, 1933, LC.
23. James Landis, COHC, p. 197.
24. FF to TGC, October 7, 1933, LC.
25. FDR to James Landis, November 14, 1933, LC.
26. James Landis to BVC, October 30, 1933; James Landis, COHC; and BVC, AJC OH.
27. TGC to FF, December 30, 1933, LC.
28. BVC to FF, January 1, 1934, LC.
29. FF to FDR, December 10, 1933, in *Roosevelt and Frankfurter,* pp. 174–76.
30. TGC to FF, October 11, 1933, LC.
31. Ibid.
32. BVC to FF, November 8, 1933, LC.
33. LDB to FF, November 16, 1933, and November 24, 1933, LC.
34. FF to FDR, December 12, 1933, in *Roosevelt and Frankfurter,* p. 176.
35. TGC to FF, December 30, 1933, LC.
36. Arthur Schlesinger, Jr., *The Coming of the New Deal* (Boston, 1958), p. 242.
37. Dean Acheson to FF, January 26, 1934, LC.
38. FF to John Maynard Keynes, December 9, 1933, LC.
39. FDR to FF, December 22, 1933, in *Roosevelt and Frankfurter,* p. 153.

40. BVC to FF, January 1, 1934, LC.
41. TGC to FF, December 30, 1933, LC.

XIII. *Frankfurter's "Happy Hot Dogs"*

1. Max Lowenthal to FF, October 26, 1933, LC.
2. FF to TGC, January 10, 1934, LC.
3. Max Lowenthal to FF, October 18, 1933, LC.
4. Max Lowenthal to FF, October 26, 1933, LC.
5. TGC to FF, November 13, 1933, LC.
6. Max Lowenthal to FF, October 26, 1933, LC.
7. FF to Senator Couzens, December 7, 1933, LC.
8. BVC to FF, January 1, 1934, LC.
9. James Landis to FF, December 13, 1933, LC.
10. BVC to FF, October 9, 1933, LC.
11. Dean Acheson to FF, January 26, 1934, LC.
12. *After Seven Years,* p. 284.
13. Interview with Telford Taylor, 1984.
14. James Landis to FF, January 26, 1934, LC.
15. FF to TGC, February 8, 1934, LC.
16. Donald A. Ritchie, *James M. Landis* (Cambridge, 1980), pp. 53, 54.
17. Max Lowenthal to FF, April 17, 1934, LC.
18. Interview with Telford Taylor.
19. James Landis, COHC.
20. LDB to FF, January 25, 1934, and February 11, 1934, LC.
21. TGC to FF, February 11, 1934, LC.
22. FF to TGC, February 14, 1943, in *Roosevelt and Frankfurter,* pp. 192–93.
23. *Roosevelt and Frankfurter,* p. 178.
24. Adolph A. Berle, *Navigating the Rapids* (New York, 1973), December 9, 1933.
25. LDB to FF, March 4, 1934, and April 1, 1934, LC.
26. Ritchie, *Landis,* p. 95; and BVC, AJC OH, p. 46.
27. FF to FDR, February 22, 1934, in *Roosevelt and Frankfurter,* p. 196; and John T. Flynn, "The Marines Land on Wall Street," *Harper's,* July 1934.
28. James Landis, COHC.
29. "Notes."
30. *Newsweek,* March 10, 1934, p. 25; and BVC, AJC OH.
31. FF to Alfred E. Cohn, LC.
32. James Landis to FF, March 6, 1934, LC.
33. John Dickinson to FF, March 5, 1934; FF to John Dickinson, March 6, 1934; and Max Lowenthal to FF, April 17, 1934, LC.
34. BVC, AJC OH, 50.
35. Ibid.
36. Raymond Moley to FF, March 27, 1934, LC; and FDR *PPA,* 1934, March 26, 1934.
37. BVC, AJC OH, 52.
38. *Congressional Record,* 73rd Congress, 2nd sess., 7693–7696; 7943–7944, 8013.
39. James Landis, COHC, 186.
40. Flynn, "Marines Land."
41. Quoted by Monica Niznick, "Thomas G. Corcoran" (Ph.D. diss., Notre Dame

University, 1981), p. 108; TGC and BVC to FF, April 22, 1934; and TGC to FF, May 11, 1934, LC.

42. *After Seven Years,* fn. p. 181.

43. Flynn, "Marines Land."

44. BVC to FF, May 11, 1934, LC.

45. Dwight Donough, *Mr. Sam* (New York, 1962), p. 430.

46. Joseph Alsop and Robert Kintner, *Men Around the President,* (New York, 1939), interview August 5, 1938, LC.

47. "Notes," December 12, 1979, LC.

XIV. *Competition for Roosevelt's Ear*

1. June 6, 1934, date Roosevelt signed the bill.

2. Donald A. Ritchie, *James M. Landis* (Cambridge, 1980), p. 59; and John T. Flynn, "The Marines Land on Wall Street," *Harper's,* July 1934.

3. *After Seven Years,* p. 286.

4. FF to TGC, May 7, 1934, LC; FF to FDR, May 22, 1934, in *Roosevelt and Frankfurter,* p. 220.

5. Julian Mack to FDR, June 6, 1934, FDRL.

6. BVC to Jane Harris, June 26, 1934, and July 26, 1934.

7. *After Seven Years,* pp. 289, 290.

8. Marvin McIntyre to FDR, July 12, 1934, FDRL; and BVC to Jane Harris, June 26, 1934.

9. James Landis, COHC.

10. BVC to Jane Harris, July 26, 1934.

11. TGC to FF, December 11, 1933, LC; and "Unofficial Observer" (Jay Franklin Carter), *The New Dealers* (New York, 1934), p. 85.

12. Raymond Moley, *The First New Deal* (New York, 1966), p. 134; New York *Times,* March 24, 1934; and *Time,* April 23, 1934.

13. TGC to FF, April 23, 1934, in Monica Niznick, "Thomas G. Corcoran" (Ph.D. diss., Notre Dame University Press, 1981), p. 116; and RGT diary, April 8, 1934, FDRL.

14. FF to FDR, May 7, 1934, in *Roosevelt and Frankfurter,* pp. 213–14.

15. Washington *Post,* April 21, 1934.

16. Max Stern, *Today,* May 19, 1934; and New York *Times,* April 22, 1934.

17. FF to TGC, May 15, 1934, LC.

18. Berle, *Navigating the Rapids* (New York, 1973), April 23, 1934.

19. FDR to Adolph Berle, April 25, 1934, FDRL.

20. LDB to FF, May 11, 1934, LC.

21. FF to FDR, June 8, 1934; and FDR to FF, June 11, 1934, in *Roosevelt and Frankfurter.*

22. TGC and BVC to FF, June 18, 1934, LC; and FF to LDB, July 24, 1934, LC.

23. LDB to FF, July 7, 1934, LC; and FF to LDB, July 24, 1934, LC.

24. TGC to Charles Wyzanski, August 4, 1934, LC.

25. BVC to Jane Harris, August 26, 1934.

26. Jerome Frank, COHC; and BVC, AJC OH, p. 56.

27. "Notes," "Folio for Chapters 4–8," LC.

28. James Landis, COHC.

29. "The Legend of Landis," *Fortune,* August 1934; Ritchie, *James M. Landis,* p.

64; Drew Pearson, "Merry-Go-Round," October 1, 1934; BVC to FF, October 2, 1934, LC; and FF to James Landis, October 9, 1934, LC.

30. Chicago *Tribune,* September 19, 1934; LDB to FF, September 19, 1934, LC; FF to FDR, September 20, 1934, in *Roosevelt and Frankfurter;* and LDB to FF, September 22, 1934, and September 25, 1934, LC.

31. Paul Freund to FF, December 11, 1934, LC.

32. *Secret Diary,* I, pp. 195–97; Charles Wyzanski to JPL, March 9, 1985; and LDB to FF, September 29, 1934, LC.

33. FF to LDB, July 29, 1934, LC.

34. Morgenthau diaries, Jr., September 6, 1934, FDRL.

35. BVC, AJC OH, 58.

36. Paul Freund to FF, December 11, 1934, LC.

37. FDRL, January 16, 1935.

XV. *The "Death Sentence"*

1. Gardner Jackson to Richard Rovere, December 18, 1946; Rovere papers on Jerome Frank, FDRL; RGT diary, November 26, 1934, FDRL.

2. Calvin Hoover to RGT in 1953, reproduced in RGT diary, November 1934, FDRL.

3. RGT to Jerome Frank, August 16, 1934.

4. Cited by Michael F. Parrish, *Securities Regulation and the New Deal* (New Haven, 1970), p. 2.

5. "Notes," LC.

6. RGT diary, November 24, 1934, FDRL.

7. Ibid.

8. Morgenthau diaries, December 19, 1934, 2:332, FDRL.

9. FF to William O. Douglas, January 16, 1934, in Parrish, *Securities Regulation,* p. 156; and Adolph Berle to BVC, December 8, 1934, NPPC, NA.

10. RGT diary, November 24, 1934, FDRL.

11. David Lilienthal, *Journals of David Lilienthal* (New York, 1964), vol. 1, p. 45.

12. BVC memorandum to Harold Ickes, January 7, 1935, NPPC.

13. Philip Funigiello, *Towards A National Power Policy* (Pittsburgh, 1973), p. 201.

14. TGC to Ferdinand Pecora, March 21, 1935, LC.

15. FF to LDB, January 22, 1935, LC.

16. Lilienthal, *Journals,* vol. 1, p. 47.

17. BVC to Funigiello, in Funigiello, *National Power Policy,* p. 207; Wendell Willkie's recollection of the episode in Steve Neal, *Dark Horse* (New York, 1984), p. 29; and BVC to Harold Ickes, February 8, 1935, NPPC.

18. *Ambassador's Dodd, Diary: 1933–1938* (New York, 1941), pp. 211, 214.

19. RGT diary, February 2, 1935, FDRL.

20. Dodd, *Diary,* pp. 213, 214.

21. FDR *PPA,* March 12, 1935, p. 98.

22. Burton Wheeler, *Yankee from the West* (Garden City, 1962), p. 307; FF to BVC, May 21, 1935, LC; and FDR *PPA,* 1931, p. 101.

23. Moley in *Today,* January 26, 1935; and BVC to Celeste Jedel, March 4, 1935, NPPC.

24. Wheeler, *Yankee,* p. 82.

25. House Interstate and Foreign Commerce Committee, *Public Utility Holding*

Companies, 74 Cong., 1st sess., March 15, 1935; and Wendell Willkie to BVC, March 18, 1935, and March 20, 1935, in Cohen papers, LC.
26. TGC to David Corcoran, March 27, 1935, LC; and Thomas P. Corcoran to TGC, March 16, 1935, LC.
27. James Bonbright to BVC, April 8, 1935, and BVC reply, NPPC.
28. Wheeler, *Yankee,* p. viii; and "Notes," LC.
29. Dillon, *Wendell Willkie,* p. 65, cited by Monica Niznick, "Thomas L. Corcoran" (Ph.D. diss. Notre Dame University, 1981), p. 172.
30. Wendell Willkie to BVC, April 26, 1935, NPPC.
31. BVC to James Bonbright, April 10, 1935, NPPC.
32. TGC to Ferdinand Pecora, March 25, 1935, LC.
33. BVC described the episode a year later to FF on March 9, 1936, and March 19, 1936, LC.
34. "Notes," pp. 8–10, LC.
35. FF to Burton Wheeler, June 12, 1935, cited by Niznick, "Corcoran."
36. *Congressional Record,* 74th Congress, 1st sess., 9184.
37. Arthur Krock, New York *Times,* June 20, 1935.
38. David Niles to FF, April 22, 1935, LC; and FF to FDR, May 16, 1935, in *Roosevelt and Frankfurter,* p. 271.
39. Arthur Krock, *Memoirs* (New York, 1938), pp. 169–71.
40. Corcoran papers, LC.
41. Funigiello, *National Power Policy,* p. 113.
42. FDR press conference, June 28, 1935.
43. FF to FDR, September 11, 1934, FDRL; *Congressional Record,* 74th Congress, 1st sess., 10659-10660; New York *Times,* July 8, 1935; TGC statement to House Rules Committee, *Investigation of Lobbying,* 74 Cong., 1st sess., July 9, 1935; Rodney Dutcher, July 19, 1935, in Corcoran papers; and TGC to FDR, July 9, 1935, FDRL.
44. TGC to President Lyndon Johnson, March 6, 1966, LC.
45. BVC to FF, March 30, 1936, LC.
46. Arthur Schlesinger, Jr., *The Politics of Upheaval* (Boston, 1960), pp. 316–24.
47. TGC to Harry Storin, December 30, 1935, LC.

XVI. *Tugwellians vs. Happy Hot Dogs*

1. *Today,* September 6, 1935.
2. *Today,* July 27, 1935, and September 6, 1935.
3. RGT diary, September 10, 1934, FDRL.
4. Adolph A. Berle, *Navigating the Rapids* (New York, 1973), September 12, 1934, p. 104.
5. Diary of Homer Cummings, February 26, 1935, at the Alderman Library, University of Virginia, Charlottesville, Virginia; and RGT diary, September 10, 1935, FDRL.
6. *Secret Diary,* I, February 20, 1935, p. 302.
7. FF to Jerome Frank, September 29, 1933, LC; and Jerome Frank, COHC, 131.
8. Gardner Jackson, COHC, 474; and Jerome Frank, COHC, 137.
9. Jerome Frank, COHC; and Adlai Stevenson, *Letters* (Boston, 1972), vol. 1, pp. 267–69.
10. Jerome Frank, COHC, 149, 155.
11. Gardner Jackson, COHC, 411.
12. Jerome Frank, COHC, 88.

13. Peter H. Irons, *The New Deal Lawyers* (Princeton, 1982), p. 140; and Thomas Powell's letter to FF, November 27, 1933, and FF to Thomas Powell, December 18, 1933, Harvard Law School papers.
14. Pat Jackson, COHC, p. 86.
15. RGT diary, 1934, p. 14, FDRL.
16. Jackson, COHC.
17. Irons, *New Deal Lawyers,* p. 175.
18. Jerome Frank, COHC, 180.
19. Pat Jackson, COHC, 621.
20. RGT diary, February 10, 1935, FDRL.
21. Ibid., February 27, 1935, FDRL.
22. Jerome Frank to Raymond Moley, May 23, 1934, in Frank papers, Yale University; and Jerome Frank to Raymond Moley, June 28, 1934, Yale University.
23. TGC and BVC to FF, April 22, 1934, LC.
24. Jerome Frank, COHC, p. 167.
25. FF to Jerome Frank, March 15, 1933, Yale University.
26. Pat Jackson, COHC, 423, 589.
27. FF to Jerome Frank, January 18, 1935; June 10, 1935; December 2, 1935; December 6, 1935; and January 18, 1936, Frank papers, Yale University.
28. Jerome Frank to FF, January 26, 1936, Yale University.
29. *Herald Tribune,* October 27, 1935.
30. FF to FDR, March 19, 1935, FDRL.
31. "Notes," LC, pp. 8, 13–14.
32. FF to M. A. LeHand, March 29, 1935, in *Roosevelt and Frankfurter,* p. 258.
33. "Notes," LC, p. 19.
34. FF to FDR, August 21, 1935, in *Roosevelt and Frankfurter,* pp. 284–85.

XVII. *Price Was the Key and the Key Jammed*

1. Leon Henderson memo, June 27, 1934, copy in Frank papers, Yale University.
2. James P. Warburg, *It's Up to Us* (New York, 1934), reviewed by BVC in *Today,* September 29, 1934.
3. RGT to FDR, September 28, 1934, FDRL; Gardiner Means, "Industrial Prices and Their Relative Inflexibility," U.S. Senate Document, 74th Cong., 1st sess., January, 1935.
4. Jerome Frank to Gardiner Means, first letter undated, second, April 28, 1935, Yale University.
5. FF to Raymond Moley, November 16, 1935, Frankfurter papers, Harvard University.
6. Gardiner Means, *The Corporate Revolution in America* (New York, 1962), pp. 30, 31.
7. Joel Seligman, *The Transformation of Wall Street* (Boston, 1982).
8. RGT diary, January 27, 1935, FDRL.
9. Ibid., 1934, p. 22, FDRL.
10. *Secret Diary,* I, p. 461.
11. Marriner Eccles, *Beckoning Frontiers* (New York, 1951), pp. 126, 127.
12. RGT diary, 1934, p. 25, FDRL.
13. Eccles, *Beckoning Frontiers,* p. 214.
14. Ibid., pp. 173–75, 193.
15. FDR *PPA,* April 28, 1935.
16. Eccles, *Beckoning Frontiers,* p. 214.
17. Chandler quoted in John Kenneth Galbraith's *Money* (Boston, 1975), p. 241.

18. RGT diary, November 5, 1934; December 5, 1934; December 17, 1934; December 31, 1934; and fn., January 16, 1935, FDRL.

19. RGT diary, March 24, 1935, FDRL.

20. FDR *PPA*, May 1, 1935, pp. 143–44.

21. RGT diary, April 29, 1935, FDRL.

22. *After Seven Years*, p. 300; and RGT diary, April 29, 1935, FDRL.

23. *Secret Diary*, I, pp. 342, 433.

24. Paul Samuelson and William D. Nordhaus, *Economics*, 12th ed. (New York, 1985), pp. 330–31; and John Kenneth Galbraith, *The Affluent Society* (Boston, 1958), p. 248.

25. RGT diary, May 9, 1935, and September 10, 1935, FDRL.

XVIII. *The Eclipse of Tugwell*

1. RGT diary, May 9, 1935, FDRL.

2. "Notes," March 1, 1979, LC.

3. United States v. Belcher 294 U.S. 736 (1935).

4. Blackwell Smith to TGC, April 5, 1935, TGC papers, LC.

5. *Secret Diary*, I, p. 247; and FDR telegram, April 3, 1935, FDRL.

6. "Notes"; and TGC to FDR, FDRL.

7. Cummings diary, April 20, 1934; and "Notes," "Pack" segment, C7-9, LC.

8. Peter H. Irons, *The New Deal Lawyers* (Princeton, 1982), p. 101.

9. FF to Stanley Reed, May 7, 1935, LC.

10. "Notes," "Pack," LC.

11. Ibid.

12. Cummings diary, May 27, 1935, and May 28, 1935.

13. RGT diary, May 19, 1935; May 30, 1935; and May 31, 1935, FDRL.

14. FDR *PPA*, May 31, 1935, pp. 200–22; *Today*, June 1, 1935; *Secret Diary*, I, p. 342; and RGT diary, June 5, 1935, FDRL.

15. Raymond Moley, *Today*, June 1, 1935, and August 13, 1935.

16. Walter Lippmann, *Interpretations: 1933–1935* (New York, 1936), pp. 288–90.

17. Cummings diary, November 15, 1935.

18. *Secret Diary*, I, p. 467.

19. Ibid., p. 462.

20. Copy of invitation, November 21, 1935, in Frank papers, Yale University.

21. *Secret Diary*, I, p. 435.

22. Adolph A. Berle, *Navigating the Rapids* (New York, 1975), p. 111; and pp. 114–15 reprint of his *New Republic* review of Bernard Sternsher's book on Tugwell.

23. Interview with BVC, April 8, 1974.

24. Copy in Corcoran papers, LC.

25. Rexford G. Tugwell, *To the Lesser Heights of Morningside* (Philadelphia, 1982), p. 35; and RGT diary, May 30, 1935, FDRL.

XIX. *The 1936 Mandate*

1. BVC, AJC OH.

2. *Secret Diary*, I, p. 517.

3. *After Seven Years*, pp. 330, 343.

4. FDR *PPA*, 1936, pp. 13, 16.

5. "Notes," May 4, 1979, LC, p. 9.

6. United States v. Butler 279 U.S. 1 78-88 (1936).

7. FDR *PPA*, 1936, pp. 43, 44.

8. Stephen Early to FDR, January 9, 1936; *FDR: His Personal Letters,* 1928–1945 I, (New York, 1950), February 13, 1936, 534; and *Secret Diary,* I, p. 534.

9. FDR to James Landis, January 9, 1936, LC.

10. Cummings diary, January 13, 1936.

11. *Roosevelt and Frankfurter,* pp. 312–13.

12. Interview with BVC, September 20, 1982; and *Secret Diary,* I, pp. 530–31.

13. TGC to Archibald MacLeish, December 7, 1936, LC.

14. BVC, AJC OH.

15. Felix Frankfurter and Adrian Fisher, "The Business of the Supreme Court," *Harvard Law Review* 51, no. 4 (February 1938).

16. Ashwander v. Tennessee Valley Authority 297 U.S. 228 (1936); David Lilienthal, *Journals of David Lilienthal,* vol. 1, (New York, 1964), p. 59; Guffey-Snyder Coal Act ruling 298 U.S. 238 (1936); and Morehead v. New York, 198 U.S. 589 (1936).

17. Quoted in Arthur Schlesinger, Jr., *The Coming of the New Deal* (Boston, 1959), p. 483.

18. FDR *PPA*, June 2, 1936, pp. 191, 192.

19. FDR to G. F. Peabody, February 19, 1936, Roosevelt *Letters,* I, p. 559; and Raymond Moley, *Today,* February 29, 1936.

20. Norman Hapgood to FDR and FDR's reply, February 24, 1936; Roosevelt *Letters,* vol. 1, p. 651; and "Unofficial Observer" (Jay Franklin Carter), *Today,* November 2, 1935.

21. FDR *PPA*, 1936, pp. 178, 182.

22. *After Seven Years,* p. 335.

23. Leon Henderson memo, December 30, 1935.

24. FDR *PPA*, June 10, 1936, p. 196.

25. *After Seven Years,* pp. 335, 343; and TGC "Rough Notes," LC.

26. Joseph Alsop and Robert Kintner, *Men Around the President* (New York, 1939), p. 104; and Samuel I. Rosenman, *Working with Roosevelt* (New York, 1952), p. 105.

27. "Notes," LC, p. 2; and Adolph A. Berle, *Navigating the Rapids* (New York, 1973).

28. FF to FDR, June 13, 1926, in *Roosevelt and Frankfurter,* pp. 314, 315; and *After Seven Years,* p. 582.

29. *Secret Diary,* II; and FDR to Robert Wagner, June 26, 1936, FDRL.

30. Samuel Beer, Transactions of the Royal Historical Society, "Two Models of Public Opinion," read at the society's conference 17 September 1973.

31. "Notes," LC; and *Secret Diary,* II, pp. 230–36.

32. Rosenman, *Roosevelt,* p. 160.

33. BVC, AJC OH; and Corcoran, "Notes."

34. Washington *Herald,* September 21, 1936.

35. "Notes," LC.

36. TGC to FF, July 3, 1936, LC; and FF to TGC, undated letter, LC.

37. TGC to M. A. LeHand, September 4, 1936, and September 5, 1936, LC.

38. FDR *PPA*, 1936, p. 383; and FF to FDR, June 13, 1936, in *Roosevelt and Frankfurter,* pp. 344–45.

39. Rosenman, *Roosevelt,* p. 160.

40. "Notes," insert B, March 8, 1979, LC.

41. Morgenthau diaries, pp. 24–27, 42; Byrd L. Jones, "Lauchlin Currie and the Causes of the 1937 Recession," *History of Political Economy* 12, no. 3 (1980):304; and Lauchlin Currie memo, December 22, 1936.

42. "Notes," The Court Plan, March 6, 1979, LC.

43. "My Day," November 15, 1936; and Eleanor Roosevelt to FDR, November 14, 1936, FDRL.

44. Lauchlin Currie comment in unpublished memoir, 1953, p. 98; and Rosenman, *Roosevelt,* p. 114.

XX. *The New Chief Advisers*

1. Stanley High, *Roosevelt and Then* (New York, 1937), pp. 7, 14.

2. TGC to Howard Corcoran, n.d., LC.

3. Mrs. Corcoran to TGC, LC; and "Notes," "Lame Duck," March 5, 1979, LC.

4. Morgenthau diaries, January 4, 1937, 51:16, FDRL.

5. "Notes," "Lame Duck," LC.

6. TGC interview with J. B. Frantz for Lyndon Johnson Library, August 20, 1978, copy in LC.

7. "Notes," "Lame Duck," LC.

8. BVC to FF, March 9, 1936, LC; and FDR to BVC, Roosevelt *Personal Letters,* (New York, 1952), vol. 1, May 14, 1936, p. 593.

9. BVC to FF, March 9, 1936, LC, and FF reply, March 10, 1936; BVC to FF, March 19, 1936; FF to George Roberts, March 21, 1936; Wendell Willkie to FF, March 26, 1936; and BVC to FF, March 31, 1936, and enclosure, LC.

10. Joel Seligman, *The Transformation of Wall Street* (Boston, 1982), p. 135; and New York *Times,* July 1, 1936, and November 13, 1936.

11. FDR *PPA,* 1937, p. 60.

12. Supplied the writer by Mrs. Boris L. Bittner, Prof. Bittner was Judge Frank's first law clerk.

13. T. Voorhees to David Corcoran, December 31, 1936, LC.

14. "Notes."

15. William S. Youngman, Jr., to TGC, November 5, 1936, LC.

XXI. *Roosevelt's Court Reform Play*

1. Interview with BVC, September 16, 1974.

2. BVC to FF, January 6, 1937, LC.

3. Interview with BVC, September 16, 1974; and "Notes," tape 2, LC.

4. Cummings diary, January 24, 1937.

5. FDR to FF, January 15, 1937, in *Roosevelt and Frankfurter,* and FF's reply, January 18, 1937.

6. Joseph Rauh in Katie Louchheim, ed., *The Making of the New Deal* (Cambridge, 1985).

7. BVC to Harold Laski, February 7, 1937, LC.

8. Robert Sherwood, *Roosevelt and Hopkins* (New York, 1948), pp. 89, 90.

9. Paul Freund in Louchheim, *New Deal,* p. 98.

10. Interview with BVC, September 16, 1974; and FF to FDR, February 15, 1937, and February 18, 1937, in *Roosevelt and Frankfurter,* pp. 380–81.

11. Paul Freund in Louchheim, *New Deal,* p. 98.

12. FDR to FF, February 9, 1937; and FF to FDR, February 15, 1937, and February 18, 1937, in *Roosevelt and Frankfurter,* pp. 381–82, 384.

13. Edward Corwin to TGC, April 18, 1937, LC; Milton Katz to TGC, March 30, 1937, LC; and Louchheim, *New Deal,* p. 128.

14. Account in "Notes," LC; Burt Wheeler, *Yankee from the West* (Garden City, 1962), pp. 319, 322; and Charles Michelson, *The Ghost Talks* (New York, 1944), p. 167.

15. Michelson, *Ghost Talks,* p. 178; and Wheeler, *Yankee,* p. 167.

16. Interview with BVC, September 16, 1974.

17. LDB to Willis Van Devanter, March 2, 1935, LC; and Van Devanter to his sisters, June 23, 1934, quoted by Paul Freund, "Charles Evans Hughes as Chief Justice," *Harvard Law Review,* 1967.

18. Interview with BVC, September 20, 1974.

19. Interview with BVC, September 20, 1982.

20. FDR *PPA,* 1937, p. LXV, p. 113.

21. FDR to FF, February 18, 1937, and FF reply, February 23, 1937, in *Roosevelt and Frankfurter;* and TGC to Stuart Chase, March 6, 1937, LC.

22. Joseph Rauh in Louchheim, *New Deal,* p. 58.

23. FF to FDR, April 12, 1937, in *Roosevelt and Frankfurter.*

24. Calvert Magruder to BVC and BVC's reply, April 15, and April 16, 1937, LC.

25. Nebbia v. New York, 291 U.S. 502(1934).

26. Joseph Rauh in Louchheim, *New Deal,* p. 59.

27. BVC to Leon Green, July 29, 1937, LC.

28. TGC to BVC, March 26, 1937, LC.

29. Wheeler, *Yankee,* p. 336.

30. Interview with BVC, September 18, 1974; and FDR *PPA,* May 25, 1937, p. 220.

31. FF to TGC, April 28, 1937, LC.

32. Interview with BVC, September 20, 1982.

33. FF to LDB, March 31, 1937, LC.

34. FF to "Dear Boys," May 15, 1937, LC.

35. BVC to FF, July 9, 1937, LC.

36. Alva Johnston, "White House Tommy," *The Saturday Evening Post,* July 31, 1937.

37. Franklyn Waltman, Washington *Post,* July 31, 1937; John T. Flynn, *The New Republic,* August 18, 1937; and FF to TGC, "Thursday," LC.

38. FF to TGC, "Sunday," July 22, 1937; BVC to LDB, July 30, 1937, LC; FF to BVC, August 7, 1937; and LDB to BVC, August 1, 1937.

39. FF's analysis of reasons for defeat of Court bill, Frankfurter papers, LC.

40. FF to FDR, August 9, 1937, in *Roosevelt and Frankfurter,* pp. 404–6.

41. Samuel I. Rosenman, *Working with Roosevelt* (New York, 1952), p. 163.

42. FDR *PPA,* 1937, pp. 360–61.

43. FF notes to TGC on a successor to Supreme Court vacancy that was supposed to go to Senator Joseph Robinson, Corcoran papers, LC; and Cummings diary, August 11, 1937.

44. "Notes," p. 5.

45. BVC to FF, October 11, 1937, LC.

46. Richard L. Stokes, St. Louis *Dispatch,* September 21, 1937.

47. FF to FDR, March 31, 1937, in *Roosevelt and Frankfurter,* p. 428.

48. "Notes," LC.

49. Beverly Smith, "Corcoran and Cohen," *American Magazine,* August 1937.

XXII. *Crisis in Economic Theory: Spenders vs. Budget-Balancers*

1. Lauchlin Currie, unpublished autobiography.

2. Interview with Leon Keyserling, September 29, 1982; and Joseph Pechman, 1982.

3. FDR *PPA,* 1936, p. 643.

4. Blum, *From the Morgenthau Diaries, 1928–1938* (Boston, 1959), p. 386; and *Secret Diary,* II, pp. 220, 235.

5. *Secret Diary,* II, pp. 240, 243.

6. Lauchlin Currie memorandum in TGC papers, November 8, 1937, LC; Isidore Lubin, COHC; and Currie, unpublished autobiography.

7. Herbert Stein, *The Fiscal Revolution in America* (Chicago, 1969), chapter on "The Struggle for the Soul of FDR."

8. Ernest Cuneo recollections in Corcoran papers, LC.

9. Adolph A. Berle, *Navigating the Rapids* (New York, 1973), p. 141.

10. Ibid., p. 148.

11. TGC to FF, December 15, n. d., LC.

12. Joseph Alsop and Robert Kintner, *Men Around the President* (New York, 1939), p. 135; and Robert Jackson, COHC.

13. *Secret Diary,* II, pp. 261, 264.

14. Robert Jackson, COHC; *Secret Diary,* II, pp. 287–88; and Ernest Cuneo's account of Jackson candidacy for governorship, written for TGC, LC.

15. Currie, unpublished autobiography, pp. 98, 99.

16. Berle, *Navigating,* p. 158; *Secret Diary,* II, p. 295; and Robert Jackson, COHC.

17. *Secret Diary,* II, p. 317.

18. Berle, *Navigating,* pp. 155, 160, 163.

19. Lauchlin Currie, unpublished memorandum, "The Causes of the Recession of 1937"; and interview with Lauchlin Currie, September 20, 1985.

20. John Maynard Keynes to FDR, February 1, 1938, FDRL.

21. Alsop and Kintner, *Men.*

22. I have followed Robert Blum's account in *Roosevelt and Morgenthau* (Boston, 1972), pp. 196–201, which is based on the Morgenthau diaries.

23. Samuel I. Rosenman, *Working with Roosevelt* (New York, 1952), p. 171.

24. FDR *PPA,* 1938, p. 242; and Rosenman, *Working,* p. 175.

25. Currie, unpublished autobiography.

26. Ibid.

27. Lauchlin Currie to Dwight Israelson, August 24, 1983, in Currie's possession; and James Roosevelt to FDR, Roosevelt, *Personal Letters,* vol. 2, February 2, 1959, p. 857.

28. Lauchlin Currie at meeting of the American Economic Association, 1971, as reported in the proceedings and published separately under the title, "The Second Crisis of Economic Theory," December 27–29, 1971, foreword by John Kenneth Galbraith.

XXIII. *The Safety Net Strengthened*

1. "Notes," LC.
2. Corcoran papers, speech file, LC.
3. Robert Jackson, COHC; Homer Cummings diary, August 1, 1937.
4. *Congressional Record,* 75 Cong., 1st sess., July 2, 1937, p. 11; Paul Freund in Katie Louchheim, *The Making of the New Deal* (Cambridge, 1983), p. 96.
5. *Congressional Record,* 75 Cong., 1st sess., June 15, 1937, p. 7.
6. BVC to Jane Harris, August 1, 1937.
7. FF undated letter. TGC papers, LC.
8. *Secret Diary,* II, p. 389.
9. Interview with Judge Reilly, May 8, 1984; and Robert Jackson, COHC, p. 470.
10. Robert Jackson, COHC, p. 461.
11. FF to "Dear Boys," n.d.; and BVC to Jane Harris, August 19, 1937.
12. Interview with Judge Reilly.
13. Ibid.
14. Frances Perkins, *The Roosevelt I Knew* (New York, 1946), pp. 265–67.
15. Robert Jackson, COHC, 466; Sar A. Levitan and Isaac Shapiro, New York *Times,* January 16, 1986; and Isidore Lubin, COHC, 67.

XXIV. *"New Deal Washington Was Out En Masse . . ."*

1. FDR to BVC, May 14, 1936; and FDR *Personal Letters* (New York, 1950), vol. 1, p. 590.
2. Interview with Joseph Rauh; and Joseph Rauh in Katie Louchheim, *The Making of the New Deal* (Cambridge, 1983), p. 57.
3. Joseph Rauh, *Harvard Law Review* 96 (1983): 947.
4. Joseph Rauh in *Louchheim,* 112; and Joseph Rauh, *Harvard Law Review* 96 (1983): 957.
5. A. J. Priest to BVC, in Cohen papers, LC.
6. Donald Ritchie, *James M. Landis* (Cambridge, 1980), p. 70.
7. BVC to Wendell Willkie, September 7, 1937; Wendell Willkie to BVC, September 10, 1937; BVC to Wendell Willkie, October 13, 1937; Wendell Willkie to BVC, October 10, 1937; BVC to Wendell Willkie, October 22, 1937; Wendell Willkie to BVC, October 30, 1937; and BVC to Wendell Willkie, November 9, 1937, Cohen papers, LC.
8. Interview with Joseph Rauh.
9. FF to BVC, November 8, 1937, LC.
10. *Secret Diary,* II, p. 314.
11. David Ginsberg to FF, February 12, 1938, LC.
12. John I. Wheeler to TGC, March 16, 1938; and Peggy Dowd to John I. Wheeler, March 30, 1938, LC.

XXV. *Drafting Roosevelt for a Third Term*

1. Amos Pinchot to FDR, May 17, 1938; and FDR to Marvin McIntyre, May 18, 1938, FDRL.
2. Robert Jackson, COHC, p. 615.
3. Ernest Cuneo to TGC, LC; and Robert Jackson, COHC, p. 619.
4. Edward J. Flynn, *You're the Boss* (New York, 1947), p. 151.

5. James A. Farley, *Jim Farley's Story* (New York, 1947), p. 151.
6. *Time,* September 12, 1938; and Robert Jackson, COHC, p. 465.
7. Samuel I. Rosenman, *Working with Roosevelt* (New York, 1982), p. 178; and FDR *PP4,* 1938.
8. *Time,* September 12, 1938.
9. New York *Times,* June 11, 1938; Robert Jackson, COHC, p. 619; and New York *Times,* September 30, 1938.
10. BVC to Jane Harris, September 4, 1938.
11. *Secret Diary,* II, p. 510.
12. BVC to M. A. LeHand, October 13, 1938, LC.
13. FDR *PPA,* November 23, 1938; and FF to FDR, November 25, 1938, in *Roosevelt and Frankfurter,* p. 466.
14. *Time,* September 12, 1938.
15. William O. Douglas, *Go East, Young Man* (New York, 1974), p. 427.
16. "Notes," "Hopkins Supplementary Notes," LC, pp. 3, 4.
17. *Secret Diary,* II, pp. 417, 419, 423; FDR to James Roosevelt, July 15, 1938, FDRL; and TGC to FDR, August 11, 1938, LC.
18. "Notes"; and Flynn, *Boss,* p. 151.
19. "Notes," March 12, 1980, LC, pp. 9, 10; and *Secret Diary,* II, p. 425.
20. "Notes," "Hopkins Supplementary Notes," 5, 6, 7; and "Notes," "Death and Resurrection," March 12, 1979, 1, LC.
21. "Notes," March 12, 1980, 2, LC; and *Secret Diary,* II, p. 424.
22. Adolph A. Berle, *Navigating the Rapids* (New York, 1973), pp. 174–75; and Cummings diary, July 4, 1938.
23. Cummings diary, September 3, 1938; and *Secret Diary,* II, p. 394.
24. John A. Salmond, *A Southern Rebel* (North Carolina, 1983), p. 98.
25. *Time,* September 12, 1938.
26. Robert Sherwood, *Roosevelt and Hopkins* (New York, 1948), p. 93.
27. "Notes," LC.
28. Douglas, *Go East,* p. xii.
29. Cummings diary, October 15, 1938; and *Secret Diary,* II, pp. 459, 463.
30. *Secret Diary,* II, p. 456.
31. Ibid., p. 464.
32. Interview with BVC, November 9, 1982, and September 16, 1974.
33. Berle, *Navigating,* pp. 180, 193, 194.
34. *Secret Diary,* II, p. 528.
35. Ibid., p. 508. *The Saturday Evening Post* articles by Joseph Alsop and Robert Kintner were published in 1939 in *Men Around the President* (New York, 1939).

XXVI. *The New Deal and the Approach of War*

1. Adolph A. Berle, *Navigating the Rapids* (New York, 1973), pp. 197–98.
2. Heywood Broun, *World-Telegram,* February 24, 1938.
3. Joseph P. Lash, *Love, Eleanor* (New York, 1982), p. 275.
4. TGC to Fay Welch, March 2, 1939; Fay Welch to TGC, March 15, 1938; and TGC to Fay Welch, May 16, 1939, LC.
5. Interview with Cornelia Wickenden, April 3, 1985.
6. FDR press conference, September 12, 1939.
7. Joseph P. Lash, *A Friend's Memoir* (New York, 1964), p. 70.
8. Berle, *Navigating.*

9. FDR *PPA,* 1938.

10. Arthur Krock, New York *Times,* March 31, 1939; and Leon Henderson, March 21, 1939, FDRL.

11. Mordecai Ezekiel, "After the New Deal," *The New Republic,* August 23, 1939.

12. Blaisdell papers, NA.

13. Mordecai Ezekiel at "Town Meeting of the Air," April 1, 1937, Ezekiel papers, FDRL.

14. "Notes," Tape 1, 22, LC; and Lauchlin Currie to BVC, July 15, 1938, TNEC file, NA.

15. BVC to Leon Henderson, June 12, 1939; and Corwin Edwards to Leon Henderson, April 22, 1939, TNEC file, NA.

16. Raymond Moley, *The Saturday Evening Post,* March 30, April 6, and April 30, 1940; Stuart Chase, *Harper's,* February 1940; and Adolph Berle's testimony in *Navigating,* p. 216.

17. FDR to Senator O'Mahoney, May 16, 1939, FDRL.

18. Lauchlin Currie at the American Economic Association; JPL with Currie, September 20, 1985; and Berle, *Navigating,* August 1, 1939.

19. Lauchlin Currie to FDR, March 18, 1940, FDRL.

20. E. Cary Brown, "Fiscal Policy in the Thirties; A Reappraisal," *American Economic Review* 46, (December 1956): pp. 857–79.

21. Herbert Stein, ed., *The Fiscal Revolution in America* (Chicago, 1969), p. 131.

22. New York *Times,* June 10, 1939.

23. *Secret Diary,* II, p. 633; BVC to M. A. LeHand, March 27, 1939, FDRL; and Robert Sherwood, *Roosevelt and Hopkins* (New York, 1948), p. 130.

24. *Secret Diary,* II, p. 670; Samuel I. Rosenman, *Working with Roosevelt* (New York, 1952), p. 115; and FDR *PPA,* 1939, September 21, 1939.

25. Jerome Frank to Senator O'Mahoney, November 26, 1938, TNEC, NA.

26. Sherwood, *Roosevelt and Hopkins,* p. 133; and Berle, *Navigating,* p. 225.

27. Berle, *Navigating,* p. 240.

28. *Secret Diary,* II, p. 705; TGC to E. I. McClintock, August 30, 1939, LC; Berle, *Navigating,* p. 241; *Secret Diary,* II, p. 713; William O. Douglas, *Go East, Young Man* (New York, 1974), p. 443; and Eleanor Roosevelt, "My Day," September 1, 1939, FDRL.

29. Interview with BVC; *Secret Diary,* II, p. 559; and FF to TGC and BVC, January 4, 1939, LC.

30. *American Hebrew,* February 8, 1938; and Judge Mack to FDR, undated letter, LC.

31. TGC to Thomas Patrick Corcoran, January 16, 1939, LC.

32. Cummings diary, July 4, 1938; and Jerome Frank to TGC, January 23, 1939, and March 12, 1939, LC.

33. Cummings diary, December 15, 1938.

34. "Unofficial Observer" (Jay Franklin Carter), *The New Dealers* (New York, 1934), p. 322.

35. FDR to C. C. Burlingham, February 6, 1936, (in Frankfurter papers, Harvard Law School), cited by Jerold S. Auerbach, *Unequal Justice* (New York, 1976), p. 187; and Samuel I. Rosenman, AJC OH.

36. Jerome Frank to TGC, March 17, 1939, LC; and Jerome Frank to TGC, March 23, 1939, LC.

37. Jerome Frank to BVC, September 26, 1939, LC.

38. TGC to David Corcoran, October 21, 1939, LC.

39. Berle, *Navigating,* p. 252.

40. Stephen Early to TGC, September 11, 1939, LC; *Secret Diary,* III, p. 6 and FDR press conference, September 12, 1939.

41. *Secret Diary,* II, pp. 718, 721.

42. Interview with BVC, September 8, 1974; and *Secret Diary,* II, p. 681.

43. Berle, *Navigating,* p. 225; Currie int. *ibid.;* Berle, *ibid.,* pp. 224, 236.

44. Berle, *Navigating,* p. 225.

45. Rosenman, *Roosevelt,* pp. 188–91.

XXVII. *Whose New Deal Is It? Tugwellism without Tugwell*

1. Robert Sherwood, *Roosevelt and Hopkins* (New York, 1948), p. 1.

2. RGT diary, November 17, 1939, FDRL; and *Secret Diary,* III, p. 6.

3. RGT diary, November 17, 1939.

4. Testimony of Robert Nathan, David Ginsburg, and Kenneth Galbraith, "World War II and the Problems of the Eighties." Hearings before House Committee on Banking and Finance, Urban Affairs, 96 Cong., 2d sess., September 23, 1980. Serial No. 96-66.

5. Interview with BVC, April 8, 1974.

6. *Ibid.;* and *Secret Diary,* III, p. 199.

7. FF to TGC and BVC, Corcoran papers, LC; and FF to TGC, December 21, 1939, LC.

8. *Secret Diary,* III, p. 107.

9. RGT diary, March 25, 1940.

10. Adolph A. Berle, *Navigating the Rapids* (New York, 1973), p. 288.

11. *Secret Diary,* II, p. 688.

12. Berle, *Navigating,* pp. 299, 305.

13. *Secret Diary,* III, pp. 158, 160–61, 169, 172.

14. Berle, *Navigating,* pp. 314–15.

15. *Secret Diary,* III, p. 204.

16. Ibid., p. 174.

17. FDR *PPA,* 1940, p. 202; and *Secret Diary,* III, p. 178.

18. Richard Gilbert memorandum, "National Defense and Fiscal Policy," [June 1940,] FDRL.

19. Joseph P. Lash, *A Friend's Memoir* (New York, 1964), pp. 104–5.

20. *Secret Diary,* III, p. 182.

21. Burt Wheeler, *Yankee from the West* (Garden City, 1962), p. 353; and BVC to FF, October 27, 1941, NPPC NA.

22. RGT diary, March 25, 1940, FDRL.

23. Edward J. Flynn, *You're the Boss* (New York, 1947), pp. 155, 157; and Wallace diaries, vol. 5, p. 990.

24. James F. Byrnes, *All in One Lifetime* (New York, 1958).

25. Wheeler, *Yankee,* p. 364.

26. *Secret Diary,* III, p. 235.

27. Flynn, *Boss,* p. 156; and Lash, *Memoir,* p. 139.

28. Samuel I. Rosenman, *Working with Roosevelt* (New York, 1952), pp. 213, 219.

29. *Secret Diary,* III, pp. 241, 266.

30. Rosenman, *Roosevelt,* p. 277.

31. Flynn, *Boss,* p. 161; and FDA *PPA,* 1940, 297.

32. Morgenthau diaries, July 25, 1940, p. 0627, FDRL.

33. *Secret Diary,* III, p. 204.

34. Ibid., pp. 207, 289.

35. Ibid., p. 271.

36. BVC memo to FDR, June 6, 1940, LC; and Oscar Cox to BVC, July 18, 1940, FDRL.

37. FDR to Frank Knox, July 22, 1940, FDRL.

38. Stimson diary, August 15, 1940, Yale University.

39. BVC, AJC OH.

40. *Congressional Record,* 76th Cong. 2d sess., June 21, 1940, p. 11314.

41. C. C. Burlingham to BVC, August 27, 1940, LC.

42. *Secret Diary,* III, p. 304.

43. Rosenman, *Roosevelt,* p. 223; and Lauchin Currie to American Economic Association, 1971, Proceedings published under title, "The Second Crisis of Economic Theory," December 27–29, 1971.

44. *Secret Diary,* III, p. 304.

45. "Notes," September 1, 1979, LC, pp. 14, 15.

46. RGT diary, January 4, 1941, FDRL.

47. Interview with BVC, April 8, 1974.

48. Rosenman, *Roosevelt,* p. 263; and RGT diary, January 9, 1941, FDRL.

XXVIII. *Blacks and the New Deal*

1. Frankfurter papers, LC.

2. Will Alexander, COHC.

3. Ibid.

4. Walter White, *A Man Called White* (New York, 1948), pp. 179–80.

5. Nancy J. Weiss, *Farewell to the Party of Lincoln* (Princeton, 1983), p. 35. I have made extensive use of Professor Weiss's book in this chapter.

6. Ibid., p. 40.

7. Elizabeth Wickenden, remarks at the New York Public Library, October 8, 1986.

8. Weiss, *Farewell,* p. 142.

9. Max Lowenthal to TGC, October 8, 1936, Corcoran papers, LC.

10. Weiss, *Farewell,* p. 208.

11. Ibid., p. 142.

12. Ibid., pp. 254, 167.

13. John Salmond, "Aubrey Williams Remembers," *Alabama Review* 25 (January 1972): 68–69.

14. Weiss, *Farewell,* p. 237.

15. David K. Niles to Harry Hopkins, February 2, 1939, Hopkins papers, FDRL.

16. Joseph P. Lash, *Eleanor and Franklin* (New York, 1971), pp. 526–28; interview with Joseph Rauh, June 10, 1986; and *Secret Diary,* III, p. 65.

17. Aubrey Williams to Walter White, September 1, 1939, Williams Papers, FDRL; FDR presidential press conferences, #649 A, June 5, 1940.

18. Joseph P. Lash, *A Friend's Memoir* (New York, 1964), p. 172.

19. *Secret Diary,* III, p. 361.

20. Weiss, *Farewell,* p. 232.

XXIX. *Labor's Magna Carta*

1. *The Second Crisis of Economic Theory,* papers and proceedings at American Economic Association meetings, John Kenneth Galbraith, editor, December 27 29, 1971, p. 135.

2. Leon Keyserling to JPL, October 19, 1984.

3. Interview with Walter Salant, October 15, 1986; and interview with Thomas Blaisdell, July 26, 1986.

4. Leon Keyserling, "The Wagner Act: Its Origins and Current Significance," *George Washington Law Review* 29, no. 2 (December 1960): 206.

5. Joseph J. Huthmacher, *Senator Robert F. Wagner and the Rise of Urban Liberalism* (New York, 1968), pp. 170, 171.

6. Interview with Lloyd Garrison, April 25, 1985.

7. Ibid; and Lloyd Garrison to General Hugh Johnson, August 18, 1934, FDRL.

8. Thomas Emerson in Katie Louchheim, *The Making of the New Deal* (Cambridge, 1985), p. 228; and Peter H. Irons, *The New Deal Lawyers* (Princeton, 1982), p. 224.

9. Keyserling, "The Wagner Act," p. 218.

10. Arthur Schlesinger, Jr., *The Coming of the New Deal* (Boston, 1958), p. 403; and FDR *PPA,* July 5, 1935, pp. 294–95.

11. Irons, *New Deal Lawyers,* p. 231.

12. Keyserling, "The Wagner Act," p. 213; and Irons, *New Deal Lawyers,* p. 234.

13. Peter Irons on Nathan Witt, in Irons, *New Deal Lawyers,* p. 235.

14. Thomas Emerson, in Louchheim, *New Deal,* p. 92; and Irons, *New Deal Lawyers,* p. 239.

15. Charles A. Horsky, in Louchheim, *New Deal,* pp. 84, 85.

16. Charles Wyzanski to FF, in Irons, *New Deal Lawyers,* p. 286.

17. Ibid., pp. 286, 287; and *Associated Press v. MLRB,* 301 U.S. 1, 30(1937).

18. Charles Wyzanski to FF, April 14, 1937, LC.

19. Interviews with Ida Klaus, August 29, 1982; August 28, 1985; and August 22, 1986.

20. Keyserling, "The Wagner Act," p. 204; and interview with Ida Klaus, August 22, 1986.

XXX. *Communists and New Dealers*

1. Interview with Louis Jaffe, September 4, 1982.

2. James Landis to FF, June 1, 1932, LC; and Peter H. Irons, *The New Deal Lawyers* (Princeton, 1982), p. 253.

3. Interview with Hope Dale Davis, September 16, 1986; Hope Davis "Revisiting the Red Decade," *New Leader,* February 6, 1984; and Hope Davis, "Looking Back at My Years in the Party," *New Leader,* February 11, 1980.

4. Herbert Fuchs in testimony before the House Un-American Activities Committee, December 13, 1955, Chicago hearings.

5. Interview with Joseph Clark, November 12, 1986.

6. Interview with Hope Davis, September 16, 1986.

7. Gardner Jackson, COHC, p. 612ff.

8. Gardner Jackson, COHC, p. 588; Frank Watson in Katie Louchheim, *The Making of the New Deal* (Cambridge, 1985), p. 110; and TGC and BVC to FF, June 18, 1934, in *Roosevelt and Frankfurter,* p. 223.

9. *Congressional Record,* 73rd Congress, 2nd sess., 7085-7087; and Arthur Schlesinger, Jr., *The Coming of the New Deal,* (Boston, 1958), p. 463.

10. New York *Times,* July 11, 1935.

11. Herbert Fuchs, testimony, December 13, 1955.

12. Davis, "Looking Back," February 11, 1980.

13. Interview with Ida Klaus, September 6, 1982.

14. Earl Latham, *The Communist Controversy in Washington* (Cambridge, 1966), p. 140.

15. Adolph A. Berle, *Navigating the Rapids,* (New York, 1973), pp. 250, 298, 583.

16. Michael Straight, *After Long Silence* (New York, 1983), pp. 134–57.

17. Interview with Walter Salant, October 15, 1986.

18. Berle, *Navigating,* p. 373.

XXXI. *Ministers without Portfolio*

1. "Notes," November 26, 1979, LC.

2. Sophie Nack to Peggy Corcoran, April 1, 1940, LC.

3. "Memoirs"; and "Notes," LC.

4. Interview with James Rowe, April 18, 1984.

5. TGC to Thomas Patrick Corcoran, February 5, 1941, LC.

6. Corcoran papers, LC.

7. James Rowe to Peggy Corcoran, January 24, 1941, LC.

8. FDR to TGC, January 20, 1941, LC.

9. Robert Nathan, Hearings before the House Committee on Banking, "World War II and the Problems of the Eighties," 76th Cong., 2nd sess., September 24, 1980.

10. Henderson-Lubin draft statement, March 29, 1941, TNEC papers, NA.

11. "Memoirs," LC.

12. James Rowe to FDR, June 25, 1941, FDRL.

13. "Memoirs," LC.

14. FF to BVC, October 21, 1941, Cohen papers, LC; and FF unmailed letter dated October 1, 1941, Cohen papers, LC.

15. "Memoirs," LC.

16. Interview with BVC, April 8, 1974.

17. *Secret Diary,* III, pp. 429, 446; John Winant to BVC, October 30, 1941, LC.

18. Interview with Jane Harris, November 4, 1983; Cohen papers, LC, on relations with Julius and Henry Simon; TGC to Celeste Jedel, July 19, 1933, LC; and Mrs. Morris Heller to JPL, September 18, 1983, and October 8, 1984, on BVC's relationship with Celeste Jedel.

19. Interviews with Jane Harris, December 6, 1982, and November 4, 1983; interview with Jean Pennypacker who had been married to Robert Kintner.

20. Henry Herman papers in Cohen papers, LC; and interview with Joseph Rauh, June 10, 1986.

21. James Rowe to FDR, April 15, 1941, FDRL.

22. BVC to Rabbi Stephen Wise, October 29, 1941, LC.

23. *Secret Diary,* III, p. 541.

24. Interview with Lauchlin Currie, September 20, 1985.

25. Copies of correspondence between Walter Salant and John Maynard Keynes and materials relating to Richard Gilbert in Salant's possession.

26. Joseph Rowe's interview with John Herling, May 21, 1974.

27. Interview with Joseph Rauh, June 10, 1986.

28. *Secret Diary,* III, p. 560.

29. James Rowe to FDR, October 2, 1941, FDRL.

30. Robert Kintner to BVC, August 4, 1941, LC.

31. FF to BVC, September 1941, LC.

32. Wendell Willkie to FDR, October 19, 1941; interview with Joseph Rauh, November 16, 1983; and FDR to Wendell Willkie, October 31, 1941, FDRL.

33. *Secret Diary,* III, p. 625.

34. FDR to BVC, September 4, 1941, LC; and James Rowe to FDR, November 15, 1941, FDRL.

35. *Secret Diary,* III, p. 856.

36. Morgenthau diary, April 12, 1941.

37. Interview with Lauchlin Currie, September 20, 1985.

38. Washington *News,* December 17, 1941.

39. *Secret Diary,* III, p. 437.

40. Senate Committee Investigating Nat'l Defense Program, 77th Cong., 1st sess., p. 3871.

41. RGT diary, January 28, 1941, and February 6, 1941, FDRL.

42. FDR press conference, December 18, 1943, in FDR *PPA,* 1943, pp. 569–75; Eleanor Roosevelt, New York *Times,* January 3, 1944; and Eleanor Roosevelt to JPL, July 18, 1944.

Epilogue

1. Proceedings at the Federal City Club, January 22, 1971, TGC papers, LC.

Index